The Linux Programmer's Toolbox

Prentice Hall
Open Source Software Development Series

Arnold Robbins, Series Editor

"Real world code from real world applications"

Open Source technology has revolutionized the computing world. Many large-scale projects are in production use worldwide, such as Apache, MySQL, and Postgres, with programmers writing applications in a variety of languages including Perl, Python, and PHP. These technologies are in use on many different systems, ranging from proprietary systems, to Linux systems, to traditional UNIX systems, to mainframes.

The **Prentice Hall Open Source Software Development Series** is designed to bring you the best of these Open Source technologies. Not only will you learn how to use them for your projects, but you will learn *from* them. By seeing real code from real applications, you will learn the best practices of Open Source developers the world over.

Titles currently in the series include:

Linux® Debugging and Performance Tuning: Tips and Techniques
Steve Best
0131492470, Paper, © 2006

Understanding AJAX: Using JavaScript to Create Rich Internet Applications
Joshua Eichorn
0132216353, Paper, © 2007

Embedded Linux Primer
Christopher Hallinan
0131679848, Paper, © 2007

SELinux by Example
Frank Mayer, David Caplan, Karl MacMillan
0131963694, Paper, © 2007

UNIX to Linux® Porting
Alfredo Mendoza, Chakarat Skawratananond, Artis Walker
0131871099, Paper, © 2006

Linux Programming by Example: The Fundamentals
Arnold Robbins
0131429647, Paper, © 2004

The Linux® Kernel Primer: A Top-Down Approach for x86 and PowerPC Architectures
Claudia Salzberg, Gordon Fischer, Steven Smolski
0131181637, Paper, © 2006

The Linux Programmer's Toolbox

John Fusco

PRENTICE
HALL

Upper Saddle River, NJ • Boston • Indianapolis • San Francisco
New York • Toronto • Montreal • London • Munich • Paris • Madrid
Cape Town • Sydney • Tokyo • Singapore • Mexico City

Many of the designations used by manufacturers and sellers to distinguish their products are claimed as trademarks. Where those designations appear in this book, and the publisher was aware of a trademark claim, the designations have been printed with initial capital letters or in all capitals.

The author and publisher have taken care in the preparation of this book, but make no expressed or implied warranty of any kind and assume no responsibility for errors or omissions. No liability is assumed for incidental or consequential damages in connection with or arising out of the use of the information or programs contained herein.

The publisher offers excellent discounts on this book when ordered in quantity for bulk purchases or special sales, which may include electronic versions and/or custom covers and content particular to your business, training goals, marketing focus, and branding interests. For more information, please contact:

> U.S. Corporate and Government Sales
> (800) 382-3419
> corpsales@pearsontechgroup.com

For sales outside the United States, please contact:

> International Sales
> international@pearsoned.com

Visit us on the Web: www.prenhallprofessional.com

This Book Is Safari Enabled

The Safari® Enabled icon on the cover of your favorite technology book means the book is available through Safari Bookshelf. When you buy this book, you get free access to the online edition for 45 days.

Safari Bookshelf is an electronic reference library that lets you easily search thousands of technical books, find code samples, download chapters, and access technical information whenever and wherever you need it.

To gain 45-day Safari Enabled access to this book:

- Go to http://www.prenhallprofessional.com/safarienabled
- Complete the brief registration form
- Enter the coupon code MXAB-JIAB-EPDD-Z4B5-7I24

If you have difficulty registering on Safari Bookshelf or accessing the online edition, please e-mail customer-service@safaribooksonline.com.

Library of Congress Cataloging-in-Publication Data

Fusco, John.
  The Linux programmer's toolbox / John Fusco.
      p. cm.
  Includes bibliographical references and index.
  ISBN 0-13-219857-6 (pbk. : alk. paper)
  1. Linux. 2. Operating systems (Computers) I. Title.
  QA76.76.O63F875 2007
  005.4'32—dc22
                                                    2006039343

ISBN 0-13-219857-6
Text printed in the United States on recycled paper at Courier in Stoughton, Massachusetts.
First printing, March 2007

To my wife, Lisa, and my children, Andrew, Alex, and Samantha.

Contents

Foreword

OK, so you've mastered the basics of Linux. You can run ls, grep, find, and sort, and as a C or C++ programmer, you know how to use the Linux system calls. You know that there's much more to life than "point and click" and that Linux will give it to you. You're just not sure yet how. So you ask yourself, "What's next?"

This book gives you the answer. John's knowledge is broad, and he shows the no-longer-novice Linux user how to climb up the next part of the learning curve toward mastery.

From command-line tools for debugging and performance analysis to the range of files in /proc, John shows you how to use all of them to make your day-to-day life with Linux easier and more productive.

Besides a lot of "what" (what tools, what options, what files), there's a lot of "why" here. John shows you why things work the way they do. In turn, this lets you understand why the "what" is effective and internalize the Zen of Linux (and Unix!).

There's a ton of great stuff in this book. I hope you learn a lot. I know I did, and that's saying something.

Enjoy,

Arnold Robbins
Series Editor

Preface

Linux has no shortage of tools. Many are inherited from Unix, with cryptic two-letter names that conjure up images of developers trying to preserve space on a punch card. Happily, those days are long gone, but the legacy remains.

Many of those old tools are still quite useful. Most are highly specialized. Each may do only one thing but does it very well. Highly specialized tools often have many options that can make them intimidating to use. Consider the first time you used `grep` and learned what a regular expression was. Perhaps you haven't mastered regular expression syntax yet (don't worry; no one else has, either). That's not important, because you don't need to be a master of regular expressions to put `grep` to good use.

If there's one thing that I hope you learn from this book, it's that there are many tools out there that you can use without having to master them. You don't need to invest an enormous amount of time reading manuals before you can be productive. I hope you will discover new tools that you may not have been familiar with. Some of the tools this book looks at are quite old and some are new. All of them are useful. As you learn more about each tool, you will find more uses for it.

I use the term *tool* loosely in this book. To me, creating tools is as important as using tools, so I have included various APIs that are not usually covered in much detail in other books. In addition, this book provides some background on the internal workings of the Linux kernel that are necessary to understand what some tools are trying to tell you. I present a unique perspective on the kernel: the user's point of view. You will find enough information to allow you to understand the ground rules that the kernel sets for every process, and I promise you will not have to read a single line of kernel source code.

What you will not find in this book is reconstituted man pages or other documentation stitched into the text. The GNU and Linux developers have done a great job of documenting their work, but that documentation can be hard to find for the inexperienced user. Rather than reprint documentation that will be out of date by the time you read this, I show you some ingenious ways to find the most up-to-date documentation.

GNU/Linux documentation is abundant, but it's not always easy to read. You can read a 10,000-word document for a tool and still not have a clue what the tool does or how to use it. This is where I have tried to fill in the missing pieces. I have tried to explain not just how to use each tool, but also why you would want to use it. Wherever possible, I have provided simple, brief examples that you can type and modify yourself to enhance your understanding of the tools and Linux itself.

What all the tools in this book have in common is that they are available at no cost. Most come with standard Linux distributions, and for those that may not, I have included URLs so that you can download them yourself.

As much as possible, I tried to keep the material interesting and fun.

Who Should Read This Book

This book is written for intermediate to advanced Linux programmers who wish to become more productive and gain a better understanding of the Linux programming environment. If you're an experienced Windows programmer who feels like a fish out of water in the Linux environment, then this book is for you, too.

Non-programmers should also find this book useful because many of the tools and topics I cover have applications beyond programming. If you are a system administrator, or just a Linux enthusiast, then there's something for you in this book, too.

The Purpose of This Book

I wrote this book as a follow-up to an article I wrote for the *Linux Journal* entitled "Ten Commands Every Linux Developer Should Know." The inspiration for this article came from my own experience as a Linux programmer. In my daily work I make it a point to invest some of my time in learning something new, even if it means a temporary lull in progress on my project. Invariably this strategy has paid off. I have always been amazed at how many times I learned about a tool or feature that I concluded would not be useful, only to find a use for it shortly afterward. This has always been a powerful motivation for me to keep learning. I hope that by reading this book, you will follow my example and enhance your skills on a regular basis.

It's also just plain fun to learn about this stuff. If you are like me, you enjoy working with Linux. Motivating yourself to learn more has never been a problem. Because Linux is open source, you have the opportunity to understand all of its inner workings, which is not possible with closed source environments like Windows. In this book I present several freely available resources available to help you learn more.

How to Read This Book

The chapters are presented such that each chapter can stand on its own. Later chapters require some background knowledge that is presented in the earlier chapters. Wherever possible, I have cross-referenced the material to help you find the necessary background information.

I believe the best way to learn is by example, so I have tried to provide simple examples wherever possible. I encourage the reader to try the examples and experiment.

How This Book Is Organized

Chapter 1, Downloading and Installing Open Source Tools, covers the mechanisms used to distribute open source code. I discuss the various package formats used by different distributions and the advantages and disadvantages of each. I present several tools used to maintain packages and how to use them.

Chapter 2, Building from Source, covers the basics of building an open source project. I present some of the tools used to build software and alternatives that are emerging. There are several tips and tricks in this chapter that you can use to master your use of `make`. I also show you how to configure projects that are distributed with GNU's `autoconf` tools so that you can customize them to meet your needs. Finally, I cover the stages of the build that are often misunderstood by many programmers. I look at some of the errors and warnings you are likely to encounter and how to interpret them.

Chapter 3, Finding Help, looks at the various documentation formats tucked away in your Linux distribution that you may not know about. I look at the tools used to read these formats and discuss effective ways to use them.

Chapter 4, Editing and Maintaining Source Files, discusses the various text editors available for programmers as well as the advantages and disadvantages of each. I present a set of features that every programmer should look for in an editor and measure each editor against these. This chapter also covers the basics of revision control, which is vital for software project management.

Chapter 5, What Every Developer Should Know about the Kernel, looks at the kernel from a user's perspective. In this chapter you will find the necessary background information required to understand the workings of a Linux system. I introduce several tools that allow you to see how your code interacts with the kernel.

Chapter 6, Understanding Processes, focuses on processes, their characteristics, and how to manage them. I cover a good deal of background required to introduce the tools in this chapter and understand why they are useful. In addition, this chapter introduces several programming APIs that you can use to create your own tools.

Chapter 7, Communication Between Processes, introduces the concepts behind inter-process communication (IPC). This chapter contains mostly background information required for Chapter 8. Along with each IPC mechanism, I introduce the APIs required to use it along with a working example.

Chapter 8, Debugging IPC with Shell Commands, presents several tools available to debug applications that use IPC. It builds on the information from Chapter 7 to help you interpret the output of these tools, which can be difficult to understand.

Chapter 9, Performance Tuning, introduces tools to measure the performance of your system as well as the performance of individual applications. I present several examples to illustrate how programming can impact performance. I also discuss some of the performance issues that are unique to multi-core processors.

Chapter 10, Debugging, presents several tools and techniques that you can use to debug applications. I look at some open source memory debugging tools including Valgrind and Electric Fence. I also take an in-depth look at the capabilities of gdb, and how to use it effectively.

Acknowledgments

I would like to thank my wife, Lisa, without whom this book would not have been possible. Too often, she had to be a single mom while I worked in seclusion. Without her support, I would never have been able to take advantage of this opportunity. Thanks also to my children—Andrew, Alex, and Samantha—who had to spend too much time without their dad during the course of this work.

My thanks also go to Arnold Robbins, who provided wonderful advice and oversight. His experience and authoritative knowledge were invaluable to me during the course of this work. Thanks for making this an enjoyable learning experience for me.

Thanks also to Debra Williams Cauley for her patience and diligence putting up with my missed deadlines and schedule slips. This first-time author is grateful to you for keeping everything on track.

Finally, I would like to thank Mark Taub for recruiting me and giving me this wonderful opportunity.

About the Author

John Fusco is a software developer for GE Healthcare, based in Waukesha, Wisconsin, specializing in Linux applications and device drivers. John has worked on Unix software for more than ten years and has been developing applications for Linux since kernel version 2.0. John has written articles for *Embedded Systems Programming* and *Linux Journal*. This is his first book.

Chapter 1

Downloading and Installing Open Source Tools

1.1 Introduction

In this chapter, I discuss the different formats for distributing free software, how to manipulate them, and where to find them. I examine archive files and package files in detail, as well as the most common tools commands used to manipulate them.

It can be dangerous to accept software from strangers. I cover various security issues that you should be aware of and things you can do to protect yourself. I introduce the concept of authentication and trust, and discuss how it applies to security. For those times when authentication is not possible, I show you how to inspect packages and archives.

Finally, I introduce some tools for managing packages on package-based distributions and how to get the most out of them.

1.2   What Is Open Source?

The term *open source* is a marketing term for free software, created by the Open Source Initiative (OSI).[1] This organization was founded to promote the principles of free software that had its roots in the GNU Project, founded by Richard Stallman. One goal of OSI is to counter some of the negative stereotypes about free software and promote the free sharing of source code.

At first, many businesses were afraid of using open source software. No doubt the marketing departments of some large software companies had something to do with it. Conventional wisdom says, "You get what you pay for." Some feared that the licenses (like the GNU Public License) would act like a virus so that by creating projects using free software, they, too, would have to make their source code public.

Fortunately, most of those fears have subsided. Many large businesses are freely using and promoting open source code in their own projects. Some have even based entire products on open source software. The genie is out of the bottle.

1.3   What Does Open Source Mean to You?

To most people, open source software simply means a lot of high-quality software available at no cost. Unfortunately, a lot of not-so-high-quality software is available as well, but that's part of the process. Good project ideas flourish and improve, while bad ones wither and die. Picking open source software is a bit like picking fruit: It takes some experience to know when it's ripe.

A natural selection process is going on at many levels. At the source code level, features and code are selected (based on patches) so that only the best code gets in. As a consumer, you select the projects to download, which drives the vitality of a project. No one wants to develop code for a project that no one is using. Fewer downloads attract fewer developers. More downloads mean more developers, which in turn means more code to choose among and, thus, better code. Sometimes selecting a project to try is a gamble, but the only things at stake are your time and effort. It's inevitable that you will make some regrettable choices once in a while, but take heart: It's all part of the process.

For some people, not knowing what you are getting is part of the fun. It's like opening a birthday gift. For others, it's a nuisance and a waste of time. If you're

---

1.   www.opensource.org

looking for the convenience of shrink-wrapped software that just installs and runs, there are open source projects for you—just not as many. Fortunately, there are many resources on the Internet to help you make good choices.

1.3.1 Finding Tools

The first place you should look before you start trolling the Internet is your distribution CDs. Assuming that you installed Linux from a set of CDs or a DVD, you probably have a lot of tools that were not installed. Most distributions ship with much more software on the CDs than is installed in a default installation. Typically, you are given a choice when you install the OS as to what kind of system you want to create. This results in an arbitrary set of packages being installed to your system, based on someone's idea of what a "workstation" or a "server" is.

You can always add to the set of installed software manually by locating the raw packages on the installation CDs. The drawback here is that the packages usually are not arranged in any particular order, so you have to know what you are looking for. Some distributions have graphical interfaces that arrange the packages into categories to help you pick which software to install.

If you don't know what you are looking for, the Internet should be your next destination. Several Web sites serve as clearinghouses for open source software. One such site is www.freshmeat.net. Here, you will find software arranged by categories so that it's easy to find what you're looking for. While writing this book, for example, I searched Freshmeat for the term *word processors* and found 71 projects available. Imagine having to choose among 71 different word processors!

Freshmeat allows you to filter your results to help you narrow down your choices. My results included various operating systems besides Linux and projects in various stages of development. So I chose to limit my search to projects that have Linux support, that are mature, and that use an OSI-approved Open Source license. (Freshmeat results include commercial software as well.) This reduced the number to 12 projects—a much more manageable number. A closer look revealed that several of these projects were not what I was looking for, given the broad interpretation of the term *word processor*. After trying a few more filters, I was able to uncover a few well-known, high-quality projects, such as AbiWord, and a few I never heard of before. There were some notable absences, such as OpenOffice, which I am using to write this book. It turns out that the reason I didn't find OpenOffice was because it was filed under "Office/Business :: Office Suites," not "word processors." The moral of the story is that if you don't find what you are looking for, keep looking.

1.3.2   Distribution Formats

Now that you've found some software that you are interested in, you probably have some more choices to make. Mature projects usually offer ready-to-install packages in one or more package formats. Less mature projects often offer only source code or binary files in an archive file. Often, this is a good indicator of what you are getting into. Downloading a software package file can be like buying a new car: You don't need to know how it works; you just turn the key, and it starts. By contrast, downloading an archive of source or binaries can be like buying a used car: It helps if you know something about cars; otherwise, you won't know what you're getting into.

Usually, when a project provides an installable package, it's a sign that the project has matured. It is also a sign that the release cycle of the project is stable. If the project were delivering new releases every week, it probably wouldn't bother making packages. With a software package file and a little luck, you might be able to install it and run. But as with a new car, it is possible to get a lemon once in a while.

The alternative to a package file is an archive file, which for Linux-based projects is usually a compressed `tar` file. An *archive file* is a collection of files packed into a single file using an archiving tool such as the `tar` command. Usually, the files are compressed with the `gzip` program to save space; often, they are referred to as *tar files* or *tarballs*.

Tar files are the preferred format for distributing source code for projects. They are easy to create and use, and every programmer is familiar with the `tar` program. Less often, you will find tar files that have binary executables in them. This is a quick-and-dirty alternative to packaging and should be avoided unless you know what you are doing. In general, tar files are for people who have some knowledge of programming and system administration.

1.4   An Introduction to Archive Files

At some point in the process of downloading and installing open source software, you are going to encounter an archive file of one sort or another. An *archive file* is any file that contains a collection of other files. If you are a Windows user, you are no doubt familiar with the predominant Windows archiver, PKZip. Linux archive utilities function similarly except that unlike PKZip, they do not include compression. Instead, Linux archive tools concentrate on archiving and leave the compression to another tool (typically, `gzip` or `bzip2`). That's the UNIX philosophy.

Naturally, because this is Linux, you have more than one choice of archivers, but as an open source consumer, you have to take what you're given. So even though you are most likely to encounter `tar` files exclusively, it's good at least to know that other tools are available.

An archive utility has some special requirements beyond just preserving filenames and data. In addition to a file's pathname and data, the archive has to preserve each file's metadata. *Metadata* includes the file's owner, group, and other attributes (such as read/write/execute permissions). The archiver records all this information such that a file can be deleted from the file system and restored later from the archive with no loss of information. If you archive an executable file and then delete it from your file system, that file should still be executable when you restore it. In Windows, the filename would indicate whether the file is executable via the extension (such as .exe). Linux uses the file's metadata to indicate whether it is executable, so this data must be stored by the archiver to be preserved.

The most common archive tools used in Linux are listed in Table 1-1. By far the most popular archive format is `tar`. The name *tar* comes from a contraction of *tape archive,* which is a legacy from its days as a tape backup utility. These days, `tar` is most commonly used as a general-purpose tool to archive groups of files into a single file. An alternative to `tar` that you may run into less frequently is `cpio`, which uses a very different syntax to accomplish the same task. There's also the POSIX standard archive utility `pax`, which can understand `tar` files, `cpio` files, or its own format. I have never seen anything distributed in `pax` format, but I mention it here for completeness.

One last archive utility worth mentioning is `ar`, which is most frequently used to create object code libraries used in software development, but it is also used to create package files used by the Debian distribution.

TABLE 1-1   Most Common Archive Tools

Tool	Notes
`tar`	Most popular.
`cpio`	Used internally by the RPM format; not used extensively elsewhere.
`ar`	Used internally by Debian packager; otherwise, used only for software development libraries. `ar` files have no path information.

TABLE 1-2   Archive Naming Conventions

Extensions	Type
`.tar`	`tar` archive, uncompressed
`.tar.gz .tgz`	`tar` archive, compressed with `gzip`
`.tar.bz2`	`tar` archive, compressed with `bzip2`
`.tar.Z .taz`	`tar` archive, compressed with the UNIX `compress` command
`.ar .a`	`ar` archive, generally used only for software development
`.cpio`	`cpio` archive, uncompressed

You can also find utilities to handle `.zip` files created with PKZip as well as some lesser-known compressed archive utilities, such as lha. Open source programs for Linux are virtually never distributed in these formats, however. If you see a `.zip` archive, it's a good bet that it's intended for a Microsoft operating system.

For the most part, you need to know two things about each format: how to query the archive for its contents and how to extract files from the archive. Unlike Windows archivers, which have all kinds of dangerous bells and whistles, Linux archivers focus on the basics. So it's generally safe to query and extract files from an archive, especially if you are not the root user. It's always wise to query an archive before extracting files so that you don't inadvertently overwrite files on your system that may have the same names.

1.4.1   Identifying Archive Files

When you download an archive from the Internet, it most likely has been compressed to save bandwidth. There are some file-naming conventions for compressed files; some of these are shown in Table 1-2.

When in doubt, remember the `file` command. This tool does a good job of identifying what you are looking at when the filename gives you no clue. This is useful when your Web browser or other tool munges the filename into something unrecognizable. Suppose that I have a compressed tar archive named `foo.x`, for example. The name tells me nothing about the contents of this file. Then I try the following command:

```
$ file foo.x
foo.x: gzip compressed data, from UNIX, max compression
```

Now I know that the file was compressed with `gzip`, but I still don't know whether it's a `tar` file. I can try unzipping it with `gzip` and try the `file` command again. Or I can just use the `-z` option of the command:

```
$ file -z foo.x
foo.x: tar archive (gzip compressed data, from UNIX, max compression)
```

Now I know exactly what I'm looking at.

Normally, people follow some intuitive file-naming conventions, and the file-name does a good job of identifying the archive type and what processing has been done.

1.4.2   Querying an Archive File

Archive files keep track of the files they contain with a table of contents, which (conveniently enough) is accessed with a `-t` flag for all the archivers I mentioned earlier. Following is a sample from a tar file for the Debian `cron` installation:

```
$ tar -tzvf data.tar.gz
drwxr-xr-x root/root           0 2001-10-01 07:53:19 ./
drwxr-xr-x root/root           0 2001-10-01 07:53:15 ./usr/
drwxr-xr-x root/root           0 2001-10-01 07:53:18 ./usr/bin/
-rwsr-xr-x root/root       22460 2001-10-01 07:53:18 ./usr/bin/crontab
drwxr-xr-x root/root           0 2001-10-01 07:53:18 ./usr/sbin/
-rwxr-xr-x root/root       25116 2001-10-01 07:53:18 ./usr/sbin/cron
```

The example above added the `-v` option to include additional information similar to a *long* listing from the `ls` command. The output includes the file permissions in the first column, followed by the ownership in the second column. The file size (in bytes) is shown next, with directories listed as having a size of `0`. When inspecting archives, you should pay careful attention to the ownership and permissions of each file.

The basic commands to list the contents of an archive for the various formats are listed in Table 1-3. All three formats produce essentially the same output.

TABLE 1-3   Archive Query Commands

Format	Command	Notes
`tar`	`tar -tvf filename`	
`tar` archive compressed with `gzip`	`tar -tzvf filename`	
`tar` archive compressed with `bzip2`	`tar -tjvf filename`	
`cpio` archive	`cpio -tv < filename`	`cpio` uses `stdin` and `stdout` as binary streams.

Reading the symbolic representation of a file's permissions is fairly straightforward when you get used to it. You should be familiar with the tricks that are used to represent additional information above and beyond the usual read/write/execute permissions.

Let's start with the permission string itself. This is represented with a ten-character string. The first character indicates the type of file, whereas the remaining three groups of three characters summarize the file owner's permission, the group members' permissions, and everyone else's permissions, respectively.

The type of file is indicated with a single character. The valid values for this character and their meanings are listed in Table 1-4.

The next nine characters can be grouped into three groups of three bits. Each bit represents the read, write, or execute permissions of the file, respectively, represented as `r`, `w`, and `x`. A - in a bit position indicates that that permission is not set. A - in the `w` position, for example, indicates that the file is not writeable. Some examples are shown in Table 1-5.

The last things to know about permissions are the *setuid, setgid,* and *sticky* bits. These bits are not listed directly, because they affect the file's behavior only when executing.

When the setuid bit is set, the code in the file will execute, using the file's owner as the effective user ID. This means that the program can do anything that the file's owner has permission to do. If a file is owned by root and the setuid bit is set, the code has permission to modify or delete any file in the system, no matter which user starts the program. Sounds dangerous, doesn't it? Programs with the setuid bit have been the subject of attacks in the past.

TABLE 1-4 File Types in an Archive Listing

Character	Meaning	Notes
-	regular file	Includes text files, data files, executable, etc.
d	directory	
c	character device	A special file used to communicate with a *character* device driver. These files traditionally are restricted to the /dev directory; you usually don't see them in archives.
b	block device	A special file used to communicate with a *block* device driver. These files traditionally are restricted to the /dev directory; you usually don't see them in archives.
l	symbolic link	A filename that points to another filename. The file it points to may reside on a different file system or may be nonexistent.

TABLE 1-5 Examples of File Permission Bits

Permissions	
rwx	File is readable, writeable, and executable.
rw-	File is readable and writeable but not executable.
r-x	File is readable and executable but not writeable.
--x	File is executable but not writeable or readable.

The setgid bit does the same thing, except that the code executes with the privileges of the group to which the file belongs. Normally, a program executes with the privileges of the group of the user who started the program. When the setgid bit is set, the program runs with privileges as though the user belonged to the same group.

You can recognize a file with the setuid or setgid bit set by looking at the x bit in the permissions string. Normally, an x in this position means that the file is executable, whereas a - indicates that the file is not executable.

The setuid and setgid bits add two more possible values for this character. A lowercase s instead of an x in the owner's permissions means that the file is executable by the owner and the setuid bit is set. An uppercase S means that the setuid bit is set, but the owner does not have execute permission. It seems odd, but it is allowed and just as dangerous. The file could be owned by root, for example, but root has no permission to execute the file. Linux gives root execute permission if *anyone* has execute permission. So even if the execute bit for root is not set, as long as the current user has execute permission, the code will execute with root privileges.

Like the setuid bit, the setgid bit is indicated by modifying the x position in the group permissions. A lowercase s here indicates that the file's setgid bit is set and that members of the group have permission to execute this file. An uppercase S indicates that the setgid bit is set, but members of the group do not have permission to execute the file.

You can see in the cron package output, shown earlier in this chapter, that the crontab program is a setuid program owned by root. Some more permissions and their meanings are shown in Table 1-6.

TABLE 1-6   Some Examples of Permissions and Their Meanings

Permission String	Execute Permission	Effective User ID	Effective Group ID
-rwxr-xr-x	All users can execute this file.	Current user	Current user
-rw-r-xr-x	All members of the file's group can execute this file except the owner; everyone else except the owner can execute this file.	Current user	Current user
-rwsr-xr-x	All users can execute this file.	File owner	Current user
-rwSr-xr-x	Everyone except the owner can execute this file.	File owner	Current user
-rwxr-sr-x	All users can execute this file.	Current user	Group owner
-rwsr-sr-x	All users can execute this file.	File owner	Group owner
-rwsr-Sr-x	All users can execute this file, including the owner, but not members of the file's group.	File owner	Group owner

The sticky bit is something of a relic. The original intent of the sticky bit was to make sure that certain executable programs would load faster by keeping the code pages on the swap disk. In Linux, the sticky bit is used only in directories, where it has a completely different meaning. Normally, when you give write and execute permission to other users in a directory that you own, those users are free to create and delete files in that directory. One privilege you may not want them to have is the ability to delete other users' files in that directory. Normally, if a user has write permission in a directory, that user can delete any file in that directory, not just the files he owns. You can revoke this privilege by setting the sticky bit on the directory. When the directory has the sticky bit set, users can delete only files that belong to them. As usual, the directory's owner and root can delete any files. The `/tmp` directory on most systems has the sticky bit set for this purpose.

A directory with the sticky bit set is indicated with a t or a T in the execute permission for others. For example:

`-rwxrwxrwt`   All users can read and write in this directory, and the sticky bit is set.

`-rwxrwx--T`   Only the owner and group members can read or write, and the sticky bit is set.

1.4.3   Extracting Files from an Archive File

Now that you know how to inspect an archive file's contents, it's time to extract the files to have a closer look. The basic commands are listed in Table 1-7.

Although it's generally safe to extract files from an archive, you need to pay attention to the pathnames to avoid clobbering any data on your system. In particular, `cpio` has the ability to store absolute paths from the root directory. This means that if you try to extract a `cpio` archive that happens to have a bunch of files in `/etc`, you could clobber vital files inadvertently. Consider a `cpio` archive that contains a copy of `/etc/hosts`, among other things. If you try to extract files from this archive, it will try to overwrite your copy of `/etc/hosts`. You can see this by querying the archive

```
cpio -t < foo.cpio
/etc/hosts
```

TABLE 1-7   Archive Extraction Commands

Format	Command	Notes
`tar`	`tar -xf filename`	This command extracts files to the current directory by default.
`tar` archive compressed with `gzip`	`tar -xzf filename`	
`tar` archive compressed with `bzip2`	`tar -xjf filename`	
`cpio` archive	`cpio -i -d < filename`	Beware of absolute pathnames.
`ar` archive	`ar x filename`	Files have no path information.

The leading / is your clue that the archive wants to restore *the* copy of /etc/hosts and not some other copy. So if you are extracting files for inspection, you probably don't want to overwrite your copies of the same file (yet). You will want to make sure that you use the GNU option `--no-absolute-filenames` so that the hosts file will be extracted to

`./etc/hosts`

Fortunately, the only time you are likely to encounter a `cpio` archive is as part of an RPM package file, and RPM always uses pathnames relative to the current directory, so there is no chance of overwriting system files unless you want to.

Note that the version of tar found in some versions of UNIX also allows absolute pathnames. The GNU version of tar found in Linux automatically strips the leading / from files extracted from a tar archive. So if you happen upon a tar file that comes from one of these other flavors of UNIX, GNU tar will watch your back. GNU tar also strips the leading / from the pathnames in archives that it creates.

1.5   Know Your Package Manager

Package managers are sophisticated tools used to install and maintain software on your system. They help you keep track of what software is installed and where the files are located. A package manager can keep track of dependencies to make sure that new software you install is compatible with the software you have already installed. If you wanted to install a KDE package on a GNOME machine, for example, the package manager would protest, indicating that you don't have the required runtime libraries. This is preferable to installing the package only to scratch your head trying to figure out why it won't work.

One of the most valuable features that a package manager offers is the ability to uninstall. This allows you to install a piece of software and try it out, and then uninstall it if you don't like it. After you uninstall the package, your system is back to the same configuration it had before you installed the package. Uninstalling a package is one way to upgrade it. You remove the old version and install the new one. Most package managers have a special *upgrade* command so that this can be done in a single step.

The package manager creates a centralized database to keep track of installed applications. This database is also a valuable source of information on the state of your system. You can list the applications currently installed on your computer, for example, or you can verify that a particular application has not been tampered with since installation. Sometimes, just browsing the database can be an educational experience, as you discover software you didn't know you had.

Two of the most common package formats are RPM (RPM Package Manager[2]) and the Debian Package format. Some additional examples are listed in Table 1-8. As you might guess, RPM is used on Red Hat and Fedora distributions, but also on Suse and others. Likewise, the Debian format is used on the Debian distribution and also on several popular distributions (Knoppix, Ubuntu, and others). Other package managers include `pkgtool`, which is used by the Slackware distribution, and `portage`, which is used by the Gentoo distribution.

The decision about which package manager to use is not yours to make (unless you want to create your own distribution). Each Linux distribution chooses a single tool to manage the installed software. It makes no sense to have two package managers in your system. If you don't like the package manager your distribution uses, you would be well advised to choose a different distribution rather than try to convert to a different package manager.

---

2. Formerly the Red Hat Package Manager.

TABLE 1-8   Some Popular Linux Distributions and the Package Formats They Use

Distribution	Package Format
Red Hat	RPM
Fedora	RPM
Debian	Deb
Knoppix	Deb
Ubuntu	Deb
Gentoo	portage
Xandros	Deb
Mandriva (formerly Mandrake)	RPM
mepis	Deb
Slackware	pkgtool

When you've identified the format you want to download, there usually is one more choice. Because this is open source we're talking about, after all, it only makes sense that you have the choice of downloading the source.

1.5.1   Choosing Source or Binary

If you are running Linux on an Intel-compatible 32-bit processor, you are likely to have the opportunity to download software in the form of precompiled binaries. Most often, binaries are available in a package format and less frequently in `tar` archive format. If you choose to download and install software from precompiled binaries, you won't need to touch any source code unless you want to.

If you are running Linux on anything other than an Intel-compatible processor, your only choice may be to download the source and build it yourself. On occasion, you may want to build from source even when a compatible binary is available. Developers deliberately generate binaries for the most compatible architecture to reach the widest audience possible. If you are using the latest and greatest CPU, you may want to recompile the package to target your machine instead of using an older compatible architecture, which may not run as fast.

Using Intel as an example, you are likely to find plenty of binary executables for the i386 architecture. The i386 refers to the 80386, which is the lowest common denominator of 32-bit Intel architectures. These days, when a package has been labeled i386, it more likely means Pentium or later. Many packages use the i586 label, which more specifically refers to the Pentium processor. Nevertheless, code compiled and optimized for a Pentium won't necessarily be optimal on a Pentium 4 or Xeon.

Whether or not you will see a performance increase by compiling for a newer processor depends on the application. There is no guarantee that the performance advantages of compiling for a newer processor will be perceptible in every application.

Table 1-9 lists some of the most common architecture names used for RPM packages. Although these labels are in many cases identical to the labels used by the GNU compiler, don't assume that they are the same. The label is often arbitrarily chosen by the packager and may not reflect the actual build contents. Most often, you will see packages labeled as i386 when they actually are compiled for Pentium or Pentium II. Because few people actually run Linux on an 80386 these days, no one complains.

TABLE 1-9   Overview of Architectures

Label	Description
i386	Most common architecture you will find, although in gcc, i386 refers specifically to 80386. When you see this in a package, you should assume that it requires at least a Pentium I CPU.
i486	Not very common. It probably is safe to assume that a package labeled with this architecture is compatible with an 80486 (or compatible).
i586	Becoming more common. The GNU compiler uses i586 to describe the Pentium I CPU. Expect this to work on any Pentium or later processor.
i686	The GNU compiler uses i686 to describe the Pentium Pro CPU, which served as the basis for the Pentium II and later processors. Assume that this requires a Pentium II or later CPU.
ix86	Not very common, but it should be safe to assume Pentium or better.

continues

TABLE 1-9   *Continued*

Label	Description
x86_64	AMD Opteron and Intel Pentium 4 with EM64T extensions. These are the latest processors that both have both 32-bit and 64-bit capability. This code is compiled to run in 64-bit mode, which means that it will not be compatible with a 32-bit processor; neither will it run on an Opteron or EM64T CPU running a 32-bit Linux kernel.
IA64	This refers specifically to the 64-bit Itanium processor. This is a one-of-a-kind architecture from Intel and Hewlett-Packard, found only on very expensive workstations and supercomputers.
ppc	PowerPC G2, G3, and G4 processors found in some Apple Macintosh and Apple iMac computers.
ppc64	PowerPC G5, found in the Apple iMac.
sparc	SPARC processor, used in Sun workstations.
sparc64	64-bit SPARC processor, used in Sun workstations.
mipseb	MIPS processor, most often found in SGI workstations.

Building from source is not necessarily difficult. For a relatively simple project, such as a text-based utility, building from source can be easy. For more complex projects, such as a Web browser or word processor, it can be a real headache. Generally speaking, the larger the project, the more supporting development libraries are required. Large GUI projects, for example, typically rely on several different development libraries, which most likely are not installed on your system. Tracking down the right versions of all these packages can be a time-consuming exercise in futility. In Chapter 2, I discuss more about how to build projects from source. In general, when looking for software, you will want to take the binary when you can get it.

1.5.2   Working with Packages

Many newer Linux distributions try to make things easy on the user, so it is possible to run Linux without being aware that there is a package manager behind the scenes. Nevertheless, it makes sense to understand how these tools work if you plan to venture outside the sandbox provided by your distribution. Knowing your way around the package management tools is very useful when things go wrong. The basic features that you can expect to find in a package manager include

- Installs new software on your system

- Removes (or uninstalls) software on your system

- Verifies—makes sure installed files have not been corrupted or tampered with

- Upgrades the installed versions of software on your system

- Queries the software installed (for example, "What package installed this file?")

- Extracts—inspects the contents of a package before you install

1.6   Some Words about Security and Packages

Just about every computer user has had some firsthand experience with *malware* (malicious software). If you are a Linux user, surely you've received some strange e-mails from your friends using Windows, the result of the latest Microsoft virus spreading across the Internet.

Malware includes more than just e-mail viruses, though: It also includes just about any software that is introduced to your system and executes without your consent. It includes viruses, spyware, and any other destructive software that finds its way into your system. Microsoft Windows defenders argue that Windows is targeted by malware writers because there are many more Windows machines out there than Linux machines. Although that may be true, it's also true that Windows is simply a much easier target. A key vulnerability in Windows 98, Windows ME, and the "home" version of Windows XP, for example, is that any user can touch any file and make systemwide changes. So just by clicking an e-mail attachment, an unseasoned Windows user can turn the computer into part of a zombie horde in a distributed denial-of-service attack or just delete the contents of drive C.

The motives for malware are varied and range from organized crime to revenge to just plain vandalism. Don't assume that you are not a target.

Linux users tend to think that their systems are immune to malware, but that is not true. The JBellz MP3, for example, was a Trojan horse that exploited a vulnerability in the `mpg123` program—an open source MP3 player for Linux. In this case, the malware wasn't even an executable file but a music file in MP3 format. When the user tried to play this file in a different program, it appeared as though the file had been corrupted and would not play. In actuality, it was a clever piece of malware that targeted a specific vulnerability in the mpg123 program. The mpg123 program contained a buffer overflow such that a corrupted MP3 file could contain arbitrary script code that would then be executed. In this particular instance, the author decided that it would be clever to delete the contents of the user's home directory.

Although your Linux machine is not likely to spread viruses on the scale of Microsoft Windows, there are still vulnerabilities. It's basically impossible to see something like the JBellz Trojan coming, so the only thing you can do is pay attention to security alerts and take them seriously. In the case of JBellz, the damage was restricted to a single user, but at least the system was not compromised, although it could have been if that user had been the root user.

There have been other instances of malware creeping into the source code of widely used packages. One such instance was the OpenSSH source code.[3] In this instance, the OpenSSH source code was compromised on the host site, created a back door for someone to get in, using the privileges of the person who compiled the source. So if you downloaded the compromised source for OpenSSH, built it, and installed it, a back door would be open that would allow an intruder to execute code with your privileges.

Linux has no equivalent of an antivirus program to scan programs for viruses; instead, it relies on trust and authentication. It's the difference between being proactive and reactive to virus threats. The Windows paradigm is decidedly reactive, but there is still a good deal of trust involved. When you download a Windows program, you trust that your virus definitions are up to date and that you are not one of the first people to encounter a new virus. By contrast, the Linux approach is to "trust but verify," using authentication and trusted third parties. (I discuss authentication in the next section.)

In the interest of good security, Linux does not allow unprivileged users to install system software. When you install software on your system, you must do so with root privileges, which means that you log in as root or use a program like sudo. This is when your system is vulnerable, because most programs require scripts to execute during installation and removal. Whether you realize it or not, you are placing a great deal of trust in the package provider that the scripts will not compromise the security of your system. Authenticating the package author is a key step in making sure the software is legitimate.

---

3.   Refer to http://www.cert.org/advisories/CA-2002-24.html

1.6.1   The Need for Authentication

With security, it's not just what you run, but also when you run it. A Linux user can create any kind of malicious program he wants, but without superuser privileges, he can't compromise the whole computer. So it's important to know that all package formats allow package files to contain scripts that execute during package installation and removal. These typically are Bourne shell scripts that execute with root privileges and, therefore, can do absolutely anything. Such scripts are potential hiding places for malware in a Trojan-horse package, which is one reason why you should always authenticate software before you install it, not just before you run it.

You should always be reluctant to use any tool that requires superuser privileges, but the package manager is one exception. The package database is the central hub of a typical distribution, and as such, it is accessible only with root privileges. There are several ways to authenticate a package. The rpm tool, for example, has authentication features built in. For others, such as Debian, authentication is a separate step.

1.6.2   Basic Package Authentication

The most basic form of package authentication involves using a hashing function. The idea is similar to a checksum, which tries to identify a set of data uniquely by using the sum of all the bytes in the data. A simple checksum of all the bytes in the file is not enough to guarantee security, however. Many different datasets can have the same checksum, and it is easy to manipulate the data while preserving the checksum. Simple checksums are never used to authenticate packages, because such a signature is easy to forge.

The value produced by a hashing function is called a *hash*. Like a checksum, the hash characterizes an arbitrarily large dataset with a single fixed-length piece of data. Unlike a checksum, the hash output is very unpredictable, making it extremely difficult to modify the data and produce the same hash. Most hashing algorithms use a large key (for example, 128 bits), so the probability of producing the same hash twice is so remote that it isn't worth trying. If you download a file from an unknown source but have the hash from a trusted source, you can have faith in two things:

- The chance of getting a modified file that has the same hash is extremely remote.

- The chance that a malicious programmer can take that file, modify it according to his wishes, and produce the same hash is infinitesimal.

One popular tool for creating hashes is md5sum, based on the MD5 algorithm,[4] which produces a 128-bit hash. The md5sum program can generate hashes or verify them. You generate the hashes by specifying the names of files on the command line. Then the program produces one line for each file containing the resulting hash and the filename:

```
$ md5sum foo.tar bar.tar
af8e7b3117b93df1ef2ad8336976574f *foo.tar
2b1999f965e4abba2811d4e99e879f04 *bar.tar
```

You can use the same data as input to the md5sum program to verify the hashes:

```
$ md5sum foo.tar bar.tar > md5.sums
$ md5sum --check md5.sums
foo.tar: OK
bar.tar: OK
```

Each hash is represented with a 32-digit hexadecimal number. (For you nongeeks, each hexadecimal digit is 4 bits.) You can check this hash against a value posted by a trusted source to see whether your data is correct. If the MD5 hash matches, you can be virtually certain that the file is unchanged from the time when the MD5 hash was created. The only catch is whether you can trust the MD5 hash that you checked it against. Ideally, you should get the MD5 sum from a trusted site that is not the same place from where you downloaded the package. If the file you downloaded is a Trojan from a compromised site, you can rest assured that any MD5 hashes from this site have also been modified.

Suppose that you want to download the latest and greatest version of OpenOffice from OpenOffice.org. The official site will refer you to one of many mirrors, so how do you know that the site you were referred to has not been compromised and that the package you download has not been replaced with a Trojan-horse package? The trick is to go back to the official site and look for the MD5 sum for the file. In this example, the OpenOffice.org site posts the MD5 sums for all the files available for download, so after you download the file, you can verify it against the MD5 hash posted on the OpenOffice.org site. Sometimes, you can download a file for input to the md5sum program, or you must make one yourself by cutting and pasting from

---

4. *MD5* stands for *Message Digest algorithm number 5.*

your Web browser. In this example, I cut and pasted the sum for the file I down-loaded into a file called `md5.sum`, as follows:

```
cf2d0beb6cae98acae81e4d690d63094  Ooo_1.1.4_LinuxIntel_install.tar.gz
```

Note that the `md5sum` program is a little picky about white space. It expects no white space before the hash and exactly two spaces between the hash and the file-name. Anything else will cause it to complain.

When you have your md5.sum file, you can check the file you downloaded as follows:

```
$ md5sum --check md5.sum
OOo_1.1.4_LinuxIntel_install.tar.gz: OK
```

As you can see in the example above, the program prints an unambiguous mes-sage indicating that the MD5 sum is correct. This means that the file you down-loaded from an unfamiliar mirror matches the MD5 sum that was posted on the OpenOffice.org site. Now you can rest assured that you have authenticated your copy of the file (provided that the OpenOffice.org site hasn't been compromised).

1.6.3   Package Authentication with Digital Signatures

A digital signature is another kind of hash like MD5, except that you do not need to know anything unique about the data you want to authenticate. All you need to authenticate a digital signature is a single public key from the person or organiza-tion you are trying to authenticate. When you have the public key, you can authen-ticate any data signed by that person. So even though each signature produced by that person is a unique hash, you need only a single public key to verify the authen-ticity of any data signed by that person.

The person who wants to sign data produces a pair of keys: one public and one private. The keys are based on a passphrase that only the originator knows. The originator keeps the private key and the passphrase secret, while the public key is made available to whoever wants it. If either the private key or the data changes, authentication will fail. The odds of creating a valid signature with the same public key but a different passphrase and private key are extremely remote. The chance of being able to forge a signature for a legitimate public key is infinitesimal.

This method is based on trust. You trust that certain individuals and organizations will not sign data that is infected with malware. You trust that they will take adequate measures to keep their private keys and passphrases secret. You also have to trust the sources of the public keys you use. Given that your trust is well placed, you can rest assured of the authenticity of data you validate with the public keys.

The tool most often used for digital signatures of Open Source code is GNU Privacy Guard (GPG). The process of signing data with GPG is depicted in Figure 1-1.

1.6.4   GPG Signatures with RPM

The RPM package format allows the option of a GPG signature for authentication. The RPM format also uses other hashes, including MD5, for each file in the RPM. These hashes can be used to verify that the RPM hasn't been corrupted during transfer and to confirm that the files haven't been tampered with since installation, but they do not provide any authentication. Only the GPG signature authenticates the RPM. Alternatively, you could authenticate the RPM manually, using the MD5 hash for the package file provided by a trusted source.

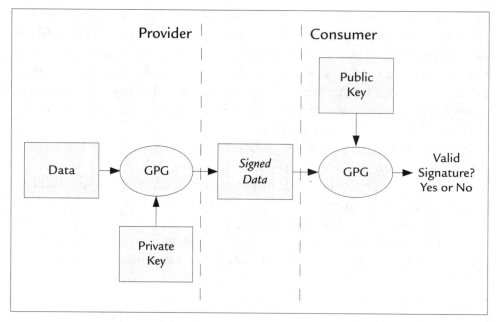

FIGURE 1-1   GPG Signing Process

The `rpm` utility has a `--checksig` flag, which unfortunately lumps all the hashes together in one line. So if a file does not have a GPG signature, `rpm` will still report that it has a good MD5 sum. If it does have a GPG signature, it simply includes an additional `gpg ok` in the output line. Consider the following output:

```
$ rpm -checksig *.rpm
abiword-2.2.7-1.fc3.i386.rpm: sha1 md5 OK
abiword-plugins-impexp-2.2.7-1.fc3.i386.rpm: sha1 md5 OK

abiword-plugins-tools-2.2.7-1.fc2.i386.rpm: sha1 md5 OK
firefox-1.0-2.fc3.i386.rpm: (sha1) dsa sha1 md5 gpg OK
dpkg-1.10.21-1mdk.i586.rpm: (SHA1) DSA sha1 md5 (GPG) NOT OK (MISSING KEYS:
GPG#26752624)
```

Notice that five RPM package files are listed, but only the `firefox` and `dpkg` packages have a GPG signature. I have a public key for `firefox` but not for `dpkg`. Therefore, `firefox` is the only package in this group that can be considered authenticated, but `rpm` doesn't highlight that fact in any way. Too bad. The `dpkg` RPM is signed with a GPG signature, but I don't have a public key for it. So even though it is signed, I don't have any way to know whether the signature is valid. In this case, at least `rpm` does produce a more ominous warning.

The signature for the `firefox` package above was recognized because it was signed by Red Hat and I ran it on a Fedora installation. The Fedora distribution includes several public keys that are used by Red Hat to sign the packages that it makes available. These are copied to the hard drive when you install the distribution. If you download an RPM, and the signature can be verified using one of these keys, you can be assured that the package is the same one that is provided by Red Hat and not infected with any malware. The public key for the dpkg RPM was not found because the RPM came from a Mandrake distribution, so the public key is not available on my Fedora installation. I'll have to track that key down myself.

If you download a package that has an invalid signature or requires an unknown public key, like the `dpkg` package above, `rpm` will warn you when you install it. Unfortunately, even with an unauthenticated signature, `rpm` version 4.3.2 lets you install the package anyway without any challenge. This is unfortunate, because your system is vulnerable during the install process when you are running scripts as root. GPG does not try to distinguish between a forged key and a missing public key. It cannot. Just as with real signatures, two people can have the same name but don't have the same signature, but that doesn't make one of them a forger. Likewise, two people with the same name will have unique public keys. The only thing GPG will tell you when it can't authenticate a signature is that it does not have a public key for it.

Tracking Down a Missing Public Key

There are several resources on the Web for tracking down GPG public keys, but usually, it's best to go to the source. In this example, I am missing a public key from the Mandrake distribution. A simple query confirms this:

```
$ rpm -qip dpkg-1.10.21-1mdk.i586.rpm
Name         : dpkg
Version      : 1.10.21              Vendor: Mandrakesoft
Release      : 1mdk                 Build Date: Thu May 20 07:03:20 2004

Host: n1.mandrakesoft.com
Packager     : Michael Scherer <misc@mandrake.org>
URL          : http://packages.debian.org/unstable/base/dpkg.html
Summary      : Package maintenance system for Debian
```

There are a few clues here for finding a trusted public key. The URLs mandrakesoft.com and mandrake.org are good starting points. The package shows that it was created in 2004, which is a long time ago in Internet years. Since Mandrake became Mandriva, these sites have been taken offline. This is not going to be easy. I need one more piece of information to know what I am looking for: the key ID.

```
$ rpm --checksig dpkg-1.10.21-1mdk.i586.rpm
dpkg-1.10.21-1mdk.i586.rpm: ...
 ... (GPG) NOT OK (MISSING KEYS: GPG 78d019f5)
```

This shows me the ID that I am looking for.

The next stop is the Mandriva Web page. A Google search takes me to http://mandriva.com. A site search for *public keys* shows me some hashes and a single public key, which is not the one I want. A few more searches turn up no leads. It looks as though Mandriva's Web page is a dead end.

Next, I try a Google search for *public keys*, and this turns up several sites that maintain public keys. After some trial and error, I finally find the key at www.keys.pgp.net by doing a key search for *0x78d019f5*, which turns up the missing key.

```
Search results for '0x78d019f5'

Type bits/keyID    cr. time    exp time    key expir

pub  1024D/78D019F5 2003-12-10

uid MandrakeContrib <cooker@linux-mandrake.com>
sig  sig3  78D019F5 2003-12-10 _____ _____   [selfsig]
sig  sig3  70771FF3 2003-12-10 _____ _____   Mandrake Linux
<mandrake@mandrakesoft.com>
```

```
sig  sig3  26752624 2003-12-10 _____ _____ MandrakeCooker <cooker@linux-
mandrake.com>
sig  sig3  45D5857E 2004-09-22 _____ _____ Fabio Pasquarelli (Lavorro)
<fabiopasquarelli@tin.it>
sig  sig3  17A0F9A0 2004-09-22 _____ _____ Fafo (Personale)
<rec.r96@tin.it>

sub  1024g/4EE127FA 2003-12-10
sig  sbind  78D019F5 2003-12-10 _____ _____ []
```

A search for *Mandrake* also turns up this key in a list of several other Mandrake keys. Clicking the hyperlinked 78D019F5 takes me to the PGP key, which is plain text. To import this key, I must save this to a file named 78D019F5.txt, and I can import it to the RPM keyring as follows:

```
rpm --import 78D019F5.txt
```

If the text contains a valid public key, I should see no errors. Finally, I can check the validity of the original package as follows:

```
rpm --checksig dpkg-1.10.21-1mdk.i586.rpm
dpkg-1.10.21-1mdk.i586.rpm: (sha1) dsa sha1 md5 gpg OK
```

The understated "gpg OK" is what I'm looking for.

Before I leave this topic, I'll discuss trust. I got the signature from the pgp.net domain. I am trusting that the proprietors of this database have taken reasonable precautions to verify that the public key came from a legitimate source. In the end, it all comes down to trust.

Be wary of any package that is signed but has a signature that your system doesn't recognize (that is, it doesn't have a public key for it). If you need to search for a public key, get it from a different site from the one where you got the RPM—one that is not referenced by that site. You shouldn't trust any keys from a site that the provider points you to, because those sites could be shams. This is common sense. You wouldn't hire a contractor just because he has a license hanging on the wall; you need to check his credentials for yourself. Likewise, you shouldn't trust his references, either; for all you know, they're his partners and family members.

1.6.5   When You Can't Authenticate a Package

Users should think twice before installing any package that isn't authenticated, but I'm willing to admit that I'm not religious about this when it comes to installing packages on my old clunker hobby PC. It's a different story when you are deploying packages across a large enterprise. With my clunker, there's not much to lose if I get burned, but in a large enterprise, the result could be disastrous.

Sometimes, the author doesn't provide any authentication information. The odds of getting a Trojan Linux package these days are fairly low, but that can change. Here are some practical steps you can take when you can't authenticate a package with a signature:

- Build from source.

  This is not foolproof, as mentioned in the discussion of the OpenSSH incident earlier in this chapter. Nevertheless, understand that building from source may be easy, or it could be difficult. Every project is different, and you won't know until you try. The initial download usually is small enough, but give yourself a deadline, after which you will resort to other means. Simply trying to build an unfamiliar project can become a time vacuum as you search for all the required development packages. I discuss building from source in detail in Chapter 2.

- Inspect the install scripts.

  These are the scripts that pose the most immediate danger, because they run with root privileges when you install the package, before you ever run any of the installed software. I'll discuss how to do this for each package format.

- Inspect the contents.

  Look at the binary files that are being installed. A typical user application should not need binaries in /usr/sbin or /sbin, because these directories are reserved for system daemons and system administration tools. Be wary of any files with the setuid or setgid bit set, especially if they are owned by root. These files can execute with the permissions of the file owner, which may be a hiding place for malware. Only a few system programs need this capability; anything else is suspicious.

Whatever technique you choose, keep in mind that this is still a matter of trust. Instead of trusting an authenticated source, you are trusting your skills at identifying malware by inspection.

1.7   Inspecting Package Contents

There are a few basic things you may want to inspect in any package you download before installing it. Most package formats consist of the following key pieces:

- An archive of files that will be installed on your system. This may be in `tar` format, `cpio` format, or something else.

- Scripts that will execute during the installation and removal of the package.

- Dependency information for the install tool to determine whether your system meets the requirements for this package.

- Some textual information about the package itself.

The amount of descriptive information in a package is largely up to the person packaging the file. Typically, it will include some basic information about the author, the date of packaging, and the licensing terms. A thoughtful packager will include some information about what the software actually does, but too often, this is not the case.

Package dependencies may be extensive, or they may be sparse or nonexistent. Packages for Slackware-based distributions, for example, don't have any dependency information in them. You install the package and cross your fingers as to whether it's going to work. RPM is at the other extreme. When you're building an RPM package, the tools can automatically detect dependencies that will be listed in the package. The packager can also opt to specify exact dependencies or to specify no dependencies at all (à la Slackware).

Each package format provides some method of running scripts at installation and removal time. Installation scripts should be scrutinized closely. Even if you don't suspect malware, an immature project may contain some defective install scripts that could damage your system. If the script is too complex for you to understand, I recommend that you find some way to authenticate the package before installing it.

Installation scripts usually are broken down into these categories:

- **Preinstall**—This script is run before any data is unpacked from the archive.

- **Postinstall**—This script is run after the data is unpacked from the archive. Typically, these scripts will do minor tasks to customize the installation, such as patching or creating configuration files.

- **Preuninstall**—This script will run when you choose to remove the package but before any files are removed from the system.

- **Postuninstall**—This script runs after the primary files have been removed from the system.

The textual information that comes with a package varies from one format to the next. Often, it contains additional authenticating information, such as a project page on SourceForge.net. Dependency information contained in the package also varies from one package format to the next. This may be names of other packages or names of executable programs that the package requires.

1.7.1   How to Inspect Packages

You probably will need to inspect a package both before and after it is installed. Before it is installed, you will be inspecting a package file, which may have any legitimate Linux filename. The filename usually, but not always, is derived from the *official* package name—that is, the name that will show up in the package database after it is installed. The package name is encoded inside the package file and should be visible with a basic package file query. Although package creators are careful to include the package name as part of the filename, don't assume that the filename and the package name are the same. After the package is installed, it can be referred to only by the name specified inside the package file, so querying a package file for its official name is a good first query. You may be installing a gcc compiler RPM, for example, but for some reason, the file was named foo.rpm. You can query the contents of this RPM file with

```
$ rpm -qip foo.rpm
```

but after you install it, the same query becomes

```
$ rpm -qi gcc
```

The rpm command normally queries the RPM database, but the -p option specifies that a package *file* is the target of the query. The same package can have any filename, but when it's installed in the database, it has only one name.

As mentioned, the basic information contained in a package includes things such as its name, version, author, copyright, and dependencies. Additional information includes the list of files to be installed, as well as any scripts that will run during install and removal. You usually are interested in these things before you install the package. Table 1-10 shows a list of basic queries for both RPM and Debian package files.

There are several reasons why you might want to query the package database. You may want to list all the packages that are installed in the system, for example, or you may want to know what version of a particular package is installed. A useful thing to do is verify the contents of an installed package to make sure that none of the files has been tampered with since installation. The query format changes slightly on installed packages versus package files. Some examples are shown in Table 1-11.

TABLE 1-10   Queries on Package Files

Query	RPM	Debian
Basic information	rpm -qpi filename	dpkg -s filename
List of files to be installed	rpm -qpl filename	dpkg -L filename
Dump install/uninstall scripts	rpm -qp -scripts filename	dpkg -e
Verify authentication information	rpm --checksig filename	not available
Show what other packages this package requires	rpm -qp --requires filename	dpkg -I
Show what package this file provides (for example, the name and version as they will appear in the database)	rpm -qp --provides filename	dpkg -I

TABLE 1-11   Queries of Installed Packages

Query	RPM	Debian
Basic information about a particular package	rpm -qi name	dpkg -s name
List all the packages installed	rpm -qa	dpkg --list
List all files installed by a particular package	rpm -ql name	dpkg -L name

continues

TABLE 1-11   *Continued*

Query	RPM	Debian

Verify files installed by a particular package	`rpm -V name`	`cd /;`
		`md5sum -c <`
		`/var/lib/dpkg/info/name.md5sums`

Which package does this file belong to?	`rpm -qf filename`	`dpkg -S filename`
What version of package X is currently installed?	`rpm -q X`	`dpkg-query -W X`

1.7.2   A Closer Look at RPM Packages

RPM is one of the most comprehensive package formats you are likely to find in Linux. An RPM package can contain a great deal of information, but it can be difficult to extract. To help you get at this additional data, the `rpm` tool comes with a `--queryformat` option (`--qf` for short). Most of the tags used by the `--qf` option are not documented in the manual, but you can get a list of them by typing

```
$ rpm --querytags
HEADERIMAGE
HEADERSIGNATURES
HEADERIMMUTABLE
HEADERREGIONS
HEADERI18NTABLE
SIGSIZE
SIGPGP
SIGMD5
SIGGPG
PUBKEYS
...
```

Note that query tags are case insensitive, although the output from `rpm` lists them all in uppercase. If you want to get an idea of who provides the packages for your distribution, for example, try this query:

```
$ rpm -qa --qf '%{vendor}' | sort | uniq -c
      1 Adobe Systems, Incorporated
     12 (none)
      1 RealNetworks, Inc
    838 Red Hat, Inc.
      1 Sun Microsystems, Inc.
```

This query on my Fedora Core 3 system shows that 838 packages are provided by Red Hat, and 12 are provided by unidentified sources. It turns out that the unidentified packages are actually GPG public keys. Each public key shows up as a separate package in the database, and typically, these have no "vendor" ID.

Another useful query is to check the install scripts that come with an RPM package. An example is shown below:

```
$ rpm -qp --scripts gawk-3.1.3-9.i386.rpm

postinstall scriptlet (through /bin/sh):
if [ -f /usr/share/info/gawk.info.gz ]; then
    /sbin/install-info /usr/share/info/gawk.info.gz
/usr/share/info/dir
fi
preuninstall scriptlet (through /bin/sh):
if [ $1 = 0 -a -f /usr/share/info/gawk.info.gz ]; then
    /sbin/install-info --delete /usr/share/info/gawk.info.gz
/usr/share/info/dirfi
```

The output includes a single line identifying the purpose of the script (post-install, etc.) and the type of script (for example, /bin/sh). This allows you to inspect the scripts visually before they execute.

You can get at the contents of the archive file in an RPM by using a command called rpm2cpio. This converts any RPM package file you give it to a cpio archive, which is what the RPM format uses internally. cpio is an archive format like tar with a slightly different syntax. The output of rpm2cpio goes to stdout by default. This is how cpio normally works, unlike tar. To extract the files in an RPM to the current directory without installing the package, use the following command:

```
rpm2cpio filename.rpm | cpio -i --no-absolute-filenames
```

Notice that I use the --no-absolute-filenames option to cpio to ensure that I don't clobber any valuable system files. In fact, RPM packages don't allow absolute filenames in the cpio archive. In any case, you can never be too safe.

1.7.3 A Closer Look at Debian Packages

Debian packages have a simpler format than RPM, and the dpkg tool lacks many of the features that the rpm utility has. As a result, this requires some more effort on your part to inspect these packages. A Debian package filename typically has a .deb extension, although it is actually an archive created with the ar program. You can inspect the contents of a Debian package with the `ar` command, but that doesn't tell you much. For example:

```
$ ar -t cron_3.0pl1-72_i386.deb
debian-binary
control.tar.gz
data.tar.gz
```

The file named `debian-binary` contains a single line of ASCII text indicating the version of the format used for the package. The file named `control.tar.gz` is a compressed tar archive that contains the install scripts as well as some other useful information. The file named `data.tar.gz` file is a compressed tar archive that contains the program install files. To extract these files for further inspection, use the `ar` command:

```
$ ar -x filename.deb
```

Now let's look at some more details from the sample file above. The file `data.tar.gz` contains the files required for the program to operate. Sometimes, you can just extract these files and have a working installation, but I don't recommend it. In this example, the list looks like the following:

```
$ tar -tzf data.tar.gz
./
./usr/
./usr/bin/
./usr/bin/crontab
./usr/sbin/
./usr/sbin/cron
./usr/sbin/checksecurity
./usr/share/
./usr/share/man/
./usr/share/man/man1/
...
```

The `control.tar.gz` file contains more files required for package installation, removal, and maintenance. You can extract these files by using the `dpkg` command with the `-e` option, for example:

```
$ dpkg -e cron_3.0pl1-72_i386.deb
$ ls ./DEBIAN/*
./DEBIAN/conffiles
./DEBIAN/control
./DEBIAN/md5sums
./DEBIAN/postinst
```

```
./DEBIAN/postrm
./DEBIAN/preinst
./DEBIAN/prerm
```

As you might have guessed, the `preinst` and `postinst` files are the preinstall and postinstall scripts described earlier in this chapter. Likewise, the `prerm` and `postrm` files are the preuninstall and postuninstall scripts, respectively.

The `md5sums` file contains the list of MD5 hashes that can be used to check the integrity of the files in `data.tar.gz`. This file can be used as input to the `md5sum` program, but these hashes are verification only—not authentication. You can use the `md5sums` file to verify that the package has not been corrupted before you install it and to verify that the installed files were not tampered with after installation, but it tells you nothing about the authenticity of the source of the files. Nevertheless, periodically verifying the contents of an installed package via its `md5sums` is a good idea.

The `md5sums` file does not include all the files that are installed, because often, a package requires configuration files that are intended to be modified after installation. It is expected that these files will *not* match the original contents after installation. Such files are excluded from checking by listing them in `conffiles`. Any file listed in `conffiles` is ignored when the integrity of the installation is checked.

1.8   Keeping Packages up to Date

A package updater helps take some of the work out of tracking down package files and their dependencies one by one. Suppose that you want to install package X, but it requires three other packages that you don't have installed. You will have to install these three packages before you can install package X. But it's also possible that these packages require other packages you don't have, and those in turn could require others, and so on, and so on.

This is where package updaters come in handy. With a package updater, you simply request package X; the tool determines what other packages are required to install the package and then downloads and installs those as well.

The package updater works by keeping a list of package repositories that it can search when you request a package. Typically, these repositories reside on the Internet and are maintained by the distributor (for example, Red Hat). The repository is a distributor's way of making fixes and security updates available, but they usually include general updates as well.

A repository can also reside on a local file system, such as a CD or another computer located inside your firewall, which is useful if you have to maintain many machines on a LAN. You can retrieve required packages from the Internet and make them available internally for faster updating of your client machines, for example.

For Debian-based distributions, the tool of choice is Apt, which stands for *Advanced Package Tool.* This is actually a set of command-line tools used to maintain the packages in your distribution. Apt has been ported for use on RPM-based distributions. It remains to be seen whether Apt will become the preferred tool for package management for RPM users.

For RPM-based distributions, two major tools are worth mentioning. The first is up2date, which is designed by Red Hat for its Enterprise Server and Fedora Core distributions. The other is yum, which stands for Yellowdog Updater Modified.[5]

Some claim that Apt and yum can upgrade an entire installation—for example, take it from Red Hat 8.0 to Red Hat 9.0 without having to reinstall the OS. I would be extremely hesitant before trying this myself.[6]

Don't expect the package updater to do everything you need. Because package updaters rely on a select few repositories to search for packages, you can expect your choices of software and versions to be somewhat limited. Official repositories tend to favor established tools with stable versions. They may have a bias for particular tools or versions, based on the distributions they support or on the whims of the repository's maintainers. Don't believe anyone who says, "If it's not in my repository, you don't need it." There is a lot of good work going on that is not part of a distribution or repository. If you want to work with the latest bleeding-edge version of a package, or to try something new or unusual, you probably will have to bypass the package updater.

If you do some searching, you are likely to find bug reports and complaints about every package updater. Trying to keep hundreds of interdependent software packages up to date and functioning is an extremely complicated task. Bugs are unavoidable while developers gain more experience with the problem. The good news is that there is a great deal of activity in this area, so things can only get better with time.

1.8.1   Apt: Advanced Package Tool

Apt is one of the more mature tools for managing packages in Debian distributions and is now available for RPM distributions. An excellent feature of Apt is that

---

5. It was called yup when it was part of the Yellowdog distribution for PowerPC, but since then, it has been adapted by other RPM-based distributions and modified.
6. Possible side effects include headaches, ear infections, anxiety, nausea, and vomiting.

unlike the basic `dpkg` tool, Apt will automatically authenticate packages signed with GPG signatures. Remember that RPM already supports GPG signatures. Furthermore, Apt will check with you before installing a package that it cannot authenticate, so you don't need to worry about repositories being compromised and loaded with Trojan-horse packages.

Just like `dpkg`, Apt is not a single command but a set of commands. The two most commonly used Apt commands are `apt-get` and `apt-cache`. To get started, you probably will be interested in the `apt-get` command. This is the workhorse that will retrieve and install packages for you. The `apt-cache` command allows you to query the list of available packages downloaded to the local cache, which is faster than repeatedly querying repositories on the Internet. This list includes all available packages, including those you have not installed as well as updates to what you have installed.

The `apt-key` command allows you to add public signatures from a trusted source to your database, as well as to inspect the ones you already have. This allows you to authenticate packages that are signed by that source. The `apt-setup` command allows you to specify the preferred repositories that Apt should search when looking for packages. On my Ubuntu distribution, `aptsetup` allows only Ubuntu mirrors; Debian repositories are not allowed. In this case, you can still edit the `/etc/apt/sources.list` file by hand to include more agnostic repositories. `/etc/apt/sources.list` can point to sites on the Internet or to local directories on your system or on your LAN. The only thing Apt requires is that the files be available via a URL.

1.8.2   Yum: Yellowdog Updater Modified

Yum currently is the tool of choice for RPM-based systems. It is a command-line utility that functions much like Apt. Like Apt, Yum keeps a cache containing information about available packages. Unlike Apt, yum queries each repository every time it runs by default. This is much more time consuming than using a cache like Apt.

The `yum` command is used to install, query, and update packages. The `-C` option tells `yum` to use the cache for the initial request. If yum decides to install software based on the request, it will update the cache before doing so.

With Yum, authentication is optional via GPG signatures. This is controlled for each repository via the configuration files in `/etc/yum.conf` and `/etc/yum.repos.d`. If the flag `gpgcheck=1` is set, the `yum` command will not install unauthenticated packages. Just as with Apt, you can create your own repository in a directory anywhere that can be accessed via a URL.

The options for the `yum` command are fairly intuitive. To show all the packages currently installed that have updates available, for example, the command is

```
$ yum list updates
```

This produces a simple list of packages that are available for update. The closest equivalent for Apt is the less intuitive `apt-get --dry-run -u dist-upgrade`, which produces a lot of cluttered additional output.

1.8.3 Synaptic: The GUI Front End for APT

Synaptic isn't even at version 1.0 at this writing, yet it is an extremely useful GUI for maintaining packages via Apt. On my Ubuntu machine, 861 packages are installed as I write this. At any given time, dozens of these are available for update. This is a task that cries out for a GUI. Synaptic groups packages by category so that you can easily locate and inspect updates for the software you use the most. As a developer, you probably want to know when gcc goes from version 3.3 to 3.4, but perhaps you don't care that FreeCell has been updated from version 1.0.1 to version 1.0.2. You can also use the categories to look for software that may be new or for something you just never installed. As a software developer, I regularly browse the development tools to see whether any cool new projects are available. You can see an example of Synaptic in action in Figure 1-2.

Like Apt, Synaptic will not install an unauthenticated package without your explicit consent. One nice feature of Synaptic is that it is easy to see the potential consequences of my actions before having to endure a long wait while the tool downloads dozens of packages I didn't ask for. If I browse to the Games and Amusements section, and select `kasteroids` for installation, there is a little problem: Ubuntu uses Gnome by default, and `kasteroids` is a KDE application. So if I want to install `kasteroids`, I will need to install ten more packages as well. Although Synaptic will gladly install these packages for me, it warns me first that there are ten more packages required to install, requiring several megabytes to download. So now I know that if I'm in a hurry, it's probably not a good idea to install `kasteroids` right now.

Unfortunately, there is no way to identify which package updates include security fixes. In general, how do you know whether you really want to upgrade `gcalctool` from version 5.5.41-0 to 5.5.41-1? Intuitively, this looks like a minor change, maybe a bug fix, but is it a security fix? Who knows? This is something that the open source community should deal with eventually.

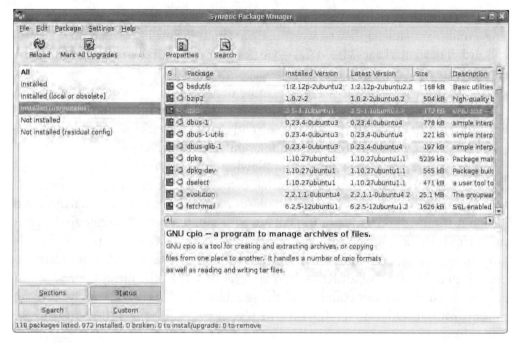

FIGURE 1-2   An Example of the Synaptic GUI

Another useful feature is the filter, which allows you to query the volumes of update data you are presented with so that you can find the updates you are interested in. Synaptic is still early in development (version 0.56 at this writing), and this feature still needs work. Currently, there is no way to filter out major from minor changes, for example. A minor change most likely includes bug fixes and security fixes; major changes typically include new features.

Synaptic is still very useful and should be the GUI of choice for Debian-based systems. It could become popular on RPM-based distributions as well. Currently, very few RPM repositories are compatible with Apt and Synaptic.

1.8.4   up2date: The Red Hat Package Updater

Red Hat provides the `up2date` GUI for use with Yum repositories. This tool can operate from the command line as well. With no options, `up2date` presents a list of files available for update, which can number in the hundreds, and asks you to select which ones to update from this list.

The default output does not include packages that you don't have installed, so if a new tool is available, up2date won't tell you about it. Just like Synaptic, up2date will authenticate packages via GPG signatures and won't install packages that it can't authenticate.

The GUI for up2date leaves much to be desired. The function is minimal, in that it only updates existing packages; it does not show you new ones, and it does not allow you to browse and uninstall currently installed packages. This is a shame, because on the command line, it is quite useful and intuitive.

up2date tries to be a chameleon by allowing access to Yum, Apt, and up2date repositories. The default configuration that comes with the Fedora Core 4 distribution directs you to a comprehensive list of Yum repositories. This seems like a good idea, but it causes your updates to take longer—much longer. A better approach is to track down a few repositories yourself and add them directly to the file /etc/sysconfig/rhn/sources. A nice feature of up2date is that you can also point it to a directory full of RPMs and let it figure out all the messy dependencies. As long as your directory contains all the required RPMs, it works nicely. You can mount your installation DVD on /mnt/dvd and add the following line to /etc/sysconfig/rhn/sources:

```
dir fc-dvd /mnt/dvd/Fedora/RPMS
```

Now you can install packages from your CD and let up2date worry about the dependencies. From the command line, an example might look like this:

```
$ up2date --install gcc
```

I have not had any luck using the up2date GUI. I once thought I would try up2date on my Fedora Core 3 system to update a handful of carefully selected packages from the list of 200 or more that were available for update. I clicked Ok, and the GUI went to sleep to ponder my selections over my broadband connection. Unresponsive, and with no indication of any progress, it looked like the tool was stuck. About 15 minutes later, the tool came back and told me that I had the wrong kernel for two of the packages; therefore, none of my selected packages would be updated. Thank you; come again!

One of the main reasons for the slowness appeared to be that /etc/syscsonfig/rhn/sources pointed to the yum repositories located in

/etc/yum.repos.d, which contained about six repository entries, each with a mirror list. The mirror list, which resides on the repository host, appears to slow the tool to a crawl. One list numbered 65 mirrors! It looks as though the GUI is using this information very inefficiently, whereas specific command-line interactions don't. So before you get discouraged using up2date, try the command line.

1.9 Summary

This chapter covered some of the basics of open source software. Specifically, I looked at the various distribution formats and tools to use them. I discussed at length the archive file, which is at the core of every distribution format and in some cases *is* the distribution format.

I reviewed some of the basic security measures that are available to ensure that you do not download malware when you look for software. I discussed the basics of authentication and the common-sense measures you can take to protect yourself.

Finally, I looked at some of the tools that are built on top of the packaging tools. These are tools to manage all the packages in the system. Each has advantages and drawbacks.

1.9.1 Tools Used in This Chapter

- dpkg—the main tool used to install and query packages in the Debian package format used by the Debian distribution and its derivatives, such as Ubuntu.

- gpg—the GNU encryption and signing tool. This is a general-purpose tool that is used with packages to enhance security with digital signatures.

- gzip, bzip2—GNU compression utilities, most often used in conjunction with archive files.

- rpm—the main tool for installing and querying software packaged in the Red Hat Package Manager (RPM) format. In addition to Red Hat, RPM is used by Suse and other distributions.

- tar, cpio, ar—the UNIX archive tools that are at the core of most package formats.

1.9.2   Online References

- www.debian.org—the home page of the Debian distribution, including a FAQ that discusses the packaging format, among other things

- www.gnupg.org—the home page of the GNU Privacy Guard project, which created the gpg tool

- www.pgp.net—a repository of public keys used by gpg and others

- www.rpm.org—the home page of the RPM project

Chapter 2

Building from Source

2.1 Introduction

In this chapter, I discuss the tools used to build software as well as the things you need to know to build software distributed in source code form. Despite its shortcomings, the make program is still the core tool used to build Linux software. Every developer has had at least some exposure to the make program, but I cover some important details that not every developer knows.

I look at how GNU source is distributed with the GNU build tools, which are used on many other open source projects. I also touch on some emerging build environments that are emerging as alternatives to make.

I'll look at some common errors and warnings you will encounter while working with build tools.

2.2 Build Tools

Developing software is an iterative process. You edit source code, compile, run the code, find some bugs, and start all over again. Although this is not an efficient process, your build tools should make it as efficient as possible. The `make` program is the workhorse of the Linux build environment. It was the first tool to support the iterative build process used by software developers. Although many programmers hate it, to date, there has been no compelling alternative to `make`. As a result, every Linux programmer should be intimately familiar with it.

2.2.1   Background

In its original form, `make` is a rather primitive tool. The UNIX version of `make` has no support for conditional constructs and does not support any language to speak of. `make` relies instead on a few simple expression types that control its interaction with the shell. During the build, the shell does the real work. `make` is just a supervisor.

The simplicity of `make` is both a feature and a drawback. The lack of any real scripting ability is a problem for developers who want to deploy common source code to multiple platforms. As a result, you sometimes see source distributions that contain several `Makefiles`—one for each target. Besides being messy and inelegant, it's a maintenance headache.

Several variants of `make` have sprouted up over the years to address its shortcomings. These keep the basic `make` syntax but often add keywords to support features that are missing. Unfortunately, there is no guarantee that a script built for one `make` variant will work on another `make` variant, so this is a disincentive for developers to switch to a new flavor of `make`. GNU `make` is one of these variants—which, being the version of `make` on Linux, has a lot going for it. I will look at some of GNU `make`'s features in detail.

There are also tools that have been built on top of `make` to work around its shortcomings. These tools generate `Makefiles` from a higher-level description of the project.

2.2.1.1   Imake

One of the first tools developed to generate `Makefiles` is the `imake` program. `imake` came out of the X Window project as a way to build X Window source on various UNIX platforms. It uses the C preprocessor to parse its build script (called an `imakefile`) and generates a `Makefile` for use by `make`. This enhances portability by encapsulating system-specific gobbledygook in preprocessor macros and conditional constructs. A side benefit is that the `imakefiles` are concise and simple.

imake never really caught on, however, and has shortcomings of its own. One of these is the fact that each build target requires a detailed set of macros. If your target system does not have a set of these descriptions, you can't use imake. This prevents projects using imake from being deployed on diverse and cutting-edge systems.

Although it worked well for building X Window on UNIX systems, the only place you are likely to encounter an imakefile today is in a legacy X Window project.

2.2.1.2   GNU Build Tools

Seeking a portable way to build software on various architectures, the GNU Project created its own suite of build tools to enhance the make program. The approach is similar to imake except that instead of the C preprocessor, the GNU build tools use the m4 program, which has more capabilities than the C preprocessor. The GNU build tools are used to create source distributions that can be built on a wide variety of machines. An individual building the project from a source distribution needs only a working shell and make program. The GNU build tools have become the de facto standard for distributing source.

Although these tools make life easy for the open source consumer, they are difficult for the developers who create the distributions. For one thing, the m4 syntax is unfamiliar to most programmers, and syntax errors are common. In addition, the tools continue to evolve and mature as new features are added, and some features break along the way.

Another drawback to the GNU build system (as well as imake) is that it adds an extra step to the build process. With the GNU build tools in particular, this configuration step can consume more time than the build itself. This has inspired some developers to think of better ways to build source.

2.2.1.3   Alternative Approaches

Alternative build tools are at a disadvantage, because most people don't have the patience to deal with a build tool that is still under development. A developer has enough to worry about without dealing with the aggravation of bugs in his build tool or wondering whether his build scripts will work with the next release of the tool. Using the GNU build tools as the benchmark, any alternative should be simpler to use and as fast or faster.

One project that is up to the challenge is Cons.[1] Cons is based on Perl,[2] which is where its build scripts borrow their syntax. So it's easier to use than the GNU build tools, because a developer is more likely to be familiar with Perl. It replaces all the GNU build tools, and the sundry files that are associated with them, with a single file used by a single tool in a single step. A disadvantage of this approach is that the time penalty incurred by the `configure` stage of a GNU build is incurred every single time you run the build. For someone downloading the source, who will only build it once, this is no big deal. But for a developer who has to build repeatedly, it is a problem. Another drawback is that the individuals downloading the source distribution must have the correct version of Perl installed, as well as the appropriate Cons tool. This forced developers to stick with older versions of Perl, which can be difficult. Although Cons introduced some good ideas, it never really caught on, and the project appears to be dead today.

Some programmers decided that the ideas behind Cons were solid, but that shortcomings of Perl were holding it back. They took the same design and implemented it in Python.[3] This is Scons.[4] Python has some advantages over Perl, including the fact that it is object-oriented by design and is more strongly typed. Although Python is in its second major version as of this writing, the basic syntax and grammar are virtually unchanged from the original, so writing backward-compatible scripts is not as painful as it is in Perl. Scons developers target Python 1.5, which covers a very wide audience, so Python compatibility is not a big issue. Scons suffers from the same time penalty as Cons. Although there are many favorable reviews of Scons, and a handful of projects use it in their source distributions, it has yet to catch on in a big way.

Perhaps an alternative to `make` will catch on, but until then, it behooves you to understand `make`.

2.2.2   Understanding make

`make` is an excellent tool to enhance your productivity. A well-written `Makefile` can make a huge difference in the speed of your development. Unfortunately, many developers have learned to use `make` through trial and error without ever reading

---

1. *Cons* (www.gnu.org/software/cons/dev/cons.html) is short for *Construction System*.
2. www.perl.org
3. www.python.org
4. www.scons.org

any documentation. These individuals rely a great deal on intuition and luck, and that shows in their `Makefiles`. Chances are that you are one of them, so I will start with some basics and work into some very useful GNU extensions.

2.2.2.1   Makefile Basics: Rules and Dependencies

Unlike traditional scripts, which execute commands sequentially, `Makefiles` contain a mixture of rules and instructions. `Makefile` rules have the following very simple form:

```
target: prerequisite
    commands
```

The rule asserts a dependency that says that the target depends on the prerequisite. In the simplest form, the target consists of a single filename, and the prerequisite contains one or more filenames. If the target is older than any of its prerequisites, the commands associated with the rule are executed. Typically, the commands contain instructions to build the target. A trivial example looks like the following:

```
foo: foo.c
    gcc -o foo foo.c
```

Here, `foo` is the target, and `foo.c` is the prerequisite. If `foo.c` is newer than `foo`, or if `foo` doesn't exist, `make` executes the command `gcc -o foo foo.c`. If `foo` is newer than `foo.c`, nothing happens. This is how `make` saves you time—by not building targets that don't need to be built.

In a more complicated example, the prerequisite of one rule can be the target in another rule. In that case, those other dependencies must be evaluated before the current dependency is evaluated. Consider this contrived example:

```
# Rule 1
program: object.o
        gcc -o program object.o

# Rule 2
source.c:
        echo 'main() {}' > $@

# Rule 3
object.o: source.c
        gcc -c source.c -o $@

# Rule 4
program2: program2.c
        gcc -o program2 program2.c
```

Starting with an empty directory, if you run make with no arguments, you will see the following output:

```
$ make
echo 'main() {}' > source.c
gcc -c source.c -o object.o
gcc -o program object.o
```

make evaluates the first rule it encounters in the Makefile and stops when the dependency is satisfied. Other rules are evaluated only if they are required to satisfy rule 1. The parsing takes place something like this:

- **rule 1:** program requires object.o.

  - object.o is the target of rule 3; evaluate rule 3 before checking the file date.

  - If object.o is newer than program, build program with gcc.

- **rule 3:** object.o requires source.c.

  - source.c is the target of rule 2; evaluate rule 2 before checking the file date.

  - If source.c is newer than object.o, build object.o with gcc.

- **rule 2:** source.c doesn't have any prerequisites.

  - If source.c doesn't exist, build it with an echo command.

Notice that the dependencies determine the order in which the commands execute. Other than the first rule, the order of the rules in the Makefile have no impact. We could, for example, swap the order of rules 2 and 3 in the Makefile, and it will make no difference in the behavior.

Notice also that rule 4 has no impact on the build. When the target for the first rule is determined to be up to date, make stops. Because this does not need anything from rule 4, program2 is never built, and program2.c is not needed. That doesn't mean that rule 4 is superfluous or useless. You could just as easily type make program2 to tell make to evaluate rule 4. Makefile rules can be independent of one another and still be useful.

make can also build specific targets in the Makefile, which allows you to bypass the default rule. This technique is the preferred way to build a single object in a project during development, for example. Suppose that you've just modified `program2.c` and want to see whether it compiles without warnings. You could type

```
$ make program2.o
```

Assuming the dependencies for `program2.o` are straightforward, this compiles `program2.c` and nothing else.

`make` can also build so called *pseudotargets*, which are targets that do not represent filenames. A pseudotarget can have any arbitrary name, but there are conventions that are commonly followed. A common convention, for example, is to use the pseudotarget `all` as the first rule in a `Makefile`. To understand the need for pseudotargets, consider this example, in which you have two programs you want to build as part of your `Makefile`:

```
program1: a.o b.o
    gcc -o program1 a.o b.o

program2: c.o d.o
    gcc -o program2 c.o d.o
```

If you ran `make` with no arguments, it would build `program1` and stop. To get around this, you could require the user to specify both programs on the command line, as follows:

```
$ make program1 program2
```

This works, but being able to run `make` with no arguments is a nice way to make your code easy to build. To fix this, add a pseudotarget named `all` as the first rule in the `Makefile` with `program1` and `program2` as the prerequisites, as follows:

```
all: program1 program2

program1: a.o b.o
    gcc -o program1 a.o b.o

program2: c.o d.o
    gcc -o program2 c.o d.o
```

This allows you to type `make` or `make all`, which will build both `program1` and `program2`. Although `all` is a common convention, you could have called your pseudotarget `fred` or anything else. As long as it's the first target, it will be evaluated when you run `make` with no arguments. Because it is a pseudotarget, the name of the target is irrelevant.

Typically, no commands are associated with a rule that contains a pseudotarget, and the name of the pseudotarget is chosen so that it doesn't conflict with any of the files in the build. Just in case, GNU make has a built-in pseudotarget that you can use to give make a clue, as follows:

```
.PHONY: all
```

This tells make not to search for a file named all and to assume that this target is always obsolete.

2.2.2.2 Makefile Basics: Defining Variables

make allows build options to be specified using variables. The syntax for defining a variable is straightforward:

```
VAR = value
VAR := value
```

The two types of definitions are equivalent except that the := form allows variables to reference themselves without recursion. This comes up when you want to append text to a variable:

```
VAR = value

# Wrong!  Causes infinite recursion
VAR = $(VAR) more

# Okay, the := prevents recursion
VAR := $(VAR) more

# A GNU extension that does the same thing
VAR = value
VAR += more
```

GNU make allows an alternative syntax for defining variables using two keywords: define and endef. The GNU equivalent syntax looks like the following:

```
define VAR
value
endef
```

The newlines before and after the keywords are required and are not part of the variable definition.

The convention for variable names is to use uppercase letters, although this is not required. The value of the variable may contain any ASCII text, but the text is stored literally and has no meaning until it is used in context. One common pattern, for example, is to use backticks to switch the contents of the variable with the output from a shell command. The backticks are a shell trick and have no special meaning inside the `Makefile`, so you are not assigning the variable with the contents of a shell command. Instead, the variable contains literal text that can be passed to the shell. The following variable works as expected because it's used in the shell:

```
SOMEFILE = `date +%02d%02m%02y`.dat

all:
      @echo $(SOMEFILE)

$ make
290505.dat
```

Because the variable is used in a shell context, the backticks behave as expected, echoing today's date followed by the `.dat` extension. It's a clever trick, but it would fail miserably if you tried to use it as a prerequisite or a target. For example:

```
all: $(SOMEFILE)
      @echo $(SOMEFILE)

290505.dat:
      touch 290505.dat

$ make
make: *** No rule to make target ``date', needed by `all'.  Stop.
```

This fails because `make` isn't looking for a target named `290505.dat`. Because the backticks have no meaning to `make`, the white space in this variable makes it look like two ugly targets:

```
0        `date
1        +%02d%02m%02y`.dat
```

The first target is the one that causes `make` to fail, and this appears in the cryptic error message. GNU `make` provides a fix for this specific situation, which I will discuss later.

White Space and Newlines in Variables

make automatically removes leading and trailing white space from your variable values when you use the traditional syntax. Specifically, any spaces following the = do not appear in the variable contents, and any spaces before the newline are removed as well. By contrast, when you use the `define` syntax, leading and trailing spaces are preserved, as the following `Makefile` illustrates:

```
TRAD=                    Hello World
define DEFD
                         Hello World

endef

all:
    @echo "'$(DEFD)'"
    @echo "'$(TRAD)'"
```

The extra quotes in the `echo` command help illustrate in the output just where your spaces are (or aren't). When you run `make`, you will see the following:

```
$ make
'                        Hello World     '
'Hello World'
```

Notice that the value of `$(DEFD)` contains spaces following `Hello World`, which you can't see in the `Makefile` listing. If you want to preserve spaces with the traditional syntax, you can use the built-in empty variable `$()` as follows:

```
TRAD=$()                 Hello World    $()
```

Limiting the length of your lines keeps your `Makefile` readable. This can be difficult using the traditional syntax, because the entire declaration must appear on one line. Fortunately, `make` allows you to break long lines using the backslash character (\) as the last character on a line. But beware, because `make` compresses white space before and after the backslash. Consider the following variable declaration:

```
FOO=Hello                 \
        World
```

When used in the `Makefile`, the value of FOO will contain simply

```
Hello World
```

As you may have noticed, it is not possible to embed newlines in a variable using the traditional syntax. GNU `make` allows you to embed newlines with the `define` syntax, but beware. Variables with embedded newlines have limited uses, as the following example illustrates:

```
define FOO
Hello
World
endef
```

This particular variable is essentially useless. If you try to use it as a command, the newline will break it into two commands. So if you wanted to echo the contents to the screen, for example, it would not work. The error you get comes from the shell (not make), as follows:

```
echo Hello
Hello
World
make: World: Command not found
```

Variables with embedded newlines can be used to encapsulate sequences of independent shell commands. But because each command in a rule is its own shell, you can't write an entire script in a variable that contains embedded newlines. The following trivial bit of shell script does not work as written:

```
define FOO
if [ -e file ]; then
        echo file exists
fi
enddef

all:
        $(FOO) # Does not work!

$ make
if [ -e file ]; then
Syntax error: end of file unexpected (expecting "fi")
```

Here are some points to remember about white space in variables:

- Leading and trailing white space does not appear in variables defined using the traditional syntax.
- White space before and after a backslash is compressed when using the traditional syntax.
- Leading and trailing white space can be preserved with the traditional syntax by using the predefined $() variable.
- The define syntax preserves all white space, including newlines, but variables with newlines have limited uses.

2.2.2.3   Makefile Basics: Referencing and Modifying Variables

As you have seen, the syntax for referencing a variable requires that you enclose the name in parentheses or braces, as follows:

```
$(MACRO)          # this is most common
${MACRO}          # less common but still okay
```

Strictly speaking, this applies only to variable names with more than one letter, which ideally is the case for all your variables. A variable named with a single letter does not require parentheses or braces.

Unlike variables in a script, which change value during the course of execution, `Makefile` variables are assigned once and never change value during the course of the build.[5] This trips up many people working with `Makefiles`, who think intuitively that variable assignments take place in order in which they appear in the `Makefile` or that they have a scope and lifetime. All variables in a `Makefile` have global scope, and their lifetime is the duration of the build. A variable can be defined many times in the `Makefile`, but only the last definition in the `Makefile` determines its value. Consider the following `Makefile`:

```
FLAGS = first

all:
        @echo FLAGS=$(FLAGS)

FLAGS = second

other:
        @echo FLAGS=$(FLAGS)
```

You might think that the variable `FLAGS` will have one value for the `all` target and another value for the `other` target, but you would be wrong. The definition of `FLAGS` is fixed before any rules are evaluated. When `FLAGS` is defined, `make` will discard old definitions as new ones are encountered so that the last definition in the file is the only one that matters.

2.2.2.4   Minimal Makefiles Using Implicit Rules

As you write more `Makefiles`, it quickly becomes apparent that many rules follow a few simple patterns. In large `Makefiles`, it is possible to have many rules that are identical except for the target and prerequisite. This leads to a great deal of copying

---

5.   The only exceptions are the so-called "automatic" variables, which I discuss later.

and pasting with the text editor—which, as every developer knows, leads to dumb mistakes.

Fortunately, make provides implicit rules that allow you to describe these patterns without having to copy and paste rules. make comes with numerous predefined implicit rules that cover many patterns commonly found in Makefiles. Thanks to the built-in implicit rules, it is possible to write rules without any instructions. It's even possible to use make without a Makefile! Just for fun, try this in an empty directory:

```
$ echo "main() {}" > foo.c
$ make foo
cc     foo.c    -o foo
```

Just by using implicit rules, make is able to figure out that you wanted to create a program named foo from foo.c.

Implicit rules are there to keep your Makefiles short and make your job easier. GNU make comes with many implicit rules to do almost everything you need. You should exploit implicit rules every chance you get.

One way to define implicit rules is to use suffix rules. As an example, the suffix rule GNU make uses to create to object files from C source files looks like this:

```
.c.o:
        $(COMPILE.c) $(OUTPUT_OPTION) $<
```

This says, "If you see a target with an .o extension, and there is no explicit rule for it, look for a file with the same base and the .c extension. If you find it, run these commands." As shown here, the commands for implicit rules typically are enclosed in variables, which allow you to exploit these rules further.

You can examine all the built-in variables and implicit rules by typing make -p. Using this to examine COMPILE.c, you can see that it is defined by using additional variables:

```
COMPILE.c = $(CC) $(CFLAGS) $(CPPFLAGS) $(TARGET_ARCH) -c
CC = gcc
```

Interestingly, only one of these additional variables (CC) is actually defined; the others are quietly replaced with empty strings. make allows you refer to undefined variables without producing an error. You can exploit this in a minimal Makefile just by including the following line:

```
CFLAGS = -g
```

You can use this one-line `Makefile` to compile objects with debugging enabled. But because `make` allows you to define variables on the command line, you could skip the `Makefile` or override `CFLAGS` on the command line as follows:

```
$ make CFLAGS=-g foo
gcc -g    foo.c    -o foo
```

Variables provided on the command line override all definitions in the `Makefile`. So whether you have a complicated `Makefile` or none at all, you can exert a great deal of control over the build from the command line. Table 2-1 lists several variables commonly used in implicit rules that can be overridden on the command line.

Given the flexibility of implicit rules for object code, you may never need to write explicit rules for object files. There are implicit rules for C, C++, Fortran, and many others. I list some of the most common ones in Table 2-2, but you can use `make` `-p` to check, or check the `make` manual for others.

TABLE 2-1   Common Variables Used in Implicit Rules

Variable	Default	Description
CC	gcc	C compiler.
CXX	g++	C++ compiler.
CFLAGS	none	Flags passed to the C compiler with implicit rules.
CXXFLAGS	none	Flags passed to the C++ compiler with implicit rules.
CPPFLAGS	none	Flags passed to the C preprocessor used with implicit rules, including C++, C, some assembly language rules, and several others. Typical flags include -I, -D, and -U.

TABLE 2-2   Default Suffix Rules to Create Object Code

Language	Extensions	Command
C	.c	$(CC) -c $(CPPFLAGS) $(CFLAGS)
C++	.cpp .cc .C	$(CXX) -c $(CPPFLAGS) $(CXXFLAGS)
Assembler	.s	$(AS) $(ASFLAGS)
Assembler[6]	.S	$(CPP) $(CPPFLAGS)

---

6. This rule doesn't create object code directly but preprocesses the .S file into an .s file, which is then compiled by the rule above.

Language	Extensions	Command
Pascal	.p	$(PC) -c $(PFLAGS)
Fortran	.f	$(FC) -c $(FFLAGS)
Fortran	.F	$(FC) -c $(FFLAGS) $(CPPFLAGS)

Defining Custom Implicit Rules

Although GNU make defines numerous implicit rules that cover the most common cases, there are likely to be cases where you can't find an implicit rule that works for you. In this case, you can write an explicit rule or define your own implicit rule.

Suppose that you have a bunch of C++ modules to compile, all of which have the .cxx extension. This is not one of the three C++ extensions recognized by GNU make.[7] You could rename all the files or create explicit rules for each of them, but creating a new implicit rule is trivial. In this example, you simply need two lines:

```
.SUFFIXES: .cxx # let make know that this is a new extension

.cxx.o:
        $(CXX) -c $(CPPFLAGS) $(CXXFLAGS) $<
```

Without the .SUFFIXES: pseudotarget, make will not use your implicit rule, because it does not recognize files that end with .cxx. The suffix rule I used above is compatible with other versions of make, as are the variables I used to define it. GNU make offers an alternative syntax, which is more flexible and less picky about suffixes, called *pattern rules*. A pattern rule for my .cxx source files would look like this:

```
%.o : %.cxx
        $(CXX) -c $(CPPFLAGS) $(CXXFLAGS) $<
```

Pattern rules produce less clutter than suffix rules because they don't require the .SUFFIXES: pseudotarget. It also looks more like a normal rule than a suffix rule because it contains a target on the left and a prerequisite on the right. Instead of specific filenames for targets and prerequisites, the pattern rule uses a % character to match filenames or targets in the Makefile, much like a wildcard character used to match filenames in the shell. When make encounters a target (or filename) that matches the pattern, it uses the part of the target name matched by % to look for a prerequisite.

continues

---

7. The extensions for C++ that make recognizes are .C, .cpp, and .cc.

Defining Custom Implicit Rules *(Continued)*

Let's look at an example using a `Makefile` that contains only the previous two-line pattern rule. If we try to build a file that doesn't exist, `make` behaves as though the pattern rule did not exist:

```
$ make foo.o
make: *** No rule to make target `foo.o'.  Stop.
```

Notice that `make` doesn't say that it can't find `foo.cxx`; it just says there's no rule. That's because although our target (`foo.o`) matches our pattern rule, there is no file or target that matches the prerequisite (`foo.cxx`). There may be dozens of other pattern rules that match the same target, but without any explicit targets or filenames to work with, `make` cannot make any assumptions. So the answer `make` provides is the safe answer.

Now suppose that we create a file named `foo.cxx` in our current directory, and we run this command again:

```
$ make foo.o
g++ -c   foo.cxx
```

This time, `make` is able to apply the implicit rule, because it sees that the target (`foo.o`) satisfies our target pattern and is able to find a file (`foo.cxx`) that matches our prerequisite pattern. The implicit rule is satisfied, so the associated commands can run.

The matching prerequisite could have also been an explicit target instead of a file. Let's remove `foo.cxx` and add a single explicit rule to our `Makefile`, as follows:

```
foo.cxx:
        @echo Hello World
```

This rule does nothing but print a message to let us know it triggered. It does not create any files, so expect `make` to fail. Now when we run the same `make` command, we get a different result:

```
$ make foo.o
Hello World
g++ -c   foo.cxx
g++: foo.cxx: No such file or directory
g++: no input files
make: *** [foo.o] Error 1
```

Because there is no file named `foo.cxx`, `gcc` fails as expected. The rule that should have created `foo.cxx` simply prints `Hello World` to the screen instead. The point is that an explicit target was enough to satisfy our implicit rule without any files at all.

Although the previous example used the GNU pattern rules, `make` behaves exactly the same way with traditional suffix rules. Each time `make` searches for a specific target, it searches the explicit rules first. Only if it cannot find a match does it attempt to apply the implicit rules.

2.2.2.5   Using Automatic Variables to Improve Readability

Because implicit rules and pattern rules work without specific filenames, `make` provides *automatic variables* that help define the commands for these rules. In earlier examples, I used `$<`, which is an automatic variable that takes on the value of the first prerequisite in the rule. Unlike other `make` variables, automatic variables have unique values for every rule. Table 2-3 shows some of the most useful automatic variables used in implicit rules.

As you have seen, user-defined variables can contain other variables. What may not be obvious is that variables can also contain automatic variables, which means

TABLE 2-3   Some Useful Automatic Variables in GNU make

Variable	Value
`$@`	Filename of the target.
`$^`	The names of all prerequisites with duplicate names removed.
`$+`	The names of all prerequisites, including duplicates.
`$<`	The name of the first prerequisite in the rule.
`$?`	The names of all prerequisites newer than the target.
`$*`	With a suffix rule, this is the base name (or stem) of the target. If the rule is `.c.o:`, for example, and the matching target is `foo.o`, this value is `foo`. With some pattern rules, this value may not be what you expect.

that their value can change over the course of the build. Automatic variables are vital for implicit rules but can be very useful in explicit rules as well. Consider this common `Makefile` pattern for creating a program:

```
program: $(OBJS)
        $(CC) -o $@ $^
```

The command portion consists of a predefined variable (`CC`) as well as two automatic variables. Unfortunately, there is no way to encapsulate this in an implicit rule because there isn't a clear pattern. The `program` can be any name, and the `OBJS` can contain any number of arbitrarily named objects. As far as `make` is concerned, there is no pattern to follow.

If you want to use this same rule to create additional programs in the same `Makefile`, you are resigned to cutting and pasting these commands for every program, as follows:

```
program1: $(PROG1_OBJS)
        $(CC) -o $@ $^

program2: $(PROG2_OBJS)
        $(CC) -o $@ $^
# etc...
```

At least with the use of automatic variables, you can cut and paste with no modifications to the command portion of the rule. It is a little cryptic, but you can do better. By embedding the automatic variables in a more intuitively named variable, you can `make` the pattern easier to follow. For example:

```
build_C_program=$(CC) -o $@ $^

program1: mod1.o mod2.o
        $(build_C_program)

program2: mod3.o mod4.o
        $(build_C_program)
```

Now the ugly automatic variables are part of the definition for `build_C_program`, but they behave as expected when `build_C_program` appears as a command. The rule is a little easier to follow, and other developers don't need to know what `build_C_program` looks like unless they want to.

2.2.2.6   Manipulating Variables

To understand why you need to manipulate variable values, let's look at a typical example of a text substitution pattern used in UNIX `make`:

```
SRCS=foo.c bar.c
OBJS=$(SRCS:.c=.o)
```

This syntax is called a *substitution reference* and is available in all flavors of `make`. Here, we take a list of source files and use it to create a list of object files. In this example, we take the value of the `SRCS` variable, substitute `.o` for all the `.c` extensions, and store the result in the `OBJS` variable. Because we have two source modules, named `foo.c` and `bar.c`, we would like `OBJS` to contain `foo.o` and `bar.o`. The text substitution is preferable to typing every name again on a second line, which would be tedious and error prone. `Makefiles` usually contain many such lists, making text substitutions indispensable.

The substitution reference works in this example because all the source modules have the same extension. What if you have mixed C and C++ sources in your `SRCS` variable? For example:

```
SRCS=foo.c bar.cpp
OBJS=$(SRCS:.c=.o)
```

The substitution reference syntax does not allow more than one file extension pattern. So in our example, the substitution does not take place for `bar.cpp` because it doesn't match the `.c` pattern. `OBJS` then contains `foo.o bar.cpp`, which is not what you want.

A typical solution in UNIX `make` would be to create an additional variable as follows:

```
CSRCS=foo.c
CXXSRCS=foo.cpp
OBJS=$(CSRCS:.c=.o) $(CXXSRCS:.cpp=.o)
```

This technique tends to increase clutter, especially when you are dealing with numerous lists.

Next, I will look at the GNU function extensions, which are much more flexible.

2.2.2.7   Manipulating Variables with Functions

As you have seen, the substitution reference syntax can be very handy, but it is a bit limited. GNU make's function extensions are versatile tools for manipulating variable contents. Here are two ways to do the same thing:

```
OBJS=$(SRCS:.c=.o)
OBJS:=$(patsubst %.c, %.o, $(SRCS)))
```

The first line uses the familiar substitution reference. The second line is the equivalent of the substitution reference using the patsubst function. The patsubst function has the same limitations as the substitution reference: Only one extension at a time is supported. Functions can be nested, however, which is something that you can't do with a substitution reference. To include additional extensions, for example, you can use the following syntax:

```
OBJS:=$(patsubst %.cpp, %.o, $(patsubst %.c, %.o, $(SRCS)))
```

Now we can transform multiple file extensions without having to create extra variables.

Here is another technique using different functions. It is a bit more concise and generic:

```
OBJS:=$(addsuffix .o, $(basename $(SRCS)))
```

The basename function takes a list of filenames (in this case, the contents of SRCS) and strips the extension from each of them. It doesn't matter what the extension is; basename just strips off all the characters following the last period in the text. We take the output and glue .o to the end of each basename, using the addsuffix function. This gives us the list of objects we want.

Another useful function is the shell function. Recall the earlier example in which we used backticks to create a filename based on the date and time:

```
NAME = `date +%02d%02m%02y`.dat
```

You saw how this pattern fails when it is used as a prerequisite or a target. GNU make provides the shell function as an alternative to do what we want:

```
NAME = $(shell date +%02d%02m%02y).dat
```

Unlike the backticks, this variable is safe to use as a prerequisite or a target because GNU `make` evaluates the shell command when the variable is initialized, before any rules are evaluated. In this particular example, this is exactly what we want. There may be situations in which you still want to use the backticks. Consider a rule like the following:

```
CURRENT_TIME=$(shell date +%T)
something:
        @echo started  $(CURRENT_TIME)
        sleep 5
        @echo finished $(CURRENT_TIME)
```

When you run this, you will see the following:

```
$ make
started  9:49:45
sleep 5
finished 9:49:45
```

This probably is not what you had in mind. The problem is that the shell command `date +%T` is evaluated only once, at the beginning of the build, so every time we use it during the build, it has the same value. If you want the value to change over time, you will have to call the shell each time, which is what the backticks do. For example:

```
CURRENT_TIME=`date +%T`
```

This gives us the output we expect:

```
$ make
started  9:49:45
sleep 5
finished 9:49:50
```

Note again that the value of CURRENT_TIME is a variable and that its value remains fixed in both examples. In the first example, CURRENT_TIME contains the output of a shell command that ran at the beginning of the build. In the second example, CURRENT_TIME contains the text of a shell command that is executed during the build. It is the output from the shell command that is changing, not the contents of the variable.

A complete list of functions can be found in the info `page` for `make`. Table 2-4 contains a list of some of the more useful functions.

TABLE 2-4   Functions for Manipulating Text

Function	Usage	Description
subst	$(subst *from, to, text*)	Returns the contents of the text argument with all occurrences of the from argument replaced with the contents of the to argument.
patsubst	$(patsubst *from-pattern, to-pattern, filenames*)	Returns a white space–separated list of filenames with the filename patterns replaced. The pattern syntax is the same syntax used for pattern rules. The function is intended for filenames, but it will work for any text.
strip	$(strip *string*)	Removes leading and trailing white space from the string argument.
findstring	$(findstring *match, string*)	Returns the match argument if it can be found in the string argument; otherwise, it returns an empty string.
filter	$(filter *patterns, filenames*)	Returns a white space–separated list of files found in the filenames argument that match the patterns argument. The patterns argument may contain multiple patterns separated by white space and uses the same syntax used for pattern rules.
filter-out	$(filter-out *patterns, filenames*)	Returns a white space–separated list of files from the filenames argument that do not match the patterns argument. The patterns argument may contain multiple patterns separated by white space and uses the same syntax used for pattern rules.
sort	$(sort *text*)	Returns the white space–separated list in the text argument sorted in lexical order.

Function	Usage	Description
word	$(word n, text)	Returns the *n*th word found in the text argument. The word count starts with 1.
wordlist	$(wordlist first, last, text)	Returns the set of words in the text argument starting with first and ending with last.
words	$(words text)	Returns the number of words in the text argument.
error	$(error message)	Used within a conditional (discussed later). Stops the build with the given error message.

2.2.2.8   Defining and Using Your Own Functions

In the unlikely event that you cannot find a built-in function to suit your needs, GNU make allows you to define your own functions. User-defined functions are accessed via the call built-in function, as follows:

```
$(call myfunction, arg1, arg2)
```

Notice that the user-defined function call don't look like other function calls. You must use the call built-in function with your function name passed as an argument. Additional arguments are separated by commas. The definition of myfunction looks just like a variable except that it now has access to positional arguments. Here's a more complete example:

```
myfunction = @echo $(1) $(2)

all:
        $(call myfunction,hello,world)
```

When you run this Makefile, it produces the following output:

```
$ make
hello world
```

The term *function* is a little misleading. make is not a programming language, and it provides only minimal error checking. Just like variables, make is happy to return empty strings when you make mistakes. Because a function definition looks no different from a variable definition, for example, you can still use a function as a variable. This seems weird, but it is consistent, given the syntax used for functions. When you use a function as a variable, it behaves as though the function were called with no arguments. For example:

```
$(call myfunction) # is the same as...
$(myfunction)
```

In both cases, the positional arguments—$(1), $(2), and so on—are replaced with empty strings.

2.2.2.9   Conditional Constructs

Conditional constructs are another useful GNU extension for controlling make behavior. There are only four types of conditionals supported in GNU make, and these are listed in Table 2-5.

There really are only two tests and their complements: if equal and if defined. Because make does not have a not operator, it is necessary to have separate keywords for equal and not equal, as well as for defined and not defined.

Each conditional block may have an optional else clause but must be terminated by an endif. The basic syntax is as follows:

```
conditional test
makefile text evaluated when test is true
else
makefile text evaluated when test is false
endif
```

TABLE 2-5   Conditionals Available in GNU Make

Conditional	Usage
ifeq	Test if two values are equal
ifneq	Test if two values are not equal
ifdef	Test if a variable is defined
ifndef	Test if a variable is not defined

The text that appears inside the conditional clause may be any valid `make` lines, but conditionals may not be used inside the command section of rules or inside variable/function definitions. This places some restrictions on how conditionals may be used.

Let's start with a simple example using the `ifeq` conditional:

```
ifeq ($(shell uname -o),GNU/Linux)
      CPPFLAGS += -DLINUX
endif
```

Here, we use the `ifeq` conditional to test for the type of OS. It uses the output of the shell command `uname -o` to indicate the type of operating system, which is `GNU/Linux` on my Linux system. So when this appears in a `Makefile` on a Linux system, the `CPPFLAGS` variable will include the `-DLINUX` flag. Recall that `CPPFLAGS` is used in implicit rules for targets that are built with tools that use the C preprocessor. This is one technique for using conditionals to support multiple build environments.

Adding an `else` clause is straightforward:

```
ifeq ($(shell uname -o),GNU/Linux)
      CPPFLAGS += -DLINUX
else
      CPPFLAGS += -DOS_UNKNOWN
endif
```

You can also wrap conditional clauses around rules as well, so the following syntax is valid:

```
ifeq ($(shell uname -o),GNU/Linux)
      all: linux_programs
else
      all: bsd_programs
endif
```

The command portion of the rule can be inside or outside the conditional clause.

One thing worth noting is that conditionals are evaluated in line with variable assignments, as illustrated by this silly example:

```
ifeq ($(A),0)   # A isn't defined yet
all:
    @echo $(A) == 0
else
all:
    @echo $(A) != 0
endif

A=0
```

Now when you run this `Makefile`, you see the following illogical output:

```
$ make
0 != 0
```

The problem is that the macro A is not defined until after the conditional, so the `ifeq` test fails (it's false). See what I mean about no error checking?

The `ifdef` clause tests for variable definitions, which can be useful for using variables as command-line options. For example:

```
ifdef (debug)
      CFLAGS += -g
else
      CFLAGS += -O2
endif
```

Recall that `CFLAGS` is the built-in variable used for implicitly building an object from C source code. In this example, the default setting for `CFLAGS` is to include optimization with the `-O2` switch. If you want to compile for debugging, invoke `make` with `debug` defined on the command line as follows:

```
$ make debug=1
```

In large, complicated `Makefiles`, you might use `ifdef` to make sure that a necessary variable is set:

```
ifndef (A_VITAL_VARIABLE)
$(error A_VITAL_VARIABLE is not set)
endif
```

2.2.2.10 Pulling Source from Various Places

Very often, projects with many source files will locate them in a single directory and build them in a different one. This reduces clutter by keeping one type of file in a directory. Traditionally, this is accomplished with the VPATH variable. As usual, however, GNU `make` extends this functionality in many useful ways.

In principle, the VPATH variable works much like the shell PATH variable. It contains a list of directories separated by colons, in which it searches for targets and prerequisites. You might have a project with two directories: `src` for source files and `bin` for objects. In this case, the `Makefile` usually would reside in the `./bin` directory and would look something like this:

```
VPATH=../src

foo: foo.c
        $(CC) -o $@ $^
```

VPATH indicates that make should search for targets and prerequisites in the ../src directory as well as the current directory. It's not necessary to specify the location of foo.c when it appears as a prerequisite. make will substitute the correct path. So assuming that foo.c resides in the ../src directory, the output would look like this:

```
$ make
gcc -o foo ../src/foo.c
```

If you have a copy of foo.c in the current directory, of course, make will still pick up that one, which can be a problem. make will always search the current working directory first. So if you are in the unfortunate situation of having two different files with the same name in two places, VPATH may not solve your problem.

GNU make adds an extension to the VPATH with the vpath directive (note the use of lowercase). With the vpath directive, you can specify filename patterns so that make will search only for particular type of files in particular directories. As a contrived example, you could put C++ source in a directory named /cxxsrc and C source in a directory named /csrc. The Makefile for this could look like this:

```
vpath %.cpp ./cxxsrc
vpath %.c ./csrc
```

In general, most projects of modest size do not need to resort to the vpath directive or even use a VPATH variable. Things can get very confusing when you use these features. These features are used with very large projects or to work around some inherited limitations of the build environment. Some of the source distributed with GNU projects require you to build in an empty directory. These projects rely on the vpath feature to read the source from a read-only location.

2.2.3 How Programs Are Linked

Most developers are blissfully unaware of the linker, because the compiler normally does most of the work. Although there is a linker command (ld), this command is almost never called directly. All we worry about are the names and locations of the libraries we want to link with. In fact, many little details must be provided to the linker. Fortunately, the compiler already knows about these and passes these arguments behind the scenes.

To get a peek at the sausage grinder, you can use the -v option of the C compiler. Here is what it looks like on my machine with the clutter removed (if you can believe that):

```
$ gcc -v -o hello hello.c

 /usr/libexec/gcc/i386-redhat-linux/4.0.1/cc1 -quiet -v hello.c -quiet -dumpbase
hello.c -auxbase hello -version -o /tmp/ccoxYr4k.s

 as -V -Qy -o /tmp/ccw3IciH.o /tmp/ccoxYr4k.s

 /usr/libexec/gcc/i386-redhat-linux/4.0.1/collect2 --eh-frame-hdr -m elf_i386
-dynamic-linker /lib/ld-linux.so.2 -o hello /usr/lib/gcc/i386-redhat-
linux/4.0.1/../../../crt1.o /usr/lib/gcc/i386-redhat-linux/4.0.1/../../../crti.o
/usr/lib/gcc/i386-redhat-linux/4.0.1/crtbegin.o -L/usr/lib/gcc/i386-redhat-
linux/4.0.1 -L/usr/lib/gcc/i386-redhat-linux/4.0.1 -L/usr/lib/gcc/i386-redhat-
linux/4.0.1/../../.. /tmp/ccw3IciH.o -lgcc --as-needed -lgcc_s --no-as-needed
-lc -lgcc --as-needed -lgcc_s --no-as-needed /usr/lib/gcc/i386-redhat-
linux/4.0.1/crtend.o /usr/lib/gcc/i386-redhat-linux/4.0.1/../../../crtn.o
```

There are three stages that the compiler goes through. The first stage converts the source code to assembly language. The second stage runs the assembler to create an object file. The third, and ugliest, stage is the linker. Although the command is `collect2`, it actually calls `ld` with the same options.

The C and C++ compilers have two basic modes of operation: with and without linking. When you specify the -c flag, you are compiling without linking. The compiler produces object files, and that's it. Without the -c option, the compiler produces object files and calls the linker to link the resulting objects into a program.

It should be apparent from the previous example that there is more to your program than the objects you create. Several objects that you never heard of, with names that begin with crt,[8] are linked with your program in addition to your object files. In addition, the C standard library is linked by default. This goes on behind the scenes, of course, so you don't have to link with these things explicitly. When you are compiling with dynamic libraries (which I will discuss shortly), the evidence is there to see. For example:

```
$ ldd hello
        libc.so.6 => /lib/tls/libc.so.6 (0x009f4000)
        /lib/ld-linux.so.2 (0x009db000)
```

---

8. crt in this context is an abbreviation for *C Runtime*.

The ldd[9] command shows you the dynamic libraries that a particular program needs. Here, you can see that my `hello` program requires `libc.so.6`—also known as the C standard library. The other requirement is `/lib/ld-linux.so.2`, which is the dynamic linker itself.

2.2.4 Understanding Libraries

A *library* is a container that holds reusable object code. When you make a POSIX function call, for example, you have to link your code with the POSIX library for it to work. Many libraries are available for different functions. Some, like the C standard library, are required; most others are optional. By encapsulating functions in libraries, developers can keep the program footprint (and the executable file) small by picking only the libraries that are absolutely necessary for the program to run.

Libraries come in two flavors: dynamic and static. A *static library* is just an archive of object files created with the `ar` command. The linker reads the object files contained in the archive one by one when it tries to resolve external symbols. The linker is free to discard any object files that are not required. So although a static library may contain hundreds of objects and megabytes of object code, your code may pull in only one or two objects and have a much smaller footprint. If you are ever inclined to peek inside a static library, you are likely to find that it contains many modules with only one function per module. This gives the linker maximum opportunities to remove unnecessary code. The key feature of static libraries is that only the person building the executable needs a copy of the library. To achieve this, some or all of the object code in the library will be copied to your executable file. If an executable is linked only with static libraries, we say that it is statically linked. This means you can take a copy of that executable to another system and execute it without requiring any additional files.

Unlike a static library, which is just an archive of object files, a *dynamic library* is itself an object file. Dynamic libraries are created by the linker, unlike static libraries, which are created by the compiler and the `ar` command. When you link with a dynamic library, the compiler does not copy any object code into your executable file. Instead, it records information about the dynamic library in your executable so that it can be *dynamically linked* at runtime. This means that part of the link process is deferred until runtime. This has several advantages over a static library. For one

---

9. `ldd` stands for *List Dynamic Dependencies.*

thing, it makes your executable file smaller, because the linker is not copying object code into it. Another advantage is that only one copy of the library code needs to reside in memory. This saves memory, because all the programs that use the library point to the same physical memory.

Patching is easier with shared libraries because you can update the shared library with a bug fix and simultaneously fix every program in the system that uses the library. If the same library were static, you would have to rebuild every program that uses it to deploy the same bug fix.

When a dynamically linked program executes, the program performs the final linking stages before it enters main. It searches for the required dynamic libraries and exits with an error if it can't find any of them. This can be a problem when you want to ship binary files to different machines, because all the machines must have all the required shared libraries; otherwise, the program won't run.

Let's create a dynamically linked executable to illustrate some of these issues. We'll need two modules: `hello.c` for the main program and `empty.c`, which will be an empty shared object.

```
$ cat <<EOF > hello.c
#include <stdio.h>
int main() { printf("Hello World\n"); }
EOF
$ cat /dev/null > empty.c
```

`empty.c` is an empty file, which can be compiled in to an object or shared object just like any other source file. We don't need any code here to illustrate our point, but we will create a shared object:

```
$ gcc -shared -fpic -o empty.so empty.c
```

The `-shared` flag tells the compiler to link the object but to create a shared object instead of an executable object. To link `hello` with this shared object, specify it on the command line like any other object file, but the result is different:

```
$ gcc -o hello hello.c empty.so
```

There's a surprise in store when you try to run this:

```
$ ./hello
./hello: error while loading shared libraries: empty.so: cannot open shared
object file: No such file or directory
```

The dynamic linker is looking for `empty.so` and can't find it. We have to help it out with an environment variable:

```
$ LD_LIBRARY_PATH=. ./hello
Hello World
```

This illustrates one of the downsides to shared objects: If the object is not in a predefined location, the program will not execute. There are other downsides as well. For one thing, if your shared library takes up large amounts of space for code, so will any process that runs your executable. Recall that static libraries are just archives of object files. When the linker sees a static library, it is free to pull in only the object files that your program actually needs, which keeps the executable as small as possible. When your code links with a shared object, however, it's all or nothing. The dynamic linker cannot discard pieces of the shared object, so your process's memory will map all the code contained in the shared object, whether it calls it or not.

With a virtual memory system, this is not such a big problem, because code that is never used may never consume any physical memory. Regardless, the additional code consumes virtual addresses, which can be a problem in large applications that require large data sets, particularly on 32-bit architectures. Shared libraries can rob you of virtual memory that you could put to better use.

Static and Dynamic Linking: A Closer Look

For this example, we will create a new shared object that does nothing but consume memory. Let's call it `piggy.c`:

```
$ cat <<EOF > piggy.c
char bank[0x100000];
EOF
```

This declares a global buffer of 1MB. For the main module, we'll use the trivial `hello.c` program that just waits for us to press Ctrl+C so we can examine it while it runs:

```
$ cat <<EOF > hello.c
#include <unistd.h>
int main(){ pause(); }
EOF
```

continues

<hr>

Static and Dynamic Linking: A Closer Look *(Continued)*

There are several ways to link these two modules into a program, each with advantages and disadvantages. The simplest way is to link them as two objects:

```
$ gcc -o hello hello.c piggy.c
$ size hello
   text    data    bss     dec    hex filename
   1117     264 1048608 1049989  100585 hello
$ nm -S hello | grep bank
080496c0 00100000 B bank
```

When the modules are linked like this, the memory consumption is visible with the `size` command. The `nm` command shows that the array `bank` is present and consuming 1MB of space. When `piggy.o` is part of a static library that is linked with the executable, the situation changes:

```
$ gcc -c piggy.c
$ ar clq libpig.a piggy.o
$ gcc -o hello hello.c -L ./ -lpig
$ size hello
   text    data    bss     dec    hex filename
   1117     264      4    1385     569 hello
$ nm -S hello | grep bank
```

This time, the size of the executable is noticeably smaller because the `bank` array is not included, which tells us that the `piggy.o` module was excluded. The linker is able to determine that there are no references to `piggy.o`, so it does not link it with the executable.

Finally, we'll create a shared object:

```
$ gcc -shared -o piggy.so piggy.c
$ gcc -o hello hello.c ./piggy.so
$ size hello
$ size ./hello
   text    data    bss     dec    hex filename
   1349     272      4    1625     659 ./hello
$ nm -S hello | grep bank
```

The size is roughly the same as the executable linked with the static library, and there is no trace of the `bank` array. This time, we'll run it using the `pmap` command to get a look at the process's memory map:

```
$ ./hello &
$ jobs -x pmap -q %1
7382:   ./hello
08048000      4K r-x--  /hello
08049000      4K rw---  /hello
```

```
b7dab000      4K rw---    [ anon ]
b7dac000   1160K r-x--  /libc-2.3.2.so
b7ece000     36K rw---  /libc-2.3.2.so
b7ed7000      8K rw---    [ anon ]
b7ee7000      4K r-x--  /piggy.so
b7ee8000      4K rw---  /piggy.so
b7ee9000   1032K rw---    [ anon ]
b7feb000     84K r-x--  /ld-2.3.2.so
b8000000      4K rw---  /ld-2.3.2.so
bffeb000     84K rw---    [ stack ]
ffffe000      4K -----    [ anon ]
```

It looks like `piggy.so` is consuming only 8K, but tucked away in this output is an *anonymous* mapping of 1032K. This is storage that was allocated for the `bank` array.

So linking with a shared object can force you to consume virtual memory that you otherwise would not use. If this data is truly unused, it may never actually consume physical memory or swap, although this range of virtual addresses is not usable by your process. This can become a problem if your process needs to allocate large blocks of memory.

By default, the compiler uses dynamic linking, which means that if it can choose between a static library and a dynamic library, it will choose the dynamic library. If you want to link exclusively with static objects, you must specify the `-static` option to `gcc/g++`. Most development libraries come with copies of both a dynamic library and a static library for this purpose. The linker cannot statically link an executable with a dynamic library, or vice versa.

Library Naming Convention

Dynamic libraries typically are identified by the `.so` extension of the filename. In Linux (and UNIX), dynamic libraries are also known as shared libraries or, more generically, as shared objects. This is where the .so extension comes from. Static libraries use the `.a` extension, which they inherited from the `ar` archive program with which they are created. To differentiate an `ar` archive (which is hardly used elsewhere) from a static library, library filenames are prefixed with the string `"lib"`. So to create a static library named `foo`, name the file `libfoo.a`.

When the linker sees an argument such as `-lfoo`, it automatically searches for a file named `libfoo.a` in a predefined search path. In keeping with tradition, dynamic libraries also use the `lib` prefix, so the linker will search for either `libfoo.a` or `libfoo.so`.

2.3   The Build Process

Now that you have an understanding of the tools used to create projects, let's take a step back and examine how these tools work together. To keep it simple, we will focus on projects built with the C and/or C++ programming languages. C is most common because it generally is more portable than C++. Although C++ is suitable for most projects, developers who want to reach the widest range of target systems will choose C. Believe it or not, there are even some programmers out there who don't know C++.

Although the GNU compilers are commonly available on Linux systems, they are not necessarily required to build from source. Open source projects, and GNU projects in particular, emphasize portability, so they don't necessarily require GNU compilers or Linux. The same code that builds and runs on Linux can also build and run on Solaris, IRIX, Free BSD, and even Windows. Portability isn't just a nice-to-have feature for anal-retentive developers; it's also vital to the survival of an open source project. More platforms means more users and more developers looking at the code. That is a recipe for a better application.

2.3.1   The GNU Build Tools

The GNU build system is the de facto standard build tool for open source projects. It is a complex set of tools used by developers to generate source distributions that are easy to build and install. A typical source distribution created with the GNU build tools includes a `configure` script, which is used by the end user to create a `Makefile`. As an end user, you don't need to know that these tools exist. You need only remember three simple steps to build any GNU program:

```
$ ./configure
$ make
$ make install
```

It isn't always that simple. Sometimes, you will need to customize something to meet your needs. Worse, any of these three steps could fail. I will focus on the GNU build tools from an end-user perspective. A complete understanding of the GNU build tools is out of the scope of this book, but many fine resources on the Web can help you, as well as documentation that comes with the GNU tools distribution.

2.3.2   The configure Stage

The `configure` stage deals with all the messy details that are too complicated to deal with in a `Makefile` alone. GNU build tools are designed to create tools that install on any POSIX-compliant system, so it makes very few assumptions about your system. The `configure` script can take a long time to run, as it checks for installed libraries and tools. It may also generate C header files to communicate system information to the compiler.

For some small projects, the developers may choose to provide a simple `Makefile` instead of using the `configure` script. You can recognize this by the presence or absence of a `Makefile` in the source archive. If there is no `Makefile`, there will be a file named `Makefile.in` that is read by the `configure` script to create the `Makefile`.

The `configure` script looks at your system and determines whether you have the necessary tools to compile the project, such as a working compiler. The GNU tools used to create the `configure` script give the developer a great deal of flexibility to check for all kinds of little details. This reassures you that the project will build before you invest a lot of time trying to build it. It can be a drawback, because the `configure` stage can take a considerable amount of time, particularly for smaller projects.

The `configure` script produced by the GNU build tools has several options that are common to all projects. Developers can add more options, but there is no requirement that these be documented, which is unfortunate. This can make building a project something of a black art, but it doesn't need to be so.

Some of the basic options common to all `configure` scripts focus on fine-tuning the installation of the program (Table 2-6).

TABLE 2-6   Common Options for the configure Command

Option	Usage
`--prefix`	Determines the root of the installation, typically `/usr/local`.
`--bindir`	Determines the location of files that otherwise will be installed in `${prefix}/bin`. This directory is for executables that will be run by regular users.
`--sbindir`	Determines the location of files that otherwise will be installed in `${prefix}/sbin`. This directory is for executables that will be run by administrators or system daemons.
`--datadir`	Determines the location of ancillary data files; defaults to `${prefix}/share`.
`--libdir`	Determines the location of shared libraries; defaults to `${prefix}/lib`.

continues

TABLE 2-6   *Continued*

Option	Usage
`--mandir`	Determines the location to install `man` pages; defaults to `${prefix}/man`.
`--program-prefix`	Adds a prefix to executable files stored in `${bindir}` and `${sbindir}`. Sometimes, this is used to install multiple versions of the same program, because it allows the use of a unique prefix for each version.
`--program-suffix`	Like `--program-prefix` except that it adds a suffix to the program.

There are various versions of the GNU build tools in circulation, and the options tend to vary slightly. To see what options are available with a particular project, you can always type

```
$ ./configure --help
```

In addition to the common options listed in Table 2-6, `configure` scripts always allow user-defined options of the form

```
--enable-X
--disable-X
--with-X
--without-X (also --with-X=no)
```

The X can be anything the developer wants, but these options are not always documented. To make matters more confusing, the `configure` script will accept any X even if there is no such feature. `configure --with-fries`, for example, runs without errors on any project, but don't open the ketchup just yet.

Consider the `gcc` project. If you download the source from the Free Software Foundation, you will need to follow the same three steps I discussed earlier. The `configure` step in particular has a large number of options that are not documented by the help function and are scarcely documented anywhere else. Some important options include the ability to enable only certain languages with the `--enable-languages` option. If you are looking for only a C and C++ compiler, for example, you will want to configure it with `--enable-languages=c,c++`. Without this, `gcc` builds in support for Fortran, Java, and whatever else that version supports, which makes the build take longer and consume more space. You won't find this in the README or any of the FAQs that come with the source, although it is widely documented in other sources on the Web.

One way to check for yourself is to examine configure.in (sometimes configure.ac) and look for script code that uses variable names beginning with enable_ or with_. These are Bourne shell variables that are set by the configure options --enable-X and --with-X. In the gcc configure.in script, for example, you will find several references to variables named enable_languages, with_newlib, and others. Generally speaking, when these are not documented in a README file or help message, they are not intended to be used by nondevelopers. But sometimes, you have to improvise.

2.3.3   The Build Stage: make

The build stage is started by running make with no arguments. This builds all the object files and links them into one or more programs. The default target in this case is a pseudotarget named all, but the GNU build tools create other pseudotargets that can be used on the command line (Table 2-7). Normally, you don't need to know about these, but in the event that your build fails and you find yourself fixing source code, these are good to know about.

TABLE 2-7   Some Useful Targets in an automake-Generated Makefile

Target	Usage
all	Default target; builds all libraries and executables.
clean	Removes object files and libraries that are built by the all target.
distclean	Removes all files created during configure and make. Ideally, what you are left with is only the files that were in the original tar archive. After building the distclean target, you will not have a Makefile and will have to run configure again before you can rebuild.
mostlyclean	Like clean, except that selected libraries are not removed, including those that the developers determined are seldom changed and should not need rebuilding.
install	Installs programs in the directories determined when configure was run. Be careful; there is not always an uninstall target.
uninstall	If present, removes programs installed by the install target.

When your build completes without errors, you are ready for the next stage in the process, which is the install stage.

2.3.4   The Install Stage: make install

If you want to install a program for all to use, the default configuration usually is sufficient. You will have to have root privileges to do so. The default location usually is `/usr/local/bin`, which is relatively safe. It won't conflict with or overwrite system programs that usually reside in `/usr/bin`. Still, `/usr/local` is used by many other programs, so it's always wise to check the installation first by installing in a test directory that you own. To do this, you will have to re-run the `configure` script with the `--prefix` option. One idea is to use `~/usr` as the prefix, in which case you would configure the package as follows:

```
$ ./configure -prefix ~/usr
```

This allows you to try out new software before making it publicly available to other users on your system. This technique can also be useful if you are working on a multiuser machine on which you are not the administrator. If you want to install the program just for yourself, perhaps this is all you need to do.

You should use this technique to test the `uninstall` target to make sure that it does what it is supposed to do before you put files in a public directory. The `uninstall` target is important. Without it, you can accumulate clutter in your system that can interfere with other programs as time goes on. For simple projects, `install` and `uninstall` are trivial, but for large projects, they can get quite complicated. You should be very reluctant to install a program in public directories unless you are certain that the `uninstall` target works correctly.

2.4   Understanding Errors and Warnings

In this section, I discuss how to interpret errors and warning messages that come from the various build tools and how you can fix them. I look at some common errors that may not have an error or warning associated with them. `Makefiles` are especially prone to this type of error, causing many a developer to struggle to understand why his build doesn't behave the way it is supposed to.

2.4.1   Common Makefile Mistakes

The language of dependencies and prerequisites that make uses is not always intuitive. The build flow is not sequential and not always obvious. Makefile rules can be simple, but the interactions of rules and dependencies can get wildly complicated. Although understanding the basics I discussed earlier goes a long way, even experienced developers get tripped up once in a while.

2.4.1.1   Shell Commands

The default shell used by make in the command portion of a rule is the Bourne shell. To be more specific, Makefile commands are executed using the command listed in the SHELL variable, which defaults to /bin/sh. In theory, you could change this to whatever shell you like, but no one does. That's probably because all the implicit rules are written for the Bourne shell. If you change the shell, you may not be able to use the implicit rules.

Another good reason for not mucking with the default shell is less obvious. When make executes the command portion of a rule, each line of the commands is spawned as a new shell. So when you assign a shell variable on one line of your commands, it is forgotten on the next line. This makes it impossible to write a script unless you can fit the entire script on one line. Fortunately, one-line scripts are a Bourne shell specialty.[10]

Programmers run into trouble, however, when they try to compress as much stuff as they can on one line. If it's a script you want, create a script file and call it from your Makefile. You can write the script in the language you're most comfortable with; ideally, it will be more readable. Just make sure that your script returns a valid exit status so that make will be informed when your script encounters an error.

2.4.1.2   Missing Tabs

It's unfortunate that the designer of make decided to give an invisible character an important meaning. The tab is required before all commands in the command portion of the rule. make uses this to differentiate among commands, targets, and variable assignments.

---

10. Note that you can use line-continuation characters, but no newlines are passed to the shell. This can be tricky to get right.

You cannot replace the leading tab with spaces; that's an error. You may put spaces after the tab but not before it. Because tabs are invisible, it's not obvious when they are replaced by spaces, as some text editors are apt to do. What is worse is the uninformative error you get when this happens, as in the following `Makefile`:

```
all:
@echo Look Ma! No Tabs!
```

Here is what GNU `make` has to say:

```
$ make
Makefile:2: *** missing separator.  Stop.
```

Not the most helpful message, is it?

The problem is that there is no requirement to have commands following a target. `make` must infer whether the line following a target contains commands, a variable assignment, or another target. The separator is what `make` uses to determine the type of line it's looking at. This could be a tab, colon, equal sign, etc. `make` doesn't try to guess what *ought* to be there, but when you see this error, 99 percent of the time it's a command line that hasn't been prefixed with a tab.

That was lucky. Our command didn't happen to have a separator, so at least we got an error message. Consider this case, in which the command is missing a leading tab but contains a different separator:

```
all:
env FOO="Look Ma! No Tabs!" printenv FOO
```

Guess what happens when you run this `Makefile`?

```
$ make
make: Nothing to be done for 'all'.
```

The problem is that `make` saw the separator = and then determined that this is a variable assignment. In case you're wondering, the variable that was assigned is named `$(env FOO)`. Yes, variable identifiers can contain white space, which is why you need those parentheses.

2.4.1.3   VPATH Confusion

Earlier, I introduced the `VPATH` feature of `make`. This feature is very useful for large projects but can be a source of confusion. The main problem occurs when your project has name clashes, such as multiple source files with the same name (a bad idea, but it happens). When this happens, you can end up pulling in a different module than the one you intended.

No matter what you set VPATH to, make always searches the current directory before anyplace else. When make finds a match in the current directory, it does not search any other directories. VPATH is always the second choice for make.

Another problem that can arise with VPATH is actually a C preprocessor issue. It's natural to assume that the C preprocessor will automatically search the current working directory for #include files, but the search path depends on the syntax. When the filename appears in quotes, such as

```
#include "foo.h"
```

the preprocessor automatically searches the directory where the source file resides. Under normal circumstances, both files reside in the current directory, but with a VPATH, the source modules may reside somewhere else. In this case, the preprocessor will search that directory, not the current one. If the #include filename appears in brackets, such as

```
#include <foo.h>
```

the preprocessor searches the standard include directories as well as any directories specified with -I flags, but nowhere else. When you are using a VPATH, this may be the preferable syntax, because you can exert more control over where the source comes from.

Consider a case in which you have a name clash among your header files. If the include statement uses quotes, the C preprocessor will always prefer the copy that resides where the source file resides, regardless of the -I options you use.[11] Suppose that you have multiple builds of the same source code. The source code resides in a directory named /src, and each build is in a separate subdirectory (build1, build2, and so on). Each subdirectory could contain a file named config.h that determines the options for each build. Each directory would also have a Makefile with a VPATH that points to ../src. If the /src directory contains a file named config.h, none of the other config.h files will be used. The C preprocessor will always use the one that resides where the source resides.

---

11. Even GNU's -nostdinc and -include options don't change this behavior.

VPATH gets even more confusing when you have many paths, presenting many opportunities for name clashes. This is where the GNU vpath syntax is preferable, because it allows you to pick only specific source patterns from specific directories.

2.4.2 Errors during the configure Stage

In a project that uses the GNU build tools, the most likely step to fail is the configure step. At least, this is the way it is supposed to work. The idea is to prevent you from wasting time trying to build when you don't have the required tools and libraries. When the configure stage passes, you have a much higher confidence level that your build will complete without errors. When it fails, it should tell you what you need instead of requiring you to guess.

A well-written autoconf script can provide a clear message indicating that you need xyz to build this project and even where to find it. More typically, you will see something like can't find xyz. If you want to build the project, you have little choice but to track down xyz and install it on your system.

In large projects with many configurable options, certain development tools may be required for one feature but not for others. In this case, it's up to the developer to define the configure script so that it correctly identifies the tools that are needed. Because this requires human input, you can rest assured that there will be mistakes. When this happens, you are not likely to realize it unless you are intimately familiar with the project. If you are not an expert in the project (or in autoconf), it's usually easier to appease the configure script than to try to debug it.

There are some occasions where configure complains that you don't have xyz when in fact you do. This can happen if xyz is located in an unexpected place. Usually, configure does a good job of searching for these things. If a required tool is in your path, it will find it. If you have required library or include files installed in a nonstandard place, you must inform the configure script. For some reason, the only way to inform configure about nonstandard directories is via environment variables rather than command-line options. The environment variables used for this purpose are:

CPPFLAGS—indicates nonstandard include paths with additional -I flags

LDFLAGS—indicates nonstandard library directories with additional -L flags

Let's look at an example. Suppose that you are an unprivileged user on a university network, trying to build an open source project named Homer, which uses the

GNU build tools. You run the `configure` script, and it informs you that it requires a particular development library named `Marge`. You track down the source for the `Marge` library—which, luckily, is another GNU build project. Because you are an unprivileged user, you cannot simply install the `Marge` library using the default installation settings. You have to install it under your home directory, so you choose to install it in `~/usr/local/lib`. The entire process for building the `Marge` library would look something like this:

```
$ configure --prefix=~/usr
$ make
$ make install
```

Now to build the `Homer` project, you have to inform `Homer`'s `configure` script where to find the `Marge` library. You do this with the `LDFLAGS` environment variable, as follows:[12]

```
$ LDFLAGS='-L ~/usr/lib' ./configure
```

Typically, a development library provides header files that you need to build code that uses the library. The compiler needs to know where to find these files. Given the prefix from before, `Marge`'s include files would reside in `~/usr/include`. You should indicate this via the `CPPFLAGS` environment variable, as follows:

```
$ LDFLAGS='-L ~/usr/lib' CPPFLAGS='-I  ~/usr/include' ./configure
```

Notice that `LDFLAGS` contains options that are passed to the linker—in this case, the `-L` option. Likewise, `CPPFLAGS` contains flags used by the preprocessor.

2.4.3 Errors during the Build Stage

The job of the `configure` script is to check for all the required development tools and libraries, and depending on the project, it may generate the `Makefile`. An advantage of a project that uses the `configure` script to generate the `Makefile` is that the `Makefile` is not touched by human hands, so in theory, it should be free of syntax errors. You can identify such a project by looking at the distribution archive. When the `configure` script generates the `Makefile`, the archive will not contain a `Makefile`; instead, it will have a file named `Makefile.in`.

---

12. Note that the space before the tilde is required for the shell to expand it properly. The presence of the space requires the use of quotes to set the environment variables properly.

Errors during the build can be broken into two categories: errors in the `Makefile` and errors detected during the build.

2.4.3.1   Errors in the Makefile

Although GNU build tools generate `Makefiles` that are unlikely to have syntax errors, there are ways to introduce syntax errors into an automatically generated `Makefile`. A developer can use the `include` keyword to insert text into the output `Makefile` verbatim, for example. This presents an opportunity to introduce syntax errors into the output `Makefile`.

If the project you are building is not using an automatically generated `Makefile`, you should consult any README files in the project to see what magic is required to build the project. Sometimes, developers use nondefault targets to build the project or require you to specify a variable on the command line manually.

It's usually safe to assume that the person packaging the source code made sure that it built before posting it on the Web. If you can't find a logical explanation for a syntax error in the `Makefile`, perhaps it's an indicator of the quality of the rest of the code. It may not be worth your time to continue in this case.

2.4.3.2   Errors Detected by make

When your `Makefile` is free of syntax errors, any build errors will be in the commands section of the rules. `make` checks the return status of every command it executes and stops when it encounters an error. Developers can choose to ignore errors from specific commands, but this is the exception.

The errors you will see during a build can be broken down as shown in Table 2-8.

I discuss compiler and linker errors in detail later; now I focus on the "other" category.

TABLE 2-8   Build Errors by Category

Error Category	Sources
Compiler errors	Preprocessor errors, syntax errors
Linker errors	Unresolved symbols
Other command errors	Write permission errors, file not found, shell syntax errors, latent syntax errors

Shell syntax errors are not uncommon in `Makefiles`, especially when developers try to cram as much script as they can into a single line. Detecting these errors can be difficult. Consider this defective bit of script inside a `make` rule:

```
t1 t2 t3:
    @if [ "$@"="t1" ]; then echo $@ is target 1; else echo $@ is not target 1;
fi
```

This combines three targets in a single rule—`t1`, `t2`, and `t3`—with no prerequisites. A funny thing happens when you run this:

```
$ make t1 t2 t3
t1 is target 1
t2 is target 1
t3 is target 1
```

Can you spot the error in the script? Because this is not a lesson in scripting, I'll give you the answer: The problem is inside the brackets. The brackets are a shell alias for the `test` command, which requires white space between every operator and tokens. Because there is no white space around the = in this example, the `test` command sees one continuous string but no operators. In this case, test returns zero, which is what `if` considers to be `true`.

Thanks to the @ in front of the script, you won't see this script printed on `stdout` when the rule executes. You can change this behavior in two ways. One is to use the `-n` option of `make`, which shows you a dry run—that is, it prints the commands but does not execute them. Even commands hidden with @ are printed, so the preceding `Makefile` produces the following output:

```
$ make -n t1 t2 t3
if [ "t1"="t1" ]; then echo t1 is target 1; else echo t1 is not target 1; fi
if [ "t2"="t1" ]; then echo t2 is target 1; else echo t2 is not target 1; fi
if [ "t3"="t1" ]; then echo t3 is target 1; else echo t3 is not target 1; fi
```

Now you can see the offending script, which might otherwise be embedded inside several variables and difficult to find inside the `Makefile`. By using the `-n` option, you can see the text that gets passed to the shell verbatim. For tricky problems, you can also redirect this output to a file and run it as a plain script. This is helpful when your compile lines have grown huge, and you need to track down an option that is causing the compiler grief. You can use the output to create a script file that you can tweak until you get it right. When the problem is fixed, you can make that same change inside the `Makefile`.

Another technique for debugging shell commands from a `Makefile` is to change the shell options to include `-x`. This prints out commands as they are executed. You can do this on the command line by modifying the `SHELL` variable as follows:

```
$ make SHELL="/bin/sh -x" t1 t2 t3
+ [ t1=t1 ]
+ echo t1 is target 1
t1 is target 1
+ [ t2=t1 ]
+ echo t2 is target 1
t2 is target 1
+ [ t3=t1 ]
+ echo t3 is target 1
t3 is target 1
```

This causes the shell to print out commands as they are being executed. It shows you only the parts of the script that are being executed, minus the shell keywords. In this example, the test inside the brackets tends to stand out a little more, which may clue you in faster than looking at the raw script. Every case is different, so if one technique doesn't work for you, try the other.

2.4.4   Understanding Compiler Errors

Compilers have gotten better over the years at reporting errors and warnings. In the old days, a simple thing like a missing semicolon in a C program would produce a totally misleading error message. Modern C/C++ compilers are much better at producing error messages that can be parsed automatically.

Let's start with a trivial example of a defective program:

```
1 void foo()
2 {
3        int x,y,z;
4
5        x=1
6        y=2;
7        z=3;
8 }
```

The assignment in line 5 is missing a semicolon. The basic error output from the compiler looks like the following:

```
$ gcc -c foo.c
foo.c: In function 'foo':
foo.c:6: error: parse error before "y"
```

The message format is designed for easy parsing from within an Integrated Development Environment (IDE) or from a text editor, such as Emacs and Vim. The error message consists of three parts separated by colons: the filename, the line number, and a textual message. This is how IDEs and text editors can direct you to the offending source code when it detects an error. The output is human readable, so you don't need any tools to parse this output. As you noticed earlier, the error is on line 5, but the compiler sees an error on line 6. That's because the compiler couldn't determine that the semicolon was missing until line 6.

Interestingly enough, the same code compiled by the C++ compiler produces a more helpful error message:

```
$ g++ -c foo.c
foo.c: In function 'int foo()':
foo.c:6: error: expected ';' before "y"
```

Well-written C code should compile fine with the C++ compiler, which can provide better warnings and strictly enforce the use of prototypes. You could do a quick switch with the offending object and see whether you get a better error message. For example:

```
$ make CC=g++ foo.o
```

Open source projects usually don't use the C++ compiler to compile C code. One reason is that there is no guarantee in the C++ standard that code written in C++ can be called from C. This rules out using C++ to compile development libraries that will be used by C clients. There's also an implicit expectation that code written in C should require only a C compiler.

Errors in the source have a tendency to cascade down, so a single error can cause the compiler to report errors on subsequent lines of code that otherwise would be correct. A best practice when tracking down errors is to start with the first error reported in the module and work your way down. Often, the first error is the only error you have to fix.

A classic example of this is the missing include file, which is something you will encounter often when you build open source code. Every development library uses header files to define the interface, so if you have the wrong version of a required library or none at all, you are likely to encounter a missing include file error.

When the C compiler encounters a missing include file, it produces only one error message indicating a missing include file. This is often followed by dozens or even hundreds of error messages caused by the missing declarations that otherwise would be found in the missing include file. The following code illustrates the error:

```
 1 // foo.h contains the following two lines:
 2 // typedef int type1;
 3 // typedef int type2;
 4
 5 #include "foo.h"
 6
 7 void foo()
 8 {
 9      type1 x;
10      type2 y;
11
12      x = 1;
13      y = 2;
14 }
```

If you compile this file without access to foo.h, the compiler spews out the following errors:

```
$ gcc -c foo.c
foo.c:5:17: foo.h: No such file or directory
foo.c: In function 'foo':
foo.c:9: error: 'type1' undeclared (first use in this function)
foo.c:9: error: (Each undeclared identifier is reported only once
foo.c:9: error: for each function it appears in.)
foo.c:9: error: syntax error before "x"
foo.c:10: error: 'type2' undeclared (first use in this function)
foo.c:12: error: 'x' undeclared (first use in this function)
foo.c:13: error: 'y' undeclared (first use in this function)
```

If you start with the first error, you see that it reports that it can't find foo.h. There is no point in debugging any further errors until you resolve this one. In this case, you know that the only error is that foo.h is missing, but the compiler doesn't know that. The compiler tries to continue as far as possible in the presence of errors. In practice, a preprocessor error is worth stopping for.

2.4.5   Understanding Compiler Warnings

Sometimes, warnings are a welcome opportunity to improve your code. At other times, they can be just a nuisance. In the old days, programmers had to run a program called lint just to get warnings. lint would examine your source code and produce a list of warnings that read like a phone book. The fact that lint was an extra step meant that the user probably was committed to following up on the warnings. Most of these same warnings can now be generated by compiler, so programmers tend to take them for granted or to view them as a nuisance. Perhaps that's why warnings are disabled by default in the GNU compiler.

One excuse for not turning on warnings is as old as the `lint` program. The complaint is that for every warning message that points to a serious problem, there are ten or more messages that are just nitpicking. The nitpicky warnings include things like unused variables, unsigned versus signed integer comparisons, and `printf` formats. Many warnings raise portability concerns, which leads some programmers to think that these warnings don't apply to them. Even if you don't ever plan to support anything but Linux on IA32, you may want to upgrade your compiler at some point. The same portability issues that occur when moving between processors or operating systems can be problems when upgrading from one version of a compiler to the next. Warnings are not hard to fix, and fixing them makes your code more robust.

The easiest way to turn on warnings with the GNU C/C++ compiler is to use the `-Wall` option, which turns on a select set of warnings chosen by the GNU team. These represent a conservative set of warnings, none of which will generate an error. There are dozens of command-line options to control warnings that the GNU compiler supports. Virtually every individual type of warning produced with `-Wall` can be disabled, and additional warnings can be enabled as well.

Typically, projects built with the GNU build tools ship with warnings turned off. Perhaps this is because the options to turn on warnings are not standard across compilers. This is unfortunate, but you can turn on warnings in a project that uses the GNU build tools with the following `configure` command:

```
$ CFLAGS=-Wall ./configure
```

You usually can assume that a mature project compiled without warnings when it was released. It's possible that although it compiled cleanly for IA32, there could be warnings when it compiles for x86_64. Also, different versions of the compiler warn about different things, so you may see new warnings pop up when you compile with a newer compiler than the developers are using. If you are digging into the source and trying to fix a bug, turning on warnings is a good place to start.

2.4.5.1   Warnings: Implicit Declarations

With `-Wall`, the compiler warns you when it encounters implicitly defined variables or functions in C code. (In C++, this is simply an error.) Most experienced programmers know not to compile code with these warnings. If you see one of these warnings, it is probably a sign of some very old legacy code that has not been touched in ages or of an inexperienced programmer at work.

An implicitly defined variable is a variable that appears on the left side of an assignment expression before it appears in a declaration. Such a variable is implicitly defined to be an int. Traditional C allows this for global variables, and gcc is very permissive about it. For example:

```
$ echo "x=1;" > foo.c
$ gcc -c -Wall foo.c
foo.c:1: warning: type defaults to 'int' in declaration of 'x'
foo.c:1: warning: data definition has no type or storage class
```

Even with the -ansi option, this still compiles. The only way to force an error for implicit variable declarations is to use the -pedantic option, but this could cause the compiler to complain about other code. Use this option carefully.

Likewise, an implicitly defined function is one that is used without a preceding function declaration or prototype. When a function is defined implicitly, the compiler assumes that it returns an int and makes no assumptions about the number or type of arguments the function takes. This is equivalent to the following function declaration:

```
int foo(); // Function declaration - no info about arguments
```

Note that a function declaration is not the same as a function prototype. A function declaration is a legacy that predates the ANSI standard. It informs the compiler about the return type, but tells the compiler nothing about the arguments. When the compiler sees a function with no prototype, it accepts any number of arguments of any type. This allows legacy C code to compile but has no place in modern code. A prototype specifies the exact number and type of arguments for a function in addition to its return value.

The problem is that either a function prototype or a function declaration will satisfy the C compiler when using -Wall. If you want to see warnings when a function is used without a prototype, use -Wstrict-prototypes. When the compiler encounters a function declaration, gcc (3.4.4) prints the following message:

```
foo.c:2: warning: function declaration isn't a prototype
```

Now that you know all about function declarations and prototypes, you will actually understand what this warning means when you see it.

2.4.5.2   Format Warnings

One of the checks turned on with the -Wall flag is format checking. The GNU compiler checks the format strings of the printf family of functions, looking for the correct number of arguments and verifying that the argument type matches the format. Format checking is done for all the functions listed in Table 2-9.

Format checking can uncover very-hard-to-find errors. The %s format in a printf statement, for example, can cause a segmentation violation if you give it an invalid pointer. The compiler warns you, for example, if you inadvertently use a %s format with an argument that isn't a char *. This kind of mistake is easy to make, particularly with format strings that have many arguments. The following trivial example illustrates the warning:

```
1 #include <stdio.h>
2 void foo(int x)
3 {
4       printf("%s", x);
5 }
```

When you compile this with -Wall, you see the following message:

```
$ gcc -c -Wall foo.c
foo.c: In function 'foo':
foo.c:4: warning: format argument is not a pointer (arg 2)
```

TABLE 2-9   Functions That Have Format Checking

printf Variants		scanf Variants	
printf	vprintf	scanf	vscanf
fprintf	vfprintf	fscanf	vfscanf
sprintf	vsprintf	sscanf	vsscanf
snprintf	vsnprintf		

This tells you that the format calls for a pointer, but the argument (in this case, the second argument to `printf`) is not a pointer. A `%s` format requires a `char *` pointer specifically, If you pass the wrong kind of pointer—for example, `int *`—you will see a warning as well. Such warnings are core dumps waiting to happen.

There are similar messages for other format mismatches, but not all such mistakes can crash your code. In particular, the IA32 architecture rarely crashes when the wrong type of argument is passed to an integer format. The IA32 is very permissive about data alignment; typically, the worst thing that happens is that you see garbled output. Other CPU architectures are not so forgiving, and mismatching the types in your `printf` formats can cause your code to crash.

It's not unusual to see format warnings in code, especially if you are turning warnings on for the first time. IA32 programmers can be complacent and may ignore warnings that they think don't apply to them. In particular, many have gotten used to substituting `long int` and `int` types as equivalent. The compiler warns when you use pass a `long` integer to a `%d` format (the correct format for a `long` integer is `%ld`). On an IA32, this is not a problem, because a `long` is the same size as an `int`. On a 64-bit machine, these are not the same size. On the x86_64 platform (for example, Opteron and Xeon/EM64T), an `int` continues to be 32 bits, and a `long` is 64-bits. This is becoming more important as 64-bit architectures become more popular.

Although `printf` is a relatively safe function to call, `scanf` is much more dangerous. Whatever the architecture, a bad `scanf` argument can crash your program. Because the arguments are pointers into program memory, a type mismatch here can result in a buffer overrun and corrupt memory. All warnings about `scanf` formats should be taken seriously.

Two other options can be added for format checking beyond those turned on by `-Wall`:

- `-Wformat-nonliteral`—This issues a warning when the compiler encounters a format string that is a variable instead of a string literal. This means that the format cannot be checked. Worse, because the format can change at runtime, this presents opportunities at runtime for bugs that can crash your code.

- `-Wformat-y2k`—Applies to the `strftime` and `strptime` functions, which use a format syntax similar to that of `printf`. You will see a warning whenever it sees a two-digit year format.

2.4.5.3   Other Warnings the GNU C Compiler Emits

In addition to format warnings, the GNU compilers can produce many other warnings. Each type of warning can be turned on individually or turned on when selected features are enabled:

- **Null pointer arguments**—Check pointer arguments of selected functions for null at compile time. This does not guarantee that null arguments will not be passed at runtime. As of `glibc` 3.4.4, there is almost no checking for this in the C/C++ standard library.

- **Missing parentheses**—Warn you when an assignment is used in a Boolean context, such as an `if` statement. Often, this is unintentional. For example:

```
if ( x = y ) //versus...
if ( x == y )
```

Line 1 is both an assignment and a Boolean test, but it could also be a typographical error. Perhaps line 2 is what you intended. This is a very common form of typographical error, so the compiler will warn you about it. An extra set of parentheses clears up the ambiguity, as follows:

```
if ( (x = y) )
```

- **Missing braces**—Warn you when your `if`/`else` statements do not use braces. This can be a source of errors, as follows:

```
1 void foo(int x, int y, int *z)

2 {
3       if ( x == y )
4               if ( y == *z ) *z = 0.0;
5       else
6               *z = 1.0;
7 }
```

The indentation in this example suggests that the `else` statement on line 5 belongs to the `if` statement on line 3, but the lack of braces dictates that this `else` statement belongs to the `if` on line 4. The warning suggests that you use braces in case this is an error:

```
$gcc -c -Wall foo.c
paren.c: In function 'foo':
paren.c:3: warning: suggest explicit braces to avoid ambiguous 'else'
```

To correct this, add braces to each `if` and `else` clause, as follows:

```
1 if (x == y) {
2     if (y == *z) {
3         *z = 0.0;
4     }
5 }
6 else
7 {
8     *z = 1.0;
9 }
```

- **Uninitialized variables**—Warn you when variables may be used before being initialized. These can be false alarms, but the problems are easy to spot when the compiler points them out. You see these warnings only when compiling with optimization. For example:

```
1 int foo(int y)
2 {
3     int x;
4     if ( y > 0 ) {
5         x = 1;
6     }
7     return x;
8 }
```

Here, the variable x is not initialized if y <= 0. In this case, the function returns an undefined value. Compiling without optimization produces no warning, but adding optimization (with -O1, -O2, and so on) produces a warning, as follows:

```
$ gcc -Wall -c -O2 uninit.c
uninit.c: In function 'foo':
uninit.c:3: warning: 'x' might be used uninitialized in this function
```

The code is just as defective without optimization, but the compiler doesn't have access to the same information when it isn't optimizing. The information it needs comes from analyzing the code flow, which is part of the optimization process.

The list of warnings the `gcc` compiler is capable of showing is long. Most warnings can be enabled and disabled on an individual basis. It is worth studying the `gcc` manual to learn more.

2.4.5.4   C++ Specific Warnings from the GNU Compiler

C++ has increased type safety over C, and many of the warnings in C (such as missing prototypes) are errors in C++. Despite this, there are plenty of new and object-oriented ways to screw up your code. The GNU compiler provides several warnings specific to C++. Some notable warnings that are turned on with `-Wall` include the following:

- **Nonvirtual destructors**—Warn you when a polymorphic class has a nonvirtual destructor. This can be a source of runtime errors due to memory leaks and resources not being released as a result of the wrong destructor being called. For example:

```
1 class Base {
2       char *m_ptr;
3 public:
4       Base() : m_ptr(0) { m_ptr = new char[1024]; };
5       virtual char *ptr() { return m_ptr; };
6       ~Base() { delete [] m_ptr; } ;
7 };
8
9 class Foo : public Base {
10      char *foo_ptr;
11 public:
12      Foo() { foo_ptr = new char[1024]; };
13      virtual char *ptr() { return foo_ptr; };
14      virtual ~Foo() { delete [] foo_ptr; } ;
15 };
```

```
$ gcc -Wall -c polymorph.cpp
polymorph.cpp:1: warning: 'class Base' has virtual functions but non-
virtual destructor
```

  The destructor in class `Base` must be declared virtual, or it will never be called when we delete a pointer of type `Foo  *`. Note the fact that the derived class destructor `~Foo` is virtual does not help. The `Base` class is still defective.

- **Reordered initializers**—Warn you when you define your initializers in a different order from the order in which they were declared. The standard calls for the compiler to initialize members in the same order in which the members are declared. The order in which the initializers appear in the code is irrelevant,

which can be misleading. Here's an example of how the initializers can fool
you into creating a bug:

```
 1 struct Foo {
 2     int m_two;              // declaration
 3     int m_one;
 4     Foo( int one )
 5     : m_one(one),           // initializer
 6       m_two(m_one+1) {};
 7 };
 8
 9 #include <iostream>
10
11 int main(int argc, char **argv[])
12 {
13     Foo f(1);
14     std::cout << f.m_one << std::endl;
15     std::cout << f.m_two << std::endl;
16 }

$ gcc -c -Wall order.cpp
order.cpp: In constructor 'Foo::Foo(int)':
order.cpp:3: warning: 'Foo::m_one' will be initialized after
order.cpp:2: warning:   'int Foo::m_two'
order.cpp:6: warning:   when initialized here
```

The initializers appear on lines 5 and 6 above. If you look at only the two initializers, you may see nothing wrong. Look again, and you realize that m_two
was defined first and therefore is initialized first. This is a problem, because
m_two is initialized using the value of m_one, which is uninitialized when
m_two is initialized. To solve the problem, you must reorder the declarations
so that m_two is declared after m_one.

• **Deprecated features**—Emit warnings for modules that use deprecated features
  such as using old-style Standard Template Library (STL) headers (for example,
  iostream.h instead of <iostream>). The warning you will see looks like the
  following:

```
warning: #warning This file includes at least one deprecated or antiquated
header. Please consider using one of the 32 headers found in section
17.4.1.2 of the C++ standard. Examples include substituting the <X> header
for the <X.h> header for C++ includes, or <iostream> instead of the
deprecated header <iostream.h>. To disable this warning use -Wno-
deprecated.
```

This warning pops up even when you compile without warnings enabled. If you follow the suggestion, you will change the #include statements to use the new-style headers—but not so fast. Along with the new headers comes much stricter namespace enforcement. In particular, any references to symbols in namespace std will not compile unless you add the appropriate namespace qualifier or a using statement. You are likely to see this only in legacy code that predates the C++ standard or in code you may be porting from a system with a more permissive C++ compiler. You have three choices here:

1. Easiest—Ignore it and/or turn it off using -Wno-deprecated.

2. Easy—Fix the offending headers and add the statement using namespace std to the module body *(but not in any header files).*[13]

3. More work—Fix the offending headers and use appropriate namespace qualifiers.

- **Incompatible ABI**—This warning is not part of -Wall but is turned on with the -Wabi flag. *ABI* stands for *Application Binary Interface*, and it is the convention used for calling functions that allows multiple programming languages to live in the same program. You may be writing a C++ program that calls a library written in Fortran, and even though you don't have a Fortran compiler, your program works. This is possible because the Fortran compiler follows a particular ABI. The ABI tells the compiler how to call a function and how to pass arguments.

  The ABI is unique for each combination of processor and operating system, because each has unique requirements and capabilities. Most procedural languages have no issues conforming to a common ABI, so ABIs typically are language neutral. C++, however, is sufficiently complicated that it requires the ABI to be extended in ways that are unique to the C++ language. The lack of a standard ABI requires each compiler to make arbitrary extensions to the C ABI to support C++. As a result, for example, you may not be able to link code created by GNU C++ with a library compiled by a commercial vendor because

---

13. *Never* put using namespace std in a header file. This pollutes the namespace of any module that uses it and can cause difficult-to-find bugs.

the ABIs may not be compatible. For that matter, you cannot link C++ code compiled with version *3.x* of the GNU compiler with a library created with version *2.x*, because the ABI changed between those two versions.

Today, there still is no universally standard C++ ABI, but GNU follows a published ABI that allegedly is vendor neutral.[14] As of g++ 3.4.4, the GNU compiler itself has some issues with this common ABI. This warning informs you when your code has run into one of these issues. Here's an example from the g++ info page:

```
$ cat <<EOF > foo.cpp
struct A {};

struct B {
    A a;
    virtual void f ();
};
EOF
$ gcc -Wall -Wabi -c foo.cpp
foo.cpp:4: warning: 'B::a' contains empty classes which may cause base
classes to be placed at different locations in a future version of GCC
```

If you see this warning, it means that you may have issues if you try to link with C++ libraries that are compiled with a third-party compiler or perhaps a slightly different version of g++.

Finally, there is one more C++ warning feature worth mentioning: The -Weffc++ flag warns when your code violates style guidelines from Scott Meyer's *Effective C++* book. You don't need the book to learn from the warnings. Try this feature on your own code when you have time to improve your skills. This produces some very informative warnings about your coding style that could lead to bugs down the road.

2.4.6   Understanding Linker Errors

Given a correctly formatted linker command line, the most likely linker error you will encounter is a missing symbol. A missing symbol can be a function or a global

---

14. www.codesourcery.com/cxx-abi/abi.html

variable that an object file refers to but does not declare. This can happen, for example, when you try to build a project using an incompatible version of a library. A missing symbol is reported as an undefined reference and looks like the following:

```
$ g++ -Wall -o main main.o -lfoo
main.o(.text+0x11): In function 'main':
: undefined reference to 'bar()'
```

When an undefined reference occurs in a C program, it means that you are missing a library or object file on your link line or that you have an incompatible version of the library that doesn't define the particular symbol.

Undefined references can also show up with C++ programs and libraries because of a difference in name mangling between your compiler and the one that built the library. *Name mangling* is a technique that C++ compilers use to rename functions based on their signature. Because the linker knows nothing about C++, the compiler must append data to function names to give them unique signatures that the linker can understand. Typically, the compiler appends extra characters to the function names to indicate the number and types of arguments.

When this happens, it can be frustrating, because you usually see an unresolved symbol like the preceding example. You don't have any clue that the name mangling is incompatible. The nm command can help here. Using the above example, you can see what the mangled name of bar() looks like by using the following command:

```
$ nm -u main.o | grep bar
         U _Z3barv
```

The string _Z3barv is how g++ 3.3.5 mangles the function signature void bar(void). If libfoo is compiled with a different incompatible compiler, the signature might be completely different. This is due to the fact that there is no standard way to mangle names in C++. If you installed a binary package that was built with an incompatible compiler, you may see such errors. Unfortunately, the only way to resolve this is to compile both your code and the library with the same compiler.

Another thing to be aware of is the fact that the linker is picky about the order of libraries specified on the linker command line. I will illustrate this by creating two libraries and one main module, as follows:

```
main.c
1 extern void two();
2 int main(int argc, char *argv[]) { two(); }

one.c
1 void one(void) { }

two.c
1 extern void one(void);
2 void two(void) { one(); }
```

Now I create two libraries and try to link as follows:

```
$ ar -clq libone.a one.o
$ ar -clq libtwo.a two.o
$ gcc -o main main.c -L. -lone -ltwo
./libtwo.a(two.o)(.text+0x7): In function 'two':
/home/john/src/linker/two.c:5: undefined reference to 'one'
collect2: ld returned 1 exit status
```

In this example, the function `two()` calls `one()`, and these functions reside in `libtwo.a` and `libone.a`, respectively. The linker sees `libone.a` first, because it is the first `-l` option on the command line. At this point, it is looking to resolve the reference to `two()` from `main()`. Because there are no references to `one()` yet, the linker assumes that it is safe to discard the module containing `one()`. Next, it processes `libtwo.a` and resolves the reference to `two()` from `main()`. But now it has an unresolved reference to `one()`. Because it has already discarded that module, the link will fail with an unresolved reference to `one()`.

The solution is simple. Just switch the order of the libraries on the command line as follows:

```
$ gcc -o main main.c -L. -ltwo -lone
```

Now the linker is satisfied. The dependencies are resolved from left to right—that is, the libraries on the left require the libraries on the right.

2.5   Summary

This chapter introduced the tools used to build open source code. The `make` tool is the most commonly used among open source projects written in C and C++. For this reason, I devoted quite a bit of coverage of `make` and how to use it.

2.5.1   Tools Used in This Chapter

- `configure`—a script that comes with each GNU project, which generates the `Makefile` to be used by `make`.

- `cons`—a build system based on the Perl scripting language that attempted to replace `make`.

- `make`—the most common UNIX build tool for C and C++ code.

- `scons`—an attempt to reimplement `cons` in the Python scripting language and overcome `cons`'s shortcomings.

2.5.2   Online References

- www.gnu.org/software/autoconf—the GNU `autoconf` project used to distribute GNU source

- www.gnu.org/software/make—the GNU home page for the `make` project

- www.python.org—the home page for the Python scripting language

- www.scons.org—the home page of the `scons` tool

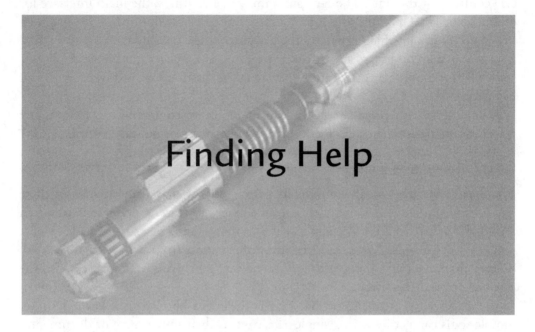

Chapter 3

Finding Help

3.1 Introduction

There's an old joke that goes something like this: "Programmers shouldn't document their code. It should be as difficult to use as it was to write." Intentional or not, the fact is that open source code often lives up to these expectations.

Although most tools do a good job of providing documentation and making it easy to find, many don't. Sometimes, you just need to know where to look.

3.2 Online Help Tools

An important innovation of UNIX was the use of online[1] help. This was a welcome alternative to keeping a shelf full of printed manuals at your disposal, which was

---

1. The term *online* here refers to documentation in electronic format as opposed to hard copy, not the modern definition that implies the Internet.

also common at the time. The man program was, and still is, the main interface for online help. The GNU project, looking for a more flexible online format, invented the Texinfo format, which generates the documentation used by the info program. Some tools may neglect to provide man pages or info pages, and instead provide some plain text or other format tucked away in the distribution, just waiting for you to find it.

Although man and info are the formats of choice for command-line tools, many GUIs choose to use their help menus as the only source of online documentation.

3.2.1   The man Page

The idea of viewing documentation in a text window may seem archaic in these days of HTML and PDF, but there are advantages to reading documentation in a terminal window. This is especially true if, like many Linux developers, that is where you do most of your work. Getting the information from a man page is much quicker than opening a browser or a PDF viewer. When you want answers fast, the man page is what you want.

man pages have a concise format that is meant to be read in a linear fashion. Simple tools can get by with a single man page as their only source of documentation; more complicated tools and programming libraries rely on a suite of man pages for documentation. Perl even created its own manual section containing hundreds of pages covering various aspects of Perl.

In the past, man pages were limited to ASCII (or ISO-8859) characters, which limited the selection of languages in which they could be written. This was largely due to the limitations of the text terminals used to display them. In the old days, text terminals were capable of handling only 7- or 8-bit character encodings, and memory constraints limited the number of available fonts. Those dumb terminals are largely a thing of the past. GUI-based terminals such as xterm are capable of handling many fonts and character encodings with no issues. The tools that create man pages allow more of a selection of character encodings, such as UTF-8, so man pages can now be written in any language.

man pages are written in an ancient markup language called troff. The troff text-formatting language, although quite old, is still very powerful. Like HTML, troff output is formatted to fit the device on which it is being presented. So in addition to viewing in a text window, the output can be formatted for printout or transformed into HTML or PDF. To format a man page for PostScript printout, for example, you can use the -t option as follows:

```
$ man -t man | lp -Pps
```

You can pipe this output to any tool that understands PostScript to manipulate the output any way you like.

There are two flavors of man in use in various distributions. Red Hat and many other RPM-based distributions use the traditional man program, whereas Debian-based distributions use a package named man-db. The difference between the two is primarily in the database that is used to index and catalog the man pages. The man-db approach has some advantages over the traditional man page database, but for the most part, both sets of tools behave the same way.

3.2.2   man Organization

The Linux manual is broken up into sections. This follows the Filesystem Hierarchy Standard,[2] which, among other things, specifies the contents of each man section. A summary of these sections is listed in Table 3-1.

TABLE 3-1   Linux Manual Sections

Section	Description
1	User commands available from the shell
2	System calls available to programs via library functions
3	Library functions available to programs
4	Devices available in /dev directory
5	Miscellaneous system files (for example, /etc)
6	Games, if any
7	Miscellaneous information
8	Commands available to administrators

2. www.pathname.com/fhs

The division of the manual into sections allows man pages to avoid name clashes. A command named sync is documented in section 1, for example, and a function named sync is documented in section 2. Both man pages are named sync. If they weren't documented in different sections, the system would have to resort to some odd naming conventions to distinguish between the two. Occasionally, you have to jump through a few hoops to get the man page you want. If you want to see the man page for the sync command, the following will do on most systems:

```
$ man sync
```

If you want the man page for the sync *function*, you need to know that sync is a system call and that it is documented in section 2. To look at this specific man page, you specify the section number before the page name, as follows:

```
$ man 2 sync
```

Another confounding factor is that some distributions take the liberty of creating their own sections. Perl is one example mentioned earlier. Another is section 3p, which comes with Fedora. This contains POSIX functions (hence, the p). This section also contains a man page for the sync function, which is virtually identical to the man page in section 2. If you are not sure, and you just want to see all the man pages the system knows about, you can type

```
$ man -a sync
```

This brings up the man pages in order, and each time you press q to exit the man page, you are presented with the next matching man page.

The convention for referring to a man page in a specific section is to put the section number in parentheses following the page name. The sync function in section 2, for example, would be referenced as sync(2), whereas the sync function in section 3p would be referenced as sync(3p). This notational convention is used throughout man pages, and I follow this convention in the footnotes of this book.

You might expect that when the section is not specified, each section is searched in sequence. But most distributions choose to search for commands before functions. That means that man searches section 8 (System Administration Commands) before section 3 (Programming Libraries). If you are a system administrator (and who isn't?), that makes sense. But as a programmer, if I am writing a socket program and need the man page for the accept function located in section 3, typing man accept will give me the man page for the accept command from the Common

UNIX Printer System package documented in section 8. If you are like me, you probably don't remember which section is which off the top of your head. That is where the whatis command comes in handy:

```
$ whatis accept
accept (8)              - accept/reject jobs sent to a destination
accept (2)              - accept a connection on a socket
```

This shows you the man pages in the order in which they are found. In this case, it's apparent that section 8 is searched before section 2. It also shows you that the man page you are looking for is in section 2.

The man page search order is determined in a system configuration file, which varies based on installation. Fedora and Ubuntu (Debian-based) use /etc/man.config, whereas Knoppix (also Debian-based) uses /etc/manpath.config. The mandb version allows you to override the settings for yourself in ~/.manpath. The traditional package, however, does not allow you to override the defaults without a command-line option or environment variable.

The command-line manual tools leave a few things to be desired. It would be nice, for example, to browse section 3 of the manual. Unfortunately, the command-line tools do not allow casual browsing of the manual; neither do they allow you simply to list all the entries in a particular section. The old xman tool, which was part of the original X11 distribution, would let you browse by section, but most newer distributions no longer include this tool. One tool that will let you browse the man pages by section is part of the KDE project. The khelpcenter program allows you to browse not only KDE documentation, but the plain old man pages as well, as you can see in Figure 3-1.

You might be asking, "What about GNOME?" As of this writing, the gnome-help tool does not support browsing of the man pages.

3.2.3   Searching the man Pages: apropos

If you can't browse the manuals, the next-best thing you can do is search them. There are two basic tools for this purpose: apropos and whatis. apropos is an unusual name for a UNIX command, not just because it has more than three letters, but also because this is a word most native English speakers haven't seen since their last high-school vocabulary quiz. The word *apropos* means *relevant*, which is the idea behind the command. You give a keyword, and it comes up with relevant results (ideally).

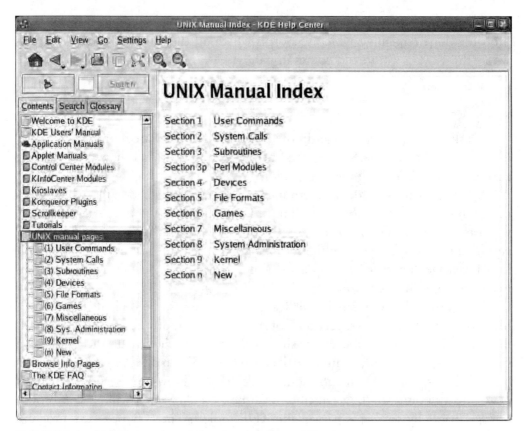

FIGURE 3-1   Using `khelpcenter` to Browse the `man` Sections

Unfortunately, the `apropos` command searches only the NAME section of the manual entries, which contains only a brief one-line description of the topic. So if your keyword doesn't show up in the NAME section, `apropos` won't help. Only one keyword at a time is searched. So if you specify two keywords, you get all the matches for the first keyword, followed by all the matches for the second keyword. By default, matching occurs anywhere in the text, so the word `man` matches the words *manual, command,* etc., as well as the word `man`. This is not a search engine. The results you get may be anything but apropos.

You also have to be careful that your keyword is not too restrictive. Searching for the word *compression,* for example, ought to show you something about compression utilities, but when I type `apropos compression`, the results are missing two of the most popular ones: `bzip2` and `gzip`. Here are the results from Fedora Core 4, for example:

```
$ apropos compression
Compress::Zlib         (3pm)  - Interface to zlib ...
pbmtopsg3              (1)    - convert PBM ...
SSL_COMP_add_compression_method (3ssl)  - handle ...
zlib                  (3)    - compression/decompression ...
```

The problem is that the term *compression* does not match the words *compress* and *compressor*, which, as it turns out, are the words used to describe `gzip` and `bzip2`, respectively. So our keyword search comes up with nothing. You can see this summary for yourself with the `whatis` command as follows:

```
$ whatis gzip bzip2
gzip (1)              - compress or expand files
bzip2 (1)            - a block-sorting file compressor, v1.0.2
```

The traditional version of `apropos`, found in Red Hat distributions, takes no options. The `mandb` version of `apropos`, found in Debian distributions, takes several, including options to restrict matches to exact matches or whole words. Both versions allow you to use regular expressions.[3] For example:

```
$ apropos 'mag[tn]'
mt (1)               - control magnetic tape drive operation
mt-gnu (1)           - control magnetic tape drive operation
rmt (8)              - remote magtape protocol module
rmt-tar (8)          - remote magtape protocol module
xmag (1x)            - magnify parts of the screen
```

The expression `mag[tn]` matches *magtape* and *magnify,* so your search results include anything that has either word. The `man-db` version of `apropos` found in Debian distributions allows you to restrict output to exact matches with the `-e` option. This allows you, for example, to look for the word *compress* without also matching the word *compressor.* Table 3-2 shows a summary of features by package.

---

3. If you need a primer on regular expressions, see `regex(7)` in the manual.

TABLE 3-2   Search Features by Package

Search Features	Traditional	mandb
Regular expressions	Yes	Yes
Exact matches		Yes
Brute-force matching	Yes	

The traditional version of man allows you to do a brute-force search for keywords by looking at every word in every single man page. The -K option (note the capitalization) of man does this and is guaranteed to be slow even on the fastest machines. When a thorough search is in order, this is the best you can do.

3.2.4   Getting the Right man Page: whatis

We saw how different sections can have man pages with the same name, which can cause you to get the wrong man page when you don't know what section to look in. If you want to look up the usage of the readdir function, for example, typing man readdir will take you to section 2 of the manual, which says:

```
This is not the function you are interested in.  Look at readdir(3) for the
POSIX conforming C library interface.  This page documents the bare kernel
system call interface, which can change, and which is superseded by getdents(2).
```

Luckily, in this case the man page is helpful enough to let you know that you are looking at a system call and not a POSIX function. It even tells you what section to look in. In the more likely event that the man page is not so helpful, the whatis command can help:

```
$ whatis readdir
readdir             (2)  - read directory entry
readdir             (3)  - read a directory
```

Because section 3 contains the man page we are looking for, we can then specify the correct man page as follows:

```
$ man 3 readdir
```

The traditional version of whatis takes no arguments, so matching is permissive. The mandb version allows regular expressions and shell-style wildcard matching. If you can't remember a command but remember that it ends with `zip`, for example, you can try the following search:

```
$ whatis -w "*zip"
funzip (1)              - filter for extracting from a ZIP ..
gunzip (1)             - compress or expand files
gzip (1)               - compress or expand files
unzip (1)              - list, test and extract compressed ...
zip (1)                - package and compress (archive) files
```

A less elegant way to get the man page you are looking for is to read all of them until you find the one you like. This is done with the -a option to man, which says, "Show me all the man pages that match." The sections are presented in the order determined by the local configuration, which can get tedious. On my Fedora Core 4 installation, for example, man -a read brings up eight man pages. Sifting through eight man pages might provide some incentive for you to remember the section number for next time.

3.2.5 Things to Look for in the man Page

A Linux man page follows the conventions that are documented in section 7 of the manual.[4] A minimal man page has a NAME section, which consists of the name of the program or topic being documented, followed by a brief description. This is the only text that is searched by the apropos command.

Most man pages consist of more than just a NAME section, of course. There are several standard sections defined by convention, but programmers are free to define additional sections as appropriate.

The SEE ALSO section is the closest thing you will get to cross-referenced documentation in a man page. Don't be surprised if this refers you to a man page that does not exist on your system (or perhaps anywhere else). Occasionally, some older man pages refer to programs that don't exist anymore. It's also possible that the man page refers to a program that just isn't installed on your system. You should always look at the SEE ALSO section and try to find the cross references. You can learn a lot more than you would by reading one man page alone.

The ENVIRONMENT section provides valuable information about how environment variables affect the program's behavior. Usually, this section covers locale

---

4. See man(7).

issues, but occasionally, there are some nice shortcuts that can be encapsulated in an environment variable. Some programs, for example, allow you to put lengthy command-line options in an environment variable to save you the trouble of typing them every time. The ENVIRONMENT section is always worth a peek.

Another section worth looking at is the CONFORMING TO section, which tells you what standards apply to the command or function. This is important when you are writing portable programs. There are many examples of multiple functions that do the same thing in Linux. This conformance should be the tie-breaker when it comes to deciding which one to use. The bcopy function does the same thing that memcpy does, for example, but if you check the CONFORMING TO section for bcopy, you will see that it conforms to 4.3BSD. The memcpy function also conforms to 4.3BSD, but it is also part of the ISO C standard (ISO 9899), so memcpy should be preferred for portability.

Near the bottom of the man page, you may see a BUGS section. Perhaps this is a misnomer, because some people say that the only difference between a bug and a feature is the documentation. Regardless, the BUGS section usually documents design limitations of the program or features that aren't fully functional. Sometimes, it contains a "to do" list to let you know what features are planned. It's an optional section, but if someone took the time to write the section, it behooves you to read it.

3.2.6   Some Recommended man Pages

Every section of the manual has an intro page that can be helpful if you forget which section is which. Though the intro pages themselves don't have much useful information,[5] they can serve as a quick reminder about section names, as follows:

```
$ whatis intro
intro               (1)  - Introduction to user commands
intro               (2)  - Introduction to system calls
intro               (3)  - Introduction to library functions
intro               (4)  - Introduction to special files
intro               (5)  - Introduction to file formats
intro               (6)  - Introduction to games
intro               (7)  - Introduction to conventions and miscellany
                           section
intro               (8)  - Introduction to administration and
                           privileged commands
```

---

5.   intro(2) is one exception here. There is a useful introduction to system calls.

If the idea of casually reading the manual seems weird, that probably means you have never spent much time reading it. There are several pages with useful information and tutorials that you would never find unless you looked for them. Many of these are in section 7, which is probably the least-read section of the manual. Table 3-3 lists a few of the selections from section 7 you may want to read.

TABLE 3-3   Recommended Reading from Section 7 of the Manual

Name	Description
ascii(7)	A short, handy page that simply lists ASCII codes in tables—very handy when you need to know silly details like the octal constant for Ctrl+G.
boot(7)	A nice overview of the kernel boot sequence. If you are trying to build distribution from scratch or just want to learn how Linux boots, this is a good read.
bootparam(7)	A nice summary of the low-level options that the kernel can take on the command line. This list is long, and it is most assuredly not complete, but it is very informative.
charsets(7)	A nice overview of character sets used in Linux, with a brief overview of the features of each. If you work on internationalized programs (i18n), this is a must read.
hier(7)	A good overview of the Filesystem Hierarchy Standard, which describes the conventions used to lay out the directories in a Linux system. It answers burning questions like "What's the difference between /bin and /usr/bin?" If you are developing an application for distribution, read this before you decide where to install your files.
man(7)	So you want to write a man page? This section tells you how, giving you just enough troff to get by as well as an explanation of the conventions used in Linux man pages.
operator(7)	Lists the C operators and their precedence. If you hate using extra parentheses in your code, you should study this man page. After reading this page, you should be able to find the bug in the following C statement: `if ( 1 & 2 == 2 ) printf("bit one is set\n");`

continues

TABLE 3-3   *Continued*

Name	Description
`regex(7)`	An introduction to regular expressions, which is a topic every programmer should master.
`suffixes(7)`	In Linux, file suffixes are conventions for the user. The OS relies on more reliable techniques to determine a file type. This man page describes many of the known conventional suffixes in use. It is not complete but can be helpful.
`units(7)`	Lists standard unit multipliers defined by SI.[6] Did you know that according to SI rules, a megabyte is actually 1,000,000 bytes and not 1,048,576 bytes (2^{20} bytes)? Disk drive manufacturers know this, and you should too. We software developers tend to use the prefixes for decimal multipliers when we mean to use the binary prefixes.
	The SI defines unique prefixes for such binary values that no one uses. Perhaps we should. By the way, 1,048,576 bytes is properly called a *mebibyte* (abbreviated MiB). Although this terminology is not likely to catch on any time soon, you must be aware of the potential for confusion when you are talking requirements with a scientist, hardware engineer, or disk drive vendor.
	There's also some nifty trivia in here, such as the prefix for a million billion billion. Impress your friends.
`uri(7)`, `url(7)`, `urn(7)`	Three keys for the same man page, describing the components of a URL and what they mean. You may think you know all the things that can go into a URL, but check this page out and see whether you learn anything.

Remember that all the man pages listed in Table 3-3 are in section 7 and that some of these names clash with those in other sections. Be sure you specify the section in order to get the correct man page.

---

6. *SI* is an abbreviation for *Système International d'unités*, the international standard for scientific measurements.

3.2.7 GNU info

When you're looking for documentation for GNU tools, the info program is the preferred tool. Very often, GNU man pages contain an abridged version of the documentation that refers you to the info program for more details.

The fact that GNU chose to use a unique tool to document its tools is something of a nuisance to UNIX folks, who are used to man pages, but info provides several features that you don't get in a man page. For one thing, info files are hyperlinked and heavily cross referenced. So when you browse the documentation for ssh, for example, it will refer to other relevant tools, such as ssh-keygen. You can follow the link in the documentation to go to the documentation for ssh-keygen and go back again, just like on a Web page. Another feature of info pages is that they are indexed so that you can locate relevant documentation more effectively than on a man page.

GNU info pages are written in a markup language called Texinfo. Like troff, Texinfo predates HTML and XML but is built upon earlier work. Texinfo evolved from the TeX formatting language (still in wide use today) and another project called scribe, which lives on today as scheme scribe. The goal of Texinfo was to mark up content, not format, which makes Texinfo documents easier to write from scratch than those in some other markup languages. Like nroff, Texinfo format can be translated into hard copy, HTML, or plain text.

Although Texinfo is a very flexible format, most binary distributions don't include Texinfo source files. Normally, a binary distribution ships with specially processed text files that are suited only for input to the info viewer. These files are created from Texinfo source with the makeinfo program. Because they do not contain any typesetting information, they don't produce the best hard copy. If you want to translate the documentation into hard copy, or if you are looking to create PDF or HTML output, you should locate the Texinfo source. It usually can be found in the source distribution or on the project's home page.

3.2.8 Viewing info Pages

The GNU info system is tightly integrated with Emacs, the flagship GNU text editor. Figure 3-2 shows what info looks like in the Emacs editor.

If you are not an Emacs user, there are a couple of alternatives. One of these is the text-based info program. People who are used to man pages have a hard time

FIGURE 3-2   Using Emacs to View `info` Pages

using the `info` browser, mainly because it does not behave anything like the `less` pager used by `man`. This can be very irritating when you have to transition between `man` pages and `info` pages. Programmers who use the `vi` text editor are comfortable with the `less` program because its key bindings are very similar to those of `vi`. The fact is that `info` borrows heavily from Emacs and behaves much like it. `info` provides `vi` key bindings for Vi users with the `--vi-keys` option, but it doesn't behave much like `vi` or `less`.

So you want to use the `info` program? You can start with the `man` page, which covers only the command-line options. If you want more in-depth information, you need to look at the `info` page—but not so fast. If you type `info info`, you get information about the `info` format, not the `info` program. For that, you have to type `info info-stnd`, which will give you the correct documentation. The `man` page ought to tell you that, but for some reason, it doesn't.

So you actually like the `info` program? You can use it as your preferred tool to look at both `man` pages and `info` pages. By default, `info` will try to find the information in `info` format and fall back to a `man` page if it does not.

There is another text-based alternative for programmers who don't use Emacs and don't care for `info`: the `pinfo` program.[7] Users who prefer `man` pages will have an easier time learning to use it. Like `info`, this is a text-based program, but it uses more advanced terminal capabilities, including color highlighting for hyperlinks. Perhaps most important, it uses `vi` keys for cursor movement.

In the realm of GUI tools are some more choices for viewing `info` pages. Some Web browsers will accept a URL of the form `info:topic`. In a GNOME system, this simply launches the `gnome-help` browser, which as of this writing does not support `man` or `info` pages. How rude!

A KDE browser sends you to `khelpcenter`, which is an excellent browser for `info` pages. You can see for yourself in Figure 3-3.

An `info` document is usually broken into sections, which makes it easier to read but can make finding exactly what you are looking for tedious. If you know the exact section you are looking for, you can bring it up with a lengthy command line like the following:

```
$ info "(make)Quick Reference"
```

There's nothing quick about having to type all that, but if it's something you refer to often, you can use a shell alias or a script to save typing. Both `pinfo` and `info` allow you to jump to specific sections with this syntax, but as of this writing, `khelpcenter` does not. If what you want is a single continuous stream of output, like a `man` page, you can coerce the `info` program to do so as follows:

```
$ info --subnodes some-topic | less
```

The `--subnodes` option forces `info` to dump the entire contents of the document to `stdout`. Piping the output to `less` gives it the look and feel of a very long `man` page.

---

7.   http://pinfo.alioth.debian.org

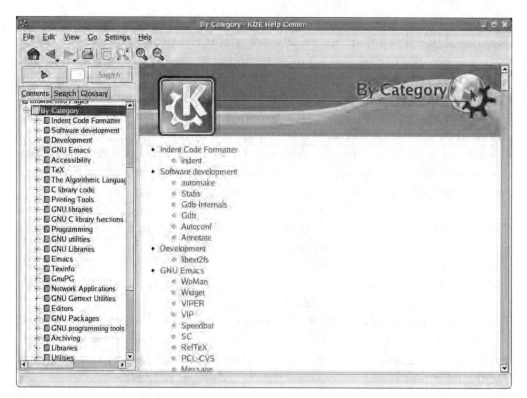

FIGURE 3-3   Using `khelpcenter` to View `info` Pages

3.2.9   Searching info Pages

You can search `info` pages like `man` pages by using the `--apropos` option to `info`. Each `info` file has an index, which can be searched with the `--apropos` option, so your search is more likely to produce output with `info` than with the `apropos` command used for `man` pages. Like `man`, the search is case insensitive and matches anywhere in the text. Unlike with `man`, you cannot use a regular expression. So although searching an index is likely to get you more relevant results, this benefit is largely offset by the lack of any filtering via regular expressions or word-based searches.

   `info` also has a `-w` option that behaves like the `whereis` command, but because there are relatively few `info` files, you are unlikely to encounter the frequent name clashes that you often can with `man`.

3.2.10 Recommended info Pages

Although most GNU tools have only terse man pages that refer you to the info documentation, GNU has made an effort to provide comprehensive man pages for some tools, such as gcc. Even these, however, are outdone by their Texinfo counterparts. The man page for gcc 3.4.4, for example, is around 54,000 words, whereas the info page comes in at nearly 158,000 words. The info file contains much more background and historical information, whereas the man page is strictly business.

When you have some time to read and learn, several topics in the info pages are worth a read. Table 3-4 lists some selected topics for you to explore in the info pages.

Although info and man cover a large number of tools, there are many more ways to document code.

TABLE 3-4   Recommended Reading

info Page	Comments
coreutils	This is some very informative light reading. It contains many of the sundry two- and three-letter commands that UNIX programmers know and love but organizes them by function. There is even a reprint of an article that Arnold Robbins wrote for *Linux Journal* in the node named "Opening the software toolbox."
cpp	This probably is one of the most misunderstood tools that every C programmer uses. The man page leaves a great deal to be desired. Given that it's a complex topic, the info format is preferred.
gcc	Provides much more information than the gcc man page, including implementation details, and is well organized for online reading.
ld	A behind-the-scenes tool that every developer uses, but developers probably don't have a clue how it works. Again, this is a complex topic that is well suited to the info format.
libc	An in-depth reference to the C standard library, with lots of background information.

3.2.11   Desktop Help Tools

In the Linux world, there are two major players in the desktop environment: GNOME and KDE. Although each desktop environment has its fans and detractors, no desktop environment would be complete without online help. GNOME's help system is provided by the `gnome-help` command (also known as `yelp`) and as of version 2.10.0 is focused exclusively on GNOME tools. What help it provides usually is not relevant to programmers. Although `gnome-help` hasn't much to offer in the way of content, it still has its uses. It makes an excellent lightweight browser for a simple HTML file, such as a README file written in HTML. Firing up Mozilla or Firefox to view a simple HTML file is like using an aircraft carrier to go water-skiing. Besides, who wants to do all that typing? Mozilla and Firefox require you to type a fully qualified URL as follows:

```
$ firefox file:///usr/share/doc/someproject/README.html
```

Remember, that's three slashes after the `file:` (and the number of slashes shall be three). `yelp` is smart enough to find files in the current working directory, and it starts up much faster than Firefox or Mozilla. So in the very likely event that you happen to be working in the directory where your documentation resides, you can use a refreshingly simple command such as:

```
$ yelp README.html
```

Because it has no plug-ins to speak of, `yelp` can pull up a simple HTML document almost as fast as `man` can pull up a `man` page.

Just like `yelp`, `khelpcenter` makes an excellent lightweight Web browser for simple HTML files. As a bonus, `khelpcenter` provides a much less myopic view of the tools than `yelp`. Although `khelpcenter` is *the* source of information on KDE tools, it also allows you to view `man` pages and GNU `info` pages. The `info` pages are hyperlinked, just as expected, but less expected is the fact that `man` pages are hyperlinked as well. Scroll down to the SEE ALSO section of a `man` page and click any of the cross-referenced `man` pages to view that document. This is a nice feature. `khelpcenter` also provides search capability, as well as a glossary. The search is a little flaky, and the glossary is sparsely populated, but it is sure to get better as the tool matures.

3.3   Other Places to Look

If you are working with a new project, chances are that it has little or no documentation in the form of a `man` or `info` page. Documentation may exist but may be hard to find. Things like README files have a way of getting lost in the packaging when a project is packaged in a binary distribution. Chances are that the help is somewhere; it's just up to you to find it.

3.3.1   /usr/share/doc

This subdirectory is part of the Filesystem Hierarchy Standard and is where many man pages and info pages are stored. It is also the preferred place to store the electronic equivalent of the writing on the back of a napkin that we call the README file.

A binary distribution typically includes a subdirectory named after each project, where it may place all sorts of sundry information. Typically, you will find release notes, change logs, copyright information, and some sort of README file.

Occasionally, developers distribute only plain text or HTML documentation without any man pages. This is the place you will usually find it. You might even find Texinfo source or some other markup, like DocBook.

Debian provides the doc-linux package, which contains many of the HOWTO documents from The Linux Documentation Project[8] (discussed later in this chapter) stored in /usr/share/doc. These files are not coupled with any installed packages; they're documentation for the sake for documentation.

3.3.2   Cross Referencing and Indexing

Cross referencing turns your documentation from a dictionary into a thesaurus. A dictionary shows you only what words you explicitly look for, whereas a thesaurus leads you to words you may not have thought of. Likewise, cross-referencing Linux documentation is important, because there is usually more than one way to do what you want, and you may not know it unless you check the cross references. Linux documentation does a fairly good job of referring to other tools despite the fact that the documentation is accumulated from many diverse sources.

For man pages, the cross-reference information can be found in the SEE ALSO section. Suppose that you are setting up a DHCP server, and you look at the dhcpd man page. This is the logical place to look, because dhcpd is the name of the DHCP daemon. If you don't look at the cross references, you may miss the dhcpd.conf page, which has more vital information. Many complex tools and servers are

---

8.   www.tldp.org

documented by more than one man page, and these elements are cross referenced in the SEE ALSO section. A typical man page cross reference looks like the following:

```
SEE ALSO
      dhclient(8), dhcrelay(8), dhcpd.conf(5), dhcpd.leases(5)
```

I described the convention for referencing man pages earlier. You can see here that the man pages themselves use this notation.

Another vital tool for cross referencing man pages is the apropos command, which I have already discussed. Beware that apropos works only when the database is indexed. This normally is done for you with a fresh installation, but as you accumulate new software with new man pages and remove others, the index gets out of sync. As a result, relevant documentation may not show up in an apropos search, or you may get hits for software that is no longer installed. To fix this problem, you need to run the appropriate indexer for the man installation. The traditional man tool uses a tool called makewhatis that is usually run as a cron job. This is a fairly time-consuming process, as the tool has to visit every man page in the system. If you have a laptop that you power up and down often, this job may never get a chance to run. When it does, you'll probably want to kill it if you are running on batteries.

The mandb version of man uses a tool named (appropriately enough) mandb. One advantage of the mandb package is that indexing with the mandb program takes much less time than makewhatis. This, too, typically is set up as a cron job. info files do a fairly good job of cross-referencing other info files via hyperlinks. The info tool also has an apropos-like function with the --apropos option. Although it is not as flexible as the apropos command, it is still useful.

GNOME and KDE use HTML and XML extensively to document their tools, and these usually are cross referenced well. Unfortunately, there is no universally accepted convention for storing and indexing HTML files to document text-based commands. These files can refer you to a man page, but they can't link to it. So when you encounter an HTML file for a command-line tool, it is not likely to have hyperlinks to locally installed documentation. Links in these HTML files are likely to point to other HTML files in the same project or to sources on the Web.

3.3.3 Package Queries

In Chapter 1, I discuss in detail how to use packages. Here's how you can put that knowledge to use. For starters, you may want just the basic information about a package. This is useful in situations when you are wondering what a particular command does. Suppose that you notice the program named `diffstat` in `/usr/bin` and wonder what it does. Perhaps you tried `man diffstat` and got nothing. The next thing you should try is a basic query, such as:

```
$ rpm -qf /usr/bin/diffstat
diffstat-1.38-2
```

This query tells you the name of the package that installed `/usr/bin/diffstat`. In this case, it reports that you have `diffstat-1.38-2` installed. Then you could query the package information to get a basic description of the package that this tool came from, such as:

```
$ rpm -qi diffstat
...
Summary     : A utility which provides statistics based on the output
              of diff.
Description : ...
```

Sometimes, this is enough to tell you what you need to know, but now that you know the name of the package, you can query the package contents to see whether you can glean any other information from it. In the list of installed files, you should look for README files or HTML documents that might give you more information. You might be on the lookout for misplaced man pages as well. These may be located in some unconventional places that you may not have checked otherwise. In the case of `diffstat-1.38-2`, someone put the man page in the wrong place:

```
$ rpm -ql diffstat
/usr/bin/diffstat
/usr/share/man/man1/man1
/usr/share/man/man1/man1/diffstat.1.gz
```

The packager mistakenly created an extra man1 subdirectory under the man1 subdirectory, so that the man command doesn't find it. Although this problem was fixed in a later version of `diffstat`, it is a useful illustration of how package queries can be helpful. Packagers are humans, too. In case you are wondering, you could still read this man page with the following command:

```
$ man /usr/share/man/man1/man1/diffstat.1.gz
```

In most distributions, when a man page cannot be found, you get nothing. In a Debian-based distribution you may encounter `undocumented(7)`, which is a generic man page describing some of the same topics covered in this section.

3.4   Documentation Formats

Linux documentation comes in many formats. Although plain text is common, several markup languages have been used over the years to produce prettier printouts or more browser-friendly output. One of the first attempts was `troff`, which is the language used to create `man` pages. `troff` generates output that can be typeset or viewed in a terminal window. Other formats such as LaTeX were designed with typeset printout in mind, but they are capable of producing browsable documentation. The preferred format of GNU, Texinfo, is designed to produce hypertext output that can be browsed or printed. Finally, there's the ubiquitous HTML which is designed exclusively for the browser. Which one are you most likely to encounter? All of them.

3.4.1   TeX/LaTeX/DVI

TeX and LaTeX markup go back a long way in UNIX history. LaTeX is an extension of the TeX markup system. Most TeX documents these days are actually LaTeX, but the two names are often used interchangeably. Primarily intended for hard-copy printout, TeX has extensive support for the special typesetting requirements of research papers that contain mathematical symbols and formulas. TeX made this easy for authors at a time when word processors were in their infancy, thereby creating a niche for itself among researchers. Despite advances in conventional word processing applications, TeX is still widely used today.

The native output format of TeX is called DVI (for Device Independent). By itself, it can be viewed using `xdvi`, `kdvi`, or `evince`, but the intended use of DVI was as an intermediate format. As a result, there are many mature tools to convert DVI files to any format under the sun. Many open source applications prefer to take advantage of this rather than reinvent the wheel, so they provide DVI or TeX output that can be manipulated further. Some tools include compressed DVI files with the binary distribution in `/usr/share/doc`. The Debian package of `gdb`, for example, includes a nifty reference card in DVI format.

Both TeX and LaTeX use the `.tex` extension for source files, which can be confusing. Documents written for TeX may not compile with the `latex` command, in which case you should try the `tex` command. In many cases, a LaTeX document consists of more than one source file, so make sure that you have all the source files before you try to create a document from LaTeX source. Sometimes, the document is complicated enough that it requires a makefile.

The `tetex-bin` package contains many programs to convert DVI files to many other formats. To keep things confusing, numerous wrapper programs allow you to shortcut the process. One such tool is `pdflatex`, which converts LaTeX source directly to PDF. It looks direct to you, but the process is essentially the same as if you compiled with LaTeX and converted the DVI file to PDF with `dvipdf`. Aside from requiring less typing, `pdflatex` will clean up some of the many intermediate files that LaTeX creates in the process of compiling.

Most desktop distributions include support for TeX and LaTeX, but some smaller ones will strip these tools out to save space, and others may not include some of the various tools. Keep this in mind when you work with TeX and LaTeX documentation.

3.4.2   Texinfo

Texinfo is the preferred format for documentation of GNU programs. The basic documentation browser for GNU documentation is the `info` program or Emacs, depending on who you ask. The files used by `info` are stored in the `/usr/share/info` directory, but these are not Texinfo files. These files are created from Texinfo source using the `makeinfo` program. Most binary distributions do not include Texinfo source files but instead provide the preformatted `info` files. These are indicated with the `.info` extension, whereas Texinfo source files usually are indicated by the `.texi` or `.texinfo` extension. As you might expect, a source distribution will include Texinfo source as well, but some binary distributions also include Texinfo source. If any Texinfo source files are provided with a binary distribution, they are most likely to be found under `/usr/share/doc`. It's worth looking, because occasionally, you will find more comprehensive documentation than is in the manual or `info` pages.

Texinfo source code is formatted with the `makeinfo` program. This allows you to convert it to `info`, HTML, DocBook, XML, or plain text. With the `--html` flag, for example, `makeinfo` creates a working Web document in a subdirectory under the current working directory. A simple example might look like the following:

```
$ makeinfo --html foo.texi
$ yelp foo/index.html
```

`makeinfo` produces several formats, including DocBook, XML, and HTML, but not DVI. For DVI, you can use the TeX formatter as long as it includes this line at the top:

```
\input texinfo
```

This line is a directive for the TeX formatter (ignored by `makeinfo`) that instructs it to import the `texinfo` package, which is what allows the TeX compiler to format Texinfo source. With this line, you can use the `tex` command to format a simple Texinfo source file to produce DVI. For most Texinfo source documents, you should use `texi2dvi` instead of the `tex` command.

3.4.3   DocBook

DocBook is an SGML[9] format for authoring documentation used by some tools. Strictly speaking, DocBook is not a file format but an SGML Document Type Definition (DTD). SGML is the predecessor and a superset of the ubiquitous XML format. DocBook follows the goals of SGML, which are to provide a storage format for documentation that separates content from style. This allows content to be searched electronically without style and markup information corrupting the search.

The DocBook DTD is valid in both SGML and XML, although DocBook files usually have the `.sgml` extension. DocBook is not a user-friendly format for writing documents from scratch. Authors are encouraged to use other tools to create formatted documentation and convert it to DocBook. `makeinfo` will generate DocBook-formatted SGML, for example. The purpose of this would be to strip the content from the Texinfo markup for the purpose of searching. The DocBook source could still be used to produce the typeset documentation in whatever format you want. KDE, for example, uses DocBook for `khelpcenter` documents.

DocBook source files can be identified by the `.sgml` or `.docbook` extension. In a binary distribution, these are most likely to be found in `/usr/share/doc`, but these may not be suitable as stand-alone documents. A DocBook file may be part of a larger scheme for online help that requires many other supporting files.

If you want to manipulate DocBook source, the `docbook-utils` package contains several programs to transform DocBook source into other formats. This requires the `jadetex` package to do its transformations using the TeX language.

---

9. *SGML* stands for *Standard Generalized Markup Language*.

This gives you access to DVI output, which means you can transform DocBook using any tool that understands DVI.

Before trying to manipulate DocBook source by hand, you should look around and see whether the files were created from other source that's easier to manipulate, such as Texinfo or `troff`.

3.4.4   HTML

Because HTML is so pervasive, many authors are more comfortable with it than with other markup languages, such as Texinfo, DocBook, and `troff`. Web pages used for project documentation are usually created by hand in a text editor like `vi` or Emacs. Often, this is only one or two plain text files with no images, JavaScript, or flashy content. Thanks to lightweight browsers like `yelp` and `khelpcenter`, you don't have to start up your bloated Web browser to read one of these HTML files. Here again, the conventional location for HTML documentation is in `/usr/share/doc`.

Some tools use HTML exclusively, without any `man` pages. The NTP (Network Time Protocol) package, for example, has extensive HTML documentation, a sample of which is shown in Figure 3-4.

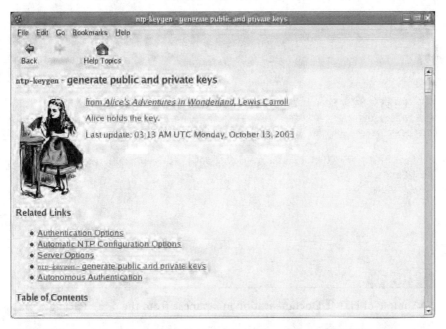

FIGURE 3-4   A Sample of HTML Documentation from the NTP Package

The downside to HTML documentation is that there are no formatting conventions to guide authors on style or content. I don't know about you, but pictures from *Alice in Wonderland* don't help me much. Don't look for HTML to replace man any time soon. There is also no convention for storing HTML documentation in any centralized fashion, so your ability to search HTML documentation is determined by the whims of the author. You won't find much, if any, cross referencing to other documentation, either.

Despite the downside, a good deal of high-quality documentation is provided in HTML format. The ability to present data with proportional and fixed-width fonts can go a long way toward making a document more readable than plain text. HTML is also better suited to internationalized documentation than plain text. Figure 3-5 shows an HTML file in Japanese from the udev package that happened to be installed on my system.

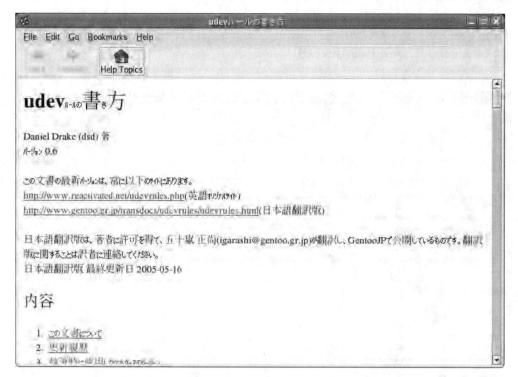

FIGURE 3-5   A Sample of HTML Documentation in Japanese from the udev Package

Depending on your system setup, your terminal may have trouble presenting plain text encoded in a non–ISO-8859 encoding. Most browsers, on the other hand, can present other encodings without much fuss.

3.4.5 PostScript

The PostScript language, created by Adobe, is the predecessor to the Portable Document Format (PDF) in wide use today. PostScript was once the dominant printer language in the UNIX world. It was common for software packages (both commercial and open source) to include documentation in PostScript format, much the same way that we use Portable Document Format (PDF) today.

At that time, PostScript printers were the preferred printers for UNIX systems. To typeset without PostScript, you would need a driver that could typeset a document on the local machine and understand how to send the proper commands to the particular printer.[10] Typically, this involved sending a large amount of data through a low-speed interface such as a serial port, parallel port, or shared Ethernet, which made printing typeset documents a very time-consuming task. As an alternative, PostScript provided a relatively concise language that allowed you to offload the typesetting task onto the printer. This made PostScript print jobs much faster but made the printers significantly more expensive.

Things have changed since then, and PostScript has faded from popularity. For one thing, the idea of a smart printer that can offload typesetting tasks is not as appealing as it used to be. The world is now full of inexpensive, dumb printers capable of producing high-quality output. A typical low-cost printer has a high-speed USB interface and is connected to a computer with horsepower and memory to spare. Although there are still top-of-the-line workgroup printers that support PostScript, it is no longer dominant in the UNIX world.

The GNU Ghostscript tools were a big enabler for using PostScript on UNIX. Ghostscript allowed those of us who couldn't afford expensive PostScript printers to print PostScript documents on less expensive printers (albeit very slowly). One thing Ghostscript allows you to do is view a PostScript file onscreen instead of

---

10. You can still see evidence of this legacy in the DVI and `groff` tools, which still provide output in HP PCL and other printer languages.

printing it. This is done via the `gs` command. The default output is to an X window, for example:

```
$ gs somedoc.ps          Displays the contents of somedoc.ps onscreen
```

When Ghostscript was introduced, viewing typeset documentation onscreen still was fairly novel. Only TeX users had that luxury with `xdvi`. With Ghostscript, anyone could view typeset documentation in PostScript format onscreen.

Ghostscript is primarily a printing tool; there are better ways to view a PostScript document onscreen. One such tool is GNOME's `evince`[11] document viewer, which can be used to view PostScript and PDF files. KDE uses `konqueror` as a front end for Ghostscript, which is a little more user-friendly than Ghostscript by itself.

3.4.6   Portable Document Format (PDF)

Although PDF is excellent for producing typeset output for printing, it is equally suitable for browsing online. One reason why it is so popular is that it saves vendors money by requiring users to print their own manuals. Although it's inconvenient to the user, this is preferable to having a single sheet of paper printed in ten languages or no manual at all.

On the more positive side, PDF is a nice way to encapsulate hyperlinked content in a single file. A well-done PDF file has a hyperlinked table of contents and index, which can make browsing the manual online much more effective than using a printed manual.

Thanks to Adobe, PDF is an open format, so open source tools can be created to view and create PDF files without royalties. Despite this, PDF documentation is not found in open source packages as commonly as it is in commercial packages. This is probably due to the tools, which have been lacking for some time, but that is changing.

Ghostscript can display PDF files but lacks the refinements of Adobe Acrobat Reader. There are no hyperlinks or table of contents, for example. The open source `xpdf`[12] program is still maturing but is slow at rendering pages. GNOME's `evince` is relatively new but is much faster at rendering pages than `xpdf`. GNOME has big plans for `evince` as a tool for viewing PostScript, PDF, and DVI.

---

11. www.gnome.org/projects/evince
12. www.foolabs.com/xpdf

Adobe has made Acrobat Reader available for Linux for a long time, although historically, the Linux version has lagged the Windows version considerably in features. Adobe recently ported Acrobat Reader 7.0 to Linux, which brings it up to date with the latest Windows version. Unfortunately, it also has much of the bloat of the Windows version. For this reason, it may be preferable to use one of the open source viewers.

3.4.7 troff

This is the native markup language of man pages. It has a long history that predates UNIX.[13] The tool used for this purpose is groff, which is the GNU version of troff, but you don't need to know that, because the man program will do most of what you need. The following two commands, for example, are equivalent:

```
$ man intro
$ gzip -dc /usr/share/man/man1/intro.1.gz | groff -man -Tascii | less
```

The man program handles the messy tasks of finding the man page and uncompressing it with gzip, of course.

Although groff can generate DVI files from troff source, it also can generate several other formats on its own. Many of these are of the printer-language variety, such as HP PCL and PostScript. No doubt this is part of its UNIX legacy. Because you can also convert your output to DVI, you can do what you like with it from there.

3.5 Internet Sources of Information

When you can't find the answers you need on your hard drive, you may be inclined to use the Internet to search for help. Using a search engine can lead you down many blind alleys and consume a great deal of your time. In this section, I discuss some resources you can use to search for information more effectively.

3.5.1 www.gnu.org

In addition to providing the source code for many of the tools that enable Linux, this site provides the manuals. Here, you will find the manuals that come with your

---

13. Interested readers are encouraged to read roff(7) in the online manual. Be advised that there are some inaccuracies.

packages, as well as some that don't. The GNU C library (`glibc`), for example, is fully documented in a manual published in two volumes and spanning more than 1,300 pages. You could purchase the two volumes for $60 each, or you could download the Texinfo source from GNU. The Texinfo source is quietly tucked away under the `glibc` link amid all the other documentation that GNU provides. You might never know that such extensive documentation was here unless you were to look. The Web page gives you no clue as to how much documentation is in each project or how good the documentation; you just have to explore and find that out for yourself. So visit the site and have a look around.

3.5.2   SourceForge.net

Many open source projects that are not sponsored by GNU are hosted by SourceForge.net, including many of the tools in your distribution that you use every day. This isn't always obvious even from the packaging information. The `strace` package that comes with the Ubuntu distribution, for example, does not give credit to the SourceForge.net Web page.

```
$ dpkg -s strace
Package: strace
Maintainer: Roland McGrath <frob@debian.org>
Description: A system call tracer
 strace is a system call tracer, i.e. a debugging tool ...
```

In fact, the only reference to SourceForge.net you will find is an email address for a mailing list on the last line of the `man` page. That's a shame, because SourceForge.net is a valuable resource for users as well as developers. RPM packages seem to do a better job of attributing credit to the original authors via the URL field of the RPM header:

```
$ rpm -qi strace
Name        : strace
Packager    : Red Hat, Inc. <http://bugzilla.redhat.com/bugzilla>
URL         : http://sourceforge.net/projects/strace/
Summary     : Tracks and displays system calls ...
```

If you have an RPM distribution, it pays to look at the information section of the RPM to see whether there is a place you can look for information. If you are using a Debian distribution, you may want to go directly to SourceForge.net and look around.

Each project on SourceForge.net has its own home page and the ability to host forums where users can discuss issues and ask questions. The forums are where you can communicate with other users and power users about a particular project you are interested in. These forums typically have very low traffic, so the "signal-to-noise" ratio is high. Just browsing the archives will be educational, and the subscribers aren't likely to flame you too badly if you post a dumb question.

3.5.3   The Linux Documentation Project

If you have never visited www.tldp.org before, you owe it to yourself to visit. TLDP is the source for the man pages that most Linux distributions use. Much of the other information here is of a more general nature, so you are unlikely to find information about a specific open source tool, for example. There is some very good reading here nonetheless. The material is arranged into a few major buckets, including HOWTOs, Guides, FAQs, and of course man pages.

Be sure to check the dates of the documents before you invest too much time reading them. Linux changes so fast that the documentation has a relatively short shelf life. These documents are written and maintained by volunteers, so they are likely to go out of date before someone has time to update them.

The HOWTO documents are often very useful, because they cover very specific topics and generally walk you through a process without requiring a great deal of background knowledge. The topic of the HOWTO is usually enough of a clue to tell you whether you want to read it. Because these are very specific topics, it's hard to find one that will waste your time.

The FAQ comes from Usenet newsgroups, where the same questions are often posted over and over.[14] The FAQ was an attempt to cut down on the noise of the same questions being posted so often. Unfortunately, FAQ is a misused term these days, because FAQs often contain questions that the author wished had been asked, rather than ones that have actually been asked. Unlike the lame, contrived FAQs you may encounter on a run-of-the mill Web page, most of the TLDP FAQs are created from real questions asked by real people (some even frequently). If you have a specific question, the FAQ is worth a look.

A good place to start is The Linux Documentation Project FAQ, located at www.tldp.org/FAQ/LDP-FAQ/index.html.

---

14. In case you didn't know, *FAQ* stands for *Frequently Asked Questions*.

3.5.4   Usenet

Usenet has a long history that predates the Internet. Usenet "newsgroups" are often more gossip and blather than news. Here, anyone can say anything, and the only repercussions are the so-called "flames" of postings by other angry readers. You will find many strong opinions and a general lack of manners.

Browsing Usenet archives via Google or another search engine is advised before actually posting a question on one of these newsgroups. There's a chance that your question has been asked before. It also helps to get to know some of the regular posters to see whether anyone is actually getting help.

Before you use any information you get from Usenet, make sure to verify it with some other source. Be skeptical of everything you read. There is no guarantee that things you read are accurate or even safe to try.

Be advised that there is no attempt to hide your e-mail address in Usenet postings, so it is out there for the world to see. Usenet groups are gold mines for spammers.

3.5.5   Mailing Lists

Of the many forum formats, this is the one that I have found to be the most valuable. What you get in a mailing list is a group of people who are passionate about the topic and generally eager to help (otherwise, they wouldn't subscribe). As with any forum, it is always advisable to do your homework before posting a question. Although people on mailing lists usually have good manners, it's rude to waste people's time with simple questions you could look up yourself.

A valuable resource for finding mailing lists is the mailing-list archive (MARC) located at http://marc.theaimsgroup.com. This site contains archives of hundreds of mailing lists on Linux as well as many other computer topics.

3.5.6   Other Forums

Many Linux Web sites host forums similar to Usenet that are targeted to Linux topics. These usually require some kind of subscription before you can post, but many allow you to read their archives without signing in. The quality of postings can vary wildly.

3.6   Finding Information about the Linux Kernel

Documenting the Linux kernel is a huge task. Several good books have been written on the topic, but the kernel is a moving target. This makes just about any book on the kernel obsolete by the time it is published. The most up-to-date documentation you are going to find is located in the kernel source tree. The kernel source, as it is distributed from http://kernel.org, contains quite a bit of documentation. In addition, many kernel modules provide helpful information embedded in the kernel objects themselves.

3.6.1 The Kernel Build

The kernel build process is well documented in many places on the Internet. Although the 2.6 series has simplified the build process significantly, there are plenty of gotchas and little details worth knowing about. The first place to look, of course, is the README file located at the root of the kernel source tree. It starts with "What Is Linux," which may make your eyes glaze over and cause you to give up prematurely. But if you stick with it, you will find that somewhere in the middle, it talks about all the targets you can build with the top-level makefile. Some of these are quite useful, and a summary can be printed at any time by typing

```
$ make help

Cleaning targets:
  clean           - remove most generated files but keep the config
  mrproper        - remove all generated files + config + various
                    backup files

Configuration targets:
  config          - Update current config utilising a line-oriented
                    program
  menuconfig      - Update current config utilising a menu based
                    program
  xconfig         - Update current config utilising a QT based front-
                    end
  gconfig         - Update current config utilising a GTK based front-
                    end
  oldconfig       - Update current config utilising a provided .config
                    as base
  randconfig      - New config with random answer to all options
  defconfig       - New config with default answer to all options
  allmodconfig    - New config selecting modules when possible
  allyesconfig    - New config where all options are accepted with yes
  allnoconfig     - New minimal config

Other generic targets:
  all             - Build all targets marked with [*]
* vmlinux         - Build the bare kernel
* modules         - Build all modules
```

```
    modules_install - Install all modules
    dir/            - Build all files in dir and below
    dir/file.[ois]  - Build specified target only
    rpm             - Build a kernel as an RPM package
    tags/TAGS       - Generate tags file for editors
    cscope          - Generate cscope index

Static analysers
    buildcheck      - List dangling references to vmlinux discarded
                      sections
                      and init sections from non-init sections
    checkstack      - Generate a list of stack hogs
    namespacecheck  - Name space analysis on compiled kernel

Kernel packaging:
    rpm-pkg         - Build the kernel as an RPM package
    binrpm-pkg      - Build an rpm package containing the compiled
                      kernel & modules
    deb-pkg         - Build the kernel as an deb package

Documentation targets:
    Linux kernel internal documentation in different formats:
    xmldocs (XML DocBook), psdocs (PostScript), pdfdocs (PDF)
    htmldocs (HTML), mandocs (man pages, use installmandocs to install)

Architecture specific targets (i386):
* bzImage         - Compressed kernel image (arch/i386/boot/bzImage)
    install         - Install kernel using
                        (your) ~/bin/installkernel or
                        (distribution) /sbin/installkernel or
                        install to $(INSTALL_PATH) and run lilo
    bzdisk          - Create a boot floppy in /dev/fd0
    fdimage         - Create a boot floppy image

    make V=0|1 [targets] 0 => quiet build (default), 1 => verbose build
    make O=dir [targets] Locate all output files in "dir", including
                         .config
    make C=1   [targets] Check all c source with $CHECK (sparse)
    make C=2   [targets] Force check of all c source with $CHECK
                         (sparse)

Execute "make" or "make all" to build all targets marked with [*]
For further info see the ./README file
```

Additionally, each selectable feature of the kernel is documented in the Kconfig files that you find in many subdirectories of the kernel source tree. These files contain the text of the help messages you see when you create a new kernel configuration via make config, make menuconfig, etc. The Kconfig files are plain text files, so you can look at them with any text editor.

3.6.2   Kernel Modules

Linux provides features for kernel modules to do a modest amount of self documentation. The modinfo command allows you to see information in the module that the author may have placed there. Specifically, modules can take parameters when loaded, much like command-line parameters. These options are shown by the modinfo command, along with whatever documentation the author provided. For most modules, the information is minimal, but for some, it is quite extensive. If the module takes a kernel parameter, it will be listed by modinfo, whether it's documented or not. Even if it's not documented, this at least gives you some direction as to what to look for in the source.

One example of how extensive the modinfo documentation can be is the aic79xx module used with Adaptec SCSI controllers. The modinfo output is shown below:

```
aic79xx:period delimited, options string.
  verbose        Enable verbose/diagnostic logging
  allow_memio    Allow device registers to be memory mapped
  debug          Bitmask of debug values to enable
  no_reset       Suppress initial bus resets
  extended       Enable extended geometry on all controllers
  periodic_otag  Send an ordered tagged transaction
                 periodically to prevent tag starvation.
                 This may be required by some older disk
                 or drives/RAID arrays.
  reverse_scan   Sort PCI devices highest Bus/Slot to lowest
  tag_info:<tag_str>    Set per-target tag depth
  global_tag_depth:<int> Global tag depth for all targets on all buses
  rd_strm:<rd_strm_masks> Set per-target read streaming setting.
  dv:<dv_settings>      Set per-controller Domain Validation Setting.
  slewrate:<slewrate_list>Set the signal slew rate (0-15).
  precomp:<pcomp_list>  Set the signal precompensation (0-7).
  amplitude:<int>    Set the signal amplitude (0-7).
  seltime:<int>      Selection Timeout:
                     (0/256ms,1/128ms,2/64ms,3/32ms)

Sample /etc/modprobe.conf line:
  Enable verbose logging
  Set tag depth on Controller 2/Target 2 to 10 tags
  Shorten the selection timeout to 128ms

options aic79xx 'aic79xx=verbose.tag_info:{{}.{}.{..10}}.seltime:1'

Sample /etc/modprobe.conf line:
  Change Read Streaming for Controller's 2 and 3


options aic79xx 'aic79xx=rd_strm:{..0xFFF0.0xC0F0}'
```

The driver takes only one parameter, named `aic79xx`, but the variable contains text that encodes dozens of details. Indeed, the `modinfo` output for the `aic79xx` module reads almost like a man page, but this is an extreme case. Most modules take no parameters and contain little or no information, but you will never know unless you try.

3.6.3   Miscellaneous Documentation

The kernel source distribution contains a treasure trove of reference material in the `Documentation` directory. The `Documentation` directory has more than 700 files, most of them plain text with a few DocBook files thrown in for good measure. The DocBook source is actually part of the kernel build. If you want to view it, there are several targets you can use to create the format you want:

```
$ make pdfdocs          # Generate PDF files
$ make mandocs          # Generate man pages
$ make psdocs           # Generate PostScript output
```

There is a great deal of diverse information here, including information for kernel hackers as well as system administrators.

3.7   Summary

This chapter introduced the main sources of documentation for Linux tools and how to use them. It looked at the various tools used to retrieve documentation and examined some of the sources of documentation. Along with the sources, the chapter looked at the formats that Linux documentation comes in. Finally, the chapter looked specifically at the kernel and the documentation that is available for various kernel modules and for the rest of the kernel.

3.7.1   Tools Used in This Chapter

- `man`—the original UNIX help tool

- `apropos`—searches the `man` headlines for keywords

- `whatis`—searches the `whatis` database of `man` pages (created by `makewhatis`) for keywords

- `info`—the GNU help tool that supports more complex documents

- `yelp`—the GNOME help tool that is also a functional Web browser

- `khelpcenter`—the KDE help tool

- `xdvi`, `kdvi`—tools for viewing documents in DVI format

- `evince`—the GNU all-purpose viewer for DVI, PDF, PostScript, and other formats

- `makeinfo`—used to render Texinfo-formatted documentation into other formats (HTML, DocBook, and others)

- `gs`—the command-line front end for Ghostscript, the GNU PostScript viewer

- `xpdf`—an open source PDF viewer for the X Window System

3.7.2 Online Resources

- www.troff.org—dedicated to the `troff` formatting language

- www.pathname.com/fhs—the Filesystem Hierarchy Standard

- http://marc.theaimsgroup.com—archives of various mailing lists

- www.foolabs.com/xpdf—the `xpdf` project home page

- www.gnome.org/projects/evince—the `evince` project home page

- pinfo.alioth.debian.org—the `pinfo` home page

Chapter 4

Editing and Maintaining Source Files

4.1   Introduction

The text editor is one tool every good developer should be intimately familiar with. Many editors have zealous followers, ready to tout their favorite text editor as the best thing since sliced bread. In this chapter, I help you sort out some of the hype from the facts and make the best choice for you.

Editing source files is only part of your task, however. A good software development process requires revision control for source files. Several open source tools and commercial tools are available for this purpose, and the number is growing. I look at the most common open source tools and some emerging ones as well.

Finally, I look at some tools to help you navigate and manipulate source files. These are particularly useful for working in teams and working with source code that is not yours.

4.2   The Text Editor

Perhaps the single most important tool you work with as a software developer is the text editor, which directly affects your productivity and quality of life. Being familiar and comfortable with your text editor can make the difference between coding for fun and coding as a chore. Because of this, the subject of text editors often evokes visceral reactions from developers. Most have strong opinions as to what defines a good text editor.

Some developers believe that a modern editor must have a GUI and be part of an Integrated Development Environment (IDE) to be useful for software development. Others want to keep their hands on the keyboard while they're typing and give the mouse a rest. What makes a good text editor is whatever works for you.

One thing you want to avoid is getting attached to a tool that is hard to find or that works in only one environment. When you work on your own system, you are free to install whatever tools you like and run whatever distribution you like. You could find an excellent editor, install it, and invest a great deal of time mastering it, only to find out that it doesn't work in your new favorite distribution. Worse, maybe it's no longer under development, and you can't get someone to work on porting it. That's an extreme case.

A more likely scenario would be if you work as a contractor for a large company. You may not have the liberty to install your favorite distribution with your favorite text editor. You may have fallen in love with KDE's Kate editor, only to find out that your new employer uses a GNOME distribution. What then? Perhaps you are working on a newly installed system you put together for a client, but you have grown so accustomed to your own editor macros and settings that you become a fish out of water without them. The client is watching, and your fumbling at the keyboard is not filling him with confidence.

Surely, there is no shortage of text editors to choose among. If anything, there are too many. As a competent developer, you should build your skills in the mainstream editors so that you can be productive in any environment. Linux text editors can be broken into the four basic categories listed in Table 4-1.

TABLE 4-1   Basic Editor Categories

Editor	Description
vi/Vim	The grandfather of UNIX text editors, vi is part of the POSIX standard. It is designed for people who know how to type, allowing you to accomplish all your tasks with your hands remaining in the home position on the keyboard at all times. Vim is the most common open source clone of vi that comes with most Linux distributions.
Emacs and clones	Emacs is the flagship GNU editor that never met a feature it didn't like. The Emacs program is extensible and has accumulated many features beyond text editing over the years. Emacs is available for every GNU/Linux distribution.
Other terminal-based clones	This category includes essentially every other terminal-based editor. Some of these editors are clones of older programs that are no longer available, such as WordStar.
GUI text editors	It may seem unfair to lump all GUI text editors into one category, but there is a good reason for this. What all GUI editors have in common is that they are all intuitive to use and modeless. The keyboard is for typing, and the mouse is for everything else.

You owe it to yourself to master one of the terminal-based editors—preferably vi or Emacs. vi is part of the POSIX standard, so if you master it, you will be able to work productively on any Linux or UNIX system. Emacs is a standard part of any open source distribution and usually will be installed on any Linux system. Although Emacs is available for most major UNIX clones, it may not be part of the standard install.

4.2.1   The Default Editor

By default, many tools that require input from a text editor bring up vi for you. As a result, most developers have some basic competency in vi. You usually can change the default editor to your editor of choice by setting the `EDITOR` environment variable. Some tools also use the `VISUAL` environment variable, if `EDITOR` is not set. Most tools will respect the choice you make here, provided that the indicated tool is installed and in the path.

4.2.2   What to Look for in a Text Editor

Ask three developers what the most important feature in a text editor is, and you are likely to get three different answers. This may partly explain why there are so many text editors out there.

Some editors seem to be created by programmers who want to scratch a particular itch at the expense of other features. If such an editor satisfies your needs, it's probably just a coincidence. Other editors are just toy projects created for the purpose of promoting one programming language or another. The text editor seems to be the project of choice for this purpose. The programming language an editor is written in shouldn't be a factor in your decision to use it.[1]

If you are looking to evaluate a new text editor or clone, you should look for several features that are geared specifically to developers. A few of these features are listed in Table 4-2.

TABLE 4-2   Common Text Editor Features

Feature	Description
Brace matching	Place your cursor on a bracing character, such as {}()[], and the editor will highlight the matching brace. Some editors allow you to move the cursor to the matching brace, which is also useful. This is extremely useful for code that is poorly indented or for writing complex expressions with multiple parentheses.
Syntax highlighting	This does more than just make the code pretty to look at; it also can alert you visually to many common types of errors, such as comments or quotes that have not been closed and preprocessor syntax errors.

---

1. The programming language should be a factor only when you have to build from source. In that case, you need to have a compiler in that language.

Feature	Description
Autocompletion	This can be a real time-saver, especially for the typing impaired. Type the first few letters of a word, and the editor will fill in the rest based on previously typed words. Some developers can't live without this feature.
Regular expressions	A regular expression is a precise syntax for searching and modifying text. It's an important feature for editing source code, particularly when you find yourself making surgical changes to a large set of source files. A less precise syntax might make unintended changes.
Automatic indenting	This seems like such a small feature that most programmers take it for granted. But extra keystrokes required to indent code really interrupt your flow and slow you down. Typically, the editor will simply indent as you type, but some editors allow you to reformat previously typed sections of code that are poorly indented.
Code browsing	Tools such as `ctags` and `etags` generate indexes for a set of source files. The editor can use this index to navigate the code. Emacs and `vi` use unique formats for tags, and most editors that support tags will use one of these formats.
Code building	The ability to build code from within the editor is more than just convenience; it's also an important development tool. A good text editor will not just run your build, but also help you track down warnings and errors.

Although the features listed in Table 4-2 can be found in most of the popular terminal-based and GUI text editors, some features that are not listed here may be important to you, as well as some that we take for granted.

One feature that we take for granted is the ability to work on multiple files. Every editor can do this, each in a different way. The generic term for this ability is *buffers,* which is used because the text you are editing need not belong to a file. The ability to open such anonymous buffers can be very useful; consequently, every editor supports this feature in some fashion.

Another feature you may be interested in and that not all Linux editors have is Windows compatibility. If you work in a Windows environment as well as in Linux, being able to work on the same text editor in both environments can improve your productivity and should be a factor in your choice. The two most popular editors for Linux (vi and Emacs) both have excellent full-featured Windows versions.

One more feature that may be important to you is internationalization (i18n for short). The ability to display text in other character sets is largely a function of your GUI, but the text editor has to be able to deal with the particular encoding as well. Most Linux text editors have no problem with Unicode UTF-8 encoding.

4.2.3   The Big Two: vi and Emacs

vi and Emacs have legacies that date back before UNIX (not just Linux). These are terminal-based editors that were around before X, when the terminal was the only interactive interface to a computer. Some programmers today resist using terminal-based editors (sometimes called text-mode editors) because they think those editors are archaic. This is not true. vi and Emacs have evolved over the years to include all the features you expect in a modern text editor, including a GUI. Nevertheless, text mode is still very important; it gives you something to work with when you can't bring up a GUI.[2]

4.2.4   Vim: vi Improved

vi is part of the POSIX standard and part of every UNIX distribution. Until recently, however, it was not open source. This led to numerous open source clones over the years. Vim is the clone that you will find in all major Linux distributions. Vim (short for vi *Improved*) implements all the features of vi, adds numerous enhancements, and addresses some of vi's shortcomings.

4.2.4.1   Vim Features

Not surprisingly, Vim has all the features listed in Table 4-2, which explains why it is the most common vi clone chosen for Linux distributions. One benefit of using an open source text editor is that the user base consists almost entirely of programmers. The people developing the code are actually using the tool as well. This is always a recipe for good software. It also means that if a useful new feature shows

---

2.   If you've never been in this situation, you're not trying hard enough.

up in another text editor, chances are that the same feature will be implemented in short order.

Table 4-3 lists a small set of features comparing vi and Vim. Vim actually has many more features—too numerous to mention here. When talking about features that are common to both vi and Vim, I will use the term vi, and I will use *Vim* to refer to features that are unique to Vim.

A key feature of vi is that it does not rely on the mouse. You accomplish everything you need to do with your hands in the home position on the keyboard instead of reaching for the mouse, as you would with a GUI editor, or contorting your fingers to press three keys at once, as you might with Emacs. To accomplish this, vi uses three basic modes: *command mode, insert mode,* and *Ex mode.* Perhaps this is something only a programmer could love (or comprehend). The modal nature of vi is both loved and despised by programmers.

4.2.4.2 Modes, Modes, Modes

vi starts in command mode, which means "Don't start typing yet!" In command mode, every key on the keyboard performs a particular function. Press a key, and something happens (maybe). Command mode is used to move the cursor, cut and paste, or do just about anything else that does not involve typing text. This is one thing that makes vi unlike any other text editor and turns away many new vi users. It's only natural to expect to be able to type after you start your editor. Before you can start typing in vi, however, you must be in *insert* mode.

Figure 4-1 illustrates the modes in vi and the methods used to change between them.

TABLE 4-3   vi vs. Vim

Feature	vi	Vim
Undo	Only one level	Multiple levels
Tab expansion	No	Yes
Number of buffers per session	Two	Limited only by system resources
GUI	No	Optional
Syntax highlighting	No	Yes
Autocompletion	No	Yes

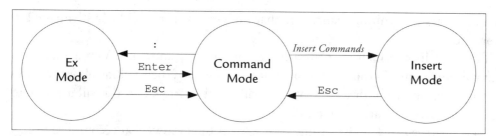

FIGURE 4-1   Modes in vi Illustrated

Notice that there are numerous ways to get from command mode to insert mode, but the only way to get out of insert mode is to press the Esc key. Also notice that all paths go through command mode. You can't go from insert mode directly into Ex mode, for example.

4.2.4.3   Command Mode

Command mode can be unnerving for new vi users. There is no status message, and there is no "Are you sure?" pop-up message. The command is executed the instant you touch the key. Press the j key in command mode, for example, and the cursor moves down one line. That's it. No fanfare or congratulations—just results. This takes some getting used to, but as you become proficient, you will find it to be a huge productivity boost.

The key mapping in command mode is a balance between easy to remember and easy to use. Most of the commands that take you to insert mode fall into the easy-to-remember category. These include commands like i for insert and a to append. Commands that involve cursor movement, on the other hand, may be more cryptic, because they are designed to be easy to use. The jkhl keys, for example, perform the same function as the arrow keys in command mode, which allows you to move the cursor with the index and middle fingers of your right hand.

Commands can be repeated by typing the number of repetitions before the command. Here again, no status is printed to the screen, and no warning is given. Just type 40j in command mode, and the cursor simply moves down 40 lines. This, too, takes some getting used to. Unintended repeats can produce some very odd behavior, which can often scare off a new vi user. Fortunately, Vim has multiple levels of undo.

4.2.4.4   Cursor Movement Commands

Table 4-4 lists some essential commands used to move the cursor in command mode. The arrow keys on the keyboard work as you would expect; in fact, each one is a unique command. But using the arrow keys requires you to move your hand from the home position. By using the `jkhl` keys, you can keep your hands in the home position.

TABLE 4-4   Cursor-Motion Commands That Can Be Used Alone or with Other Commands

Command	Description
j	Move cursor down one line.
k	Move cursor up one line.
h	Move cursor left one column.
l	Move cursor right one column.
Enter	Move cursor down one line.
G	Go to line. With no repeat count, it jumps to the end of the file. If you provide a repeat count, it jumps to that line. 50G, for example, jumps to line 50 of the file.
+	Move cursor down one line and position it at the first nonblank character on the line.
−	Move cursor up one line and position it at the first nonblank character on the line.
%	Jump to matching brace. Cursor most be positioned on a bracing character such as (){}[]; otherwise, the terminal beeps, and no movement is made.
[[	A two-character command that takes you backward to the first { in the first column. This is useful for moving between functions.
]]	Same as [[except that it moves you forward.
'{mark}	Jump to line marked by the m command with the specified mark. Marks are user defined with the m command and can be any character.

continues

TABLE 4-4   *Continued*

Command	Description
' '	Jump (return) to the last line you jumped or searched from. This command is very useful for when you accidentally jump somewhere you didn't expect, as well as for peeking at some other section of a file and returning to what you were doing.
/{expr}	Search forward. Press /, and you are prompted for a regular expression to search for. The search begins when you press Enter. The search takes place from the current line and continues until the first match. By default, the search will continue from the top of the file (that is, wrap around). See also the ws setting in Table 4-18.
?{expr}	Search backward. This command is the same as / except that the search take place from the current line to the top of the file. This, too, will wrap around and continue the search from the bottom.
n	Repeat last search in the same direction starting from the current cursor position.
N	Repeat last search in the opposite direction starting from the current cursor position.
w	Move cursor forward one word.
b	Move cursor backward one word.

There is a method to having all these cursor-movement commands. As you shall see, all the cursor-movement commands listed in Table 4-4 can be combined with other commands to make them very useful. There also are some useful movement commands that cannot be combined with other commands. Some of these commands are listed in Table 4-5.

The fact that cursor movement is done almost exclusively in command mode is a gotcha for first-time vi users. It's natural for many users to reach for the arrow keys while typing, only to be punished by a bunch of garbage spewed on the screen with each keypress. Older versions of vi could not handle arrow keys in insert mode. Vim, on the other hand, allows you to use the arrow keys while you're in insert mode, which is a nice improvement. Without this feature, you would have to go back to command mode just to move the cursor.

TABLE 4-5   Stand-Alone Cursor-Motion Commands

Command	Description
Ctrl+F	Move forward one screen.
Ctrl+B	Move backward one screen.
Ctrl+]	Jump to the tag that the cursor points to. This is used with ctags and can also be accomplished in Ex mode with :ta.
Ctrl+T	Return from the previous tag jump (like the Back button in a Web browser).

4.2.4.5   Insert and Change Commands

Aside from cursor movement, the most important commands you need to know to get started are the ones that let you start typing. These are the commands that take you into insert mode. There are many ways to get into insert mode, but most programmers pick one and stick with it. There are always circumstances where one of the other commands is preferred, but the i command is enough for most cases. Table 4-6 lists several of the most common commands for entering insert mode.

TABLE 4-6   Basic Insert Commands

Command	Description
i	Enter insert mode starting before the character under the cursor.
a	Enter insert mode starting after the character under the cursor.
I	Enter insert mode starting before the first non blank character on the line.
A	Enter insert mode starting after the last non blank character on the line.
o	Enter insert mode starting on a new line below the current cursor position.
O	Enter insert mode starting on a new line above the current cursor position.

Although it may seem unintuitive, insert commands are single commands like everything else. The entire insert, starting from the moment you press the command key until the point you press Esc, is treated as one single command regardless of the number of words. Normally, this is not important until you realize that like all other commands, inserts can be repeated, perhaps inadvertently. Because there is no feedback when you enter a repeat count, as I pointed out earlier, this type of error is easy to make. Suppose that you want to enter the following line of text, but you forget to enter insert mode:

```
50 dollars per hour is my rate, and that's a bargain at any price
```

You start typing **50**, and nothing appears. Oops! You're not in insert mode. No problem; you just press i to take you into insert mode. But there's a surprise in store. You finish typing, and press Enter and then Esc to return to command mode. Suddenly, the same line appears 49 more times. What happened was that the command you entered was not simply i, but 50i, because you forgot that you were in command mode when you started typing. vi dutifully replicates the insert you did 49 more times, for a total of 50 "inserts."

This is a kind of time bomb, because you really don't know you made the mistake until after you exit insert mode, which may be some time later. Fortunately, you have the undo command (u). It may be useful to remember that using Ctrl+C instead of Esc to exit insert mode will cancel any repeats that you specified. The insert remains intact, but you will see only one copy. Before you enter an insert command, you can clear any repeat that you may have inadvertently typed by pressing Ctrl+C or Esc first.

Without repeats, insert commands are straightforward. You press the key, enter insert mode, type to your heart's content, and then exit insert mode by pressing Esc or Ctrl+C. Change commands behave the same way, except that they are preceded by an initial deletion. The basic change commands are shown in Table 4-7.

There are no patterns to speak of for using insert commands except for the repeats I mentioned earlier. Change commands can be repeated as well. When you repeat a change command, however, vi repeats the deletion but the insert occurs only once. This behavior is more instantaneous and intuitive. There are no time bombs ticking when you use change commands.

The patterns in Table 4-8 are identical to the patterns for the delete command (d), which I will introduce in Table 4-12. In fact, in Vim, the only difference between a change and a delete is that the change leaves you in insert mode. This is another difference between vi and Vim. When you run a command like 4s to change the next four characters, for example, vi will return you to command mode after you type the fourth character. Vim, on the other hand, will remain in insert mode.

TABLE 4-7   Change Commands

Command	Description
c	Delete everything from the cursor to the end of the line; then enter insert mode. This command is the same as D (see Table 4-10) followed by A.
c{motion}	Delete text starting with the character under the cursor as determined by the motion and then enter insert mode. Valid motion commands include any of the commands listed in Table 4-4.
{N}s	Change (substitute) the next N characters from the current cursor position. This command is similar to the c command except that you specify an exact number of characters instead of a motion command. The command 5s is the same as c5l.
s	Change (substitute) the current line in its entirety. This command deletes all text on the current line (except the newline) and puts you in insert mode.

TABLE 4-8   Some Patterns for Using Change Commands

Pattern	Description
2cw	Delete two words and enter insert mode; alternatively, change the next two words.
cta	Delete everything up to the next occurrence of the letter a and then insert. This is a combination of the c command and a ta motion command.
5cta	Delete everything up to the fifth occurrence of the letter a and then insert.
5s	Delete the current line and the subsequent four lines, and enter insert mode.

4.2.4.6   Other Commands in Command Mode

You should know several miscellaneous commands that are available from command mode. Perhaps the most important is the undo command (u), because it's easy to make mistakes with vi. Vim enhances the undo feature over vi's. Standard vi allows you to undo only the most recent insert or change, whereas Vim allows numerous undo levels, like a modern word processor. In traditional vi, repeating an undo twice would simply redo the change. Because Vim allows multiple levels of undo, it had to introduce a new redo command, which is Ctrl+R in command mode. Table 4-9 lists these and other commands you should know.

Control keys are used sparingly as commands in vi because they are part of the ASCII character set. Some control keys are vitally important, such as Ctrl+M, which is a carriage return.[3] Other control keys are relics of the teletype era, such as Ctrl+R, which ASCII defines as Device Control 2. That's probably why Vim uses Ctrl+R for undo, because it isn't likely to clash with any pseudoterminal features.

TABLE 4-9   Miscellaneous Commands

Command	Description
u	Undo the most recent change or insert. This command can be used multiple times to undo multiple changes.
Ctrl+R	Redo the most recent undo (Vim only).
m{letter}	Set a bookmark at the current line, using the given letter. The letter can be any lowercase letter as defined by the current locale.
.	Repeat the last change or insert.
Ctrl+L	Redraw the screen. This command is useful when a background process prints text to the screen and garbles the output.
zt	Redraws the screen, placing the current line and the cursor at the top of the screen.
zz	Redraws the screen, placing the current line and the cursor in the middle of the screen.
zb	Redraws the screen, placing the current line and the cursor at the bottom of the screen.

---

3. See the ascii(7) man page for more details. Note that Ctrl+A is ASCII \001, Ctrl+B is ASCII \002, and so on.

4.2.4.7 Cut, Paste, and Delete Commands

Historically, vi documentation uses the term *register* to refer to what is conventionally called a clipboard today. No doubt this is part of its legacy as a programmer's text editor. Similarly, what we call *cut* and *paste* today are referred to in vi documentation as *yank* and *put*. Luckily, the term for *delete* is *delete*.

One difference between these commands and the change commands is that none of them uses insert mode. When you execute one of the commands listed in Table 4-10, you return to command mode. Like most vi commands, these commands can be repeated, so typing **5p**, for example, will paste the contents of the clipboard five times.

TABLE 4-10   Delete, Cut, and Paste Commands

Command	Description
D	Delete from the current cursor position to the end of the line. Data is saved in the default clipboard (register).
d{motion}	Delete some number of characters starting at the current cursor position. The number of characters is determined by the motion argument. Type **dd** to delete the current line. Data is saved in the default clipboard (register). Valid motion commands include any of the commands listed in Table 4-4.
y{motion}	Copy (yank) some number of characters to the clipboard (register). The number of characters is determined by the motion argument. Type **yy** to copy the current line to the default clipboard (register). Valid motion commands include any of the commands listed in Table 4-4.
p	Paste (put) the characters in the clipboard at the current cursor position, starting with the character after the character under the cursor.
P	Paste (put) the characters in the clipboard at the current cursor position, starting with the character before the character under the cursor.

The yank and delete commands take a single argument labeled motion, which tells vi how much to delete or copy. The motion argument can be any of the cursor-movement commands listed in Table 4-4, as well as the additional motion commands listed in Table 4-11.

The commands in Table 4-11 seem a bit arbitrary until you put them to use. Believe it or not, the names are mnemonic. Table 4-12 lists some basic patterns for the d and y commands that show you how to combine them with motion commands.

TABLE 4-11   Additional Movement Commands Used Only with Commands

Command	Description
f{char}	Position the cursor under the first column to the right that matches the given character.
t{char}	Same as f except that the cursor is positioned one column to the left of the matching character.
F{char}	Position the cursor under the first column to the left that matches the given character.
T{char}	Same as T except that the cursor is positioned one column to the right of the matching character.

TABLE 4-12   Some Cut-and-Paste Patterns

Pattern	Description
dfa	Delete characters from the current cursor position to the right, up to and including the first a. Stated mnemonically, *delete until you find a.*
dta	Delete characters from the current cursor position to the right, up to but not including the first a. Stated mnemonically, *delete everything up to a.*
5yta	Copy characters from the current cursor position up to the fifth occurrence of the letter a.
yy4p	Copy the current line and paste four more copies to the buffer. This is two commands: (1) yy (yank the current line) and (2) 4p (paste the default register four times).

Pattern	Description
dn	Delete characters from the current position until the first match of the most recent search. This is the d command with n as the motion command.
d'a	Delete characters from the current cursor position until the position marked a. This is a combination of a d command and 'a as the motion command.
yG	Copy all lines from the current line to the end of the file. This is a y command combined with the motion command G. Recall that the G command positions you at the end of the file.
y50G	Copy all lines between the current line and line 50, including the current line and line 50. This is a y command combined with the motion command 50G.
d5l	Delete the next five characters, starting at the current cursor position (that's a lowercase L, not a one). This is a combination of d with 5l as the motion command.
5dd	Delete the current line and the following four lines. This is a dd command preceded by a repeat count of five.

In the patterns shown in Table 4-12, the commands y and d are interchangeable. The patterns are the same for both commands, although the effects are different.

Finally, the delete, yank, and put commands can be used with multiple registers (clipboards), which I left out for clarity. Each register is user defined and designated by a single lowercase letter. The desired register is indicated by a leading quote followed by the register name. To yank (copy) the current line into a register named a, for example, type the following:

```
"ayy
```

POSIX states that register names are limited to lowercase characters as defined by the locale, which means in English that you have 26 named registers available plus a default register. When you use an uppercase letter for the register name, the text that you yank or delete is appended to the register.

To put (paste) the contents of register a into the buffer, follow the same pattern:

`"ap`

Before Vim, the user registers were the only way to copy and paste data from one file to another. Traditional `vi` clears the default register when you switch buffers, so anything you yanked or deleted is lost when you switch buffers. Vim preserves the default buffer when switching buffers, which is another enhancement over `vi`.

4.2.4.8   Ex Mode

This is where `vi` starts to look a bit like a Frankenstein's monster. Ex is the name of the line-oriented editor that `vi` is built upon, and many of the commands in Ex mode are from the original editor. It's hard to imagine that ex was once a text editor that people used to get their work done, but it was. Ex is a line-oriented editor, which means that it works with files one line at a time. It seems as though this ought to be forgotten dinosaur DNA, but many important tasks are still done in Ex mode. Because Ex is a fully functional editor, many of the tasks you can do in command mode can also be done in Ex mode. Ex mode is used to provide complex commands or commands that take arguments. In general, Ex commands fall into the easy-to-remember category.

In Figure 4-1, you can see that you enter Ex mode from command mode by pressing the colon (`:`). All the text that follows, up until you press Enter, is interpreted as an ex command. When you press Enter, the command is executed, and `vi` returns to command mode.

Ex commands all have the same basic form, which is an optional line number or range of line numbers followed by a command, as follows:

`:[firstline][,lastline]command`

The most frequently used commands typically are one or two letters, but others can be longer. The line numbers are optional. If you don't specify any, the command applies only to the current line. If you specify only one line number, the command applies to the specified line. If you want the command to affect a range of lines, you must specify a starting line and an ending line. To delete lines 25 through 30 inclusive, for example, you can use the `d` command as follows:

`:25,30d`

Several shortcuts are available as alternatives to entering specific line numbers. Some of the most common ones are shown in Table 4-13.

TABLE 4-13   `vi` Shortcuts for Specifying Line Numbers in Ex Mode

Char	Shortcut
`.`	The current line number.
`$`	The last line number in the file.
`%`	A shortcut specifying the entire file—the same as typing `1,$`.
`'a`	Location of tag a. Recall that tags are set in command mode with the `m` command.
`/{expr}/`	The next line that matches the regular expression.
`?{expr}?`	The previous line that matches the regular expression.
`\/`	The next line that matches the most recent regular expression.
`\?`	The previous line that matches the most recent regular expression.
`\&`	The next line that matches the most recent substitution.

Note that the shortcuts in Table 4-13 can apply to both the start address and the end address. You could delete a block of text starting with the word *Begin* and ending with the word *End* by using the following form:

```
:/Begin/,/End/d
```

When you are using a search instead of a line number, the search begins at the current line. In this example, I use a forward search, so the command deletes the first line that has the word *Begin* following the current line. You can mix and match line numbers and searches in commands. You could delete everything from line 1 to the first line that has the word *End* with the following command:

```
:1,/End/d
```

Like all Ex commands, the delete command may apply to one or more lines, but each line is treated equally. You can't delete from line 3, column 5 up to line 10, column 17 with a single command, for example.

A very useful shortcut listed in Table 4-13 is the marker. The apostrophe is the same key used to jump to marked lines in command mode, so it's not hard to remember when you get used to using it.

Table 4-14 lists a few of the most essential Ex commands you are likely to use in `vi`. Note that almost every command can take a range of addresses as I have specified here, whether it makes sense or not. The :w command, for example, is used to update the current file on disk. This command can take an argument to write the current buffer to a different file, but it can also take a range of addresses, such as:

```
10,20w foo.dat
```

This writes lines 10 through 20 to a file named foo.dat. Not every command allows an address or range of addresses, but most commands do. It may seem unnecessary or unusual for some commands, but it comes in handy on occasion.

TABLE 4-14   Essential Ex Commands

Command	Short Form	Description
write	:w {filename}	Write the current buffer to the given filename. The filename is optional. Without it, vi updates the current file on disk. Use :w! to force writing to a file that is marked read-only. Use :w often to update your work on disk.
quit	:q	Quit vi (does not comply if the buffer is not saved). Use :q! to force vi to quit and discard modifications. See also :e.
xit	:x	Quit vi and save unsaved data. This fails if the file is read-only. Use :x! to force writing to a file marked read-only. The :wq command can also be substituted.
edit	:e {filename}	Open the named file for editing in a new buffer. The current file is not closed. When no filename is specified, vi reopens the current file without saving any changes but will not discard edits without your permission. So if you want to lose your edits and start over, use :e!.
delete	:d	Delete the current line or range of lines.
map	:map {a} {b}	Remap the keys used in command mode. With no arguments, it prints out the current settings.
set	:set {argument}	Change default settings for Vim (see Table 4-18). This command is most useful in your .vimrc file.

Command	Short Form	Description
help	:help	Enter the Vim help system. Help can take a keyword argument and does a decent job of finding relevant information. The help is hyperlinked using vi's tags capability, which means you have to be somewhat competent with vi to get help from Vim.

It's interesting to note that many of the commands that Ex understands are also understood by the sed (stream editor) command. What you learn here can help you elsewhere in scripting tasks.

4.2.4.9   Vim Enhancements in Insert Mode

While you're in insert mode, the keyboard behaves much as you would expect. You type, and text appears. It's as simple as that—almost. This is where Vim has added some significant improvements over vi. Vim makes several commands available in insert mode, which is a capability that vi does not have. The list is too numerous to mention here, but Table 4-15 describes some of the most useful ones.

TABLE 4-15   Vim Commands in Insert Mode

Command	Description
Ctrl+N/Ctrl+P	Complete the word from existing words in the document. Unlike some editors, Vim doesn't require you to provide any letters to guess at a match, although it helps to narrow the search. Press Ctrl+N again to produce the *next* match. Press Ctrl+P to go back to the *previous* match.
Ctrl+T/Ctrl+D	(Also valid in vi) Shift current line right or left by one shiftwidth setting. This defaults to eight columns but can be changed with the set shiftwidth command.
Ctrl+R	Insert the contents of one of the special registers used by Vim into the current document. Type **:help registers** to see what registers are available. Each register has a single, arbitrarily chosen character for a name. These include things like % for the current filename and . (period) for the most recent insert.
Ctrl+V	(Also valid in vi) Enter nonprintable characters, such as control characters, that otherwise might have be interpreted as a vi command. It's not a good idea to put control characters in scripts, but see the sidebar for a useful application.

Example Use of Ctrl+V

One customization I use in my `vi` sessions is to remap the `T` key in command mode so that it will switch between the current buffer and the alternate buffer (think toggle). In other words, I define the `T` key to be equivalent to the following `ex` command:

```
:e#
```

To define (or map) keys in command mode, you use the `map` command in Ex mode. To map the `T` key the way I want, the command looks something like this:

```
:map T :e#
```

Unfortunately, this does not work. The problem is that I am trying to use an `ex` command to describe another `ex` command, but `ex` commands don't take effect until you press `Enter`. When I press `Enter` to complete the `map` command, it maps the `T` key to an incomplete `e` command. I need an additional `Enter` key to be included with the mapping for the `T` key. This is where `Ctrl+V` comes in handy.

When you type a control character preceded by `Ctrl+V`, it is *escaped*, which means that it is interpreted literally and not interpreted by the terminal. `vi` uses the `^` character to represent escaped control characters. An escaped `Ctrl+C` character, for example, is displayed as `^C`.

For this problem, I need to know that `vi` sees the `Enter` as an ASCII carriage return (`\015` or `Ctrl+M`). With this knowledge, I can enter the same `map` command followed by `Ctrl+V` and `Ctrl+M` as follows:

```
:map T :e#^M
```

Notice that the `Ctrl+V` character does not appear in the output; only the character that follows `Ctrl+V` appears. Now the mapping for `T` contains the additional carriage return that `ex` requires.

The complete list of commands includes some that seem a bit silly, such as `Ctrl+E`, which inserts the character below the cursor at the current position. This seems silly only until you find a use for it, of course.

4.2.4.10   Search and Replace

Although you can do searches in command mode, search-and-replace commands are accessible only in Ex mode. This is because Ex mode is the only mode for lengthy arguments, and regular-expression search-and-replace operations can get quite lengthy.

The basic Ex command to replace text is the `substitute` command, which can be abbreviated as `subst` or, more often, `s`. Like all Ex commands, it takes a line number or a range of line numbers with all the abbreviations listed in Table 4-13 available. The basic `substitute` command looks like this:

```
:s/search/replacement/flags
```

The search string is the only required argument. The `replacement` and `flags` parameters are optional. With no `replacement`, the search string is replaced by an empty string. By convention, all arguments are delimited with a forward slash (/), which can be a problem when you are working with filenames. `vi` requires you to *escape* the slashes with a backslash, for example, which is a nuisance. This is what a substitute command with a pathname looks like in `vi`:

```
:s/\/usr\/bin\/file1/\/usr\/bin\/file2\//
```

This is what Larry Wall, author of the Perl programming language, calls "the leaning toothpick syndrome" because of its appearance. Aesthetics aside, it is just plain difficult to type. `vi` will allow you to use just about any punctuation character as a delimiter.[4] It assumes that the first character following the command is the delimiter, and it looks for that character to parse arguments. In Vim, you can use this much-easier syntax to work with filenames:

```
:s#/usr/bin/file1#/usr/bin/file2/#
```

In this case, I chose to use the pound sign (#) to delimit the arguments, which allows me to use forward slashes in the string arguments.

By default, the `subst` command replaces the first match found on each line specified. If you want to replace every occurrence of the search string on a line, use the `g` flag to the `substitute` command as follows:

```
:s/some text/some other text/g
```

---

4. Actually, the entire family tree of tools built on `ed` allows this as well, but it's not used often.

One restriction that may be apparent is that the search string must be on one line. This is a restriction of Ex commands in general, because there is a one-line-per-command rule. Embedded newlines are not allowed in search strings, although the replacement may contain multiple lines by using escaped carriage-return characters (`Ctrl+V Ctrl+M`).

This section does not have enough space to do justice to the power of the regular expressions used in the search and replace commands. For further information, you can start with the `regex(7) man` page.

4.2.4.11   Browsing and Building Code

Vim works in conjunction with a program called `ctags`, which creates an index of your source files that can be read by Vim. Running `ctags` can be as simple as

```
$ ctags -R
```

which automatically recognizes source files in the current directory and subdirectories, and creates a single index file named `tags`. This is what Vim looks for when it starts. POSIX requires only that `ctags` and `vi` work with C and Fortran files, but Exuberant `ctags`, which comes with most Linux distributions, can index source files in many languages, including C++, Java, and Python.

Essentially, `ctags` makes your editor (in this case, `vi`/Vim) behave something like a Web browser, with your source behaving like a Web page. `ctags` does not modify your source. The only output is a single index file. But when `vi` sees this index, function calls and variable names become hyperlinks. If you are looking at a function reference, you can follow the link and be taken to the declaration of that function. Follow a link for a class instance (in C++), and you will be taken to the definition for that class. Just as you can in a Web browser, you can back out of links that you jump to, returning to the place you started. This is an excellent tool for developers.

Code browsing in `vi` can be done in command mode or Ex mode but not in insert mode. Table 4-16 lists the most useful commands for browsing code. Several of these commands are unique to Vim, which enhances `vi`'s code-browsing facilities significantly. Traditional `vi` allows only the basic jumps and has no support for multiple tag matches, which can occur in C++ code that uses function overloading or namespaces. Note that Vim maintains a tag "stack" so that you can back out of your jumps as though you were clicking the Back button in your browser.

TABLE 4-16 Commands for Browsing Code

Command	Short Form	Function
`Ctrl+]`		Jump to tag under cursor.
`:tag` *name*	`:ta`	Jump to specified tag. If no tag is specified, jump to the tag under the cursor.
`Ctrl+T`		Return from current tag to most recent jumping-off point.
`:pop`	`:po`	(Vim only) Same as `Ctrl+T` except that you can specify a count to go up multiple levels with a single command.
`:tnext`	`:tn`	(Vim only) Jump to next match when a tag produces more than one match, such as an overloaded C++ function. This does not affect the tag stack.
`:tprevious`	`:tp`	(Vim only) Same as `:tnext` but moves to previous match.
`:tselect` *name*	`:ts`	(Vim only) Show a list of matching tags you can select when a tag produces more than one match.
`:tags`		(Vim only) Show the current tag stack with one line for each tag.

The GUI version of Vim even has some pretty buttons to perform most of the functions listed in Table 4-16, which makes it look even more like a Web browser.

Seamlessly moving between building code and editing code is one of the key features of an IDE. Many developers find this to be an essential productivity tool. Vim doesn't claim to be an IDE but does have features to edit and build code simultaneously. Rather than try to take over your whole project, as many IDEs do, Vim requires you to provide a `Makefile`. Then you can call `make` from Vim with the `:make` command, which doesn't seem like much of a feature. But when you do it this way, Vim will save the output of the compilers and allow you to visit each line of source that produced an error or warning. To build your code, use the `:make` command in Ex mode as follows:

```
:make arguments
```

Use the `:make` command as you would call make from the shell. You can specify additional flags or targets, if you like. After it runs, Vim saves the warnings and error messages to allow you to navigate the source. The commands for this are listed in Table 4-17. Note that this is a Vim feature. POSIX `vi` does not have a `make` command or any of the commands listed in Table 4-17.

By default, Vim understands the errors and warnings produced by `gcc` and `g++`, but you can tweak it to understand other compilers with the `errorformat` setting.[5] Likewise, if you don't use `make` to run your builds, you can change the program that the `:make` command runs via the `makeprg` setting.

4.2.4.12 Customizing vi Settings

Many settings control the way `vi` behaves and are modified in Ex mode via the `:set` command. Historically, `vi` uses a file in your home directory named `.exrc` to read your personalized settings, but Vim prefers to use `.vimrc`. If both files are present, Vim will ignore your `.exrc` and read only your `.vimrc`. This distinction is important if you use more than one `vi` clone. You can expect all clones to read

TABLE 4-17   Vim Code Build Commands

Command	Short Form	Function
`:make arguments`	`:mak`	Run make in the current directory and capture errors and warnings.
`:cnext`	`:cn`	Jump to the source line of the next error or warning in the most recent build.
`:cprev`	`:cp`	Jump to the source line of the previous error or warning in the most recent build.
`:cfile filename`	`:cf`	Read a list of errors from the file for processing with :cnext and :cprev. This is an alternative to using :make.

---

5. Type **:help errorformat** for more information.

your `.exrc` file, but probably none of them besides Vim will look for `.vimrc`. For this case, it's a good idea to keep your vanilla `vi` settings in your `.exrc` file and then use the `source` command in your `.vimrc` to read your `.exrc` as follows:

```
:so ${HOME}/.exrc
```

In addition to this line, you can use the `.vimrc` file to include commands that are understood only by Vim. Table 4-18 contains a list of some useful settings that you may want to modify in your `.vimrc` or `.exrc` file.

TABLE 4-18   User-Modifiable Settings

Setting	Short Form	Example Usage	Description
tabstop	ts	set ts=4	Set the number of columns per tab stop (default is 8). This affects how text containing tabs is displayed or expanded.
shiftwidth	sw	set sw=4	Set the number of columns to shift with using the shift commands (default is 8). Notice that this is independent of the `tabstop` setting.
autoindent	ai	set ai	Turn automatic indenting on or off: `ai` for on and `noai` for `off` (default is off).
expandtabs	et	set et	Do not insert tabs; instead, use the number of spaces defined by `tabstop`. The default is to use hard tabs (ASCII code \011).
wrapscan	ws	set ws	Change the search behavior: When this option is turned on (the default), a forward search may find a match on preceding lines, and a backward search may find a match on a subsequent line. This applies to searches in both command mode and Ex mode.
			When turned off, a forward search searches only from the current line to the end of the file. Likewise, a backward search searches only from the current line to the beginning of the file.

continues

TABLE 4-18   *Continued*

Setting	Short Form	Example Usage	Description
`syntax`	`sy`	`sy on`	(Vim only) Turn syntax high-lighting on or off. Notice that this does not use the `set` command.
`makeprg`	`mp`	`set mp=ant`	(Vim only) Choose an alternative to make to run your build.
`errorformat`	`efm`	`set efm=%f\ %d`	(Vim only) Specify a `scanf`-like string for Vim to use to parse the error output from the compiler. For a full description of the format, see `:help efm` in the Vim help system.

Notice that some settings are made via the `:set` command; other settings are themselves commands (such as `:syntax`).

4.2.4.13   GUI Mode

Vim has a GUI available, usually as a separate program named `gvim` in GNOME systems and `kvim` in KDE.[6] The GUI is an excellent enhancement and a great way to learn `vi`. If you despise modes and for some reason still want to use Vim, use the modeless option of `gvim` (`-y`). This makes Vim behave like a typical modeless GUI editor for the faint of heart.

Each menu in GUI mode has reminders for the equivalent `vi` command to help you learn commands you may not be familiar with. The menu shows the keystrokes required to use the command without the GUI, so it is an excellent learning tool. Finding the right packages to install the GUI can be tricky, depending on your distribution. Table 4-19 lists a couple of packages for KDE and GNOME.

---

6. Interestingly, although many KDE and GNOME apps coexist peacefully, `kvim` and `gvim` cannot be installed at the same time.

TABLE 4-19   Package Names for GUI-Enabled Vim

Distribution	Package Name
Knoppix (KDE)	`vim-gtk`
Ubuntu (KDE)	`kvim`
Ubuntu (GNOME)	`vim-gnome`
Fedora (GNOME)	`vim-X11`

4.2.4.14   The Bottom Line on Vim

Recalling the list of features in Table 4-2, let's look at how to use them. Table 4-20 presents a summary of the features and how to access them.

Many more features are available in Vim. The most comprehensive help information is in Vim's own help menus. These are accessible as read-only, tagged documents, which can be opened in command mode by typing `:help` *keyword*. Unfortunately, navigating Vim's help system requires some knowledge of `vi` and tags. Just remember that to close a help page, you type `:q`.

TABLE 4-20   How to Access Core Features in Vim

Feature	How
Brace matching	In command mode, type %.
Syntax highlighting	Normally on by default. You can enable and disable it manually by typing **:syn on** or **:syn off** in Ex mode.
Autocompletion	`Ctrl+N` / `Ctrl+P` in insert mode.
Regular expressions	Available during search in command mode and via the `substitute` command in Ex mode.
Automatic indenting	Enable and disable from command mode with `:set ai` and `:set noai`.
Code browsing	In command mode, `Ctrl+]` to follow the tag of the text under the cursor and `Ctrl+T` to return from the tag.

4.2.5   Emacs

Emacs is the flagship text editor of the GNU project. As an alternative to vi, Emacs has a loyal following. Emacs comes with a script processor based on the Lisp programming language so that anyone can program extensions (anyone who knows Lisp, that is). Because the primary users of Emacs are programmers, the result is that Emacs has become something of a sandbox for developers over the years, having accumulated many features that have little or nothing to do with text editing. If these happen to be features you are looking for in a text editor, Emacs wins hands down.

4.2.5.1   Emacs Features

As you might expect, Emacs has all the features listed in Table 4-2, but finding them can be difficult. Along with the basics, Emacs has several tools for manipulating source code that you are not likely to find elsewhere. In most instances, these are shell commands that have been integrated into the editor.

4.2.5.2   Modes? What Modes?

Emacs claims to be *modeless,* which is what vi detractors consider to be vi's ugliest wart. Because Emacs is by nature a terminal-based editor, modelessness is something of an illusion. Emacs has modes. The difference is that the modes that Emacs uses typically are transient—that is, you enter the mode when you input a command, which may require additional arguments or interaction on your part. When the job is done, you return to the default mode. The Emacs default mode varies based on the type of file.

If you are a vi user, you can think of Emacs being in insert mode all the time. There is no command mode or Ex mode. Instead, Emacs relies on key combinations using the Ctrl and Meta keys on the keyboard.[7] This technique does have drawbacks, because control keys map to valid ASCII characters, some of which have important functions. Ctrl+G, for example, maps to the ASCII BEL character (\007), which causes the terminal to beep. Try it for yourself by pressing Ctrl+G in your terminal window. Ctrl+G happens to be what Emacs uses to abort a command sequence.

---

7.   On a PC, the meta key is labeled Alt.

Meta keys are also a problem if you are using a GUI terminal window like `gnome-terminal`, because your terminal may map the Meta key to some other purpose. The `gnome-terminal` happens to trap the Meta key to allow keyboard access to the GUI menus, which supersedes Emacs making it unusable in text mode.[8] In general, when you run Emacs in its own GUI window, these problems don't exist.

Another thing to know about Emacs is that the default mode can vary based on the type of file you are editing. As a programmer, you probably are interested in *CC Mode,* which is the mode Emacs uses to edit C, C++, Java, and others. CC Mode handles automatic indenting and is complex enough to have its own `info` page. By default, Emacs starts in CC Mode when it recognizes the file you are editing as source code. By contrast with `vi`, in which automatic indentation is a gentle hint, CC Mode automatic indentation is in your face. It works hard to make sure you don't deviate from your chosen indentation style. The supported styles are documented in the CC Mode `info` page and are listed in Table 4-21.

TABLE 4-21   Emacs Styles Used for Autoindentation

Style	Description
gnu	The default style used by Emacs, "blessed" by the Free Software Foundation
K&R	The style used in the Kerninghan and Ritchie examples
bsd	Also known as Allman Style; similar to K&R
whitesmith	Based on the style used with examples from the Whitesmith C compiler—a commercial compiler used on PDP-11
Stroustrup	C++ style used by Stroustrup
ellemtel	Named for Ellemtel Telecommunication Systems Laboratories, which published this style
linux	Style used in the Linux kernel
python	Style used for writing C extensions to Python
java	Style used for Java code.

---

8. You can override this by disabling the keyboard shortcuts listed in the Edit menu in `gnome-terminal`.

By default, Emacs uses the GNU style, which is the style found in the Emacs source code. This style is not found in many other places however, so you probably will want to change the style. I demonstrate how to do that in a later section.

4.2.5.3   Emacs Commands and Shortcuts

Emacs relies heavily on nonprintable key sequences to implement commands. These are keys that use the `Ctrl`, `Alt`, and `Esc` keys on the keyboard. I will use the Emacs convention for documenting commands summarized in Table 4-22. Note that Emacs documentation refers to the PC's `Alt` key as the Meta key. Some legacy systems do not use a PC keyboard and do not have an `Alt` key. The `Esc` key is used differently from the Ctrl and Meta keys, because pressing `Esc` produces an ASCII character (\033). By comparison, the `Ctrl` and `Alt` keys by themselves do not produce and output. Commands that use `Esc`, therefore, require two keystrokes. Note that on systems where there is no Meta key (or the Meta key has been assigned for other purposes), you can use the `Esc` key instead. `M-x` is equivalent to `Esc x`, for example.

Each Emacs command has a name, and most commands have a shortcut. Every command can be executed by typing **Esc x** or **M-x** followed by the command name. Because command names tend to be descriptive, they also tend to be rather long. The Backspace key, for example, is mapped to the `delete-backward-char` command. If you are a glutton for punishment, you could press the following key sequence instead of the Backspace key:

```
M-x delete-backward-char
```

TABLE 4-22   Emacs Convention for Documenting Commands

Notation	Description
C-*character*	Hold down the `Ctrl` key while you press the indicated character.
M-*character*	Hold down the `Alt` key (aka Meta key) while you press the indicated character.
Esc *character*	Press the `Esc` key and then press the indicated character or control sequence; same as `M-character`.

I will list commands by their shortcuts for the most part, especially for commands that you are not ever likely to type in this way (such as `delete-backward-char`).

When you type `M-x`, Emacs enters what it calls *minibuffer* mode. In minibuffer mode, Emacs allows you to save typing with tab completion. Type the first few letters of the command name, and press Tab. If there is an unambiguous match, Emacs will complete the command and allow you to press `Enter`. If there is more than one match, you are prompted with a list of possible matches. Minibuffer mode also keeps a history of commands, so `M-x` followed by an up or down arrow allows you to scroll through the history of your most recently used commands.

4.2.5.4   Cursor Movement

Like `vi`, Emacs allows the user to move the cursor without moving from the home position on the keyboard. The basic movements are listed in Table 4-23.

On a PC keyboard, the cursor keys also work, as well as `Page Up` and `Page Dn`. Emacs also provides the ability to repeat commands a given number of times. Repeats in Emacs are done by preceding a command with `C-u` and the number of repeats. This sequence moves the cursor five characters to the right:

```
C-u 5 M-f
```

You can apply this pattern to any Emacs command.

TABLE 4-23   Basic Cursor Movement in Emacs

Keys	Movement
C-b	Left one column (mnemonic: *back*)
C-f	Right one column (mnemonic: *forward*)
C-n	Down one column (mnemonic: *next*)
C-p	Up one column (mnemonic: *previous*)
C-v	Down one screen
M-v	Up one screen
M-f	Right one word (mnemonic: *forward*)
M-b	Left one word (mnemonic: *backward*)

4.2.5.5 Deleting, Cutting, and Pasting

Because of its age, Emacs does not use the contemporary terms for describing features such as the clipboard, cut, copy, and paste, although it has all these features. Likewise, it does not use the same terms as vi. The basic cut operation in Emacs is called *kill*, and a paste operation is called *yank*, as in "yank text from the clipboard." vi users note that this is the opposite direction from a vi yank.

To cut or copy an arbitrary region of text, you first have to set a mark. You do this by moving your cursor to one end of your region and marking it with the C-@ command. The other end of your region is defined by wherever your cursor happens to be when you call the appropriate cut or copy command. The basic commands are listed in Table 4-24.

4.2.5.6 Search and Replace

Emacs searches have two basic forms, illustrated in Table 4-25. Notice that the basic form does not use regular expressions. To get a regular expression, you precede the search command with an Esc character.

TABLE 4-24   Basic Cut and Paste Commands in Emacs

Keys		Movement
C-@	C-Space	Set a mark to define a region of text to be used with kill and copy commands
C-k		Cut text (aka kill) from the cursor position to the end of the line
M-k		Cut text from the current cursor to the end of the sentence
C-w		Cut a region of text from current cursor position to the mark set with C-@
ESC w	C-Ins	Copy a region of text from the current cursor position to the mark set with C-@
C-y		Paste (aka yank) text from the clipboard beginning at the current cursor position
C-_	C-x u	Undo

TABLE 4-25   Emacs Search-and-Replace Commands

Keys	Movement
C-s	Search forward using exact matching (no regular expressions)
C-r	Search backward using exact matching (no regular expressions)
Esc C-s	Search forward using a regular expression
Esc C-r	Search backward using a regular expression

Emacs uses an incremental mode for searching that is very useful. When you press C-s to start a forward search, you are prompted for a search string. As you type the string, Emacs finds the closest text that matches your string and moves the cursor while you type. In addition, it highlights all the matching text that is visible onscreen. When you press Backspace, the cursor moves backward as well, so if you delete the search, you are left where you started. Emacs remains in this mode until you press Return.

Before you press Return, you can press either C-s or C-r to move to the next match or previous match, respectively. Leaving the search mode leaves you at the first matching string and removes all the highlighting. After you have left search mode, you can repeat the last search again by entering the command twice—for example, C-s followed by C-s.

4.2.5.7   Browsing and Building Code with Emacs

Emacs uses the same principle as vi for browsing code. You create an index of your source code using a utility like etags, which comes with the Exuberant Ctags package. etags takes a list of source files that you want to index and creates an index file named TAGS in the current directory. This file is what Emacs uses to find its way through the source. Some useful commands for browsing code in Emacs are shown in Table 4-26.

Another useful feature is the bookmark, which allows you to mark a point in a text file with a meaningful name. To set a bookmark named review, the sequence would look like this:

```
C-x r m review
```

The name *review* is now saved for later reference. To go back to that line, you would type the following sequence:

```
C-x b m review
```

TABLE 4-26   Emacs Commands for Browsing Code

Keys		Movement
`M-.`	`Esc-.`	Jump to a tag. This command prompts you to enter a tag. Press `Return` to jump to the tag under the cursor.
`M-*`	`Esc-*`	Return from the current tag to the most recent jumping-off point.
`C-u M-.`		Find next alternative tag for most recent tag (for overloaded C++ functions, for example).
`C-u - M-.`		Go back to previous alternative tag found.
`C-x r` *name*		Set a bookmark at the current cursor position with the given name.
`C-x b` *name*		Jump to the bookmark with the given name.

Bookmarks are saved to disk. You can quit Emacs, and the next time you run it, it will remember the bookmarks that you set earlier.

4.2.5.8   Text Mode Menus

Emacs commands can be not only difficult to remember, but also downright difficult to type. The key sequences required to type Emacs commands can be especially difficult for people with repetitive-strain injuries, such as carpal tunnel syndrome. With the GUI version of Emacs, this is not a problem, because the GUI menus allow you to access most commands via the mouse. Recent versions of Emacs also allow you to access menus in text mode. To use the menu, press F10 on the keyboard, and you will be prompted for further input. It's not as convenient as a mouse but more intuitive than remembering a bunch of control sequences, and it's easier on the wrists. Figure 4-2 shows what this looks like.

GNOME users beware `gnome-terminal` intercepts the F10 key. If you want to use text-mode menus in Emacs you must disable this feature in the Keyboard Shortcuts[9] section of the Edit menu of `gnome-terminal`.

---

9. You might ask, "Why use emacs in text mode if you are running GNOME?" One occasion where this would be necessary is if you are running emacs remotely on an embedded target with no X libraries.

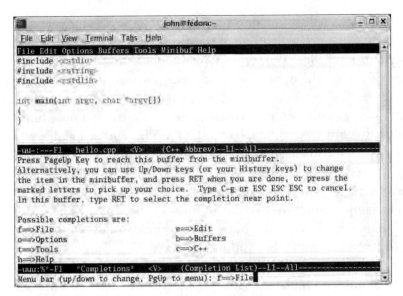

FIGURE 4-2   Emacs Editor in Text Mode Using Menus

4.2.5.9   Customizing Emacs Settings

One drawback to using Emacs is that it compels you to learn some Lisp programming. That is, if you want to customize even the simplest settings you must use Lisp syntax. When Emacs starts up it looks for a file in your home directory named .emacs. This file contains Lisp statements and functions that can be used to change the default settings of Emacs.

An introduction to Lisp is beyond the scope of this book, but there are numerous resources in the Emacs info pages and on the Web. Let's look at a simple example to demonstrate how settings are customized in Lisp, which will also illustrate the hurdles involved. You will see what it takes to change the default indentation style, which is perhaps the first thing you will want to change. I'll set it to K&R style, and while I'm at it, I'll set the tab stops at four spaces (instead of the default eight) and turn on syntax highlighting. The .emacs file for this can look like the following:

```
1. (defun my-c-style ()
2.   (c-set-style "k&r")
3.   (turn-on-font-lock)
4.   (setq c-basic-offset 4))
5.
6. (add-hook 'c-mode-common-hook 'my-c-style)
7. (setq indent-tabs-mode nil)
```

The file starts by defining a Lisp function named `my-c-style`, which will be called when we enter CC Mode. The first line of this function on line 2 is straightforward and sets style to `k&r`. Line 3 turns on syntax highlighting `font-lock` is what Emacs calls it. Finally set the number of spaces per indent to four by setting the value of `c-basic-offset` on line 4. That's it for the `my-c-style` function, which ends with a closing parenthesis. Line 6 installs `my-c-style` as a *hook* function to be called whenever Emacs sets the mode to CC Mode. This is a global setting and therefore can be done in a stand-alone expression. Finally, line 7 contains another stand-alone expression that disables the use of tabs in indentation of code by setting the value of `indent-tabs-mode` to nil.

As you can see, changing the default behavior in Emacs is not trivial. The basics of Lisp expressions are not hard to master, but can be intimidating if you are not familiar with it. Often you can find what you need on the Web ready to cut and paste into your `.emacs` file. Advanced Emacs users (who by definition are Lisp programmers) have created and accumulated many Lisp libraries to customize Emacs extensively. This cuts both ways, however. If you get too accustomed to nonstandard customizations, you could find yourself a fish out of water should you have to work on a system without access to your files. Custom hooks that make you productive are great. Just don't get too attached to them.

4.2.5.10   Emacs for `vi` Users

There is another feature of Emacs for `vi` users called Viper, which is the name for the `vi` compatibility mode for Emacs. In fact Viper has its own `info` page and is documented as though it were a separate editor. Viper can be enabled by modifying your `.emacs` file as follows:

```
(setq viper-mode t)
(require 'viper)
```

The first time you start Emacs in Viper mode, you will be greeted with a lengthy help message describing the features of Viper and asking you if you want to disable the message next time you start Viper. The next thing you are asked is to choose a *level* from 1 to 5. Level is closest to `vi` with virtually no Emacs features each increment brings you closer to Emacs nirvana. Viper does not read your `.exrc` or `.vimrc` files like `vi` and Vim. Instead, Viper stores changes in your home directory in a file named `.viper`, which contains (you guessed it) Lisp statements.

Although Viper claims to make some improvements over vi, Viper is not Vim, and many of the features listed in the previous section are not available in Viper. If you are a vi user who wants to explore Emacs, Viper is a useful alternative.

4.2.5.11   GUI Mode

Most major Linux distributions include the GUI version of Emacs (technically called Xemacs) as their default Emacs editor. Xemacs was a fork of Emacs, but now it seems these two programs have merged into one big happy executable. When compiled with a GUI, Emacs can still function in text mode but will not do so unless you explicitly specify the -nw (no windows) option (you can also run emacs-nox). Note that even if you aren't running an X server, this version of Emacs still tries to bring up the GUI, and instead of falling back to text mode, it quits with an error message.

The GUI behaves exactly like text-mode Emacs. All the same commands are accepted, but if you have trouble remembering them, there are always the mouse and menus. Emacs could be mistaken for any other GUI editor except that it doesn't typically have the look and feel of the desktop environment it is running on. The Emacs GUI is not quite as polished as some of the more modern GUI editors we will discuss.

4.2.5.12   The Bottom Line on Emacs

Emacs has much to offer a programmer looking for a text editor, but the learning curve can be difficult. If you don't mind learning something about Lisp and you like tools like CC Mode to police your editing, you really should learn Emacs. Even if you despise Emacs, it still behooves you to learn the basics. The GNU info browser borrows heavily from Emacs, particularly for the searching and navigation options. These are good skills to master the info pages have much more information than the corresponding man pages. Occasionally you may encounter a tool that borrows the Emacs command set as well. Learning the basics of Emacs will help you go a long way to being productive in other tools.

4.2.6   Attack of the Clones

Emacs and vi have loyal followings, but even the most loyal minions can point to some shortcomings in their favorite editor. The danger of creating a tool for programmers is that there is always someone out there who thinks he can do it better.

With vi, what spurred the clones was that although vi is part of the POSIX standard, the original source was proprietary until recently. This meant that vi users on operating systems other than UNIX needed an alternative. As a result several vi clones sprouted up, the most successful of which was Vim, which is available many platforms in addition to Linux. Most of the other vi clones lack the features that Vim adds but do a good job of being compatible with the original vi. They have names like Elvis, Vile, and Nvi. One unique and interesting variant is called bvi for Binary vi. This tool allows you to view and edit binary data files with a vi interface. The binary data is presented in hexadecimal bytes and you can use the familiar vi commands to navigate and modify the data. An example of bvi is shown in Figure 4-3.

In the case of Emacs, the one shortcoming that motivates cloning is its memory footprint. It's too big. Because Emacs is extensible, it makes no sense to create a clone of Emacs that has more features. It's easier to extend Emacs with Lisp programs. So it should be no surprise that all the Emacs clones are light versions of Emacs. A typical user is someone who is comfortable with the Emacs interface but who happens to be working in a low-memory environment, like an embedded system.

A few other interfaces are also popular and worth mentioning. One is WordStar, which was to DOS what vi was to UNIX. WordStar was *the* text editor for developers working on DOS machines. The interface was cloned in several other products such as Borland's Turbo Pascal and Turbo C. Many Linux users got their start on DOS-based machines and came to like the WordStar interface. It's only natural that

FIGURE 4-3   bvi in Action

this interface would find its way into some clones. You can find the WordStar interface provided by the Joe text editor. Joe is an interesting editor because it can change its behavior to be an Emacs clone or a clone of another editor called Pico, which brings us to next popular interface.

Pico was part of the very popular Pine email client, which was available on UNIX systems before the era of Web browsers. As part of an email client you might guess that Pico is easy to use, and it is. Many users came to be comfortable with it, although it lacks many features required for programming. Nevertheless, programmers use it. You can get the original source for Pine from the University of Washington[10] or you can get the GNU clone called Nano. GNU cloned Pico because the Free Software Foundation determined that the source license for Pico was not compatible with the GPL. Nano follows the same interface as Pico and adds several enhancements. Some popular clones are listed in Table 4-27. With the exception of Vim, all these clones run exclusively in text mode (there is no GUI). I will look at some GUI text editors in the next section. Table 4-28 presents a summary of available features in each clone. The list of features comes from Table 4-2.

TABLE 4-27   Some Popular Editor Clones

Editor Name	Emulates	Notes
Vim	vi	Adds many enhancements to vi.
Joe	Emacs, Pico, WordStar	Emulation is selected by the command name. The joe and jstar commands emulate WordStar; jmacs emulates Emacs; and jpico emulates Pico. These commands point to the same executable.
Zile	Emacs	*Zile* stands for *Zile Is Lossy Emacs*. Zile does not have text menus, so it's probably better suited for experienced Emacs users.
Jed	Emacs, WordStar, Others	Emulation is selected in your .jedrc file. Jed uses text menus that are the same in all modes, so it's suitable for beginners.
Nano	Pico	GNU clone of the Pico text editor with enhancements.

10. www.washington.edu/pine

TABLE 4-28   Emulator Feature Summary

Editor	Version Tested	Brace Matching	Syntax Highlighting	Auto-completion	Regular Expressions	Automatic Indenting	Code Browsing	Code Building
Vim	6.3.71	Yes	Yes	Yes	Yes	Yes	Yes	Yes
Joe	3.1	Yes	Yes		Yes	Yes	Yes	Yes
Zile	2.2	Yes			Yes	Yes		
Jed	0.99.16	Yes	Yes	Yes	Yes	Yes	Yes	Yes
Nano	1.2.4-3		Yes		Yes	Yes		

Later I look in depth at one more feature that these editors bring to the table. All the clones use less memory than their predecessors, which is one reason why they are exclusively text based. A GUI by nature consumes more memory than a text-based editor. But before I can discuss that topic, I need to take a closer look at the GUI editors.

4.2.7   Some GUI Text Editors at a Glance

Emacs and Vim aside, what all GUI text editors have in common is that they are modeless. They can do this because the mouse and GUI are used for all features that don't involve typing. There is no shortage of GUI editors available. The number of features each provides varies greatly. Some GUI editors are not intended for code development and don't have the features you would look for in a programmer's text editor. Others specifically target programmers.

In this section I look at the default editors provided with Gnome and KDE, as well as some other popular examples. There are many other fine editors including a couple written purely in Java. I chose not to include these, because most Linux distributions do not come with a Java installation. If you have a Java installation, a Java-based editor may be worth looking at. An editor written in Java is attractive if you work in Windows and Linux, you can run the same editor in both environments. Because Java uses Unicode internally, you can expect to find excellent support for internationalization.

Keep in mind that all these editors are constantly under development, so this is only a snapshot of the features available.

4.2.7.1   Kate, Kwrite

Kate is the featured text editor for the KDE environment and Kwrite is its light cousin. Both have all the features listed in Table 4-2 except code browsing. One feature Kate have not covered before is *folding* allows you to hide sections of code or comments to cut down on clutter while you work. You can see how this works in Figure 4-4 and Figure 4-5.

Kate has a plug-in mechanism to support additional features. The autocompletion feature, for example, is available as a plug-in.

Although Kwrite is supposed to be the light version of Kate, the only significant difference I have found is that Kate will open multiple files in the same window when you use tabs. By comparison, Kwrite will open one window for each file.

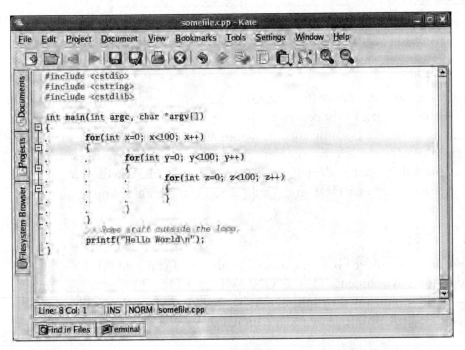

FIGURE 4-4   Kate Editor Showing the Folding Controls (Unfolded)

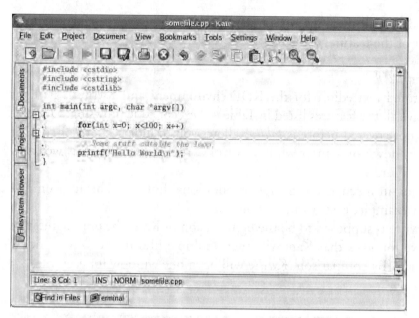

FIGURE 4-5   Kate Editor Showing the Folding Controls (Folded)

4.2.7.2   Gedit

This is the default text editor for the GNOME environment. Compared with KDE's Kate and Kwrite, Gedit comes up short on features. Of the features listed in Table 4-2, however, it lacks only code browsing and autocompletion. Syntax-highlighting implementation is very complete and supports many languages besides C and C++, including markup languages such as LaTeX and HTML and hardware design languages such as VHDL and Verilog. You can see an example of Gedit in Figure 4-6.

4.2.7.3   NEdit

NEdit is one of the older GUI text editors around and is not married to any particular desktop environment, such as GNOME or KDE. Because it uses only X libraries, it will run on any distribution that has X without many extra libraries. The controls look a little primitive by today's standards, as you can see in Figure 4-7.

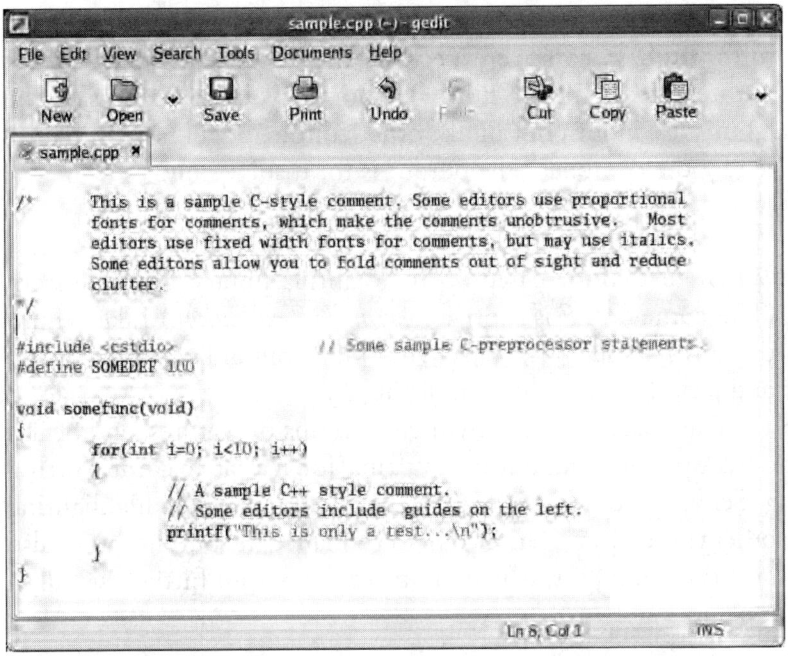

FIGURE 4-6 Gedit Editor

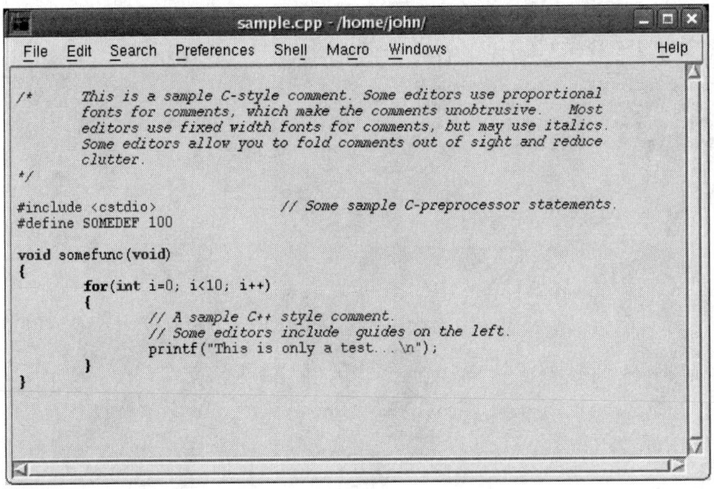

FIGURE 4-7 NEdit Editor

Don't let the simple controls fool you. NEdit is a full featured programmer's editor with all the features you have come to expect. Of the features in Table 4-2, the only thing lacking is integrated builds. NEdit will compile your code and save the error messages in an output window, but unlike other editors, it will not visit faulty lines of code reported by the compiler. The output is for display only.

4.2.7.4   SciTE

SciTE is a relatively new text editor based on the Scintilla library, available from www.scintilla.org. (The name *SciTE* is short for *Scintilla Text Editor*.) Like NEdit, SciTE is not married to any particular desktop environment, but unlike NEdit, SciTE has a modern look and feel, thanks to the Scintilla library.

As a newcomer, the bar is already set fairly high in terms of features, and SciTE delivers. SciTE has a couple of unique features going for it that make it worth a look. For one thing, SciTE produces some of the best-looking syntax highlighting you will find. Like other text editors, it uses colors to enhance the output, but it also uses proportional fonts for comments, which improves the output further (usually). You can see an example in Figure 4-8.

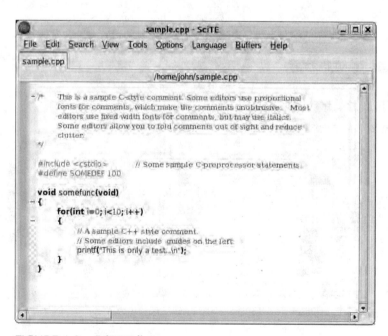

FIGURE 4-8   SciTE Editor

As if to show this off, SciTE allows you to export the text with syntax highlighting (typefaces and all) to PDF, RTF, LaTeX, HTML, or XML. You can export entire documents or just the text selected with the mouse.

Another nice feature is a split window that allows you to look at compiler output and code in a single window. You can use the mouse to click warnings, and SciTE will highlight the appropriate line of code.

Finally, SciTE has an excellent Windows version, which looks and feels exactly like the Linux version. You won't find Kate or Gedit for Windows, and NEdit will run only if you have an X server for Windows.

4.2.8   Memory Usage

Memory footprint is a big deal in some environments. On a desktop machine with hundreds of megabytes of memory, you probably don't worry too much about how much memory your text editor uses. But in an embedded system with limited memory, a slow CPU, and no swap disk, efficient memory usage is essential.

Embedded targets running Linux are becoming more common. These are systems with very little memory and often no keyboard or display. They may have just enough memory to run a small text editor but not a GUI. When working on embedded systems, it's usually most productive to do as much as you can on the target system. So any tool that conserves memory is welcome.

Even on a desktop machine, the more memory an editor uses, the more sluggish it is. If your system is low on memory, excessive memory usage causes swapping, which makes everything run slowly. Another issue is startup and shutdown time. Often, developers need to edit things in "just in time" fashion, which makes long startup times annoying and unproductive. A text editor with a small footprint usually starts up very quickly and exits just as fast.

Figure 4-9 shows the memory footprint of the editors I have discussed so far. The editors that have the biggest footprint are, not surprisingly, GUI based, whereas the smallest footprint can be found on the terminal-based editors.

These measurements were taken immediately after startup with an empty file. What is harder to compare is how these editors manage memory while running and editing large files. Suppose that you need to modify one line of a 100MB file. Does your editor read in the entire file and consume an extra 100MB, or does it read in only the pieces you need to see so as to conserve memory? That's an extremely contrived example, but you don't need such large files to run into efficiency issues on embedded targets. Some common sense as well as trial and error should help you find the right editor for the job.

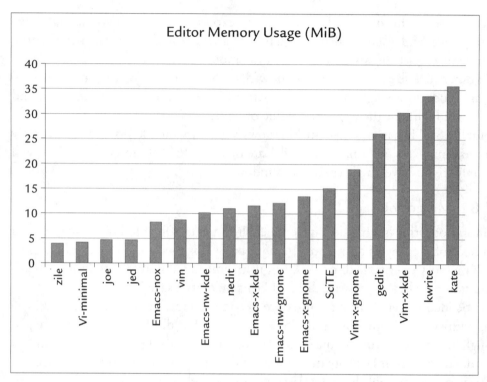

FIGURE 4-9   Memory Usage by Text Editor

4.2.9   Editor Summary

I have focused on text editor features for programmers, and the choice of features was perhaps a little arbitrary. There are many other choices offering many more features. Perhaps you would like a GUI editor that you can use in both Windows and Linux. Emacs and Vim will work, but so will SciTE and many other editors I didn't cover here.

Another feature I left out that may be important to you is internationalization (i18n for short). The i18n support in all the editors tested was surprisingly good. It used to be that terminal-based editors could not support the fonts or encodings required for i18n, but that's not true anymore. Thanks in large part to the international community of open source developers, most popular text editors, including terminal-based editors, can handle multiple encodings. All the editors tested support UTF-8, a versatile Unicode encoding that is a superset of ASCII and that can represent any written language on Earth.

Don't just look at the features listed here; also consider what special requirements you have. If you do any searching on the topic of text editors, you will discover that this has been the topic of "holy wars" in the past. Try to keep an open mind, and always be skeptical of anyone who claims that his favorite editor is the only one you'll ever need. As a programmer, your goal is to be productive, not fashionable.

4.3   Revision Control

Any good software process requires revision control. It is a key metric for any organization that claims to be mature. The ability to control what goes into a release of software and to keep track of it after it is released is vital to quality software development.

Good revision control is necessary not only for large organizations, but also for individual developers. It can be a chore, but more often than not, it is a vital tool in your development process. From a text-editing perspective, you can think of revision control as being a *super undo* function. It allows you to checkpoint your development at certain stages where features are stable, before you start to implement new features that may affect the whole project.

This section cannot do justice to all the tools that are available for revision control. Indeed, you can find several books on each of these tools. Instead, I look at some of the basic concepts of revision control that are common to all tools. Then I cover some of the features of several popular tools. You can find more information about these tools in the Online References section at the end of this chapter.

4.3.1   Revision Control Basics

Suppose that Figure 4-10 illustrates the revisions of a module you created for an open source project. Revisions A through F are the main branch, where new features are added and debugged. At revision C, you decided to release the code. While users were getting used to the features, you continued to work on new features in revisions D through F. Sometime during this development, your users discovered bugs that needed to be addressed. In order to fix these bugs without releasing unfinished features, you created a branch from revision C. This allowed you to fix the released code and work on new features at the same time. At revision F, you were able to *merge* the bug fixes into the main code, which is typical before a new release.

The pattern illustrated in Figure 4-10 is a bit oversimplified, but it is the same for virtually all revision control tools.

Until recently, there weren't many open source tools available for revision control. That has changed, and some new tools are maturing and competing for new projects. Some of the most popular tools are listed in Table 4-29.

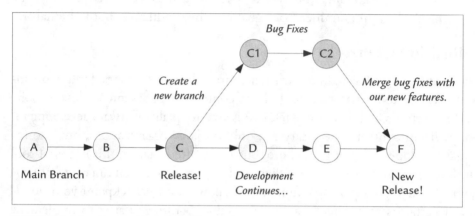

FIGURE 4-10   Simple Branching Example

TABLE 4-29   Some Popular Revision Control Tools

Name	Description
RCS	Revision Control System—the ancestor of CVS (Concurrent Version System), which served as its basis originally. RCS does not support projects and requires that files be locked to be modified.
CVS	Concurrent Version System—built on RCS; allows files to be grouped in projects and does away with the locking requirement. Developers must resolve conflicts with a merge before they are allowed to commit changes.
Subversion	A successor to CVS fixes many of its shortcomings while preserving the basic user interface.
GNU arch	An alternative to CVS that developed at about the same time as Subversion. It addresses many of the same issues that Subversion does. It remains to be seen whether it will catch on.
monotone	Takes some new approaches to revision control that may be a little controversial; uses SHA1 hashes to record changes and versions.

4.3.2   Defining Revision Control Terms

The terminology varies from one tool to the next, so I'll define some neutral terms for comparing one tool with another.

4.3.2.1   Project

Generally, this is an arbitrary grouping of files determined by the developer, although very often in practice, one project produces a single executable or library. Each open source tool, for example, has its own revision control "project."

Each file under the project has an independent history, but the project itself may have a history as well. In CVS and Subversion, a project is called a *module,* whereas GNU arch calls it an *archive* and monotone calls it a *working copy.*

4.3.2.2   Add/Remove

This is a basic feature. Developers need to be able to add and remove source files as the project evolves. All tools allow this. Most tools keep a history of removed files so that they can be restored for old versions of the source.

4.3.2.3   Check In

This is the ability to create new versions of a file. Each time you check in a file, it is a snapshot of what the file looked like at that point. No matter how many additional changes you make, you can always reproduce the file exactly as it was when you checked it in.

4.3.2.4   Check Out

This is the ability to recall a file that was checked in earlier. Depending on the tool, you may check out a file or an entire project. Most tools default to a nonlocking scheme for checking out files, with locks supported only for special circumstances. When a file is locked, no one else can work on it (check it out).

Consider RCS, which uses a locking scheme. To modify a file, you need to check it out with a lock. This gives you a writable copy of the checked-out file that you can modify. Until you check the file in, no one else can lock the file. In principle, the lock means that no one else can edit the file. This ensures that when you do check the file in there will be no other changes to your file. In this case, the check-in operation is little more than a copy operation.

Locks can be a nuisance in projects with many developers and many source files. If two developers need to modify the same source file, they cannot do it at the same time, no matter how trivial the change. This impairs the productivity of the whole team, because developers may have to synchronize their efforts.

All modern revision control tools use nonlocking schemes that allow multiple developers to modify the same file. They accomplish this by *merging* changes when the files are checked in (see below). The assumption is that two developers working on the same file will be working on different lines, such that a merge will not be difficult. When this is not the case, the merge must be done manually. It's a small price to pay for enhanced productivity.

4.3.2.5 Branch

Branching is a vital tool for revision control. It enables numerous useful patterns. One pattern for creating bug fixes is illustrated in Figure 4-10 earlier in this chapter. A branch allows you to create new versions of old source files that don't conflict with the latest development and that don't pick up any unwanted changes that aren't ready for release.

4.3.2.6 Merge

Another key enabler, this allows tools like CVS to work without locks. Instead, the tools rely on merges. The idea is that when you change a file, the tool checks to see whether anyone else made a change since you started working on it. If so, you are required to perform a merge before you can check in.

If you and another developer check out the same file, and the other developer finishes first, you are required to merge his changes with yours before you can submit them. The merge is done with the help of a merge tool and is facilitated by the revision control tool. If you circumvent the merge step, your changes will overwrite the other developer's.

4.3.2.7 Label

Revision control tools typically pick arbitrary labels for versions of files checked into the system. When you have more than one source file, odds are that they aren't all the same revision. The tools use labels like 1.1, 1.2, and so on. monotone, for example, uses a 40-character hash. These are arbitrary and probably not what you want to use to communicate release versions. A label allows you to give a bunch of files a common name like `release_1.0` so that you can keep track of all the files that went into a release with one key.

4.3.2.8   In Summary

If you are contributing to a revision-controlled project, very likely the choice of tools is out of your hands; you will have to use whatever the project maintainer decided on. If you plan to create an open source project, you should become familiar with your choices. Understand that CVS has been the workhorse of open source projects for a long time and that many developers are comfortable with it. Subversion is rapidly catching on, as it uses nearly the same syntax as CVS and addresses many of CVS's flaws.

Creating a project with an unfamiliar revision control tool is likely to discourage some developers from joining your project. Even if you think a particular tool is the best, if you want to recruit developers, you need to think about what they find most productive. Trying to get developers to change tools may create an unnecessary hurdle for you.

4.3.3   Supporting Tools

Managing changes in source code is a difficult job, and it only gets more difficult when more developers are involved. It should come as no surprise that several tools are available to make this job easier.

4.3.4   Introducing diff and patch

Most users are familiar with the basic `diff` command, which compares pairs of files. Most often, we are interested only in knowing whether two files are identical. In that case, you can use the `cmp` command. When you want to see the changes, the output from `diff` is not the most user friendly. That's because the real usefulness of the `diff` command is for creating patches that can be applied by the `patch` command. As you shall see, there are better tools than `diff` for looking at file changes, but let's look at what `diff` is good for. I'll start with an example of `diff` output with a few trivial changes:

```
$ cat -n before.txt
     1  This is a line to be deleted
     2  This is a line that will be changed
     3  This is a line that will be unchanged

$ cat -n after.txt
     1  This is a line that has been changed
     2  This is a line that will be unchanged
     3  This is a line that has been added
```

```
$ diff before.txt after.txt
1,2c1
< This is a line to be deleted
< This is a line that will be changed
---
> This is a line that has been changed
3a3
> This is a line that has been added
```

Although not particularly user friendly, the output is readable. By default, lines that are changed or deleted from the first file are indicated with a < character. Lines that have been added or changed in the second file are preceded by a > character. The extra information indicates the line numbers where the change took place, which can be used by the `patch` command.

Let's see how this output is used by the `patch` command. Suppose that you have a file identical to `before.txt` that you want to patch (call it `new.txt`). You want to take the differences between `before.txt` and `after.txt` and apply them to `new.txt`. You can do this with a patch as follows:

```
$ cp before.txt new.txt
$ diff before.txt after.txt > mypatch.txt
$ cat mypatch.txt | patch new.txt
```

After the patch is applied, `new.txt` is identical to `after.txt`. This is not a very interesting application, because you could just as easily have overwritten `new.txt` with `after.txt`. But that's not the point. The point is that if all you have is a copy of `before.txt`, all you need to create `after.txt` is `mypatch.txt`. Instead of keeping two copies of the same file, which may be very large, all you need are the original and the difference (which could be very small) in the form of a patch. This was the intended use for patches, which was very important back when a great deal of networking was done with slow modems and disk drive sizes were a couple of orders of magnitude smaller. Patches allowed you to update your source code using much smaller files instead of downloading an entire project. Despite the increasing popularity of broadband Internet and huge disks, patches are still used widely today to disseminate changes to the Linux kernel source. Many open source projects distribute changes in the form of patches as well.

Another useful feature of patches is that they can be reversed. To undo the changes you just made to `new.txt` with the `patch` command, you can use the same patch file as follows:

```
$ patch -R new.txt < mypatch.diff
```

The -R flag tells patch to apply the differences in the reverse direction or to *undo* the patch. When using the default output of the diff command, you have to tell patch exactly what files to patch. In this example, I gave the filename new.txt as an argument to patch; otherwise, it would have prompted for a file to patch. A more versatile way to create a patch is to use the -u option (for unified format), which looks like this:

```
$ diff -u before.txt after.txt | tee mypatch.diff
--- before.txt  1994-07-02 12:34:56.000000000 -0500
+++ after.txt   2004-07-02 12:34:56.000000000 -0500
@@ -1,4 +1,4 @@
-This is a line to be deleted.
-This is a line that will be changed.
+This is a line that has been changed.
 This is a line that will be unchanged.
+This is a line that has been added.
```

Notice that the output is now quite a bit different and includes both filenames as well as their creation date and time (with the time zone). It is also a bit more readable than the default diff output. Although the patch has two filenames, a given patch will modify only one file. The patch command chooses one of these two files to modify, depending upon which one exists. If only one file exists, it patches that file. If both files exist, it patches the second file (after.txt, in this example). If no files exist, the patch command fails, because there is nothing to patch.

When you use the unified format, multiple differences can be combined into a single large patch. In this way, you can patch numerous files with a single patch file. This is how many open source tools, including the Linux kernel, distribute patches.

The most common way to create a large patch is to use the diff command with the -r option to walk through directories recursively. This requires you to have two identical directory trees with identical filenames. The only differences are in the files themselves. By looking for matching pathnames, diff is able to determine which pairs of files to compare to produce the differences. When diff encounters a file that exists in only one of the two trees, the default behavior is to skip that file and print a warning to stderr. This behavior can be changed with the -N option, which causes diff to assume that a missing file is actually there but empty. In this way, a patch can include files that were created. Then applying the patch will create new files.

Let's look at another trivial example that ties this all together. First, you need a set of files to work with:

```
# Create before and after directory trees
$ mkdir old new
$ echo "This is one. It's unchanged." | tee old/one new/one
$ echo "This is two. It will change." > old/two
$ echo "This is two. It changed." > new/two
$ echo "This is three. It's new" > new/three
```

This creates two directories for the demonstration. The *new* directory contains what you want, or the latest versions of the files. The *old* directory contains what you started with, or the old versions of the files. You can create a patch as follows:

```
$ diff -Nur old new > mypatch.diff
```

This produces a patch that looks like the following:

```
diff -Nur old/three new/three
--- old/three    1969-12-31 18:00:00.000000000 -0600
+++ new/three    2005-10-30 20:40:56.296875000 -0600
@@ -0,0 +1 @@
+This is three. It's new
diff -Nur old/two new/two
--- old/two     2005-10-30 20:40:56.265625000 -0600
+++ new/two     2005-10-30 20:40:56.281250000 -0600
@@ -1 +1 @@
-This is two. It will change.
+This is two. It changed.
```

Note that patches have a *direction,* which is determined by the order of the files given to the `diff` command. In this case, the direction is from *old* to *new.* So now that you have a patch, you can transform *old* into *new,* as follows:

```
$ patch --dir old < mypatch.diff
patching file three
patching file two
```

After `patch` runs, the contents of *old* and *new* are identical. You can also reverse the direction of the patch and transform *new* into *old,* as follows:

```
$ patch --dir new -R < mypatch.diff
patching file three
patching file two
```

This is a small example of what you might do on a larger scale with the Linux kernel source or a large open source project. In the kernel, unofficial patches are available all the time, offering features that are not part of the kernel. Usually, there is good reason for this, but some good features are not ready for wide distribution. You can use a patch and be assured that if the feature turns out to be broken, you can undo the change to your source and get your kernel back the way it was.

I glossed over some details in these examples. First is the `--dir` option to `patch`, which tells the `patch` command to do a `chdir` to the specified directory before applying the patch. Another detail is the fact that the `patch` command automatically removes the leftmost directory element of the patch before applying the patch. In this case, it's the *old* or *new,* which means that the `patch` command will not look for a directory named *old* or *new* when applying the changes. You can exert more control over this behavior with the `-p` option (see `patch(1)` for details).

The `.diff` extension is one common convention for naming patch files. The Linux kernel uses filenames that start with `patch`. These files can include changes to hundreds of files in the Linux source tree.

4.3.5 Reviewing and Merging Changes

The `diff` command leaves something to be desired when it comes to reviewing changes. You could argue that the output is not intended for human consumption, but for small changes, it's adequate. The GNU `diff` command has many options to make the output more readable, but in a text terminal, there's only so much you can do.

For large changes, it's often more helpful to see formatted output so that you can zero in on exactly what has changed. When `diff` sees a single character changed on one line, it prints out the entire line (twice) to indicate the change. For example:

```
$ diff src1 src2
1c1
< const char *somechars=":,-;+.({)}";
---
> const char *somechars=":,-;+.{()}";
```

Only two characters changed on this line. Can you spot the change? This is where some other tools are more helpful. Vim, for example, is capable of showing differences that highlight single-character changes, as follows:

```
$ vim -d src1.c src2.c
```

A slightly nicer alternative is the GUI version, `gvimdiff`, which is shown in Figure 4-11. This illustrates how single-character changes are highlighted in addition to line changes. Now the difference is much easier to spot. Both `vim` and `gvimdiff` highlight changes, but the limitations of your terminal capabilities may make the GUI preferable.

Another open source GUI tool for reviewing differences is `xxdiff`,[11] available from sourceforge.net. This tool adds some nice features, including a merge utility. A GUI is especially nice to have in a merge utility, which you shall find out.

Eventually, the time comes when things get more complicated and a merge is in order. A merge situation comes up most often when you're working under revision control. Usually, the need for a merge arises when you are working with other team members or on multiple branches. To help you understand merges better, I'll introduce the GNU command-line merge tool.

The GNU merge tool used by revision control tools such as CVS and Subversion is called `diff3`. The `diff3` command gets its name because it requires three filename arguments, as follows:

```
$ diff3 myfile original yourfile
```

The order of *myfile* and *yourfile* is interchangeable, but the second filename must be the common ancestor. Figure 4-12 shows a graph of what the revision tree looks like.

To illustrate, we need a file to work with. Let's consider this trivial example:

```
1  void foo(void)
2  {
3          printf("This will be changed by me.\n");
4
5          printf("This will be unchanged.\n");
6
7          printf("This will be changed by you.\n");
8  }
```

Now suppose that I change my copy of this file so that line 3 reads

```
printf("This was changed by me.\n");
```

and you change your copy of the file so that line 7 reads

```
printf("This was changed by you.\n");
```

---

11. http://sourceforge.net/projects/xxdiff

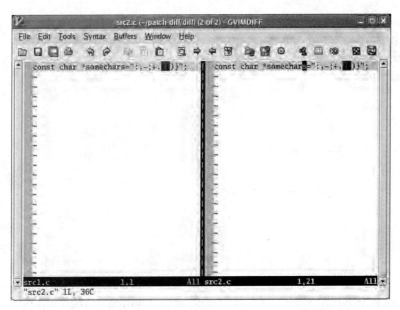

FIGURE 4-11   The Same Difference Shown with gvimdiff (Highlighted s Is the Cursor)

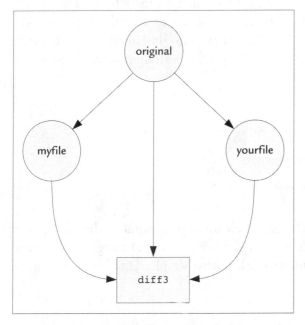

FIGURE 4-12   Graphic Illustration of a Merge using `diff3`

Now we have two different changes that need to be merged. Luckily, they're on different lines of the same file, so merging is quite easy. With no arguments, diff3 produces output that illustrates the changes but is readable only if the changes are small, as in this example:

```
$ diff3 me.c orig.c you.c
====1
1:3c
        printf("This was changed by me.\n");
2:3c
3:3c
        printf("This will be changed by me.\n");
====3
1:7c
2:7c
        printf("This will be changed by you.\n");
3:7c
        printf("This was changed by you.\n");
```

Differences are delimited by ====1 or ====3, indicating which of the modified files caused the difference against the original. Numbering is based on the argument order, so in this example, 1 is me.c, 2 is orig.c, and 3 is you.c. The line numbers, as well as the types of changes, are indicated on the left. This is not the most useful output from diff3, however. The more useful output comes with the merge option, where diff3 will attempt to do the merge for us. Because the changes are trivial in this example, diff3 produces straightforward results:

```
$ diff3 -m me.c orig.c you.c   | cat -n
1   void foo(void)
2   {
3           printf("This was changed by me.\n");
4
5           printf("This will be unchanged.\n");
6
7           printf("This was changed by you.\n");
8   }
```

Notice that both your and my changes show up in the output in the right place. Very often in a large source file, it's possible to have such trivial merges that require no input from the user, but sometimes, it's not so simple. Let's look at another example:

```
1  void foo(void)
2  {
3          printf("This will be changed by both of us.\n");
4  }
```

In this case, both you and I modify the same line of code. Instead of showing you the listings, let's see what `diff3` says:

```
$ diff3 -m me.c orig.c you.c
 1  void foo(void)
 2  {
 3  <<<<<<< me.c
 4          printf("This was changed by me.\n");
 5  ||||||| orig.c
 6          printf("This will be changed by both of us.\n");
 7  =======
 8          printf("This was changed by you.\n");
 9  >>>>>>> you.c
10  }
```

Clearly, this output is not ready to compile. Now we have some choices to make, as indicated by the delimiters. The conflict starts with the <<<<<<< characters and ends with the >>>>>>> characters. We must use a text editor to clean up everything in between, deciding which changes to keep, and which ones to loose.

CVS and Subversion look for conflicts when you try to put changes back in the repository via the `commit` command. If the tool detects that someone else has changed a file since you retrieved your copy, it will not allow you to `commit` your changes. To resolve this, you have to do an `update`, which is the command to bring your local copy up to date with the repository. When you do the update, changed files that have not been modified by you are overwritten with the new changes. At the same time, files that have been changed in the repository and by you require a merge to bring them up to date in your local copy. When you run the `update` command, the tool runs `diff3` to do whatever merges are necessary. Then it is up to you to resolve any remaining conflicts with your text editor.

Let's take one more look at `xxdiff`, which can be very helpful with merges. The same merge is shown in Figure 4-13.

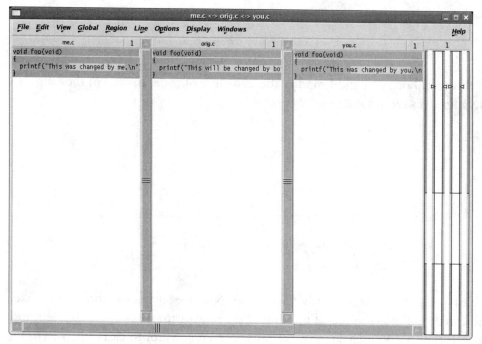

FIGURE 4-13   Using xxdiff to Do a Merge

Here, you are presented with all three files and can choose which change to take with the click of a mouse. You can even select all three changes, which can produce output that looks just like diff3. Or you can tell xxdiff to wrap each change in an #ifdef statement. For example:

```
1    void foo(void)
2    {
3    #if defined( ME )
4      printf("This was changed by me.\n");
5    #elif defined( ORIG )
6      printf("This will be changed by both of us.\n");
7    #elif defined( YOU )
8      printf("This was changed by you.\n");
9    #endif
10   }
```

One thing to notice with CVS and most revision control tools is that the person doing the merge has the power of choice. That is, if I were merging this change to a revision control system, I would get the opportunity to choose which change gets checked in: yours or mine.

4.4   Source Code Beautifiers and Browsers

I discussed how Emacs' CC Mode enforces rigid indentation rules that are hard to break. If everyone used Emacs, and used the same indentation style, there would be no issues. In reality, everyone has his or her own favorite editor with his or her own settings. As more people touch the same source file with all these different settings, what you are left with can be a mess. Some editors expand tabs to spaces; others mix tabs and spaces; and all make different assumptions about how many spaces are in a tab. What may look pretty in one editor may look like avant-garde poetry in another editor.

There are tools that will indent the code for you, but beware: Reformatting an entire module can cause problems in revision control systems. That's because you are touching virtually every line of code. Even though you are only rearranging the code, the merge tool does not know that. So when someone makes a change in an *unpretty* version of the file, trying to merge those changes with the pretty version could be unwieldy. Let's consider another contrived example. Suppose that you had a source file with a bunch of declarations on one line, as follows:

```
int i; int j; int k; int l; int m; int n; int o; int p; int q; int r;
```

You run a beautifier, which places each declaration on its own line. Now another developer checks out the same file and notices that the variable m is unused; he deletes that declaration to remove the warning. This developer is not interested in beautifying the code but just wants to commit a simple change to fix a warning. Now when you commit your beautified code, what should have been a one-line change is now a ten-line change, as follows:

```
$ diff3 -m -E me.c orig.c you.c
<<<<<<< me.c
int i;
int j;
int k;
int l;
int m;
int n;
int o;
int p;
int q;
int r;
=======
int i; int j; int k; int l; int n; int o; int p; int q; int r;
>>>>>>> you.c
```

This is an easy example, of course; it only gets uglier from here. The only advice to offer is to make sure that no unbeautified code gets merged with beautified code, which may be difficult or impossible to guarantee. Resist the temptation to beautify entire modules unless you are certain that there will be no merges after that point. If you can't be certain, you may be able to beautify small sections of code, which are less likely to conflict with other merges.

In the end, this should illustrate the importance of coding standards, in particular when it comes to indentation. If you work on an open source project, you probably will have to comply with a required indentation style. Even if you don't like something about the style, it is important to comply. Any indentation style is better than none at all.

4.4.1   The Indent Code Beautifier

UNIX had a command named `cb` that could reformat C source code. It was implemented as a filter that operated exclusively on standard input and output. This was annoying to some people, because you couldn't just turn it loose on your source code. This approach has its advantages, particularly for `vi` users, because `vi` is able to take advantage of filters. You can indent only the code between two braces, for example, as follows:

```
!%cb
```

There is another good reason for keeping code beautifiers at bay. Consider the earlier example of beautified code that has to be merged with unbeautified code. Filtering a block of code allows you to make incremental changes to a large module that might be in work by many users. Instead of reformatting an entire module and clashing with everyone else, you can fix up a single function or block of code without causing too much grief when it comes time to merge.

The Linux equivalent of the `cb` filter is the `indent` command, which is much more versatile. For one thing, `indent` can reformat C++ as well as C. It can operate as a filter like `cb` but can also indent files in place. Although doing so is not recommended, you could reformat a bunch of files with a single command, as follows:

```
$ indent *.c
```

Although `indent` does not support all the styles that Emacs supports (listed in Table 4-21 earlier in this chapter), it does include K&R, GNU, and BSD styles. You can exert precise control over every aspect of reformatting with more than 80 command-line options, however, so whatever style you like, you can tweak `indent` to support it.

Let's look at some examples. Listing 4-1 shows a pathologically indented Fibonacci function—a classic example from programming class.

LISTING 4-1   Fibonacci on Drugs

```
unsigned int fibonacci(unsigned int n)
    {
    if ( n < 2 ) {
   return n;
    }
 else
{
 return
  fibonacci( n - 1 )
   +
    fibonacci( n -2 );
     }
      }
```

Now let's run this through a few styles with `indent`. You can see two examples in Listing 4-2 and Listing 4-3.

LISTING 4-2   An Example of GNU Style Using indent

```
unsigned int
fibonacci (unsigned int n)
{
  if (n < 2)
    {
      return n;
    }
  else
    {
      return fibonacci (n - 1) + fibonacci (n - 2);
    }
}
```

LISTING 4-3   Berkeley Style Using indent

```
unsigned int
fibonacci(unsigned int n)
{
    if (n < 2) {
      return n;
    } else {
      return fibonacci(n - 1) + fibonacci(n - 2);
    }
}
```

indent is fairly aggressive in its reformatting output, so it merges and breaks lines as it sees fit. There are dozens of options to control the finer details, so you usually can start with one of the basic styles and tweak it with additional options. For example:

```
$ indent -kr -bl -bli0 -nce
```

This takes the K&R style and tells indent to put braces on their own line (-bl) with no additional indentation (-bli0). Finally, it tells indent to keep the else on its own line (-nce). These options can be combined in a file named .indent.pro, which may reside in the current directory or your home directory. All you do is place the same options in a text file. For example:

```
-kr -bl -bli0 -nce
```

If this file is in your home directory, these will be the default options, whenever you run indent. Alternatively, if you contribute to multiple projects with different indentation styles, you could put a unique .indent.pro in each project directory.

4.4.2   Astyle Artistic Style

Another promising open source beautifier is called astyle.[12] Like indent, astyle understands C and C++, but it also understands Java and (gasp) C#. Here again, astyle does not support all the formats that Emacs does, but it does have predefined formats for K&R, GNU, and Linux styles, as well as something it calls ANSI style.

---

12. http://sourceforge.net/projects/astyle

astyle is less aggressive than indent when it comes to reformatting. It will not break lines unless you explicitly tell it what kind of lines it can break. It will not consolidate statements that span more than one line into a single line. This does not work well with Listing 4-1, for example. Listing 4-4 shows the results after Listing 4-1 has been processed with astyle.

LISTING 4-4   Example of ANSI Style with astyle

```
unsigned int fibonacci(unsigned int n)
{
    if ( n < 2 ) {
        return n;
    }
    else
    {
        return
            fibonacci( n - 1 )
            +
            fibonacci( n -2 );
    }
}
```

Notice that this style is almost identical to the modified K&R style I created in the last section except that the second return statement still occupies three lines.

4.4.3   Analyzing Code with cflow

When you have to work on code that you didn't create or haven't looked at in a long time, just looking at the source is not always enough to understand the code. Fortunately, there are tools to help.

The POSIX cflow command translates your source code into a call graph that allows you to see an overview of program flow. This is very useful for looking at unfamiliar code. GNU has a version of the POSIX cflow[13] command that, although not fully POSIX compliant, is still very useful. Let's use Listing 4-5 as an example.

---

13. www.gnu.org/software/cflow

LISTING 4-5   ex4-5.c

```
 1  void zfunc(void) { afunc(); }
 2
 3  void xfunc(void) { zfunc(); }
 4
 5  void afunc(void) { afunc(); }
 6
 7  void recurs(void) { recurs(); }
 8
 9  void mainfunc()
10  {
11          xfunc();
12          recurs();
13  }
```

This module is simple enough to illustrate how `cflow` works. Using the POSIX format of cflow, you get the following:

```
$ cflow --format=posix ex4-5.c
    1 afunc: void (void), <ex4-5.c 5>
    2     afunc: 1                          afunc() calls itself
    3 mainfunc: void (), <ex4-5.c 9>
    4     xfunc: void (void), <ex4-5.c 3>   mainfunc() calls xfunc()
    5         zfunc: void (void), <ex4-5.c 1>  xfunc() calls zfunc()
    6             afunc: 1                  zfunc() calls afunc()
    7     recurs: void (void), <ex4-5.c 7>  etc...
    8         recurs: 7
    9 recurs: 7
   10 xfunc: 4
   11 zfunc: 5
```

Notice that the output looks something like an outline. Functions are listed first in alphabetical order. Under each function, `cflow` lists the functions called by that function, with one level of indentation for each level of call depth. In this example, you can find `mainfunc()` listed in alphabetical order on line 3, followed by the functions it calls. Notice that call trees are shown only once—for example, `xfunc()` is called by `mainfunc()`, and this is shown in the call tree beginning on line 3. `cflow` lists `xfunc()` on line 10 but does not show its call tree, because that was shown under `mainfunc()`.

The POSIX output format is the most concise. The default output format includes function signatures and redundant call trees, making the output a little more cluttered. For example:

```
$ cflow ex4-5.c
afunc() <void afunc (void) at ex4-5.c:5> (R):
    afunc() <void afunc (void) at ex4-5.c:5> (recursive: see 1)
mainfunc() <void mainfunc () at ex4-5.c:9>:
    xfunc() <void xfunc (void) at ex4-5.c:3>:
        zfunc() <void zfunc (void) at ex4-5.c:1>:
            afunc() <void afunc (void) at ex4-5.c:5> (R):
                afunc() <void afunc (void) at ex4-5.c:5> (recursive: see 6)
        recurs() <void recurs (void) at ex4-5.c:7> (R):
            recurs() <void recurs (void) at ex4-5.c:7> (recursive: see 8)
recurs() <void recurs (void) at ex4-5.c:7> (R):
    recurs() <void recurs (void) at ex4-5.c:7> (recursive: see 10)
xfunc() <void xfunc (void) at ex4-5.c:3>:
    zfunc() <void zfunc (void) at ex4-5.c:1>:
        afunc() <void afunc (void) at ex4-5.c:5> (R):
            afunc() <void afunc (void) at ex4-5.c:5> (recursive: see 14)
zfunc() <void zfunc (void) at ex4-5.c:1>:
    afunc() <void afunc (void) at ex4-5.c:5> (R):
        afunc() <void afunc (void) at ex4-5.c:5> (recursive: see 17)
```

Another useful format is the reverse call tree, which is something like a cross reference. Instead of listing each function and showing you the functions it calls, it shows you each function followed by a list of functions that call it. Using the more concise POSIX format, the reverse call tree of our example looks like this:

```
$ cflow --format=posix ex4-5.c -r
   1 afunc: void (void), <ex4-5.c 5>          afunc defined on line 5
   2     zfunc: void (void), <ex4-5.c 1>      afunc called by zfunc
   3         xfunc: void (void), <ex4-5.c 3>  zfunc called by xfunc
   4             mainfunc: void (), <ex4-5.c 9>  etc...
   5     afunc: 1
   6 mainfunc: 4
   7 recurs: void (void), <ex4-5.c 7>
   8     recurs: 7
   9     mainfunc: 4
  10 xfunc: 3
  11 zfunc: 2
```

You can also get a less cluttered, flat cross reference by using the --xref option to cflow. This produces a simple list of functions with one line for each time the function appears in the source. For example:

```
$ cflow  --xref ex4-5.c
afunc * ex4-5.c:5 void afunc (void)       afunc defined on line 5, denoted by "*"
afunc   ex4-5.c:1                         afunc is referenced on line 1
afunc   ex4-5.c:5                         etc...
```

```
mainfunc * ex4-5.c:9 void mainfunc ()
recurs * ex4-5.c:7 void recurs (void)
recurs    ex4-5.c:7
recurs    ex4-5.c:12
xfunc * ex4-5.c:3 void xfunc (void)
xfunc     ex4-5.c:11
zfunc * ex4-5.c:1 void zfunc (void)
zfunc     ex4-5.c:3
```

The output lists the functions in alphabetical order, as well as the filename and line where they were encountered. If the line is a function declaration, the output includes an asterisk along with the function prototype.

4.4.4   Analyzing Code with ctags

While we're talking about cross-referencing, let's revisit Exuberant Ctags. Although ctags normally produces output for your text editor, it can also produce a human-readable cross reference using the -x option. Using our trusty example again, you can see the output as follows:

```
$ ctags -x ex4-5.c
afunc           function      5 ex4-5.c        void afunc(void) { afunc(); }
mainfunc        function      9 ex4-5.c        void mainfunc()
recurs          function      7 ex4-5.c        void recurs(void) { recurs(); }
xfunc           function      3 ex4-5.c        void xfunc(void) { zfunc(); }
zfunc           function      1 ex4-5.c        void zfunc(void) { afunc(); }
```

Notice that the difference between cflow and ctags is that ctags focuses exclusively on definitions, not references. Although cflow gives you additional information about references, ctags has more features. For one thing, ctags supports numerous languages besides C and C++, whereas cflow supports only C. Another feature of ctags is that it lets you filter the output for C code using the --c--kinds option. Suppose that you wanted to see all the global variables declared in a set of modules and nothing else. You could limit the output using the following command:

```
$ ctags -x --c--kinds=v --file-scope=no
```

The --c--kinds option indicates that you want variables only (v), which normally would show every variable defined at file scope, including static definitions. The --file-scope=no flag tells ctags to exclude variables that are not global. Note that the -x option works with all the languages that ctags supports, but the --c--kinds flag applies only to C code.

Finally, the cross reference from ctags is tab separated so you can import it into a spreadsheet or table easily. This can be useful for performing simple code metrics.

4.4.5 Browsing Code with cscope

cscope is a text mode browser for looking at code. It creates its own database from a list of source files that you provide and then enters into an ncurses text menu system. You need a functional terminal emulator to use cscope. An example is shown in Figure 4-14.

The screen is broken into two halves. Each line on the top half of the screen presents a line of code that matched the most recent query. The bottom half of the screen contains entry fields for several types of queries that are supported. Each query is preceded by a straightforward description, such as "Find this C symbol." Most programmers should find these queries self explanatory. The Tab key takes you between the top and bottom halves of the screen, and the up-arrow and down-arrow keys move between lines in each half. Enter a query in the appropriate field of the bottom half of the screen, and the results appear in the top half. Move the cursor to one of the hits in the top half, and cscope will call your favorite editor and take you to that line of code.

Needless to say, this is a very interactive tool. cscope has only limited support for static output. The > character will save the current list of matches to a file, and you can append to it with >>. Make no mistake—cscope is intended to be used interactively.

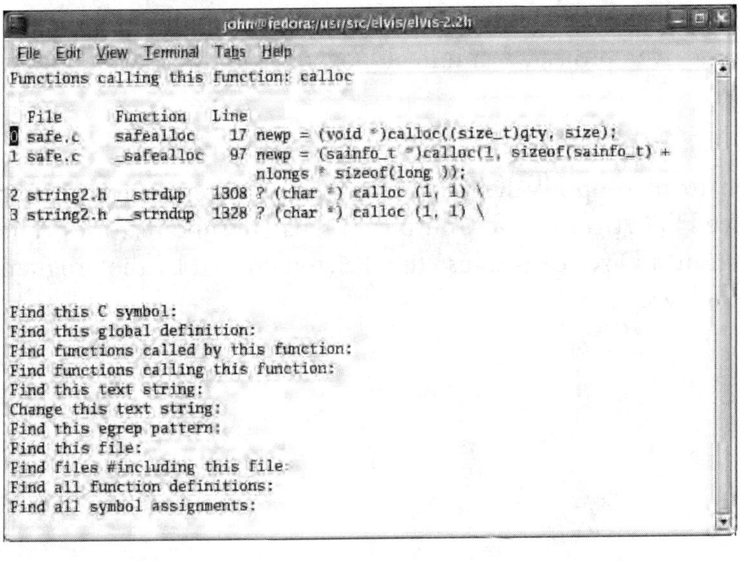

FIGURE 4-14 Cscope Menu System

4.4.6   Browsing and Documenting Code with Doxygen

Doxygen is a great tool, primarily intended for generating documentation for software projects. It is able to parse your C and C++ code and produce hyperlinked documentation (typically, HTML) for browsing. In addition, you can add some very lightweight markup to your code, and Doxygen will include it in the documentation. The following is sufficient documentation for a function:

```
/**
 ** This is a function.
 */
void func(void)
{
}
```

Java programmers will recognize this as javadoc syntax. In fact, Doxygen borrows heavily from javadoc. This is a lightweight markup syntax that lets you write comments that can be read in a text editor but can produce quality typeset text output for documentation.

Doxygen can generate output in HTML, LaTeX, PDF, RTF, and even `man` pages (for example, `troff`). It can also use the Graphviz[14] tool (`dot`) to generate complex UML diagrams for C++ classes. This is an excellent tool for verifying designs that use the UML syntax. If you start with a design in UML, you should be able to generate the same diagrams from the source code.

You start with Doxygen by creating a Doxyfile, which is the file that contains all of your preferences for a given project. A minimal Doxyfile could read as follows:

```
INPUT              =.
FILE_PATTERNS      = *.cpp
```

This tells Doxygen to pick up all the `.cpp` files in the current directory. By default, it will produce HTML and LaTeX output in separate subdirectories. The more typical way to create a Doxyfile is to use the skeleton created by the program via the `-g` option, as follows:

```
$ doxygen -g
```

---

14. www.graphviz.org

Inside the Doxyfile, you will find a lengthy list of tags that control the output. There are 127 tags in the skeleton Doxyfile that is generated by Doxygen 1.4.0. With comments, the file is 1,200 lines long. That's a lot of information. You can get a good feel for what Doxygen is capable of just by reading the comments in the skeleton. Most of these tags take a YES or NO value. The skeleton file is completely usable after you fill in the INPUT and FILE_PATTERNS tags, which are two of the few that don't take a simple YES or NO value.

Some more useful settings for your Doxyfile are shown in Table 4-30.

Doxygen is a very useful tool for generating documentation from source code. Because the documentation is the source, the odds of it being up to date are greater than keeping documentation in separate files. By keeping documentation in the source, the document revisions track the source revisions. It's still up to developers to update the contents of the documentation with each revision, but since the documentation is in plain sight, there are fewer excuses to neglect it.

TABLE 4-30   Some Useful Doxygen Tags

Tag	Purpose
USE_PDFLATEX	Produce PDF output from LaTeX; requires GENERATE_LATEX (default NO)
PDF_HYPERLINKS	Produce PDF output with hyperlinks; requires USE_PDFLATEX (default NO)
GENERATE_HTML	Generate HTML output (default YES)
GENERATE_TREEVIEW	For HTML output, produce a hierarchical view of classes (default NO)
GENERATE_LATEX	Generate LaTeX source (default YES)
GENERATE_RTF	Generate RTF output (default NO)
GENERATE_MAN	Generate man pages (default NO)
HAVE_DOT	Use the Graphvis dot program to produce collaboration diagrams (default NO)
UML_LOOK	Give collaboration diagrams a UML look (default NO)

4.4.7   Using the Compiler to Analyze Code

The GNU Compiler Collection (GCC) offers a few capabilities to analyze your source code. First and foremost is the C preprocessor. Most of the preprocessor-related options on the gcc command line are interchangeable with those on the cpp command line, but in general, it's a good idea to use gcc to interface with the pre-processor.

4.4.7.1   Dependencies

The compiler can generate dependencies for you via the -M option. By itself, the -M option includes system headers in the dependency, which produces a great deal of clutter. Most likely, you will want to show dependencies for only your source files. One way is with the -MM option. Here's a sample from the strace[15] source tree:

```
$ gcc -MM -I ./linux syscall.c
syscall.o: syscall.c defs.h ./linux/syscall.h ./linux/dummy.h \
  ./linux/syscallent.h ./linux/errnoent.h
```

Note that the output is intended to be used in a Makefile, which is why each line ends with a backslash. There aren't too many options to make this more user friendly. This output can be used to create Makefiles or supplements to Makefiles but can also give you insight as to what is going on in an unfamiliar project. The previous example shows you that syscall.c requires a file called dummy.h, even though this file is not pulled in by syscall.c; it's actually pulled in via syscall.h. The output is also dependent on your include search path, con-trolled with the I option. By default, if a required file is not found, it fails. You can change that behavior with the -MG option, which assumes that files that are not found will be generated at compile time and found in the current directory.

4.4.7.2   Macro Expansions

You can debug preprocessor macros with the -d option, which can be used only with the preprocessor (-E option). To see a list of predefined macros in no particu-lar order, you could type the following:

```
$ echo | gcc -E -dM -
```

---

15. http://sourceforge.net/projects/strace

TABLE 4-31   Flags Used with the -d Option

Option	Description
-dM	Outputs a list of #define statements from your source as well as built-in macros. The output is in no particular order.
-dD	Essentially the same as -dM. The GNU documentation says this does not include built-in macros, but in fact, it includes most of them. Macros found in the source are printed in the same order in which they are declared.
-dN	Produces the same output as -dD except that only the macro names are shown. The macro values are omitted.
-dI	In combination with -E, this flag includes the #include statements in the output; normally, they are omitted from preprocessor output.

Notice that you have to combine the -d option with the -E option and that the -d option must be followed by the letter M, D, N, or I. The usage and meanings of these letters are described in Table 4-31.

With -dM, what you get is a list of #define statements, cleaned up and printed verbatim. The white space is trimmed, but the macros printed are equivalent to what is in the code. The output is in no particular order, so you can't infer anything about where a macro is defined in the code. The -dD option produces the essentially the same information except that the line order is preserved and the output contains #line directives to direct you to the correct source line. Consider the following source file, foo.h:

```
#define A a+b+c
#define B a                     + b          +c
#define C a \
  +b                +\
  c
#define TEXT "Hello                 \
          World"
```

The output is cleaned up and presented as follows:

```
$ gcc -E -dD foo.h
...
# 1 "foo.h"
#define A a+b+c
```

```
#define B a + b +c
#define C a +b + c
```

```
#define TEXT "Hello                          World"
```

Note that although they look very different, the two sets of macros are *identical*. The only difference is in the white space that the preprocessor cleans up. This is a useful illustration of how the C preprocessor cleans up white space in your macro expressions, which has changed over various releases. This output can be very helpful if you are porting code that compiled in an earlier release of gcc. The newline between `"Hello"` and `"World"` would have been preserved in gcc 2.9x, for example, but gcc 3.x removes it.

The other two flags (`N` and `I`) don't improve the output much. Using `-dN` produces a list of macro names without their expansions. The `-dI` leaves the `#include` statements intact in the output.

4.5   Summary

This chapter focused on tools to manipulate source code. I listed some of the programmer-centric features you should look for in a text editor. I examined and compared the two most popular text editors for Linux: Vim and Emacs. I also looked at some alternatives, as well as their pros and cons.

I scratched the surface of revision control, introducing the basic concepts and some of the tools used to support revision control. I showed you how to create and apply patches, which is at the core of many revision control tools.

Finally, I looked at tools that allow you to extract information from your source code in the form of cross references, browser output, and even typeset documentation.

4.5.1   Tools Used in This Chapter

The two main text editors discussed in this chapter are

- Vim—the most widely used clone of the `vi` text editor, which is the standard text editor

- Emacs—the flagship GNU text editor

I looked at several clones of `vi` and Emacs. Most of these have fewer features but use less memory:

- `vi` clones—Elvis, nvi, Vile

- Emacs clones—Zile, joe, jed

`vi` and Emacs started out as terminal-based editors and later *acquired* GUIs. As a result, they still maintain a terminal-based look and feel. More recent editors are exclusively GUI based, and these may be more intuitive to use for those who are not familiar with `vi` or Emacs:

- GNOME—Gedit

- KDE—Kate, Kwrite

- X (generic)—NEdit, SciTE

I looked at revision control and the tools that support it:

- Tools for merging and differencing—`diff`, `diff3`, `patch`, `xxdiff`, `vimdiff`, `gvimdiff`

- Tools for managing projects—Subversion, `cvs`, monotone, GNU arch

This chapter looked at several tools for beautifying and browsing code:

- `indent`

- `astyle`

- `cflow`

- `ctags`

4.5.2 References

- Cameron, D., et al. *Learning GNU Emacs.* 3d ed. Sebastopol, Calif.: O'Reilly Media, Inc., 2004.

- Dougherty, D., and A. Robbins. *sed and awk.* 2d ed. Sebastopol, Calif.: O'Reilly Media, Inc., 1997.

- Friedl, J.E.F. *Mastering Regular Expressions.* 3d ed. Sebastopol, Calif.: O'Reilly Media, Inc., 2006.

- Lamb, L., and A. Robbins. *Learning the vi Editor.* 6th ed. Sebastopol, Calif.: O'Reilly Media, Inc., 1998.

4.5.3   Online Resources

Text Editors

- Emacs—www.gnu.org/software/emacs
- Vim—www.vim.org

Text Editor Clones

- `bvi`—http://bvi.sourceforge.net
- gedit—www.gnome.org/projects/gedit
- JED—www.jedsoft.org/jed
- joe—http://joe-editor.sourceforge.net
- Kate—www.kate-editor.org
- nano—www.gnu.org/software/nano
- NEdit—www.nedit.org
- SciTE—www.scintilla.org/SciTE.html
- vile—http://invisible-island.net/vile
- WordStar—www.wordstar.org
- Zile—http://zile.sourceforge.net

Code Browsers and Beautifiers

- astyle—http://astyle.sourceforge.net
- cflow—www.gnu.org/software/cflow
- cscope—http://cscope.sourceforge.net

- Doxygen—www.stack.nl/~dimitri/doxygen
- Exuberant Ctags—http://ctags.sourceforge.net, http://xxdiff.sourceforge.net

Revision Control Tools

- arch—www.gnuarch.org/arch
- cvs—www.nongnu.org/cvs
- monotone—http://venge.net/monotone
- Subversion—http://subversion.tigris.org
- xxdiff—http://xxdiff.sourceforge.net

Chapter 5

What Every Developer Should Know about the Kernel

5.1 Introduction

This chapter assumes you have some experience writing applications for Linux and some basic understanding of the Linux kernel. I will cover some kernel-related topics that are more often covered in books about the kernel itself. Unlike material in those books, the material in this chapter focuses on applications.

The topics covered in this chapter include a discussion of the Linux scheduler, which has undergone many changes recently. I cover process priority and preemption, their roles and real-time applications.

In the past, a 32-bit address space was sufficiently large that most applications never encountered any limits. Today, with 32-bit systems that can have more than 4GB of RAM, many programmers are running head first into these limitations without a good understanding of what they're running into. After reading this chapter, you should have a much better understanding of these issues and how to work around them.

This chapter also looks at system input and output and how it relates to processes. Perhaps you have been dazzled by the blinding clock speeds of modern processors, only to be disappointed by performance that is throttled by slow devices. I'll look at some of the inefficiencies built into the Linux programming model and how to work around them. I'll also look closely at improvements in the Linux 2.6 I/O scheduler and how to take advantage of it.

5.2   User Mode versus Kernel Mode

Processes execute in two modes: user mode and kernel mode. The code that you write and the libraries you link with execute in user mode. When your process requires services from the kernel it must execute kernel code, which runs only in kernel mode. That sounds simple, but the devil is in the details. First of all, why do we need two modes of operation?

One reason is security. When a process executes in user mode, the memory it sees is unique to it. Linux is a multiuser operating system, so one process should not be allowed to view another process's memory, which could contain passwords or sensitive information. User mode ensures that a process sees only memory that belongs to it. Moreover, if the process corrupts its internal structures, it can crash only itself; it will not take any other processes with it and certainly not the whole system. The memory that the process sees when in user mode is called *user space*.

For the system to function as a whole, the kernel needs to be able to maintain data structures to control every process in the system. To do this, it needs a region of memory that is common to all processes. Because the kernel is executed by every process in the system, every process needs access to a common memory region. To preserve security, however, the kernel code and data structures must be strictly isolated from user code and data. That is why there is a kernel mode. Only kernel code runs in kernel mode, where it can see the common kernel data and execute privileged instructions. We call the memory that the process sees in kernel mode *kernel space*. There is only one kernel space, which is seen by every process when it runs in kernel mode, unlike user space, which is unique to every process.

Figure 5-1 shows the allocation of virtual addresses among processes and the kernel. In this example, the kernel is allocated the top 1GB of virtual addresses, and the processes are allocated the rest. This split can be determined when the kernel is built, but this so-called 3G/1G split is common in many stock kernels. In this configuration, all addresses above `0xC0000000` are in the kernel. To use these addresses, the process must be executing in kernel mode.

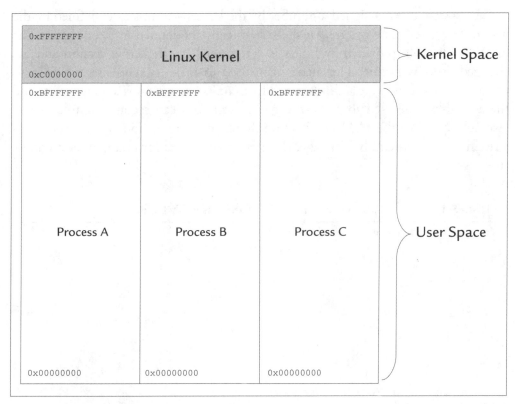

FIGURE 5-1   Virtual Addresses in a Typical 32-Bit Environment

5.2.1   System Calls

Processes enter and exit kernel mode via system calls. Many common POSIX functions are simply thin wrappers around system calls, such as `open`, `close`, `read`, `ioctl`, and `write`. Device drivers, for example, run exclusively in kernel mode. Application code cannot call a device driver function directly. Instead, applications use one of the predefined system calls to enter the driver code indirectly. The call to `read`, for example, is equivalent to the following:

```
#include <syscall.h>
...
n = syscall(SYS_read, fd, buffer, length);
```

Each system call is assigned a number by the kernel—in this case, defined by the macro SYS_read. The macros for the system calls are defined in syscall.h. The list of system calls provided by Linux is determined by the kernel version and has changed little over time. The mechanism used to make system calls, however, is unique to each processor architecture. The syscall function is a wrapper around the assembly code used to make the system call. You can see an example of this assembly code for the IA32 architecture in Listing 5-1. Although this example is written in IA32 assembly language, this pattern is typical for many other architectures as well.

LISTING 5-1   basic.S: A Basic System Call in 80x86 Assembly Language

```
# Use the C preprocessor for this example

#include "sys/syscall.h"

.data

# Contents of struct timespec {1,0}
sleeptime:
.long 1, 0

.text

# Linker uses _start as the entry point.
# Equivalent to main() in C.

.global _start
      .type    _start, @function
_start:

# Execute the nanosleep(2) syscall
# Parameters are stored in registers.
# Interrupt 0x80 takes us into kernel space.

      movl  $SYS_nanosleep, %eax   # 1st arg, system call number
      movl  $sleeptime,     %ebx   # 2nd arg, pointer to struct timespec
      int   $0x80                  # execute the system call

# Can't just return. We have to call the exit(2) system call
# with our exit status.

      movl  $SYS_exit,%eax    # 1st arg, 1 = exit()
      movl  $0,       %ebx    # 2nd arg, exit code
      int   $0x80             # execute the system call
```

Building and Running Listing 5-1

The code in Listing 5-1 shows how the system uses interrupts to switch between user mode and kernel mode. Even exiting the program requires a system call. To build and run this example, use the following commands:

```
$ gcc -o basic -nostdlib basic.S
$ strace -t ./basic
23:25:27 execve("./basic", ["./basic"], [/* 32 vars */]) = 0
23:25:27 nanosleep({1, 0}, NULL)        = 0
23:25:28 _exit(0)                       = ?
```

We cheat a little by using the C preprocessor in our assembly module. The convention for this is to name the module with the .S extension and pass that to the C compiler (not the assembler). The C compiler runs the preprocessor and sends the preprocessed output to the assembler.

The strace command is very useful for tracing system calls and demonstrates that we are doing exactly what we said we would do. Try strace on a C program sometime, and see just how many system calls it takes to print hello world.

Typically, the user code puts arguments on the stack or in predefined registers and then issues an interrupt that causes a system call handler to be called. The interrupt handler switches the process into kernel mode and calls the appropriate system call. In kernel mode, the arguments are read from registers or copied from user space using special functions. If this is unfamiliar to you, that's because it should be. Portable programs do not use system calls directly but rely on libraries to do the system calls on their behalf. System calls vary from one operating system to the next and possibly from one version to the next. Library calls insulate you from these differences.

The technique used by the Linux for the syscall is called an *Application Binary Interface* (ABI, for short), and it is not unique to Linux. The same technique is used by other operating systems and even the BIOS. Unlike an *Application Programming Interface* (API), which requires you to link with compatible functions, an ABI does not require you to link your code against the code you want to run. This is one reason why your executable program can run on many different kernels without rebuilding. Most compatibility issues with different Linux distributions are due to changes in the library APIs and not the kernel ABI. If you have a statically linked executable that runs on a Linux 2.2 kernel, for example, there's a good chance that it will still run on a 2.6 kernel, because many of the most common system call interfaces never change.

5.2.2   Moving Data between User Space and Kernel Space

Memory in kernel space is not visible in user mode, and special care must be taken in kernel mode when accessing memory in user space. As a result, passing data via system calls is tricky. Simple arguments can be passed in registers, but large blocks of memory must be copied, which is inefficient.

Listing 5-1 put a pointer to the `timespec` structure in a register, which was passed to the kernel. What you don't see is the copy of the `struct timespec` data from user space to kernel space. This is some very ugly, architecture-dependent code that is well hidden inside the kernel. In this case, the copy is trivial—two words. Some system calls (such as `read` and `write`) require a large amount of data to be passed between user space and kernel space. This extra copying is inefficient, but it is necessary to maintain separation between user space and kernel space.

Although copying is a short-term performance hit, most often it helps performance in the long run. An example of this is the file-system cache. When you write a data to a file, the data is copied to kernel space before it is written to disk. Because the data is copied, the write can complete in the background so that your application can reuse the user space buffer and continue to execute.

5.3   The Process Scheduler

Back in the days of DOS and CP/M, the typical desktop operating system ran only one process at a time. Scheduling was not an issue, because the system did only one thing at a time in the order in which it was requested. Those days are history. Today, even the humblest embedded operating system supports multitasking.

The problem that multitasking operating systems share is dividing CPU time among different tasks. The algorithm that does this is called the *scheduler.* Each operating system uses its own scheduling algorithm, maybe even more than one, because no single algorithm is perfect for all applications. A scheduler that works well for one set of processes may not be suitable for another. The Linux kernel provides several scheduling algorithms and allows the user to select at boot time the type of scheduler the system will use.

5.3.1   A Scheduling Primer

In Linux circles, the scheduler is sometimes discussed as though it were a separate process. In fact, the scheduler code is executed by every process. Whenever a process goes to sleep or blocks waiting for a device, it calls the scheduler routines to determine what process to execute next. Calls to the scheduler are often embedded in system calls and take place when it is necessary for the process to wait for an event.

A process that communicates extensively with devices will call the scheduler often. Device I/O invariably involves some amount of waiting. When the device is slow, most of the process's run time will be spent waiting. Such a process does not consume much CPU time as a proportion of overall run time. If every process were like this, the operating system could leave it up to the processes to call the scheduler, and everything would work out. Such a scheme does exist, and it's called *cooperative multitasking*.

This is illustrated in Figure 5-2. Two processes, A and B, contend for the CPU, but only one can run at a time. Transitions from one process to the next occur only when the running process gives up the CPU, which allows the other to run. In this case, Process A waits for disk and gives up the CPU, allowing Process B to run. Then Process B waits for a keystroke, which allows Process A to run again. There are also calls that allow a process to give up the CPU explicitly and be nice (so to speak). The problem with cooperative multitasking occurs when tasks don't cooperate.

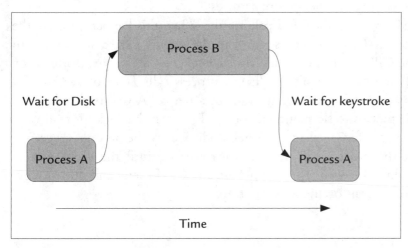

FIGURE 5-2   Cooperative Multitasking Example

A process that does no I/O, such as a number-crunching application, can consume the CPU and starve other processes of CPU time. Such a process does not provide any opportunities for the scheduler to execute, so it does not allow any other processes to run. To deal with this, operating systems use *preemptive multitasking*. A preemptive multitasking operating system interrupts (preempts) processes that do not give up the CPU so that another task can be scheduled. All UNIX variants, including Linux, use a combination of cooperative and preemptive multitasking. If a process is cooperative and gives up the CPU often, it may never be preempted. Preemption is reserved for those processes that do not give up the CPU voluntarily.

Figure 5-3 illustrates an example of preemptive multitasking. Here, Process A is a *nice* process that gives up the CPU often. The Number Cruncher does not give up the CPU, so the operating system preempts it via an interrupt. This allows the scheduler to run, which then allows Process A to run again.

5.3.2   Blocking, Preemption, and Yielding

Each Linux process is given a time slice (or *quantum*) in which to execute before it is stopped by the kernel and another process is allowed to run. When the kernel stops a process because its time slice has expired, we say that the process has been *preempted*. The kernel can also preempt a process before its time slice expires if a higher-priority process is ready to run. When this happens, we say the higher-priority process *preempts* the lower-priority process.

A process can also give up the CPU voluntarily. When this happens, we say the process has *yielded* the CPU. A process can call the sched_yield system call to explicitly yield the CPU from user code. More often, the CPU is yielded for it by other system calls the process makes. When a process calls read or write, for example, chances are that it will have to wait for a device. A well-behaved device driver will put the process to sleep and yield the CPU until the device is ready.

When a process waits for an event in kernel mode, we say the process is *blocking*. That means that the process will not be ready to run until the event occurs. Therefore, a blocking process does not consume any CPU cycles and does not get scheduled until some event occurs to wake it up.

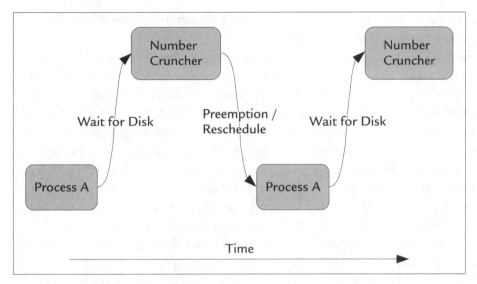

FIGURE 5-3   Preemptive Multitasking Example

One of the new features in Linux 2.6 is the preemptable kernel. This is available as a patch on some 2.4 kernels as well. In a nonpreemptable kernel, a process that is running in kernel mode cannot be preempted until it returns to user mode. So if a process is in the middle of a system call when a higher-priority process is ready to run, the higher-priority process is forced to wait until the lower-priority process finishes its system call. In a preemptable kernel, the lower-priority process can be preempted in the middle of the system call. This allows the higher-priority process to be scheduled more quickly. This is particularly useful in situations where a defective driver is causing a process to take too long in kernel mode. Although a process may be stuck in the driver, the system can still function by preempting the process. In a nonpreemptable kernel, such a process could hang the whole system.

5.3.3   Scheduling Priority and Fairness

All preemptive multitasking operating systems, including Linux, implement a priority scheme for scheduling. In simple terms, priorities resolve scheduling conflicts when more than one process is ready to run. Whenever this happens, a higher-priority process is allowed to run before a lower-priority process. Priorities can be influenced by the user, but the kernel ultimately determines a process's priority. To understand why, consider an example.

Figure 5-4 shows an example of fixed priority with three processes. Process A is the lowest priority, and perhaps it forks the other two processes: Number Cruncher A and Number Cruncher B. These two processes are always running (never waiting), so neither process gives up the CPU voluntarily. The CPU spends 100 percent of its time executing one of these two processes, and scheduling occurs only when the running process is preempted. Now suppose that the lower-priority process gets an interrupt from the keyboard (perhaps Ctrl+C). Process A will not be scheduled to run until the two number crunchers are done, because it has a lower priority. The interrupt is not delivered until the scheduler decides that Process A may run again. Until the number crunchers are done, it would appear that Process A is hung.

To prevent this situation, the Linux kernel continually upgrades or downgrades a process's priority as it runs by using *dynamic priority,* which is illustrated in Figure 5-5. When a process is identified as *interactive,* its effective priority is increased, which allows it to be scheduled even when the system is busy.

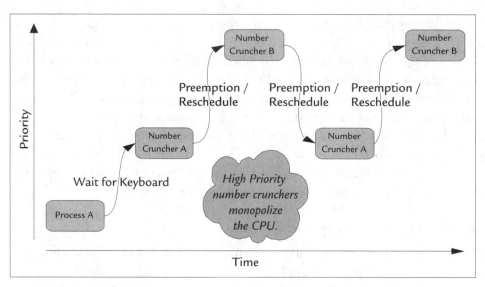

FIGURE 5-4   Fixed Priority Scheduling Can Allow Noninteractive Processes to Hog the CPU

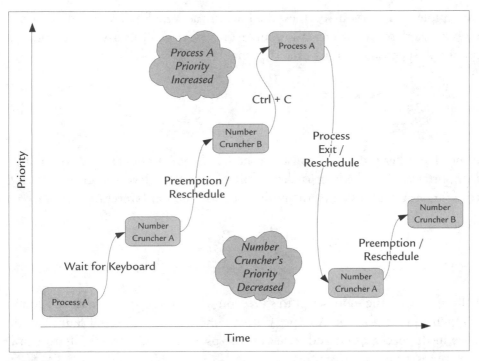

FIGURE 5-5   Dynamic Priority Allows the Operating System to Promote an Interactive Task

An overriding goal of the Linux scheduler is to see that every task gets a chance to run—that is, that no task gets starved for CPU time. The scheduler pays attention to each process's behavior so that processes that are deemed interactive have a higher priority. A keyboard input process would be a good example of an interactive process. Such a process spends most of its time waiting for input and very little time processing. It is easily identified by the scheduler because it is never preempted and consumes very little CPU time. It always gives up the CPU voluntarily. To give interactive processes a higher priority, the scheduler keeps a bonus value in addition to the process's *static priority*—the priority assigned when the process is created, which the scheduler does not change over the life of the process. The *effective priority* of a process is the sum of its static priority plus its bonus.[1] The bonus value can be positive or negative, so the effective priority can be higher or lower than the static priority.

---

1.   This ignores the nice value, which I will discuss shortly.

An example will let you see the scheduler in action. First, you'll need some processes to run, so you'll create a couple of scripts. Call one script `niceguy`, because it will spend most of its time sleeping.

```
#!/bin/sh
# The niceguy - sleeps most of the time
while true; do
      sleep .1
done
```

You need another process to consume the CPU, but it doesn't need to do anything important. The scheduler is clever, but it's not that clever. So create a script named `cruncher` that just runs the built-in `true` function forever:

```
#!/bin/sh
# The cruncher - consumes the CPU with nonsense
while true; do
      true
done
```

Finally, you need one more script to show you what's going on, because it'll probably happen too fast for you to type. Call it `runex`. This script will launch both processes in the background and then run the `ps` command periodically to show those processes' priorities over time.

```
#!/bin/sh
./cruncher &
./niceguy &

# Trap SIGINT (Ctrl+C) to clean up
trap 'echo stopping; kill %1 %2; break' SIGINT

while true; do
      ps -C niceguy -C cruncher -o etime,pid,pri,cmd
      sleep .5
done
```

Next, run the example by running the `runex` script, which launches two processes and prints out their priorities over time. The output is shown below. Pay attention to the `PRI` field in the output, which is the effective priority:

```
$ ./runex
   ELAPSED   PID PRI CMD
     00:00 17076  20 /bin/sh ./cruncher
     00:00 17077  22 /bin/sh ./niceguy
   ELAPSED   PID PRI CMD
     00:01 17076  20 /bin/sh ./cruncher
     00:01 17077  24 /bin/sh ./niceguy
```

```
ELAPSED    PID PRI CMD
  00:01 17076  19 /bin/sh ./cruncher
  00:01 17077  23 /bin/sh ./niceguy
ELAPSED    PID PRI CMD
  00:02 17076  18 /bin/sh ./cruncher
  00:02 17077  24 /bin/sh ./niceguy
ELAPSED    PID PRI CMD
  00:02 17076  17 /bin/sh ./cruncher
  00:02 17077  24 /bin/sh ./niceguy
ELAPSED    PID PRI CMD
  00:03 17076  15 /bin/sh ./cruncher
  00:03 17077  24 /bin/sh ./niceguy
ELAPSED    PID PRI CMD
  00:04 17076  14 /bin/sh ./cruncher
  00:04 17077  24 /bin/sh ./niceguy
```

Notice how the priorities of the two processes change over time. The cruncher process spends all its allotted time running; it never sleeps. This results in the scheduler's giving it negative bonus value, causing it to lower its effective priority. The niceguy process spends most of its time sleeping, which results in a positive bonus. Because of this, the scheduler raises niceguy's effective priority.

On my machine, the scheduler *lowers* the cruncher process's priority from 20 to a low of 14 after about 4 seconds. Conversely, the scheduler *raises* the niceguy process's priority from 22 to 24. In this controlled example in a controlled environment, the priorities settle into a steady state. In a real system, priorities will go up and down accordingly as other processes are activated, created, and destroyed.

A Brief Description of PS Options

This example uses some uncommon options of the ps command. The -C option tells ps to show only processes with executable names that match the argument. You specify -C multiple times to tell ps to look for more than one command name.

The -o option allows you to control the output format. It is followed by the fields you want to see in the output, which are documented in the ps man page. The fields you are looking at are:

- etime—elapsed clock time since the process started
- pid—process ID
- pri—priority
- cmd—command line used to start the process

5.3.4   Priorities and Nice Value

If you ran the example in the previous section, chances are that your system was still fairly responsive. When you pressed `Ctrl+C` to kill the program, for example, it probably terminated immediately. Just having many processes running does not necessarily mean that your system will be sluggish. In the previous example, the tasks weren't actually *doing* anything, so it seems natural that such a process will not bog down the system.

Such a trivial process *can* bog down the system if it is given the opportunity, however. One way to do so is to give it a high priority. The kernel allows users to influence the scheduler's decisions about priority, using what is called the *nice value*. Giving a process a positive nice value causes the scheduler to give it a lower priority; giving a process a negative value causes the scheduler to give it a higher priority.

The nice value is subtracted from the sum of the bonus and the static priority to create the effective priority. Any unprivileged user can set positive nice values with the `nice` command, but only the superuser can set a negative nice value. To run a command with low priority, you would use the `nice` command as follows:

```
$ nice -n 1 tar -cvf foo.tar ...# Run tar with a nice value of 1
```

In this case, the `tar` command runs normally, with no side effects other than its effective priority. The nice value of a process remains constant over the life of the process unless it is changed with the `renice` command. The `renice` command works on only one running process, as follows:

```
$ renice 1 -p 1234
1234: old priority 0, new priority 1
```

This changes the nice value of process 1234 to 1. Unprivileged users can only increase the nice value with `renice`, even if the resulting nice value is still positive.

Note that unlike the `nice` command, which allows any user to set a positive nice value, the `renice` command allows unprivileged users only to raise the nice value, not to lower it. Only root is allowed to lower a nice value, even if the resulting nice value is zero or greater.

The range of nice values is defined by POSIX to be between −20 and 19. Linux priorities used by the scheduler for *normal* processes[2] are unsigned and fall in the

---

2. A "normal" process is one that is not a real-time process, which I will describe shortly.

range 0 through 39. Looking at it differently, if the nice value is 19, the highest that the effective priority can ever go is 20. Likewise, with a nice value of –20, the lowest that the effective priority can ever go is 20.

Look at another example, using the `niceguy` script from earlier in the chapter. This example launches four different processes with four different nice values and then uses the `ps` command to see what the scheduler is up to:

```
$ for nv in 0 1 2 3; do nice -n $nv ./niceguy & done
$ ps -C niceguy -p $$ -o pid,pri,ni,cmd
  PID PRI  NI CMD
 5694  23   0 bash
 6661  23   0 /bin/sh ./niceguy            nice -n 0 ...
 6662  22   1 /bin/sh ./niceguy            nice -n 1 ...
 6663  21   2 /bin/sh ./niceguy            nice -n 2 ...
 6664  20   3 /bin/sh ./niceguy            nice -n 3 ...
```

In this example, I ran the `ps` command after a few seconds to let things settle down. New processes inherit their static priority from their parent process, which in this example is the Bash shell, running with a priority of 23. You can see that the child with a nice value of zero runs with the same priority as its parent. Notice that the processes with nonzero nice values have their priority lowered by that much. So a process with a nice value of 3 has a priority of 20, which is 3 less than the priority of the parent shell. As you might expect, the effective priority tends to go up when you use negative nice values.

This ideal behavior shows up only in an unloaded system with simple processes that do nothing. In a real system, busy with real processes, priorities shift constantly, and there is no guarantee that two processes with the same nice value will have the same priority. The only thing the nice value guarantees is that your effective priority will never go higher or lower than a certain level.

5.3.5   Real-Time Priorities

The scheduler provides a different type of scheduling for processes that have strict latency requirements. *Latency* refers to the time it takes for software to respond to external events, such as interrupts. Applications with strict latency requirements are often called *real-time applications*. These applications must guarantee that the software responds to events within a certain interval of time; otherwise, bad things happen.

A real-time application that you might encounter on your computer is your media player. When showing a video, the player must update the screen at reasonable intervals; otherwise, you're going to notice in the form of jerky motion in your favorite movie. That's what we call a *soft real-time* application, because when the software is late once in a while, it can always recover. If your media player skips a frame, it's not the end of the world. A *hard real-time* application is one that cannot be late even once. An example of a hard real-time application might be a flight-control computer that has to respond immediately to pilot control movements. Being late in this application could cost lives.

The Linux scheduler provides a real-time scheduling implementation that is very close to the POSIX 1003.1 standard. This provides an additional 100 priority levels, all of which are higher priority than the normal process priorities (0–39). Real-time processes in Linux have priorities in the range 41 to 139. (For some reason, priority 40 is unused.) Like normal priorities, higher values mean higher priority, but what makes real-time priorities different is that they never change over the life of the process. Because the priority never changes, real-time processes do not have a nice value, and there is no bonus value. The priority is what it is.

When you designate a process as a real-time process, you also must specify the scheduling policy. POSIX specifies two scheduling policies for real-time processes: *FIFO* and *round robin*.

5.3.5.1   FIFO Scheduling

The term *FIFO* stands for *first in, first out* and refers to how the processes are placed in the run queue. When two FIFO processes of the same priority are ready to run, the first that was ready is the first one to run—always. A FIFO process cannot be preempted except by another process with a higher priority, which by definition is another real-time process. If you ran the `cruncher` script as a FIFO process, you would render your system unusable. Try this with a safer example that illustrates this situation nicely. You will need the `chrt` command from the `schedutils` package:

```
#!/bin/sh

(sleep 5; kill -ALRM $$) &

while true; do
    true ;
done
```

This is a variation of the `cruncher` script that you used earlier, but it runs for only 5 seconds. You will soon find out why you went to this trouble. Call this script `chewer`. Using the `chrt` program, run this as a real-time/FIFO process, and watch what happens:

```
$ sudo chrt --fifo 50 ./chewer &
```

This launches the script in the background as a real-time process with real-time priority 50 and FIFO scheduling. You should notice that your system becomes unresponsive for 5 seconds. In fact, it will probably appear to be locked up. A typical Linux system does not have any real-time processes running, so your shell and any daemons that are running are all blocked while this dumb script runs. Fortunately, we launched a background process at the same priority to kill us after five seconds. Don't skip that line or you will need to hit the reset button.

The `chewer` process doesn't do anything; it simply consumes CPU cycles. Because it is a real-time process, it can be preempted only by a real-time process with higher priority. The only time that a lower-priority process gets to run is when `chewer` yields the CPU. Because `chewer` makes no blocking system calls while it spins in its loop, it never provides any opportunities to yield the CPU.

5.3.5.2   Round-Robin Scheduling

Round-robin scheduling is the second policy for real-time processes and is almost identical to FIFO scheduling except that round-robin processes are not allowed to run indefinitely; instead, they are given a time slice in which to run. A process running with round-robin scheduling will be preempted only when its time slice expires or when a higher-priority process is ready to run. If a round-robin process is preempted by a higher-priority process, the scheduler allows the round-robin process to consume the remainder of its time slice before scheduling any other processes at the same priority. Only when a round-robin process yields the CPU are lower-priority processes allowed to run.

Recall that normal processes have a time slice called a quantum. If a normal process consumes its entire time slice without yielding the CPU, its time slice is shortened the next time it is scheduled. Unlike a quantum, the round-robin time slice never changes. The process is given the same time slice every time.

5.3.6   Creating Real-Time Processes

You saw one way to create a real-time process using the chrt command. On the inside, chrt uses basic fork and exec calls with an additional POSIX call to set the priority. To set the real-time priority, an application can use the following POSIX functions:

```
int sched_setscheduler(pid_t pid, int pol, const struct sched_param*p);
int pthread_setschedparam(pthread_t thread, int policy,
      const struct sched_param *param);
```

The sched_setscheduler function is for use by processes and takes a process ID as its argument. The pthread_setschedparam function is used for threads and takes a thread ID instead of a process ID. Both functions require a policy and a pointer to a sched_param structure. The policy is indicated by one of the macros shown in Table 5-1.

The only value in the sched_param structure that is filled in by the user is the priority field, which must fall within a specified range of valid values. You can determine the range of allowable values with the following POSIX functions:

```
int sched_get_priority_min(int policy);
int sched_get_priority_max(int policy);
```

POSIX allows each real-time scheduling policy to have a unique range of priorities, although Linux uses the same range for both real-time policies (SCHED_FIFO and SCHED_RR). When setting a nonreal-time policy (SCHED_OTHER), sched_setscheduler does not allow you to set the priority. Any value other than zero for the priority will produce an error with errno set to EINVAL. Instead, a process can set the nice value via the nice or the setpriority system calls. Note that although the name setpriority implies that you are setting priority, it sets only the nice value.

TABLE 5-1   Macros Used for POSIX Scheduling Policy

Macro	Meaning
SCHED_FIFO	Use FIFO scheduling
SCHED_RR	Use round-robin scheduling
SCHED_OTHER	Use normal Linux scheduling

Linux uses the range 1 through 99 for POSIX real-time priorities passed to `sched_setscheduler`. This is a little confusing, because the Linux scheduler uses only one continuous range of priorities that includes both normal and real-time processes. The entire range of absolute priorities used by the scheduler extends from 0 through 139. When you assign a real-time priority of 1, for example, the scheduler uses an absolute priority of 41. For example:

```
$ chrt -f 1 ps -C ps -o pri,ni,rtprio,comm
PRI  NI RTPRIO COMMAND
 41   -      1 ps
```

This runs the `ps` command with a `SCHED_FIFO` policy and a priority value of 1. The `ps` command is instructed to show what it is doing. The `PRI` column is the absolute priority used by the scheduler, whereas the `RTPRIO` column shows the same priority represented in the real-time range. Notice that the nice value (`NI` field) is shown with a hyphen because the nice value is not valid for real-time processes. Likewise, if this were a normal process, the `RTPRIO` column would not be valid, and the nice value would be represented by a decimal number.

5.3.7 Process States

Over the life of your process, it will pass through several states. As a user, you see only the states shown via tools like `ps` or what you get from the `/proc` file system (which is what `ps` uses). The states and their abbreviations are listed in Table 5-2.

TABLE 5-2   Process States As Seen by the User

State	Abbrev	Meaning
Running	R	Running or ready to run
Interruptible	S	Blocked waiting for an event but may be awakened by a signal
Uninterruptible	D	Blocked waiting for an event and will not be awakened by a signal
Stopped	T	Stopped due to job control or external tracing (for example, `ptrace`)
Zombie	Z	Exited, but its parent has not called `wait` (not reaped)

5.3.7.1   Sleeping versus Running

When a process is in the runnable state, it does not mean that it is running; it means only that the process is not sleeping or waiting for an event. It is possible to have multiple processes in the runnable state. A number-crunching process, for example, would always be in the runnable state. You should keep this in mind when using the `ps` command, as the following example illustrates:

```
$ ./cruncher & ./cruncher & ./cruncher &
$ ps -C cruncher -p $$ -o pid,state,cmd
  PID S CMD
 2588 S bash
 2657 R /bin/sh ./cruncher
 2658 R /bin/sh ./cruncher
 2659 R /bin/sh ./cruncher
```

This example launched three cruncher processes as background tasks and then executed a `ps` command to show the process state as well as the state of the parent shell process. As you can see, the output shows that all three crunchers are in state R, which means that they are all runnable. This is expected, because they don't sleep. Because this is a single CPU system, however, only one of the processes is actually running. The output also shows that the parent shell (`bash`) is sleeping. This is expected as well. Because the shell created the process, it probably is sleeping in a `wait` system call, waiting for `ps` to exit.

The sleep state that you see in Bash in the previous example is an interruptible sleep. That means that if the Bash shell receives a signal, it will respond to the signal (that is, run its signal handler). A `SIGTERM` or `SIGQUIT` signal, for example, will cause it to terminate. Most of the time, when your code is blocking due to I/O or just sleeping, it is in an interruptible sleep.

An uninterruptible sleep occurs less frequently and used when the kernel code (most often, a device driver) decides that the process had better not be interrupted while an operation is taking place. Normally, this is a transient state that the driver uses only for short durations to ensure that the process finishes what it starts. Your driver might be flipping bits on a particular device and waiting for a response via polling, for example. The driver wants to ensure that the device is left in a known state, which cannot be guaranteed if the process is allowed to terminate during the sleep. To prevent this, the driver puts the process in an uninterruptible sleep until the hardware is back in a known state.

You can observe uninterruptible sleeps by accessing a slow device, such as a CD-ROM. Here, I use the `dd` command to read the entire contents of a CD (`/dev/cdrom`) and dump it to the bit bucket (`/dev/null`):

```
$ dd if=/dev/cdrom of=/dev/null &
```

While this runs, you can peek at the process state periodically to see what it is up to. The CD-ROM is slow enough that you should expect to see it enter an uninterruptible sleep occasionally. It may take a couple of tries, but the following command will work:

```
$ ps -C dd -o pid,state,cmd
  PID S CMD
 4606 D dd if /dev/hdc of /dev/null
```

A process in an uninterruptible state can be a dangerous thing. Under normal circumstances, it's in this state for a very short time, but when hardware or media is faulty, the uninterruptible state can be a problem. It may never arise until you encounter defective hardware or media. Consider a poorly written driver that uses uninterruptible sleeps with no timeout. When this driver tries to read from a defective device, it may never get the response it requires and can leave a process in an uninterruptible sleep indefinitely. Worse, the user has no idea why. All she knows is that her process is stuck, and she cannot kill it or wake it up.

If you ever run across a process that you can't kill, even with `kill -9`, chances are that it is stuck in an uninterruptible sleep. There is no remedy for this situation except to reboot and fix the device (or perhaps its driver).

5.3.7.2 Zombies and Wait

When a process exits, it does not disappear entirely until its parent calls one of the `wait` system calls. Until this happens, the process stays around in a so-called zombie state, waiting for its parent to acknowledge its termination. The name *zombie* is a whimsical term for a process that has terminated but stays around neither living or dead, like its undead namesake. Zombie processes don't consume memory or

processing resources,[3] but they do show up in the `ps` output. If the parent terminates without waiting for its child processes, those processes are "adopted" by the
`init` process, which calls `wait` periodically to *reap* these processes (another dark
metaphor).

In keeping with the undead analogy, create an example script to illustrate zombie processes named `romero`.[4] Write this one in Perl so that the Perl programmers
in the audience don't feel left out.[5]

```perl
#!/usr/bin/perl

use POSIX;

$pid = fork();
if ( $pid )
{
    # Parent stops
    printf("%d is the proud father of %d\n",getpid(),$pid);
    pause();
}
else
{
    # Child exits
    exit(0);
}
```

The API is virtually identical to the POSIX C API, thanks to Perl's POSIX package. You use the `fork` function to create the child just as you would in a C function. Perl's POSIX package has `wait` functions as well, but you won't use them for
this example. The parent process simply calls `pause`, which stops the process until
a signal is received. While the parent is paused, the child simply exits. Although the
child process has exited, it continues to show up in the process tables until the

---

3. They don't consume human flesh or brains, either.
4. In honor of the king of all zombie movies: George A. Romero.
5. Please don't take this to mean that Perl is a dead language or that Perl programmers are in any way
   undead.

parent acknowledges its termination. Now run the romero script in the background with the trusty ps command in the foreground to see what is happening:

```
$ ./romero &
[1] 5039
$ 5039 is the proud father of 5040
$ ps -o pid,state,cmd
  PID S CMD
 4545 S bash
 5039 S /usr/bin/perl ./romero
 5040 Z [romero] <defunct>
 5043 R ps -o pid,state,cmd
```

In this example, process ID 5039 is the parent, and 5040 is the child. The ps command indicates that the child is in state Z and indicates this further in the CMD section, where it reads defunct—a slightly more dignified description than *zombie*. Rest assured that process 5040 is consuming no processing time or memory.

Why Zombies?

You may ask, "Why bother keeping zombie processes around?" After all, the only useful information they have is their exit status.

But that's the whole point. You, the application programmer, may not care about the exit status of a process that you forked (although you should), but the kernel does not know that. The kernel assumes that the parent process is interested in knowing the result of the child process that it forked, so it sends the parent a signal (SIGCHLD) and keeps the status for the parent to collect. Until the parent retrieves the return status by calling one of the wait functions, the process continues to exist in a zombie state.

When a parent process exits before the child process, the child is *adopted* by init, which collects the status immediately, effectively removing the zombie process.

5.3.7.3   Stopped Processes

A process can be stopped for various reasons. You probably have used the shell Ctrl+Z sequence to stop a process running in the foreground. Terminals traditionally define this character as a so-called SUSP character to be used to stop a process running in the foreground. In Linux (and UNIX), pressing this key causes the pseudoterminal to send a SIGTSTP signal[6] to the process. You can define this key to be whatever you like, but the default is Ctrl+Z by convention.[7]

Several signals will cause a process to enter the stopped state; you can find a list of them in the signal(7) man page. A process will leave the stopped state and continue executing when it receives a SIGCONT signal. Otherwise, the only other way to leave the stopped state is via a termination signal. Normally, a signal received in the stopped state is recorded by the kernel, and the process does not run its signal handler until it leaves the stopped state. There are exceptions unique to Linux. SIGTERM and SIGKILL, for example, are handled immediately, even when the process is stopped.[8]

Another way processes can be stopped is by the terminal itself. A terminal manages processes using the convention of *background* and *foreground* processes. Each terminal has one—and only one—foreground process, which is the only process that receives input from the keyboard. Any other process started from that terminal is considered to be a background process. When a background process tries to read from its standard input, the terminal stops it by sending it a SIGTTIN signal because there is only one input device (the keyboard), and that device is connected to the foreground process. A process stopped by SIGTTIN does not continue until it is brought into the foreground by the fg command. Note that this concept of *foreground* and *background* processes is used only with respect to terminals. The kernel does not keep track of processes this way, but it provides these signals to facilitate the terminal's process management. Here's an example that demonstrates SIGTTIN in action:

```
$ read x &
[1] 5851
```

This example tries to run the bash built-in read command in the background. Because a background process is not allowed to take standard input from the

---

6. Not to be confused with SIGSTOP. SIGTSTP can be caught; SIGSTOP cannot.
7. Refer to stty(1).
8. SIGKILL cannot be trapped by a user-defined signal handler, but SIGTERM can.

terminal, the process receives a SIGTTIN signal, which sends it to the stopped state. The next command shows that indeed, the process is listed in state T (for *stopped*):

```
$ jobs -x ps -p %1 -o pid,state,cmd
  PID S CMD
 5851 T bash
```

When stopped by the SIGTTIN, a process can be awakened by SIGCONT but will block again when it tries to read from the standard input. Only when it is brought into the foreground can it complete its input.

The same method can be used to silence background processes and prevent them from cluttering your terminal display, which always seems to happen at the worst possible time. The terminal has a tostop (terminal output stop) setting that is off by default on most systems. When this setting is disabled, background processes are allowed to write to the terminal whenever they need to. When you enable the tostop flag with the stty command, background processes will be stopped when they try to write to the standard output. To enable the tostop setting, for example, use the stty command as follows:

```
$ stty tostop
$ echo Hello World &
$ jobs -1
[1]+  2709 Stopped (tty output)    echo Hello World
```

After enabling the tostop flag, any background process that tries to write to standard output will receive SIGTTOU, which will put it to sleep. Just as you can with a process stopped by SIGTTIN, you can wake it up with SIGCONT, but it will just go back to sleep when it tries to finish the write that was interrupted by the signal. Only when it is brought into the foreground will the process continue. Alternatively, you could disable tostop and send the process a SIGCONT.

To disable tostop, use the following command:

```
$ stty -tostop
```

In case you weren't paying attention, the only difference between this stty command and the earlier one is the dash, which indicates that the subsequent flag is to be disabled.

5.3.8   How Time Is Measured

The kernel keeps track of execution time for each process. The kernel records how much time each process spends in user mode versus kernel mode separately. The `time` command is very useful for illustrating where your process is spending its time. This feature is built into the Bash shell and some others but also is available as a command in `/bin/time`. I'll use the built-in Bash version in this example:

```
$ time sleep 1

real    0m1.042s
user    0m0.000s
sys     0m0.020s

$ time dd if=/dev/urandom of=/dev/null count=1000
1000+0 records in
1000+0 records out

real    0m0.527s
user    0m0.000s
sys     0m0.500s
```

The `sleep` command executes the sleep system call, which causes the process to block for 1 second. In this case, the process executes for 1.042 seconds total. Because the process blocked the whole time, it consumed no CPU cycles during the sleep. The `dd` command, on the other hand, runs diligently for 1,000 blocks, copying data from `/dev/urandom` to `/dev/null`. In this case, the process runs for 527 ms total, with 500 ms of that time being spent in kernel mode. This is most likely the `/dev/urandom` driver executing on behalf of the process. Aside from this, the `dd` command has little to do except copy the data, which likely accounts for the other 27 ms.

If your process is consuming too much time in user space, you can't blame it on the kernel. It might be your code or some library functions you are linking with, but it's not the kernel. There are several tools at your disposal to improve performance in user mode, including optimizing and refactoring. On the other hand, if the process is spending too much time in system calls, it may not be your fault. It could be that you are calling some particular system call more often than you need to, or it could be that the particular system call takes too long. The strace tool is excellent for tracking down these problems. Look at that dd command again with strace:

```
$ strace -c dd if=/dev/urandom of=/dev/null count=1000
1000+0 records in
1000+0 records out
% time     seconds  usecs/call     calls    errors syscall
------ ----------- ----------- --------- --------- ----------------
 88.77    0.730879         729      1003           read
 10.44    0.085947          86      1002           write
  0.68    0.005611         701         8           close
  0.04    0.000310         310         1           execve
  0.03    0.000210          18        12         6 open
  0.01    0.000079          13         6           old_mmap
  0.01    0.000064           8         8           rt_sigaction
  0.01    0.000053          27         2           munmap
  0.00    0.000039          10         4           fstat64
  0.00    0.000038          19         2           mprotect
  0.00    0.000036          18         2           mmap2
  0.00    0.000030          10         3           brk
  0.00    0.000016          16         1         1 access
  0.00    0.000013          13         1           set_thread_area
------ ----------- ----------- --------- --------- ----------------
100.00    0.823325                  2055         7 total
```

Using the -c option, strace counts the occurrences of each system call as well as the total amount of time spent executing code in the system call. Notice that strace causes the process to run more slowly, because it intercepts the system calls. The entire program took 527 ms before, but now the read calls alone take 729 ms. The process calls read and write the same number of times, yet roughly 89 percent of the time is spent in the read system call. Because you were reading from /dev/urandom, this tells you that this device is the culprit for consuming system time. Anything you can do to minimize the use of this device, therefore, will improve performance.

This is a contrived example, because /dev/urandom spends a nontrivial amount of time calculating random numbers on your behalf in kernel mode. If you had used /dev/zero, for example, the numbers would be much shorter.

A trickier problem is when your code takes too long because it is blocking. This is hard to track down, because it can be difficult to find out what is causing you to block. Look at the same thing again, using a slow device such as a CD-ROM drive:

```
$ time dd if=/dev/cdrom of=/dev/null count=1000
1000+0 records in
1000+0 records out

real    0m0.665s
user    0m0.000s
sys     0m0.060s
```

As expected, most of the time is spent blocking, as indicated by the high real-time value of 655 ms and the negligible CPU time values. In this case, it's obvious that the culprit is the CD-ROM drive, but the strace command is remarkably unhelpful here:

```
$ strace -c dd if=/dev/cdrom of=/dev/null count=1000
1000+0 records in
1000+0 records out
```

% time	seconds	usecs/call	calls	errors	syscall
51.91	0.131404	131	1003		read
44.31	0.112158	112	1002		write
3.01	0.007612	952	8		close
0.20	0.000516	43	12	6	open
0.13	0.000338	338	1		execve
0.11	0.000274	34	8		rt_sigaction
0.09	0.000231	39	6		old_mmap
0.06	0.000145	36	4		fstat64
0.04	0.000107	54	2		munmap
0.04	0.000104	35	3		brk
0.03	0.000088	44	2		mprotect
0.03	0.000082	41	2		mmap2
0.02	0.000040	40	1	1	access
0.02	0.000038	38	1		set_thread_area
------	----------	-----------	---------	---------	----------------
100.00	0.253137		2055	7	total

Again, you have the same number of calls to both read and write, but the reads and writes appear to be taking close to the same amount of time. From the kernel's perspective, they are consuming about the same number of CPU cycles, but the reads are blocking, whereas the writes are certainly not. The kernel counts only the CPU cycles used by each system call. Time spent blocking in your process is time the kernel spends doing other things.

If your code is running slowly because of a blocking device or system call, there are few options to speed your code. The most obvious is to avoid doing those calls. If that's not possible, you can try to parallelize your application with threads or asynchronous I/O.

5.3.8.1 System Time Units

POSIX defines the clock tick (clock_t) as one unit for measuring system time in user space applications. Unfortunately, this particular unit has two definitions. The ANSI definition is used with the ANSI clock function, which should not be used in Linux programs. This function returns the amount of CPU time consumed by the process, which is roughly equal to the sum of the user time and system time.

clock returns a value measured in CLOCKS_PER_SEC, which is a system-defined macro that the GNU standard library defines to be 1000000. On a Linux system, the return value of the clock function is measured in units of microseconds, although the actual tick rate will usually be much lower. The frequency of the clock tick used by functions that return a clock_t is given by the sysconf function, as follows:[9]

```
sysconf(_SC_CLK_TCK);
```

sysconf returns a value in ticks per second (or hertz), and any variable of type clock_t is related to this value. This is important if you are doing performance measurements, because it determines the precision for functions that return a value of type clock_t.

One problem with the ANSI clock function is that it will overflow within a little more than an hour. For processes that run much longer than that, the clock function is inappropriate. What's more, the clock function does not take into account CPU usage by child processes and does not differentiate between user space and kernel space. With all these problems, it does not make sense to use the clock function on Linux systems, although it is part of ANSI standard C. Fortunately, Linux provides several alternatives.

---

9. Note that the ANSI CLK_TCK macro is made obsolete by POSIX, although it is still defined as sysconf(_SC_CLK_TCK).

The POSIX `times` function also uses the `clock_t` type but defines the unit differently. Instead of `CLOCKS_PER_SEC` or microseconds, `clock_t` values returned by the `times` function are measured in system clock ticks. This makes overflow much less likely.

The prototype for the `times` function is as follows:

```
clock_t times(struct tms *buf);
```

The value returned represents the number of ticks of the wall clock since an arbitrary time in the past. Linux defines this point to be the time the system booted. For portability, the return value should be used only as a reference for relative timing, not for absolute times. The important details from `times` are stored in the `struct tms` structure, whose address is passed by the calling process. The `tms` structure is defined as follows:

```
struct tms {
        clock_t tms_utime;   /* user time */
        clock_t tms_stime;   /* system time */
        clock_t tms_cutime;  /* user time of children */
        clock_t tms_cstime;  /* system time of children */
};
```

The `tms_utime` value is the amount of time the process has spent executing user code since the process started. The `tms_stime` field is the time process spent executing kernel code since it started. The output of the ANSI `clock` function is equivalent to the sum of these two values multiplied by the tick interval. The `tms_cutime` and `tms_cstime` values are the same values except that these are measured for forked processes that have terminated and been reaped with one of the `wait` system calls.

An alternative to `times` is the `getrusage` function introduced in BSD:

```
int getrusage(int who, struct rusage *usage);
```

Unlike the `times` function, `getrusage` fetches specifically the parent or child information. The `rusage` structure contains numerous fields in addition to timing information, but the Linux kernel fills in very few of them. Two of the fields that are filled in include the user time and system time, like `times` except these are stored in a `struct timeval`:

```
struct timeval ru_utime;
struct timeval ru_stime;
```

Instead of the ambiguous `clock_t` type, the `timeval` structure stores time as two integers in seconds and microseconds:

```
struct timeval {
    long    tv_sec;          /* seconds */
    long    tv_usec;         /* microseconds */
};
```

This gives you higher precision than `times`, but although the units are in microseconds, the clock does not tick every microsecond. You might expect the clock to tick at the same rate as `clock_t`, but you would be wrong. In Linux, the frequency of the clock used by `getrusage` is determined by your running kernel. So whereas the interval for a `clock_t` may be 10 ms, the tick interval you get from `getrusage` may be 1 ms. It is not uncommon to see Linux 2.6 kernels that run with an internal tick frequency of 1,000Hz and a user tick frequency of 100Hz. In this case, the `getrusage` function will return more-precise values than the `times` function. Unfortunately, there is no API to determine the frequency of the kernel tick; therefore, you can never know how accurate the values in the `timeval` structure will be. It should be safe to assume that it is as precise as `clock_t` or even more so.

Just when you thought that there were enough clock functions, there is another one worth talking about. The POSIX real-time extensions defined in POSIX 1003.1 added the `clock_gettime` function, which has a couple of advantages. The `clock_gettime` prototype looks like the following:

```
int clock_gettime(clockid_t clk_id, struct timespec *tp);
```

The first thing to notice is yet another time structure. `timespec` defines times in units of nanoseconds as follows:

```
struct timespec {
    time_t    tv_sec;
    long      tv_nsec;
};
```

Here again, the nanosecond resolution does not mean that the clock ticks once every nanosecond. The API allows for multiple clocks, each of which may tick at a different interval and have a different reference. You must specify the clock via the `clockid_t` parameter. Unlike with `getrusage`, you can determine the clock period with the `clock_getres` function. The prototype for `clock_getres` looks like this:

```
int clock_getres( clockid_t clk_id, struct timespec *res);
```

This tells you the clock period with a `timespec` structure. Although the API allows multiple clocks, the only clock required by POSIX is `CLOCK_REALTIME`.

Table 5-3 lists several other useful clocks.

TABLE 5-3   Clocks Used with clock_gettime

ID	Description	Notes
CLOCK_REALTIME	Required by POSIX; returns seconds in Coordinated Universal Time (UTC) with a higher tick frequency than the ANSI `time` function.	Tick frequency typically is the same as `SC_CLK_TCK`.
CLOCK_MONOTONIC	A simple clock that represents an elapsed time from an arbitrary (and undefined) time in the past.	Tick frequency typically is the same as `SC_CLK_TCK`.
CLOCK_PROCESS_CPUTIME_ID	Indicates CPU time consumed by a process. As with the ANSI `clock` function, time consumed includes user and system time. For multithreaded processes, this time includes time consumed by threads.	This does not have the rollover issues that the ANSI `clock` function has. Tick frequency from `clock_getres` indicates 1 nanosecond, but I measured 1/100th of a second on my 2.6.14 kernel.
CLOCK_THREAD_CPUTIME_ID	Indicates CPU time consumed by the current thread; same as above except that in multithreaded processes, the time is measured only for the currently running thread.	Tick frequency from `clock_getres` indicates 1 nanosecond, but actual ticks are much larger. Tick frequency from `clock_getres` indicates 1 nanosecond, but I measured 1/100th of a second on my 2.6.14 kernel.

Portable code should use `clock_getres` to check the clock period as well as the availability of a particular clock before using it. The `clock_gettime` function does not take child processes into account, so the values you get are not affected by `wait` calls.

The `clock_getres(3) man` page warns that the clocks using `CLOCK_PROCESS_CPUTIME_ID` and `CLOCK_THREAD_CPUTIME_ID` typically are implemented using hardware timers in the CPU. This means that the resolution can vary from system to system, which perhaps explains why `clock_getres` says the resolution is 1 nanosecond on my system (that is, the kernel doesn't know the actual resolution). The `man` page goes on to warn that on Symmetric Multiprocessing (SMP) systems, the hardware timers may not be in sync across CPUs. That means that if a process or thread is rescheduled on a different CPU, the values returned by these timers may vary. This should give you pause (pun intended) before using either of these timers in your code. Using these timers in portable code is not advisable.

5.3.8.2   The Kernel Clock Tick

The standard unit of time in the kernel is called the *jiffy*. One jiffy represents a tick of an internal clock, which is a hardware timer programmed to generate interrupts at a specific frequency. The frequency is determined when the kernel is built and does not change. Most distributions use the default value, which is stored in a macro named `HZ`. Each architecture defines a unique default value for `HZ`. Until recently, this value was not easily configurable in the kernel. Most people were satisfied with the default value, which for IA32 was 100Hz. As if to keep things simple, this happened to be the same frequency that the GNU standard library uses for `clock_t`.

It used to be that only people concerned with real-time and multimedia performance would tweak the `HZ` value; specifically, they would increase it to increase the frequency. To understand why, consider that the tick interval is the maximum time it can take to preempt a CPU-intensive process. When a process does not give up the CPU voluntarily, it will not be preempted until the next clock tick. Each time the timer ticks, the scheduler gets an opportunity to run and preempt a running process. At 100Hz, this means that a process can monopolize the CPU for up to 10 ms. This seems like nitpicking, but 10 ms can be an eternity in real-time and multimedia applications. As you might expect, you cannot arbitrarily increase the frequency as high as you like. At some point, handling the tick interrupts and context switches will consume as much time as executing processes does.

Table 5-4 illustrates some examples of real-world timing requirements compared with the default 100Hz Linux clock.

TABLE 5-4   Some Example Timing

Application	Frequency (Hz)	Interval (ms)
Default Linux clock	100	10
One NTSC video frame	60	16.67
One PAL video frame	50	20
CRT display refresh rate (typical)	80	12.5

Starting with the 2.6 kernel, the default tick frequency changed to 1,000Hz to improve multimedia performance. Linus Torvalds admits that this value was chosen rather arbitrarily. It turns out that the change also has some undesirable side effects. One is that the increased interrupt frequency increases the CPU usage. This is not a problem on a dual Xeon machine plugged into a wall outlet, but it is a problem for a laptop running on batteries. The increase in CPU usage drains the battery faster. SMP systems with many CPUs are also adversely affected by a high system clock frequency. The overhead of delivering the interrupts to many CPUs at high frequency can be significant. Finally, embedded systems with slower CPUs can be affected by both the interrupt overhead and the extra power consumption.

For these reasons, the kernel team decided to make the system clock tick frequency configurable on several of the most popular architectures. The kernel configuration tools now give the user three choices for the system clock tick. As of 2.6.14, the default value for IA32 is 250Hz, but you can select 100, 250, or 1,000 when you build the kernel. Choose a lower frequency for a slow processor or low-power system. Use the higher frequency if you have a desktop system or plan to use many multimedia applications.

The timer frequency can be set only when the kernel is built. Figure 5-6 shows what this looks like when you create the kernel using the `menuconfig` target.

Recall that the frequency of the clock used by functions that return type `clock_t` is independent of the kernel tick. The macro `USER_HZ` determines this frequency and is determined when the kernel is built. This value is the value that is returned when you call `sysconf(_SC_CLK_TCK)`. No matter what you set the `HZ` value to in the kernel, this value will not change. Generally, it is safe to assume that the kernel tick frequency will be equal to or higher than the user tick frequency.

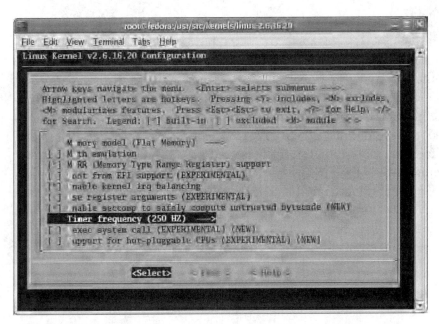

FIGURE 5-6   Changing the Timer Frequency in the Kernel Build

5.3.8.3 Timing Your Application

The Bash shell provides built-in commands to monitor the performance of your application, including `time`, which allows you to monitor the CPU usage of any command or script without having to modify the code. The time printed is measured from when the process starts to when it terminates.

Time measurements get tricky when an application forks or uses threads. Depending on the application and the functions used for timing, the time can be measured differently. Specifically, if you time an application that forks a process and then reaps it by calling any of the `wait` family of system calls, that process's time statistics will include the time consumed by its children. If the process neglects to reap any of its children, the time does not reflect their runtime, which could be misleading.

When you're timing your application from within, the `getrusage` function has explicit flags to control what data you get. You tell `getrusage` which data you want via the first argument, which can be RUSAGE_SELF or RUSAGE_CHILDREN. The time returned when you use RUSAGE_CHILDREN, however, includes only those children that the process has reaped. Until the parent process calls wait, the time returned for the children will be zero. This is not true for processes that use threads. A thread is not a child process, so time consumed by threads is considered time consumed by the process. The timing output from getrusage increases as the threads execute without any additional system calls required.

You can time your application externally from the shell with the time command. This is implemented as a Bash built-in function and as a general-purpose command in /usr/bin/time. Both accomplish the same thing except that the Bash version focuses exclusively on timing, whereas the time command also gives you access to the information from the getrusage system call. To use the built-in time command, just pass your command line as arguments to time as follows:

```
$ time sleep 1

real    0m1.007s
user    0m0.000s
sys     0m0.004s
```

You can bypass the built-in command by *escaping* the command as follows:

```
$ \time sleep 1
0.00user 0.00system 0:01.00elapsed 0%CPU (0avgtext+0avgdata 0maxresident)k
0inputs+0outputs (0major+199minor)pagefaults 0swaps
```

The output here includes much more information from the rusage structure, including much that is not filled in by Linux.

Both time commands print out three values: real, user, and system time. I discussed system and user time earlier, and as you might guess, *real time* is the time elapsed from the start of the process to the exit. This is time that you *feel* when you run an application.

When the real time exceeds the sum of the system time and user time, it means that the process is either blocking in system calls or not getting a chance to run. When the system is busy, a process will not get to run 100 percent of the time. Blocking can be caused by misuse of system calls or perhaps a slow device in the system. Running the time command is usually the first step in finding out.

5.4 Understanding Devices and Device Drivers

Every application communicates with devices at some point. Intentionally or not, it's hard not to come in contact with one or more devices on the system. You might write a sophisticated modeling algorithm that runs entirely in memory, but if you want to save the results, you'll need to save your data to a file system. Even before then, your code might swap to disk due to system load. Any printout you want to send to the console will likely require the pseudoterminal driver. So try as you might to avoid them, device drivers will be called from your process.

The Linux device driver API dates back to the early days of UNIX and has been largely unchanged since then. The POSIX standard formalizes this interface and serves as the basis for Linux.

Many devices are opened just like files on a disk. Communication with these device drivers starts by opening one of these files. The application uses a file descriptor returned by the `open` system call and uses all the system calls that take a file descriptor for an argument. It's interesting to consider that this is an object-oriented model that uses functional programming, although this was created in the 1970s—long before object-oriented programming was in vogue. Typically, a device is accessed via its file descriptor (much like an object), and there is a limited set of system calls that you can use to access the device (think methods).

A device driver may implement only the system calls that it needs, so a system call that works on one device may not work on another.[10] A driver could implement only the `open` and `close` system calls, for example, although such a driver wouldn't be very useful. When an application tries to use a system call that is not implemented by the driver, the function typically returns an error indication, and `errno` is set according to the particular system call.

5.4.1 Device Driver Types

Device drivers fall into a few basic categories. The most familiar devices are *block devices* or *character devices,* which are accessible via special files on a disk. These files are called device *nodes,* which distinguishes them from plain files and directories. Other device types include file-system drivers and network drivers, which normally

---

10. You might call that polymorphism, but maybe that's going too far.

are not accessed directly from an application but work closely with other drivers in the system.

5.4.1.1 Character Devices

A typical example of a character device is the serial port on your PC or the terminal device you use to type shell commands. Data is received and transmitted 1 byte at a time. A write to the device transmits bytes in the same order in which they were written. Imagine the confusion if the letters you typed in the terminal appeared in any arbitrary order. Likewise, a read from the device receives bytes in the same order in which they were sent.

Not all character devices read and write characters this way, however. Character devices cover a wide range of hardware and functions. Some character devices can allow random access to data, much like a storage device, so their drivers can support additional system calls, such as `mmap` or `lseek`.[11]

The `mem` driver is a good example. This driver implements several devices that perform simple, loosely related functions, which are listed in Table 5-5. Some of these devices, such as `/dev/null`, don't involve any hardware at all.

5.4.1.2 Block Devices

A *block device* is a storage device with a fixed amount of space. As the name suggests, the device manages the storage in fixed-size blocks. The main application for block devices is to communicate with disk drives, although they are used with other types of storage media, such as flash drives. When a disk drive uses *logical block addressing* (LBA), there is a one-to-one correlation between blocks on the device and logical blocks on the disk. A unique feature of block devices is that they can host file systems, which requires them to interact closely with a file-system driver.

Block drivers also use system memory as cache to make the most effective use of the device. Blocks are kept in memory as long as possible to maximize opportunities for reuse. This minimizes the number of times the physical device is read or written, which improves performance. When using a file system, your code may never interact with the underlying block device at all, instead operating entirely out of cache.

---

11. Some drivers don't allow `lseek` but still implement the system call. Instead of returning -1, these drivers typically return 0 to indicate that the position has not changed, so technically, the system call completed without error.

5.4.1.3   Network Devices

Unlike block and character devices, a network device does not use a device node. Network devices are in a class by themselves. Applications rarely need to interact directly with network drivers; when they do, they use a specific name such as `eth0` passed to the `ioctl` function using an anonymous socket. I will not look at network devices in this book. If you are interested in learning more about network devices, the `netdevice(7)` man page is a good place to start.

5.4.1.4   File-System Drivers

Although technically not a device, a file system requires a driver. File-system drivers require a separate block device. Although applications interact with files all the time, they rarely need to interact with the file-system driver directly. There are some rare exceptions for particular file systems. The XFS file system, for example, allows you to preallocate file extents to improve performance. Such a command is accomplished via the `ioctl` function, using the file descriptor of an open file in the file system.

5.4.2   A Word about Kernel Modules

The kernel module is a very popular way to deliver a device driver, but *kernel module* and *device driver* are not synonymous. Modules may contain any kernel code, not just device drivers, although that's what they're most often used for. What makes modules attractive is that they can be compiled after the kernel is built and then installed in a running kernel. This enables users to try new drivers without having to rebuild the kernel or even take their system down.

This feature has matured nicely in Linux, and the 2.6 kernel makes building modules almost child's play. With a 2.6 kernel, you no longer need the full kernel source installed—just a bunch of headers that are installed by default in most distributions. A module build line looks like the following:

```
$ make -C /lib/modules/$(uname -r)/build M=$(pwd) modules
```

This command line builds against the currently running kernel, assuming that it uses the standard location for the kernel headers. The resulting module includes a signature so that it cannot be installed on a different kernel. Linux 2.6 forces users to build modules specifically for their target kernel, but in return, the kernel makes it as easy as possible to do so.

Kernel modules are denoted by the .ko extension (for *kernel object*) and can be inserted into the kernel directly with the insmod command. Many (but not all) modules can also be removed from the kernel with the rmmod command. If you decide to keep a module, you can do a more permanent installation with the following command line:

```
$ make -C /lib/modules/$(uname -r)/build M=$(pwd) modules_install
```

This places the module in an appropriate place under /lib/modules. Depending on the module, you may need to run the depmod command to update the module dependencies.

5.4.3   Device Nodes

Block devices and character devices are accessed as files on disk via device nodes. A node contains an integer that indicates a major and minor number. Traditionally, the major number identifies the device driver in the kernel, whereas the minor number is used by the driver to identify specific devices. In Linux 2.4 and earlier, the value used to store the major and minor number was a 16-bit value, with 8 bits allocated for the major number and 8 bits for the minor number. Linux 2.6 increased this value to 32 bits, allocating 12 bits for the major number and 20 bits for the minor number.

Nodes can be created on disk with the mknod command, which takes the device type (character or block) as well as the major and minor number as arguments. Because devices nodes provide an interface to device drivers, a security risk is involved. After all, you don't want just anyone to have access to the block device that contains your root file system. As a result, device nodes may be created only by the superuser. The syntax to create /dev/mem, which uses major number 1 and minor number 1, is:

```
$ mknod /dev/mem c 1 1
```

By convention, the /dev directory contains all the nodes in the system, but device nodes can be created on any file system.[12] Most distributions provide a comprehensive set of device nodes in /dev through one of a few techniques, so that

---

12. Device nodes on a file system can be rendered useless by mounting it with the nodev option; see mount (8).

a typical user never has to use the `mknod` command. You can see a list of the currently installed devices and their major numbers in `/proc/devices`:

```
$ cat /proc/devices
Character devices:
  1 mem
  4 /dev/vc/0
  4 tty
  4 ttyS
  5 /dev/tty
  5 /dev/console
  5 /dev/ptmx
...
Block devices:
  1 ramdisk
  2 fd
  3 ide0
  9 md
 22 ide1
253 device-mapper
254 mdp
```

When a process opens a device node, the kernel locates the appropriate driver using the major number. The minor number is passed to the driver and is used differently by each driver. In general, the minor number is used to distinguish between functions, devices, or both. One straightforward example is the `mem` driver, which implements several different functions based on the minor number (see Table 5-5). Each function is accessed via separate device nodes. In principle, because all the device nodes have a common major number, they all belong to the same driver.

The nodes are defined in `/dev` using the names listed in Table 5-5. When you open `/dev/mem`, for example, the kernel calls the `mem` driver's `open` function with a minor number of 1. This tells the driver that you want to look at the physical memory of the system.

In general, the driver itself does not enforce any access policy. Instead, it relies on the `open` system call to verify the permissions of the device node against the current user, the same way that it is done for every other file in the system. Looking at system memory, for example, is not something you want to let just any user do, because any user can use this device to snoop in memory for passwords or to vandalize the system. In this case, the convention is to allow only root to open `/dev/mem` and `/dev/kmem`, whereas most of the other functions of the `mem` device are open to everyone. You can see this by looking at the file permissions of each device node.

TABLE 5-5   Character Devices Implemented by the mem Driver

Device Node Name	Minor Number	Function
mem	1	Allows access to physical memory.
kmem	2	Allows access to kernel virtual memory.
null	3	A data *sink*. All data written to this device is discarded.
port	4	Allows access to I/O ports (found on some architectures).
zero	5	Reads from this device are filled with zeros.
	6	Obsolete /dev/core device replaced by /proc/kcore.
full	7	A write to this device will always fail with ENOSPC.
random	8	Reads from this device are filled with random bytes; returns only as many bytes as the driver considers random. See random(4) for more details.
urandom	9	Like random, except that this returns all the data requested, regardless of whether it is high-quality random data. See random(4) for more details.
	10	Not provided by mem driver.
kmsg	11	Allows applications to write to the kernel message log instead of using the syslog system call.

It should be apparent that for security reasons, only root is allowed to create device nodes and change the permissions of a device node. If this were not the case, any user could create a device node to point to /dev/mem or some other vulnerable device and wreak havoc with the system. Likewise, root can prevent device nodes from being recognized on user-mountable file systems such as /mnt/floppy by putting the nodev option to mount in /etc/fstab.

5.4.3.1   Device Minor Numbers

Minor numbers are used differently depending on the driver, and the convention is not always straightforward. Block devices are particularly complicated because by convention, the minor number uniquely identifies a specific drive and partition.

Consider the IDE driver (/dev/hd), for example. In Linux 2.6, the convention is to use the least significant 6 bits to encode the partition and the most significant 14 bits to encode the drive. That means that the IDE device can map up to 16,384 drives (2^{14}), and each drive can have up to 63 partitions (2^6-1); partition zero is used to address the entire drive. The naming convention for disks' device nodes is to use a unique letter to identify each drive followed by a decimal number to identify the partition. To address the entire device (partition 0), the partition number is left off. You can see this for yourself with the ls command as follows:

```
$ ls -l /dev/hd[ab]*
brw-------  1 john disk 3,   0 Dec 21 10:00 /dev/hda
brw-rw----  1 root disk 3,   1 Dec 21 03:59 /dev/hda1
brw-------  1 john disk 3,  64 Dec 21 10:00 /dev/hdb
brw-rw----  1 root disk 3,  65 Dec 21 03:59 /dev/hdb1
brw-rw----  1 root disk 3,  66 Dec 21 03:59 /dev/hdb2
```

When the ls command encounters a device node, it prints the major and minor number where it normally would print the file size. Here, you can see that the major number for the IDE driver is 3, and the first disk is labeled hda. The entire disk is accessed via a device node named /dev/hda with a major number of 3 and a minor number of 0. Partition 1 of the first drive has a node with a minor number of 1 and is named /dev/hda1. In this example, hda has only 1 partition. The second drive's device node is named hdb, and its minor numbers start at 64. This is dissected further in Table 5-6.

The SCSI driver follows the same convention as the IDE driver, except that the SCSI driver uses only 4 bits of the minor number to encode the partition, allowing only 15 partitions. This leaves 16 bits to encode the drive number, which allows the SCSI driver to support up to 65,536 (2^{16}) drives. For SCSI devices, the formula for the minor number is 16 * drive + partition.

TABLE 5-6   Minor Numbers for IDE Devices Dissected (Linux 2.6 and Later)

Drive	Partition	Minor No. = 64 * Drive + Partition	Node Name
0	0	0	/dev/hda
0	1	1	/dev/hda1
1	0	64	/dev/hdb
1	1	65	/dev/hdb1
1	2	66	/dev/hdb2

5.4.3.2   Device Major Numbers

Normally, the major number along with the driver type (character or block) identifies one—and only one—device driver. When a major number is assigned to a character device driver, for example, no other character device driver can use that major number. The device driver assigned to a major number owns all the minor numbers, whether it needs them or not. The mem driver, for example, provides several pseudodevices with the same major number. If it weren't for that, each device would have to consume a unique major number.

This was a serious issue on kernels before Linux 2.6, which allowed only 256 major numbers to be used in the system at any time. Although no one really needs that many device drivers in a single system, the problem is that many major numbers are statically defined so that they don't change from one system to the next. That limits the total number of possible devices.

Linux 2.6 addresses this in two ways. One, which I've already discussed, is the increase of allowable major numbers to 1,024. Another improvement is that drivers can now register for only a range of minor numbers. Having many minor numbers comes in handy for a disk driver, but many drivers don't have the potential to use more than a few minor numbers. One example is the NVRAM driver, which looks at the battery-backed RAM in your PC. This driver sees only one NVRAM, so it should need only one minor number. This particular driver uses major number 10, which is described as "Miscellaneous." At this writing, 230 devices are defined that use major number 10, including the NVRAM driver.

A list of permanently assigned major numbers is maintained at www.lanana.org/docs/devicelist. A snapshot of this list is distributed with each release of the kernel source in `Documentation/devices.txt`. The use of permanently assigned major numbers is a headache for custom driver writers. If you are writing a one-of-a kind driver or just experimenting, you don't want to apply for a major number just to print "hello world". But, you cannot borrow a major number without the possibility of creating havoc in your system. Even if you don't have an IDE drive in your system, for example, you can't borrow the IDE driver's major number (3) for your custom driver. The IDE driver is often compiled into the kernel, so your driver will fail when it tries to register for major number 3.

The reason that drivers, such as the IDE driver, are given fixed major numbers is consistency. Virtually every x86 motherboard chipset includes an IDE interface. Imagine if every chipset driver used an arbitrarily chosen major number. The values in `/dev` would have to be unique for every system configuration. Fortunately, that is not the case, and distributions can create a default set of nodes in `/dev` that will work in all configurations. The permanent assignment of major numbers probably will be around forever.

One curiosity is an artifact of these permanent major number assignments combined with the 16-bit value used for major/minor identification: The SCSI driver has not 1 but 16 major numbers assigned to it. This is a workaround to allow the SCSI driver to address more drives in systems with large disk arrays. In a Linux 2.4 system, the SCSI driver can address 256 disk drives by consuming 16 major numbers. In a Linux 2.6 system, a single major number can address 65,536 drives. Because the major numbers are still assigned, the SCSI driver theoretically can address up to 1,048,576 drives (2^{20}).

For custom driver writers, Linux allows a driver to be assigned a major number from a pool of permanently unused numbers. These are major numbers that are reserved and will never be assigned permanently to any device. Assignment is first come, first served, so there is no guarantee that a driver will get the same number every time. This creates a new problem: Because the major number is no longer fixed, you have to re-create the device node each time the driver is loaded to accommodate the fact that the major number can change. This is a nuisance, but it is manageable.

5.4.3.3   Where Device Nodes Come From

Many distributions based on Linux 2.4 and earlier include a single package that contains hundreds or maybe thousands of device nodes to be extracted to /dev. If you have a device that is not described by one of these nodes, you have to add the node yourself. If you should ever look in this directory, you are likely to see hundreds of nodes that point to drivers you don't have and probably never plan to. This is an inelegant, brute-force solution that rubbed many Linux users the wrong way and inspired some alternative solutions. The first one, called devfs, was implemented as a file-system driver to create a pseudo file system on /dev. It populates the /dev directory dynamically with only the nodes that are actually present in the system. So instead of thousands of nodes in your /dev directory, you see only the ones that have drivers installed in your system. Nodes are created and deleted as devices are added to and removed from the system.

devfs was abandoned because of lack of a maintainer as well as some serious flaws in the design. One major drawback of devfs was that it hard-coded node names in the kernel (and/or modules). This sort of policy enforcement in the kernel is one of the taboos of Linux kernel development. Linux kernel developers believe that the kernel has no business telling users what their device nodes should be named or where they should reside.

Although it provided an alternative to the brute-force archiving of thousands of device nodes, devfs was doomed due to philosophical problems. A more palatable implementation was found in udev, which places the naming and location of device nodes in user space using helper programs. udev is built on top of another feature called hotplug, which arose at the same time.

udev and hotplug

The hotplug feature of the kernel is primarily responsible for locating and loading driver modules for hardware as they come online and go offline. The hotplug implementation relies on minimal intervention from the kernel; the bulk of the work is done in user space. All the kernel does is recognize when a piece of hardware becomes available or unavailable and, in response, spawn a user-space process to handle the event. The user-space process handles the job of recognizing the device, finding a driver module for it, and loading the module.

By default, the kernel looks for `/sbin/hotplug`[13] to execute when a `hotplug` event is handled, but it can be replaced by any script or program as required. The program name for the `hotplug` handler process is stored in `/proc/sys/kernel/hotplug` and can be overridden by writing a new filename to it. `udev`, for example, replaces the default `hotplug` handler with `/sbin/udevsend`.

The primary function of `udev` is to populate the `/dev` directory with device nodes that accurately reflect the devices currently available in the system. It was natural to implement this as an extension of the `hotplug` feature.[14]

To see how this works, look at a module that usually isn't loaded by default. The `nvram` module is used to access the nonvolatile memory in your computer and typically uses the node `/dev/nvram`. This module is categorized by www.lanana.org as a "miscellaneous" device, which means that it uses major number 10. It is assigned to minor number 144. After loading the module on a system with `udev`, the device node appears immediately after the module is loaded. For example:

```
$ ls -l /dev/nvram
ls: /dev/nvram: No such file or directory
$ modprobe nvram
$ ls -l /dev/nvram
crw-rw----  1 root root 10, 144 Aug 13 16:14 /dev/nvram
```

Similarly, when you remove the module with `rmmod`, the device node is removed. How does this happen? The rules for `udev` are contained in `/etc/udev/rules.d`. There, you will find a file named `50-udev.rules`,[15] which contains default rules provided by the `udev` package. In the case of the `nvram` module, the rule looks like this:

```
KERNEL=="nvram", MODE="0660"
```

---

13. Part of the `hotplug` package at http://linux-hotplug.sourceforge.net.
14. www.kernel.org/pub/linux/utils/kernel/hotplug/udev.html
15. The 50 indicates priority. (Low numbers have higher priority.) Multiple files may reside here with different numbers, and rules can be defined more than once. The highest-priority rule is the one that applies.

This KERNEL field tells the udev daemon to match the kernel module name (nvram) to apply this rule. The MODE field tells it what permissions to apply to the device node. The name of the device node defaults to the same name that is used in the kernel. To illustrate further, change the name of the device node from nvram to cmos. All you need to do is create a file in /etc/udev/rules.d that contains the new rule.

```
$ cat <<EOF >/etc/udev/rules.d/25-cmos.rules
> KERNEL="nvram", MODE="0660", NAME="cmos"
> EOF
```

To override the default rule, you need to give it higher priority, so name it 25-cmos.rules. The leading number and the .rules extension are required, but everything in between is arbitrary. All you do is copy the existing rule and add a NAME parameter with the name cmos:

```
$ modprobe nvram
$ ls -l /dev/cmos /dev/nvram
ls: /dev/nvram: No such file or directory
crw-rw----  1 root root 10, 144 Aug 13 16:37 /dev/cmos
```

A complete explanation of the udev rules is contained in the udev(8) man page.

sysfs

sysfs is a new feature key to the hotplug implementation and is worth discussing a little at this point because it will come up again later. sysfs is a memory-based file system like procfs that contains text files with system information. It is based on kernel objects (kobjects), which is new to the 2.6 kernel, so sysfs is not available on 2.4 or earlier kernels.

By convention, sysfs is mounted on a directory named /sys so that user-space applications can find it easily. This mount point is a rigid convention that many tools depend on, much the way /proc is used with procfs. In many ways, sysfs overlaps procfs, although sysfs has a much more intuitive format and does not add much (if any) additional code to modules and drivers to support it. procfs, for example, requires device-driver writers to add callbacks to support procfs entries, and driver writers must provide the information from scratch. There are few conventions in procfs as to where files and directories can be located or what the contents of the files should be. Not every driver provides information in /proc, and when one does, the format is often whatever the author dreamed up. sysfs makes it very easy for device-driver writers to add entries into /sys with a trivial amount of code. Many driver entries show up with no additional code in the driver. The /sys/bus/scsi directory, for example, describes the SCSI buses in the system based on information already in the kernel from kobjects.

Whereas procfs typically contains flat files with a great deal of information, sysfs contains a hierarchy of small files, each containing a minimal amount of information. In many cases, the directory structure itself conveys information about the system. For example:

```
$ ls /sys/bus/pci*/devices
/sys/bus/pci/devices:
0000:00:00.0  0000:00:07.0  0000:00:07.2  0000:00:0f.0  0000:00:11.0
0000:00:01.0  0000:00:07.1  0000:00:07.3  0000:00:10.0  0000:00:12.0

/sys/bus/pci_express/devices:
```

Here, you can see that my system has ten PCI devices and no PCI-Express devices. Each one of the names listed is actually a directory. The names themselves contain useful information if you are a device-driver writer.

sysfs tries to create a directory hierarchy that closely mimics the system hardware. Through symbolic links, it is often possible to get the same information from several points of view. Suppose that you want to look at SCSI devices by bus. In this case, you will find what you want to know in /sys/bus/scsi/devices. Perhaps you want to know what SCSI device is mapped to block device sda. In that case, you can look at /sys/block/sda/device. Both of these are links to the same directory, which contains various information about the device.

The SCSI bus is a good example of how procfs and sysfs differ. Using procfs, you will find a directory named /proc/scsi that contains a directory for each host adapter, which usually contains a file for each SCSI bus (named 0, 1, 2, and so on). Inside this file is whatever the driver writer thought would be useful. Unfortunately, the people who wrote the Adaptec driver didn't talk to the people who wrote the LSI driver, who never spoke to the people who wrote the BusLogic driver. As a result, each driver produces similar information in a completely

different format. Here's a small example from the aic79xx SCSI module, which
shows a system attached to an Ultra 320 disk array:

```
$ cat /proc/scsi/aic79xx/0
Adaptec AIC79xx driver version: 1.3.11
Adaptec AIC7902 Ultra320 SCSI adapter
aic7902: Ultra320 Wide Channel A, SCSI Id=7, PCI-X 67-100Mhz, 512 SCBs
Allocated SCBs: 36, SG List Length: 128


Serial EEPROM:
0x17c8 0x17c8 0x17c8 0x17c8 0x17c8 0x17c8 0x17c8 0x17c8
0x17c8 0x17c8 0x17c8 0x17c8 0x17c8 0x17c8 0x17c8 0x17c8
0x09f4 0x0146 0x2807 0x0010 0xffff 0xffff 0xffff 0xffff
0xffff 0xffff 0xffff 0xffff 0xffff 0xffff 0x0430 0xb3f7


Target 0 Negotiation Settings
        User: 320.000MB/s transfers (160.000MHz DT|IU|QAS, 16bit)
Target 1 Negotiation Settings
        User: 320.000MB/s transfers (160.000MHz DT|IU|QAS, 16bit)
        Goal: 320.000MB/s transfers (160.000MHz DT|IU|QAS, 16bit)
        Curr: 320.000MB/s transfers (160.000MHz DT|IU|QAS, 16bit)
        Transmission Errors 0
        Channel A Target 1 Lun 0 Settings
                Commands Queued 1333
                Commands Active 0
                Command Openings 32
                Max Tagged Openings 32
                Device Queue Frozen Count 0
...
```

There's a lot of information here. Other drivers have similar files in a similar
location but formatted completely differently. The equivalent file connected to a
BusLogic adapter might show up under /proc/scsi/BusLogic/0 but would
look completely different. The only thing these procfs files have in common is
that each one tells you information about the devices on the bus, but each one provides a different amount of detail with a unique format. There's no guarantee that
the driver will tell you anything in particular. An important tuning parameter for
SCSI drives is the command queue depth (listed by the aic79xx driver as
"Command Openings"). This is the length of the queue used for SCSI commands,

which is the number of commands that can be active simultaneously. It's a very useful tuning parameter, but there's no guarantee that a different driver will present this information, and if it does, you can rest assured that it will be in a different format.

The sysfs approach is a bit more intuitive and manageable. Under /sys, you will find /sys/bus/scsi, which lists devices by host adapter number, channel number, device number, and logical unit number. All that information is encoded in the directory name. Inside each directory, you will find various SCSI parameters in the form of unique files. To get the queue depth for a drive, you can look at the file named queue_depth. For example:

```
$ ls /sys/bus/scsi/devices/0:0:1:0
block          device_blocked model queue_depth scsi_level timeout  vendor
detach_state generic          power rev          state      type

$ cat /sys/bus/scsi/devices/0:0:1:0/queue_depth
32
```

Translating this directory name (0:0:1:0) into SCSI jargon, you are looking at host 0, channel 0, device 1, and logical unit 0. The queue depth is 32, which in this case is in decimal. This structure and format are the same for all drives, regardless of the driver. This is an improvement over procfs, but what if you don't know the SCSI device ID of a particular drive? Suppose that you want to verify the queue depth of the SCSI drive mapped to block device /dev/sda. In this case, you don't need to know anything about the SCSI device information. All you need to know is the block device name. Use the following command:

```
$ cat /sys/block/sda/device/queue_depth
32
```

The directory /sys/bus/scsi/devices/0:0:1:0 and the directory /sys/block/sda/device are both symbolic links to a common directory. This technique is used in many places in the sysfs file system. It allows you to look at the system from many points of view.

All this is available whether you have an Adaptec SCSI controller, LSI, or whatever. The data will be in the same place and in the same format all the time.

What Makes sysfs Unique?

Consider at a small example of just how easy it is to use sysfs. For this book, I used this trivial module to keep track of the internal clocks as I fiddled with various kernels, because there is no system call to get this information.

hz.c

```
#include "linux/module.h"
// Store the USER_HZ macro in a variable
int user_hz=USER_HZ;

// Store the HZ macro in a variable
int hz=HZ;

// This is all it takes to make it visible in /sys!!!
// I specify the name, the type and file permissions.
module_param(user_hz,int,0444);
module_param(hz,int,0444);
```

The Makefile for this module is equally trivial, thanks to the 2.6 build system.

```
Makefile:
    all::
        make -C /lib/modules/`uname -r`/build M=`pwd`    modules

        obj-m+=hz.o
```

To build and install this module, I type the following command:

```
$ make
$ insmod ./hz.ko
```

Now comes the interesting part. I can look at these variables from user space with a simple cat command:

```
$ cat /sys/module/hz/parameters/hz
1000
$ cat /sys/module/hz/parameters/user_hz
100
```

So I have a useful module in about four lines of code. Not bad.

5.4.4   Devices and I/O

Normally, before any data can touch your application buffers, it must pass through kernel space. A typical read from a device, for example, results in the data being copied at least twice—once to a kernel buffer and then once again to your user buffer. This is the price we pay for reliability and security. To prevent one process from crashing the kernel or crashing other processes, all input and output must be handled by the kernel, which acts as the security checkpoint.

This might come as a surprise to some of you, considering that UNIX and Linux are viewed as being high-performance operating systems. In fact, as you shall see, the extra copying is to your advantage. Understanding the rules and reasons for this can help you use I/O most efficiently.

5.4.4.1   I/O and Character Devices

For a slow serial port, the extra time required for copying is insignificant. For high-speed devices, these extra copies can be a serious performance issue.

For custom hardware, the character device is often the driver of choice because it is the most straightforward. Reads and writes are synchronous, which means that typically when the process calls `read` or `write`, it blocks and does not return from the system call until the operation is complete.[16] When you write to a character device, the driver may copy the data directly from your user-space buffer to the device. This means that the driver cannot allow you to continue until it is finished with that memory. Your process blocks, waiting for the write to complete. Time waiting for the device is time you could spend executing code, so this usually is undesirable. I can illustrate this with the `/dev/tty` device, which is a character device representing the current terminal, as follows:

```
$ time dd if=/dev/zero of=/dev/tty count=1000
1000+0 records in
1000+0 records out

real    0m0.442s
user    0m0.000s
sys     0m0.020s
```

I just wrote a bunch of NULs to the terminal, which does nothing to the terminal except consume time. Here, you can see that the command took 442 ms to execute but spent only 20 ms of CPU time. Where did all the time go? It was spent waiting for the driver (blocking). What little CPU time the process consumed was used by the driver (listed here as `sys`).

---

16. It's a little more subtle than that, but this is the default behavior of most character devices.

The terminal, like the serial port, is a streaming device. Random access on a streaming device is not possible. So the read and write system calls are the only ones you can use to interact with this device.

Devices that allow random access often support the mmap system call. This allows an application to see all the data the device has to offer as one big region of memory. A character device driver can support mmap exclusively and not allow read and write calls. When a driver does not support mmap, the system call returns with a value of MAP_FAILED, and errno is set to ENODEV.

With mmap, reading and writing from the device is almost as simple as allocating a large block of memory. With a character device, using mmap allows you to access the data with fewer system calls, because you don't need to call read or write to manipulate the data. This is especially important when you're working with large amounts of data (see the sidebar "A Simple mmap Example").

5.4.4.2   Block Devices, File Systems, and I/O

Block devices are the basis for disks and other storage devices that can use a file system. For this reason, you can access a block device in two ways: directly or through a file system. Often, the only time you use a block device directly is when you partition it or create a file system.

A file system can be created on any block device or partition of a block device. The floppy driver is unique in that it does not allow partitioning, although the floppy media can support partitions. Instead of partitions, the minor numbers used by the floppy driver enumerate the many flavors of floppy drives that have come and gone over the life of the PC. Most of them don't exist anymore, but the support is there if you need it.[17]

To create a file system, you can use the mkfs command and specify the file-system type with the -t option. To format a floppy disk that you can use with Windows, for example, you can type

```
$ mkfs -t vfat /dev/fd0
```

mkfs is a wrapper that calls a file system–specific helper program. In this case, it calls mkfs.vfat, which you can call directly if you want. Most file systems support

---

17. Refer to the fd(4) man page.

A Simple mmap Example

The following code snippet shows the basic usage of mmap. It helps to think of it as a memory allocation like `malloc`, which is how the GNU standard C library implements many `malloc` calls.

```c
#include <stdio.h>
#include <stdlib.h>
#include <string.h>
#include <unistd.h>
#include <sys/file.h>
#include <sys/mman.h>

#define ERROR(x) do { perror(x);\
    exit(EXIT_FAILURE); } while(0)

int main(int argc, char *argv[])
{
  const int nbytes = 4096;
  void *ptr;

  int fd = open("/dev/zero", O_RDWR);
  if (fd == -1) ERROR("open");

  /* /dev/zero allocates memory on our behalf. */
  ptr = mmap(0, nbytes, PROT_READ | PROT_WRITE,
             MAP_PRIVATE, fd, 0);
  if (ptr == MAP_FAILED) ERROR("mmap");

  /* We are free to use it just like a malloc call. */
  memset(ptr, 1, nbytes);

  /* Equivalent of free() */
  munmap(ptr,nbytes);

  return 0;
}
```

In this example, I use /dev/zero to do the mmap. You may recall that /dev/zero is a character device that returns buffers of zeros, but another feature is that mmap calls to /dev/zero will allocate memory for you. You could get the same thing by using the MAP_ANONYMOUS flag, which does not use the file descriptor at all.

To support the mmap system call, a device must be able to allow random access. This rules out streaming character devices. All block devices can support mmap.

multiple options when they are created, and the most common file-system options are documented in the mkfs(8) man page. More up-to-date details for a specific file system, such as mkfs.vfat(8), are available in the helper program's man page.

When the block device has a file system, it can be mounted on a directory with the mount command:

```
$ mount -t vfat /dev/fd0 /mnt/floppy
```

Usually, the mount command can figure out what kind of file system is on the device, so the -t option is optional. After the block device is mounted, you can look at it in two ways: through the device node (for example, /dev/fd0) or through its mount point (for example, /mnt/floppy). Reading from the device node will give you raw data that includes everything in the file system and then some. This may seem useless, but you can do useful things with it. One idea is to use it for archiving. It's usually a very inefficient method for archiving a file system, but dumping the raw device saves data that an archive utility like tar cannot. Although tar can create an archive of every file and directory in the file system with all the metadata preserved, it cannot save the boot block, which is not part of the file system. To get an exact copy of every byte on a floppy, including the boot block, you need to copy the data from the device node. For example:

```
$ cp /dev/fd0 floppy.img
```

Note that what gets copied is the data in the device, not the device node. This is a unique property of device nodes. This technique is used to copy bootable floppy images that are used more often these days to create bootable CDs than they are for floppies. If this were a hard disk, copying the entire block device would preserve the partition tables and master boot record (if any).

As mentioned earlier, this is not an efficient way to archive data. The block device has no idea how much data is valid and how much is empty space. Only the file system knows that. As a result, every floppy image will be 1,440K, regardless of how many files are on the disk. An archive, on the other hand, will contain only the files in use, so potentially, it can be much smaller.

5.4.4.3   The Role of the Buffer Cache and File-System Cache

One way block devices differ from character devices is that they use system memory as cache. Linux supports many generic caches through data structures in memory, but the most interesting to application programmers are the buffer cache and the file-system cache.[18]

The *buffer cache* is the storage used for blocks written and read from block devices. When a process writes to a block device, the data is first copied to a block in the buffer cache. The block driver is not actually called until the kernel determines that it is time to write the block to the device, which may be some time later. The kernel saves a copy of each block read and written in the buffer cache for as long as possible. For physical devices, such as disks, it means that the data may not make it to the disk for some time after the write occurs. The advantage of this is that the data is available for any process that wants to read from that section of the disk later. The disadvantage is that if the system crashes or loses power before the data is written to the device, the data is lost.

Caching improves performance in several ways. One way is that by keeping data in memory, the system avoids rereading from devices such as disk drives, which are many orders of magnitude slower than the memory. It also allows the kernel to coalesce adjacent blocks of data written to cache into a single large disk write instead of several small ones, which usually makes more efficient use of the disk. The cache also cuts down on redundant writes to disk, because if a block is updated before it is written to disk, the kernel needs to perform only one write to disk instead of two. All this comes at the cost of extra copies, which in many applications is insignificant compared with the time that could be lost due to inefficient use of the disk.

The file-system cache works exactly the same way as the buffer cache except that the data is managed by the file-system driver. Data written to the disk is copied to the file-system cache before it is written to the disk. Likewise, the kernel will try to read data from the file-system cache before it reads from disk, and every read from disk is copied to the file-system cache.

The beauty of this is that it all takes place without any intervention from the application programmer or the device-driver writer. Linux uses the same mechanisms for all block drivers and file systems, and consumes any unused memory for use as cache. So if you have gigabytes of memory in your system but few processes, you usually can rest assured that the extra memory is being put to good use.

---

18. Most disk drives include a hardware cache, but this is effectively invisible to the Linux kernel.

You can see the cache in action with the `vmstat` command:

```
$ vmstat
procs -----------memory---------- ...
 r  b   swpd   free  buff  cache
 1  0      0  93412  5736  38096
```

Write 4MB to the ramdisk.
```
$ dd if=/dev/zero of=/dev/ram0 bs=1k count=4096
4096+0 records in
4096+0 records out
```

```
$ vmstat
procs -----------memory---------- ...
 r  b   swpd   free  buff  cache
 0  0      0  89272  9832  38096
```
4MB is added to the buffers.

The `vmstat` command provides more information, but for now, I'll focus on the memory information.[19] Here, I copied 4MB from `/dev/zero` (a character device) into the `ramdisk` device `/dev/ram0` (a block device). Because I am interacting directly with the block device, it must allocate storage from the buffer cache to accommodate the writes. You can see that in the `vmstat` output, the size of the buffer cache went from 5,736K to 9,832K—an increase of exactly 4,096K. One feature of the `ramdisk` device is that once it allocates memory, that memory is never freed, which is why the buffers continue to show up in the buffer cache. Not all block devices do this.

In the following example, you see what happens when you put a file system on this device and mount it:

```
$ mkfs -t ext2 /dev/ram0                Create the file system.
mke2fs 1.37 (21-Mar-2005)
Filesystem label=
OS type: Linux
Block size=1024 (log=0)
Fragment size=1024 (log=0)
4096 inodes, 16384 blocks
...
```

---

19. See also `free(1)`, which is part of the same `procps` package. Also see `/proc/meminfo`.

```
$ vmstat                                    Get a baseline for cache usage.
procs -----------memory----------
  r  b   swpd   free   buff   cache
  1  0      0  88792  10164   38272


$ mount /dev/ram0 /mnt/tmp                  Mount the file system.

$ vmstat                                    There is no significant increase in cache usage.
procs -----------memory----------
  r  b   swpd   free   buff   cache
  0  0      0  88792  10168   38272
                                            Create a 2MB file in the file system.
$ dd if=/dev/zero of=/mnt/tmp/zero.dat bs=1k count=2048
2048+0 records in
2048+0 records out

$ vmstat                                    File-system cache usage goes up by roughly that amount.
procs -----------memory----------
  r  b   swpd   free   buff   cache
  1  0      0  86572  10200   40324
```

Notice that when you create the 2MB file in the file system, the file-system cache size (listed as cache) increases by 2,052K, which is just slightly more than the 2,048K you created. The "free" memory decreases by about this amount as well. Notice also that the buffer cache is virtually unchanged—an increase of only 32K. Keep in mind that cache numbers are not static, so the results are not always exact. Another factor is that the file system requires additional space to store file-system information on the disk, which increases the numbers slightly.

The file that you created will sit in the cache until one of the following things happens:

- It is kicked out by newer data in the cache.

- The file is deleted.

- The file system is unmounted.

- The kernel flushes it to free memory for processes.

- An application explicitly flushes the data with sync or fdatasync.

Until one of these events occurs, the data is not written to disk.

One thing I haven't emphasized so far is that the caches contend with processes for system memory. From the point of view of a process, the buffer cache and file-system cache are free memory, because they can be flushed to make room for more process memory. A system that is doing intensive I/O operations can consume most of system memory as buffer cache or file-system cache. If processes request more memory than is currently free, the system must free up space somehow. To free up memory, the kernel can reclaim cache by flushing blocks.

Under normal circumstances, the kernel will take space from the cache by flushing the oldest blocks to disk. Blocks that belong to a file on disk can be written to disk and the memory reclaimed by the kernel. So-called clean blocks can be reclaimed immediately without any disk I/O. A *clean block* is one that has been read from disk and not modified, or one that has been written to disk but not reclaimed. Likewise, a *dirty block* is one that has been modified (or created), and the changes have not yet been written to disk.

---

ramdisk versus tmpfs

One feature of the `ramdisk` device is that it does not allow its memory to be reclaimed, so `ramdisk` blocks will always consume free memory until the system is rebooted. Because the blocks it consumes from the buffer cache are never returned to the system, a `ramdisk` device cannot be resized or removed. This allows you to unmount and remount the `ramdisk` without losing any data.

A disadvantage of this is that when you create a file system on a `ramdisk` device, it consumes both buffer cache and file-system cache, so in theory, it can consume twice as much RAM as a disk file system. Instead of the `ramdisk` device, most applications that require temporary storage in RAM use the `tmpfs` file system.

The `tmpfs` file system is unique in that it does not require a block device for storage. The data in a `tmpfs` file system exists entirely in the file-system cache. This memory is also allowed to swap, so you can get the benefits of a high-speed RAM disk and the flexibility of virtual memory at the same time.

`tmpfs` is the default file system for the shared memory device (`/dev/shm`) in virtually all distributions.

5.4.4.4 How the Kernel Manages the File-System Cache

Normally, the kernel relies on user processes to execute much of the code required for system maintenance. This is unreliable for things that must occur on a periodic basis, which is why most systems have daemon processes that run in the background for critical functions. One such daemon is `pdflush`, which is responsible for making sure that data does not sit in the cache too long without being written to disk.

Suppose that you have an idle system, and you write 1MB of data to a file. This results in 1MB of dirty cache blocks in memory. If the system remains idle, this data could sit in memory indefinitely. This situation is undesirable, because a power failure or system crash could result in lost data or data corruption of your physical media. To prevent this from happening, `pdflush` executes periodically and writes all the dirty cache blocks to the block device within a certain amount of time. This interval defaults to 30 seconds in most Linux distributions.

Kernel Threads

One unique aspect of the `pdflush` daemon is that technically, it is not a process but a kernel thread. Recall that a process lives in two worlds, so to speak: user space and kernel space. A *kernel thread* is a process that has no user space and runs entirely in kernel space. Because it has no user space, the code for a kernel thread must reside entirely in the kernel. Unlike a user-space daemon, which typically is executed by the `init` process from an executable file on disk, a kernel thread is started directly by the kernel via functions defined in the kernel and has no executable file.

Kernel threads look and behave like ordinary processes, but their lack of user space gives them away. One simple way to detect a kernel thread is to look at `/proc/PID/maps`, which in a normal process shows its virtual memory map. Because it has no user space, a kernel thread's `maps` file will always be empty.

Blocks may be written to the device earlier by the kernel when it needs to free up memory. In this case, buffers are reclaimed oldest first—or, more specifically, "least recently used." Because dirty blocks are more likely to be recently used, it's unlikely that the kernel will flush these blocks, but in systems that are doing lots of I/O, it is possible. In this case, `pdflush` may never need to do anything. When this happens, the job of writing the dirty buffers to disk is done by the currently running process.

Applications can also force the blocks of a particular file to be written early via the `fsync`, `fdatasync`, and `sync` system calls. The `sync` command allows users to call the `sync` system call from the shell. These system calls allow applications (or users) to exert more control over the file-system cache by forcing disk I/O to occur at a particular time rather than wait until the `pdflush` daemon runs.

5.5   The I/O Scheduler

An important final piece of I/O management is the I/O scheduler. When blocks are written to or read from a device, the requests are placed in a queue to be completed later. Each block device has its own queue. The I/O scheduler is responsible for keeping these queues sorted to make the most efficient use of the media. On a disk drive, this is very important, because it can cut down on excessive head movement, which is one of the most time-consuming operations in any system. Even on other media, such as flash drive, ordering the I/O operations makes the most efficient use of the device.

The default I/O scheduling algorithm in Linux is called an *elevator* algorithm because the problem of scheduling reads and writes to a disk is very similar to scheduling stops on an elevator. Disk drive heads move back and forth across tracks in much the same way that an elevator moves up and down in a building. Just as an elevator stops on various floors to pick up or drop off passengers, the drive head stops on cylinders to read or write data. The scheduling problem is the same for both. If requests are handled simply in the order in which they come in, the result will be very inefficient use of the hardware.

Figure 5-7 shows a hypothetical example of a head moving across a disk. In this example the head starts at track 8, then moves to track 6 and then moves back to track 8 again. The total amount of head movement is shown as a dashed line. Figure 5-8 shows the same I/O operations after sorting with an elevator algorithm. The dashed line illustrates how this cuts down the amount of head travel dramatically.

For this to work, the kernel must force some I/O requests to wait so as to make most effective use of the disk. The kernel must decide how many requests it will queue up before it starts to execute them. There is no ideal solution to this problem, which is why Linux offers several different algorithms for queuing I/O.

5.5.1   The Linus Elevator (aka noop)

Before 2.4, there was only one I/O scheduler, sometimes called the Linus Elevator. This scheduler sorts I/O requests like an elevator, and as new requests come in, it merges contiguous requests so that it can keep requests from the same part of the media together. Requests that can't be merged with one of the existing I/O requests are placed in the back of the queue.

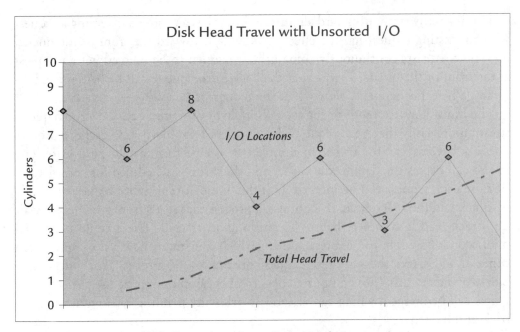

FIGURE 5-7 Unsorted I/O Operations Cause Extra Head Movement

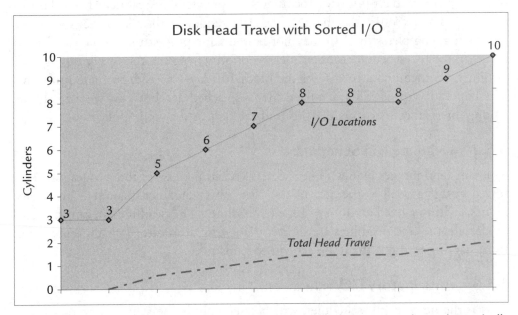

FIGURE 5-8 Sorting I/O Operations (Elevator Algorithm) Reduces Head Travel Drastically

This is a fairly straightforward algorithm, but it has a problem: Merging a request with an existing request has the effect of moving it toward the front of the queue. So if new requests continuously come in that happen to be merged with a request at the front of the queue, a request at the back of the queue can be held off indefinitely. When this happens, we say that the request is *starved.*

The Linus Elevator tends to starve reads in favor of writes, because write requests stream more easily than read requests do. Thanks to the file-system cache, a process does not have to wait for a write to complete before performing the next write. The write call copies the data to the cache, and the write is scheduled for completion. Because each request can be merged with the one before it, write requests can pile up quickly in the I/O queue. By contrast, a process that reads from a file has to wait until each read is complete before it can do another read. There could be several milliseconds between read requests, during which time many new write requests can come in and starve the next read request. In this way, a process that writes large blocks of data to disk (not an unusual occurrence) can monopolize the device. Large writes will be merged, which can effectively push any pending read requests to the back of the queue.

It may seem odd, but a process's priority has no impact on where its requests go in the I/O queue. A high-priority process gets no preferential treatment from the I/O scheduler. The reason is that because the data resides in the file-system cache, the process that completes the I/O may not be the same process that wrote the data to cache. So the I/O scheduler cannot infer the priority from the currently running task.

Linux 2.6 included a rewrite of the block I/O layer to address these problems. The Linus Elevator is still available as the noop scheduler, but now you can choose among three other I/O schedulers to find the best fit for your application.

5.5.2   Deadline I/O Scheduler

This sorts and merges requests like the noop scheduler except that requests are also sorted by age as well as the area of the disk. This scheduler guarantees to service requests within a fixed amount of time (a deadline). The deadlines are tunable, and by default, the read deadlines are shorter than write deadlines. This prevents writes from starving reads, as the noop scheduler tends to do.

5.5.3   Anticipatory I/O Scheduler

This is the new default scheduler, which essentially is the same as the deadline scheduler except that it waits 6 ms after the last read before continuing with other

I/O requests. In this way, it *anticipates* a new read request coming from the application. This improves read performance at the expense of some write performance.

5.5.4   Complete Fair Queuing I/O Scheduler

This is the newest I/O scheduler to be added to the kernel. It gives I/O requests a priority, much the same way that the processes have. The I/O priority of the request is independent of the process priority, so reads and writes from a high priority process do not automatically inherit high I/O priority.

5.5.5   Selecting an I/O Scheduler

In Linux 2.4 and early versions of 2.6, you could choose only one scheduler for all I/O queues, and this scheduler had to be selected at boot time via the `elevator` boot parameter. This is passed as a boot parameter to the kernel (typically in `lilo.conf` or `grub.conf`). Valid values at this writing are listed in Table 5-7 and can be found in `Documentation/kernel-parameters.txt`.

In later versions of 2.6, it is no longer necessary to use the `elevator` option at boot time. Now you can choose the scheduler for each block device and change it on the fly. The current scheduler in use for each block device is listed in `/sys/block/{device}/queue/scheduler`. For example:

```
$ cat /sys/block/hdb/queue/scheduler
noop [anticipatory] deadline cfq
```

TABLE 5-7   I/O Schedulers Available in Linux 2.6

Parameter	Description
`noop`	The Linus Elevator from Linux 2.4 and earlier. Requests are sorted and new requests are merged to minimize disk seeks.
`deadline`	Similar to `noop` except that it enforces a deadline for I/O to complete.
`as`	Anticipatory I/O scheduler; same as `deadline` except that reads are followed by a 6 ms pause.
`cfq`	Complete Fair Queuing scheduler; same as `deadline` except that I/O requests have a priority, much like a process.

In this case, device `hdb` is using the anticipatory I/O scheduler. You can change the scheduler for that device by writing a different value to the file. To change the scheduler to the `cfq` scheduler, for example, you would use the following command:

```
$ echo cfq > /sys/block/hdb/queue/scheduler
```

The choice of scheduler is based on the application. Real-time applications working with disks will want the `deadline` or `cfq` scheduler. An embedded system working with RAM and flash devices, however, might do just fine with the `noop` scheduler.

5.6   Memory Management in User Space

One of the nice things about a protected memory operating system like Linux is the fact that programmers don't need to be concerned about things like where their code is located in memory or, for that matter where the memory comes from. Everything falls into place with no intervention from the programmer. Most programmers don't appreciate just how much goes on behind the scenes in the kernel, in the libraries, and in the startup code.

This section focuses on 32-bit processors, which present unique challenges for applications that work with large data sets. At this writing, 32-bit processors are the most common platforms for running Linux. For 64-bit processors, the problems are the same, but the boundaries change. The boundaries with 64-bit architectures are large enough that most of the challenges encountered in 32-bit processors become moot for the foreseeable future.

5.6.1   Virtual Memory Explained

The core concept behind *virtual memory* is that the memory addresses used by your code have nothing to do with the physical location of the data. The data in your application may not be in physical memory at all but may be saved to disk *(swapped)* to allow some other process to have memory. What looks like a block of contiguous data in virtual memory is most likely scattered in pieces in various locations in physical memory or perhaps on the swap disk. This is illustrated in Figure 5-9.

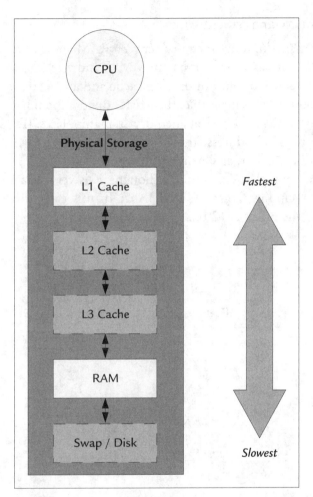

FIGURE 5-9   Physical Storage as Seen by the Processor

Using virtual memory allows Linux to provide each process its own unique data, protected from other processes. Each process runs as though it were the only process on the machine. In user space, address A of one process points to a different physical memory location than address A of another process. Any time the CPU issues a load or store to memory, the virtual address used by software must be translated into a physical address. The job of translating virtual addresses into physical addresses belongs to the *Memory Management Unit* (MMU).

5.6.1.1   The Role of the Memory Management Unit

The MMU works closely with the caches to move memory between RAM and cache as required. In general, if your processor has a cache, it has an MMU, and vice versa. All modern desktop processors have some amount of on-chip cache and an MMU.

To make the job of translating addresses manageable, the MMU divides memory into pages, which are the smallest units of physical memory it manipulates. To translate a virtual address into a physical address, the MMU breaks it into two pieces: the page frame number and the offset, as illustrated in Figure 5-10.

The size of a page is determined by each architecture, although 4K is very common among many architectures, including PowerPC and IA32. In this case, the page frame number is 20 bits, and the offset is 12 bits.

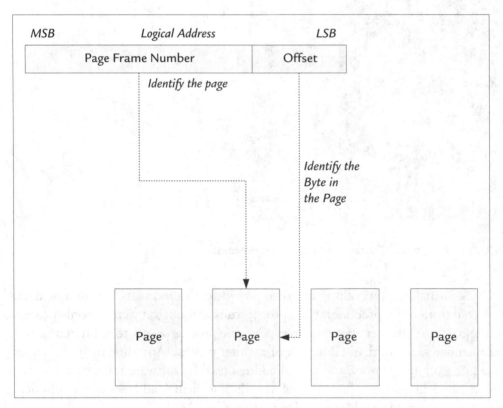

FIGURE 5-10   Logical Address Broken into a Page Frame Number and Offset

Given the page frame number, the MMU can determine the physical address of the page by using a *page table,* which is created by the kernel. The offset taken from the virtual address is added to the physical address of the page to produce a complete physical address.

Every time the processor issues a load or store instruction, the virtual address is translated by the MMU. If the MMU does not find an address in the page table, the result is called a *page fault.* This can happen when a page is not located in memory or when the process uses an invalid logical address. If the page fault is caused by an invalid address, the kernel sends the process a *segmentation violation* signal (SIGSEGV). Page faults also can occur when the requested page has been swapped to disk. In this case, the kernel must use the disk device to retrieve the page into physical memory and update the page table to point to the new physical location.

Page faults that involve disk I/O are what Linux calls *major* page faults. Linux also keeps track of what it calls *minor* page faults, which occur when the requested page is in physical RAM but not in on-chip cache. In this case, the system incurs some small latency caused by the time it takes to move the page from RAM to cache, but because it is handled entirely in hardware, the page fault is considered to be minor.

This discussion is a bit oversimplified, because each architecture adds various twists to this design, but it is the basic way most processors work. Fortunately, a complete understanding of the MMU is not necessary for application programming.

5.6.1.2   The Translation Lookaside Buffer

Because every process on the system has its own virtual addresses, each process must have a unique page table. An important part of the context switch from one process to another involves changing the page tables to point to the appropriate virtual memory. It's actually very sophisticated, but I'll explain some of the details.

Any time the CPU accesses memory, the MMU must translate the address using the page tables before it can complete the operation, but page tables are stored in memory as well. That means that in the worst case, every load or store can require two memory transactions: a read from the page table followed by the actual load or store.

If the page tables were stored exclusively in memory, this would bring the system to a crawl. Page tables can get quite large, and there is no upper limit on the number of processes an operating system can support, so storing the page tables entirely on chip is not an option either.

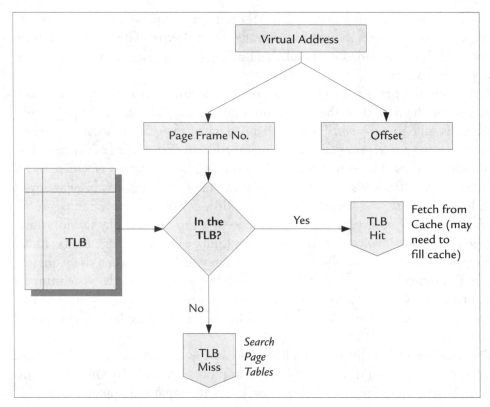

FIGURE 5-11   TLB Lookup Flow Chart

As a compromise, the CPU keeps a cache of page table entries called the *Translation Lookaside Buffer* (TLB). The TLB makes it possible for a process to operate on a large region of memory while keeping the critical address translation information on chip. The TLB needs to be large enough to cover the entire CPU cache. So a processor with 512K of cache and a page size of 4K needs 128 TLB entries to be effective. Figure 5-11 shows an example of how the processor translates a virtual address using the TLB.

Because the TLB contains a cache of page table entries from the running process, you might expect that it is flushed when a context switch occurs. Flushing and refilling the TLB is expensive, however, so the kernel avoids flushing the TLB at all costs to keep the context switch time low. This is sometimes called *lazy TLB flushing*. This is feasible because kernel virtual memory is common to all processes, so it is possible to reuse the kernel portion of the TLB from one process to the next. This is particularly

useful in a preemptable kernel, where the kernel can switch from one process in kernel mode to another process in kernel mode. Avoiding the TLB flush until the last
possible moment gives the kernel opportunities to avoid unnecessary TLB flushes.

5.6.1.3   The CPU Cache

Because the speed of processors has far outstripped the speed of DRAM devices, all
modern processors have some amount of cache memory to allow the processors to
run at high clock rates without being slowed by the RAM devices. Creating memory that can run at gigahertz clock frequencies consumes many transistors and a
great deal of power. To compromise, many designs include several levels of cache, as
shown in Figure 5-9 earlier in this chapter.

   The cache closest to the processor is called the *L1 cache,* which resides on the chip
and usually is relatively small (8K to 32K is common) but runs with zero latency.
That means that a load or store to these memory locations can be completed in only
one clock cycle. Stated another way, the L1 cache runs as fast as the CPU. On some
architectures, this may be the only cache that the processor has. Some low-cost versions of the x86 processors, for example, implement only an L1 cache.

   To increase the cache size, many architectures include additional levels that are
larger but progressively slower. The *L2 cache* is the next level and is larger than the
L1 cache but has some latency that will cause a load or store instruction to take
more than one clock cycle. In older designs, the L1 cache resided on chip, whereas
the L2 cache lived outside—on the motherboard or on a daughter card.[20] External
cache invariably runs slower than the internal clock of the CPU. As CPUs got faster,
it became more difficult to have fast-enough cache outside the CPU, so most high-
performance processors include both L1 and L2 cache on the chip. The on-chip L2
cache may or may not be slower than the L1 cache, but there surely is a latency
penalty for using it—that is, delays are incurred on certain address boundaries.
Some vendors claim that their L2 cache runs at the same frequency as the CPU,
which may be true. What they don't tell you is that the cache cannot run continuously at that frequency—only in bursts. Otherwise, it would be an L1 cache.

   When the L2 cache moved on chip, chipmakers invented the term *L3 cache* to
refer to cache memory that resides outside the chip. Recently, Intel has begun to
integrate L3 cache into its Xeon processors. Perhaps this trend will continue, and
we'll see systems with L4 and L5 caches in the future.

---

20. The first Pentium II processors came on a daughter card that included L2 cache.

A full discussion of cache is beyond the scope of this book, and fortunately, most programmers don't need to know much about cache beyond the basics. The following sections discuss the basic concepts that you should know about.

Cache Lines

The CPU never reads or writes bytes or even words from DRAM. Every read or write from the CPU to DRAM must first go into L1 cache, which reads or writes to the DRAM in units of lines. The cache line is the unit of all cache transactions with the DRAM. Although a typical virtual-memory page may be 4K, a typical cache line is on the order of 32 or 64 bytes. Both the page size and the cache line size are unique to the make and model of the processor in use.

Figure 5-12 shows a simplified flow chart of how this works. To execute a simple line of code that reads a single byte from memory, the CPU may end up reading an entire cache line (perhaps 64 bytes). If subsequent instructions also read from the same line of cache, the line fill was worthwhile; otherwise, the extra cycles spent filling the cache line were wasted. An L1 cache miss isn't always that costly, either. It is possible that the data is in L2 or L3 cache, in which case the fill is much faster than reading from RAM. Usually, the memory on the motherboard is laid out so that a burst from the DRAM is the same size as the cache line. This way, cache line fills from RAM are as efficient as possible.

Even if the code in Figure 5-12 were writing to memory, the flow would be exactly the same—that is, to write a single byte of memory you have to fill the entire cache line. When it's time to write this line of cache back to memory, the CPU will write the entire line even if only 1 byte was changed.

This is the safe way to proceed, but it is inefficient. If, for example, the application is going to overwrite a large block of data, the CPU will need to fill every cache line before modifying it. The cycles spent filling the cache lines are a waste of time, because the lines are only going to be overwritten. For this reason, most processors have assembly-language instructions to instruct the processor to skip the cache line fill because you plan to overwrite it. Unfortunately, there is no portable way to include these instructions in your high-level language code.[21] This is one justifiable use of inline assembly in your application.

---

21. POSIX has the `madvise` function, which can cause the processor to fill in advance, but there is no way to tell it to skip the fill.

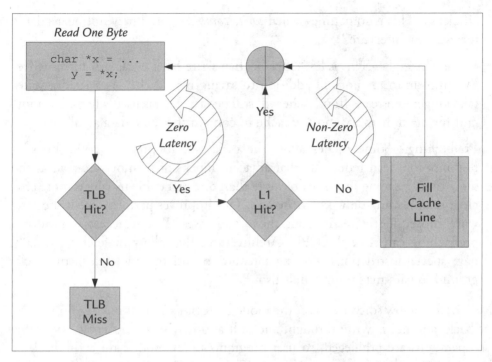

FIGURE 5-12   Cache Miss: Reading a Single Byte Can Cause a Cache Line Fill

This may seem like nitpicking when you are working with processors that run at 3GHz, but the extra clock cycles add up, particularly if you are using large amounts of data.

Write Back, Write Through, and Prefetching

Caches have different modes of operation, and each CPU architecture has its own idiosyncrasies. The basic modes that they have in common are

Write Back—This is the highest-performance mode and the most typical. In write-back mode, the cache is not written to memory until a newer cache entry flushes it out or the software explicitly flushes it. This enhances performance because the CPU can avoid extra writes to memory when a line of cache is modified more than once. Also, although cache lines may be written in random order, they may be flushed in sequential order, which may improve efficiency. This is sometimes called *write combining* and may not be available for every architecture.[22]

Write Through—This is less efficient than write-back because it forces writes to complete to memory in addition to saving it in cache. As a result, writes take longer, but reads from cache will still be fast. This is used when it's important for main memory and the cache to contain the same data at all times.

Prefetching—Some caches allow the processor to prefetch cache lines in response to a read request so that adjacent blocks of memory are read at the same time. Reading in a burst of more than one cache line usually is more efficient than reading only one cache line. This improves performance if the software subsequently reads from those addresses. But if access is random, prefetching can slow the CPU. Architectures that allow prefetching usually have special instructions allowing software to initiate a prefetch in the background to gain maximum parallelism.[23]

Most caches allow software to set the mode by regions so that one region may be write-back, another is write-through, and still another is noncacheable. Typically, these operations are privileged, so user programs never modify the write-back or write-through modes of the cache directly. This kind of control usually is required only by device drivers.

5.6.1.4   Programming Cache Hints

Prefetching can be controlled by software through so-called cache hints with the `madvise` function. This API allows you to tell the operating system how you plan to use a block of memory. There are no guarantees that the operating system will take your advice, but when it does, it can improve performance, given the right circumstances. To tell the OS that prefetching would be a good idea, you would use this pattern:

```
madvise( pointer, size, MADV_WILLNEED | MADV_SEQUENTIAL);
```

---

22. Write combining is similar to merging I/O requests in the I/O scheduler discussed earlier in the chapter.
23. Some newer BIOSes allow you to enable or disable cache line prefetching at the system level.

These two flags tell the OS that you will be using the memory shortly and that you will be doing sequential access. Prefetching can be a liability if you are accessing data in a random fashion, so the same API allows you to tell the OS that prefetching is a bad idea. For example:

```
madvise( pointer, size, MADV_RANDOM );
```

The `madvise` function has other flags to suggest that flushing or syncing would be a good idea, but the `msync` function usually is more appropriate for this purpose.

5.6.1.5   Memory Coherency

Memory coherency refers to the unique problem that multiprocessor systems have in keeping their caches up to date. When one processor modifies a memory location in cache, the second processor will not see it until that cache is written back to memory. In theory, if the second processor reads that location, it will get the incorrect value. In reality, modern processors have elaborate mechanisms in hardware to ensure that this doesn't happen. Under normal circumstances, this is transparent to software, particularly in user space. In a *Symmetric Multiprocessing System (SMP),* the hardware is responsible for keeping the cache coherent between CPUs.

Even in a single-processor system, memory coherency can be an issue because some peripheral hardware can take the place of other processors. Any hardware that can access system memory via *Direct Memory Access (DMA)* can read or write memory without the processor's knowledge. Most PCI cards, for example, have DMA controllers. When a controller writes to system memory via DMA, there is a chance that some of those locations are sitting in the CPU cache. If so, the data in cache will be invalid. Likewise, if the necessary data is sitting in cache when a device reads from memory via DMA, the device will get the wrong data. It is the job of the operating system (typically, a device driver) to manage the DMA transfers and the cache to prevent this. If the device driver allows `mmap`, it may be up to the application to manage the memory coherency.

When the data in cache is older than the data in memory, we say that it is *stale.* If the software initiates a DMA transfer from a device to RAM, the software must tell the CPU that the cached entries must be discarded. On some systems, this is called *invalidating* the cache entries.

When the data in cache is newer than the data in RAM, we say that it is *dirty*. Before a device driver can allow a device to read from memory via DMA, it must make sure that all dirty entries are written to memory. This is called *flushing* or *synchronizing* the cache.

Fortunately, most application programmers are shielded from cache-coherency problems by the hardware and the operating system. Only specific drivers may present this problem to the application when it uses the mmap system call. One example is a memory-mapped file. If a process makes a shared mapping of a file, changes to that file are not reflected immediately to other processes. The process must synchronize the memory explicitly with the file before other processes can see its changes.

For this reason, POSIX provides the msync function, which allows the application to do the equivalent of a flush or invalidate. To update the file with the changes in memory (that is, flush), use the following pattern:

```
msync( ptr, size, MS_SYNC );
```

The MS_SYNC flag indicates that the msync operation should complete before the msync function returns. Without this flag, the operation will be scheduled by the operating system but may not be complete when the function returns.

This synchronization is between the currently running process and the file on disk. Other processes may have copies of the data in memory, which will be out of sync. To make sure that other processes invalidate these copies, msync provides the MS_INVALIDATE flag. This flag tells the kernel to make sure that any *other* process that has mapped this particular file will invalidate its pages so that the next access to the data will read from the file and update the data in memory.

5.6.1.6   The Role of Swap

Adding swap space has the effect of adding more memory to your system. The idea is that much of the memory allocated by processes is not needed most of the time. With this in mind, it makes sense to remove these blocks of memory from DRAM and store them temporarily on disk so that you can free up the DRAM for other uses. When the memory is needed again, the data can be read from disk and placed back in memory, while perhaps another unused block of memory is removed from memory and put on disk. The two blocks of memory swap places, which is where the name *swap* comes from. Programmers often use the word *swap* as both a noun and a verb. We call the region of the disk used to store these pages the *swap* space, but *swap* is also the word we use to describe the operation of moving data to and from the swap partition. In operating system circles, *swap* is never used as a verb. The action of moving data from memory to the swap partition is simply called *paging*.

Paging occurs in the background with no intervention from the application. The application experiences only the side effect of increased latency, which is the technical way to say that everything slows down. Determining the appropriate swap size for your system is more art than science. The rule of thumb used to be to allocate twice as much swap as DRAM. Depending on the application and the amount of RAM you have, you may not need that much swap. Most systems should have a swap partition, but some systems can function without a swap partition. Most embedded Linux devices have no swap partition at all, for example.

One problem that occurs with swap is called *thrashing*, which occurs when several running processes are simultaneously accessing more memory than is physically available. The system must swap pages in and out with each context switch, which means that it spends more time moving pages in and out than it does running code. This brings your system to a crawl, as the CPU is consumed with the task of moving data on and off the swap disk. The alternative, however, is to kill off processes via the *out-of-memory killer* (also called *OOM;* more on this subject later in the chapter).

Another issue can occur when the system is under heavy I/O load. In this case, the file-system cache may be consuming the majority of memory while running processes are trying to request more memory. If a process requests a large block of memory, and the request can't be filled immediately, the system has to decide between swapping and reclaiming file-system cache buffers. The kernel doesn't factor in device speed when deciding to free up cache or page to disk. This small decision can have big consequences if you have a very fast disk array and a relatively slow swap disk. The kernel thinks both transactions are equal, but in this example, paging to disk would be much more time consuming than freeing cache blocks. This is one example in which turning off the swap partitions may be a good idea.

You can disable swap at any time by using the `swapon` and `swapoff` commands. Linux allows you to have more than one swap partition, so these commands allow you to enable or disable specific partitions. You also can disable them all by using the -a option, which applies the command to all partitions in /etc/fstab listed as swap partitions.

Swap devices need not be disk partitions. The mkswap command is used to format a swap partition but will format a plain file as well. To create a 4MB swap file, for example, you can use the following commands:

```
$ dd if=/dev/zero of=/tmp/swap.dat bs=1k count=4096
4096+0 records in
4096+0 records out

$ mkswap /tmp/swap.dat
Setting up swapspace version 1, size = 4190 kB
...
$ swapon /tmp/swap.dat

$ swapon -s
Filename                          Type          Size      Used     Priority

/dev/mapper/VolGroup00-LogVol01   partition     327672    0        -1
/tmp/swap.dat                     file          4088      0        -3
```

Just-in-time swap files like this can be useful if it becomes necessary to increase swap space temporarily. You can do so without repartitioning your drives.

5.6.1.7 Processes and Virtual Memory

From a programmer's point of view, each process in Linux has its own virtual memory. The kernel space is common to all processes so that when processes run in kernel mode, they all see the same memory. This is necessary because it allows the kernel to delegate tasks to the currently running process. There is a trade-off here, because there is a finite amount of address space that must be divided into kernel space and user space.

User-space addresses start at zero and extend up to a fixed upper limit. The upper limit marks the maximum theoretical size of the memory seen by a user-space process. All kernel virtual addresses start at this address and cannot be seen in user mode. The most common default for 32-bit architectures is to reserve 3GB for user space and 1GB for kernel space. This boundary is configured when the kernel is built and cannot be changed without rebuilding the kernel.

In theory, a 32-bit process can allocate up to 3GB of memory. In reality, a good deal of memory used by a simple C program is consumed by the standard library and any other libraries you include, as well as dynamic memory. Listing 5-2 shows an example.

LISTING 5-2   pause.c: A Trivial Program to Illustrate Memory Usage

```
int main()
{
    return pause();
}
```

The program in Listing 5-2 does nothing but stop so that you can examine it. You can run it in the shell in the background and then look at its memory maps. You can view each process's (user space) memory map by looking at the file /proc/PID/maps, but you can see more user-friendly output with the pmap command, which is part of the procps package:

```
$ ./pause &
[1] 6321
$ pmap 6321
6321:   ./pause
004d0000    104K r-x--  /lib/ld-2.3.5.so
004ea000      4K r----  /lib/ld-2.3.5.so
004eb000      4K rw---  /lib/ld-2.3.5.so
004ee000   1168K r-x--  /lib/libc-2.3.5.so
00612000      8K r----  /lib/libc-2.3.5.so
00614000      8K rw---  /lib/libc-2.3.5.so
00616000      8K rw---     [ anon ]
08048000      4K r-x--  /home/john/examples/mm/pause
08049000      4K rw---  /home/john/examples/mm/pause
b7f08000      4K rw---     [ anon ]
b7f1a000      4K rw---     [ anon ]
bfb05000     88K rw---     [ stack ]
ffffe000      4K -----     [ anon ]
 total     1412K
```

The pmap command lists the virtual addresses and sizes of various segments of virtual memory. As you can see, each memory region has a set of permissions like a file. Next to each region, `pmap` lists the file associated with the mapping, if any. You can see from this output that the process that does nothing consumes about 1.4MB of virtual memory, most of which is consumed by the C standard library (`/lib/libc-2.3.5.so`). Another big culprit is the dynamic linker (`ld-2.3.5.so`), which consumes 112K. My trivial code occupies only 4K, which is a single page of memory—the smallest possible size. I should point out that although `libc` consumes 1.1MB of virtual memory, the read-only sections are shared among all processes in the system that use it—that is, the library consumes only 1.1MB of physical storage in the entire system. This is one of the main advantages of using shared libraries.

Another thing to notice about the map is that there can be big gaps in the virtual-memory addresses, which means that the amount of contiguous virtual memory you can allocate in your process is less than it would be if those regions were contiguous. One such gap occurs between the region located at address 616000 and the executable segment located at 8048000 (approximately 122MB). In most applications, this is not a problem, but if your application needs to keep a large amount of data in memory, these gaps can be an issue.

Now look at the same example using assembly language. For simplicity, I'll use an 80x86 assembly, but the results should be similar on any platform. Listing 5-3 is the same program as Listing 5-2 written in 80x86 assembly language. The difference is that this uses hand-coded system calls and does not use the standard C library.

LISTING 5-3   pause.s: Trivial 80x86 Assembly-Language Program

```
.text

# Linker uses _start as the entry point.
.global _start
        .type    _start, @function

# Signal handler. Does nothing

sighdlr:
        ret

_start:
```

```
# Use the BSD signal() syscall; same as : signal(SIGCONT,sighdlr)

        movl  $sighdlr, %ecx      # 3rd arg, sighdlr
        movl  $18, %ebx           # 2nd arg, 18 = SIGCONT
        movl  $48, %eax           # 1st arg, 48 = BSD signal() system call
        int   $0x80               # execute the system call

# Execute the pause() syscall

        movl  $29, %eax           # 1st arg, 29 = pause() system call
        int   $0x80               # execute the system call

# Exit system call
# We only get here if you send SIGCONT.

        movl  $0,%ebx             # 2nd arg, exit code
        movl  $1,%eax             # 1st arg, 1 = exit()
        int   $0x80               # execute the system call
```

You can build this program with the following command:

```
$ gcc -nostdlib -o pause pause.s
```

Now when you run this, you'll see a much smaller memory map:

```
$ ./pause &
[1] 6992
$ pmap 6992
6992:   ./pause
08048000      4K r-x--  /home/john/examples/mm/pause
08049000      4K rwx--  /home/john/examples/mm/pause
bf8f5000     88K rwx--   [ stack ]
ffffe000      4K -----   [ anon ]
 total      100K
```

What you see here was only what the linker and the Linux exec system call created. The linker added a writable data section because you did not specify one. exec mapped the code into a single read-only page at address 8049000. The permission bits are very similar to the file permission bits and show that code in this page may be read and executed. Next to the permission bits, pmap lists the executable name so that you know where this page came from. exec also allocated a single writable page for your data segment. Finally, exec created a stack, which is the largest piece of the map at 88K. The *anonymous* mapping at ffffe000 is used in Linux 2.6 as part of a new, more efficient mechanism for system calls on IA32. This example uses the old method.

A Look at Intel's Physical Address Extension (PAE)

The amount of RAM you can install on your computer is not limited just by the number of DIMM slots on your motherboard. It's also limited to the amount of physical memory that your processor is capable of addressing. At one time, this limit was determined by the word size of the CPU. A 32-bit machine, for example, could store only 32-bit pointers; therefore, the physical address limit was 2^{32} bytes, or 4GB. When the first 32-bit processors came out, the idea that anyone could need, much less afford, 4GB of RAM seemed improbable.

Time went on; DRAMs got denser; and soon it became possible to produce systems with 4GB of RAM for a reasonable cost. It wasn't hard for software to figure out ways to consume all this memory, and soon, users were demanding more. One obvious solution would have been to switch to a 64-bit architecture. But at that time, switching to a 64-bit processor meant porting all your applications to a new platform. This was a costly solution, especially considering that what most customers wanted was more processes, not bigger processes. This led Intel to implement a technique to expand the physical memory without requiring a costly transition to a 64-bit processor architecture.

Intel's *Physical Address Extensions (PAE)* allow the processor to address up to 64GB (2^{36} bytes) of RAM by enlarging the page address from 20 bits to 24 bits. The page size does not change, so the offset still requires 12 bits. That means that the effective physical address is 36 bits. Because the logical address must fit in a 32-bit register, individual processes still can address only 4GB of virtual memory.

The MMU and the operating system use page addresses exclusively for manipulating pages, so the operating system is free to use the 24-bit page address when allocating pages to cache or processes. Therefore, cumulative virtual memory available to the system is effectively 64 GB (2^{36}).

This is occasionally a source of misunderstanding among programmers who intuitively assume that a process can see as much virtual memory as the whole system can address physically. Indeed, until recently this assumption was still baked into parts of the Linux kernel long after support for PAE was implemented. Luckily, it affected only certain device drivers, and only then in a system with more than 4GB of RAM.

5.6.2 Running out of Memory

Any system is constantly in flux, allocating and deallocating memory at all times. Many processes allocate small chunks of memory for short periods; other processes allocate memory once and never free it. A process can run out of memory even though the system has plenty, and the system can run out of memory while some processes continue to run without error. Everything depends on the circumstances.

The standard library and the swap partition conspire to confuse the average programmer when he tries to get a handle on just how much memory is available. The swap disk makes your system look as though it has more physical memory than it does. So when you want to know how much memory is available, the answer usually is fuzzy. Meanwhile, the standard library employs some tricks that can make it look as though your process has just allocated far more memory than the system can allow it to have. To make matters more confusing, the process may not even crash.

5.6.2.1 When a Process Runs out of Memory

Processes can run out of memory in one of two ways: They can run out of virtual addresses, or they can run out of physical storage. Running out of virtual addresses may seem to be improbable. After all, if you have only 1GB of DRAM and no swap disk, wouldn't `malloc` fail long before you ran out of virtual addresses? The program in Listing 5-4 illustrates that this is not the case. This program allocates memory in 1MB chunks until `malloc` fails.

LISTING 5-4   crazy-malloc.c: Allocate As Much Memory As Possible

```
#include <stdio.h>
#include <string.h>
#include <stdlib.h>

int main(int argc, char *argv[])
{
  void *ptr;
  int n = 0;

  while (1) {
    // Allocate in 1 MB chunks
    ptr = malloc(0x100000);
```

continues

```
   // Stop when we can't allocate any more
   if (ptr == NULL)
     break;

   n++;
 }
 // How much did we get?
 printf("malloced %d MB\n", n);

 // Stop so we can look at the damage.
 pause();
}
```

I ran the program in Listing 5-4 on a 32-bit machine with 160MB of RAM and swap disabled. Care to guess what happened? `malloc` did *not* fail until the process allocated almost 3GB of RAM! I included the `pause` call, so that you can look at the memory map:

```
$ ./crazy-malloc &
[1] 2817
malloced 3056 MB
$ jobs -x pmap %1
2823:   ./crazy-malloc
000cc000    4112K rw---     [ anon ]
004d0000     104K r-x--   /lib/ld-2.3.5.so
004ea000      4K r----   /lib/ld-2.3.5.so
004eb000      4K rw---   /lib/ld-2.3.5.so
004ee000    1168K r-x--   /lib/libc-2.3.5.so
00612000      8K r----   /lib/libc-2.3.5.so
00614000      8K rw---   /lib/libc-2.3.5.so
00616000      8K rw---     [ anon ]
006cf000 124388K rw---     [ anon ]
08048000      4K r-x--   /home/john/examples/mm/crazy-malloc
08049000      4K rw---   /home/john/examples/mm/crazy-malloc
08051000 2882516K rw---     [ anon ]
b7f56000 125424K rw---     [ anon ]
bfa43000     84K rw---     [ stack ]
bfa58000   5140K rw---     [ anon ]
ffffe000      4K -----     [ anon ]
 total  3142980K
```

Recall that the typical kernel split between user space and process space is 3GB, which is true for this particular kernel as well. As expected, the total memory allocated by this process, as reported by `pmap`, cannot exceed this limit and is very close to it.[24] The discrepancy is due to holes in the memory map that were not big enough to fit the 1MB allocations, so they remain unused. You can see these in the `pmap` output if you look for them. One such hole is at virtual address `618000` and is 732 KB—too small for a 1MB block but still useful for smaller blocks. Although `pmap` does not highlight this, it starts immediately after the 8K block at `616000` and stops at the next block, which is at `6CF000`.

If you've never seen this behavior before, you may wonder how this is possible. There are two culprits at work here. The first is the GNU C standard library's implementation of the heap; the other is the Linux virtual-memory subsystem.

The GNU Standard C Library and the Heap

The heap is the term used to describe the pool of memory used by C and C++ programs for dynamic memory allocations. There are several ways to implement a heap, and the GNU standard library seems to use all of them. The classic method, described in *The C Programming Language,* by Kernighan and Ritchie (Prentice Hall PTR), involves allocating a large pool of memory and keeping track of free blocks with a linked list in that pool. This has the drawback that your process may consume memory that it doesn't need. For efficiency, most heap implementations will allocate heap only as necessary via the `brk` system call. This allows the application to start with a small heap that can grow in response to additional requests for dynamic memory. Once allocated, this memory is seldom returned to the system.

Another drawback is that a monolithic pool of memory will tend to get *fragmented* over time. This occurs when small blocks are allocated and not immediately freed, as illustrated in Figure 5-13. When small blocks are allocated and not freed, such as blocks 2 and 4 in the illustration, they have the effect of splitting larger blocks. When we first allocate block 1, the size of the allocation is limited only by the size of the memory pool. After four allocations and two frees, the maximum size of the next allocation is much less than the total memory available. The small blocks allocated in blocks 2 and 4 have fragmented the memory pool. In a system without virtual memory, this can continue indefinitely until allocations start to fail. Fortunately, the standard library takes many steps to prevent fragmentation.

---

24. 3GB is exactly 3,145,728K.

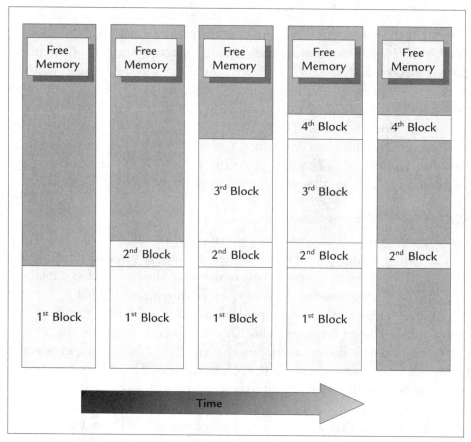

FIGURE 5-13   Memory Fragmentation Illustrated

A complete discussion of the heap is beyond the scope of this book, but I'll describe one trick the GNU standard library uses to avoid fragmentation, which is at work in the program in Listing 5-5 later in this chapter.

The GNU standard C library uses a conventional pool of memory for small allocations but uses the mmap system call to allocate large blocks of memory. This tends to prevent the kind of fragmentation illustrated in Figure 5-13 because it separates the small and large blocks into different pools.[25] For most applications, the virtual-memory pool is much larger than you would ever want your heap to be, so there

---

25. This also confounds some heap-checking tools, which are unaware of this trick.

are always enough virtual addresses to go around. For many applications, this is enough. Under the right circumstances, however, you can fragment the virtual address space just like a traditional heap. So the library allows applications some control over how mmap memory is used via the mallopt function. There is no man page for mallopt, but you can find out more about it in the GNU info page for libc as follows:

```
$ info libc mallopt
```

The mallopt function is part of the SVR4 standard, although the values that it takes can vary from system to system. A couple of useful ones defined by GNU are shown in Table 5-8.

You can use mallopt, for example, to disable the use of mmap entirely, or you can just tweak the threshold. To disable the use of mmap, use the following code:

```
#include <malloc.h>
r = mallopt(M_MMAP_MAX,0);
if ( r == 0 ) // error...
```

Unlike POSIX functions, mallopt returns zero for error and nonzero for success. Unfortunately, there is no way to determine the current value of a parameter such as M_MMAP_THRESHOLD, for example.[26]

TABLE 5-8 Tunable Parameters Defined by GNU for Use with mallopt()

Parameter	Usage
M_MMAP_THRESHOLD	Set to a threshold size in bytes. Any allocation larger than this threshold will use mmap instead of the heap.
M_MMAP_MAX	Maximum number of mmapped blocks to use at any time. When this threshold is exceeded, all allocated blocks will use the heap. Set this threshold to zero to disable the use of mmap.

---

26. There is a function named mallinfo, but it provides only statistical data on how the heap is currently being used.

Virtual Memory and the Heap

In the `crazy-malloc` example, the code allocated almost all the user space as dynamic memory on a system with only 160MB and no swap partition. The map illustrated how the standard library created *anonymous* mappings in user space via the `mmap` call. Using `strace`, you can see that each `malloc` call results in a call to `mmap` as follows:

```
mmap2(NULL,1052672,PROT_READ|PROT_WRITE,MAP_PRIVATE|MAP_ANONYMOUS,-1,0)
```

The `mmap2` system call allows a process to allocate memory by setting the `MAP_ANONYMOUS` flag. This does not require a device driver for storage, which is why the file descriptor argument is −1. For efficiency, the kernel defers finding any physical space for these pages until they are used, so `mmap2` returns a pointer to virtual memory that does not exist yet. Not until you try to use this virtual address will the physical memory be allocated. When this happens, it will cause a page fault, which will cause the kernel to find physical RAM for the page. This is a very effective technique that increases the efficiency of many operations by preventing unnecessary memory access.

If you modify the program in Listing 5-4 to modify the data that it allocates, it will force page faults to occur, and then you'll see a very different behavior, shown in Listing 5-5.

LISTING 5-5   crazy-malloc2.c: Allocate Memory and Touch It

```c
#include <stdio.h>
#include <string.h>
#include <stdlib.h>

int main(int argc, char *argv[])
{
  void *ptr;
  int n = 0;

  while (1) {
    // Allocate in 1MB chunks
    ptr = malloc(0x100000);

    // Stop when we can't allocate any more
    if (ptr == NULL)
```

```
    break;

  // Modify the data.
  memset(ptr, 1, 0x100000);
  printf("malloced %d MB\n", ++n);
  }
  // Stop so we can look at the damage.
  pause();
}
```

When the program in Listing 5-5 runs, the results may not be what you expect. Instead of pausing so you can inspect the damage, the program is killed before it gets there:

```
$ ./crazy-malloc2
malloced 1 MB
malloced 2 MB
malloced 3 MB
...
malloced 74 MB
Killed
$
```

The program was killed by the dreaded *out-of-memory killer* (often abbreviated as *OOM*). By modifying the data, you forced the *system* to run out of memory. From the process's point of view, there was plenty of memory in the form of virtual addresses. When the system runs out of storage in the form of RAM and swap, the kernel responds by killing the processes. The kernel gets a bit chatty to try to help you debug what was going on (perhaps out of guilt). Among many esoteric items you will find in /var/log/messages is the following:

```
Out of Memory: Killed process 2995 (crazy-malloc2).
```

If you're keeping score, the only time malloc failed was when it ran out of virtual memory. malloc continued to return pointers to virtual memory far beyond what the system was able to provide. You might say that malloc was writing checks it couldn't cash. Linux calls this *overcommit,* which refers to the fact that the kernel allows a process to allocate more memory than is currently available. The kernel is effectively speculating that the memory will be available when needed. You can alter this behavior if necessary.

You can force the kernel to disable overcommit by running the following command as root:

```
$ echo 2 > /proc/sys/vm/overcommit_memory
```

This forces the kernel to allow allocations based only on the physical storage that is currently available. Try it and rerun the examples to see how it changes the behavior.

These examples fly in the face of a common excuse people use for not checking pointers returned from `malloc`. Perhaps you have heard the excuse that goes something like this: "If `malloc` fails, the whole system is screwed anyway, so what's the point of trying to recover?" What we have seen is that the system takes care of itself and actively avoids getting screwed up by your process. So when `malloc` fails, it's your problem. And yes, you can recover.

5.6.2.2   When the System Runs out of Memory

You have seen how the kernel uses the out-of-memory killer to deal with processes when the system runs out of memory. Before that happens, the kernel will flush the file-system cache to free up space along with any other cache that can be flushed. After that, it will resort to swapping pages to disk if it can.

These are time-consuming operations that usually are charged to the process that is causing the problem (the one requesting all the memory). When memory gets low, however, virtually every process can cause swapping as a result of a simple context switch. This is the *thrashing* that I described earlier. It's only when the system runs out of swap that you run into the out-of-memory killer, as you did in an earlier example. Before that happens, the system can waste a great deal of time thrashing.

5.6.2.3   Locking Down Memory

Both kernel and user-space pages can page to disk, but some memory cannot be paged to disk. These pages are said to be *locked*. Memory allocated by the `ramdisk` device cannot be swapped to disk, for example. The kernel allows user-space processes to lock memory by using the `mlock` and `munlock` system calls. Locking memory consumes RAM and reduces the amount of pageable memory. Doing this can lead to thrashing, as unlocked pages have fewer physical pages to use. For this reason, only processes with superuser privileges can use the `mlock` and `munlock` system calls.

To prevent a region of memory from being swapped to disk, use the following call:

```
r = mlock( ptr , size );
```

Like all POSIX functions, `mlock` returns zero for success and -1 for error. When it returns, you are guaranteed that the pages are resident in RAM so there will be no significant latency when accessing this memory. More specifically, a page fault will never occur as a result of accessing this memory.

This is one way critical processes keep running even when the system is out of memory. Pages that are locked are above the fray when the system is thrashing. A context switch to a process that has locked most or all of its pages will not be as costly as switching to another process. That is why there is another useful function for locking pages: `mlockall`. This function takes only a flags argument, which can be a combination of `MCL_CURRENT` to lock all pages that are currently allocated or `MCL_FUTURE` to lock all future pages that are allocated by this process. An obnoxious daemon might insist on locking all its pages in memory at all times. This would be done by setting both flags:

```
r = mlockall( MCL_CURRENT | MCL_FUTURE );
```

After this call, all memory in use by the process will remain in RAM until it is unlocked. Any new pages that are created as a result of a call to `brk` (usually the result of a `malloc`) or any other that allocates new pages will also remain in RAM indefinitely. You had better hope that you don't have a memory leak.

Unlike the `mlock` function, the `mlockall` function can be called by a process without superuser privileges. The restriction is simply that the process cannot lock pages unless it has superuser privileges. An unprivileged process can call `mlockall` (`MCL_FUTURE`), which does not lock any of the pages currently allocated but tells the kernel to lock any new pages that are allocated by this process. If the process does not have superuser privilege, when this happens, this allocation will fail. If a `malloc` results in a `brk` system call, for example, the `brk` call will fail, which in turn will result in `malloc` returning a `NULL` pointer. This is one way to test your error handling for out-of-memory conditions.

As you might expect, `mlock` and `mlockall` have counterparts to unlock pages, intuitively named `munlock` and `munlockall`. It is important to lock pages only when necessary and to unlock pages if you can to free physical memory for use by other processes.

When your system has much less memory than the virtual address space of your processor, your process isn't likely to run out of memory until the system runs out of memory. This is unfortunate, because you might be able to include some error handing in your application to deal with this situation. You can't deal with anything when the out-of-memory killer has killed your process. One workaround is available from the GNU C library, which is part of the `sysconf` library function. You can query the number of available physical pages from the system with the following call:

```
num_pages = sysconf( _SC_AVPHYS_PAGES );
```

This tells you the number of pages the system can allocate without having to flush cache or page to disk. It is roughly equal to the `MemFree` value you see in `/proc/meminfo`. Because this value does not take into account memory that could be freed by flushing pages from the file-system cache, it is a very conservative value.

Beware—the value you get by multiplying the number of available pages by the page size can overflow. This is due to the fact that both IA32 and PowerPC have memory extensions to allow the processor to see more than 4GB of RAM (see the sidebar on Intel's PAE earlier in this chapter). In case you don't already know, C does not inform you when an integer overflows; it provides an invalid result instead. The best advice is to do any math in units of pages, not bytes.

There is another line of defense when dealing with process memory usage: the `setrlimit` system call, which allows the administrator or even a user to impose limits on the amount of resources a single process can use. Listing 5-6 is the `crazy-malloc` program reworked to include a call to `setrlimit` based on the available memory in the system.

LISTING 5-6   crazy-malloc3.c: Allocate Memory with Resource Limits Set

```
1 #include <stdio.h>
2 #include <string.h>
3 #include <stdlib.h>
4 #include <limits.h>
5 #include <signal.h>
6 #include <unistd.h>
7 #include <sys/types.h>
8 #include <sys/stat.h>
```

```
 9 #include <sys/resource.h>
10
11 int main(int argc, char *argv[])
12 {
13     void *ptr;
14     int n = 0;
15     int r = 0;
16     struct rlimit rl;
17     u_long pages, max_pages, max_bytes;
18
19     pages = sysconf(_SC_AVPHYS_PAGES);
20
21     /* Calculate max_bytes, but look out for overflow */
22     max_pages = ULONG_MAX / sysconf(_SC_PAGE_SIZE);
23     if (pages > max_pages)
24         pages = max_pages;
25     max_bytes = pages * sysconf(_SC_PAGE_SIZE);
26
27     r = getrlimit(RLIMIT_AS, &rl);
28
29     printf("current hard limit is %ld MB\n",
30             (u_long) rl.rlim_max / 0x100000);
31
32     /* Modify the soft limit and don't change the hard limit. */
33     rl.rlim_cur = max_bytes;
34
35     r = setrlimit(RLIMIT_AS, &rl);
36     if (r) {
37         perror("setrlimit");
38         exit(1);
39     }
40
41     printf("limit set to %ld MB\n", max_bytes / 0x100000);
42
43     while (1) {
44         // Allocate in 1 MB chunks
45         ptr = malloc(0x100000);
46
47         // Stop when we can't allocate any more
48         if (ptr == NULL) {
49             perror("malloc");
50             break;
51         }
52
```

continues

```
53          memset(ptr, 1, 0x100000);
54          printf("malloced %d MB\n", ++n);
55      }
56      // Stop so we can look at the damage.
57      printf("paused\n");
58      raise(SIGSTOP);
59      return 0;
60 }
```

When you run `crazy-malloc3`, instead of getting killed by the OOM killer, it fails. On my system, I got the following output:

```
$ ./crazy-malloc3
current hard limit is 4095 MB
limit set to 53 MB
malloced 1 MB
malloced 2 MB
malloced 3 MB
...
malloced 50 MB
malloced 51 MB
malloc: Cannot allocate memory
paused
```

The `rlimit` structure consists of a soft and a hard limit. The hard limit typically is set at system startup; otherwise, there are no default limits. An unprivileged user can set the soft limit to any value up to, but not greater than, the hard limit. The user can also lower the hard limit for the current process and its children, but when that happens, the limit can't be raised again by this process. That's why before you call `setrlimit`, you use `getrlimit` (on line 27) so that you don't inadvertently lower the hard limit. Unprivileged processes should modify only the soft limit.

Now instead of just dying, the process can take some corrective action, attempt to recover, or just fail-safe. In this instance, the process found that 53MB was available, but it could `malloc` only 51 blocks of 1MB due to overhead from the system libraries. This is expected, based on what you've already seen.

Keep in mind that the number of available pages you get from `sysconf` is only a snapshot. On any system, this value will go up and down with demand from other processes. On a busy system, this value may be totally unreliable.

If you're tuning system memory usage at this level, chances are that you are working on an application-specific system, such as an embedded device. In this case, you have probably accounted for most of the memory usage in the system anyway, and if you haven't, you should. Only then will you know what are good values to use for `setrlimit`.

Bash allows users access to `getrlimit` and `setrlimit` via the built in `ulimit` function, which takes its name from the deprecated library function that used to serve this purpose. These limits apply only to the current shell and any children. If you want to apply limits systemwide, you should set this in `/etc/profile`, which applies to all Bash shells.

5.7 Summary

In this chapter, I took an in-depth look at how processes function in Linux. I described the concepts of user mode and kernel mode. I explored the basics of system calls and explained how many of the library functions you take for granted are actually thin wrappers around system calls.

I also looked at the Linux scheduler and how it affects your code. I described some of the user commands you can use to influence the scheduler behavior. In addition to describing the scheduler, I described how the kernel keeps track of time. I showed some of the different clocks in the system that tick at various rates. Ideally, you know which ones are most appropriate for your needs.

I described the basics of device drivers and device nodes, as well as the basics of system input and output using device drivers. I introduced the I/O schedulers and demonstrated how you can adjust and tune them at runtime.

I finished this chapter with a discussion of virtual memory and what it means to your process. Along the way, I demonstrated the various out-of-memory conditions that processes can run into and introduced the dreaded OOM killer.

5.7.1 Tools Used in This Chapter

- `mkswap`, `swapon`, `swapoff`—tools for manipulating swap partitions

- `nice`, `renice`, `chrt`—tools to influence the scheduler's behavior

- `pmap`—shows you a map of a process's virtual memory

- `ps`, `time`, `times`—used to show how much time your process spends in user space and kernel space

- `strace`—an excellent tool for analyzing the system call behavior of your program

5.7.2   APIs Discussed in This Chapter

- `clock_getres`, `clock_gettime`—high-resolution POSIX clocks

- `getrusage`, `times`—library functions to look at resource usage

- `mallopt`—a GNU API to allow you to influence how `malloc` behaves

- `mlock`, `mlockall`—allow you to lock pages in RAM

- `mmap`, `msync`, `madvise`—allow you to influence how memory is stored in RAM and on disk

- `pthread_setschedparam`—chooses a scheduling policy for a thread

- `sched_get_priority_min/max`—determines at runtime the minimum and maximum priorities for a given scheduling policy

- `sched_setscheduler`—chooses a scheduling policy for a process

- `sysconf`—tells you details about system configuration constants

5.7.3   Online References

- www.kernel.org/pub/linux/utils/kernel/hotplug/udev.html—numerous resources for learning about `udev`

- http://linux-hotplug.sourceforge.net—resources and documentation for the Linux `hotplug` features

5.7.4   References

- Cesati, M., and D.P. Bovet. *Understanding the Linux Kernel.* 3d ed. Sebastopol, Calif.: O'Reilly Media, Inc., 2005.

- Kernighan, B.W., and D. Ritchie. *The C Programming Language.* Englewood Cliffs, N.J.: Prentice Hall, 1988.

- Kroah-Hartman, G., J. Corbet, and A. Rubini. *Linux Device Drivers.* Sebastopol, Calif.: O'Reilly Media, Inc., 2005.

- Love, R. *Linux Kernel Development.* 3d ed. Indianapolis: Novell Press, 2005.

- Rodriguez, C.S., G. Fischer, and S. Smolski. *The Linux Kernel Primer: A Top-Down Approach for x86 and PowerPC Architectures.* Englewood Cliffs, N.J.: Prentice Hall, 2006.

Chapter 6

Understanding Processes

6.1 Introduction

I introduced the Linux process model in Chapter 5. Most of that discussion focused on process interaction with the kernel. In this chapter, I focus on processes in user space. I look at the life cycle of a process from `exec` to `exit` and everything in between. This chapter looks closely at the process footprint and shows you several tools and APIs that you can use to examine the resources a process consumes.

6.2 Where Processes Come From

Linux processes have a parent–child relationship. A process has one—and only one—parent, but it can have (almost) any number of children. All processes have a single common ancestor: the `init` process. `init` is the first process to run when you boot the system and remains alive until you shut it down. `init` is responsible for preserving sanity on your system by enforcing graceful startup and shutdown.

You cannot terminate the init process via a signal, even as superuser. You must politely ask it to terminate in one of several ways. When you do, it shuts down the system—gracefully, you hope.

Linux creates processes with one of three system calls. Two of these are traditional system calls provided by other UNIX variants: fork and vfork. The third is Linux specific and can create threads as well as processes. This is the clone system call.

6.2.1   fork and vfork

The fork system call is the preferred way to create a new process. When fork returns, there will be two processes: a parent and child, identical clones of each other. fork returns a process ID (pid_t) that will be either zero or nonzero. From the programmer's perspective, the only difference between parent and child is the value returned by the fork function. The parent sees a nonzero return value, which is the process ID of its child process (or –1 if there's an error). The child sees a zero return value, which indicates that it is the child. What happens next is up to the application. The most common pattern is to call one of the exec system calls (which I will discuss shortly), although that is by no means required.

The vfork system call is something of an artifact. It is virtually identical to fork except that vfork guarantees that the user-space memory will not be copied. In the bad old days, a fork call would cause all the process's user-space memory to be copied into new pages. This is especially wasteful if the only thing the child process is going to do is call exec. In that case, all that copying is done for nothing. This happens to be exactly what the init process does, for example. The children of init have no use for a copy of init's user space, so copying it is a waste of time. The idea behind vfork was to eliminate this copying step to make processes like init more efficient.

The problem with vfork is that it requires the child process to call exec immediately, without modifying any memory. This is harder than it sounds, especially if you consider that the exec call could fail. The vfork(2) man page has an interesting editorial on this topic for the interested reader.

All modern UNIX variants use a technique called *copy on write,* which makes a normal fork behave very much like a vfork, thereby making vfork not just undesirable, but also unnecessary.

6.2.2 Copy on Write

The purpose of copy on write is to improve efficiency by eliminating unnecessary copying. The idea is relatively simple. When a process forks, both processes share the same physical memory for as long as possible—that is, the kernel copies only the page table entries and marks all the pages copy on write. This causes a page fault when either process modifies the memory. When a page fault occurs due to copy on write, the kernel allocates a new page of physical storage and copies the page before allowing it to be modified. This is illustrated in Figure 6-1.

If a process forks and the child modifies only a tiny fraction of memory, this is a big win, because you save the time of copying all that data. It also conserves physical memory, because the unmodified pages reside in memory that is shared by two processes. Without copy on write, the system would need twice as much physical storage for parent and child.

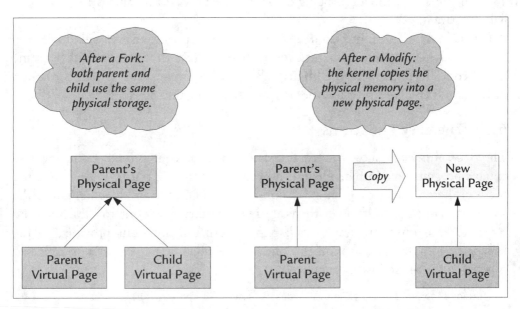

FIGURE 6-1   Copy-on-Write Flag Triggers a Page Fault When Data Is Modified

Think of how long startup would take if init had to copy all its pages each time it started a process. The basic job of the init process is to fork and exec. The child has no use for any of init's memory. Likewise, there are many system daemons whose job it is to fork and exec just like init. (These processes benefit as well.) Such daemons include xinetd, sshd, and ftpd.

6.2.3 clone

The clone system call is unique to Linux and can be used to create processes or threads. I mention it here for completeness only. Portable code should never use the clone system call. The POSIX APIs should be sufficient enough to provide what you need, be it a thread or a process.

clone is a complicated system call implemented as kind of a general-purpose fork. It gives the application full control over which parts of the child process will be shared with the parent. This makes it suitable for creating processes or threads. You can think of a thread as being a special-case process that shares its user space with its parent.

If you look at the Linux source, you will find separate system calls for fork, vfork, and clone. As you might expect, these are just wrappers around the same kernel code. To implement the library calls for fork, exec, and pthread_create in Linux, GLIBC seems to use the clone system call almost exclusively.

6.3   The exec Functions

The exec functions allow you to transfer control of your process from one executable program to another. There is no function named exec in Linux, but I use the term here to refer to a family of library calls. The calls are documented in the exec(3) man page.[1] Although there are many library functions to implement an exec, there is only one system call: execve. All the functions provided by the library are just wrappers around this one system call. The execve system call itself is accessed via the following function:

```
int execve(const char *filename, char *const  argv [], char *const envp[]);
```

---

1.   Note that the man page is in section 3 (libraries) and not section 2 (system calls).

The `execve` system call looks for the file you specify; determines whether it is executable; and, if so, tries to load it and execute it. It is unusual for a system call to do so much work, but `execve` is unique. For the purpose of this chapter, I'll use the term `execve` to refer to the specific system call. The term `exec` will refer to any of the `exec` functions listed in `exec(3)`.

The first step for the kernel is to look at the permissions on the file. The process owner must have permission to execute the file before the kernel will attempt to read it. If that test fails, `execve` returns an error (`-1`) and sets `errno` to `EPERM`.

Having passed the permission test, it's time for the kernel to look at the contents of the file and determine whether it really is an executable. In general, executable files fall into three categories: *executable scripts, executable object files,* and *miscellaneous binaries.*

6.3.1   Executable Scripts

Executable scripts are text files that direct the kernel to an interpreter, which must be an executable object file. If not, `execve` fails with `errno` set to `ENOEXEC` (exec format error). The interpreter may not be another script.

The kernel recognizes an executable script by looking at the first two characters of the file. If it sees the characters `#!`, it parses this first line into one or two additional tokens separated by white space. A typical example is a shell script, which starts with this line:

```
#!/bin/sh
```

The kernel interprets the token following `#!` as the path to an executable object file. If this file does not exist or is not an executable object file, `execve` returns `-1` to indicate an error. Otherwise, the kernel breaks line 1 of the script into three tokens and creates an `argv` vector for the interpreter as follows:

- `argv[0]`—the pathname of the interpreter executable
- `argv[1]`—all text following the name of the interpreter (the argument)
- `argv[2]`—the filename of the script

`argv[1]` consists of everything following the interpreter (white space and all) on the first line of the script, packed into a single string. This is unlike a normal command line, where each element of `argv` has no white space. This can lead to odd behavior if you're not aware of it. This script works, for example:

```
#!/bin/sh -xv                argv[1] = "-xv"
echo Hello World
```

This script, on the other hand, does not work:

```
#!/bin/sh -x -v              argv[1] = "-x -v"
echo Hello World
```

Both are legal syntax in a regular command line, but when `execve` processes the script, the latter example is equivalent to:

```
$ sh '-x -v'
sh: - : invalid option
Usage:  sh [GNU long option] [option] ...
```

The shell expects the arguments to be stripped of white space from the command line. When that is not the case, it gets confused.

The interpreter can be any program, but this technique is intended only for script interpreters. Some common choices are Perl, Python, Awk, and Sed. An `awk` script can be written as follows:

```
#!/bin/awk -f
BEGIN { print "Hello World" }
END { print "Goodbye World" }
```

Notice that the `-f` option is required so that when `awk` is called, the `argv` vector is equivalent to the following command:

```
/bin/awk -f scriptname
```

Here, you can see why the options from the first line are sandwiched into the second element of the `argv` vector. Without the `-f` option to `awk`, you can't write an `awk` script that can be executed directly. Perl, Python, and most other script interpreters don't require any additional arguments to function this way.

Linux limits the first line of a script to 128 characters,[2] including white space, after which the line is truncated and used as is. Any arguments that exist past the 128th character are silently discarded. Other systems may have larger limits.

---

2. This number is determined by BINFMT_BUF_SIZE in the kernel.

Typos and Scripts

I have made my share of typos in scripts and have seen some bizarre behavior. The shell works to hide some of these issues from you without your knowing it. Here are some antipatterns that work from the shell but not from `execve`:

`# !/bin/sh`   Note the space between # and !.

` #!/bin/sh`   Note the space before #.

When you try to execute one of these scripts with an `execve` system call, it will fail with the error `ENOEXEC`. If you happen to start one of these scripts from the shell, however, it will work.

When the shell starts one of these scripts, it calls `execve` just like you would from an application. Just like your application, the `execve` call fails. But unlike your application, the shell's child process is a perfectly functional command interpreter, so it determines that the file happens to be a text file and then proceeds to interpret the text as commands. The first line, which you thought was a parameter to `execve`, is now ignored as a shell comment, and the rest of the statements are interpreted without errors. Voilà! Your shell script works—by accident.

Bash uses a simple algorithm to determine whether a file rejected by `ENOEXEC` will be passed to the interpreter. Version 3.00.17 reads the first 80 characters or the first line (whichever is shorter), looking for non-ASCII characters. If it sees only ASCII characters, the file is passed to the shell interpreter; otherwise, it throws an error.

Another antipattern occurs when you use Windows text editors that excrete carriage returns in your file. `execve` sees the carriage return on the first line as part of the interpreter filename. As expected, it fails with `ENOENT` (no such file or directory). The shell takes this one at face value and quits. For example:

```
$ unix2dos ./busted-script
unix2dos: converting file ./busted-script to DOS format ...
$ ./busted-script
: bad interpreter: No such file or directory...
```

Thanks to your helpful text editors, it may be hard to figure out what's wrong when this happens. Both Vim and Emacs do their best to hide carriage returns from view. For Vim, you can use the `-b` option to force it to show these Windows waste products as `^M` sequences, for example:

```
#!/bin/sh^M
```

The `^M` is an abbreviation for `Ctrl+M`, which is the control key that emits an ASCII carriage return.

6.3.2   Executable Object Files

Executable object files are object files that have been linked with no unresolved references other than dynamic library references. The kernel recognizes only a limited number of formats that are allowed to be used with the execve system call. There are some variations by processor architecture, but the ELF[3] format is common. Before ELF, the common format for Linux systems was a.out (short for *assembly output*), which is still available as an option today.

Other formats might be recognized depending on your kernel and architecture. Processors that don't have a Memory Management Unit (MMU), for example, use a so-called flat format that the kernel supports. When compiled for the MIPS architecture, the kernel also allows the ECOFF format, which is a variation of the Common Object File Format that is the predecessor of ELF.

To identify an object file, the kernel looks for a signature in the file, typically called a *magic number*. ELF files, for example, have a signature in the first 4 bytes of the file—specifically, the byte 0x7f followed by the string 'ELF'. Although all ELF files have this signature, not all ELF files are executable. Compiled modules (.o files), for example, are not executable, although they are ELF binary object files. When the kernel encounters an ELF file, it also checks the ELF header in addition to the magic number to verify that it is an executable file before loading and executing it. Compilers generate object files without execute permission, so execve should never see such a file by accident.

6.3.3   Miscellaneous Binaries

The kernel allows you to extend the way execve handles executables with the BINFMT_MISC option to the kernel. This option is specified in the kernel build and allows the superuser to define helper applications that execve can call on to run programs. This is useful for running Windows applications with wine,[4] Java executables, or jar files.

Obviously, the kernel can't load and run a Windows executable, but wine executes Windows programs much like an interpreter executes a script. Likewise, Java binaries are executed in a similar fashion by the Java interpreter.

With a kernel built with the BINFMT_MISC option, you can tell the kernel how to recognize a non-native Linux file and what helper program to execute with it. All

---

3. *ELF* is short for *Executable and Linkable Format.*
4. www.winehq.org

this is done within the execve system call, so the application calling execve does not need to know that the program it is about to execute is not a native Linux file.

To start, you need to mount a special procfs entry, as follows:

```
$ mount binfmt_misc -t binfmt_misc /proc/sys/fs/binfmt_misc
```

This mounts a directory with two entries:

```
$ ls -l /proc/sys/fs/binfmt_misc/
total 0
--w-------  1 root root 0 Feb 12 15:19 register
-rw-r--r--  1 root root 0 Feb 11 20:06 status
```

The register pseudofile is for writing new rules to the kernel, and the status entry allows you to enable and disable the kernel's handling of miscellaneous binaries. You also can query the status by reading this file.

New rules can be added by writing a specially formatted string to the register pseudofile. The format consists of several tokens separated by colons:

```
:name:type:offset:magic:mask:interpreter:flags
```

The name is any name you like, which will show up under the binfmt_misc directory for later reference. The type field tells the kernel how to use this rule to recognize the file type. This field can be M for *magic number* or E for *extension*. When you're using a magic number (M), the rest of the rule will include a string of bytes to look for, as well as its location in the file. When you're using an extension (E), the rest of the rule tells the kernel what file extension to look for. This is most often used with DOS and Windows executables.

The offset, magic, and mask fields are for handling the so-called magic number. The offset is optional and indicates the first byte of the file where the magic number resides. The magic field indicates the value that kernel should look for as a magic number. The mask is optional as well. This is a bit mask that the kernel applies to the magic number (via a bitwise AND) before testing the value. This allows a single rule to specify a family of magic numbers. The number and mask may be indicated by raw ASCII characters. If necessary, binary bytes can be used, provided that they use hexadecimal escape sequences.

You can enable wine to handle Windows executables automatically by using the following rule:

```
$ echo ':Windows:M::MZ::/usr/bin/wine:' >   /proc/sys/fs/binfmt_misc/register
```

This uses a magic number of 2 bytes (M) followed by z. Because no offset is provided, the kernel reads the magic number from the beginning of the file. There is no mask, either, which means that the magic number appears as is in the file.[5]

This works, provided that your Windows program has executable file permission and that you use the complete filename; this should be sufficient to recognize the file and execute wine when it is passed to execve. Naturally, you can also double-click its icon on the desktop to run it as well.

When the rule has been enabled, you see a new file in the binfmt_misc directory:

```
$ ls -l /proc/sys/fs/binfmt_misc/
total 0
-rw-r--r--  1 root root 0 Feb 12 15:19 Windows
--w-------  1 root root 0 Feb 12 15:19 register
-rw-r--r--  1 root root 0 Feb 11 20:06 status
```

The Windows pseudofile tells you that a rule named Windows has been installed. You can see the details of the rule by reading the file:

```
$ cat /proc/sys/fs/binfmt_misc//Windows
enabled
interpreter /usr/bin/wine
flags:
offset 0
magic 4d5a
```

Notice that the magic number you specified as MZ is now represented in hexadecimal. To disable this rule, you can delete it by writing -1 to the file. For example:

```
$ echo -1 > /proc/sys/fs/binfmt_misc/Windows
```

The BINFMT_MISC driver also accepts certain flags in the rules, which are documented in the kernel source.[6] Be aware that the rules are applied in the reverse order from the order in which they were set. If you have a file that matches two rules (perhaps one by extension and one by magic number), the rule added more recently is the one that applies.

---

5. By the way, the wine RPM from Fedora comes with a startup service that handles these settings for you.
6. See Documentation/binfmt_misc.txt in the kernel source.

6.4   Process Synchronization with wait

The underlying assumption when you create a process is that you want to wait around to find out how things turned out. When a process exits, it sends the parent process a SIGCHLD signal. The default behavior for the SIGCHLD signal is to ignore the signal, although the information is not lost. The process status remains in memory until the parent collects it with one of the wait functions listed below:

```
pid_t wait(int *status);
pid_t waitpid(pid_t pid, int *status, int options);
pid_t wait3(int *status, int options, struct rusage *rusage);
pid_t wait4(pid_t pid, int *status, int options, struct rusage *rusage);
```

As I discussed in Chapter 5, the act of waiting for a child process to terminate is called *reaping* the process. When a parent process neglects to wait for a child process that has terminated, the child process goes into a so-called zombie state, where the kernel keeps around just enough information to inform the parent of the child's exit status.

In Linux (and UNIX), it does not matter whether the child process has terminated before or after the parent calls wait. The wait function behaves the same way in both cases except that it can block if the child has not terminated when the wait function is called. If a parent terminates before the child process, the child process continues normally except that it is *adopted* by the init process (pid 1). When the child process terminates, init will reap the status. Likewise, any zombie children left over by the parent when it exits are adopted and reaped by init.

Table 6-1 summarizes the features of wait functions. What these functions have in common is that they all map to the same one or two Linux system calls. Each one takes a pointer to an int variable to hold the child process's status, and they all return the process ID of the process that terminated. This is the basic function of the wait call. The waitpid and wait4 functions add a process ID to the input so that the caller can wait explicitly for one of many children to terminate. The wait and wait3 functions do not take a pid argument. These functions will return as soon as any child process terminates.

TABLE 6-1   Summary of wait Functions

Function	pid	options	rusage	
`wait`	No	No	No	Returns as soon as a child process exits or immediately if no child processes are running.
`waitpid`	Yes	Yes	No	Same as `wait` except that the caller can return immediately without blocking, if desired. Can also return when a child process is stopped.
`wait3`	No	Yes	Yes	Supports the same options as `waitpid` but takes no `pid` as an argument. Returns when any child process exits or stops as determined by the options. Also returns an `rusage struct` to indicate resource usage by the child.
`wait4`	Yes	Yes	Yes	Same as `wait3` except that it takes a `pid` as an argument.

The `waitpid`, `wait3`, and `wait4` functions take an `options` argument that can have one of two flags:

- `WNOHANG`—When set, the function does not block and returns immediately. The return status is `-1` if no process was reaped.

- `WUNTRACED`—When set, the function returns for processes that are in the stopped state and are not being traced (by a debugger, for example).

Recall when I discussed the `getrusage` function that the kernel does not provide data for child processes until they have been reaped. This is where the `WUNTRACED` option comes in handy. You can stop a child process explicitly to check on resource usage, as follows:

```
struct rusage ru;
kill(pid,SIGSTOP);                          Stop the process.
r = wait4(pid,&status,WUNTRACED,&ru);       Wait for it to get status.
if ( r == pid )kill(pid,SIGCONT);           Start it again.
```

Another thing all `wait` functions have in common is that they can all return -1 to indicate that no process was reaped. The exact reason for the -1 value can be determined by checking the value of `errno`. The value ECHILD indicates that there was no unreaped child process to wait for. This can occur if your process has not forked any children successfully. It also can happen when you use the WNOHANG option, which tells the `wait` function to return immediately, whether or not it has reaped a process.

6.5   The Process Footprint

As I discussed in Chapter 5, each process has its own unique virtual-memory space (user space). In addition, processes have several other properties, and they consume resources other than virtual memory.

When a process is created by the kernel, it is given some initial values for these properties as well as a virtual-memory space to work in. Part of this is determined by the kernel, and part is determined by the compiler and libraries. An example is shown in Figure 6-2 for an IA32 with a typical kernel.

In Figure 6-2, the kernel is compiled with a 3G/1G split, which means that the lower 3GB of virtual addresses belong to user space, while the top 1GB is kernel space shared by all processes. This division is the same for every process running under this kernel.

By now, you know that the process ID uniquely identifies each process on the system. This is the key that the kernel uses to search its internal tables to find information about a particular process.

The maps shown in Figure 6-2 are of virtual memory. Not all this memory is consumed by the process; the diagram shows its *intended* uses. Memory is not consumed until it is allocated. The stack, for example, can grow to some predefined maximum (typically, 1MB or more), but initially, the kernel allocates only a few pages. As the stack grows, more pages will be allocated. I will look at the stack in more detail later in this chapter.

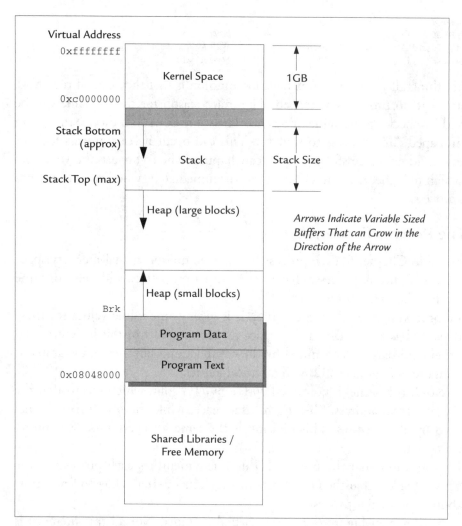

FIGURE 6-2   Typical Memory Map on IA32

All processes except `init` start life as a fork of another process—that is, they don't start with a clean slate. The memory map in Figure 6-2 is initially populated by the parent's mappings. The data is identical to the parent's until the child process modifies the memory or calls `exec`. When the child process calls `exec`, the slate is cleaned (so to speak), and the map is populated by only program text, data, and a stack. If it is a C program, the process typically populates the map with some amount of shared libraries and dynamic storage.

The kernel space story is a little different. When a child process forks, it gets a copy of the page tables in kernel space. The memory required for this is unique to the process, so although the process is an identical clone in user space, in kernel space, it is unique. The child process gets its own set of file descriptors, which initially are clones of the parent's (more on that later in this chapter).

In general, the process's footprint includes

- Page tables

- Stack (includes environment variables)

- Resident memory

- Locked memory

In addition, each process has properties, which coincidentally may be the same as those of other processes, but they are unique to each process. These include

- Root directory

- Current working directory

- File descriptors

- Terminal

- umask

- Signal mask

6.5.1 File Descriptors

File descriptors are plain integers returned by the open system call. Several system calls take file descriptors as arguments, which they use as indexes into important kernel structures. In general, the file descriptor is a simple index into a table that the kernel manages for each process.

Each process has its own set of file descriptors. When created, a process typically has three open file descriptors: 0, 1, and 2. These are, respectively, standard input, standard output, and standard error, known collectively as standard I/O. These are initially inherited from the parent process. One job of a process such as sshd is to make sure that these three file descriptors are associated with the proper pseudoterminal or socket. Before the sshd child process calls exec, it must close these file descriptors and open new ones for standard I/O.

Every file descriptor has unique properties, such as read or write permission. These are specified in the open call with the flags argument. For example:

```
fd = open("foo",O_RDONLY);          Open as read-only
fd = open("foo",O_WRONLY);          Open as write-only
fd = open("foo",O_RDWR);            Open for reading and writing
```

The flags must agree with the file permissions; otherwise, the open call fails. You cannot open a file for writing if the current user does not have permission to write to it, for example. When this happens, the open call indicates the failure by returning -1 and setting errno to EACCESS (permission denied).

When the open call succeeds, the read/write attributes are enforced exclusively by file descriptor. If the file permissions are changed during the course of the program's execution, it doesn't matter. The file's permissions are enforced only during the open call.

Each file descriptor has unique properties, even when multiple file descriptors point to the same file. Suppose that a process has two file descriptors open that point to the same file. One was opened with O_RDONLY; the other, with O_WRONLY. Any attempt to write to the read-only file descriptor will fail with EBADF (bad file descriptor). Likewise, an attempt to read from the write-only file descriptor will fail with the same error.

Just as file descriptors within a process are unique, file descriptors cannot be shared between processes. The only exception to this rule is between parent and child. When a process calls fork, all the files that were open when fork was called are still open in both the parent and the child. Moreover, writes to a file descriptor in the child affect the same file descriptor in the parent, and vice versa. This is illustrated in Listing 6-1.

LISTING 6-1   fork-file.c: An Example of File Descriptor Usage Following a Fork

```
1 #include <stdio.h>
2 #include <string.h>
3 #include <stdlib.h>
4 #include <assert.h>
5 #include <unistd.h>
6 #include <sys/file.h>
7 #include <sys/times.h>
```

```
 8 #include <sys/stat.h>
 9 #include <sys/wait.h>
10
11 // Write a NUL terminated string to an fd.
12 void writestr(int fd, char *buf)
13 {
14     int r = write(fd, buf, strlen(buf));
15     if (r == -1)
16         perror(buf);
17 }
18
19 // Simple busy-wait loop to throw off our timing.
20 void busywait(void)
21 {
22     clock_t t1 = times(NULL);
23     while (times(NULL) - t1 < 2);
24 }
25
26 int main(int argc, char *argv[])
27 {
28     int fd = open("thefile.txt",
29                   O_CREAT | O_TRUNC | O_RDWR,
30                   S_IRWXU | S_IRWXG | S_IRWXO);
31     assert(fd != -1);
32
33     writestr(fd, "This is the parent.\n");
34
35     pid_t pid = fork();
36
37     // Both parent and child do a busywait,
38     // which should throw off our timing.
39     busywait();
40
41     if (pid == 0) {
42         // Child process
43         writestr(fd, "Child write\n");
44     }
45     else {
46         // parent process writes one line and
47         // waits for the child
48         writestr(fd, "Hi it's me. I'm back.\n");
49
50         int status;
51         waitpid(pid, &status, 0);
52     }
53     close(fd);
54
55     return 0;
56 }
```

This example is a textbook pattern of a race condition because there is no synchronization between parent and child except for the `waitpid` call. As a result, the output will vary from one run to the next:

```
$ cc -o fork-file fork-file.c

$ ./fork-file && cat thefile.txt
This is the parent.
Hi it's me. I'm back.                    Parent writes before child
Child write


$ ./fork-file && cat thefile.txt
This is the parent.
Child write                              Child writes before parent
Hi it's me. I'm back.
```

As you can see, the order of the lines of text varies from one run to the next. This is illustrated further in Figure 6-3. I'll show you more about race conditions in Chapter 7. The point of this example is to illustrate how parent and child affect each other's file descriptors. Notice that both the parent's and the child's output appears in the file, and *one does not overwrite the other*. This indicates that the child's writes caused the parent's file descriptor to move forward, and vice versa.

Most of the time, this behavior is what you want, but you may not realize it. Consider any program you have written that uses the `system` library call to `fork` and `exec` a shell command for you. Because your standard input and output file descriptors are inherited by your child process, it is able to print to the same terminal as the parent process, so your program looks like a single coherent application to the user and not like Frankenstein's monster.

All the parent's file descriptors are inherited in this way across an `exec`. Many times, the child process has no use for the open files other than the standard I/O. Think about how many programs you have written. How many times have you stopped to think about how many file descriptors your process has open when it starts?

This is important for a few reasons. One is the fact that a process has a finite number of file descriptors. This number is fixed when the kernel is built and cannot be increased. Leaving file descriptors open is a bit like leaking memory. Eventually, you will run out. Depending on the nature of your application, you may never run into a problem.

Another problem is that open file descriptors can cause child processes to hold on to resources that you want to free up. A device, for example, may allow only one open file descriptor at a time. If you `fork` and `exec` with this device open, it will

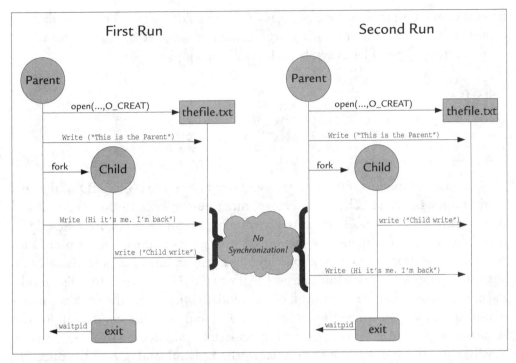

FIGURE 6-3   Timing Diagram for Listing 6-1

remain open until the child terminates, which means that simply closing it in the
parent process is not enough to free the resource.

So what's a programmer to do? You could be paranoid and close all open file
descriptors after you fork. This is called for sometimes but can be tricky. A more
proactive approach is to set the FD_CLOEXEC flag on open file descriptors. When
this flag is set, the file descriptor will be closed when exec is called. (By default, file
descriptors are not closed automatically.) You can set this flag only by using the
fcntl call, as follows:

```
fcntl( fd, FD_SETFD, FD_CLOEXEC );
```

File descriptors can point to open files, devices, or sockets. Each is copied during
the fork and remains open after exec.[7] Leaving file descriptors open, particularly

---

7. One notable exception is the file descriptor returned by shm_open, which is specified to have
    FD_CLOEXEC set.

unused ones, is a problem that can lead to bizarre side effects. There are tools to help. The /proc file entry for each process contains a subdirectory named fd, which shows currently open files as symbolic links. For example:

```
$ ls /proc/self/fd > foo.txt
$ cat foo.txt
total 4
lrwx------ 1 john john 64 Feb 16 23:08 0 -> /dev/pts/2
l-wx------ 1 john john 64 Feb 16 23:08 1 -> /home/john/foo.txt
lrwx------ 1 john john 64 Feb 16 23:08 2 -> /dev/pts/2
lr-x------ 1 john john 64 Feb 16 23:08 3 -> /proc/26186/fd
```

Note that the subdirectory self is a symbolic link to the process ID of the currently running process. The fd directory under here applies to the ls command that is currently running. There is one symbolic link for each open file descriptor inside the process. The names are just the decimal values of the file descriptor numbers inside the process. Each symbolic link points to an open file or device.

In this example, you will notice that I redirected the output to a file. The resulting output shows that file descriptor 1 (the standard output) for the current process points to the file I am redirecting to (foo.txt). Also notice that standard input and standard error file descriptors point to the current pseudoterminal (/dev/pts/2). Finally, a fourth file descriptor is required by the ls command to read the directory you are looking at.

6.5.1.1 The lsof Command

The lsof[8] command allows you to look at all the open files of all processes in the system. You need superuser permission to see everything; otherwise, you get to see only processes that you own. lsof allows you to look at much more than file descriptors. Compare the output between lsof and simply looking at /proc/pid/fd:

```
$ ls -l /proc/26231/fd
total 4
lrwx------ 1 root root 64 Feb 17 19:40 0 -> /dev/pts/0
lrwx------ 1 root root 64 Feb 17 19:40 1 -> /dev/pts/0
lrwx------ 1 root root 64 Feb 17 19:40 2 -> /dev/pts/0
lrwx------ 1 root root 64 Feb 17 19:40 255 -> /dev/pts/0
```

---

8. ftp://lsof.itap.purdue.edu/pub/tools/unix/lsof

```
$ lsof -p 26231
COMMAND     PID USER    FD    TYPE DEVICE      SIZE    NODE NAME
bash      26231 root    cwd    DIR  253,0      4096  542913 /root
bash      26231 root    rtd    DIR  253,0      4096       2 /
bash      26231 root    txt    REG  253,0    686520  415365 /bin/bash
bash      26231 root    mem    REG  253,0    126648  608855 /lib/ld-2.3.5.so
bash      26231 root    mem    REG  253,0   1489572  608856 /lib/libc-2.3.5.so
bash      26231 root    mem    REG  253,0     16244  608859 /lib/libdl...
bash      26231 root    mem    REG  253,0     12924  606897 /lib/libtermcap...
bash      26231 root    mem    REG    0,0                 0 [heap] (stat: ...
bash      26231 root    mem    REG  253,0  48501472  801788 /usr/lib/locale...
bash      26231 root    mem    REG  253,0     46552  606837 /lib/libnss_fil...
bash      26231 root    mem    REG  253,0     22294  862494 /usr/lib/gconv/...
bash      26231 root     0u    CHR  136,0                 2 /dev/pts/0
bash      26231 root     1u    CHR  136,0                 2 /dev/pts/0
bash      26231 root     2u    CHR  136,0                 2 /dev/pts/0
bash      26231 root   255u    CHR  136,0                 2 /dev/pts/0
```

Here, you can see that lsof shows much more than just file descriptors. Notice that in the FD column of the lsof output, several files are listed in addition to those that have a file descriptor. These files have the abbreviations mem and txt, which indicate that these files have been mmapped into the process's space. These files don't consume file descriptors, even though they are mapped into memory. Like other files opened with file descriptors, you can delete these files, but they will continue to take up space on the file system until no process has them open. Finally, there are the abbreviations cwd for the current working directory and rtd for the root directory. As I mentioned earlier, each process has its own unique root and current working directory (more on that later in this chapter).

lsof is a rather complicated tool with many options. In addition to the man page, a QUICKSTART file that comes with it should be installed with the lsof package. This file contains some very good tutorial information.

6.5.1.2   Limits to File Descriptor Usage

The actual number of open files allowed to each process is determined by the kernel, but you can find out at runtime with the sysconf function as follows:

```
sysconf(_SC_OPEN_MAX);
```

You have used the sysconf call before, to determine the system page size and clock tick. When called with the _SC_OPEN_MAX argument, sysconf returns the maximum number of files a single process may have open at one time. When the process reaches its limit, a subsequent call to `open` will fail with the error `EMFILE` (too many open files). It doesn't matter whether it's a file, a device, or a socket; the limit is on the number of file descriptors.

6.5.2   Stack

The stack is a region of memory in user space used by the process for temporary storage. The stack gets its name because the behavior is analogous to a stack of items. As with a real stack of objects, the last item to be placed on the stack is the first one that is taken off. This is sometimes called a LIFO (last in, first out) buffer. Placing data on the stack is called *pushing,* and removing data from the stack is called *popping.*

For programmers, the stack is where local variables are stored inside functions. A portable C/C++ program never allocates memory from stack directly, instead relying on the compiler to allocate local variables for it. This works nicely with functional programming languages, because variables can be pushed on the stack during the life of the function, and all the compiler needs to ensure is that the stack pointer is restored to its original location before the function exits. In other words, memory is allocated and freed automatically. C/C++ refers to local variables that are stored on the stack as *automatic* storage and uses the `auto` keyword to indicate this. This happens to be the default storage class for local variables, so almost no one ever uses the `auto` keyword. The alternative to automatic storage is *static* storage, which is identified with the `static` keyword. Local variables listed as `static` do not use the stack for storage but rely on permanent storage allocated by the linker and/or loader.[9]

As shown in Figure 6-2 earlier in this chapter, the base (bottom) of the stack is placed near the highest user-space virtual address, and the stack grows down from there. The maximum size of the stack is fixed at process start time. The maximum can be adjusted for new processes, but when a process starts, the maximum size of the stack cannot be changed. If the process consumes too much stack space, the result is called a *stack overflow.* Linux responds to a stack overflow with a simple `SIGSEGV` to the process.

You cannot know for sure where the stack base will be because of a couple of features in the kernel that randomize the location of the stack base (see the "Stack

---

9. The `static` keyword is notorious for being overloaded (having different meanings in different contexts). Just remember that in every context, `static` means permanent storage and limited scope.

Coloring" sidebar). So although you don't know exactly where the base of the stack is, you know it will be somewhere near the maximum user-space virtual address.

Stack Coloring

The base address of the stack (the bottom) is not the same in every process because of a technique called stack coloring. When the stack base is placed at the same virtual address every time, processes running the same executable tend to get the same virtual addresses for stack variables every time they run.

This creates performance issues on Intel processors with Hyperthreading technology. This is an Intel feature that allows a single CPU to behave like two independent CPUs on a single chip. Unlike a true dual-core CPU, which contains two independent CPUs, a CPU with Hyperthreading shares most of the processor resources between the two logical cores, including the cache.

When two threads or processes use the same virtual address for the stack, they contend for the same cache lines, causing contention and degrading performance. By randomizing the base address of the stack, multiple processes are more likely to use different cache lines and avoid thrashing.

Although stack coloring was not intended to be a security feature, it does provide a modest security enhancement. Some buffer overflow attacks rely on the fact that virtual addresses will be the same from one run to the next. Randomizing the stack base makes it less likely (but not impossible) that such an attack will succeed.

Stack size limits are determined by the `setrlimit` system call, which also can be accessed via the Bash built-in `ulimit` command. The new limit is enforced for all children of the current process.

6.5.3   Resident and Locked Memory

The use of virtual memory means that parts of a process may not be stored in RAM. These parts may be stored on the swap disk or not stored at all. Memory that has not been initialized or accessed, for example, does not need to be allocated physically. Such pages will not be allocated until a memory access causes a page fault, which causes the kernel to allocate them.

Part of a process's footprint includes the amount of RAM that it consumes, which is characterized by the amount of *resident memory*, which refers specifically to the parts of a process's memory that are stored in RAM. It does not include parts of the process that are in swap or are not stored.

A subset of the resident memory is *locked memory*, which refers to any virtual memory that has been explicitly locked into RAM by the process. A locked page cannot be swapped and is always resident in RAM. A process locks a page to prevent the latency that can occur due to swapping. Locked pages mean that less RAM is available to other processes. For this reason, only processes with root privileges are allowed to lock pages.

6.6   Setting Process Limits

The setrlimit function can be used to enforce limits on the resources a process can consume. You can examine the current limits by using the getrlimit function call. I introduced these functions in Chapter 5. These are defined as follows:

```
int setrlimit(int resource, const struct rlimit *rlim);
int getrlimit(int resource, struct rlimit *rlim);
```

Recall that the rlimit structure has a *soft* and *hard* limit. The hard limit typically is set at system startup and usually is not modified. When the hard limit is reduced, it cannot be raised for that process. The soft limit can be raised and lowered as desired but cannot exceed the hard limit. The rlimit structure is defined as follows:

```
struct rlimit {
      rlim_t rlim_cur;   /* Soft limit */
      rlim_t rlim_max;   /* Hard limit (ceiling for rlim_cur) */
};
```

Note that a process can set limits only for itself; there is no API to change the limits of a different process. A typical pattern for setting resource usage is to do so following a fork in the child process before an execve. For example:

```
pid_t pid = fork();
if ( pid == 0 ) {
      struct rlimit limits = {...};
      getrlimit( RLIMIT_..., &limits);

      Modify soft limit.

      setrlimit( RLIMIT_..., &limits );
      exec( ... );
}
```

The caller indicates the resource to be limited in the first argument. The resources that can be controlled include many that apply to the current user, not just the current process. A complete list is provided in Table 6-2.

TABLE 6-2   Resource Flags Used by setrlimit and getrlimit

Resource	Description
RLIMIT_AS	Limits the amount of virtual memory *(address space)* a process may consume. This applies to both stack and heap. When the size exceeds the soft limit, dynamic allocations (including anonymous mmaps) will fail with ENOMEM. If a stack allocation causes the limit to be exceeded, the process will be killed with SIGSEGV.
RLIMIT_CORE	Limits the size of a core file. Setting this to zero disables the generation of core files, which may be desirable for security reasons but undesirable during software development.
RLIMIT_CPU	Limits the amount of CPU time a process may consume. Input is in seconds. When the soft limit expires, the process receives SIGXCPU once per second until the hard limit, when it receives SIGKILL.
RLIMIT_DATA	Maximum size of the data segment. This affects calls to brk and sbrk, which (in theory) means that dynamic memory allocations will fail when the soft limit is reached. The errno when this occurs is ENOMEM. glibc uses mmap when brk fails, effectively neutering this feature.
RLIMIT_FSIZE	Maximum size of an individual file a process may create. When the process exceeds the soft limit, it receives SIGXFSZ, and the write and truncate system calls fail with EFBIG.
RLIMIT_LOCKS	Limits the number of locks a process may have at one time; not used in Linux 2.6.
RLIMIT_MEMLOCK	Sets the maximum number of bytes a process may have locked at one time; can be overridden by privileged users.
RLIMIT_NOFILE	Limits the number of file descriptors a process may have open at one time.
RLIMIT_NPROC	Maximum number of processes that may be created by the real user ID of the calling process. When the soft limit is reached, the fork call fails with errno set to EAGAIN.
RLIMIT_RSS	Limits the *resident set size* of a process, which is the size of all resident memory of the process; allegedly enforced in Linux but not observed in 2.6.14.

continues

TABLE 6-2   *Continued*

Resource	Description
RLIMIT_SIGPENDING	Limits the number of signals that may be queued (pending) for the given process. See Chapter 7.
RLIMIT_STACK	Sets the maximum size of the stack allowed for the process.

The behavior of the process when it attempts to exceed one of these resources depends on the resource being limited. If you are limiting stack, for example, the process will abort with a SIGSEGV when you try to allocate too much automatic storage. On the other hand, if you are limiting the number of file descriptors, the process will most likely fail in an open call by returning -1.

Checking the limits via getrlimit is one way to ensure robust operation. In theory, this would work very well with the getrusage system call. Unfortunately, this system call in Linux provides very little information about resource usage to the application. What little is provided comes after an exit call, making it largely unusable at runtime.

You may be wondering why anyone would want to impose limits on processes. There are several reasons. One might be to prevent users from crippling your system by allocating and using too much memory. A malicious (or poorly written) process can bring a system to a crawl simply by allocating lots of memory. Excessive page faulting caused by the process can cause other processes to experience excessive latency and slow everything. Another reason for limits is to disable core files, which may contain passwords or other sensitive information. Think that's a stretch? Listing 6-2 demonstrates a trivial example of how even an encrypted password can be exposed in a core file.

LISTING 6-2   insecure.c: Password Exposed in a Core File

```
#include <stdio.h>
#include <stdlib.h>

// Encrypted message, might take years to crack.
unsigned char secret_message[] = {
  0x8f, 0x9e, 0x8c, 0x8c, 0x88, 0x90, 0x8d, 0x9b, 0xc2, 0x8b, 0x90,
  0x8f, 0xdf, 0x8c, 0x9a, 0x9c, 0x8d, 0x9a, 0x8b
};

int main(int argc, char *argv[])
```

```
{
  int i;
  for (i = 0; i < sizeof(secret_message); i++) {
    // Okay maybe not years, but you get the idea.
    secret_message[i] ^= 0xff;
  }
  abort();
}
```

The password might be protected by encryption, but if the program decrypts the password into memory, it can be visible when the process dumps a core file. The data is only as secure as the core image. If the core gets dumped to disk, it can be read by anyone with permission to read it. For this reason, the kernel creates core files with restricted permissions so that only the owner can read them. This is only a modest defense against unauthorized users gaining access to sensitive information. Sometimes, the owner of the executable file may be unauthorized to see the core file.

Consider Listing 6-2, which contains a secret message. It's simply an ASCII string with all the bits toggled. This is a pitiful form of encryption, but it is enough to hide the message from a casual observer. The first thing this program does is decrypt the secret message so that it resides in memory. The subsequent abort causes the core to be written to disk, now containing the unencrypted message.

```
$ ulimit -c unlimited          Many distributions disable core files for your protection.
$ ./insecure
Aborted (core dumped)
$ strings ./core | grep password    Just looking . . .
password=top secret                  Look what I found!
```

This is a fairly contrived example, but it illustrates how easy it can be to steal private information from insecure code. Most distributions disable core file generation by default for this reason.

6.7   Processes and procfs

The `procfs` file system is a pseudo file system that presents information to the user about the system and individual processes. Some operating systems are notorious for having numerous arcane system calls to provide the information in `procfs`. With `procfs` in Linux, however, the only system calls you need are `open`, `close`, `read`, and `write`. Beware—no standards cover the contents of `procfs`. In theory, a program that reads from `procfs` may work fine on one kernel and fail on another.

By convention, `procfs` is mounted on the `/proc` directory. In this file system, there is a tree of system and process information. Much of what you find here is not available via a system call, which is often why it is here.

`procfs` was introduced in UNIX to make debugging easier. It is vital to support process monitoring commands in user space, such as `ps`. Since Linux adopted it, it has suffered from quite a bit of feature creep.

`procfs` has two basic missions in Linux today. One is the same as in UNIX, which is to provide information about each process running in the system; the other is to provide information about the system as a whole.

For the most part, the information in `procfs` is in ASCII text.

Each process has a subdirectory under `/proc` named after its process ID, so process 123 has a directory named `/proc/123`, which exists for the lifetime of the process. In addition, there is a directory named `/proc/self`, which is a link to the directory of the currently running process.

Inside each subdirectory, you will find much of the information I have discussed about the process footprint, and then some. Some of this information is quite useful, and some is esoteric. It never hurts to explore, though.

The `/proc` directory is an excellent debugging tool, allowing you to get information about system behavior with no further tools. The actual contents of the directory can vary depending on the options compiled into the kernel, as well as from one release to the next. Table 6-3 lists some of the most common entries and their uses.

TABLE 6-3   Sample Files in the /proc/PID Directory

File	Description	Format
auxv	A vector of values used by tools like `gdb`, containing information about the system.	Binary
cmdline	An ASCII string delimited with ASCII NULs (0) representing the `argv` vector that a C program would see.	ASCII
cwd	A symbolic link to the current working directory of the process.	N/A
environ	The process's environment packed into an ASCII string delimited by ASCII NULs. Each token is represented as it is in the `envp` vector passed to C programs (for example, `PATH=xyz:abc`).	ASCII

File	Description	Format
exe	A symbolic link to the file containing the code for this process.	N/A
fd	A directory containing a symbolic link for each file descriptor open by the process. These links include anything open with a file descriptor, including plain files, sockets, and pipes.	N/A
maps	A textual representation of the user space memory mapped by the process. For kernel threads, this file is empty, because kernel threads have no user space.	ASCII text
mem	A file that allows other processes to access this process's user space; used by programs like gdb.	Binary
mounts	A list of mounted file systems, like /etc/mtab. This is the same for all processes.	Text
oom_adj	Allows the user to adjust the oom_score (see below).	Text
oom_score	The process's "badness" as determined by the OOM (out of memory) killer. When the system runs out of memory, processes with high scores are killed first.	Text
root	A symbolic link to the root file system of the process; normally points to / but will be different if the process has called chroot.	N/A
smaps	Detailed list of mappings of the shared libraries used by this process. Unlike maps, this includes more details about the mappings, including the amount of clean and dirty pages.	ASCII text
stat	A one-line, scanf-friendly representation of the process status, used by the ps command.	ASCII text
statm	A summary of process memory usage, most of which is in stat.	ASCII text
status	Same information as stat in a more human-readable form.	ASCII text
wchan	Indicates the kernel function in which the process is blocking (if applicable).	Text

Technically, `procfs` is not required to run a Linux system, although many tools depend on the contents of `/proc`. You might be surprised by what doesn't work if you try to run a system without it.

6.8   Tools for Managing Processes

The `procps` project[10] contains many tools for mining the `procfs` file system and is included with most distributions. Some of the tools included with the package, such as the `ps` command, are part of the POSIX standard. Other tools are non-standard yet very useful. Often, it is more convenient to use these commands than to plod through the `/proc` directories yourself. Before you write a script to go through the `/proc` directories, check here first.

6.8.1   Displaying Process Information with ps

The `ps` command from the `procps` package implements the features specified by POSIX standard, as well as several other standards. While these standards are converging, they each have their own argument conventions, which cannot be changed easily without affecting a large body of client code (scripts). As a result, you will find that `ps` usually has at least two ways to do the same thing, two names for each field, and so on. Not surprisingly, the man page for the `ps` command is a bit dense.

Typing **ps** with no arguments shows you only processes that are owned by the current user and attached to the current terminal. This generally includes all the processes that were started in the currently running shell, although it has nothing to do with the shell's concept of background and foreground processes. Recall that the shell keeps track of processes as *jobs* running in the foreground or background. Two different shells can use the same terminal, but the jobs listed include only the currently running shell, whereas the default `ps` output includes processes started from both shells. For example:

```
$ tty                          What is the name of our terminal?
/dev/pts/1
$ ps
```

---

10. http://procps.sourceforge.net

```
  PID TTY          TIME CMD
21563 pts/1     00:00:00 bash
21589 pts/1     00:00:00 ps                    Only two processes are running on this terminal.

$ sleep 1000 &
[1] 21590                                       Background job 1, process ID 21590
$ jobs -l
[1]+ 21590 Running   sleep 1000 &
$ ps
  PID TTY          TIME CMD
21563 pts/1     00:00:00 bash
21590 pts/1     00:00:00 sleep
21591 pts/1     00:00:00 ps                     New process is listed by the ps and jobs commands.

$ bash                                          Start a new shell in the same terminal.
$ jobs                                          The list of jobs is now empty because it's a new shell.
$ ps                                            ps shows processes from both shells.
  PID TTY          TIME CMD
21563 pts/1     00:00:00 bash
21590 pts/1     00:00:00 sleep
21592 pts/1     00:00:00 bash
21609 pts/1     00:00:00 ps
```

Most often, you want to see more information than the default output from ps. Either you are interested in what's happening outside your terminal, or you want to see more information about the state of your process. The -l option is a good place to start. This provides a longer list of process properties. For example:

```
$ ps -l
F S   UID   PID  PPID  C PRI  NI ADDR SZ WCHAN  TTY          TIME CMD
0 S   500 21563 21562  0  75   0  - 1128 wait   pts/1    00:00:00 bash
0 S   500 21590 21563  0  76   0  -  974 -      pts/1    00:00:00 sleep
0 R   500 21623 21563 96  85   0  - 1082 -      pts/1    00:00:26 cruncher
0 R   500 21626 21563  0  75   0  - 1109 -      pts/1    00:00:00 ps
```

The field headings provide a brief, sometimes cryptic description of the columns in the output. Reading from left to right, the column descriptions from the default long output are listed in Table 6-4.

Chances are that this output has more than you're interested in or is missing something you want. Fortunately, ps allows you to customize your output to show you exactly what you want to know.

TABLE 6-4   Output Columns of the ps Long Format

Column Header	Description
F	Flags (see `sched.h`)
S	The process state:
	R—running
	S—sleeping (interruptible)
	T—stopped
	D—sleeping (uninterruptible)
	Z—terminated but not reaped
UID	Effective user ID of the process
PID	Process ID
PPID	Parent process ID
C	CPU utilization percentage
PRI	Process's priority
NI	Process's nice value
ADDR	Unused in Linux
SZ	Approximate virtual-memory size of the process, in pages
WCHAN	System call or kernel function that is causing the process to sleep (if any)
TTY	Controlling terminal
TIME	Amount of CPU time consumed by the process
CMD	Command name as listed in `/proc/stat` (truncated to 15 characters)

6.8.2   Advanced Process Information Using Formats

The `procps` package is intended for use in operating systems besides Linux, and nowhere is this more apparent than the `ps` command. In particular, the formatting fields used by the `-o` option are a motley bunch of mnemonics derived from various flavors of UNIX over the years. Many of these are synonyms, due to the fact that each vendor happened to choose a slightly different name. SGI came up with one mnemonic, Sun came up with another, and Hewlett-Packard with yet another. As of `procps` version 3.2.6, the `ps` command recognizes 236 different formatting options.[11] Only a few are documented in the `man` page.

I have used this feature in some earlier examples; now I'll show it in detail. To illustrate the formatting options at work, you can use the following command to see how much time your process has been running and how much CPU time it has consumed:

```
$ sleep 10000 &
[1] 23849
$ ps -o etime,time -p 23849
    ELAPSED     TIME
      00:06 00:00:00
```

The `etime` format option shows the elapsed time since the process began, and the `time` format option shows the CPU time consumed by the process in seconds.

Table 6-5 shows a listing of the most useful formats. In many instances, there are several formats to tell you the same information. Sometimes, the output format is slightly different; at other times, there are multiple aliases for the identical format.

If you are using this feature in a script that will run in multiple operating systems, beware: Not all these formats are supported in all (non-`procps`) versions of `ps`. The `procps` source code complains about many ambiguities in the standards that apply.

---

11. Of these, 86 options produce no useful data!

TABLE 6-5   Format Options Supported by ps

	Format	Description
Time related	start, start_time, lstart, bsdstart	The time and date when the process started. Each format produces slightly different output. Some formats includes the date; some include the seconds; all include the hour and minutes.
	etime	Elapsed time from the start of the process.
	time, cputime, atime, bsdtime	Cumulative CPU time consumed by the process in hours, minutes, and seconds. bsdtime is minutes and seconds only.
Memory related	size	Approximate total swappable process memory; includes stack and heap.
	m_size	Virtual-memory size of the process as reported by the kernel; not exactly the same as size.
	pmem, %mem	The process's resident memory, expressed as a percentage of total physical memory in the system.
	majflt, maj_flt, pagein	The number of *major* page faults as defined by the kernel.
	minflt, min_flt	The number of *minor* page faults as defined by the kernel.
	sz, vsz, vsize	Total virtual memory used by the process. sz is reported in pages; vsz and vsize are reported in K.
	rss, rssize, rsz	Total process memory resident in RAM, expressed in K.
	lim	Process limit on rss set by setrlimit.
	stackp	The lowest address of allocated stack; fixed until more stack is allocated.

	Format	Description
Scheduler related	cpu	On SMP systems, identifies the CPU that the processes is executing on; prints – for uniprocessor systems.
	policy, class, cls, sched	Indicate the scheduler class of the process as a number or a mnemonic, defined as follows: TS (0)—Normal, time sliced FF (1)—Real time, FIFO RR (2)—Real time, round robin
	cp, %cpu, c, util	CPU utilization of the process, expressed as a percentage.
	pri	Priority listed as a positive integer, with higher values indicating higher priority (0–39 normal, 41–99 real time; priority 40 is unused by Linux). These are the same values you would see in the kernel.
	priority	Priority using lower numbers to indicate higher priority (39–0 normal, -1– -99 real time). These are the same values found in /proc/PID/stat/.
	opri, intpri	Inverted version of priority format (-39– -0 normal, 1–99 real time). Positive numbers are used for real-time processes, and negative numbers are normal processes.
	s, state, stat	Process state. state is D, R, S, T, or Z. stat adds a character for more information.
	tid, spid, lwp	For multithreaded processes, indicates the thread ID of multiple threads. Threads are shown only with the -T option.
	wchan, wname	Name of system call or kernel function causing the process to block; – if process is not sleeping.

6.8.3 Finding Processes by Name with ps and pgrep

Occasionally, you need to find what's going on with a command you launched from another terminal or perhaps during startup. You might know the command name, but you don't know the process ID. The typical pattern is

```
$ ps -ef | grep myprogram
```

It's so common that it was added to the `ps` command with the `-C` option—a feature I have used repeatedly in the examples in this book. When you use this option, the command name you provide must match exactly. Then the `ps` command will apply to all processes that match. When you don't know the exact command (or don't want to type it), the `pgrep` command is a nice alternative. As you might expect, the argument to `pgrep` is a regular expression that matches anywhere in the string, just like `grep`. Unlike the `ps` command, however, the default output consists of unadorned `pids`, which makes it suitable for generating a list of `pids` that can be used by other programs. For example:

```
$ ./myproc &
[1] 5357
$ cat /proc/$(pgrep myproc)/stat        # Embed pid of myproc in the /proc filename.
5357 (myproc) T 3681 5357 3681 34817 ...
```

`pgrep` has some peculiar behavior for processes with names longer than 16 characters due to the fact that it allocates only 16 characters to store the command name. This can be dangerous when used in combination with commands like `kill` (something that is not advisable anyway). For more examples, see the discussion of `skill` and `pkill` later in this chapter. These commands have the same issue, but for a different reason.

Other useful options for `pgrep` include the `-x` option, which forces an exact match, and the `-l` option, which provides some additional information similar to the default output from `ps`. This saves you the trouble of having to send the output of `pgrep` to the `ps` command.

Finally, `pgrep` has several options that allow you to filter output based on terminal name, user ID, group ID, and so on. One very useful option is the `-n` option, which shows you only the most recently executed command that matches. If you want to know what the most recently spawned `telnetd` process is, you could use the following:

```
$ pgrep -n telnetd
```

The `telnetd` process forks a new copy for each terminal that logs in. This tells you which process is the most recent.

A similar but less flexible program is `pidof`, which also takes a command name as an argument. This is not part of `procps` but is part of the `SysVinit` package, which is used for startup scripts. This command lives in `/sbin` and is intended for use by startup scripts. Not every distribution uses the `SysVinit` package, so it's probably wise to avoid it if portability is a concern.

6.8.4 Watching Process Memory Usage with pmap

I have used the `pmap` command before to look at processes. This information is contained in `/proc/PID/maps`, which shows a map of a process's virtual memory. For example:

```
$ cat &
[1] 3989
$ cat /proc/3989/maps
009db000-009f0000 r-xp 00000000 fd:00 773010      /lib/ld-2.3.3.so
009f0000-009f1000 r-xp 00014000 fd:00 773010      /lib/ld-2.3.3.so
009f1000-009f2000 rwxp 00015000 fd:00 773010      /lib/ld-2.3.3.so
009f4000-00b15000 r-xp 00000000 fd:00 773011      /lib/tls/libc-2.3.3.so
00b15000-00b17000 r-xp 00120000 fd:00 773011      /lib/tls/libc-2.3.3.so
00b17000-00b19000 rwxp 00122000 fd:00 773011      /lib/tls/libc-2.3.3.so
00b19000-00b1b000 rwxp 00b19000 00:00 0
08048000-0804c000 r-xp 00000000 fd:00 4702239     /bin/cat
0804c000-0804d000 rwxp 00003000 fd:00 4702239     /bin/cat
0804d000-0806e000 rwxp 0804d000 00:00 0           [heap]
b7d1e000-b7f1e000 r-xp 00000000 fd:00 1232413     /usr/../locale-archive
b7f1e000-b7f20000 rwxp b7f1e000 00:00 0
bfd1b000-bfd31000 rw-p bfd1b000 00:00 0           [stack]
ffffe000-fffff000 ---p 00000000 00:00 0           [vdso]
```

This is a little hard to read, but the format is described fully in the `proc(5)` man page. Each line is a range of virtual memory. The range of addresses is shown on the left in the first column. The second column shows the permissions and an s or p to indicate shared and private mappings. The next column indicates the device offset, such as would be used for an equivalent mmap call. For anonymous memory maps, this is the same as the virtual address. If the virtual memory is mapped to a file or device, the subsequent fields indicate the device identifier in major/minor format, followed by the inode[12] and finally the file/device name.

The equivalent map produced by the pmap command is a bit more user friendly:

```
$ pmap 3989
3989:   cat
009db000      84K r-x--  /lib/ld-2.3.3.so
009f0000       4K r-x--  /lib/ld-2.3.3.so
009f1000       4K rwx--  /lib/ld-2.3.3.so
009f4000    1156K r-x--  /lib/tls/libc-2.3.3.so
00b15000       8K r-x--  /lib/tls/libc-2.3.3.so
00b17000       8K rwx--  /lib/tls/libc-2.3.3.so
00b19000       8K rwx--     [ anon ]
08048000      16K r-x--  /bin/cat
0804c000       4K rwx--  /bin/cat
0804d000     132K rwx--     [ anon ]
b7d1e000    2048K r-x--  /usr/lib/locale/locale-archive
b7f1e000       8K rwx--     [ anon ]
bfd1b000      88K rw---     [ stack ]
ffffe000       4K -----     [ anon ]
 total     3572K
```

This tells you more of what you probably want to know, such as the total amount of memory mapped. Each region is presented only with the base address and size, along with the permissions and device name. For nondevice mappings, an appropriate substitute is provided. If you want to see more device information from /proc/PID/maps, use the -d option.

6.8.5   Sending Signals to Processes by Name

The skill and pkill commands function like the kill command, except that they try to match process names instead of a process ID. Treat these commands like loaded weapons. *Use with caution.*

skill takes a process name as an argument and looks only for exact matches. It uses the contents of /proc/PID/stat to match. Linux stores only the first 15 characters of the command name in /proc/PID/stat,[13] so if you are looking for a process with an unusually long command name, you won't find it with skill.

---

12. I discuss inodes in more detail in Chapter 7.
13. Defined by TASK_COMM_LEN in the kernel.

Things can get weird if you have commands that are exactly 15 characters and commands that are longer with the same first 15 characters. For example:

```
$ ./image_generator &              Exactly 15 characters
[1] ...
$ ./image_generator1 &             Exactly 16 characters
[2] ...
$ skill image_generator            Kills both!
[1] Terminated ./image_generator
[2] Terminated ./image_generator1
```

pkill works on a similar principle except that it uses a regular expression for the process name. This is even more dangerous, because it will match anywhere in the command string. Unlike skill, pkill uses /proc/cmdline, which stores the entire argv vector as -is. If not careful, the unwary user is likely to kill unintended processes. For example:

```
$ ./proc_abc &
[1] ...
$ ./abc_proc &
[2] ...

$ pkill abc                        Kills both!
$ pkill ^abc                       Kills only abc_proc.
$ pkill abc\$                      Kills only proc_abc. ($ is escaped with a backslash.)
```

Because the argument is a regular expression, the first command in the previous example kills both processes because the term abc is found in both commands. To be more specific, you could specify the entire command, or you could use the regular-expression syntax to be more precise. That is what the two subsequent commands do. The regular expression ^abc indicates that the command must begin with the letters abc, which prevents it from killing proc_abc. Similarly, the regular expression abc$ indicates that the command must end with the letters abc, which prevents it from killing abc_proc.

6.9   Summary

This chapter focused on the user-space aspects of processes. I took a detailed look at how exec occurs and some of the tricks that Linux uses to execute various kinds of code. I also illustrated a few pitfalls associated with exec.

I looked in detail at the various resources that processes consume and how to look for them. Finally, I looked at some of the tools you can use to manage processes from the shell.

6.9.1   System Calls and APIs Used in This Chapter

- `execve`—Linux system call to initialize a process's user space and execute program code. POSIX defines several functions with similar signatures, but they all use this system call. This is usually called after a call to `fork`. Refer to `exec(3)`.

- `fcntl`—used to set flags on file descriptors. I used this function to set the `FD_CLOEXEC` flag.

- `fork`—system call to create a clone of the currently running process. This is the first step in creating a new process.

- `kill`—system call to send a signal to a running process.

- `setrlimit, getrlimit`—functions to test and set process resource limits.

- `sysconf`—returns system constants that can be used at runtime.

- `wait, waitpid, wait3, wait4`—allow a parent to synchronize with a child process.

6.9.2   Tools Used in This Chapter

- `pgrep`—finds processes that match a regular expression

- `pmap`—prints a process's memory map

- `ps`—the well-known process status command

- `ulimit`—Bash built-in function to test and set process resource limits

6.9.3   Online Resources

- http://procps.sourceforge.net—the home page for the `procps` project, which provides many useful tools for tracking process and system resources

- www.unix.org—publishes the Single UNIX Specification

- www.unix.org and www.opengroup.org—publish the POSIX standard (IEEE Standard 1003.2) and many others (registration required)

## Chapter 7

Communication between Processes

7.1 Introduction

Because each process has its own separate address space, communication between processes is not always easy. There are several techniques for interprocess communication (IPC), each with benefits and drawbacks.

A central problem that arises in applications with multiple processes or threads is the race condition. A *race condition* describes any situation in which multiple processes (or threads) attempt to modify the same data at the same time. Without synchronization, there is no guarantee that one process isn't going to clobber the output of another. Perhaps more important, race conditions make the output unpredictable.

In general, race conditions are caused by a lack of synchronization, which can result in output that changes based on system load or other factors. You saw some simple examples in Chapter 6, where the text from parent and child processes varied from one run to the next. Race conditions are almost never this obvious. Many times, a race condition may not exhibit itself until after the code is released.

IPC is vital to preventing race conditions. When you use it improperly, however, you may introduce race conditions rather than prevent them. This chapter will help you understand how to use IPC properly and will show you some tools you can use to debug processes using IPC.

7.2   IPC Using Plain Files

Plain files are a primitive but effective way to communicate between processes. When two processes that don't execute simultaneously must communicate, a file is perhaps your only choice for IPC. An example of this is the C compiler. When you compile a program with gcc, for example, it generates an assembly-language file, which is passed to the assembler. The intermediate file is deleted after assembly, so you normally don't see it, but you can see it for yourself with the -v option to gcc:

```
$ gcc -v -c hello.c
...
.../cc1 ... hello.c ... -o /tmp/ccPrPSPE.s     Compiler generates a temporary file.
...
as -V -Qy -o hello.o /tmp/ccPrPSPE.s           Assembler uses temporary file for input.
```

This works for the C compiler because it must work in a serial fashion—that is, the compiler must finish before the assembler can start. So although these are different processes, they don't run simultaneously.

You can use files for IPC between processes that are running simultaneously, but the opportunity for race conditions looms. When two processes communicate via file, there is no guarantee that one isn't writing while the other is reading, or vice versa. That means you can read a message that is half written or read an old message when you were expecting a new one. One such naïve—and seriously flawed—implementation is shown in Listing 7-1.

LISTING 7-1   file-ipc-naive.c: Naïve IPC Using a File

```
 1 #include <stdio.h>
 2 #include <string.h>
 3 #include <stdlib.h>
 4 #include <unistd.h>
 5 #include <sched.h>
 6 #include <sys/wait.h>
 7
 8 // This is the file parent and child will use for IPC.
 9 const char *filename = "messagebuf.dat";
10
11 void error_out(const char *msg)
12 {
13     perror(msg);
```

```
14      exit(EXIT_FAILURE);
15 }
16
17 void child(void)
18 {
19     // Child reads from the file.
20     FILE *fp = fopen(filename, "r");
21     if (fp == NULL)
22         error_out("child:fopen");
23
24     // Read from the file
25     char buf[32];
26     fread(buf, sizeof(buf), 1, fp);
27
28     printf("child read %s\n", buf);
29     fclose(fp);
30 }
31
32 void parent(void)
33 {
34     // Parent creates the file
35     FILE *fp = fopen(filename, "w");
36     if (fp == NULL)
37         error_out("parent:fopen");
38
39     // Write a message to the file.
40     fprintf(fp, "Hello World\n");
41     fclose(fp);
42 }
43
44 int main(int argc, char *argv[])
45 {
46     pid_t pid = fork();
47
48     if (pid == 0) {
49         child();
50     }
51     else {
52         parent();
53
54         // Wait for the child to finish.
55         int status = 0;
56         int r = wait(&status);
57         if (r == -1)
58             error_out("parent:wait");
59
60         // Child returns non-zero status on failure.
61         printf("child status=%d\n", WEXITSTATUS(status));
62         unlink(filename);
63     }
64     exit(0);
65 }
```

Listing 7-1 runs with no synchronization whatsoever, so the output is unpredictable for the most part, but on my machine it fails almost every time:

```
$ ./file-ipc-naive
child:fopen: No such file or directory
child status=1
```

Can you spot the race condition? You may be inclined to use strace to find it, but you could be in for a surprise. Again on my machine, I observed the following:

```
$ strace -o strace.out -f ./file-ipc-naive
child read Hello World                        The #$!% thing works now!
child status=0
```

Monitoring with strace interfered with the timing enough to cause the program to produce the expected result. This is where a less experienced programmer is likely to put a sleep call with a comment like "Don't remove this!" That's a sure sign that the programmer encountered a race condition and didn't know how to deal with it. Also, it's usually very inefficient.

So how do you fix this code? Well, one thing I won't show you is where to put the sleep calls. There are several elegant solutions to the problem, but basically, you need to synchronize access to the file between the parent and the child processes. One simple way to do this is by using the lockf function. An example of this is shown in Listing 7-2.

LISTING 7-2   file-ipc-better.c: IPC Using Files and Synchronization with lockf

```
 1 #include <stdio.h>
 2 #include <string.h>
 3 #include <stdlib.h>
 4 #include <unistd.h>
 5 #include <sched.h>
 6 #include <sys/wait.h>
 7 #include <sys/file.h>
 8 #include <sys/stat.h>
 9
10 const char *filename = "messagebuf.dat";
11
12 void error_out(const char *msg)
13 {
14     perror(msg);
15     exit(EXIT_FAILURE);
16 }
17
18 void child(void)
19 {
```

```
20      // With mandatory locks we block here until the parent unlocks the file.
21      FILE *fp = fopen(filename, "r+");
22      if (fp == NULL)
23          error_out("child:fopen");
24
25      // With advisory locks we block here until the parent unlocks the file.
26      int r = lockf(fileno(fp), F_LOCK, 0);
27      if (r == -1)
28          error_out("parent:lockf");
29
30      // Now we know the data is valid.
31      char buf[32];
32      fread(buf, sizeof(buf), 1, fp);
33      if (ferror(fp))
34          error_out("fread");
35
36      printf("child read '%s'\n", buf);
37  }
38
39  void parent(FILE * fp)
40  {
41      // Write our PID to the file.
42      fprintf(fp, "%#x", getpid());
43
44      // Flush the user-space buffers to the
45      // filesystem before unlocking.
46      fflush(fp);
47
48      // As soon as the data on the filesystem is up-to-date
49      // we can unlock the file and let the child read it.
50      int r = lockf(fileno(fp), F_ULOCK, 0);
51      if (r == -1)
52          error_out("lockf:F_ULOCK");
53
54      fclose(fp);
55  }
56
57  int main(int argc, char *argv[])
58  {
59      int r;
60
61      // Create the file before the fork
62      int fd =
63          open(filename, O_CREAT | O_TRUNC | O_RDWR,
64              0666 /*|S_ISGID */ );
65
66      FILE *fp = fdopen(fd, "r+");
67      if (fp == NULL)
68          error_out("parent:fopen");
69
```

continues

```
70      // Put an exclusive lock on the file.
71      r = lockf(fileno(fp), F_LOCK, 0);
72      if (r == -1)
73          error_out("parent:lockf");
74
75      // Now we fork with the file locked.
76      pid_t pid = fork();
77
78      if (pid == 0) {
79          // Run the child-only code.
80          child();
81          exit(0);
82      }
83      else {
84          // Run the parent-only code and wait for the child to finish.
85          int status = 0;
86          parent(fp);
87          wait(&status);
88
89          // Child returns non-zero status on failure.
90          printf("child status=%d\n", WEXITSTATUS(status));
91      }
92      unlink(filename);
93      exit(0);
94  }
```

A Note about the Examples

Notice that these examples use `fopen` instead of `open`, but the `fopen` call is implemented on top of `open`. So underneath, there is still a file descriptor. See `fileno(3)` for more information.

The new, improved version of the program creates the file before forking and then locks it using `lockf`. When the child opens the file, it locks the file before reading from it, which causes it to block until the parent unlocks the file. By keeping the file locked, the parent can ensure that the contents are valid before the child reads from it. The parent unlocks the file after it ensures that the file has been written. Now you have a robust implementation that is free of race conditions.

7.2.1   File Locking

There are two kinds of locks: advisory and mandatory. *Advisory locks* work when every process calls `lockf` to lock the file before reading or writing. If a process neglects to call `lockf`, the lock will be ignored. *Mandatory locks* address this problem by causing any process that accesses a locked file to block in the read or write call. The locking is enforced by the kernel, so you don't need to worry about uncooperative processes ignoring your advisory lock. To use mandatory locking, GNU/Linux requires that the file system be mounted with the `mand` flag and that the file be created with the group execute bit off and the `setgid` bit set. If any of these conditions is not met, mandatory locking is not enforced.

7.2.2   Drawbacks of Using Files for IPC

There are several drawbacks to using files for IPC. Using a file means that you are likely to encounter latency caused by the underlying media. A large file-system cache can insulate you from this to some extent, but you are likely to encounter it just when you least expect it.

   Another problem with using files for IPC is security. Placing unencrypted data in a file makes it vulnerable to prying eyes. If your data contains sensitive information, storing it unencrypted in a file is not a good idea. For noncritical user tasks, however, a file can be a very simple means of IPC.

7.3   Shared Memory

As you know, processes cannot simply expose their memory to other processes for reading and writing, thanks to memory-protection mechanisms in Linux. A pointer to a memory location in a process is a virtual address, so it does not necessarily refer to a physical location in memory. Passing this address to another process accomplishes nothing except maybe crashing the other process. A virtual address has meaning only in the process that created it.

   Linux and all UNIX operating systems allow memory to be shared between processes via the *shared memory* facilities. There are two basic APIs for sharing memory between processes: System V and POSIX. Both use the same principles, with different functions. The core idea is that any memory to be shared must be explicitly allocated as such. That means that you cannot simply take a variable from the stack or the heap and share it with another process. To share memory between processes, you must allocate it as shared memory, using the special functions provided.

   Both APIs use keys or names to create or attach to shared memory regions. Processes that want to share memory must agree on a naming convention so that they can map the correct shared regions into memory. The System V API uses keys, which are application-defined integers. The POSIX API uses symbolic names that follow the same rules as filenames.

7.3.1   Shared Memory with the POSIX API

The POSIX shared memory API is arguably the more intuitive of the two. Table 7-1 shows an overview of the API. The functions `shm_open` and `shm_unlink` behave much like the `open` and `unlink` system calls provided for regular files. These even return file descriptors that work with the regular system calls like `read` and `write`. In fact, `shm_open` and `shm_unlink` aren't strictly required in Linux, but if you are writing portable applications, you should use them instead of some other shortcut.

   Because the API is based on file descriptors, there is no need to reinvent new APIs to support additional operations. Any system call that use file descriptors can be used for this purpose. Listing 7-3 shows a complete example of how to create a shared memory region that can be seen by other processes.

TABLE 7-1   POSIX Shared-Memory API

Function	Usage
shm_open	Create a shared memory region or attach to an existing shared memory region. Regions are specified by name, and the function returns a file descriptor, just like the `open` system call.
shm_unlink	Delete a shared memory region using the file descriptor returned by `shm_open`. As with the `unlink` system call used for files, the region is not removed until all processes unlink from it. No new processes can attach to this region after `shm_unlink` has been called, however.
mmap	Map a file into the process's memory. The input includes a file descriptor provided by `shm_open`. The function returns a pointer to the newly mapped memory. `mmap` can also use file descriptors that belong to plain files and some other devices.
munmap	Unmap a region of memory that was mapped by a `mmap` call. The amount of memory unmapped can be less than or equal to the amount of memory mapped with the `mmap` call, provided that the region to be unmapped satisfies all the alignment and size requirements of the operating system.
msync	Synchronize access to a region of memory mapped with `mmap` and writes any cached data to the physical memory (or other device) so that other processes can see the changes.

LISTING 7-3   posix-shm.c: POSIX Shared Memory Example

```
 1 /* posix-shm.c : gcc -o posix posix.c -lrt */
 2 #include <stdio.h>
 3 #include <string.h>
 4 #include <stdlib.h>
 5 #include <unistd.h>          // POSIX
 6 #include <sys/file.h>        // Pulls in open(2) and friends.
 7 #include <sys/mman.h>        // Pulls in mmap(2) and friends.
 8 #include <sys/wait.h>
 9
10 void error_out(const char *msg)
11 {
12     perror(msg);
13     exit(EXIT_FAILURE);
14 }
15
16 int main(int argc, char *argv[])
17 {
18     int r;
19
20     // shm_open recommends using a leading '/' in
21     // the region name for portability, but Linux
22     // doesn't require it.
23     const char *memname = "/mymem";
24
25     // Use one page for this example
26     const size_t region_size = sysconf(_SC_PAGE_SIZE);
27
28     // Create the shared memory region.
29     // Notice the args are identical to open(2).
30     int fd = shm_open(memname, O_CREAT | O_TRUNC | O_RDWR, 0666);
31     if (fd == -1)
32         error_out("shm_open");
33
34     // Allocate some memory in the region. We use ftruncate, but
35     // write(2) would work just as well.
36     r = ftruncate(fd, region_size);
37     if (r != 0)
38         error_out("ftruncate");
39
40     // Map the region into memory.
41     void *ptr =
42         mmap(0, region_size, PROT_READ | PROT_WRITE, MAP_SHARED, fd,
43             0);
44     if (ptr == MAP_FAILED)
45         error_out("mmap");
46
47     // Don't need the fd after the mmmap call.
```

continues

```
48      close(fd);
49
50      pid_t pid = fork();
51
52      if (pid == 0) {
53          // Child process inherits the shared memory mapping.
54          u_long *d = (u_long *) ptr;
55          *d = 0xdeadbeef;
56          exit(0);
57      }
58      else {
59          // Synchronize with the child process.
60          int status;
61          waitpid(pid, &status, 0);
62
63          // Parent process sees the same memory.
64          printf("child wrote %#lx\n", *(u_long *) ptr);
65      }
66
67      // Done with the memory, umap it.
68      r = munmap(ptr, region_size);
69      if (r != 0)
70          error_out("munmap");
71
72      // Remove the shared memory region.
73      r = shm_unlink(memname);
74      if (r != 0)
75          error_out("shm_unlink");
76
77      return 0;
78 }
```

shm_open creates a shared memory region exactly as you would create a file. Just like a file, the region is empty when you create it. Allocating space in a newly created shared memory region is exactly the same as filling a file with data. You can write to it with the write system call, but with shared memory, it's often more convenient to use the ftruncate system call. Finally, shared memory regions persist just like files—that is, they don't disappear when a process terminates but must be explicitly removed.

Listing 7-3 creates a peer process via a fork call. Although it may seem like cheating, this does illustrate an important point. Shared memory mappings are inherited across forks. So unlike any stack or dynamic memory mappings, which are cloned using copy on write semantics, a shared memory mapping will point to the same physical storage in both parent and child.

```
$ gcc -o posix-shm posix-shm.c -lrt
$ ./posix-shm
$ child wrote 0xdeadbeef
```

You can share memory between processes that do not have a parent–child relationship, such as peer processes. A peer process that needs to connect to this shared memory region would use virtually the same code as Listing 7-3. The only difference is that the peer does not need to create or truncate the region, so you would remove the O_CREAT flag in the shm_open call and the call to ftruncate.

Processes must take measures to ensure proper synchronization to avoid race conditions. I noted that the wait call in Listing 7-3 synchronizes parent and child. Without this synchronization, there would be a race condition. The value printed out by the parent would depend on which process executed first: parent or child. By inserting the waitpid call, you force the child to finish first, which ensures that your value is valid. This is a simple method that works for this example, but you will see later how to use more sophisticated synchronization.

Inside POSIX Shared Memory in Linux

The Linux implementation of shared memory is dependent on the shared memory file system, which by convention is mounted on /dev/shm. If this mount point does not exist, shm_open will fail. Any file system will work, but most distributions mount the tmpfs file system by default. Even if tmpfs is not mounted on /dev/shm, shm_open will use the underlying disk file system. You might not notice if this happens, because depending on the size of the memory regions, the memory could spend most of its time in the file-system cache. Recall that tmpfs is basically a file system with a cache and no media.

Because shm_open creates files in /dev/shm, each shared memory region is visible as a file in the directory. The filename is the same that was used by the process that created the region. This is a very useful debugging feature, because all the tools available for debugging files are also available for debugging shared memory.

7.3.2 Shared Memory with the System V API

The System V API is still widely used by X Window System, and by extension, many X applications use it. For most other applications, the POSIX shared memory interface is preferred. Table 7-2 shows the API at a glance. This same API is also used for semaphores and message queues, both of which I discuss later in this chapter.

TABLE 7-2   System V Shared Memory API at a Glance

Function	Usage
shmget	Create a shared memory region or attach to an existing one (like shm_open)
shmat	Get a pointer to a shared memory region (like mmap)
shmdt	Unmap a region of shared memory mapped with shmat (like munmap)
shmctl	Many uses, including unlinking a shared memory region created with shmget (like shm_unlink)

A complete example using the System V API equivalent of Listing 7-3 is shown in Listing 7-4. The steps are essentially the same except that the shmget function both creates and allocates the shared memory region, so no truncation step is required.

LISTING 7-4   sysv-shm.c: Shared Memory Example Using System V

```
 1 #include <stdio.h>
 2 #include <string.h>
 3 #include <stdlib.h>
 4 #include <unistd.h>
 5 #include <sys/ipc.h>
 6 #include <sys/shm.h>
 7 #include <sys/wait.h>
 8
 9 void error_out(const char *msg)
10 {
11     perror(msg);
12     exit(EXIT_FAILURE);
13 }
14
15 int main(int argc, char *argv[])
16 {
17
18     // Application-defined key, like the filename in shm_open()
19     key_t mykey = 12345678;
20
21     // Use one page for this example
22     const size_t region_size = sysconf(_SC_PAGE_SIZE);
23
24     // Create the shared memory region.
25     int smid = shmget(mykey, region_size, IPC_CREAT | 0666);
26     if (smid == -1)
```

```
27          error_out("shmget");
28
29      // Map the region into memory.
30      void *ptr;
31      ptr = shmat(smid, NULL, 0);
32      if (ptr == (void *) -1)
33          error_out("shmat");
34
35      pid_t pid = fork();
36
37      if (pid == 0) {
38          // Child process inherits the shared memory mapping.
39          u_long *d = (u_long *) ptr;
40          *d = 0xdeadbeef;
41          exit(0);
42      }
43      else {
44          // Synchronize with the child process.
45          int status;
46          waitpid(pid, &status, 0);
47
48          // Parent process sees the same memory.
49          printf("child wrote %#lx\n", *(u_long *) ptr);
50      }
51
52      // Done with the memory, umap it.
53      int r = shmdt(ptr);
54      if (r == -1)
55          error_out("shmdt");
56
57      // Remove the shared memory region.
58      r = shmctl(smid, IPC_RMID, NULL);
59      if (r == -1)
60          error_out("shmdt");
61
62      return 0;
63 }
```

The key used by shmget is functionally equivalent to the filename used by shm_open. The shmid returned by shmget is functionally equivalent to the file descriptor returned by shm_open. In each case, one is defined by the application, and the other is defined by the operating system. Listing 7-4 is almost identical to Listing 7-3, so as you might expect, the output is the same:

```
$ gcc -o sysv-shm sysv-shm.c
$ ./sysv-shm
child wrote 0xdeadbeef
```

Unlike memory created with the POSIX API, memory created with the System V API is not visible in any file system. The `ipcs` command is designed specifically for manipulating System V shared memory objects. I discuss this tool later in the chapter.

7.4   Signals

Arnold Robbins goes to great lengths in his book[1] to decry the use of signals for IPC, so I won't belabor the point. One problem with signals is that signal handlers are not free to call every standard library function that is available. You cannot predict when a signal will arrive, so when it does, the operating system interrupts the running process to handle the signal with no regard to what the process is doing at the time. That means that the libraries are in an unknown state when your signal handler runs. Your process might have been in the middle of a `malloc` or `printf` call when it was interrupted by the signal handler, for example. When that happens, any global or static variables may be in an inconsistent state. If the signal handler were to call the library function, it might use these values incorrectly and cause your process to crash. Such functions are unsafe to call from a signal handler. The POSIX standard specifies which functions must be safe to call from a signal handler. These are listed in the `signal(2)` man page.

Making matters worse, functions called from a signal handler don't know that they're in a signal handler. So there's no way for a function that is not *signal safe* to fail safe—that is return an error status when called from a signal handler. Instead, the function behaves unpredictably. Your program may crash, produce garbage, or seem to work fine. This places several constraints on the things a signal handler can safely do.

Typically, signals are used to handle exception conditions (not IPC), so that even if the signal handler calls an unsafe function, it happens infrequently enough that the likelihood of finding the bug is low. That's no excuse for poor programming, but the signal API is complicated and full of pitfalls to trap even experienced programmers.

Suppose that you decide to use signals as an IPC framework. Presumably, the frequency of signals in your system will be much higher than if you used them only

---

1. *Linux Programming by Example: The Fundamentals*

for exceptions. This provides many more opportunities to discover a signal handler that is using an unsafe function. You'll find out only when it crashes. Unless you know what you are doing and are prepared to take a risk, it probably is best to avoid using signals for IPC.

7.4.1 Sending Signals to a Process

Signals have been around since UNIX was created, and although the API has evolved, the signal mechanism is still fairly simple. When a process receives a signal, an internal flag is set to indicate that the signal has been received. When the kernel gets around to scheduling the process, instead of resuming the process where it left off, it calls the signal handler. When the signal handler is called, the flag is cleared.

A process sends a signal to another process using the `kill` system call, which takes a process ID and signal number as its arguments:

```
int kill( pid_t pid, int signal );
```

Each signal is represented by a unique integer, so the `kill` system call can send only one signal at a time. The signal value of 0 means no signal, which is a useful trick to test for a process's existence, as in this example:

```
int r = kill(pid,0);                     Using a signal of 0 has no effect on the process.
if ( r == 0 )
        /* process exists! */
else if ( errno == ESRCH )               Must check errno before drawing any conclusions.
        /* process does not exist */
```

Like all POSIX functions, `kill` returns -1 when it fails and sets `errno`. In this case, when it returns 0, it simply means that the process existed at the time the signal was sent. Because the signal was 0, no signal was sent, so all it tells you is that the process existed when you checked. When `kill` returns -1 and the value of `errno` is `ESRCH`, it means that there is no process with the given process ID.

7.4.2 Handling a Signal

There are two basic APIs for handling signals: POSIX and System V. The POSIX API was inherited from BSD and is the preferred technique because it is more flexible and more immune to race conditions. The System V API is the one chosen by ANSI for the standard C library. It's simpler but less flexible than the POSIX API.

Both POSIX and System V allow you to define one of the following behaviors for each signal:

- Call a user-defined function
- Ignore the signal
- Return to the default signal behavior

The POSIX API also allows you to block and unblock individual signals without changing the underlying signal handler. This is key to preventing race conditions. Note that the signals SIGKILL and SIGSTOP cannot be handled, blocked, or ignored, because these are vital for process control.

The process must tell the operating system about user-defined signal handlers using either API. The ANSI function for setting signal handlers is the signal system call, which is defined as follows:

```
typedef void (*sighandler_t)(int);
sighandler_t signal(int signum, sighandler_t handler);
```

The signal function takes as an argument a pointer to the function to be used as a handler. GNU provides a type definition (typedef) for this argument called sighander_t. I included the definition of sighandler_t above because this type is not defined by any standard,[2] and it makes the prototype easier to read.

The POSIX system call is sigaction and is defined as follows:

```
int sigaction(int signo, struct sigaction *new, struct sigaction *old);
```

The sigaction function requires a pointer to a sigaction structure (which I will look at shortly) to define the new signal handler. Both functions return the current signal handler, which your application can use to restore the signal handler at a later time. Another use for the old signal handler is to allow the new signal handler to call it before returning.

Table 7-3 shows the patterns you can use to determine the signal-handling behavior discussed earlier.

---

2. GNU defines this type for you only when you specify -D_GNU_SOURCE on the command line.

TABLE 7-3 Setting Signal Behavior

Action	System V Pattern	POSIX Pattern
Call a user-defined function	`old = signal(signo,handler)`	`sigaction(signo,new,old)`
Ignore the signal	`old = signal(signo,SIG_IGN)`	`sigaction(signo,new,old)`
(Re)set to default handler	`old = signal(signo,SIG_DFL)`	`sigaction(signo,new,old)`

7.4.3 The Signal Mask and Signal Handling

The *signal mask* is what the kernel uses to determine how to deliver signals to a process. Conceptually, this is just a very large word with 1 bit per signal. If a process sets the mask for a particular signal, that signal is not delivered to the process. When a signal is masked, we also say that it is *blocked*.

POSIX defines `sigset_t` to manage the signal mask. For portability, you should never modify a `sigset_t` directly but use these functions:

```
int sigemptyset(sigset_t *set);              Clears all signals in the mask
int sigfillset(sigset_t *set);               Sets all signals in the mask
int sigaddset(sigset_t *set, int signum);    Sets one signal in the mask
int sigdelset(sigset_t *set, int signum);    Clears one signal in the mask
int sigismember(sigset_t *set, int signum);  Returns 1 if signum is set in the mask and 0 otherwise
```

`sigaddset`, `sigdelset`, and `sigismember` take a single signal number as an argument. Thus, each function affects only one signal in the mask. A process must call one of these functions once for each signal it wants to modify. Note that these functions operate only on the `sigset_t` argument; they do not affect signal handling.

When a process finishes modifying the mask, it passes the mask to the `sigprocmask` function to change the process's signal mask. This allows an application to affect all signals simultaneously, using a single system call to avoid race conditions. The prototype for `sigprocmask` is as follows:

```
int sigprocmask(int how, const sigset_t *set, sigset_t *oldset);
```

The function takes two pointers to a `sigset_t`. The first is the new mask to be applied, and the second is the old mask, which can be used to restore the signal mask to its original state at some later point. The how argument indicates how to apply the input signal mask to the process's signal mask. This value can be one of the following:

- SIG_BLOCK—Add any set signals from the input signal mask to the process's signal mask. The signals indicated in the input signal mask will be blocked in addition to the currently blocked signals.

- SIG_UNBLOCK—Remove any set signals in the input signal mask from the process's signal mask. The signals indicated in the input signal mask will be unblocked, but the rest of the process's signal mask will remain unchanged.

- SIG_SET—Overwrite the current signal mask with the value of the input signal mask. Only the signals listed in the input mask will be blocked. Any other signals will be unblocked, and the current signal mask will be discarded.

You should notice that the sigprocmask function does not take a signal handler as an argument. Blocking a signal only delays the delivery of the signal; it does not discard the signals that have been sent to the process. The example in Listing 7-5 should illustrate.

LISTING 7-5   sigprocmask.c: Using sigprocmask to Delay Delivery of a Signal

```
 1 #include <stdio.h>
 2 #include <string.h>
 3 #include <stdlib.h>
 4 #include <signal.h>
 5 #include <unistd.h>
 6
 7 volatile int done = 0;
 8
 9 // Signal handler
10 void handler(int sig)
11 {
12     // Ref signal(2) - write() is safe, printf() is not.
13     const char *str = "handled...\n";
14     write(1, str, strlen(str));
15     done = 1;
16 }
17
18 void child(void)
19 {
20     // Child process exits immediately, and generates SIGCHLD to the parent
```

```
21      printf("child exiting\n");
22      exit(0);
23  }
24
25  int main(int argc, char *argv[])
26  {
27      // Handle SIGCHLD when child process exits.
28      signal(SIGCHLD, handler);
29      sigset_t newset, oldset;
30
31      // Set all signals in the set
32      sigfillset(&newset);
33
34      // Block all signals and save the old signal mask
35      // so we can restore it later
36      sigprocmask(SIG_BLOCK, &newset, &oldset);
37
38      // Fork a child process
39      pid_t pid = fork();
40      if (pid == 0)
41          child();
42
43      printf("parent sleeping\n");
44
45      // Sleep with all signals blocked.
46      int r = sleep(3);
47
48      // r == 0 indicates that we slept the full duration.
49      printf("woke up! r=%d\n", r);
50
51      // Restore the old signal mask,
52      // which will result in our handler being called.
53      sigprocmask(SIG_SETMASK, &oldset, NULL);
54
55      // Wait for signal handler to run.
56      while (!done) {
57      };
58
59      printf("exiting\n");
60      exit(0);
61  }
```

The program in Listing 7-5 forks a child process that exits immediately. This results in the parent process's receiving a SIGCHLD signal. Before you fork, however, you install a signal handler for SIGCHLD and block the SIGCHLD signal for 3 seconds. Immediately after you return from the sleep, you restore the original signal handler, which unblocks SIGCHLD. Then the signal handler executes, demonstrating that the signal was delivered:

```
$ ./sigprocmask
child exiting          This is when SIGCHLD is sent to the parent.
parent sleeping        SIGCHLD is blocked, so the parent goes to sleep.
woke up! r=0           The return of 0 indicates we slept for 3 seconds; still no signal.
handled...             Signal is delivered after the signal mask is restored.
exiting
```

The POSIX API includes a couple of additional functions for dealing with signal masks while signals are blocked. The prototypes are

```
int sigpending(sigset_t *set);
int sigsuspend(const sigset_t *mask);
```

sigpending allows you to examine signals that have been sent but not delivered. In Listing 7-5, you could have tested the signal mask before going to sleep and possibly would have seen the signal. There is no guarantee, however, because sigpending does not wait for signals; it simply takes a snapshot of the signals and presents them to the caller. This technique is also called *polling*. If you want to wait for a specific set of signals and no other signals, the sigsuspend function is what you want. This function temporarily overwrites the signal mask with the input mask until the desired signal is delivered. Before returning, it restores the signal mask to its original state.

7.4.4 Real-Time Signals

Astute readers may notice a few issues that arise as a result of blocking signals. What happens, for example, if more than one signal is sent while a signal is blocked? When a single signal arrives while signals are blocked, the value remains set in the kernel, so the signal is not lost; it is delivered immediately when the process unmasks the signal. If the same signal is sent twice while it is blocked, the second signal normally is discarded. When the signal is unmasked, the signal handler is called only once.

POSIX introduced real-time signals to provide applications the ability to receive a signal multiple times, even when that signal is blocked. When a real-time signal is blocked, the kernel will keep track of the number of times the signal is received and call the signal handler that many times when the signal is unblocked.

Real-time signals are identified by a range of signal numbers. This range is identified by the macros SIGRTMIN and SIGRTMAX. If you specify a signal number between these two values, the signal will be queued. Listing 7-6 shows an example.

LISTING 7-6 rt-sig.c: Blocking and Real-Time Signals

```
1 #include <stdio.h>
2 #include <string.h>
3 #include <stdlib.h>
4 #include <signal.h>
5 #include <unistd.h>
6
7 volatile int done = 0;
8
9 // Signal handler
10 void handler(int sig)
11 {
12     // Ref signal(2) - write() is safe, printf() is not.
13     const char *str = "handled...\n";
14     write(1, str, strlen(str));
15     done = 1;
16 }
17
18 void child(void)
19 {
20     int i;
21     for (i = 0; i < 3; i++) {
22         // Send rapid fire signals to parent.
23         kill(getppid(), SIGRTMIN);
24         printf("child - BANG!\n");
25     }
26     exit(0);
27 }
28
29 int main(int argc, char *argv[])
30 {
31     // Handle SIGRTMIN from child
32     signal(SIGRTMIN, handler);
33     sigset_t newset, oldset;
34
35     // Block all signals and save the old signal mask
36     // so we can restore it later
37     sigfillset(&newset);
38     sigprocmask(SIG_BLOCK, &newset, &oldset);
39
40     // Fork a child process
41     pid_t pid = fork();
42     if (pid == 0)
43         child();
44
45     printf("parent sleeping\n");
46
47     // Sleep with all signals blocked.
48     int r = sleep(3);
```

continues

```
49
50    // r == 0 indicates that we slept the full duration.
51    printf("woke up! r=%d\n", r);
52
53    // Restore the old signal mask,
54    // which will result in our handler being called.
55    sigprocmask(SIG_SETMASK, &oldset, NULL);
56
57    // Wait for signal handler to run.
58    while (!done) {
59    };
60
61    printf("exiting\n");
62    exit(0);
63 }
```

Listing 7-6 is very similar to Listing 7-5 except that it uses SIGRTMIN as the signal instead of SIGCHLD, and the child now sends this signal to the parent three times before exiting. There are no special flags required to use queued signals. The signal number tells the kernel to use queued signals. Running this example shows how it works:

```
$ ./rt-sig
child - BANG!
child - BANG!
child - BANG!
parent sleeping
woke up! r=0
handled...
handled...
handled...
exiting
```

Here again, you see that the parent is not interrupted by the signals until after the signal mask is restored. When the signal mask is restored, the handler is called three times—once for each time the child called kill.

7.4.5   Advanced Signals with sigqueue and sigaction

Finally, we come to an alternative to the kill system call named sigqueue. The prototype is shown below and looks much like the kill system call except that it takes an additional argument:

```
int sigqueue(pid_t pid, int sig, const union sigval value);
```

The `pid` and `sig` arguments are identical to the `kill` system call, but the `value` argument actually lets you include data with the signal. Recall that non–real time signals are not queued, so only when you use a signal number between `RTSIGMIN` and `RTSIGMAX` will the signals be queued with their associated information.

The additional information provided by the `sigqueue` function can be retrieved only by a handler installed with the `sigaction` function, which I introduced earlier as an alternative to the `signal` system call. Installing a handler with `sigaction` is a bit more involved. Using Listing 7-6 as an example, the `signal` function could be replaced by `sigaction` as follows:

```
struct sigaction sa = {          Using C99 structure initializer syntax . . .
    .sa_handler = handler,       Same handler as before
    .sa_flags = SA_RESTART       Rearm the signal handler after it's called . . .
};
sigemptyset(&sa.sa_mask);        Create an empty signal mask

sigaction(SIGRTMIN,&sa,NULL);    Discard the old action via NULL
```

Filling in the `sigaction` structure is an extra step required to use the `sigaction` function. The `sa_mask` field is a signal mask that is used while the signal handler runs. Normally, when the signal handler is called, the signal being handled is blocked. The mask specified here indicates additional signals to be blocked while the handler runs. The handler in the `sigaction` structure is a pointer to a function. This is actually a union containing pointers to two different handler types. `sa_handler` points to a System V style signal handler, used above. `sa_sigaction` points to a new-style handler that has the following prototype:

```
void handler(int sig, struct siginfo *si, void *ptr)
```

To take full advantage of `sigqueue`, you should define a new-style handler. To indicate that you are using a new-style handler, you set the `SA_SIGINFO` flag in the `sa_flags` field as follows:

```
struct sigaction sa = {                    Using C99 structure initializer . . .
    .sa_sigaction = handler,               Use new-style handler
    .sa_flags = SA_RESTART|SA_SIGINFO      DON'T FORGET THIS!
};
sigemptyset(&sa.sa_mask);
```

When the kernel sees the `SA_SIGINFO` flag, it puts different arguments on the stack for the signal handler. Without this, your signal handler will be called with the wrong arguments and probably will cause your application to crash with a `SIGSEGV`.

Now that you have a new-style handler, you can replace the `kill` function with `sigqueue` as follows:

```
union sigval sv = {
        .sival_int = 42                      Any user-defined number will do.
};
sigqueue(getppid(), SIGRTMIN, sv);        You can use any signal, but only RT signals are queued.
```

Looking at the handler again, the `siginfo` structure contains various things defined by different standards. Following are the set of values used in Linux and their POSIX definitions:

int	si_signo	*Signal number – SIGINT and so on*
int	si_code	*Signal code (see text)*
int	si_errno	*If nonzero, an errno value associated with this signal*
pid_t	si_pid	*Sending process ID*
uid_t	si_uid	*Real user ID of sending process*
void	*si_addr	*(see text)*
int	si_status	*Exit value or signal*
long	si_band	*Band event for SIGPOLL*
union sigval	si_value	*Signal value*

As the annotation above suggests, several signal-specific fields in the `siginfo` structure are not defined under all circumstances. Of all the fields defined, only the `si_signo`, `si_errno`, and `si_code` fields contain valid data all the time, according to POSIX. If the signal is sent by another process, `si_pid` and `si_uid` indicate the process ID and user ID of the process that sent the signal.

The `si_code` takes one of the values defined in Table 7-4 and indicates some details about the source of the signal and the reason for it. A signal that was the result of another process or a call to the `raise` function results in an `si_code` value of `SI_USER`. A signal that is sent with the `sigqueue` function has an `si_code` value of `SI_QUEUE`.

An example of a context-sensitive field is the `si_value` field, which is defined only if the caller used `sigqueue` to send the signal. When this is true, `si_value` contains a copy of the `sigval` that was sent by the function. Most of the other fields deal with various exception conditions that have nothing to do with IPC and come from the current process.

Another context-sensitive field, `si_errno` may be nonzero if an error is associated with this signal. `si_band` is defined only for `SIGPOLL`, which can be useful in certain IPC applications.

TABLE 7-4   Values Defined si_code

si_code	Meaning
SI_USER	Signal sent via kill() or raise()
SI_KERNEL	Signal sent from the kernel
SI_QUEUE	Signal sent via sigqueue()
SI_TIMER	POSIX timer expired
SI_MESGQ	POSIX message queue state changed
SI_ASYNCIO	Asynchronous I/O (AIO) completed
SI_SIGIO	Queued SIGIO (not used in Linux)
SI_TKILL	Signal sent via tkill() or tgkill(); Linux only

7.5   Pipes

Pipes are simple to create and use. They come in two varieties: an unnamed pipe for use between a parent and a child process, and a named pipe for use between peer processes on the same computer. You can create an unnamed pipe in a process with the pipe system call, which returns a pair of file descriptors. The prototype for the pipe function looks like the following:

```
int pipe(int filedes[2]);
```

The caller passes an array of two integers, which will hold two file descriptors upon successful return. The first file descriptor in the array is read-only, and the second is write-only. Unnamed pipes are useful only for communication between a parent and a child process. Because the child inherits the same file descriptors as the parent, the parent can create the pipe before forking to create a communication channel between parent and child. Following is a typical pattern:

```
int fd[2];
r = pipe(fd);
if ( r == -1 )                          Check for errors.

pid_t pid = fork();
if ( pid == 0 )                         Child writes to fd[1] inherited from parent.
{
    write(fd[1], "Hello World", 11);
    ...
}

int n = read(fd[0],buf,11);             Parent reads from fd[0].
```

Linux and UNIX allow named pipes, which are identified by special files on disk created with the `mkfifo` or `mknod` function:

```
int mkfifo(const char *pathname, mode_t mode);
```

Both `mkfifo` and `mknod` are also available as shell commands. A named pipe can be opened, read, and written just like a regular file with the familiar `open`, `read`, and `write` system calls. The file on disk is used only for naming; no data is ever written to the file system.

Normally, when a process opens a named pipe for reading, the process blocks until another process opens the named pipe for writing, or vice versa. This makes named pipes useful for synchronizing with other processes as well. The following demonstrates a named pipe with some simple shell commands:

```
$ mkfifo myfifo                          Create the fifo.
$ cat < myfifo &                         cat command blocks until we write to the pipe.
[1] 29668
$ echo Hello World > myfifo              Write to the pipe.
Hello World                              cat command completes.
[1]+  Done ...

$ echo Hello World > myfifo &            echo command blocks until we read from the pipe.
[1] 29670
$ cat myfifo                             Read from pipe.
Hello World
[1]+  Done ...                           echo command completes.
```

If you are opening for reading, you can avoid the blocking by using the `O_NONBLOCK` flag to open it in nonblocking mode. Linux does not allow you to open a named pipe for writing in nonblocking mode.

7.6   Sockets

Sockets are general-purpose tools for communication between processes; they can be used locally or across a network. Sockets behave very much like pipes except that unlike pipes, sockets are bidirectional. When you need to distribute processes across processors in a network, the socket allows you to use the same API to communicate among all processes, whether they are local or not.

A full tutorial on sockets is beyond the scope of this book,[3] but I'll discuss some basic examples.

---

3.   A good tutorial is available on the `glibc info` page: `info libc sockets`.

7.6.1 Creating Sockets

The system call for creating general-purpose sockets is the `socket` function, which creates sockets that can be used for local or network connections. There is also the `socketpair` function, which creates a local connection exclusively. Following are the prototypes for both functions:

```
int socket(int domain, int type, int protocol);
int socketpair(int domain, int type, int protocol, int fd[2]);
```

Both these functions require that you specify a *domain, type,* and *protocol* for the socket, which I will discuss shortly. The `socketpair` function returns an array of two file descriptors, just like the `pipe` system call.

7.6.1.1 Socket Domains

The socket domain parameter helps determine the interface the socket can use— that is, it determines whether the socket will use the network interface, a local interface, or some other interface. *Domain* is the term used by POSIX, but GNU refers to it as the *namespace* to avoid overloading the term *domain,* which has many other meanings. The POSIX constants defined for this parameter use the prefix `PF` (for *protocol family*). Table 7-5 provides a partial list of these constants. The ones you are likely to encounter are `PF_UNIX` and `PF_INET`. `PF_UNIX` is used for communication between processes on the same computer, and `PF_INET` is used for communication across an IP network.[4]

TABLE 7-5   Some Domains Used for Socket Functions

Domain	Protocol/Usage
`PF_UNSPEC`	Unspecified. OS decides. Defined as zero.
`PF_UNIX, PF_LOCAL`	Communication between processes on the same computer.
`PF_INET`	Use IPv4 Internet protocols.
`PF_INET6`	Use IPv6 Internet protocols.
`PF_NETLINK`	Kernel user interface device.
`PF_PACKET`	Low-level packet interface to allow direct access to a device.

---

4.   More precisely, an IPv4 network. IPv4 is the original IP protocol, with 32 bits per address, whereas IPv6 uses 128 bits for addressing.

7.6.1.2   Socket Types

The *type* of socket is the second argument required by the socket functions, indicating the type of service the application is looking for. Table 7-6 provides a more detailed explanation. Perhaps the most common and easiest to use is the `SOCK_STREAM` type. This type requires a *connection,* which essentially means that a running process must have each end of the socket open to function; otherwise, it's considered to be an error. The reliability of the connection is determined by the third argument: the *protocol.*

7.6.1.3   Socket Protocols

Each protocol has different capabilities, and not all protocols support all socket types. POSIX defines a set of protocols that all socket implementations must support (Table 7-7). The macros for these protocols are defined in `<netinet/in.h>`. Other protocols may be supported, but these may be nonstandard. Either way, a list of known protocols is maintained in `/etc/protocols`. To specify a protocol by the name listed in `/etc/protocols`, you would use one of the `getprotoent(3)` family of library calls and use the value returned to designate the protocol.

TABLE 7-6   Socket Types

Socket Type	Description
`SOCK_STREAM`	"Reliable" connection-based data transfer. The underlying protocol guarantees that data is read in the same order it is transmitted. The protocol may support "out of band" data.
`SOCK_DGRAM`	"Unreliable" connectionless transfer, with no guarantees about delivery or delivery order.
`SOCK_SEQPACKET`	Similar to `SOCK_STREAM`, but reader is required to read entire packets at a time.
`SOCK_RAW`	Allows access to raw network packets.
`SOCK_RDM`	Similar to `SOCK_STREAM` except that there are no guarantees with respect to delivery ordering.

TABLE 7-7 Socket Protocols

Macro	Protocol Name	Description
IPPROTO_IP	ip	Internet protocol, technically not a protocol. This macro is used for local sockets of any type and can be used with connectionless network and local sockets.
IPPROTO_ICMP	icmp	Internet Control Message Protocol, used by applications such as the ping command.
IPPROTO_TCP	tcp	Transmission Control Protocol, a connection-based, reliable protocol for use with SOCK_STREAM sockets.
IPPROTO_UDP	udp	User Datagram Protocol, a connectionless, unreliable protocol used for IPC that provides low latency at the expense of reliability and is most often used with sockets of type SOCK_DGRAM.
IPPROTO_IPV6	ipv6	Like IP, technically not a protocol but does specify that packets should use IPv6 addressing.
IPPROTO_RAW	raw	Allows an application to receive raw packets; usually not available to unprivileged users.

The pseudoprotocol ip has a value of 0, which is the value used for all local sockets (PF_LOCAL). As a result, many programmers just use 0 for the protocol when they want a local socket.

7.6.2 Local Socket Example Using socketpair

The simplest way to create a local socket is to use the socketpair function, which is illustrated in Listing 7-7.

LISTING 7-7 socketpair.c: Sockets Example Using socketpair

```
1 #include <stdio.h>
2 #include <string.h>
3 #include <stdlib.h>
4 #include <errno.h>
5 #include <unistd.h>
6 #include <sys/types.h>
7 #include <sys/socket.h>
```

continues

```
 8 #include <sys/wait.h>
 9 #include <netdb.h>
10
11 int main(int argc, char *argv[])
12 {
13     int fd[2];
14
15     // ref. socketpair(2)
16     // domain (aka Protocol Family) = PF_LOCAL (same as PF_UNIX)
17     // type = SOCK_STREAM (see table)
18     // protocol = zero (use default protocol)
19     int r = socketpair(PF_LOCAL, SOCK_STREAM, 0, fd);
20     if (r == -1) {
21         perror("socketpair");
22     }
23
24     pid_t pid = fork();
25
26     if (pid == 0) {
27         // Child process reads.
28         char buf[32];
29         int n = read(fd[1], buf, sizeof(buf));
30         if (n == -1) {
31             perror("read");
32         }
33         printf("read %d bytes '%s'\n", n, buf);
34     }
35     else {
36         // Parent process writes.
37         char msg[] = "Hello World";
38         int n = write(fd[0], msg, sizeof(msg));
39         if (n == -1) {
40             perror("write");
41         }
42
43         // Wait for child to finish.
44         int status;
45         wait(&status);
46     }
47
48     exit(0);
49     return 0;
50 }
```

Listing 7-7 illustrates the basics of creating a socket via the `socketpair` function. As mentioned earlier, this is much like a pipe except that the socket is a bidirectional link, unlike a pipe. Recall that a pipe provides two file descriptors—one for writing and one for reading. If you want bidirectional communication between two processes via pipes, you must create one pipe for each direction. Because the socket is bidirectional by design, only one socket is required to provide a full-duplex communication path between two processes.

7.6.3 Client/Server Example Using Local Sockets

Sockets are most often used in client/server applications, which require the use of the more general-purpose `socket` system call. Unlike `socketpair`, which returns a pair of file descriptors, `socket` returns a single file descriptor. `socketpair` shields the programmer from many of the gory details of sockets, but it can be used only between a parent and a child process.

Before you can use the `socket` function, you need to introduce some additional functions. Figure 7-1 shows a flow chart for a basic client and server. Notice that the `socketpair` function provides a convenient shortcut for all the additional API calls required for a general-purpose client and server.

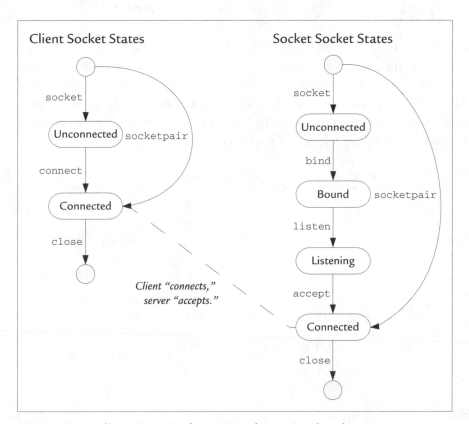

FIGURE 7-1   Client/Server Sockets API and Associated Socket States

All these functions have comprehensive man pages in Linux, so I won't go into detail here; instead, I will provide some working examples. First, however, I'll introduce one more function not listed in Figure 7-1: select. select is used to wait on multiple file descriptors with an optional timeout.[5] It's used with many file descriptors other than sockets, but writing a sockets program without it is hard. select is defined as follows:

```
int select(int n, fd_set *readfds, fd_set *writefds, fd_set *exceptfds,
       struct timeval *timeout);
```

The fd_set type is how the application tells select which file descriptors to monitor. Each fd_set can be manipulated with a group of macros defined as follows:

FD_SET(int fd, fd_set *set)	*Add* fd *to the* fd_set.
FD_CLR(int fd, fd_set *set)	*Remove* fd *from the* fd_set.
FD_ISSET(int fd, fd_set *set)	*Test for the presence of* fd *in the* fd_set.
FD_ZERO(fd_set *set)	*Remove all* fds *from the* fd_set.

A complete example will illustrate how all these functions work together. Listing 7-8 is a simple server using sockets. Notice that the socket file descriptor returned by socket is passed to listen, which transforms it into a so-called listen socket. *Listen sockets* are used by servers to accept connections. The accept function takes a listen socket as input and waits for a client to connect. At this point, it returns a new file descriptor, which is a socket connected to the client.

LISTING 7-8   server_un.c: Socket Server Using a Local Socket

```
 1 #include <stdio.h>
 2 #include <string.h>
 3 #include <signal.h>
 4 #include <stdlib.h>
 5 #include <unistd.h>
 6 #include <sys/types.h>
 7 #include <sys/socket.h>
 8 #include <sys/un.h>
 9
10 // Call perror and exit if return value from system call is -1
11 #define ASSERTNOERR(x,msg) do {\
12     if ((x) == -1) { perror(msg); exit(1); }} while(0)
13
```

---

5. A function related to select is poll.

```
14  // Local sockets require a named file, this must be unlinked later
15  #define SOCKNAME "localsock"
16
17  int main(int argc, char *argv[])
18  {
19      // ref. socket(2)
20      // Create a local stream socket
21      // domain (aka Protocol Family) = PF_LOCAL (same as PF_UNIX)
22      // type = SOCK_STREAM (see table)
23      // protocol = zero (use default protocol)
24      int s = socket(PF_LOCAL, SOCK_STREAM, 0);
25
26      ASSERTNOERR(s, "socket");
27
28      // Local sockets are given a name that resides on a filesystem.
29      struct sockaddr_un sa = {
30          .sun_family = AF_LOCAL,
31          .sun_path = SOCKNAME
32      };
33
34      // This creates the file.
35      // If file exists it fails with EADDRINUSE,
36      // so don't forget to unlink when done!
37      int r = bind(s, (struct sockaddr *) &sa, sizeof(sa));
38
39      ASSERTNOERR(r, "bind");
40
41      // Allow clients to connect. Allow a backlog of one.
42      // This call does not block. That occurs during accept.
43      r = listen(s, 0);
44
45      ASSERTNOERR(r, "listen");
46
47      // We use struct sockaddr_un for the Unix socket address.
48      // This requires a path to a file in a mounted filesystem.
49      struct sockaddr_un asa;
50      size_t addrlen = sizeof(asa);
51
52      // Block until a client connects. Returns the file descriptor
53      // of the new connection as well as its address.
54      int fd = accept(s, (struct sockaddr *) &asa, &addrlen);
55
56      ASSERTNOERR(fd, "accept");
57
58      while (1) {
59          char buf[32];
60          fd_set fds;
61
62          // Use select to wait for data from the client.
63          FD_ZERO(&fds);
```

continues

```
64          FD_SET(fd, &fds);
65          int r = select(fd + 1, &fds, NULL, NULL, NULL);
66
67          ASSERTNOERR(r, "select");
68
69          // Read the data
70          int n = read(fd, buf, sizeof(buf));
71          printf("server read %d bytes\n", n);
72
73          // Zero length read means client closed the socket.
74          if (n == 0)
75              break;
76      }
77
78      // Plain unlink system call is sufficient.
79      unlink(SOCKNAME);
80
81      return 0;
82  }
```

Listing 7-9 is a simple client for use with the server in Listing 7-8. Here, the file descriptor used by socket is passed to connect, which returns after the socket is connected to the server.

LISTING 7-9   client_un.c: Simple Client Using Local Sockets

```
 1 #include <stdio.h>
 2 #include <string.h>
 3 #include <stdlib.h>
 4 #include <signal.h>
 5 #include <unistd.h>
 6 #include <sys/types.h>
 7 #include <sys/socket.h>
 8 #include <sys/un.h>
 9
10 #define ASSERTNOERR(x,msg) do {\
11     if ((x) == -1) { perror(msg); exit(1); }} while(0)
12
13 // Name must match the server we want to connect to.
14 #define SOCKNAME "localsock"
15
16 int main(int argc, char *argv[])
17 {
18     // Options ust match server_un.c
19     int s = socket(PF_LOCAL, SOCK_STREAM, 0);
20
21     ASSERTNOERR(s, "socket");
22
```

```
23      // Socket address takes AF_ macros
24      struct sockaddr_un sa = {
25          .sun_family = AF_LOCAL,
26          .sun_path = SOCKNAME
27      };
28
29      // Returns -1 if failed.
30      int r = connect(s, (struct sockaddr *) &sa, sizeof(sa));
31
32      ASSERTNOERR(r, "connect");
33
34      const char data[] = "Hello World";
35      r = write(s, data, sizeof(data));
36
37      printf("client wrote %d bytes\n", r);
38
39      return 0;
40 }
```

When the server runs, it creates a file in the local directory named `localsock`. This is required for a UNIX domain socket and is specified in the `sockaddr_un` structure. Both the client and server specify the socket name, but only the server creates the socket. A local socket is visible via the `ls` command and can be identified by the `s` in first column of the permissions, as in this example:

```
$ ./server_un &
$ ls -l localsock
srwxrwxr-x  1 john john 0 Apr 29 22:28 localsock
```

A client using local sockets is fairly simple, as shown in Listing 7-9 earlier in the chapter. Running the client (after the server) produces the following output:

```
$ ./client_un
client wrote 12 bytes
server read 12 bytes
server read 0 bytes
[1]+ Done                    ./server_un
```

I deliberately glossed over a few details in these examples. The `listen` system call, for example, requires a *backlog* argument, which determines how many connections the operating system will accept on your behalf. Each pending connection requires the server to call `accept`, but a pending connection causes the client to block until the server code calls `accept`. I specified a backlog of zero, which means that only one connection can be active at a time. As long as this connection is open, any clients that try to connect to the server will be refused.

As soon as you close this connection, the operating system may initiate a new connection before you have a chance to close the listen socket. The shutdown system call prevents the kernel from accepting any new connections while the server terminates gracefully.

7.6.4   Client Server Using Network Sockets

Luckily, a network client and server are not much different from the local client and server created in Listing 7-9 and Listing 7-8. I will highlight the differences here. Essentially, the difference is in the protocol family and address used. Other than that, the code is virtually identical.

- Replace the include file sys/un.h with netinet/in.h.

- The protocol family passed to the socket function changes from PF_LOCAL to a network protocol family. (PF_INET is typical.)

- The socket address structure changes from sockaddr_un to sockaddr_in. It has a network address family (AF_INET is typical) and is initialized with a network address and a port.

- You do not unlink the socket when you are done. A network socket does not persist after the server exits.

The socket address is slightly different for client and server and is worth a closer look. Because it is a network address, it must be specified using an address and a numeric port. The server can allow connections on any interface using the special address macro INADDR_ANY. When initializing the structure, you need to be aware of network byte order as well. The code to initialize a server address port address of 5000 looks like the following:

```
struct sockaddr_in sa = {
    .sin_family = AF_INET,
    .sin_port=htons(5000),
    .sin_addr = {INADDR_ANY} };
```

The macro htons stands for *host to network short* and converts the byte order of the port ID to network byte order.[6] Instead of INADDR_ANY, you can specify a

---

6.   Refer to inet(3).

specific interface address in the `sin_addr` field and use a struct `in_addr`, which can be initialized using the following pattern:

```
struct in_addr ifaddr;
int r = inet_aton("192.168.163.128",&ifaddr);
```

Then you can use the value of `ifaddr` to initialize `sin_addr` in the struct `sockaddr`. The same changes apply to the client except that a client typically uses a specific address instead of `INADDR_ANY`.

7.7 Message Queues

Message queues are yet another way to transfer data between two processes. As you might expect, there are two ways to create a message queue: the System V method and the POSIX method. Each method is a little different, but the principle is the same.

Both types of message queues emphasize fixed-size, priority-based messages. A receiver must read exactly the number of bytes transmitted; otherwise, the read from the message queue will fail. This provides an application some degree of assurance that a process it is communicating with uses the same version of a message structure.

Each API implements priority slightly differently. The System V API allows the receiver a bit more flexibility in prioritizing incoming messages, whereas the POSIX API enforces strict prioritization.

7.7.1 The System V Message Queue

The function for creating or attaching to a message queue is `msgget`, which takes an integer value as a user-defined key for the message queue, just like the System V API for shared memory. The function returns a system-defined key for the queue, which is used for subsequent reads and writes to the queue. Following is the prototype for `msgget`:

```
int msgget(key_t key, int msgflg);
```

As I mentioned earlier in the chapter, the `key` argument can be an application-defined key that never changes. The value returned by `msgget` is the system-defined message queue identifier that is used for all reads and writes by this process. The key can be replaced by the macro `IPC_PRIVATE`. Using this value for the key will always create a new message queue. The message queue IDs returned by msgget are valid across processes, unlike file descriptors. So the message queue ID can be shared between parent and child as well as between peer processes.

The msgflag argument to msgget is very similar to the flags passed to the open system call. In fact, the lower 9 bits are the same permission bits used by the open call. Other flags allowed are IPC_CREAT and IPC_EXCL. IPC_CREAT is used to create a new message queue; if the message queue exists, it will return a message queue ID for the existing queue. When IPC_CREAT is specified with IPC_EXCL, it causes the msgget to fail if the message queue exists. This behavior is the same as the O_CREAT and O_EXCL flags used with the open(2) system call.

There is no equivalent to a close function for the message queue, because queue IDs do not consume file descriptors. The IDs are visible to all processes, and the operating system does not keep track of message queues by process.

A process can remove a message queue with the msgctl function, which, as the name suggests, does many things besides removing message queues:

```
int msgctl(int msqid, int cmd, struct msqid_ds *buf);
```

The cmd argument to remove a message queue is IPC_RMID, in which case the buf argument may be NULL. Refer to msgctl(2) for more details.

Reading and writing to a message queue are accomplished with the following two functions:

```
int msgsnd(int qid, void *msg, size_t msgsz, int msgflg);
ssize_t msgrcv(int qid, void *msg, size_t msgsz, long typ, int msgflg);
```

System V message queues allow messages to have a variable length, provided that the sender and receiver agree on the size. The message *type* doubles as the message priority. So depending on the application, you can choose to prioritize messages in the queue, use the priority to identify the message type, or some combination of both.

You can see a demonstration of all these techniques in Listing 7-10.

LISTING 7-10   sysv-msgq-example.c: Message Queue Example Using System V API

```
1 #include <stdio.h>
2 #include <string.h>
3 #include <stdlib.h>
4 #include <unistd.h>
5 #include <sys/wait.h>
6 #include <sys/stat.h>
7 #include <sys/file.h>
```

```
 8 #include <sys/msg.h>
 9 #include <sys/ipc.h>
10
11 // Fixed-size message to keep things simple.
12 struct message {
13     long int mtype;
14     char mtext[128];
15 };
16
17 // Stuff text into a message and send it.
18 int send_msg(int qid, int mtype, const char text[])
19 {
20     struct message msg = {
21         .mtype = mtype
22     };
23     strncpy(msg.mtext, text, sizeof(msg.mtext));
24
25     int r = msgsnd(qid, &msg, sizeof(msg), 0);
26     if (r == -1) {
27         perror("msgsnd");
28     }
29     return r;
30 }
31
32 // Read message from queue into a message struct.
33 int recv_msg(int qid, int mtype, struct message *msg)
34 {
35     int r = msgrcv(qid, msg, sizeof(struct message), mtype, 0);
36     switch (r) {
37     case sizeof(struct message):
38         /* okay */
39         break;
40     case -1:
41         perror("msgrcv");
42         break;
43     default:
44         printf("only received %d bytes\n", r);
45     }
46     return r;
47 }
48
49 void producer(int mqid)
50 {
51     // Pay attention to the order we are sending these messages.
52     send_msg(mqid, 1, "type 1 - first");
53     send_msg(mqid, 2, "type 2 - second");
54     send_msg(mqid, 1, "type 1 - third");
55 }
56
57 void consumer(int qid)
```

continues

```
58 {
59     struct message msg;
60     int r;
61     int i;
62     for (i = 0; i < 3; i++) {
63         // -2 accepts messages of type 2 or less.
64         r = msgrcv(qid, &msg, sizeof(struct message), -2, 0);
65         printf("'%s'\n", msg.mtext);
66     }
67 }
68
69 int main(int argc, char *argv[])
70 {
71     // Create a private (unnamed) message queue.
72     int mqid;
73     mqid = msgget(IPC_PRIVATE, S_IREAD | S_IWRITE);
74     if (mqid == -1) {
75         perror("msgget");
76         exit(1);
77     }
78
79     pid_t pid = fork();
80     if (pid == 0) {
81         consumer(mqid);
82         exit(0);
83     }
84     else {
85         int status;
86         producer(mqid);
87         wait(&status);
88     }
89     // Remove the message queue.
90     int r = msgctl(mqid, IPC_RMID, 0);
91     if (r)
92         perror("msgctl");
93     return 0;
94 }
```

Some things to point out in this example are that it uses an unnamed message queue and fixed-length messages. The receiver uses a feature of msgrcv that I have not discussed. By specifying the acceptable message type as -2, it indicates that any message of type 2 or lower may be accepted. This produces some interesting output when you run the program:

```
$ cc -o sysv-msgq-example sysv-msgq-example.c
$ ./sysv-msgq-example
'type 1 - first'
'type 1 - third'
'type 2 - second'
```

Notice that the type 1 messages were received first. Lower numbers are higher priority and received first. As a result, you received your messages in a different order from the order in which they were sent. To receive the messages in the same order in which they were sent (FIFO), use a zero for the `type` argument in `msgrcv`.

When the `type` argument of `msgrcv` has a nonzero value, the messages are received by priority, as follows:

- Positive—Only messages of that type are accepted.

- Negative—Only messages of the absolute value of the type specified or lower values are accepted.

Linux also adds a `MSG_EXCEPT` flag, which is not part of any standard. When the type is positive and `MSG_EXCEPT` is set in the flags argument of `msgrcv`, this has the effect of inverting the selection—that is, instead of message type N, `msgrcv` will accept anything but message type N.

7.7.2   The POSIX Message Queue

The POSIX API is functionally very similar to the System V API except that message queues are modeled closely after the POSIX file model. As in the file model, message queues have names, which must obey the same rules as filenames. Message queues can be opened, closed, created, and unlinked, just like files. In Linux, these message queues consume file descriptors, just like open files. The POSIX message queue API should be very intuitive for a programmer who is comfortable with the POSIX API for files.

7.7.2.1   Creating, Opening, Closing, and Removing POSIX Message Queues

POSIX does not provide a `creat` function for creating message queues. Instead, message queues are created by using the `mq_open` function with the `O_CREAT` flag. `mq_open` is defined as follows:

```
mqd_t mq_open(const char *name, int oflag, ...);
```

The function signature looks a lot like the `open` system call. The POSIX standard allows (but does not require) the return value to be a file descriptor. In Linux, it is a file descriptor. It should come as no surprise, then, that the `oflag` argument takes the same arguments as the `open` system call, including `O_CREAT`, `O_READ`, `O_WRITE`, and `O_RDWR`. When the caller sets the `O_CREAT` flag, however, `mq_open` requires two additional arguments to create the message queue. The third argument is the mode, just like the open call, and determines the read/write permissions of the message queue. This takes the same values as the permission flags (such as S_IREAD) and is enforced by subsequent calls to mq_open on that message queue. The fourth argument to mq_open, required by O_CREAT, is a pointer to a mq_attr structure, which is defined as follows:

```
struct mq_attr
{
  long int mq_flags;          Implementation-defined flags, including O_NONBLOCK
  long int mq_maxmsg;         Maximum number of messages pending in the queue
  long int mq_msgsize;        Maximum size of each message in the queue
  long int mq_curmsgs;        Number of messages currently in the queue
  long int __pad[4];
};
```

The mq_attr argument is optional and can be omitted, in which case the system will use implementation-defined default values for the attributes. You can't use a message queue with unknown attributes, so POSIX provides the function mq_getattr to retrieve this structure for a given message queue. There is also a function named mq_setattr that allows you to adjust the flags of the queue. Both these functions are defined as follows:

```
int mq_setattr(mqd_t mqdes, const struct mq_attr *iattr, struct mq_attr *oattr);
int mq_getattr(mqd_t mqdes, struct mq_attr *oattr);
```

The mq_maxmsg and mq_msgsize fields are used only by the mq_open call when the message queue is created. These fields determine the maximum number of messages the queue will hold and the size of each message, respectively. These values are fixed for the lifetime of the queue, so they are ignored by mq_setattr. Similarly, the mq_curmsgs field has no meaning when passed as input to mq_open or mq_setattr but is filled in only by the mq_getattr call and the output of the mq_getattr call.

Because the message queue ID returned by the Linux version of mq_open is a file descriptor, you need a close function to free up the file descriptor and any associated resources. POSIX defines the mq_close function for this purpose:

```
int mq_close(mqd_t mqdes);
```

As you might guess, the Linux version of mq_close is just an alias for the close system call. To delete a message queue permanently, use the mq_unlink function, which is patterned after the unlink system call, as follows:

```
int mq_unlink(const char *name);
```

As with a regular file, the message queue is not removed until the reference count goes to zero. Any processes that have the message queue open when it is unlinked will continue to be able to use it.

7.7.2.2 Reading and Writing to a POSIX Message Queue

The functions for reading and writing the message look much like the System V equivalents. Following are the prototypes for `mq_send` and `mq_receive`, slightly abbreviated to conserve space:

```
int mq_send(mqd_t mqdes, char *ptr, size_t len, unsigned prio);
ssize_t mq_receive(mqd_t mqdes, char *ptr, size_t len, unsigned *prio);
```

Like the System V calls, these functions include a priority, but unlike System V, POSIX places an upper limit on the size of messages. The `mq_send` function takes arguments much like a `write` system call, with the addition of a priority argument. `mq_send` will write messages that are smaller than the maximum allowed for the message queue. `mq_receive` requires the receiver to provide enough space for the maximum message size and returns the actual size of the message received.

By default, reading from an empty message queue blocks your process until a message is available. Likewise, writing to a full message queue causes your process to block as well. You can specify the `O_NONBLOCK` flag when you open the message queue to change this behavior. You also can change this flag dynamically with the `mq_setattr` function.

7.7.2.3 A Complete Example Using POSIX Message Queues

Now let's look at a complete example of a program that uses a POSIX message queue. Listing 7-11 shows a basic usage of POSIX message queues. Here again, you have a producer and a consumer process.

LISTING 7-11   posix-msgq-ex.c: Example of POSIX Message Queue

```
 1 #include <stdio.h>
 2 #include <string.h>
 3 #include <stdlib.h>
 4 #include <unistd.h>
 5 #include <mqueue.h>
 6 #include <sys/stat.h>
 7 #include <sys/wait.h>
 8
```

continues

```
 9 // Simple message wrapper.
10 struct message {
11     char mtext[128];
12 };
13
14 int send_msg(int qid, int pri, const char text[])
15 {
16     int r = mq_send(qid, text, strlen(text) + 1, pri);
17     if (r == -1) {
18         perror("mq_send");
19     }
20     return r;
21 }
22
23 void producer(mqd_t qid)
24 {
25     // Low priority messages
26     send_msg(qid, 1, "This is my first message.");
27     send_msg(qid, 1, "This is my second message.");
28
29     // High priority message...
30     send_msg(qid, 3, "No more messages.");
31 }
32
33 void consumer(mqd_t qid)
34 {
35     struct mq_attr mattr;
36
37     // We assume the producer is finished at this point.
38     do {
39         u_int pri;
40         struct message msg;
41         ssize_t len;
42
43         len = mq_receive(qid, (char *) &msg, sizeof(msg), &pri);
44         if (len == -1) {
45             perror("mq_receive");
46             break;
47         }
48         printf("got pri %d '%s' len=%d\n", pri, msg.mtext, len);
49
50         // Check for more messages in the queue.
51         int r = mq_getattr(qid, &mattr);
52         if (r == -1) {
53             perror("mq_getattr");
54             break;
55         }
56     } while (mattr.mq_curmsgs); // Stop when no more messages
57 }
58
```

```
59 int main(int argc, char *argv[])
60 {
61     // Allow up to 10 messages before blocking.
62     // Message size is 128 bytes (see above).
63     struct mq_attr mattr = {
64         .mq_maxmsg = 10,
65         .mq_msgsize = sizeof(struct message)
66     };
67
68     mqd_t mqid = mq_open("/myq",
69                         O_CREAT | O_RDWR,
70                         S_IREAD | S_IWRITE,
71                         &mattr);
72
73     if (mqid == (mqd_t) -1) {
74         perror("mq_open");
75         exit(1);
76     }
77
78     // Fork a producer process, we'll be the consumer.
79     pid_t pid = fork();
80     if (pid == 0) {
81         producer(mqid);
82         mq_close(mqid);
83         exit(0);
84     }
85     else {
86         // Wait for the producer to send all messages so
87         // we can illustrate priority.
88         int status;
89         wait(&status);
90
91         consumer(mqid);
92         mq_close(mqid);
93     }
94
95     mq_unlink("/myq");
96     return 0;
97 }
```

When the program runs, it forks a producer process, which sends three messages in sequence. The last message is given a higher priority than the first two for the purpose of illustrating priority. The consumer process (the parent) waits for the producer to finish—not because it has to, but for illustration. This demonstration shows that the message queue can hold messages until they can be delivered, even if the sender has exited. By allowing the messages to sit in the queue, you receive the messages in priority order, not in sequence:

```
$ ./posix-msgq-ex
got pri 3 'No more messages.' len=18
got pri 1 'This is my first message.' len=26
got pri 1 'This is my second message.' len=27
```

Note that you did not need to synchronize with the `wait` function. You could have just as easily synchronized with `mq_receive`, but then the order of the messages would be undefined. They could come in the same order or in sequence. The actual results would depend on the implementation and the OS scheduler.

7.7.3   Difference between POSIX Message Queues and System V Message Queues

There are some significant differences in behavior between System V and POSIX messages queues. System V allows the size of a message to vary as long as the value read matches the value written. POSIX message queues, however, allow the sender to write variable-length messages, although the reader must provide enough room for the fixed message size—that is, a call to `msg_receive` fails if the size given is not large enough to hold a full message.

Another difference is that whereas System V allows the reader to do some rudimentary filtering of messages based on a particular priority, POSIX messages are delivered in strict priority order—that is, the reader cannot pick which priority to read or block until a message of a particular priority is available. A read from a POSIX message queue will always retrieve the highest-priority message available. If more than one message of a given priority is available in the queue, the first message queued is the first message read (like a FIFO).

7.8   Semaphores

When two processes share resources, it is important that they maintain orderly access to the shared resources; otherwise, chaos can erupt in the form of garbled output and program crashes. The word *semaphore* in computer terms refers to a special type of flag that is used to synchronize concurrent processes. Semaphores are like traffic lights for concurrent processes.

Here again, you have two APIs for using semaphores: the System V API and the POSIX API. The basic semaphore is a counter. Conceptually, the counter keeps track of some finite resource. A very common pattern is to use one semaphore per resource so that the counter never increments more than 1. This sometimes is called a *binary semaphore*, because the value of the semaphore count is always 1 or 0.

A complete explanation of semaphores and concurrency is beyond the scope of this book, but consider an example using the POSIX API. Listing 7-12 is a contrived example of two processes that are trying to send two halves of the same message to the standard output. In this case, the standard output is the shared resource that must be *protected* with a semaphore.

LISTING 7-12   hello-unsync.c: Two Unsynchronized Processes Trying to Write to Standard Output

```
 1 #include <stdio.h>
 2 #include <string.h>
 3 #include <stdlib.h>
 4 #include <unistd.h>
 5 #include <sys/file.h>
 6 #include <sys/times.h>
 7 #include <sys/stat.h>
 8 #include <semaphore.h>
 9 #include <assert.h>
10
11 // Simple busy-wait loop to throw off our timing.
12 void busywait(void)
13 {
14     clock_t t1 = times(NULL);
15     while (times(NULL) - t1 < 2);
16 }
17
18 /*
19 ** Simple message. 1st half printed by one process
20 ** 2nd half printed by the other. No synchronization
21 ** so the output is designed to be garbage.
22 */
23 int main(int argc, char *argv[])
24 {
25     const char *message = "Hello World\n";
26     int n = strlen(message) / 2;
27
28     pid_t pid = fork();
29     int i0 = (pid == 0) ? 0 : n;
30     int i;
31
32     for (i = 0; i < n; i++) {
33         write(1, message + i0 + i, 1);
34         busywait();
35     }
36 }
```

When you run the program in Listing 7-12, you invariably will see garbage. Note that I included a `busywait` routine to randomize the runtime just a little. Otherwise, the scheduler can unintentionally allow this program to run in the correct order:

```
$ cc -o hello-unsync hello-unsync.c
$ $ ./hello-unsync
HWelolo rld                        Garbage caused by out-of-sync access to the standard output
```

The timing of Listing 7-12 is illustrated in Figure 7-2. The basic problem is that both `write` calls can occur in any order. I deliberately made things worse by writing 1 byte at a time. To clean this up, you need a traffic cop to prevent more than one process from accessing the standard output at a time. Listing 7-13 shows how to use a semaphore to do this using the POSIX API.

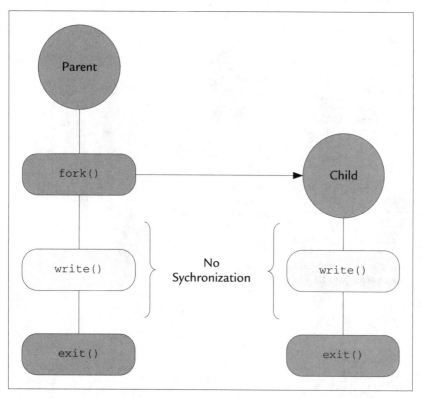

FIGURE 7-2   Timing of Listing 7-12: Unsynchronized Code Produces Garbage

LISTING 7-13   hello-sync.c: Orderly Output with Two Processes

```
 1 #include <stdio.h>
 2 #include <string.h>
 3 #include <stdlib.h>
 4 #include <unistd.h>
 5 #include <sys/file.h>
 6 #include <sys/times.h>
 7 #include <sys/stat.h>
 8 #include <semaphore.h>
 9 #include <assert.h>
10
11 // Simple busy-wait loop to throw off our timing.
12 void busywait(void)
13 {
14     clock_t t1 = times(NULL);
15     while (times(NULL) - t1 < 2);
16 }
17
18 /*
19 ** Simple message. 1st half printed by one process
20 ** 2nd half printed by the other. Synchronized
21 ** with a semaphore.
22 */
23 int main(int argc, char *argv[])
24 {
25     const char *message = "Hello World\n";
26     int n = strlen(message) / 2;
27
28     // Create the semaphore.
29     sem_t *sem = sem_open("/thesem", O_CREAT, S_IRUSR | S_IWUSR);
30     assert(sem != NULL);
31
32     // Initialize the semaphore count to zero.
33     int r = sem_init(sem, 1, 0);
34     assert(r == 0);
35
36     pid_t pid = fork();
37     int i0 = (pid == 0) ? 0 : n;
38     int i;
39
40     // Parent waits for semaphore to increment.
41     if (pid)
42         sem_wait(sem);
43
44     for (i = 0; i < n; i++) {
45         write(1, message + i0 + i, 1);
46         busywait();
47     }
48
49     // Child increments the semaphore when done.
50     if (pid == 0)
51         sem_post(sem);
52 }
```

The fixed-up timing is shown in Figure 7-3. I'll look at the POSIX API in more detail shortly, but the example is about as simple as it gets with semaphores. You initialize the semaphore count with zero so that any process that wants to wait for the semaphore (to go nonzero) will block. I chose to allow the parent to block for this example and let the child print the first half of the message. So the first thing the parent does is wait for the semaphore with the `sem_wait` function, which causes it to block.

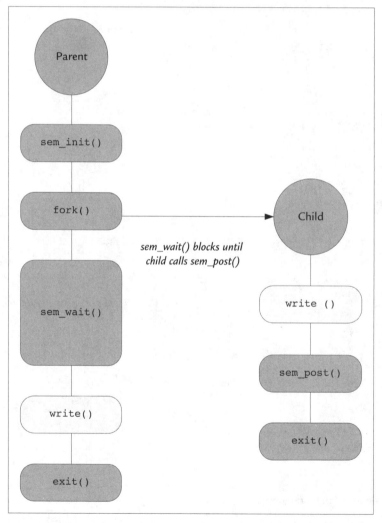

FIGURE 7-3   Timing of Listing 7-13: Semaphore Acts as Traffic Cop

When the child is done, it increments the semaphore using the POSIX sem_post function. This has the effect of unblocking the parent process, which allows it to print the second half of the message. Now the message comes out correctly every time:

```
$ cc -o hello-sync hello-sync.c
$ ./hello-sync
Hello World
```

Astute readers may have noticed that I could have used a wait system call to get the same effect. In this trivial example, that's true, but semaphores are much more useful. Notice that the POSIX API uses the terms *wait* and *post* to refer to decrementing and incrementing the semaphore, respectively. This may suggest that no counting is going on, but these are counting semaphores.

7.8.1 Semaphores with the POSIX API

You saw one complete example of a semaphore between parent and child in Listing 7-13. POSIX semaphores have names that are visible throughout the system. A semaphore exists from the time it is created until the time it is unlinked or the system reboots, as the program in Listing 7-14 illustrates.

LISTING 7-14 posix_sem.c: Simple POSIX Semaphore Program

```
 1 #include <stdio.h>
 2 #include <string.h>
 3 #include <stdlib.h>
 4 #include <assert.h>
 5 #include <errno.h>
 6 #include <unistd.h>
 7 #include <sys/file.h>
 8 #include <sys/stat.h>
 9 #include <semaphore.h>
10
11 int main(int argc, char *argv[])
12 {
13     const char *semname = "/mysem";
14
15     // Create the semaphore, and initialize count to zero.
16     // Since we use O_EXCL, this will Fail if the
17     // semaphore exists with EEXIST.
18     sem_t *sem = sem_open(semname,
```

continues

```
19                      O_CREAT | O_EXCL,
20                      S_IRUSR | S_IWUSR,
21                      0);
22     if (sem != SEM_FAILED) {
23         printf("created new semaphore\n");
24     }
25     else if (errno == EEXIST) {
26         // Semaphore exists, so open it without O_EXCL
27         printf("semaphore exists\n");
28         sem = sem_open(semname, 0);
29     }
30
31     assert(sem != SEM_FAILED);
32
33     int op = 0;
34
35     // User argument : zero, positive or negative
36     if (argc > 1)
37         op = atoi(argv[1]);
38
39     if (op > 0) {
40         printf("incrementing semaphore\n");
41         sem_post(sem);
42     }
43     else if (op < 0) {
44         printf("decrementing semaphore\n");
45         sem_wait(sem);
46     }
47     else {
48         printf("not modifying semaphore\n");
49     }
50     int val;
51     sem_getvalue(sem, &val);
52     printf("semaphore value is %d\n", val);
53
54     return 0;
55 }
```

The semaphore is created the first time the program is run using the sem_open function. The first three arguments to sem_open are identical to the open(2) system call. The fourth argument is used only when the semaphore is created, and that contains the semaphore count. The prototype is as follows:

```
sem_t *sem_open( const char *name, int oflag, ...);
```

I used the O_EXCL flag to force sem_open to fail when the semaphore exists. This is not necessary, and I could have left it out. The flag is there so that you can print a different message when the semaphore is created.

This program does a single semaphore operation based on the user argument. The user can increment the semaphore by using a positive integer for an argument or decrement the semaphore by using a negative argument. For example:

```
$ cc -o posix_sem posix_sem.c -lrt
$ ./posix_sem 1                      Create and increment the semaphore.
created new semaphore
incrementing semaphore
semaphore value is 1

$ ./posix_sem 1                      Increment the semaphore again.
semaphore exists
incrementing semaphore
semaphore value is 2                 Semaphore value reflects the number of sem_post calls.

$ ./posix_sem -1                     Now let's decrement.
semaphore exists
decrementing semaphore
semaphore value is 1

$ ./posix_sem 0                      No operation
semaphore exists
not modifying semaphore
semaphore value is 1                 Value = 2 x sem_post – 1 x sem_wait

$ ./posix_sem -1
semaphore exists
decrementing semaphore
semaphore value is 0

$ ./posix_sem -1
semaphore exists
decrementing semaphore                Semaphore blocks!
```

Listing 7-14 uses a named semaphore. I neglected to call sem_close in this example, which, as you would expect, frees up the user-space resources consumed by the semaphore. Likewise, there is a sem_unlink function that removes a semaphore from the system and frees up any system resources that the semaphore consumed.

The POSIX API also allows unnamed semaphores, but beware: Unnamed semaphores in Linux work only with threads. An unnamed semaphore is defined without using sem_open, which requires a name. Instead, the application calls sem_init, which has the following prototype:

```
int sem_init( sem_t *sem, int pshared, int value );
```

POSIX states that a nonzero pshared argument indicates that the semaphore may be shared between processes. Linux does not implement this, which means that unnamed semaphores may be used only between threads in a process. One pattern to initialize an unnamed semaphore looks like the following:

```
sem_t mysem;                              User-defined storage
int r = sem_init( &mysem, 0, 0 );        Initialize to zero pshared=0
...
sem_destroy(&mysem);                      Do this to reclaim storage.
```

Note that the sem_destroy call is required before the storage can be reclaimed; otherwise, memory corruption may result. If you use unnamed semaphores, it's safest to allocate them for the life of the application instead of putting them on the stack or heap.

7.8.2   Semaphores with the System V API

The System V API for semaphores is consistent with the APIs used for shared memory and message queues—that is, the application defines a key and the system assigns an ID when the semaphore is created. An equivalent example to Listing 7-14 is shown in Listing 7-15.

LISTING 7-15   sysv_sem.c: Example Using System V Semaphores

```
 1 #include <stdio.h>
 2 #include <string.h>
 3 #include <stdlib.h>
 4 #include <assert.h>
 5 #include <errno.h>
 6 #include <unistd.h>
 7 #include <sys/stat.h>
 8 #include <sys/sem.h>
 9
10 int main(int argc, char *argv[])
11 {
```

```
12      // Make a key using ftok
13      key_t semkey = ftok("/tmp", 'a');
14
15      // Create the semaphore - an "array" of length 1.
16      // Since we use IPC_EXCL, this will fail if the
17      // semaphore exists with EEXIST.
18      int semid =
19          semget(semkey, 1, IPC_CREAT | IPC_EXCL | S_IRUSR | S_IWUSR);
20      if (semid != -1) {
21          printf("created new semaphore\n");
22      }
23      else if (errno == EEXIST) {
24          // Semaphore exists, so open it without IPC_EXCL
25          printf("semaphore exists\n");
26          semid = semget(semkey, 1, 0);
27      }
28
29      assert(semid != -1);
30
31      // Note: zero is a legitimate Sys V semaphore operation
32      // So we only do an operation if we have an argument
33      if (argc == 2) {
34          int op = atoi(argv[1]);
35
36          // Initialize the operations structure,
37          // which applies to an array of semaphores.
38          // but in this case we are using only one.
39          struct sembuf sb = {
40              .sem_num = 0,      // index into the array.
41              .sem_op = op,      // value summed with the count
42              .sem_flg = 0       // flags (e.g. IPC_NOWAIT)
43          };
44
45          // One call does it all!
46          int r = semop(semid, &sb, 1);
47
48          assert(r != -1);
49          printf("operation %d done\n", op);
50      }
51      else {
52          printf("no operation\n");
53      }
54
55      printf("semid %d value %d\n", semid, semctl(semid, 0, GETVAL));
56
57      return 0;
58  }
```

The functions map almost one for one to the POSIX API, with a few important differences. For one thing, the System V API uses only the `semop` function for both the equivalent `wait` and `post` operations. Also, the System V API includes a "wait for zero" operation, which does not modify the semaphore value but blocks the caller until the semaphore count goes to zero. Let's look at this:

```
$ cc -Wall  -lrt  sysv_sem.c   -o sysv_sem

$ ./sysv_sem 0                  Create semaphore
created new semaphore
operation 0 done
semid 360448 value 0

$ ./sysv_sem 1                  Increment the semaphore
semaphore exists
operation 1 done
semid 360448 value 1

$ ./sysv_sem 0 &                Launch a background task to wait for zero
[1] 32475
semaphore exists               Process blocks

$ ./sysv_sem -1
semaphore exists
operation -1 done
semid 360448 value 0
operation 0 done               Background job wakes up
semid 360448 value 0
```

The wait-for-zero operation is unique to System V semaphores. Just like POSIX semaphores, decrementing a semaphore will also block if the semaphore value is zero.

7.9   Summary

This chapter introduced the basics of interprocess communication. I introduced several APIs and basic examples of each. In most cases, there are at least two APIs for doing the same thing. I discussed the history and rationale behind these, which ideally should give you enough background to make an intelligent choice of API.

7.9.1   System Calls and APIs Used in This Chapter

I covered many APIs in this chapter in several categories.

7.9.1.1   Miscellaneous

- `flock`—places an advisory lock on a file
- `ftok`—creates unique keys for use with System V IPC
- `lockf`—places a mandatory lock on a file
- `select`—function for blocking on or polling multiple file descriptors

7.9.1.2   Shared Memory

- `shm_open`, `shm_unlink`, `mmap`—POSIX shared memory routines
- `shmget`, `shmat`, `shmdt`, `shmctl`—System V shared memory routines

7.9.1.3   Signals

- `kill`, `sigqueue`—functions for sending signals
- `sigaction`, `signal`—functions for defining signal handlers
- `sigpending`, `sigsuspend`—functions for waiting on signals
- `sigprocmask`, `sigemtpyset`, `sigfillset`, `sigaddset`, `sigdelset`, `sigismember`—functions for manipulating signal masks

7.9.1.4   Pipes

- `mkfifo`—create a named pipe
- `pipe`—create an unnamed pipe

7.9.1.5   Sockets

- `bind`, `listen`, `accept`, `close`—vital functions for creating connection-oriented servers
- `connect`—client function for connecting to a server socket
- `socket`—main function for creating sockets

7.9.1.6 Message Queues

- `mq_open, mq_close, mq_unlink, mq_send, mq_receive, mq_setattr, mq_getattr`—POSIX message queue functions

- `msgget, msgsend, msgrcv, msgctl`—System V message queue functions

7.9.1.7 Semaphores

- `sem_open, sem_close, sem_post, sem_wait`—POSIX semaphore functions

- `semget, semop`—System V semaphore functions

7.9.2 References

- Gallmeister, B. *POSIX 4 Programmers Guide*. Sebastopol, Calif.: O'Reilly Media, Inc., 1995.

- Robbins, A. *Linux Programming by Example, The Fundamentals*. Englewood Cliffs, N.J.: Prentice Hall, 2004.

- Stevens, W. R., et al. *UNIX Network Programming*. Boston, Mass.: Addison-Wesley, 2004.

7.9.3 Online Resources

- www.opengroup.org—publishes the POSIX standard (IEEE Standard 1003.2) and many others (registration required)

- www.unix.org—publishes the Single UNIX Specification

Chapter 8

Debugging IPC with Shell Commands

8.1   Introduction

In this chapter, I look at techniques and commands you can use from the shell for debugging interprocess communication (IPC). When you are debugging communication between processes, it's always nice to have a neutral third party to intervene when things go wrong.

8.2   Tools for Working with Open Files

Processes that leave files open can cause problems. File descriptors can be "leaked" like memory, for example, consuming resources unnecessarily. Each process has a finite number of file descriptors it may keep open, so if some broken code continues to open file descriptors without closing them, eventually it will fail with an errno value of EMFILE. If you have some thoughtful error handling in your code, it will be obvious what has happened. But then what?

The procfs file system is very useful for debugging such problems. You can see all the open files of a particular process in the directory /proc/PID/fd. Each open file here shows up as a symbolic link. The name of the link is the file descriptor number, and the link points to the open file. Following is an example:

```
$ stty tostop                                Force background task to stop on output.
$ echo hello | cat ~/.bashrc 2>/dev/null &   Run cat in the background.
[1] 16894                                     It's stopped.
$ ls -l /proc/16894/fd                        Let's see what files it has open.
total 4
lr-x------  1 john john 64 Apr  9 12:15 0 -> pipe:[176626]
lrwx------  1 john john 64 Apr  9 12:15 1 -> /dev/pts/2
l-wx------  1 john john 64 Apr  9 12:15 2 -> /dev/null
lr-x------  1 john john 64 Apr  9 12:15 3 -> /home/john/.bashrc
```

Here, I piped the output of echo to the cat command, which shows up as a pipe for file descriptor zero (standard input). The standard output points to the current terminal, and I redirected the standard error (file descriptor 2) to /dev/null. Finally, the file I am trying to print shows up in file descriptor 3. All this shows fairly clearly in the output.

8.2.1   lsof

You can see a more comprehensive listing by using the lsof command. With no arguments, lsof will show all open files in the system, which can be overwhelming. Even then, it will show you only what you have permission to see. You can restrict output to a single process with the -p option, as follows:

```
$ lsof -p 16894
COMMAND    PID USER   FD    TYPE DEVICE     SIZE   NODE NAME
cat      16894 john   cwd    DIR  253,0     4096 575355 /home/john
cat      16894 john   rtd    DIR  253,0     4096      2 /
cat      16894 john   txt    REG  253,0    21104 159711 /bin/cat
cat      16894 john   mem    REG  253,0   126648 608855 /lib/ld-2.3.5.so
cat      16894 john   mem    REG  253,0  1489572 608856 /lib/libc-2.3.5.so
cat      16894 john   mem    REG    0,0             0 [heap]
cat      16894 john   mem    REG  253,0 48501472 801788 .../locale-archive
cat      16894 john    0r   FIFO    0,5          176626 pipe
cat      16894 john    1u    CHR  136,2               4 /dev/pts/2
cat      16894 john    2w    CHR    1,3            1510 /dev/null
cat      16894 john    3r    REG  253,0      167 575649 /home/john/.bashrc
```

This output shows not only file descriptors, but memory-mapped files as well. The FD heading tells you whether the output is a file descriptor or a mapping. A mapping does not require a file descriptor after mmap has been called, so the FD column includes some text for each mapping to indicate the type of mapping. File descriptors are shown by number as well as the type of access, as summarized in Table 8-1.

You also can use `lsof` to discover which process has a particular file open by providing the filename as an argument. There are many more options to the `lsof` command; see `lsof(8)` for details.

8.2.2 fuser

Another utility for tracking down open files is the `fuser` command. Suppose that you need to track down a process that is writing a huge file that is filling up your file system. You could use `fuser` as follows:

```
$ fuser some-huge-file.txt              What process has this file open?
some-huge-file.txt:  17005
```

If that's all you care about, you could go ahead and kill the process. `fuser` allows you to do this with the `-k` option as follows:

```
]$ fuser -k -KILL some-huge-file.txt
some-huge-file.txt:  17005
[1]+  Killed                  cat some-huge-file.txt
```

TABLE 8-1   Text Used in the FD Column of lsof Output

Identifier	Meaning
cwd	Current working directory
ltx	Shared library text (code and data)
mem	Memory-mapped file
mmap	Memory-mapped device
pd	Parent directory
rtd	Root directory
txt	Program text (code and data)
{digit}r	File descriptor opened read-only
{digit}w	File descriptor opened write-only
{digit}u	File descriptor opened read/write.

This sends the SIGKILL signal to any and all processes that have this file open. Another time fuser comes in handy is when you are trying to unmount a file system but can't because a process has a file open. In this case, the -m option is very helpful:

```
$ fuser -m /mnt/flash            What process has files open on this file system?
/mnt/flash:            17118
```

Now you can decide whether you want to kill the process or let it finish what it needs to do. fuser has more options that are documented in the fuser(1) man page.

8.2.3   ls

You will be interested in the *long* listing available with the -l option. No doubt you are aware that this gives you the filename, permissions, and size of the file. The output also tells you what kind of file you are looking at. For example:

```
$ ls -l /dev/log /dev/initctl /dev/sda /dev/zero
prw-------  1 root root    0 Oct  8 09:13 /dev/initctl    A pipe (p)
srw-rw-rw-  1 root root    0 Oct  8 09:10 /dev/log        A socket (s)
brw-r-----  1 root disk 8, 0 Oct  8 04:09 /dev/sda        A block device (b)
crw-rw-rw-  1 root root 1, 5 Oct  8 04:09 /dev/zero       A char device (c)
```

For files other than plain files, the first column indicates the type of file you are looking at. You can also use the -F option for a more concise listing that uses unique suffixes for special files:

```
$ ls -F /dev/log /dev/initctl /dev/zero /dev/sda
/dev/initctl|  /dev/log=  /dev/sda  /dev/zero
```

A pipe is indicated by adding a | to the filename, and a socket is indicated by adding a = to the filename. The -F option does not use any unique character to identify block or character devices, however.

8.2.4   file

This simple utility can tell you in a very user-friendly way the type of file you are looking at. For example:

```
file /dev/log /dev/initctl /dev/sda /dev/zero
/dev/log:      socket
/dev/initctl: fifo (named pipe)
/dev/sda:      block special (8/0)       Includes major/minor numbers
/dev/zero:     character special (1/5)   Includes major/minor numbers
```

Each file is listed with a simple, human-readable description of its type. The `file` command can also recognize many plain file types, such as ELF files and image files. It maintains an extensive database of magic numbers to recognize file types. This database can be extended by the user as well. See `file(1)` for more information.

8.2.5   stat

The `stat` command is a wrapper for the `stat` system that can be used from the shell. The output consists of all the data you would get from the `stat` system call in human-readable format. For example:

```
stat /dev/sda
  File: `/dev/sda'
  Size: 0               Blocks: 0          IO Block: 4096   block special file
Device: eh/14d  Inode: 1137          Links: 1      Device type: 8,0
Access: (0640/brw-r-----)  Uid: (   0/   root)   Gid: (   6/   disk)
Access: 2006-10-08 04:09:34.750000000 -0500
Modify: 2006-10-08 04:09:34.750000000 -0500
Change: 2006-10-08 04:09:50.000000000 -0500
```

`stat` also allows formatting like the `printf` function, using specially defined format characters defined in the `stat(1) man` page. To see only the name of each file followed by its access rights in human-readable form and octal, you could use the following command:

```
stat --format="%-15n %A,%a" /dev/log /dev/initctl /dev/sda /dev/zero
/dev/log        srw-rw-rw-,666
/dev/initctl    prw-------,600
/dev/sda        brw-r-----,640
/dev/zero       crw-rw-rw-,666
```

`stat` can be very useful in scripts to monitor particular files on disk. During debugging, such scripts can act like watchdogs. You can watch a UNIX socket to look for periods of inactivity as follows:

```
while [ true ]; do
        ta=$(stat -c %X $filename)    # Time of most recent activity
        tnow=$(date +%s)              # Current time

        if [ $(($tnow - $ta)) -gt 5 ]; then
                echo No activity on $filename in the last 5 seconds.
        fi
        sleep 1
done
```

In this example, the script checks a file every second for the most recent access to the file, which is given with the %X format option to stat. Whenever a process writes to the socket, the time is updated, so the difference between the current time and the time from the stat command is the amount of elapsed time (in seconds) since the last write or read from the socket.

8.3   Dumping Data from a File

You probably are familiar with a few tools for this purpose, including your favorite text editor for looking at text files. All the regular text processing tools are at your disposal for working with ASCII text files. Some of these tools have the ability to work with additional encodings—if not through a command-line option, maybe via the locale setting. For example:

```
$ wc -w konnichiwa.txt                          Contains the Japanese phrase "konnichiwa" (one word).
0 konnichiwa.txt                                wc reports 0 words based on current locale.
$ LANG=ja_JP.UTF-8 wc -w konnichiwa.txt
1 konnichiwa.txt                                Forced Japanese locale gives us the correct answer.
```

Several tools can help with looking at binary data, but not all of them help interpret the data. To appreciate the differences among tools, you'll need an example (Listing 8-1).

LISTING 8-1   filedat.c: A Program That Creates a Data File with Mixed Formats

```
 1 #include <stdio.h>
 2 #include <string.h>
 3 #include <stdlib.h>
 4 const char message[] = { // UTF-8 message
 5     0xbf, 0xe3, 0x81, 0x93, 0xe3, 0x82, 0x93, 0xe3, 0x81, 0xab,
 6     0xe3, 0x81, 0xa1, 0xe3, 0x81, 0xaf, '\r', 0x20, 0x20, 0x20,
 7     0x20, 0x20, 0x20, 0x20, 0x20, 0x20, 0x20, 0x0a, 0x0a, 0
 8 };
 9
10 int main(int argc, char *argv[])
11 {
12     const char *filename = "floats-ints.dat";
13     FILE *fp = fopen(filename, "wb");
14
15     /* error checking omitted. */
16
17     fprintf(fp, "Hello World\r%12s\n", "");
18     fwrite(message, sizeof(message), 1, fp);
19
20     /* write 250 zeros to the file. */
```

```
21      char *zeros = calloc(250, 1);
22      fwrite(zeros, 250, 1, fp);
23
24      int i;
25
26      /* Write four ints to the file 90000, 90001, ... */
27      for (i = 0; i < 4; i++) {
28          int idatum = i + 90000;
29          fwrite((char *) &idatum, sizeof(idatum), 1, fp);
30      }
31
32      /* Write four floats to the file 90000, 90001, ... */
33      for (i = 0; i < 4; i++) {
34          float fdatum = (float) i + 90000.0;
35          fwrite((char *) &fdatum, sizeof(fdatum), 1, fp);
36      }
37      printf("wrote %s\n", filename);
38      fclose(fp);
39 }
```

Listing 8-1 creates a file that contains a mix of ASCII, UTF-8, and binary data. The binary data is in native integer format (32 bits on my machine) and IEEE float (also 32 bits). A simple `cat` command produces nothing but garbage:

```
$ ./filedat
wrote floats-ints.dat
$ cat floats-ints.dat
```

floats-ints.dat____È ̄GÈ ̄GÉ ̄GÉ ̄G$ *Not even "Hello World" is printed!*

The problem, of course, is that `cat` just streams bytes out to the terminal, which then interprets those bytes as whatever encoding the locale is using. In the "`Hello World`" string on line 17 of Listing 8-1, I included a carriage return followed by 12 spaces. This has the effect of writing "`Hello World`" but then overwriting it with 12 spaces, which effectively makes the string invisible on the terminal.

You could use a text editor on this file, but the results may vary based on your text editor. Earlier, I looked at the `bvi` editor, which is a Vi clone for files with binary data.

Figure 8-1 shows that `bvi` does a good job of representing raw bytes and ASCII strings, and even lets you modify the data, but it is not able to represent data encoded in UTF-8, IEEE floats, or native integers. For that, you'll need other tools.

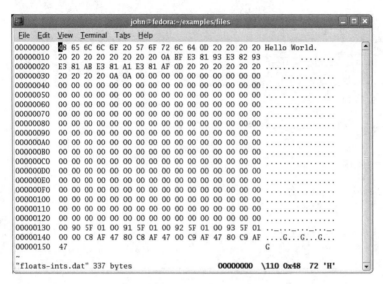

FIGURE 8-1   The Output from Listing 8-1 As Seen in `bvi`

8.3.1   The strings Command

Often, the text strings in a data file can give you a clue as to its contents. Sometimes, the text can tell you all you need to know. When the text is embedded in a bunch of binary data, however, you need something better than a simple `cat` command.

Looking back at the output of Listing 8-1, you can use the `strings` command to look at the text strings in this data:

```
$ strings floats-ints.dat
Hello World
```
Invisible characters? Newlines? Who knows?
```
$
```

Now you can see `Hello World` and the spaces, but something is still missing. Remember that `message` array on line 18? It's actually UTF-8 text I encoded in binary. `strings` can look for 8-bit encodings (that is, non-ASCII) when you use the `-e` option as follows:

```
$ strings -eS floats-ints.dat          Tell strings to look for 8-bit encodings (-eS)

Hello World
```

こんにちは   *Japanese "konnichiwa," "good day" in UTF-8*

óG⬚óG   *Our floats and ints produce this gobbledygook.*
ɰG⬚ɰG

The example above shows that the UTF-8 output is in Japanese, but I glossed over one detail: To show this on your screen, your terminal must support UTF-8 characters. Technically, you also need the correct font to go with it, but it seems that most UTF-8 font sets have the Hiragana[1] characters required for the message above. With `gnome-terminal`, you can get the required support by setting the character encoding to UTF-8. This is visible below Terminal on the menu bar. Not every terminal supports UTF-8; check your documentation.

By default, `strings` limits the output to strings of four characters or more; anything smaller is ignored. You can override this with the `-n` option, which indicates the smallest string to look for. To see the binary data in your file, you will need other tools.

8.3.2   The xxd Command

`xxd` is part of Vim and produces output very similar to `bvi`. The difference is that `xxd` is not a text editor. Like `bvi`, `xxd` shows data in hexadecimal and shows only ASCII characters:

```
$ xxd floats-ints.dat
0000000: 4865 6c6c 6f20 576f 726c 640d 2020 2020  Hello World.
0000010: 2020 2020 2020 2020 0abf e381 93e3 8293      ........
0000020: e381 abe3 81a1 e381 af0d 2020 2020 2020  ..........
0000030: 2020 2020 0a0a 0000 0000 0000 0000 0000  ............
0000040: 0000 0000 0000 0000 0000 0000 0000 0000  ................
0000050: 0000 0000 0000 0000 0000 0000 0000 0000  ................
0000060: 0000 0000 0000 0000 0000 0000 0000 0000  ................
0000070: 0000 0000 0000 0000 0000 0000 0000 0000  ................
0000080: 0000 0000 0000 0000 0000 0000 0000 0000  ................
0000090: 0000 0000 0000 0000 0000 0000 0000 0000  ................
00000a0: 0000 0000 0000 0000 0000 0000 0000 0000  ................
00000b0: 0000 0000 0000 0000 0000 0000 0000 0000  ................
00000c0: 0000 0000 0000 0000 0000 0000 0000 0000  ................
00000d0: 0000 0000 0000 0000 0000 0000 0000 0000  ................
00000e0: 0000 0000 0000 0000 0000 0000 0000 0000  ................
00000f0: 0000 0000 0000 0000 0000 0000 0000 0000  ................
0000100: 0000 0000 0000 0000 0000 0000 0000 0000  ................
0000110: 0000 0000 0000 0000 0000 0000 0000 0000  ................
0000120: 0000 0000 0000 0000 0000 0000 0000 0000  ................
0000130: 0090 5f01 0091 5f01 0092 5f01 0093 5f01  .._..._..._..._.
0000140: 0000 c8af 4780 c8af 4700 c9af 4780 c9af  ....G...G...G...
0000150: 47                                       G
```

---

1.   Hiragana is one of three sets of characters required to render Japanese text.

xxd defaults to 16-bit words, but you can adjust this with the -g option. To see the data in groups of 4 bytes, for example, use -g4. Make sure, however, that the groups preserve the byte order in the file. This means that 32-bit words printed on an IA32 will be incorrect. IA32 stores words with the least significant byte first, which is the reverse of the byte order in memory. This is sometimes called *Little Endian* byte order. To display the correct words, you must reverse the order of the bytes, which xxd does not do.

This can come in handy on some occasions. If you need to look at *Big Endian* data on a Little Endian machine, for example, you do not want to rearrange the bytes. Network protocols use the so-called network byte order for data transfer, which happens to be the same as Big Endian. So if you happen to be looking at a file that contains protocol headers from a socket, you would want a tool like xxd that does not swap the bytes.

8.3.3   The hexdump Command

As the name suggests, hexdump allows you to dump a file's contents in hexadecimal. As with xxd, the default format from hexdump is 16-bit hexadecimal, however, the byte order is adjusted on Little Endian architectures, so the output can differ between xxd and hexdump.

hexdump is better suited for terminal output than xxd because hexdump eliminates duplicate lines of data skipped to avoid cluttering the screen. hexdump can produce many other output formats besides 16-bit hexadecimal, but using them can difficult. Because the hexdump(1) man page does such a rotten job of explaining this feature, here's an example using 32-bit hexadecimal output:

```
$ hexdump -e '6/4 "%8X "' -e '"\n"'  floats-ints.dat
6C6C6548 6F57206F   D646C72 20202020 20202020 20202020
81E3BF0A 9382E393 E3AB81E3 81E3A181 20200DAF 20202020
20202020      A0A        0        0        0        0
       0        0        0        0        0        0
*
       0        0        0        0 15F9000  15F9100
15F9200  15F9300 AFC80000 AFC88047 AFC90047 AFC98047
      47
```

Notice that I included two -e options. The first tells hexdump that I want 6 values per line, each with a width of 4 bytes (32 bits). Then I included a space, followed by the printf-like format in double quotes. hexdump looks for the double quotes and spaces in the format arguments, and will complain if it does not find them. That is why I needed to enclose the entire expression in single quotes.

Still looking at this first argument, I had to include a space following the %8X to separate the values. I could have used a comma or semicolon or whatever, but hexdump interprets this format verbatim. If you neglect to include a separator, all the digits will appear as one long string.

Finally, I told hexdump how to separate each line of output (every six words) by including a second -e option, which for some reason must be enclosed in double quotes. If you can't tell, I find hexdump to be a nuisance to use, but many programmers use it. The alternatives to hexdump are xxd and od.

8.3.4 The od Command

od is the traditional UNIX *octal dump* command. Despite the name, od is capable of representing data in many other formats and word sizes. The -t option is the general-purpose switch for changing the output data type and element size (although there are aliases based on legacy options). You can see the earlier text file as follows:

```
$ od -tc floats-ints.dat                    Output data as ASCII characters
0000000   H   e   l   l   o       W   o   r   l   d  \r
0000020                                      \n 277 343 201 223 343 202 223
0000040 343 201 253 343 201 241 343 201 257  \r
0000060                          \n  \n  \0  \0  \0  \0  \0  \0  \0  \0  \0  \0
0000100  \0  \0  \0  \0  \0  \0  \0  \0  \0  \0  \0  \0  \0  \0  \0  \0

*        Duplicate lines are skipped (indicated with "*").

0000460  \0 220   _ 001  \0 221   _ 001  \0 222   _ 001  \0 223   _ 001
0000500  \0  \0 310 257   G 200 310 257   G  \0 311 257   G 200 311 257
0000520   G
0000521
```

This output is comparable to what you've already seen with other tools. By default, the offsets on the left are printed in octal (in keeping with the name). You can change the base of the offsets with the -A option. -Ax, for example, prints the offsets in hexadecimal.

od's treatment of strings is similar to that of xxd and bvi. It recognizes ASCII for display on the terminal but treats everything else as raw binary. What od can do that the others can't is rearrange the bytes *when necessary* to represent data in native format. Recall that the data from Listing 8-1 has IEEE floats and integers in the data. To see the integers in decimal, you can use the `-td` option, but you must tell `od` where the data starts. In this case, the float data starts at offset `0x131` in the file, so use the `-j` option as follows:

```
$ od -td4 -j0x131 floats-ints.dat                    Show me 4-byte words in decimal.
0000461      90000       90001       90002       90003
0000501  1202702336  1202702464  1202702592  1202702720 Float data (gibberish)
0000521
```

Now you can see the four consecutive decimal numbers we stored, starting with `90000`. If you do not specify the offset to the data, the output will be incorrect. The float and integer data in this case starts on an odd boundary. The float data starts at offset `0x141`, so you must use the `-j` option again to see your floats:

```
$ od -tf4 -j0x141 floats-ints.dat
0000501   9.000000e+04   9.000100e+04   9.000200e+04   9.000300e+04
0000521
```

I stored four consecutive float values starting with `90000`. Notice that in this case, I qualified the type as `-tf4`. I used IEEE floats in the program, which are 4 bytes each. The default for the `-tf` option is to display IEEE doubles, which are 8 bytes each. If you do not specify IEEE floats, you would see garbage.

Note that `od` adjusts the byte order only when necessary. As long as your data is in native byte order, `od` will produce correct results. If you are looking at data that you know is in network byte order (that is, Big Endian), `od` will show you incorrect answers on a Little Endian machine such as IA32.

8.4   Shell Tools for System V IPC

The preferred tools for working with System V IPC objects are the `ipcs` and `ipcrm` commands. `ipcs` is a generic tool for all the System V IPC objects I've discussed. `ipcrm` is used to remove IPC objects that may be left behind after a process exits or crashes.

8.4.1   System V Shared Memory

For shared memory objects, the `ipcs` command will show you the application-defined key (if any), as well as the system-defined ID for each key. It will also show you whether any processes are attached to the shared memory. The X Window system uses System V IPC shared memory extensively, so a spot check on your system is likely to reveal many shared memory objects in use. For example:

```
$ ipcs -m                        -m indicates that only shared memory objects should be shown.

------ Shared Memory Segments --------
key          shmid    owner    perms    bytes    nattch    status
0x00000000 163840     john     600      196608   2         dest
0x66c8f395 32769      john     600      1        0
0x237378db 65538      john     600      1        0
0x5190ec46 98307      john     600      1        0
0x31c16fd1 131076     john     600      1        0
0x00000000 196613     john     600      393216   2         dest
0x00000000 229382     john     600      393216   2         dest
0x00000000 262151     john     600      196608   2         dest
0x00000000 294920     john     600      393216   2         dest
0x00000000 327689     john     600      393216   2         dest
0x00000000 360458     john     600      196608   2         dest
0x00000000 393227     john     600      393216   2         dest
0x00000000 425996     john     600      196608   2         dest
0x00000000 884749     john     600      12288    2         dest
0x00000000 2031630    john     600      393216   2         dest
0x00000000 2064399    john     600      196608   2         dest
0x00000000 2097168    john     600      16384    2         dest
```

Here, you see a mix of private and public shared memory objects. Private objects have a `key` of zero, although every object has a unique `shmid`. The `nattch` column tells you how many processes currently are attached to the shared memory object. The `-p` option of `ipcs` shows you the process ID of the object's creator and the process ID of the process that most recently attached to or detached from each shared object. For example:

```
$ ipcs -m -p

------ Shared Memory Creator/Last-op --------
shmid      owner    cpid     lpid
163840     john     2790     2906
32769      john     2788     0
65538      john     2788     0
98307      john     2788     0
131076     john     2788     0
196613     john     2897     2754
229382     john     2899     2921
262151     john     2899     2921
294920     john     2907     2754
327689     john     2921     2923
360458     john     2893     2754
393227     john     2893     2754
425996     john     2921     2754
884749     john     2893     2754
2031630    john     8961     9392
2064399    john     8961     9392
2097168    john     8961     9392
```

The creator's PID is listed as `cpid` and the last `PID` to attach or detach is listed as `lpid`. You may think that as long as `nattch` is 2, these are the only processes. Don't forget that there is no guarantee that the object creator is still attached (or still running). Likewise, the last process to attach or detach to the object doesn't tell you much.

If `nattch` is zero, and neither process listed by `ipcs` is running, it *may* be safe to delete the object with the `icprm` command. What `ipcs` does not answer is "Who has this memory mapped *now?*" You can answer this question with a brute-force search using the `lsof` command. Consider the following example:

```
$ ipcs -m

------ Shared Memory Segments --------
key         shmid        owner      perms      bytes       nattch      status
...
0xdeadbeef 2752529      john       666        1048576     3
```

> *There are three processes attached to this object, but what are they?*

```
$ ipcs -m -p

------ Shared Memory Creator/Last-op --------
shmid       owner      cpid      lpid
2752529     john       10155     10160
```

> *Process 10155 and 10160 are suspects. `lsof` to the rescue.*

```
$ lsof | head -1 ; lsof | grep 2752529
COMMAND       PID     USER    FD    TYPE    DEVICE   SIZE     NODE NAME
sysv-shm  10155     john    DEL    REG     0,7              2752529 /SYSVdeadbeef
sysv-clie 10158     john    DEL    REG     0,7              2752529 /SYSVdeadbeef
sysv-clie 10160     john    DEL    REG     0,7              2752529 /SYSVdeadbeef
```

The `lsof` command produces a great deal of output, but you can `grep` for the `shmid` to see which processes are still using this object. Notice that `lsof` indicates the key in the NAME column in hexadecimal. You could have used this as the search key as well.

If no running process is attached to the shared memory, you probably can assume that this object is just code droppings and can be removed.

You can get more information about a shared memory object by using the -i
option to ipcs. When you've decided that it's safe to remove a System V shared
memory object, you need to use the shmid of the object (not the key). For example:

```
$ ipcs -m -i 32769                                   Tell me about this shmid.

Shared memory Segment shmid=32769
uid=500 gid=500 cuid=500          cgid=500
mode=0600        access_perms=0600
bytes=1 lpid=0 cpid=2406          nattch=0           Created by process 2406...
att_time=Not set
det_time=Not set
change_time=Sat Apr  8 15:48:24 2006

$ kill -0 2406                                       Is this process still running?
bash: kill: (2406) - No such process                Not running

$ ipcrm -m 32769                                     Let's delete the shared memory.
```

Notice that you must indicate that you are deleting a shared memory object with
-m. ipcs is used for all types of IPC objects, not just shared memory. The shmid
alone does not tell the system about the type of object; nothing prevents a message
queue and a shared memory object from using the same identifier.

8.4.2   System V Message Queues

You can use the ipcs command to list all the System V message queues by using
the -q option as follows:

```
$ ipcs -q
------ Message Queues --------
key        msqid       owner      perms      used-bytes   messages
0x00000000 131072      john       600        0            0
0x00000000 163841      john       600        0            0
0x00000000 196610      john       600        0            0
0x00000000 229379      john       600        132          1
```

The values listed in the key column are the application-defined keys, whereas the
values listed under msqid are the system-defined keys. As you might expect, the system-defined keys are unique. The application-defined keys in this case are all 0,
which means these message queues were created with the IPC_PRIVATE key.

One of the queues listed above (msgqid 229379) has data in it, which you can
see below the headings used-bytes and messages. This could be a symptom of a

problem, because most applications don't let messages sit in queues for very long. Again, the -i option of ipcs is helpful:

```
$ ipcs -q -i 229379

Message Queue msqid=229379
uid=500 gid=500 cuid=500        cgid=500         mode=0600
cbytes=132      qbytes=16384    qnum=1  lspid=12641    lrpid=0
send_time=Sun Oct 22 15:25:53 2006
rcv_time=Not set
change_time=Sun Oct 22 15:25:53 2006
```

Notice that the lspid and lrpid fields contain the *last sender PID* and the *last receiver PID*, respectively. If you can determine that this queue is no longer needed, you can delete it by using the message queue ID as follows:

```
$ ipcrm -q 229379
```

Again, the ipcrm command applies to more than just message queues, so you indicate the system ID of the object as well as the fact that it is a message queue with the -q option.

8.4.3   System V Semaphores

Just as with message queues and shared memory, the ipcs command can be used to list all the semaphores in the system with the -s option, as follows:

```
$ ipcs -s

------ Semaphore Arrays --------
key         semid     owner     perms     nsems
0x6100f981 360448     john      600       1
```

Recall that System V semaphores are declared as arrays. The length of the array is shown in the nsems column. The output is very similar to the output for message queues. Likewise, you can remove the semaphore with the ipcrm command as follows:

```
$ ipcrm -s 360448
```

Here again, you specify the system semaphore ID (not the key) to remove the semaphore. Additional information can be retrieved with the -i option:

```
$ ipcs -s -i 393216

Semaphore Array semid=393216
uid=500  gid=500           cuid=500          cgid=500
mode=0600, access_perms=0600
nsems = 1
otime = Tue May  9 22:23:30 2006
ctime = Tue May  9 22:22:23 2006
semnum     value      ncount     zcount      pid
0          3          0          1           32578
```

The output is similar to the `stat` command for files except that there is additional information specific to the semaphore. The `ncount` is the number of processes blocking on the semaphore, waiting for it to increment. The `zcount` is the number of processes blocking on the semaphore, waiting for it to go to zero. The `pid` column identifies the most recent process to *complete* a semaphore operation; it does not identify processes *waiting* on the semaphore.

The `ps` command can help identify processes waiting on a semaphore. The `wchan` format option shows what system function is blocking a process. For a process blocking on a semaphore, it looks as follows:

```
$ ps -o wchan -p 32746
WCHAN
semtimedop
```

The `semtimedop` is the system call that is used for the semaphore operation. Unfortunately, there is no way to identify which process is waiting on which semaphore. The process maps and file descriptors do not give away the semaphore IDs.

8.5   Tools for Working with POSIX IPC

POSIX IPC uses file descriptors for every object. The POSIX pattern is that every file descriptor has a file or device associated with it, and Linux extends this with special file systems for IPC. Because each IPC object can be traced to a plain file, the tools we use for working with plain files are often sufficient for working with POSIX IPC objects.

8.5.1   POSIX Shared Memory

There are no tools specifically for POSIX shared memory. In Linux, POSIX shared memory objects reside on the `tmpfs` pseudo file system, which typically is mounted on `/dev/shm`. That means that you can use all the normal file-handling tools at your disposal to debug these objects. Everything that I mentioned in the section on working with open files applies here. The only difference is that all the files you will need to look at are on a single file system.

As a result of the Linux implementation, it is possible to create and use shared memory with only standard system calls: `open`, `close`, `mmap`, `unlink`, and so on. Just keep in mind that this is all Linux specific. The POSIX standard seems to encourage this particular implementation, but it does not require it, so portable code should stick to the POSIX shared memory system calls.

Just to illustrate this point, let's walk through an example of some shell commands mixed with a little pseudocode. I'll create a shared memory segment from the shell that a POSIX program can map:

```
$ dd if=/dev/zero of=/dev/shm/foo.shm count=100        Create /foo.shm
100+0 records in
100+0 records out
$ ls -lh /dev/shm/foo.shm
-rw-rw-r--  1 john john 50K Apr  9 21:01 /dev/shm/foo.shm
```

Now a POSIX shared memory program can attach to this shared memory, using the name `/foo.shm`:[2]

```
int fd = shm_open("/foo.shm",O_RDWR,0);
```

Creating a shared memory segment this way is not portable but can be very useful for unit testing and debugging. One idea for a unit test environment is to create a wrapper script that creates required shared memory segments to simulate other running processes while running the process under test.

8.5.2   POSIX Message Queues

Linux shows POSIX message queues via the `mqueue` pseudo file system. Unfortunately, there is no standard mount point for this file system. If you need to debug POSIX message queues from the shell, you will have to mount the file system manually. To mount this on a directory named `/mnt/mqs`, for example, you can use the following command:

```
$ mkdir /mnt/mqs
$ mount -t mqueue none /mnt/mqs                    Must be the root user to use mount
```

---

2. The leading slash is not strictly required, but it is recommended.

When the file system is mounted, you can see an entry for each POSIX message queue in the system. These are not regular files, however. If you `cat` the file, you will see not messages, but a summary of the queue properties. For example:

```
$ ls -l /mnt/mqs
total 0
-rw-------  1 john john 80 Apr  9 00:20 myq

$ cat /mnt/mqs/myq
QSIZE:6         NOTIFY:0    SIGNO:0     NOTIFY_PID:0
```

The `QSIZE` field tells you how many bytes are in the queue. A nonzero value here may be indication of a deadlock or some other problem. The fields `NOTIFY`, `SIGNO`, and `NOTIFY_PID` are used with the `mq_notify` function, which I do not cover in this book.

To remove a POSIX message queue from the system using the shell, simply use the `rm` command from the shell and remove it from the `mqueue` file system by name.

8.5.3   POSIX Semaphores

Named POSIX semaphores in Linux are implemented as files in `tmpfs`, just like shared memory. Unlike in the System V API, there is no system call in Linux to create a POSIX semaphore. Semaphores are implemented mostly in user space, using existing system calls. That means that the implementation is determined largely by the GNU real-time library (`librt`) that comes with the `glibc` package.

Fortunately, the real-time library makes some fairly predictable choices that are easy to follow. In `glibc` 2.3.5, named semaphores are created as files in `/dev/shm`. A semaphore named `mysem` shows up as `/dev/shm/sem.mysem`. Because the POSIX API uses file descriptors, you can see semaphores in use as open files in `procfs`; therefore, tools such as `lsof` and `fuser` can see them as well.

You can't see the count of a POSIX semaphore directly. The `sem_t` type that GNU exposes to the application contains no useful data elements—just an array of `ints`. It's reasonable to assume, however, that the semaphore count is embedded in this data. Using the `posix_sem.c` program from Listing 7-14 in Chapter 7, for example:

```
$ ./posix_sem 1                          Create and increment the semaphore.
created new semaphore
incrementing semaphore
semaphore value is 1
```

```
$ ./posix_sem 1                              Increment the semaphore again.
semaphore exists
incrementing semaphore
semaphore value is 2
$ od -tx4 /dev/shm/sem.mysem                  Dump the file to dump the count.
0000000 00000002 ...
```

Although you can use tools like `lsof` to find processes using a semaphore, remember that just because a process is *using* a semaphore doesn't mean that it's blocking on it. One way to determine whether a process is blocking on a particular semaphore is to use `ltrace`. For example:

```
$ lsof /dev/shm/sem.mysem                    Identify the process using a named semaphore...
COMMAND PID USER  FD   TYPE DEVICE SIZE   NODE NAME
pdecr   661 john mem    REG   0,16   16 1138124 /dev/shm/sem.mysem

$ ltrace -p 661                              Find out what it is doing...
__errno_location()                                          = 0xb7f95b60
sem_wait(0xb7fa1000, 0x503268, 0xbffa3968, 0x804852f, 0x613ff4 <unfinished ...>
```

Process is blocking in a `sem_wait` call on a semaphore located at 0xb7a1000...

```
$ pmap -d 661 | grep mysem
b7fa1000       4 rw-s- 0000000000000000 000:00010 sem.mysem
```

This address is mapped to a file named `sem.mysem`! This process is blocking on our semaphore.

This is a bit of work, but you get your answer. Note that for this to work, your program must handle interrupted system calls. I did not do that in the examples, but the pattern looks like this:

```
do {
        r = sem_wait(mysem);                 Returns -1 with errno == EINTR if interrupted
} while ( r == -1 && errno == EINTR );
```

This is required because tools like `ltrace` and `strace` stop your process with SIGSTOP. This results in a semaphore function returning with `-1` and `errno` set to EINTR.

8.6   Tools for Working with Signals

One useful command for debugging signals from the shell is the `ps` command, which allows you to examine a process's signal mask as well as any pending (unhandled) signals. You can also see which signals have user-defined handlers and which don't.

By now, you may have guessed that the -o option can be used to view the signal masks as follows:

```
$ ps -o pending,blocked,ignored,caught
          PENDING           BLOCKED          IGNORED          CAUGHT
0000000000000000 0000000000010000 0000000000384004 000000004b813efb
0000000000000000 0000000000000000 0000000000000000 0000000073d3fef9
```

A more concise equivalent uses the BSD syntax, which is a little unconventional because it does not use a dash to denote arguments. Nevertheless, it's easy to use and provides more output for you:

```
$ ps s          Notice there's no dash before the s.
  UID    PID   PENDING   BLOCKED   IGNORED   CAUGHT ...

  500   6487  00000000  00000000  00384004  4b813efb ...
  500   6549  00000000  00000000  00384004  4b813efb ...
  500  12121  00000000  00010000  00384004  4b813efb ...
  500  17027  00000000  00000000  00000000  08080002 ...
  500  17814  00000000  00010000  00384004  4b813efb ...
  500  17851  00000000  00000000  00000000  73d3fef9 ...
```

The four values shown for each process are referred to as *masks*, although the kernel stores only one mask, which is listed here under the BLOCKED signals. The other masks are, in fact, derived from other data in the system. Each mask contains 1 or 0 for each signal N in bit position N-1, as follows:

- Caught—Signals that have a nondefault handler

- Ignored—Signals that are explicitly ignored via signal(N,SIG_IGN)

- Blocked—Signals that are explicitly blocked via sigprocmask

- Pending—Signals that were sent to the process but have not yet been handled

Let's spawn a shell that ignores SIGILL (4) and look at the results:

```
$ bash -c 'trap "" SIGILL; read '&
[1] 4697
$ jobs -x ps s %1
  UID    PID   PENDING   BLOCKED   IGNORED    CAUGHT STAT ...
  500   4692  00000000  00000000  0000000c  00010000 T    ...
```

You ignore SIGILL by using the built-in trap command in Bash. The value for SIGILL is 4, so you expect to see bit 3 set under the IGNORED heading. There,

indeed, you see a value of 0xc—bits 2 and 3. Now this job is stopped, and you know
that if you send a SIGINT to a stopped job, it won't wake up, so see what happens:

```
$ kill -INT %1
[1]+  Stopped                    bash -c 'trap "" SIGILL; read '
$ jobs -x ps s %1
  UID   PID  PENDING   BLOCKED   IGNORED   CAUGHT STAT ...
  500  5084  00000002  00000000  0000000c  00010000 T    ...
```

Now you can see a value of 2 (bit 1) under the PENDING heading. This is the
SIGINT (2) you just sent. The handler will not be called until the process is
restarted.

Another useful tool for working with signals is the strace command. strace
shows transitions from user mode to kernel mode in a running process while listing
the system call or signal that caused the transition. strace is a very flexible tool,
but it is a bit limited in what it can tell you about signals.

For one thing, strace can only inform you when the user/kernel transition takes
place. Therefore, it can only tell you when a signal is delivered, not when it was sent.
Also, queued signals look exactly like regular signals; none of the sender's information is available from strace. To get a taste of what strace is capable of, look at
the rt-sig program from Listing 76 in Chapter 7 when you run it with strace.

```
$ strace -f -e trace=signal ./rt-sig > /dev/null
rt_sigaction(SIGRT_2, {0x8048628, [RT_2], SA_RESTART}, {SIG_DFL}, 8) = 0
rt_sigprocmask(SIG_BLOCK, ~[RTMIN RT_1], [], 8) = 0
Process 18460 attached
[pid 18459] rt_sigprocmask(SIG_BLOCK, [CHLD], ~[KILL STOP RTMIN RT_1], 8) = 0
[pid 18460] kill(18459, SIGRT_2)         = 0
[pid 18460] kill(18459, SIGRT_2)         = 0
[pid 18460] kill(18459, SIGRT_2)         = 0
Process 18460 detached
rt_sigprocmask(SIG_SETMASK, [], NULL, 8) = 0
--- SIGCHLD (Child exited) @ 0 (0) ---
--- SIGRT_2 (Real-time signal 0) @ 0 (0) ---
sigreturn()                              = ? (mask now [])
--- SIGRT_2 (Real-time signal 0) @ 0 (0) ---
sigreturn()                              = ? (mask now [])
--- SIGRT_2 (Real-time signal 0) @ 0 (0) ---
sigreturn()                              = ? (mask now [])
```

I cheated a little here. Because rt-sig forks, I can trace both processes with the
-f option, which follows forks. This allows me to see the sender and receiver in
one trace.

`strace` normally produces a great deal of output that has little to do with what you are interested in. It is common to use a filter, specified with the `-e` option, to limit the output to what you are interested in. In this case, you would use the `trace=signal` filter to limit the output to the results of signals and signal-related system calls.

8.7 Tools for Working with Pipes and Sockets

The preferred user-space tool for debugging sockets is `netstat`, which relies heavily on the information in the `/proc/net` directory. Pipes and FIFOs are trickier, because there is no single location you can look at to track down their existence. The only indication of a pipe's or FIFO's existence is given by the `/proc/pid/fd` directory of the process using the pipe or FIFO.

8.7.1 Pipes and FIFOs

The `/proc/pid/fd` directory lists pipes and FIFOs by inode number. Here is a running program that has called `pipe` to create a pair of file descriptors (one write-only and one read-only):

```
$ ls -l !$
ls -l /proc/19991/fd
total 5
lrwx------  1 john john 64 Apr 12 23:33 0 -> /dev/pts/4
lrwx------  1 john john 64 Apr 12 23:33 1 -> /dev/pts/4
lrwx------  1 john john 64 Apr 12 23:33 2 -> /dev/pts/4
lr-x------  1 john john 64 Apr 12 23:33 3 -> pipe:[318960]
l-wx------  1 john john 64 Apr 12 23:33 4 -> pipe:[318960]
```

The name of the "file" in this case is `pipe:[318960]`, where `318960` is the inode number of the pipe. Notice that although two file descriptors are returned by the `pipe` function, there is only one inode number, which identifies the pipe. I discuss inodes in more detail later in this chapter.

The `lsof` function can be helpful for tracking down processes with pipes. In this case, if you want to know what other process has this pipe open, you can search for the inode number:

```
$ lsof | head -1 && lsof | grep 318960
COMMAND  PID    USER    FD    TYPE    DEVICE    SIZE      NODE NAME
ppipe  19991    john    3r    FIFO      0,5              318960 pipe
ppipe  19991    john    4w    FIFO      0,5              318960 pipe
ppipe  19992    john    3r    FIFO      0,5              318960 pipe
ppipe  19992    john    4w    FIFO      0,5              318960 pipe
```

As of `lsof` version 4.76, there is no command-line option to search for pipes and FIFOs, so you resort to `grep`. Notice that in the `TYPE` column, `lsof` does not distinguish between pipes and FIFOs; both are listed as `FIFO`. Likewise, in the `NAME` column, both are listed as `pipe`.

8.7.2 Sockets

Two of the most useful user tools for debugging sockets are `netstat` and `lsof`. `netstat` is most useful for the big-picture view of the system use of sockets. To get a view of all TCP connections in the system, for example:

```
$ netstat --tcp -n
Active Internet connections (w/o servers)
Proto Recv-Q Send-Q Local Address         Foreign Address          State
tcp        0     48 ::ffff:192.168.163.128:22  ::ffff:192.168.163.1:1344  ESTABLISHED
```

Following is the same command using `lsof`:

```
$ lsof -n -i tcp
COMMAND      PID    USER   FD   TYPE DEVICE SIZE NODE NAME
portmap     1853     rpc    4u   IPv4   4847       TCP *:sunrpc (LISTEN)
rpc.statd   1871 rpcuser    6u   IPv4   4881       TCP *:32769 (LISTEN)
smbd        2120    root   20u   IPv4   5410       TCP *:microsoft-ds (LISTEN)
smbd        2120    root   21u   IPv4   5411       TCP *:netbios-ssn (LISTEN)
X           2371    root    1u   IPv6   6310       TCP *:x11 (LISTEN)
X           2371    root    3u   IPv4   6311       TCP *:x11 (LISTEN)
xinetd     20338    root    5u   IPv4 341172       TCP *:telnet (LISTEN)
sshd       23444    root    3u   IPv6 487790       TCP *:ssh (LISTEN)
sshd       23555    root    3u   IPv6 502673       ...
        TCP 192.168.163.128:ssh->192.168.163.1:1344 (ESTABLISHED)
sshd       23557    john    3u   IPv6 502673       ...
        TCP 192.168.163.128:ssh->192.168.163.1:1344 (ESTABLISHED)
```

The `lsof` output contains PIDs for each socket listed. It shows the same socket twice, because two `sshd` processes are sharing a file descriptor. Notice that the default output of `lsof` includes listening sockets, whereas by default, `netstat` does not.

`lsof` does not show sockets that don't belong to any process. These are TCP sockets that are in one of the so-called *wait* states that occur when sockets are closed. When a process dies, for example, its connections may enter the `TIME_WAIT` state. In this case, `lsof` will not show this socket because it no longer belongs to a process. `netstat` on the other hand, will show it. To see all TCP sockets, use the `--tcp` option to `netstat` as follows:

```
$ netstat -n --tcp
Active Internet connections (w/o servers)
Proto Recv-Q Send-Q Local Address      Foreign Address      State
tcp        0      0 127.0.0.1:60526    127.0.0.1:5000       TIME_WAIT
```

When using these tools to look at sockets, note that every socket has an inode number, just like a file. This is true for both network sockets and local sockets, but it is more important for local sockets, because the inode often is the only unique identifier for the socket. Consider this output from `netstat` for local sockets:

```
Active UNIX domain sockets (w/o servers)
Proto RefCnt Flags       Type       State         I-Node Path
unix  2      [ ]         DGRAM                     3478   @udevd
unix  2      [ ]         DGRAM                     5448   @/var/run/...
unix  8      [ ]         DGRAM                     4819   /dev/log
unix  3      [ ]         STREAM     CONNECTED      642738
unix  3      [ ]         STREAM     CONNECTED      642737
unix  2      [ ]         DGRAM                     487450
unix  2      [ ]         DGRAM                     341168
unix  3      [ ]         STREAM     CONNECTED      7633
unix  3      [ ]         STREAM     CONNECTED      7632
```

This is just a small piece of the output. I'll zoom in on something specific that I can talk about in more detail. The GNOME session manager, for example, creates a listen socket in the `/tmp/.ICE-unix` directory. The name of the socket is the process ID of the `gnome-session` process. A look at this file with `lsof` shows that this file is open by several processes:

```
lsof /tmp/.ICE-unix/*
COMMAND    PID USER   FD   TYPE     DEVICE SIZE NODE NAME
gnome-ses 2408 john   15u  unix 0xc3562540      6830 /tmp/.ICE-unix/2408
gnome-ses 2408 john   19u  unix 0xc2709cc0      7036 /tmp/.ICE-unix/2408
gnome-ses 2408 john   20u  unix 0xc27094c0      7054 /tmp/.ICE-unix/2408
gnome-ses 2408 john   22u  unix 0xc2193100      7072 /tmp/.ICE-unix/2408
gnome-ses 2408 john   23u  unix 0xc1d3ddc0      7103 /tmp/.ICE-unix/2408
gnome-ses 2408 john   24u  unix 0xc1831840      7138 /tmp/.ICE-unix/2408
gnome-ses 2408 john   25u  unix 0xc069b1c0      7437 /tmp/.ICE-unix/2408
gnome-ses 2408 john   26u  unix 0xc3567880      7600 /tmp/.ICE-unix/2408
bonobo-ac 2471 john   15u  unix 0xc3562540      6830 /tmp/.ICE-unix/2408
gnome-set 2473 john   15u  unix 0xc3562540      6830 /tmp/.ICE-unix/2408
wnck-appl 2528 john   15u  unix 0xc3562540      6830 /tmp/.ICE-unix/2408
gnome-vfs 2531 john   15u  unix 0xc3562540      6830 /tmp/.ICE-unix/2408
notificat 2537 john   15u  unix 0xc3562540      6830 /tmp/.ICE-unix/2408
clock-app 2541 john   15u  unix 0xc3562540      6830 /tmp/.ICE-unix/2408
mixer_app 2543 john   15u  unix 0xc3562540      6830 /tmp/.ICE-unix/2408
```

The first thing to notice is that most of these have unique inodes, although they all point to the same file on disk. Each time the server accepts a connection, a new file descriptor is allocated. This file descriptor continues to point to the same file (the listen socket), although it has a unique inode number.

A little intuition and some corroborating evidence tell you that the server is the gnome-session process—PID 2408. In this case, the filename of the socket is a dead giveaway as well. The server is listening on file descriptor 15 (inode number 6830). Several other processes are using file descriptor 15 and inode number 6830. Based on what you know about fork, these processes appear to be children or grandchildren of gnome-session. Most likely, they inherited the file descriptor and neglected to close it.

To locate the server using netstat, try using -l to restrict the output to listen sockets and -p to print the process identification, as follows:

```
$ netstat --unix -lp | grep /tmp/.ICE-unix/
unix 2 [ACC] STREAM LISTENING 7600 2408/gnome-session /tmp/.ICE-unix/2408
```

Notice that the duplicate file descriptors are omitted, and only one server is shown. To see the accepted connections, omit the -l option (by default, netstat omits listen sockets):

```
netstat -n --unix -p | grep /tmp/.ICE-unix/2408
Proto RefCnt/Flags/Type/State/I-Node/PID/Program name Path
unix 3 [ ] STREAM CONNECTED 7600 2408/gnome-session  /tmp/.ICEunix/2408
unix 3 [ ] STREAM CONNECTED 7437 2408/gnome-session  /tmp/.ICEunix/2408
unix 3 [ ] STREAM CONNECTED 7138 2408/gnome-session  /tmp/.ICEunix/2408
unix 3 [ ] STREAM CONNECTED 7103 2408/gnome-session  /tmp/.ICEunix/2408
unix 3 [ ] STREAM CONNECTED 7072 2408/gnome-session  /tmp/.ICEunix/2408
unix 3 [ ] STREAM CONNECTED 7054 2408/gnome-session  /tmp/.ICEunix/2408
unix 3 [ ] STREAM CONNECTED 7036 2408/gnome-session  /tmp/.ICEunix/2408
```

Unlike lsof, the netstat command does not show the inherited file descriptors that are unused.

8.8   Using Inodes to Identify Files and IPC Objects

Linux provides a virtual file system (vfs) that is common to all file systems. It enables file systems that are not associated with a physical device (such as tmpfs and procfs) and at the same time provides an API for physical disks. As a result, virtual files are indistinguishable from files that reside on a disk.

The term *inode* comes from UNIX file-system terminology. It refers to the structure saved on disk that contains a file's accounting data—the file-size permissions and so on. Each object in a file system has a unique inode, which you see in user space as a unique integer. In general, you can assume that anything in Linux that has a file descriptor has an inode.

Inode numbers can be useful for objects that don't have filenames, including network sockets and pipes. Inode numbers are unique within a file system but are not guaranteed to be unique across different file systems. Although network sockets can be identified uniquely by their port numbers and IP addresses, pipes cannot. To identify two processes that are using the same pipe, you need to match the inode number.

`lsof` prints the inode number for all the file descriptors it reports. For most files and other objects, this is reported in the NODE column. `netstat` also prints inode numbers for UNIX domain sockets only. This is natural, because UNIX-domain listen sockets are represented by files on disk.

Network sockets are treated differently, however. In Linux, network sockets have inodes, although `lsof` and `netstat` (which run under operating systems in addition to Linux) pretend that they don't. Although `netstat` will not show you an inode number for a network socket, `lsof` does show the `inode` number in the DEVICE column. Look at the TCP sockets open by the `xinetd` daemon (you must be the `root` user to do this):

```
$ lsof -i tcp -a -p $(pgrep xinetd)
COMMAND  PID USER    FD    TYPE DEVICE SIZE NODE NAME
xinetd  2838 root    5u   IPv4  28178      TCP *:telnet (LISTEN)
```

Here, you can see that `xinetd` is listening on the telnet socket (port 23). Although the NODE column contains only the word TCP, the DEVICE column contains the inode number. You also can find the inode for network sockets listed in various places in `procfs`. For example:

```
$ ls -l /proc/$(pgrep xinetd)/fd
total 7
lr-x------ 1 root root 64 Oct 22 22:24 0 -> /dev/null
lr-x------ 1 root root 64 Oct 22 22:24 1 -> /dev/null
lr-x------ 1 root root 64 Oct 22 22:24 2 -> /dev/null
lr-x------ 1 root root 64 Oct 22 22:24 3 -> pipe:[28172]
l-wx------ 1 root root 64 Oct 22 22:24 4 -> pipe:[28172]
lrwx------ 1 root root 64 Oct 22 22:24 5 -> socket:[28178]
lrwx------ 1 root root 64 Oct 22 22:24 7 -> socket:[28175]
```

Now `procfs` uses the same number for file descriptor 5 as `lsof`, although it appears inside the filename between brackets. It's still not obvious that this is the inode, however, because both `lsof` and `procfs` are pretty cryptic about reporting it. To prove that this is really the inode, use the `stat` command, which is a wrapper for the `stat` system call:

```
$ stat -L /proc/$(pgrep xinetd)/fd/5
  File: `/proc/2838/fd/5'
  Size: 0           Blocks: 0          IO Block: 1024    socket
Device: 4h/4d   Inode: 28178    Links: 1
Access: (0777/srwxrwxrwx)  Uid: (    0/    root)   Gid: (    0/    root)
Access: 1969-12-31 18:00:00.000000000 -0600
Modify: 1969-12-31 18:00:00.000000000 -0600
Change: 1969-12-31 18:00:00.000000000 -0600
```

Finally, the inode is unambiguously indicated in the output.[3] Notice that I used the `-L` option to the `stat` command, because the file-descriptor files in `procfs` are symbolic links. This tells `stat` to use the `lstat` system call instead of `stat`.

8.9   Summary

This chapter introduced several tools and techniques for debugging various IPC mechanisms, including plain files. Although System V IPC requires special tools, POSIX IPC lends itself to debugging with the same tools used for plain files.

8.9.1   Tools Used in This Chapter

- `ipcs`, `ipcrm`—command-line utilities for System V IPC
- `lsof`, `fuser`—tools for looking for open files and file descriptor usage
- `ltrace`—traces a process's calls to functions in shared objects
- `pmap`—user-friendly look at a process's memory map
- `strace`—traces the system call usage of a process

---

3. Another place to look is `/proc/net/tcp`. The inode is unambiguous, but the rest of the output is not very user friendly.

8.9.2   Online Resources

- http://procps.sourceforge.net—the `procps` home page, source of the `pmap` command
- http://sourceforge.net/projects/strace—the `strace` home page

Chapter 9

Performance Tuning

9.1 Introduction

In this chapter, I look at performance issues from both a system perspective and an application perspective. Sometimes, your slow application will not be helped much by faster CPUs, faster memory, or faster disk drives. After reading this chapter, you should be able to figure out the difference between an application that is slow because it is inefficient and one that is bogged down by slow hardware.

9.2 System Performance

When system performance is not optimal, it affects all processes. The system users feel it, whether it's a slow window update or slow connections to a server. Many tools can show you system performance. Unfortunately, some of these tools are burdened with so much detail that they're often unused because of it. With a basic understanding of system performance issues, these details won't be so unfamiliar.

9.2.1   Memory Issues

It's a shopworn tech-support tip that has lost all meaning: "You need more memory." Why should adding more memory fix anything? As far as performance goes, it doesn't increase your CPU's clock frequency; it doesn't increase your computer's bus speed. So why should you expect that adding more memory is going to make your computer run faster?

Adding more memory sometimes can address performance issues, but no one wants to waste money by throwing RAM at a problem only to find that it didn't solve anything. Besides, there are only so many DIMM slots in a motherboard, so throwing RAM at a problem may not be an option anyway. Being able to predict that more RAM will fix a problem takes more than guesswork. You need to understand how the system uses memory to understand whether memory is your performance problem.

9.2.1.1   Page Faults

Counting the number of page faults, therefore, can be a good measure of how efficiently your system is using memory. Recall that a page fault occurs when the CPU requests a page of memory that doesn't reside in RAM. Normally, this happens either because the page hasn't been initialized yet or because it has been kicked out of RAM and stored on the swap device.

When the system is generating many page faults, it affects every process in the system. A couple of simple programs can illustrate this situation. First is a program that will allocate a chunk of memory just for the sake of consuming it. This program will touch the memory once and not use it. This program, appropriately named `hog`, is illustrated in Listing 9-1; it allocates the memory via `malloc`, modifies 1 byte in each page, and then goes to sleep.

It's worth noting here that you need to read or write to at least 1 byte in each page of an allocated region to consume the page from memory. Linux is smart enough not to commit any physical storage to a page that has not been touched. It's interesting that all it takes is 1 byte!

```
$ free -m                  Report memory usage in megabytes (MB).
                total       used       free     shared    buffers     cached
Mem:              250        118        131          0          0          9
-/+ buffers/cache:          108        141
Swap:             511          0        511
                Note 131MB free and no swap space in use.
```

```
$ ./hog 127 &              Consume 127MB of memory.
[1] 4513
$ allocated 127 mb

$ free -m
             total      used      free    shared   buffers    cached
Mem:           250       245         4         0         0         9
-/+ buffers/cache:        235        14
Swap:          511         0       511
```

Note that free memory decreased by exactly 127MB and still no swap in use.

I deliberately used less than the total available free space in this example to avoid paging. Linux will not allow the free space to go to zero, so it will use the swap partition to page out the least recently used pages when it needs to increase the free memory. If you were to launch a second hog process, you would observe paging taking place, because there is not enough free memory to accommodate the allocations. I will look at that topic in more detail later in this chapter.

You can see evidence of the page faults by using the GNU `time` command. Recall that this is not the same as the Bash built-in `time` command. Use a backslash to get the GNU version, as follows:

```
$ \time ./hog 127
allocated 127 mb
Command terminated by signal 2
0.01user 0.32system 0:01.17elapsed 28%CPU (0avgtext+0avgdata 0maxresident)k
0inputs+0outputs (0major+32626minor)pagefaults 0swaps
```

Here, I have highlighted the useful information, which is the number of minor page faults. A *major* page fault is a page fault that requires input and/or output to disk, and a *minor* page fault is any other page fault.

In more precise terms, when the hog program requests memory with `malloc`, the kernel creates page table mappings for the process's user space. At this point, no storage has been allocated; only the mapping has been created. It is not until the process tries to read or write the memory for the first time that a *page fault* occurs, requiring the kernel to find storage for the page. This mechanism is the method that the kernel uses to allocate new storage for processes.

The example above allocates 127MB, which requires 32,512 pages on an IA32 with 4K pages. The `time` command shows that hog caused 32,626 minor page faults, which agrees nicely with my prediction. The difference is caused by additional pages required to load the program code and data.

LISTING 9-1   hog.c: A Program That Allocates Memory but Doesn't Use It

```
1 #include <stdio.h>
2 #include <string.h>
3 #include <stdlib.h>
4 #include <unistd.h>
5
6 int main(int argc, char *argv[])
7 {
8     if (argc != 2)
9         exit(0);
10
11    size_t mb = strtoul(argv[1], NULL, 0);
12
13    // Allocate the memory
14    size_t nbytes = mb * 0x100000;
15
16    char *ptr = (char *) malloc(nbytes);
17    if (ptr == NULL) {
18        perror("malloc");
19        exit(EXIT_FAILURE);
20    }
21
22    // Touch the memory (could also use calloc())
23    size_t i;
24    const size_t stride = sysconf(_SC_PAGE_SIZE);
25    for (i = 0; i < nbytes; i += stride) {
26        ptr[i] = 0;
27    }
28
29    printf("allocated %d mb\n", mb);
30    pause();
31    return 0;
32 }
```

9.2.1.2   Swapping

Until now, plenty of free memory was available, so the new pages were taken from free memory, and the latency was low. If you run this process again with inadequate free memory to meet your needs, the kernel will be forced to store pages to the swap partition with each page fault. Specifically, it stores the least recently used pages (sometimes abbreviated LRU) to the swap partition.

Paging and swapping are among the worst things that can happen when performance is critical. When the system is forced to page, a load or store to memory that normally takes a few nanoseconds to complete now takes tens of milliseconds or more. When the system needs to page in or out a few pages, the effect is not so severe; if it has to move many pages, it can slow your system to a crawl.

To illustrate, I'll revisit the hog program, this time allocating enough memory to cause paging:

```
$ free -m
              total        used        free      shared     buffers      cached
Mem:            250         109         140           0           0          11
-/+ buffers/cache:           97         152
Swap:           511           0         511
```

Note 250MB total RAM, 140MB free, 0MB swap when we start

```
$ \time ./hog 200
allocated 200 mb
Command terminated by signal 2
0.03user 0.61system 0:03.94elapsed 16%CPU (0avgtext+0avgdata 0maxresident)k
0inputs+0outputs (0major+51313minor)pagefaults 0swaps
```

Note 51,313 minor page faults, but no major page faults!

```
$ free -m
              total        used        free      shared     buffers      cached
Mem:            250          48         201           0           0           6
-/+ buffers/cache:           42         208
Swap:           511          68         443
```

Yet we paged out 68MB to disk!

Here, you see that the hog program caused 68MB of memory to get paged to disk, yet the time command reports that it saw no major page faults. This is misleading, but it's not an error. A major page fault occurs when a process requests a page that resides on disk. In this case, the pages did not exist; therefore, they did not reside on disk and thus do not count as major page faults. Although the hog process caused the system to write pages to disk, it did not actually write those pages to disk. The actual writes were done by kswapd.

The kswapd kernel thread takes care of the dirty work of moving the data from memory to disk. Only when the process that owns those pages tries to use them again will a major page fault occur. That page fault will be charged to the process that requested the data as a *major* page fault. This may seem like a bit of Enron-style accounting[1] going on here, but usually, things aren't so unbalanced. Before I show you another example, I'll introduce a new tool.

The top Command

Yet another useful tool from the `procps` package is the `top` command. This command uses the `ncurses` library, which makes the most of a text terminal.[2] The output is very much like the formats you can get from the `ps` command except that `top` includes many fields that `ps` does not support. The output from `top` is refreshed periodically, so you usually set aside one window for `top` display and do your thing in another. Following is a typical `top` window:

```
top - 20:27:24 up  3:06,  4 users,  load average: 0.17, 0.27, 0.41
Tasks:  64 total,   3 running,  61 sleeping,   0 stopped,   0 zombie
Cpu(s):  6.8% us,   5.1% sy,  0.8% ni, 80.8% id,  6.2% wa,  0.3% hi,  0.0% si
Mem:    158600k total,    30736k used,   127864k free,     1796k buffers
Swap:   327672k total,    10616k used,   317056k free,    16252k cached

  PID USER      PR  NI  VIRT  RES  SHR S %CPU %MEM   TIME+  COMMAND
    1 root      16   0  1744   96   72 R  0.0  0.1  0:00.89 init
    2 root      34  19     0    0    0 S  0.0  0.0  0:00.00 ksoftirqd/0
    3 root      RT   0     0    0    0 S  0.0  0.0  0:00.00 watchdog/0
    4 root      10  -5     0    0    0 S  0.0  0.0  0:00.10 events/0
    5 root      13  -5     0    0    0 S  0.0  0.0  0:00.03 khelper
    6 root      10  -5     0    0    0 S  0.0  0.0  0:00.00 kthread
    8 root      20  -5     0    0    0 S  0.0  0.0  0:00.00 kacpid
   61 root      10  -5     0    0    0 S  0.0  0.0  0:01.37 kblockd/0
   64 root      10  -5     0    0    0 S  0.0  0.0  0:00.00 khubd
...
```

Because there is so much information to display, `top` breaks it into four screens full of information called *field groups*. Pressing `Shift+G` in the main screen prompts you with the following:

```
Choose field group (1 - 4):
```

As the prompt indicates, you can choose among four screens of information. This is necessary because it's not possible to fit all the possible columns onto one text terminal screen. You can still see all four screens at the same time by breaking across

---

1. Enron was the notorious American company that defrauded investors by (among other things) hiding losses in subsidiaries that existed solely for the purpose of hiding losses.
2. There is also GNOME `gtop`, which in Fedora is `gnome-system-monitor`. You don't get as many options with the GUI.

rows. You do this by pressing Shift+A, which sacrifices some rows to show more screens. For example:

```
1:Def - 22:26:14 up  1:41,  3 users,  load average: 0.02, 0.01, 0.10
Tasks:  69 total,   1 running,  68 sleeping,   0 stopped,   0 zombie
Cpu(s):  0.7% us,  0.0% sy,  0.0% ni, 99.3% id,  0.0% wa,  0.0% hi,  0.0% si
Mem:    256292k total,   174760k used,    81532k free,    8860k buffers
Swap:   524280k total,    28120k used,   496160k free,   113608k cached

1  PID USER       PR  NI  VIRT  RES  SHR S %CPU %MEM    TIME+  COMMAND
   4026 john       15   0 42232  11m 6504 S  0.7  4.7  0:05.13 gnome-terminal
  30696 john       16   0  1936  956  764 R  0.3  0.4  0:00.01 top
   3583 john       15   0  7056  660  396 S  0.0  0.3  0:04.98 sshd
2  PID PPID    TIME+  %CPU %MEM  PR  NI S  VIRT SWAP   RES  UID COMMAND
  30696 4034  0:00.01  0.3  0.4  16   0 R  1936  980   956  500 top
   4054 4026  0:00.03  0.0  0.3  16   0 S  4276 3600   676  500 bash
   4034 4026  0:00.09  0.0  0.3  15   0 S  4276 3484   792  500 bash
   4033 4026  0:00.00  0.0  0.1  16   0 S  2068 1920   148  500 gnome-pty-helpe
3  PID %MEM  VIRT SWAP  RES CODE DATA  SHR nFLT nDRT S  PR  NI %CPU COMMAND
   4026  4.7 42232  29m  11m  256  17m 6504  542    0 S  15   0  0.7 gnome-termin
   4030  0.5  4576 3248 1328   48 1604  896   47    0 S  16   0  0.0 gconfd-2
  30696  0.4  1936  980  956   48  268  764    0    0 R  16   0  0.3 top
   3588  0.3  4276 3460  816  580  260  624   10    0 S  16   0  0.0 bash
4  PID PPID  UID USER      RUSER     TTY          TIME+  %CPU %MEM S COMMAND
   4026 3588  500 john      john      pts/1     0:05.13   0.7  4.7 S gnome-termina
   4030    1  500 john      john      pts/1     0:00.32   0.0  0.5 S gconfd-2
  30696 4034  500 john      john      pts/2     0:00.01   0.3  0.4 R top
   3588 3583  500 john      john      pts/1     0:00.29   0.0  0.3 S bash
```

top is very permissive about terminal dimensions and will gladly truncate the output to fit the terminal window. For those of you who have limited terminal space, you can eliminate or change columns to make the output fit whatever window you are working in. The options are a bit overwhelming at first, but when you get used to them, they're easy to remember.

You can change fields interactively by typing f in the main screen while top is running. This brings up a new screen full of options for you to choose among. After you select the fields you want to see, you can return to the main screen by pressing Enter. If you want to keep the changes as your defaults, you can save the settings by typing W in the main screen.

Using top to Track Down Hogs

I need another program similar to hog.c in Listing 9-1 to show some timing information and gain more control of its behavior. This program, which I'll call son-of-hog.c, is shown in Listing 9-2. I'm going to do a couple of tricks with this program so that you can better see the action in `top`. To build this example, do the following:

```
$ cc -O2 -o son-of-hog son-of-hog.c -lrt      librt required for clock_gettime
$ ln -s son-of-hog hog-a                       Give it two different names that we can see in top.
$ ln -s son-of-hog hog-b
```

Now for the tricky part. Empty the swap partition so you can get a better picture of what is going on. You do this with the `swapon` and `swapoff` commands, as follows:

```
$ free -m
              total         used         free       shared      buffers       cached
Mem:            250          246            3            0           14          165
-/+ buffers/cache:            66          183
Swap:           511            4          507
```

4MB swap in use

```
$ sudo swapoff -a       Turn off all swap partitions (must be root); pull all swapped pages into RAM.
```

```
$ sudo swapon -a        Turn on all swap partitions again.
```

```
$ free -m
              total         used         free       shared      buffers       cached
Mem:            250          246            3            0           14          160
-/+ buffers/cache:            71          178
Swap:           511            0          511
```

On my system, about 178MB RAM can be used without paging. This shows up in the output from the `free` command in the `+/- buffers/cache` row. Buffers and cache represent storage that can be reclaimed without sending it to the swap partition.[3] Next, tell `hog-a` to use 150MB, which should be safe to prevent resorting to paging:

```
$ ./hog-a 150 &
[1] 30825
$ touched 150 mb; in 0.361459 sec

$ free -m
              total         used         free       shared      buffers       cached
Mem:            250          246            3            0           11           17
-/+ buffers/cache:           217           32
Swap:           511            0          511
```

---

3. This is an ideal number. In reality, there are several complicating factors, but in rough numbers, this is OK.

Notice that you were able to touch 150MB of pages in a reasonable amount of time (about 361 ms). No paging was required, but a great deal of data in cache needed to be reclaimed. Give the process a SIGUSR1, which will cause it to wake up and touch its memory again:

```
$ kill -USR1 %1
$ touched 150 mb; in 0.009929 sec
```

Notice that the same job took only 9 ms! The second time you touched the buffer, all the pages should have been in RAM, so there were no page faults to handle. Now launch another hog and see what happens:

```
$ ./hog-b 150 &
[2] 30830
$ touched 150 mb; in 5.013068 sec
$ free -m
                 total      used      free    shared   buffers    cached
Mem:               250       246         3         0         0        10
-/+ buffers/cache:           235        14
Swap:              511       136       375
```

What a difference paging makes! What took only 361 ms before now takes more than 5 seconds. This is as expected, because you knew that hog-b would have to kick out many of the pages from hog-a to free up space. More precisely, the free command tells you that hog-b forced 136MB to disk. No wonder it was so slow! A second pass here should run much faster:

```
$ pkill -USR1 hog-b
touched 150 mb; in 0.019061 sec
```

Not surprisingly, it's very close to the value you saw for hog-a's second run. Now see what top has to say about all this. Launch top using the -p option to show only the hog processes, as follows:

```
$ top -p $(pgrep hog-a) -p $(pgrep hog-b)
```

Then you can show all four windows with Shift+A. The output looks like the following:

```
1:Def - 23:21:16 up  2:36,  2 users,  load average: 0.00, 0.02, 0.01
Tasks:   2 total,   0 running,   2 sleeping,   0 stopped,   0 zombie
Cpu(s):  0.0% us,  0.0% sy,  0.0% ni, 100.0% id,  0.0% wa,  0.0% hi,  0.0% si
Mem:    256292k total,   252048k used,     4244k free,      692k buffers
Swap:   524280k total,   139760k used,   384520k free,    11908k cached
```

```
1  PID USER       PR  NI  VIRT  RES  SHR S %CPU %MEM   TIME+   COMMAND
  30825 john       16   0  151m  63m  172 S  0.0 25.3   0:00.36 hog-a
  30830 john       16   0  151m 150m  296 S  0.0 60.1   0:00.57 hog-b
2  PID PPID     TIME+  %CPU %MEM  PR  NI S  VIRT SWAP  RES  UID COMMAND
  30830 4054   0:00.57  0.0 60.1  16   0 S  151m 1160 150m  500 hog-b
  30825 4054   0:00.36  0.0 25.3  16   0 S  151m  88m  63m  500 hog-a
3  PID %MEM  VIRT SWAP  RES CODE DATA  SHR nFLT nDRT S  PR  NI %CPU COMMAND
  30830 60.1 151m 1160 150m    4 150m  296    9    0 S  16   0  0.0 hog-b
  30825 25.3 151m  88m  63m    4 150m  172    2    0 S  16   0  0.0 hog-a
4  PID PPID  UID USER    RUSER    TTY        TIME+  %CPU %MEM S COMMAND
  30830 4054  500 john     john    pts/3   0:00.57  0.0 60.1 S hog-b
  30825 4054  500 john     john    pts/3   0:00.36  0.0 25.3 S hog-a
```

Notice that both processes have a virtual-memory footprint of 151MB, as indicated by the VIRT column in screen 1. After swapping 130MB to disk, both hogs show fewer than ten major faults, as indicated in the nFLT column in screen 3. The RES column (screens 1 and 2) indicates how much of that is present in RAM (that is, resident). There is also a SWAP column, which indicates how much of that process resides on disk.

LISTING 9-2   son-of-hog.c: A Modified hog.c

```
 1 #include <stdio.h>
 2 #include <string.h>
 3 #include <stdlib.h>
 4 #include <signal.h>
 5 #include <time.h>
 6 #include <unistd.h>
 7 #include <sys/time.h>
 8
 9 void handler(int sig)
10 {
11     // Does nothing
12 }
13
14 // convert a struct timespec to double for easier use.
15 #define TIMESPEC2FLOAT(tv) ((double)(tv).tv_sec + (double)(tv).tv_nsec *
1e-9)
16
17 int main(int argc, char *argv[])
18 {
19     if (argc != 2)
20         exit(0);
21
22     // Dummy signal handler.
23     signal(SIGUSR1, handler);
24
25     size_t mb = strtoul(argv[1], NULL, 0);
26
```

```
27      // Allocate the memory
28      size_t nbytes = mb * 0x100000;
29      char *ptr = (char *) malloc(nbytes);
30      if (ptr == NULL) {
31          perror("malloc");
32          exit(EXIT_FAILURE);
33      }
34
35      int val = 0;
36      const size_t stride = sysconf(_SC_PAGE_SIZE);
37
38      // Each loop touches memory, then stops and wait for a SIGUSR1
39      while (1) {
40          int i;
41          struct timespec t1, t2;
42
43          // t1 - when we started to touch memory
44          clock_gettime(CLOCK_REALTIME, &t1);
45
46          // All it takes is one byte per page!
47          for (i = 0; i < nbytes; i += stride) {
48              ptr[i] = val;
49          }
50          val++;
51
52          // t2 - when we finished touching memory
53          clock_gettime(CLOCK_REALTIME, &t2);
54
55          printf("touched %d mb; in %.6f sec\n", mb,
56                  TIMESPEC2FLOAT(t2) - TIMESPEC2FLOAT(t1));
57
58          // Wait for a signal.
59          pause();
60      }
61      return 0;
62 }
```

As a final illustration of how processes can cause one another to run slow, alternate signals between hog-a and hog-b to deliberately cause the system to write to
disk. Whenever the system is spending more time paging to disk than it is executing user code, we say that it's *thrashing*. If you're running this example, you can
watch the action in your top window, but I won't show that here:

```
$ pkill -USR1 hog-a                          hog-b was the last one we signaled.
$ touched 150 mb; in 14.286939 sec
$ pkill -USR1 hog-b                          hog-b is now mostly on disk.
$ touched 150 mb; in 16.731990 sec
pkill -USR1 hog-a
$ touched 150 mb; in 16.944799 sec
```

I'll wrap up this section on swapping by putting things in perspective. Each `hog` is using 150MB of memory but touching 1 byte per page. This example ran on a Pentium 4 with a page size of 4K, which means that there are 38,400 pages total. Stated another way, it took as much as 17 seconds to modify 37K of memory. The speed of the memory in this example is largely irrelevant; the time for each pass is dominated entirely by the speed of the swap device.

When you can point to paging as a cause for performance issues, it is likely that more RAM will alleviate the problem. If you are writing an application that is causing excessive paging, it may be possible to rework your code to use memory more efficiently rather than to add more RAM. Using the tools in this section, you should be able to determine the right course of action.

9.2.2   CPU Utilization and Bus Contention

In the previous section, I looked at paging, which is caused when processes contend for a limited amount of RAM. Likewise, there are other scarce resources in the system that processes contend for. One of these resources is bus bandwidth.

Figure 9-1 shows a simplified bus layout of a typical PC using PCI Express (PCIe). The *frontside bus* (FSB) is the point of entry for all data going into and out of the CPU. The DRAM may have one or multiple paths because it may be accessed via the CPU or peripherals, or (in some systems) the video controller. More often, the video controller has a decent amount of memory, as well as its own high-speed bus (PCIe or AGP) so that it doesn't have to contend for the DRAM bus.

9.2.2.1   Multiprocessing and the Frontside Bus

The speed of the FSB is always a major factor in computer performance because in personal computers today, the FSB is significantly slower than the CPU clock. The speed of the FSB determines the upper limit of I/O in the system.

With the rise of multiprocessor systems, the FSB is becoming a significant bottleneck. A typical multiprocessor system looks exactly like Figure 9-1, except that the block labeled CPU contains not just one but two or more processors, all sharing a single FSB. This means that instead of one fast CPU waiting for a slower FSB, you now have two. So the problem of FSB contention gets worse with more CPUs.

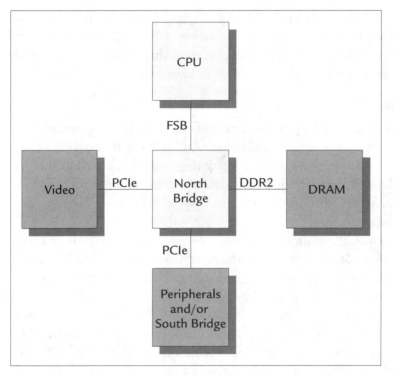

FIGURE 9-1   Typical PC Architecture Using Intel Architecture CPU and PCI Express

This type of multiprocessing computer is called a Symmetric Multiprocessing (SMP) computer. These computers have been around for some time in high-end servers and workstations. Linux has had support for SMP since Linux 2.0. Recently, multicore CPUs have become available for desktop computers, making SMP available to more users. A computer with a single multicore processor is functionally identical to an SMP computer except that the processors reside in a single chip instead of multiple chips.

So now FSB contention is a problem on the desktop as well as in servers and workstations. FSB contention exhibits itself as increased instruction latency. Code that relies heavily on the FSB runs slower when it has to contend for the FSB with another processor—that is, the same instructions take longer to execute because of FSB contention.

You can get an idea of how much of the FSB a process uses by counting the number of page faults. This is not the whole picture, however. A process uses the memory bus when it tries to read or write a memory location that is not in cache, which does not always result in a page fault but, rather, a *cache miss.*

9.2.2.2   CPU Utilization versus Efficiency

In principle, CPU utilization refers to percentage of the time the CPU spends running code. A CPU that is 100 percent utilized is running code all the time. While the system is up, of course, the CPU is always running code. Each architecture has its own `cpu_idle` function, which Linux calls when the scheduler cannot find any other process to run. Utilization can be expressed as any time the CPU runs code that is not part of the `cpu_idle` function.

Many tools can show CPU utilization, as you have seen already. What you have looked at mostly was utilization by process—the percentage of time the CPU spends executing one particular process. Utilization does not tell the whole story, however. What utilization doesn't tell you is how *efficiently* the CPU is being utilized.

I have already demonstrated how something as simple as modifying a few kilobytes of RAM can run at dramatically different speeds. In each case, the same instructions run at different speeds. In every case, the CPU utilization is 100 percent. CPU utilization is not enough to characterize the efficiency of a process or the system.

The issue of processor efficiency is not hard to understand. You encounter the same problems in real life. Think of the last time you went to buy groceries. Even if you are the most efficient person in the world, you could still be held up by a long line at the checkout counter. Either way, you are devoting 100 percent of your time to your errands, but your efficiency is largely out of your control. In a computer, the long lines come in the form of increased instruction latency. Increased latency can be caused by contention for a resource (such as another processor or device), or by a slow resource (such as DRAM).

The kernel scheduler is somewhat handicapped in its ability to detect inefficient processes. Just like in real life, it's not necessarily the fault of the process; the process is a victim of circumstances. The scheduler relies primarily on utilization to adjust process priorities. Processor hogs have their effective priority lowered,[4] whereas so-called interactive processes (ones that spend most of their time waiting) are given a higher priority.

---

4. If they are not real-time processes.

Many processors include additional performance monitoring registers to monitor code efficiency. But these registers are not available on all processors that run Linux, and to date, they are not used by the scheduler. This is somewhat subjective, after all. Just because a task is inefficient doesn't mean it's not important.

This is where we users have some value to add. In the following sections, I look at tools that can help determine code efficiency. The Intel architecture has a rich set of performance-monitoring registers for this purpose, and a few tools are available to make use of them. As a result, many tools are available only on the Intel architecture.

9.2.3 Devices and Interrupts

When you think of devices and performance, you probably think the devices are independent of the rest of the system—that is, a device doesn't affect processes that aren't using it. Very often, that's true, but devices have a way of creating side effects you may not be aware of.

9.2.3.1 Bus Contention

Most conventional computer designs today, regardless of the CPU architecture, rely on the PCI bus for peripherals. I'll use PCI as the example, although the same issues apply whether the bus is SBUS, ISA, VME, or whatever. What all these buses have in common is that they are parallel buses, which means that the devices share the same wires. Devices that want to talk to the CPU must negotiate time on the bus to do so. Bus bandwidth is fixed and must be shared among the different devices on the bus. Just like multiple CPUs sharing a common FSB, devices on a peripheral bus contend with one another for time on the bus.

The PCI bus allows computers to break the bus into segments in a treelike fashion. As illustrated in Figure 9-2, these segments form a hierarchy, with the north bridge at the top. Two devices on different segments don't contend with each other for bandwidth on their own bus segments. If these devices need to access the CPU or memory, they contend with each other for bandwidth at the north bridge. It's unlikely, but the most efficient use of such a bus scheme occurs when two devices communicate with each other without involving the CPU. In this case, depending on the bus layout, there may be no contention for bandwidth, because each segment is separate.

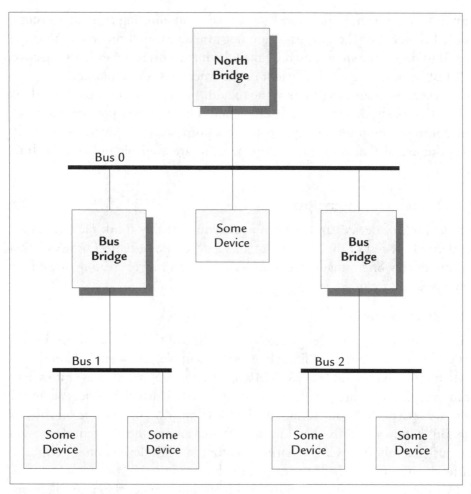

FIGURE 9-2   A Hypothetical Bus Hierarchy

Recently, manufacturers have been moving away from parallel buses to high-speed serial connections that are point to point. Two examples are Intel's PCI Express (PCIe) and AMD's Hypertransport. These are point-to-point connections, so there is no contention for the link. In principle, however, this is similar to the bus segments I just discussed. You can think of each device as having a dedicated bus segment that it does not have to share. These so-called *switched fabric* architectures are similar in concept to a conventional Ethernet network. In such a configuration, each bridge (including the north bridge) functions more like a switch than a bridge. PCIe devices contend with other devices at each bridge they must cross. For traffic that must cross the north bridge (such as a memory access), a PCIe device must contend with every other PCIe device in the system.

9.2.3.2   Interrupts

In the bad old days before USB and FireWire, peripherals like scanners and frame grabbers required special adapters to be installed on the ISA bus. What all adapter cards have in common is that they require an interrupt line to the CPU. In a legacy PC, there are only 15 usable interrupts total, and many of those are already dedicated to system functions, leaving them unavailable for use by additional devices. To work around this, the hardware can share an interrupt with another card, provided that the driver is written to allow this. This has an adverse effect on performance because it requires the operating system to call each driver in turn until one handles the interrupt. Worse, some poorly written drivers don't work with shared interrupts, so if you are out of interrupts, you are out of luck. The lack of interrupts in a typical PC architecture has been made moot by the development of buses like USB and FireWire, which make it possible to add peripherals without adding adapter cards. Nevertheless, some systems require additional adapter cards—maybe additional network cards. In this case, finding interrupts for these cards may be an issue.

You can see the status of interrupts and drivers in the pseudofile /proc/interrupts. Here, you can see exactly which device is assigned to which interrupt. The pseudofile also displays a count next to each interrupt, which is the number of times that interrupt had been handled since the system started. For example:

```
$ cat /proc/interrupts
          CPU0
   0:     27037        XT-PIC   timer
   1:        10        XT-PIC   i8042
   2:         0        XT-PIC   cascade
   7:         1        XT-PIC   parport0
   8:         1        XT-PIC   rtc
   9:         0        XT-PIC   acpi
  11:      1184        XT-PIC   uhci_hcd:usb1, uhci_hcd:usb2, uhci_hcd:usb3, eth0
  12:         0        XT-PIC   VIA8233
  14:      6534        XT-PIC   ide0
  15:       269        XT-PIC   ide1
 NMI:         0
 LOC:     27008
 ERR:         0
 MIS:         0
```

Almost always, you will see the timer interrupt with the most counts, incremented for every system tick. Recall that the tick frequency is determined when you configure the kernel. If you configured the kernel with a tick frequency of 250, this counter will increment 250 times per second.

In this example, you can see that my USB peripherals share a common interrupt, which is assigned to the root hub. Also, the Ethernet adapter shares the same interrupt. Because these are onboard peripherals, I can't do anything about this. Otherwise, it might be possible to move the adapter to a different slot to use a different interrupt.

9.2.3.3   PIC versus APIC

The interrupt architecture is one of the few remaining bits of ISA legacy left in the desktop PC of today. Most PC chipsets contain an implementation of the old 8259 *Programmable Interrupt Controller (PIC)* embedded in the south bridge (refer to Figure 9-1). Interrupts that are delivered by the 8259 must travel across two bridges to reach the CPU. These two bridges must be crossed again to acknowledge the interrupt. The extra "hops" across the bridges increase the latency of the interrupts, which can affect system performance.

Pentium processors come with a built-in interrupt controller called an *Advanced Programmable Interrupt Controller (APIC)*, which allows system designers to provide a low-latency path for interrupts to the processor. Intel also defines an interface to an external APIC that is required for multiprocessor systems. This will be present only if you have a motherboard that can support two or more CPUs. The onboard APIC usually is referred to as the *Local APIC (or LAPIC)*, whereas the external APIC generally is referred to as the *I/O APIC*.

Neither of these APICs is required in a single-processor system, and each can be disabled in software. Many BIOSes disable the APIC for compatibility and fall back on the old-fashioned 8259 PIC in the south bridge. If this is the case, Linux will run with the old PIC. You might see a message in /var/log/messages like the following:

```
localhost kernel: Local APIC disabled by BIOS -- you can enable it with "lapic"
```

As the message says, to enable the local APIC that has been disabled by the BIOS, you must specify it on the boot line with the lapic parameter. The resulting entry in /etc/grub.conf might look like this:

```
Fedora Core (2.6.16np)
      root (hd1,0)
      kernel /vmlinuz-2.6.16np ro root=/dev/VolGroup00/LogVol00 rhgb quiet lapic
      initrd /initrd-2.6.16np.img
```

Enabling the APIC will improve interrupt latency, which can be an issue in real-time applications. It also provides significantly more interrupts than the old-fashioned PIC. So enabling the APIC means that cards don't have to share an interrupt, which I will discuss shortly.

The APIC has been blamed for breaking some drivers. If your BIOS has enabled the APIC, and you want to disable it, you can do so with the `nolapic` option. An SMP system requires an I/O APIC, so by default, this is enabled when you run an SMP kernel—and ideally by the BIOS as well.

9.2.3.4 Devices and Slots

If you have adapters installed in slots on the motherboard, you should be aware of a few things. As I mentioned earlier, the slot often determines which interrupt a card will use. If your card is sharing an interrupt with another device, moving to a different slot may prevent the sharing. Sharing may not be a problem, but it is not optimal for performance.

Parallel buses like PCI and PCI-X must divide the available bus cycles between installed cards. A slow card mixed with a fast card can slow both cards. PCI-X allows both 66MHz cards and 133MHz-capable cards to reside on the same PCI-X bus, for example, but the bus runs only as fast as the slowest card. Likewise, motherboards that can support 133 MHz PCI-X cards will tune the clock frequency based on the number of cards installed. The motherboard may provide two PCI-X slots capable of 133MHz, but due to signal-quality issues, you may slow the clock if you populate both slots. This is entirely dependent on the motherboard design and the BIOS; every one will be different.

PCIe is unique in that it uses a point-to-point connection that eliminates many of the signal-quality issues associated with parallel buses. PCIe bandwidth is expressed in *lanes* of fixed bandwidth (2.5GB/s per lane). The physical slot dimension determines the maximum number of lanes an installed card can have. So an x8 slot can support cards with up to 8 lanes (20 GB/s). The PCIe spec allows manufacturers to provide slots that are physically *wider* than the motherboard can support. The slot may be x8 physically, for example, but the motherboard provides only four lanes. In this case, the card still works, but at half the speed.

Just remember that all slots are not created equal. The specific configurations are unique for every motherboard, and for quality motherboards, these are documented for the concerned user. It always pays to read the manual.

9.2.3.5   Tools for Dealing with Slots and Devices

A very useful tool for determining slot configuration is the `lspci` utility, which can show common bus segments that are shared by more than one device. Sometimes, you find that a particular slot shares a common bus segment with a device soldered to the motherboard. In this case, you may be slowing your bandwidth without realizing it.

With no options, `lspci` lists the devices on the PCI bus. Each PCI device has a vendor ID and a device ID. The vendor ID is a 16-bit number that identifies the manufacturer. This ID is assigned by the PCI-SIG,[5] which maintains the PCI specifications. Each manufacturer assigns its own device IDs to the parts it ships, which, together with the vendor ID, uniquely identify devices. `lspci` includes a table of vendors and devices so that it can report accurate device information in human-readable format. For example:

```
$ lspci
00:00.0 Host bridge: Intel Corporation E7501 Memory Controller Hub (rev 01)
    Subsystem: Intel Corporation Unknown device 341a
    Flags: bus master, fast devsel, latency 0
    Capabilities: <access denied>

00:00.1 Class ff00: Intel Corporation E7500/E7501 Host RASUM Controller (rev 01)
    Subsystem: Intel Corporation Unknown device 341a
    Flags: fast devsel

00:03.0 PCI bridge: Intel Corporation E7500/E7501 Hub Interface C PCI-to-PCI
Bridge (rev 01) (prog-if 00 [Normal decode])
    Flags: bus master, 66MHz, fast devsel, latency 64
    Bus: primary=00, secondary=02, subordinate=04, sec-latency=0
    I/O behind bridge: 00002000-00005fff
    Memory behind bridge: eff00000-feafffff
    Prefetchable memory behind bridge: eda00000-edcfffff

00:03.1 Class ff00: Intel Corporation E7500/E7501 Hub Interface C RASUM
Controller (rev 01)
    Subsystem: Intel Corporation Unknown device 341a
    Flags: fast devsel
...
```

---

5.   www.pcisig.com

Each device in this listing includes a number that identifies the device's logical location on the bus. The default format, listed above, is

```
bus : slot . function
```

PCI is a parallel bus, which means that cards must share a common set of signals. The bus field indicates the bus number. PCI allows multiple buses with the use of bridges. Bus 0 is closest to the processor (the north bridge). Each bridge creates a new bus segment with a higher number. You can see this graphically with the -t option to lspci:

```
-[0000:00]-+-00.0
           +-00.1
           +-03.0-[0000:02-04]--+-1c.0
           |                    +-1d.0-[0000:04]--+-07.0
           |                    |                 +-07.1
           |                    |                 +-09.0
           |                    |                 +-09.1
           |                    |                 +-0a.0
           |                    |                 \-0a.1
           |                    +-1e.0
           |                    \-1f.0-[0000:03]--+-07.0
           |                                      +-07.1
           |                                      \-0a.0
           |
           +-03.1
           +-1d.0
           +-1d.1
           +-1e.0-[0000:01]----0c.0
           +-1f.0
           +-1f.1
           \-1f.3
```

In this output, only the slot and function identifiers are shown to conserve space. The bus is identified by the two-digit number in the brackets.[6] The slot numbers are unique within a bus segment but not unique across bus segments. You will notice that there is a slot labeled 1e on buses 2 and 0, for example.

The point of this output is to see where your cards lie in the bus hierarchy. Quality computer hardware usually comes with a bus diagram pasted to the inside cover of the box. For those times when you don't have access to such a diagram or aren't physically present at the hardware lspci helps you see for yourself what's going on inside the box.

---

6.   The four-digit number is the PCI domain. Most PCI motherboards have only one domain.

In the example above, bus segment 4 has three slots occupied. In this case, it happens to be populated by an onboard SCSI controller and two dual-channel network cards. Here's the plain `lspci` output:

```
$ lspci -s 04:          Show all the cards on bus segment 04.

04:07.0 SCSI storage controller: Adaptec AIC-7902 U320 (rev 03)
04:07.1 SCSI storage controller: Adaptec AIC-7902 U320 (rev 03)
04:09.0 Ethernet controller: Intel Corporation 82546GB Gigabit Ethernet Controller (rev 03)
04:09.1 Ethernet controller: Intel Corporation 82546GB Gigabit Ethernet Controller (rev 03)
04:0a.0 Ethernet controller: Intel Corporation 82546GB Gigabit Ethernet Controller (rev 03)
04:0a.1 Ethernet controller: Intel Corporation 82546GB Gigabit Ethernet Controller (rev 03)
```

This illustrates another use for this tool: It allows you to see when your cards are sharing a bus segment with a device that is soldered onto the motherboard. Here, you see that two dual-port Ethernet adapters (devices 9 and 0xa) are sharing bus 4 with the onboard SCSI controller. In this case, each card happens to be capable of operating at 133MHz, but there's no way that the BIOS is going to allow such a full bus segment to run that fast. To improve performance here, you would need to find another slot for at least one of the Ethernet cards.

Because a PCI bus segment runs only as fast as the slowest card on the bus segment, you could inadvertently slow your onboard SCSI controller just by putting a slow card in one of these slots! Unfortunately, `lspci` does not tell you how fast your bus segment is running or the capability of your cards. Some intuition, however, along with some trial and error, is enough to uncover issues due to overpopulated bus segments. `lspci` is extremely useful for this purpose.

Although `lspci` cannot tell you exactly how fast a parallel PCI device is operating, it can tell you about PCIe devices. To get this information, you need to use the `-vv` option (doubly verbose). Buried in the copious output, you will find the card's capability as well as the current settings. Following is the output from a system with an eight-lane PCI device installed in an eight-lane slot:

```
$ lspci -vv
...
04:00.0 InfiniBand: Mellanox Technologies MT25204 [InfiniHost III Lx HCA] (rev a0)
        Subsystem: Mellanox Technologies MT25204 [InfiniHost III Lx HCA]
...
        Capabilities: [60] Express Endpoint IRQ 0
                Device: Supported: MaxPayload 128 bytes, PhantFunc 0, ExtTag-
                Device: Latency L0s <64ns, L1 unlimited
                Device: AtnBtn- AtnInd- PwrInd-
```

```
Device: Errors: Correctable+ Non-Fatal+ Fatal+ Unsupported-
Device: RlxdOrd- ExtTag- PhantFunc- AuxPwr- NoSnoop-
Device: MaxPayload 128 bytes, MaxReadReq 128 bytes
Link: Supported Speed 2.5Gb/s, Width x8, ASPM L0s, Port 8
Link: Latency L0s unlimited, L1 unlimited
Link: ASPM Disabled RCB 64 bytes CommClk- ExtSynch-
Link: Speed 2.5Gb/s, Width x8
```

Supported Speed represents the capabilities of the card. The actual speed is the second highlighted line, which represents the speed of the slot where the card resides.

9.2.4   Tools for Finding System Performance Issues

You have several tools at your disposal for tracking down processes that are causing your system to run slow. In an earlier section, I used the top command with some detailed examples. In this section, I show you some other tools that can help illustrate what your system is doing. Most of the features in these tools overlap. What makes one tool more useful than another often depends on the application.

9.2.4.1   Virtual-Memory Status and More with vmstat

I used vmstat in an earlier chapter to illustrate the system use of disk cache. This is a familiar tool that has been around for a long time. One appeal of vmstat is its simplicity; just type **vmstat**, and you get one line of dense but useful information. Type **vmstat 1** to get that information printed every second. For example:

```
$ vmstat 1
procs -----------memory---------- ---swap-- -----io---- --system-- ----cpu----
 r  b   swpd   free   buff  cache   si   so    bi    bo   in    cs us sy id wa
 1  1      0   3940  14740 147440    0    0    51    15  263    91  1  8 90  1
 0  1      0   3764  15236 145516    0    0  2952     0  534   606  3 10  0 87
 0  1      0  12368  16320 132804    0    0  1576     0  565   644  0  9  0 91
 0  1      0   8216  16728 135116    0    0  2768     0  455   430  2  5  0 93
 0  1      0   3984  16732 139260    0    0  4164     0  402   354  1  5  0 94
 0  1      0  14452  16764 128484    0    0  3596  1020  438   397  1  5  0 94
 0  1      0  11236  17796 129696    0    0  2196     0  588   695  2  9  0 89
 0  1      0   8028  18724 130944    0    0  2220     0  556   610  2  7  0 91
 0  1      0   4040  19604 132240    0    0  2180     0  532   601  1 12  0 87
 1  1      0   4140  19744 131624    0    0  2964     0  491   506  1  5  0 94
 0  1      0   4368  20024 131004    0    0  3484   932  481   488  1  6  0 93
 0  1      0   9748  20212 124968    0    0  3840     0  502   535  1  8  0 91
```

The default output is plain text and fits on an 80-column text display. Aside from the column headers, that's as fancy as it gets. The output is dynamic and can change with every sample. Each line of output is one sample (in this case, one per second). The following sections look at some of the details.

Process Information from vmstat

The only process-specific information from the default vmstat output is listed in the r and b columns under the heading procs. The r column lists the number of processes that are in the *runnable* state at that time, and the b column lists the number of processes in an uninterruptible sleep.

You may have seen or used the system *load* as a metric of how busy the system is. The term *load* usually is defined as some kind of average of the number of processes in the run queue (that is, that are runnable) over time. In some applications, load is a useful metric. In a general-purpose server or a desktop, this value is not always the most helpful.

Processes that are in an uninterruptible sleep are blocked in a system call (most likely, a device driver). The most common reason for an uninterruptible sleep is to wait for I/O. So a frequent nonzero number in the b column is an indicator of a process that is being blocked by a slow device.

Memory Usage Information from vmstat

Under the heading memory are four columns labeled swpd, free, buff, and cache. These are the current values of the amount of memory swapped to disk, free, in system buffers, or in cache, respectively. All values are in kilobytes by default. You can change this with the -S option (see vmstat(8) for details).

Periodic output from vmstat is a good way to look for trends. When you're looking for memory leaks, the value of the swpd column will tend to go up as one or more processes neglect to free memory. The free column is not as helpful as you may think, because it represents the amount of RAM the kernel can use for allocations without resorting to swapping pages or flushing cache buffers.

The amount of RAM available to applications without swapping is more accurately reflected by the sum of free memory plus the buffers and the cache. This is how the free program represents the same information.

I/O Information from vmstat

I/O is shown under two headings from the default output. The swap heading shows the rate of memory going to and from the swap device. These are the *major* page faults I discussed earlier in the chapter. The si column indicates the rate of reads from the swap device (page in), and the so column indicates the rate of writes to the swap device (page out). The values here are expressed in units of KB/sec by default. Optimal values for both columns are zero, of course. The upper limit of these values is determined by the speed and capability of the swap device.

Next to the swap heading, labeled simply io, is the rest of the system I/O. This includes reads and writes to or from disk other than swap. This includes any I/O, not just I/O caused by the read and write system calls, but page faults due to mappings created by mmap calls as well. The bi column contains the input rate, and the bo column contains the output rate. Here again, the values are measured in KB/sec by default.

Other Information from vmstat

The final two headings in the default output are labeled system and cpu. Under the system heading, the in column indicates the number of interrupts per second. This value is always in interrupts per second regardless of the reporting interval specified on the command line. On an idle system, this value should be very close to the system clock tick, which requires one interrupt per tick.

The cs column indicates the number of context switches per second. A context switch requires a certain amount of overhead, but this overhead has been reduced by techniques such as lazy TLB flushing, which I discussed in Chapter 5. By itself, the context switch rate does not mean much, but with the other data, it can provide some useful insight into the system behavior.

Finally, the cpu heading lists the percentage of time the system spent in user mode (us), kernel mode (sy), and idle (id). The last column (wa) indicates the amount of time the system spends waiting for I/O. This value is printed in all versions of vmstat but is valid only in 2.6-series kernels. In 2.4 and earlier kernels, this value is always zero; the amount of time spent waiting for I/O is not available and is included as *idle* time.

This value in the wa column is a very useful value, because if the kernel is spending a great deal of time waiting for I/O, processes are contending for I/O. Exactly what device they are contending for is another story.

9.2.4.2   Tools from the sysstat Package

The syststat package is a vital package that comes with virtually every distribution. The tools here allow you to monitor system performance interactively and retrospectively. The primary tool in this package is sar, which is short for *system activity reporting.* The data it provides is similar to the output of vmstat except that sar has many more options. The ability to collect system data over time and review it later is unique to sar.

Introducing sar

sar takes an interval and count argument, like vmstat. The default output, however, tells you only about CPU utilization. For example:

```
$ sar 1 4
Linux 2.6.16np (redhat)         06/01/2006

09:41:05 PM        CPU     %user    %nice   %system    %iowait    %steal     %idle
09:41:06 PM        all      6.00     0.00     11.00      83.00      0.00      0.00
09:41:07 PM        all      0.99     0.00      8.91      90.10      0.00      0.00
09:41:08 PM        all     95.92     0.00      1.02       3.06      0.00      0.00
09:41:09 PM        all      5.94     0.00      8.91      85.15      0.00      0.00
Average:           all     26.75     0.00      7.50      65.75      0.00      0.00
```

This command tells sar to report statistics four times, once per second. Each line shows basic CPU utilization information along with the time of day of each sample. These values reflect an average taken over the interval specified (1 second, in this case). This is essentially the same output that vmstat provides except that there are additional fields labeled %nice and %steal. The %nice column indicates the percentage of time spent executing processes with a positive nice value (that is, lower priority). The %steal column shows the percentage of time forced to wait by the hypervisor[7] on a virtual machine.

Virtual-Memory Information from sar

The -r option provides virtual-memory information like vmstat, only with more details:

```
$ sar -r 1 4
Linux 2.6.16np (redhat)         05/31/2006

11:04:54 PM kbmemfree kbmemused %memused kbbuffers  kbcached kbswpfree kbswpused  %swpused kbswpcad
11:04:55 PM      5504    250120    97.85     20708    128008    524280         0      0.00        0
11:04:56 PM      5504    250120    97.85     20708    128008    524280         0      0.00        0
11:04:57 PM      5504    250120    97.85     20708    128008    524280         0      0.00        0
11:04:58 PM      5504    250120    97.85     20708    128008    524280         0      0.00        0
Average:         5504    250120    97.85     20708    128008    524280         0      0.00        0
```

---

7. A *hypervisor* is software used to run an OS in a virtual machine. Open source examples include Xen, QEMU, and Bochs.

You can also see paging and virtual-memory activity by using the -B option as follows:

```
$ sar -B 1 5
Linux 2.6.16np (redhat)         05/31/2006

11:08:53 PM   pgpgin/s pgpgout/s   fault/s  majflt/s
11:08:54 PM      0.00      0.00     53.00      0.00
11:08:55 PM      0.00      0.00     31.00      0.00
11:08:56 PM      0.00      0.00     11.00      0.00
11:08:57 PM      0.00      0.00     11.00      0.00
11:08:58 PM      0.00     48.00     11.00      0.00
Average:         0.00      9.60     23.40      0.00
```

Unlike that of vmstat, the output is in units of pages (or faults) per second and cannot be changed. You can get similar output for each block device in the system or for specific devices as well.

Process Information from sar

You can see utilization by process, as with the top command, by using the -x option. This takes a single argument, which can be a single process ID, or you can specify multiple process IDs with multiple -x options as follows:

```
$ jobs -x sar -x 3942 -x 3970 1 1
Linux 2.6.16np (redhat)         06/01/2006

10:04:09 PM     PID  minflt/s  majflt/s    %user   %system   nswap/s   CPU
10:04:10 PM    3942 43231.00      0.00     5.00     48.00      0.00     0
10:04:10 PM    3970     0.00      0.00    46.00      0.00      0.00     0

Average:        PID  minflt/s  majflt/s    %user   %system   nswap/s
Average:       3942 43231.00      0.00     5.00     48.00      0.00
Average:       3970     0.00      0.00    46.00      0.00      0.00
```

One nice thing about the sar command is that the output units are always unambiguous. These units should be familiar to you by now. Output consists of minflt/s (minor faults per second), majflt/s (major faults per second), and columns for percentage of time spent in user space (%user) and kernel space (%system). The nswap/s column is valid only in 2.4 and earlier kernels. The CPU column identifies the CPU with which the runtime is associated. In this example, it's a uniprocessor machine, so the output is always CPU 0. Even on an SMP machine, however, the output lists only one CPU, even if the process migrates between CPUs. SMP support is a fairly recent addition to sar, and it appears to need more work.

The lowercase x option above shows usage only for the processes listed, whereas an uppercase X shows the statistics for *only* the children of the processes listed. If a process has no children, the output will be all 0. One use for this is when you want to look at processes as they are being forked, which may occur too fast for you to type. By tracing a common parent process with X, you can see the usage of child processes currently executing, as well as any new processes as they are forked.

sar comes with the sysstat package,[8] which includes mpstat and iostat. The Fedora distribution includes a startup service named sysstat that periodically logs the system activity into log files stored in a directory named /var/log/sa. These files are available for postmortem debugging of system activity.

I/O Information from sar

sar can show detailed information on block devices and network devices. In addition, you can see the interrupt activity over time. Ideally, there is only device per interrupt line, although as I discussed earlier, that is not always the case.

For block devices, the output is all or nothing. You cannot choose which block devices to monitor, but the output is useful if you are trying to debug disk utilization. Here, I use the -p option to show device names instead of major/minor numbers. For example:

```
$ sar -d -p 1 1
Linux 2.6.16np (redhat)        06/01/2006


10:40:12 PM     DEV      tps  rd_sec/s  wr_sec/s  avgrq-sz  avgqu-sz     await    svctm    %util
10:40:13 PM     hda     0.00      0.00      0.00      0.00      0.00      0.00     0.00     0.00
10:40:13 PM     hdb   457.00      8.00   8248.00     18.07      1.00      2.19     2.18    99.60
10:40:13 PM     hdc     0.00      0.00      0.00      0.00      0.00      0.00     0.00     0.00
10:40:13 PM   nodev  1037.00      8.00   8288.00      8.00      3.54      3.41     0.96    99.60
10:40:13 PM   nodev     0.00      0.00      0.00      0.00      0.00      0.00     0.00     0.00
```

sar allows you to monitor network device usage with the -n option, which requires a single argument. This argument allows you to report specific types of network objects defined by the sar program. This argument can take one of the following values:

- DEV—Ethernet device statistics

- EDEV—Ethernet device error statistics

---

8. http://perso.wanadoo.fr/sebastien.godard

- NFS—NFS client statistics

- NFSD—NFS server statistics

- SOCK—socket statistics

- ALL—all of the above

As with block devices, the statistics are all or nothing with respect to specific Ethernet ports, so the output can be dense. Here is a sample of Ethernet statistics from my machine:

```
$ sar -n DEV 1 1
Linux 2.6.16np (redhat)          06/01/2006


10:57:43 PM     IFACE   rxpck/s   txpck/s   rxbyt/s   txbyt/s   rxcmp/s   txcmp/s   rxmcst/s
10:57:44 PM        lo    15.00     15.00  11068.00  11068.00      0.00      0.00      0.00
10:57:44 PM      eth0    14.00     15.00   1186.00  18082.00      0.00      0.00      0.00
```

Interrupt activity can be an important indicator of system activity. sar allows you to monitor interrupt activity with the -I option. For example:

```
$ sar -I 0 1 1
Linux 2.6.16np (redhat)          06/01/2006

11:00:52 PM      INTR    intr/s
11:00:53 PM         0    250.00
Average:            0    250.00
```

In this case, I chose interrupt 0, which happens to be the timer interrupt. The output matches the system clock tick, which is 250Hz on this system. You must specify a specific interrupt to monitor or ALL to show all interrupts. If you need to know which interrupt belongs to which device, look at the contents of /proc/interrupts.

Some Concluding Comments on sar

The most common use for sar is for looking at performance retroactively. The system can create a cron job to run the sysstat service periodically and save the results to a file. The cron job that comes with the sysstat package is stored in /etc/cron.d/sysstat and contains commented-out entries that you can use.

The sysstat script uses a couple of helper programs to store the output in files. The naming convention for these files is sa followed by a two-digit day. To prevent the files from being unwieldy, process information is not stored in the files. Everything I discussed in this section is available except processes.

If, for example, you wanted to check on server utilization on the 13th from 3 AM to 4 AM, you could use the following query:

```
$ sar -f sa13 -s 03:00:00 -e 04:00:00
Linux 2.6.7 (somemachine)        06/13/06

03:00:00          CPU    %user    %nice    %system   %iowait    %idle
03:10:00          all    2.19     0.34     4.35      0.06       93.06
03:20:00          all    2.31     0.21     4.33      0.10       93.06
03:30:00          all    1.98     0.00     4.11      0.06       93.85
03:40:00          all    2.25     0.20     4.34      0.08       93.12
03:50:00          all    5.29     0.01     4.96      0.34       89.41
04:00:00          all    2.10     0.00     4.34      0.06       93.49
Average:          all    2.69     0.13     4.40      0.12       92.67
```

By default, `sysstat` is configured to save statistics at 10-minute intervals. You could run `sar` manually as well with shorter intervals to track system behavior over a shorter time. As the interval gets shorter, of course, the file gets larger and the overhead gets bigger. Use your judgment.

9.2.4.3   iostat and mpstat

The `sysstat` package comes with two more useful tools for looking at system performance: `iostat` and `mpstat`. The data that these tools provide is also available from `sar`, but these tools are for command-line use exclusively. They do not store or retrieve archived system information, but they may be easier to use than remembering a bunch of options.

The output is similar to the `-d` output of `sar` except that you can target a single device with the `-p` option. Typing **iostat** with no arguments, for example, gives you system information on I/O devices since the system was booted:

```
# iostat
Linux 2.6.16np (redhat)        06/03/2006

avg-cpu:   %user    %nice %system %iowait   %steal    %idle
           4.56     0.42    1.55    1.65     0.00    91.83

Device:            tps    Blk_read/s    Blk_wrtn/s    Blk_read    Blk_wrtn
hda                0.01        0.04          0.00         201           0
hdb                5.66      169.67         39.79      833342      195444
hdc                0.00        0.01          0.00          28           0
dm-0               9.42      169.51         39.60      832570      194512
dm-1               0.03        0.01          0.19          72         928
```

As with `sar`, the units are self explanatory. You can get a periodic update every second by providing the interval in seconds as the first argument. When periodic updates are requested, the first sample always contains the cumulative statistics since boot time. Subsequent samples reflect the current I/O activity.

The `mpstat` program shows activity for multiple processors in an SMP system. Because this functionality has been integrated into `sar`, the `mpstat` command doesn't offer much. The output is virtually identical to the default output from `sar`.

9.3 Application Performance

You have seen how to monitor the performance of the system as a whole, but what happens when you want to focus on a single application? Perhaps you have narrowed a system issue down to a single unruly process. What then? There are tools to help, but sometimes, they can be difficult to decipher. It helps to understand the architecture of the system and CPU you are working on.

Tools are available on all platforms, but if you are working on an Intel architecture processor, you're in luck: Several sophisticated tools are available that use the built-in performance monitoring registers to debug performance issues. In this section, I look in detail at tools that work on all architectures, as well as some that work only on the Intel architecture.

9.3.1 The First Step with the time Command

When you're tuning performance, the `time` command is perhaps the quickest and easiest way to get some basic answers. I have used this command extensively in earlier examples, so I won't dwell on it here except to say that this command should be your first step when debugging performance issues.

I'll begin with a simple example using the `dd` command, which reads from a device and writes to another device. In this case, I'll read the random numbers from `/dev/urandom` and write them to the bit bucket:

```
$ time dd if=/dev/zero of=/dev/null count=1000
1000+0 records in
1000+0 records out

real    0m0.226s
user    0m0.000s
sys     0m0.212s
```

You may recall that `bash` has a built-in `time` command that provides only timing information, which is what you see above. GNU provides a stand-alone `time` command that implements the POSIX standard features, as well as many additional ones. This command is provided with most Linux distributions. You can specify the stand-alone command by escaping the `time` command with a single backslash, as follows:

```
$ \time dd if=/dev/zero of=/dev/null count=1000
1000+0 records in
1000+0 records out
0.00user 0.22system 0:00.22elapsed 96%CPU (0avgtext+0avgdata 0maxresident)k
0inputs+0outputs (0major+161minor)pagefaults 0swaps
```

This version of the `time` command provides additional useful information regarding CPU utilization, page faults, and swapping, as well as the elapsed time. The default output is fairly dense, as you can see. The GNU version, however, allows you to zoom in on the relevant details by using formats. The format string is given with the `f` option, and specific formats are documented in the `time(1)` man page. To look at minor page faults, for example, you could use `%R` format with the following command:

```
$ \time -f "%R" bash -c "read -n 4096 x" < /dev/zero
286
$ \time -f "%R" bash -c "read -n 40960 x" < /dev/zero
295
```

Here, you can see that minor faults go up with the number of bytes read by the Bash `read` function. There are many additional formats to allow you to focus on whatever measurement you are interested in.

9.3.2 Understanding Your Processor Architecture with x86info

x86info[9] summarizes your processor configuration based on the information provided by the `cpuid` instruction defined on the Intel architecture. Most distributions come with this tool, but the Intel architecture is a moving target. If your distribution is older than your processor, it's likely that the information it provides will be incomplete or just wrong.

---

9. http://sourceforge.net/projects/x86info

One problem in particular is the way the Intel architecture describes the cache. For example:

```
$ x86info
x86info v1.17.  Dave Jones 2001-2005
Feedback to <davej@redhat.com>.

Found 1 CPU
--------------------------------------------------------------------
Found unknown cache descriptors: 64 80 91 102 112 122
Family: 15 Model: 1 Stepping: 2 Type: 0 Brand: 8
CPU Model: Pentium 4 (Willamette) [D0] Original OEM
Processor name string: Intel(R) Pentium(R) 4 CPU 1.70GHz

Feature flags:
 fpu vme de pse tsc msr pae mce cx8 apic sep mtrr pge mca cmov pat pse36 clflsh
ds acpi mmx fxsr sse sse2 ss ht tm
Extended feature flags:

Instruction trace cache:
        Size: 12K uOps  8-way associative.
L1 Data cache:
        Size: 8KB       Sectored, 4-way associative.
        line size=64 bytes.
L2 unified cache:
        Size: 256KB     Sectored, 8-way associative.
        line size=64 bytes.
Instruction TLB: 4K, 2MB or 4MB pages, fully associative, 64 entries.
Found unknown cache descriptors: 64 80 91 102 112 122
Data TLB: 4KB or 4MB pages, fully associative, 64 entries.
The physical package supports 1 logical processors
```

This is my humble 1.7 GHz Pentium 4, which is getting a bit old. Still, x86info says it doesn't recognize several of the cache descriptors. For Intel processors, cache descriptors are described in Intel Application note 485,[10] which is updated frequently.

In this case, it appears to be a bug in x86info, because these cache descriptors are reported correctly but the tool still says they're unknown. Generally speaking, the specific information provided by x86info usually is correct, especially for mature processors. Beware if you have a newer processor, and if in doubt, check the application note to be sure.

Another place to look is /proc/cpuinfo, but this information is baked into the kernel. Chances are that this information is even more out of date. If your processor

---

10. http://developer.intel.com

is newer than your kernel, the information here is likely to be incomplete or wrong. Furthermore, the information here is much less specific than x86info. In particular, /proc/cpuinfo does not distinguish among level 1, 2, or 3 caches. Again, using my humble P4 as an example:

```
$ cat /proc/cpuinfo
processor       : 0
vendor_id       : GenuineIntel
cpu family      : 15
model           : 1
model name      : Intel(R) Pentium(R) 4 CPU 1.70GHz
stepping        : 2
cpu MHz         : 1700.381
cache size      : 256 KB
fdiv_bug        : no
hlt_bug         : no
f00f_bug        : no
coma_bug        : no
fpu             : yes
fpu_exception   : yes
cpuid level     : 2
wp              : yes
flags           : fpu vme de pse tsc msr pae mce cx8 apic sep mtrr pge mca cmov
pat pse36 clflush dts acpi mmx fxsr sse sse2 ss ht tm
bogomips        : 3406.70
```

Now that you have this information, it's time to put it to use. First, you need an example program to work with: cache-miss.c, shown in Listing 9-3.

LISTING 9-3   cache-miss.c: A Program to Demonstrate Tools That Monitor Cache Hits and Misses

```
 1 #include <stdio.h>
 2 #include <string.h>
 3 #include <stdlib.h>
 4 #include <unistd.h>
 5 #include <malloc.h>
 6 #include <assert.h>
 7
 8 int main(int argc, char *argv[])
 9 {
10     // Default to 64 TLBs (max on my processor).
11     int num_pages = 64;
12
13     // User can specify any number of pages.
```

```
14      if (argc > 1) {
15          num_pages = atoi(argv[1]);
16      }
17
18      const size_t page_size = sysconf(_SC_PAGESIZE);
19
20      int num_bytes = num_pages * page_size;
21      int alloc_bytes = num_bytes;
22
23      if (alloc_bytes == 0) {
24          // allocate one page, just for a baseline.
25          // we won't use it though.
26          alloc_bytes = page_size;
27      }
28
29      // Allocate memory aligned on a page boundary
30      char *buf = memalign(page_size, alloc_bytes);
31      assert(buf != NULL);
32
33      printf("%d pages %d KB\n", num_pages, num_bytes / 1024);
34
35      // User requested zero pages. We allocated one page, but
36      // did not touch it, therefore we caused no additional page faults.
37      if (num_pages == 0) {
38          exit(0);
39      }
40
41      // Need a place to store the bytes that we will read.
42      static volatile char store;
43
44      /*
45       ** We read one byte from the base of each page
46       ** until we've done 1,000,000 reads.
47       */
48
49      int i;
50      char *c = buf;
51
52      for (i = 0; i < 1000000; i++) {
53          store = *c;
54          c += page_size;
55          if (c - buf >= num_bytes)
56              c = buf;
57      }
58
59      return 0;
60  }
```

Note that this program reads 1 byte from each page allocated until it does 1 million reads. It writes the byte to a variable so that the compiler doesn't discard the read instructions due to optimization. Now I'll use this example to demonstrate some tools.

9.3.3   Using Valgrind to Examine Instruction Efficiency

Valgrind is available on Intel architectures (IA32 and X86_64) as well as PowerPC 32-bit architectures. It is actually a suite of tools for checking memory leaks and memory corruption. Here, I'll focus on the tool named `cachegrind`, which reports the cache efficiency of your code. Compile the example from Listing 9-3:

```
$ cc -O2 -o cache-miss cache-miss.c
```

You need to compile with optimization to get the best results. This program takes a single argument, which is the number of pages to allocate. When it runs, the program does 1 million reads—one per page, cycling through the pages as necessary. First, run this with an argument of 0 pages, which will give you a baseline against which you can compare. The command to invoke Valgrind with the `cachegrind` tool is

```
$ valgrind --tool=cachegrind ./cache-miss 0

==18902== Cachegrind, an I1/D1/L2 cache profiler.
==18902== Copyright (C) 2002-2005, and GNU GPL'd, by Nicholas Nethercote et al.
==18902== Using LibVEX rev 1471, a library for dynamic binary translation.
==18902== Copyright (C) 2004-2005, and GNU GPL'd, by OpenWorks LLP.
==18902== Using valgrind-3.1.0, a dynamic binary instrumentation framework.
==18902== Copyright (C) 2000-2005, and GNU GPL'd, by Julian Seward et al.
==18902== For more details, rerun with: -v
==18902==
--18902-- warning: Pentium 4 with 12 KB micro-op instruction trace cache
--18902--          Simulating a 16 KB I-cache with 32 B lines
0 pages 0 KB
==18902==
==18902== I   refs:       137,569                        Instruction cache
==18902== I1  misses:       1,216
==18902== L2i misses:         694
==18902== I1  miss rate:     0.88%
==18902== L2i miss rate:     0.50%
==18902==
==18902== D   refs:        62,808  (47,271 rd + 15,537 wr)  Data cache – L1 and L2
==18902== D1  misses:       2,253  ( 1,969 rd +    284 wr)
==18902== L2d misses:       1,251  ( 1,041 rd +    210 wr)
==18902== D1  miss rate:      3.5% (    4.1%  +    1.8%  )
==18902== L2d miss rate:      1.9% (    2.2%  +    1.3%  )
```

```
==18902==
==18902== L2 refs:          3,469  ( 3,185 rd +     284 wr)   Data cache – L2 only
==18902== L2 misses:        1,945  ( 1,735 rd +     210 wr)
==18902== L2 miss rate:       0.9% (   0.9%   +     1.3%  )
```

That's a lot of output, but I've highlighted the important parts. It helps to know what you're looking for to see through the noise. In this case, the program exits immediately, so most of the activity you see is generated by the process of loading the application. Given the same input parameters, the output will be the same for every run (except for the `pid`, of course).

In this case, you can see that there were 62,808 data references. Of these, 47,271 were read requests, and the other 15,537 were writes. The interesting part is on the next line, which tells you that there were 2,253 cache misses in the L1 data cache (abbreviated as `D1`). A *cache miss* is a read or write that requested data that wasn't in the cache. A cache miss occurs on the first read or write of a cache line. Because this example reads only 1 byte from each page, this is the only read it is counting.

When a cache miss occurs, the instruction *stalls* while the cache line is filled. This in turn causes the instruction to take more clock cycles and possibly delay other instructions from completing. You can see a summary on the lines labeled `miss rate`, where the misses are reflected as a percentage of the total. Here, you see that the read miss rate was 3.5 percent.

Now see what happens when you run this while the program actually does something. Run it with only two pages so that the data access fits inside the L1 cache:

```
$ valgrind --tool=cachegrind ./cache-miss 2          Allocate two pages.

==18908== Cachegrind, an I1/D1/L2 cache profiler.
...
1 pages 4 KB
==18908==
==18908== I    refs:       10,136,737
==18908== I1   misses:          1,213
==18908== L2i  misses:            692
==18908== I1   miss rate:        0.01%
==18908== L2i  miss rate:        0.00%
==18908==
==18908== D    refs:        2,062,373  (1,046,952 rd + 1,015,421 wr)
==18908== D1   misses:          2,236  (    1,951 rd +       285 wr)
==18908== L2d  misses:          1,252  (    1,041 rd +       211 wr)
==18908== D1   miss rate:         0.1% (     0.1%  +       0.0%  )
==18908== L2d  miss rate:         0.0% (     0.0%  +       0.0%  )
==18908==
==18908== L2 refs:             3,449  (    3,164 rd +       285 wr)
==18908== L2 misses:           1,944  (    1,733 rd +       211 wr)
==18908== L2 miss rate:          0.0% (     0.0%  +       0.0%  )
```

Notice that you see just over 2 million data references. This is the application reading and writing 1 million times, as planned. Because the data fits in cache, the number of L1 data cache misses does not go up. In fact, the number of read misses goes down—from 1,969 read misses to 1,951. Most likely, this is due to read prefetching going on inside the cache controller, although there is no way to know for sure. The number of write misses goes up by only 1—from 284 to 285. With so many references hitting the cache, the misses are negligible compared with the hits, so the miss rate is effectively zero.

Now I'll make it interesting. This processor has 256K of cache (64 pages), so allocate the full L2 cache and see what it looks like:

```
$ valgrind --tool=cachegrind ./cache-miss 64
...
64 pages 256 KB
==18914==
==18914== I   refs:       9,152,148
==18914== I1  misses:         1,176
==18914== L2i misses:           670
==18914== I1  miss rate:       0.01%
==18914== L2i miss rate:       0.00%
==18914==
==18914== D   refs:       2,062,236  (1,046,866 rd + 1,015,370 wr)
==18914== D1  misses:     1,002,231  (1,001,947 rd +       284 wr)
==18914== L2d misses:         1,315  (    1,105 rd +       210 wr)
==18914== D1  miss rate:      48.5% (     95.7% +       0.0%  )
==18914== L2d miss rate:       0.0% (      0.1% +       0.0%  )
==18914==
==18914== L2 refs:        1,003,407  (1,003,123 rd +       284 wr)
==18914== L2 misses:          1,985  (    1,775 rd +       210 wr)
==18914== L2 miss rate:        0.0% (      0.0% +       0.0%  )
```

Now virtually all the L1 data cache reads are misses, and the majority of the L1 writes are hits. That's because the read buffer no longer fits in the L1 data cache, but because you are writing to the same memory location all the time, the writes always hit the cache. At 256K, however, the data still fits in the L2 data cache, as you can see in the output that follows the L1 data cache statistics.

The L2 cache on this processor is *unified,* which means that the same cache is used for both instructions and data. Here, you see that 1,003,407 references went to the L2 cache controller, whereas before, there were only 3,449 references. This number includes both instruction fetches and data reads. The processor does not distinguish between the two types of references, but it does distinguish between the two types of misses. The ones you are interested in are the data cache misses, listed as `L2d misses`.

The vast majority of the L2 references were reads, which is as expected. The number of misses was negligible, which tells you that most of the reads were hits. This is reflected in an effective L2 miss rate of 0 percent. Finally, see what this output looks like when the data no longer fits in L2:

```
$ valgrind --tool=cachegrind ./cache-miss 256
...
256 pages 1024 KB
==18918==
==18918== I   refs:        9,140,561
==18918== I1  misses:          1,176
==18918== L2i misses:            670
==18918== I1  miss rate:        0.01%
==18918== L2i miss rate:        0.00%
==18918==
==18918== D   refs:        2,062,295  (1,046,911 rd + 1,015,384 wr)
==18918== D1  misses:      1,002,230  (1,001,946 rd +       284 wr)
==18918== L2d misses:      1,001,251  (1,001,041 rd +       210 wr)
==18918== D1  miss rate:       48.5% (     95.7%  +      0.0%  )
==18918== L2d miss rate:       48.5% (     95.6%  +      0.0%  )
==18918==
==18918== L2 refs:         1,003,406  (1,003,122 rd +       284 wr)
==18918== L2 misses:       1,001,921  (1,001,711 rd +       210 wr)
==18918== L2 miss rate:         8.9% (      9.8%  +      0.0%  )
```

This run uses 256 pages, which is four times the size of the L2 cache. You expect that every read from the block of memory will produce a cache miss. In fact, the output shows that the total number of L2 data misses exceeds 1 million. Valgrind expresses the miss rate as a percentage of total data references, which is listed as `D refs`. This includes reads that were issued to load the code, so the result in this example comes out to 95.6 percent instead of 100 percent.

The overall L2 data miss rate (`L2d miss rate`) is reported as only 48.5 percent because it includes both reads and writes. Recall that the program does just as many reads as writes, except that the writes are all to a single page that certainly never leaves the cache.

Likewise, the L2 miss rate is somewhat misleading for this example. Here, it shows 8.9 percent, which is the relationship of L2 misses (both instruction and data) against all reads and writes (9,140,561). If you look at this number, it looks like the program is not so bad. This number is misleading because the instruction fetches that occur inside a tight loop are all cache hits, which tend to drive down the overall average miss rate.

Valgrind has other tools that are worth exploring. It is an excellent tool that is being improved continually and should be in every developer's toolbox. The answers that Valgrind produces are useful even when your target architecture is not supported by Valgrind. As long as you can port your code to a supported platform and run it there, you can use the answers from Valgrind to fix your source code.

9.3.4   Introducing ltrace

ltrace traces an application's use of library calls. Like strace, which I've used in earlier examples, ltrace can show which functions are called, as well as their arguments. The difference is that strace shows you system calls only, whereas ltrace is able to show you library calls. In C and C++, system calls are made via standard library wrappers, so ltrace can show you the same information as well.

For performance, it can be useful to see a histogram of calls with the -c option:

```
$ ltrace -c dd if=/dev/urandom of=/dev/null count=1000
1000+0 records in
1000+0 records out
% time     seconds  usecs/call     calls      function
------ ----------- ----------- --------- --------------------
 94.44    2.298177        2298      1000 read
  3.35    0.081500          81      1000 write
  2.04    0.049663          49      1000 memcpy
  0.04    0.000869         434         2 dcgettext
  0.03    0.000674          84         8 sigaction
  0.02    0.000582         582         1 setlocale
  0.02    0.000450         225         2 fprintf
  0.02    0.000369          92         4 close
  0.01    0.000279          93         3 strchr
  0.01    0.000250          62         4 sigemptyset
  0.01    0.000201         100         2 open64
  0.00    0.000115          57         2 malloc
  0.00    0.000098          49         2 free
  0.00    0.000061          61         1 __strtoull_internal
  0.00    0.000059          59         1 bindtextdomain
  0.00    0.000055          55         1 __errno_location
  0.00    0.000054          54         1 textdomain
  0.00    0.000051          51         1 getpagesize
  0.00    0.000050          50         1 __ctype_b_loc
  0.00    0.000050          50         1 __cxa_atexit
------ ----------- ----------- --------- --------------------
100.00    2.433607                  3037 total
```

With the -c option, ltrace prints the library calls made by the process, sorted by the time spent in each call. The example above reads from the urandom device, which generates random numbers, and writes to the null device, which discards everything written. Intuitively, you should expect that it takes virtually no time to write to a null device. Likewise, it takes some amount of time in kernel mode to generate the random numbers required by the read. Therefore, the reads should take significantly longer than the writes. Because virtually all that this process does is read and write, the reads should dominate the runtime. That is, in fact, what the output shows, with the read function dominating 94 percent of the runtime.

The catch to using ltrace is that the program takes significantly longer to run. ltrace works much like attaching to a process with a debugger, which accounts for the extra time it takes. Each function call is like a breakpoint, which causes ltrace to store timing statistics.

By default, ltrace produces detailed output of all library calls. You can filter the list with the -e option to show only functions of interest. You also can trace the duration of each individual function call with the -T option. For example:

```
$ ltrace -T -e read,write dd if=/dev/urandom of=/dev/null count=1
read(0,
"\007\354\037\024b\316\t\255\001\322\2220\b\251\224\335\357w\302\351\207\323\n$\
032\342\211\315\2459\006{"..., 512) = 512 <0.000327>
write(1,
"\007\354\037\024b\316\t\255\001\322\2220\b\251\224\335\357w\302\351\207\323\n$\
032\342\211\315\2459\006{"..., 512) = 512 <0.000111>
1+0 records in
1+0 records out
+++ exited (status 0) +++
```

Here, you can see additional information about each call, but the -T option adds the duration of the call (indicated within the angle brackets). Here, too, you can see that the read takes longer than the write, but only by three times. The precise output can vary based on the overhead consumed by the program. Beware of reading too much into these numbers.

The limitation of ltrace is that it can trace only dynamic library calls—not calls to functions in statically linked libraries.

9.3.5   Using strace to Monitor Program Performance

strace and ltrace take many of the same options and can be used in much the same way. The difference is that strace tracks system calls exclusively. Unlike ltrace, however, strace does not require a dynamic library to trace system calls. Calls are traced whether or not they use wrapper functions, because system calls use interrupts to transition between user mode and kernel mode. This results in less overhead than ltrace, even though strace slows your program execution. It's not as extreme a penalty as ltrace.

You should not take timing results from strace too seriously, however. An unfortunate side effect of the way strace monitors program execution is that it tends to underestimate system time severely. Consider the earlier example in which ltrace indicated that the read function (which is a system call) took 94 percent of the overall runtime, and see what strace has to say:

```
$ strace -c dd if=/dev/urandom of=/dev/null count=1000
1000+0 records in
1000+0 records out
Process 22820 detached
% time     seconds  usecs/call     calls    errors syscall
------ ----------- ----------- --------- --------- ----------------
100.00    0.013654          14      1003           read
  0.00    0.000000           0      1002           write
  0.00    0.000000           0        12         6 open
  0.00    0.000000           0         8           close
  0.00    0.000000           0         1           execve
  0.00    0.000000           0         1         1 access
  0.00    0.000000           0         3           brk
  0.00    0.000000           0         6           old_mmap
  0.00    0.000000           0         2           munmap
  0.00    0.000000           0         1           uname
  0.00    0.000000           0         2           mprotect
  0.00    0.000000           0         8           rt_sigaction
  0.00    0.000000           0         2           mmap2
  0.00    0.000000           0         4           fstat64
  0.00    0.000000           0         1           set_thread_area
------ ----------- ----------- --------- --------- ----------------
100.00    0.013654                   2056         7 total
```

According to strace, the program just got 16 times faster, but don't believe everything you read! Notice that although there were 1,002 write calls, they are listed as 0 percent of the time, which doesn't mean that they took no time to execute—just that strace couldn't measure them. More important, the read calls, which you know are slow, consumed only 13 ms. This is not possible if the output from the time command is to be believed.

This discrepancy is an artifact of the way strace traces work. strace forks and executes your process on your behalf, so there actually are two processes running. A certain amount of system time that would be consumed by the process being traced is charged to `strace`. You can see this for yourself by timing `strace` with the `time` command:

```
$ time strace -c dd if=/dev/urandom of=/dev/null count=1000
...
  0.00    0.000000          0          1           set_thread_area
------ ----------- ----------- --------- --------- ----------------
100.00    0.013590                  2056         7 total

real    0m0.318s
user    0m0.016s
sys     0m0.292s
```

Despite the timing discrepancies, `strace` is still useful for profiling because it can give you a count of the system calls a process makes. The ranking of system calls usually is accurate, as it is in this example, and it can steer you to system calls in your application that may be causing performance issues.

The ability to attach to running processes is a very useful technique as well. This comes in handy when you have a process that appears to be hung. You can attach to the process with `strace -p`, for example:

```
$ strace -ttt -p 23210
Process 23210 attached - interrupt to quit
1149372951.205663 write(1, "H", 1)       = 1
1149372951.206036 select(0, NULL, NULL, NULL, {1, 0}) = 0 (Timeout)
1149372952.209712 write(1, "e", 1)       = 1
1149372952.210045 select(0, NULL, NULL, NULL, {1, 0}) = 0 (Timeout)
1149372953.213802 write(1, "l", 1)       = 1
1149372953.214133 select(0, NULL, NULL, NULL, {1, 0}) = 0 (Timeout)
1149372954.217911 write(1, "l", 1)       = 1
1149372954.218244 select(0, NULL, NULL, NULL, {1, 0}) = 0 (Timeout)
1149372955.221994 write(1, "o", 1)       = 1
Process 23210 detached
```

In this contrived example, I created a process that writes `Hello World` 1 byte at a time with a sleep in between. It's silly, but it illustrates what the output looks like. You also can use the `-c` option to get a histogram in this mode.

9.3.6 Traditional Performance Tuning Tools: gcov and gprof

These tools have origins that go back to UNIX and are useful but somewhat hard to use. One problem with these tools is that they require you to instrument your executable, which can be tricky and also degrades your performance. Optimization can make the output challenging to read, as the source code may not accurately reflect what the CPU is doing. Turning off optimization and turning on debugging ensure that each line of source code has machine instructions associated with it. Running an executable without optimization, however, is unacceptable in many applications. Fortunately, GNU has done a great deal to make sure that you can optimize your code and still produce usable results.

9.3.6.1   Using gprof

gprof is a tool for profiling your executable, which means that it helps you determine where your program is spending most of its time. The catch is that it measures only code that has been instrumented by the compiler. This instrumentation is generated when you compile with the -pg flag using gcc. Any code that is not instrumented is not measured, so any modules that you do not compile with -pg will not be measured. This usually is the case with the libraries that you link with. If your code calls a library function that is taking quite a bit of time, the time is charged to the calling function, leaving it up to you to figure out what is causing your function to consume so much time.

Listing 9-4 is a simple example that illustrates how the profiler can help, as well as some of its limitations.

LISTING 9-4   profme.c: Simple Profiling Demonstration Program

```
 1 #include <stdio.h>
 2 #include <string.h>
 3 #include <stdlib.h>
 4 #include <math.h>
 5
 6 /* Raise x to the power of something. Not very fast. */
 7 double slow(double x)
 8 {
 9     return pow(x, 1.12345);
10 }
11
12 /* Floating point division - very slow. */
13 double slower(double x)
14 {
15     return 1.0 / x;
16 }
17
18 /* Square root - perhaps the slowest. */
19 double slowest(double x)
```

```
20 {
21      return sqrt(x);
22 }
23
24 int main(int argc, char *argv[])
25 {
26      int i;
27      double x;
28
29      /* Need a large number here to get a good sample. */
30      for (i = 0; i < 3000000; i++) {
31          x = 100.0;
32          x = slow(x);
33          x = slower(x);
34          x = slowest(x);
35      }
36 }
```

Before you can use the profiler, you must build and link your code with the -pg option. Other than that, you should use the same flags that you normally compile with. If you normally compile with optimization, compile with optimization; if not, don't turn on optimization. If you change the flags just for profiling, what you profile may not represent what you normally run. To build this example, use -O2 and -pg as follows:

```
$ cc -pg -O2 -o profme profme.c -lm
$ ./profme
```

Each time you run this program, it creates a file named gmon.out in the current directory. This, along with the instrumented executable, is the input to the gprof program. The simplest and most useful output from gprof is the flat profile. This is the default:

```
$ gprof ./profme
Flat profile:

Each sample counts as 0.01 seconds.
  %   cumulative   self              self     total
 time   seconds   seconds    calls  ns/call  ns/call  name
46.88     0.15      0.15  3000000    50.00    50.00  slowest
37.50     0.27      0.12  3000000    40.00    40.00  slower
12.50     0.31      0.04                            main
 3.12     0.32      0.01  3000000     3.33     3.33  slow
...
```

I truncated the output to highlight the important points. Notice that the `slow` function is the fastest function in the group. In fact, `main` takes almost as long to run. These are so close that from one run to the next, they will likely exchange places. Based on what you know about the application, the only thing `main` does is loop and call functions; the time spent in `main` is pure overhead. The fact that the `slow` function is practically tied with `main` tells you that it probably is not that slow after all. To get a better picture, you can accumulate multiple `gmon.out` files and feed them to `gprof` as follows:

```
$ export GMON_OUT_PREFIX=gmon.out        Causes GLIBC to create mon.out with the PID as the suffix.
                                         (This feature is not documented.)
$ ./profme                               Creates a file named gmon.out.PID.
$ ./profme                               Repeat three more times.
$ ./profme
$ ./profme

$ gprof ./profme gmon.out.*              Generate profile based on four runs.
Flat profile:

Each sample counts as 0.01 seconds.
   %   cumulative   self              self     total
 time   seconds   seconds    calls  ns/call  ns/call  name
 55.22     0.74      0.74 12000000    61.67    61.67  slowest
 32.84     1.18      0.44 12000000    36.67    36.67  slower
  6.72     1.27      0.09 12000000     7.50     7.50  slow
  5.22     1.34      0.07                            main
...
```

Notice that `slow` now runs a little slower than `main` in the timing produced with the additional samples. Also notice that the `calls` column reflects the total function calls produced by all the runs of the program. This is about as straightforward as it gets with `gprof`. More often, the output can be hard to interpret. In this trivial example, I wrapped several standard library functions, which helps profiling but perhaps impedes performance. If I had not done this, however, `gprof` would have charged all the runtime to `main`, because that would be the only function it had instrumented. Standard library calls like `pow` and `sqrt` are not instrumented and, therefore, do not show up in the profile.[11] To get around this, `gprof` allows you to produce a line-by-line profile with the `-l` option. To use this option, however, your

---

11. Some distributions provide profiled versions of the libraries.

executable must be compiled with debugging enabled (-g) for line-number information. After recompiling with the debugging flag, the output for the example looks like this:

```
Each sample counts as 0.01 seconds.
  %    cumulative  self              self    total
 time   seconds   seconds   calls  ns/call  ns/call  name
54.55     0.18     0.18                               slowest (profme.c:21 @ 8048546)
24.24     0.26     0.08                               slower (profme.c:16 @ 8048535)
 6.06     0.28     0.02                               main (profme.c:34 @ 8048592)
 6.06     0.30     0.02                               slowest (profme.c:22 @ 804855c)
 3.03     0.31     0.01  3000000    3.33     3.33     slow (profme.c:8 @ 8048504)
 3.03     0.32     0.01  3000000    3.33     3.33     slowest (profme.c:20 @ 8048538)
 3.03     0.33     0.01                               main (profme.c:33 @ 8048587)
 0.00     0.33     0.00  3000000    0.00     0.00     slower (profme.c:14 @ 8048528)
```

This output can get hard to read when you have a great deal of code. But you can compile only selected modules with profiling (-pg) so that only those modules will be included in the profiling output. As long as you include the -pg option on the link line, your executable will produce an appropriate gmon.out file.

gprof can also produce annotated source, similar to gcov, for modules compiled with debugging. This also can be a useful tool for performance tuning.

9.3.6.2   Using gcov with gprof for profiling

Normally, gcov is for determining *code coverage*—that is, how much of your code has executed during a particular run. Code coverage is a good predictor of how well your code has been tested, but it also can help in optimization, particularly with unfamiliar code.

Suppose that you have an application that was written by a summer intern, who has left to go back to school. The application is useful but slow. Throwing compiler optimizations at the code does not improve performance significantly; your intern has stumped the optimizer. In this case, you have to dive into the code and do some hand optimization. Upon doing so, you find that in addition to being inefficient, the source code is incomprehensible. This is where gcov can help.

Instead of poring over thousands of lines of code, trying to reverse-engineer a design that may not exist, it probably makes more sense to target your effort at the lines of code that execute most often. These lines are not necessarily where the application is spending most of its time, but they're a good place to start. Hand optimization should combine both coverage testing and profiling.

Listing 9-5 shows the hypothetical intern's work.

LISTING 9-5   summer-proj.c: Example to Illustrate Profiling and Coverage

```
 1 #include <stdio.h>
 2 #include <string.h>
 3 #include <stdlib.h>
 4 #include <time.h>
 5 #include <math.h>
 6
 7 volatile double x;
 8
 9 int main(int argc, char *argv[])
10 {
11     int i;
12     for (i = 0; i < 16000000; i++) {
13         x = 1000.0;
14
15         /* 0 <= r < 16 */
16         int r = i & 0xf;
17
18         if (r <= 8) {
19             x = pow(x, 1.234);   /* called 9/16 of the time. */
20         }
21         else if (r <= 11) {
22             x = sqrt(x);         /* called 3/16 of the time. */
23         }
24         else {
25             x = 1.0 / x;         /* called 4/16 of the time. */
26         }
27     }
28 }
```

To enable coverage testing, you have to compile with two special flags for this purpose:

```
$ cc -g -O2 -ftest-coverage -fprofile-arcs summer-proj.c -o summer-proj -pg -lm
```

For the purpose of coverage testing, it is preferable to leave optimization off, because this preserves the line structure of the code more accurately. For your purposes, you don't care, so you turn on optimization. Compiling with the -ftest-coverage flag causes the compiler to produce a file named summer-proj.gcno in addition to the executable. The -fprofile-arcs causes your executable to produce a file named summer-proj.gcda when it runs. Both files are used as input to the gcov program.[12] Finally, you kept the -pg option so

---

12. The .gcda file can also be used as feedback to the compiler to optimize based on branch probabilities with the -fbranch-probabilities option.

that you can use `gprof` as well. You must run the program at least once before you can run `gcov`:

```
$ ./summer-proj                          Produces summer-proj.gcda
$ gcov ./summer-proj                     Produces summer-proj.c.gcov
File 'summer-proj.c'
Lines executed:100.00% of 9
summer-proj.c:creating 'summer-proj.c.gcov'
```

Not surprisingly in this example, you have 100 percent coverage, which means that all the lines of code that are executable were executed during this run. That's not what you're interested in, however. You need to look at the counts, which are contained inside `summer-proj.c.gcov`, to see what happened. This is shown in Listing 9-6.

LISTING 9-6   summer-proj.c.gcov: Example of gcov Output

```
        -:    0:Source:summer-proj.c
        -:    0:Graph:summer-proj.gcno
        -:    0:Data:summer-proj.gcda
        -:    0:Runs:1
        -:    0:Programs:1
        -:    1:#include <stdio.h>
        -:    2:#include <string.h>
        -:    3:#include <stdlib.h>
        -:    4:#include <time.h>
        -:    5:#include <math.h>
        -:    6:
        -:    7:volatile double x;
        -:    8:
        -:    9:int main(int argc, char *argv[])
        1:   10:{
        -:   11:    int i;
16000000:   12:    for (i = 0; i < 16000000; i++) {
16000000:   13:        x = 1000.0;
        -:   14:
        -:   15:        /* 0 <= r < 16 */
16000000:   16:        int r = i & 0xf;
        -:   17:
16000000:   18:        if (r <= 8) {
 9000000:   19:            x = pow(x, 1.234);   /* called 9/16 of the time. */
        -:   20:        }
 7000000:   21:        else if (r <= 11) {
 3000000:   22:            x = sqrt(x);         /* called 3/16 of the time. */
        -:   23:        }
        -:   24:        else {
 4000000:   25:            x = 1.0 / x;         /* called 4/16 of the time. */
        -:   26:        }
        -:   27:    }
        -:   28:}
```

Notice that the counts line up nicely with the predictions in the comments. Because most code doesn't come with such helpful comments, tools like gcov are available. Based on this output, it's clear that line 19 is called most often. Recall that lines 19, 22, and 25 are the same as the slow, slower, and slowest functions used in Listing 9-4, but without the wrappers. Based on that output, you know that sqrt is significantly slower than the other two. But where is this program spending its time? Here again, gprof comes to the rescue:

```
$ gprof --no-graph -l summer-proj| head -10
Flat profile:

Each sample counts as 0.01 seconds.
  %   cumulative   self              self     total
 time   seconds   seconds    calls  Ts/call  Ts/call  name
34.00      0.17      0.17                              main (summer-proj.c:22 @ 8048926)
20.00      0.27      0.10                              main (summer-proj.c:25 @ 8048879)
16.00      0.35      0.08                              main (summer-proj.c:19 @ 80488c6)
11.00      0.41      0.06                              main (summer-proj.c:18 @ 80488b3)
 6.00      0.43      0.03                              main (summer-proj.c:21 @ 8048870)
...
```

Note that because this program does not call any instrumented functions, you have to specify the option nograph to gprof. Otherwise, you will get nothing but the following complaint:

```
gprof: gmon.out file is missing call-graph data
```

In the output, you can see that the lines are ranked by the amount of time spent on each line. Now it is clear that although the most counts occurred on line 19, the program spends most of its time on line 22 (sqrt). So in this case, the line counts from gcov were misleading. In larger, more complicated programs, the output of gcov tends to be a good indicator of where your code is spending most of its time. The annotated listings often are easier to interpret than the output of gprof. One more tool, however, can do both of these jobs, and with less interference: OProfile.

9.3.7   Introducing OProfile

A recent addition to the Linux kernel is a built-in profiler called OProfile. Your kernel must be compiled with OProfile support enabled for this to work.[13] OProfile is a very complex tool but has numerous advantages over gcov and gprof.

---

13. This flag can be found when you configure the kernel. Look under *Instrumentation Support*; then select *Profiling Support*. When you enable profiling, you will be prompted with an *OProfile* option.

Although OProfile is most useful to kernel developers to determine where the kernel is spending its time, it's also very useful for programmers, because it can tell you what's going on in user space as well. What's more, you can operate exclusively in user space if you want to. You don't need kernel source or instrumented object files either in the kernel or user space. In other words, you don't need to rebuild your code to profile it.

There's no such thing as a free lunch, of course. Running the profiler (oprofiled) requires root privilege. When it runs, your code will run a little slower, but the impact is much less than instrumenting the object files with compiler flags. The following sections show OProfile in action.

OProfile consists of a package of user-space tools, including a daemon as well as some command-line tools, which I will discuss shortly. These tools, however, work only with a kernel that has been built with OProfile support enabled.

The command-line tools include

- opcontrol—starts and stops the oprofiled daemon

- opreport—prints a report based on the most recent oprofiled statistics

- opgprof—produces a gmon.out file that can be used by gprof

- opannotate—produces annotated source from profile data

The opcontrol program is the central tool for managing the oprofiled daemon that does the work of collecting the statistics.

Controlling the Profiler with opcontrol

opcontrol comes with numerous defaults to make the job of profiling as easy as possible. There are numerous options as well, which are there for when you are ready for more advanced work. In addition, opcontrol saves the command-line options from each run, so that these become defaults the next time you run opcontrol.

To start the daemon, you need to call opcontrol with the start option. The first time you call opcontrol, you must tell it whether you want to profile the kernel or just user space. Because you will be working in user space for these examples, you will use the --no-vmlinux option to exclude kernel profiling as follows:

```
$ sudo opcontrol --start --no-vmlinux
Using default event: GLOBAL_POWER_EVENTS:100000:1:1:1
Using 2.6+ OProfile kernel interface.
Using log file /var/lib/oprofile/oprofiled.log
Daemon started.
Profiler running.
```

opcontrol saves your most recent settings in your home directory in a directory named .oprofile. The next time you start OProfile, you won't need any options other than --start, because the tool stores these options in your home directory. Only root can start and stop the daemon, so this information is stored in root's home directory. Ordinary users can only dump statistics with the --dump option—but I'm getting ahead of myself.

When the daemon is running, it collects statistics from everything that runs in the system—*everything*. This can be overwhelming the first time you look at it. The output is available to any user, but first, you must tell the oprofiled to dump the statistics with the --dump option. After you dump the statistics, you can view them with opreport, opgprof, or opannotate. Any user can dump statistics or call opreport, not just root. Here's an example of how this is done:

```
$ opcontrol --dump
$ opreport | head -15
CPU: P4 / Xeon, speed 1700.38 MHz (estimated)
Counted GLOBAL_POWER_EVENTS events (time during which processor is not stopped)
with a unit mask of 0x01 (mandatory) count 100000
GLOBAL_POWER_E...|
  samples|      %|
------------------
   29141 62.2445 no-vmlinux                          Placeholder for kernel events
    3380  7.2196 libc-2.3.3.so
    2641  5.6411 libglib-2.0.so.0.400.8
    2234  4.7718 libgobject-2.0.so.0.400.8
    1824  3.8960 libgdk-x11-2.0.so.0.400.13
    1076  2.2983 libvte.so.4.4.0
     911  1.9459 libgtk-x11-2.0.so.0.400.13
     861  1.8391 libcrypto.so.0.9.7a
     738  1.5764 libpthread-2.3.3.so
     659  1.4076 libX11.so.6.2
...
```

The output appears as a list of object files containing the code that was running when the profiler took each sample. The files are listed with the most frequently encountered file at the top. Because you are not profiling the kernel, any samples that occurred in kernel mode show up listed as no-vmlinux. This output format is not the most useful for application programmers, however.

Notice that the output indicates that it counted GLOBAL_POWER_EVENTS. This is the default on IA32. OProfile uses performance counters that are embedded in the

CPU, which is how it is able to have such a small impact on the system. Each processor supports different set of events, but all IA32 processors have a common set of events that can be trapped. This particular event counts everything that occurs while the processor is not powered off.

`oprofiled` records everything from the time you call `opcontrol --start`. By calling `opcontrol --dump`, you produce a snapshot of the statistics, but `oprofiled` continues to collect and accumulate data. Subsequent calls to `opcontrol --dump` will make the newly accumulated data available for inspection. Only when you call `opcontrol --stop` does `oprofiled` stop collecting data.

Profiling an Application with OProfile

The steps to profiling an application are straightforward but must be followed exactly if you are to get useful results. Because `oprofiled` accumulates data continuously, it's important to clear and dump the statistics at the appropriate times. To get accurate results, it's also important to work on an idle system; otherwise, other running processes may affect your results. In general, the steps are

- Start the daemon/start collecting data

- Reset the statistics (if necessary)

- Run the application

- Dump the statistics and/or stop the daemon

After you have collected statistics with your application, you can use the reporting tools. You can profile an application that has not been compiled with any special flags. You can compile Listing 9-4 with optimization and no other flags, for example, and get useful results:

```
$ cc -o profme -O2 -lm
$ opcontrol --start -no-vmlinux                 Start collecting statistics.
Using default event: GLOBAL_POWER_EVENTS:100000:1:1:1
Using 2.6+ OProfile kernel interface.
Using log file /var/lib/oprofile/oprofiled.log
Daemon started.
Profiler running.
$ ./profme                                      Run our application to be profiled.
$ opcontrol dump                                Write a snapshot of the statistics so we can run opreport.
$ opreport
```

```
Counted GLOBAL_POWER_EVENTS events (time during which processor is not stopped)
with a unit mask of 0x01 (mandatory) count 100000
GLOBAL_POWER_E...|
  samples|       %|
------------------
   16477 52.9807 libm-2.3.3.so
   11597 37.2894 profme
    1795  5.7717 no-vmlinux
     325  1.0450 libc-2.3.3.so
     162  0.5209 bash
     140  0.4502 libglib-2.0.so.0.400.8
     103  0.3312 oprofiled
```

The output of `opreport` shows that the application spends most of its time in
`libm`, the standard math library. This makes sense, because you already know that
the slowest functions reside there. The difference is that you are running a fully
optimized executable that you have not instrumented in any way.

That's not all you can do, however. The OProfile package comes with another
tool called `opgprof`, which creates a `gmon.out` file that can be used by `gprof`. It's
just an extra step, as follows:

```
$ opgprof profme             Create gmon.out from saved statistics.
$ gprof --no-graph profme    Resulting gmon.out does not have call graph data.
Flat profile:

Each sample counts as 1 samples.
  %   cumulative   self              self     total
 time   samples   samples   calls  T1/call  T1/call  name
 70.37   8161.00   8161.00                            slow
 22.78  10803.00   2642.00                            slower
  5.40  11429.00    626.00                            slowest
  1.41  11593.00    164.00                            main
  0.03  11597.00      4.00                            _init
...
```

There are a few things to notice about this output. One is that there is no timing. Everything is based on sample counts exclusively. Because these samples (and
the percentage of time) reflect everything that is going on in the system, they may
not accurately reflect how much time your code is taking. If you were to collect this
data on a busy system with your process running at a low priority, this profile could
be misleading.

Notice also that there is no call count in the output. You know that the
`oprofiled` collected 8,161 samples when the CPU was running the `slow` function,

but you don't know how many times the `slow` function was actually called. That is a side effect of the fact that OProfile is looking at the entire system, not just one process.

Finally, you had to use the `--no-graph` option again because the `gmon.out` file produced by `opgprof` does not have call graph information. As with a normally instrumented program, if you want line-by-line profiling, you must compile the executable with debugging (`-g`). To see this, look again at Listing 9-5:

```
$ cc -g -O2 -o summer-proj summer-proj.c -lm
$ opcontrol --reset                              Clear statistics.
Signalling daemon... done
$ opcontrol --start
Profiler running.
$ ./summer-proj                                  Run our code.
$ opcontrol --dump                               Tell daemon to dump stats.
$ opgprof ./summer-proj                          Create gmon.out for gprof.
$ gprof --no-graph -l ./summer-proj | head
Flat profile:

Each sample counts as 1 samples.
  %   cumulative   self              self     total
 time   samples   samples   calls  T1/call  T1/call  name
 46.81   3496.00   3496.00                            main (summer-proj.c:19 @ 8 048444)
 20.10   4997.00   1501.00                            main (summer-proj.c:12 @ 8 0483fb)
 14.82   6104.00   1107.00                            main (summer-proj.c:19 @ 8 04842c)
  8.19   6716.00    612.00                            main (summer-proj.c:22 @ 8 048410)
  4.69   7066.00    350.00                            main (summer-proj.c:21 @ 8 0483ea)
```

This produces the familiar line-by-line profile. Again, there is no timing information—just sample counts. But OProfile does `gprof` one better by providing annotated source listings with `opannotate`. This does not even require the `opgprof` step:

```
$ opannotate --source ./summer-proj              Output goes to stdout (below).

/*
 * Command line: opannotate --source ./summer-proj
 *
 * Interpretation of command line:
 * Output annotated source file with samples
 * Output all files
 *
 * CPU: P4 / Xeon, speed 1700.38 MHz (estimated)
 * Counted GLOBAL_POWER_EVENTS events (time during which processor is not
stopped) with a unit mask of 0x01 (mandatory) count 100000
 */
/*
```

```
 * Total samples for file : "/home/john/examples/ch-07/prof/summer-proj.c"
 *
 *    7458 99.8527
 */

                    :#include <stdio.h>
                    :#include <string.h>
                    :#include <stdlib.h>
                    :#include <time.h>
                    :#include <math.h>
                    :
                    :volatile double x;
                    :
                    :int main(int argc, char *argv[])
                    :{ /* main total:   7458 99.8527 */
                    :    int i;
 1554 20.8060 :      for (i = 0; i < 16000000; i++) {
   27  0.3615 :          x = 1000.0;
                    :
                    :          /* 0 <= r < 16 */
    6  0.0803 :          int r = i & 0xf;
                    :
  115  1.5397 :          if (r <= 8) {
 4678 62.6322 :              x = pow(x, 1.234);   /* called 9/16 of the time. */
                    :          }
  350  4.6860 :          else if (r <= 11) {
  612  8.1939 :              x = sqrt(x);         /* called 3/16 of the time. */
                    :          }
                    :          else {
  116  1.5531 :              x = 1.0 / x;         /* called 4/16 of the time. */
                    :          }
                    :      }
                    :}
```

Here, you see the best of gcov and gprof. Each line is annotated with a sample count—the number of times the oprofiled caught the processor executing this code. Next to the sample count is the percentage of time spent on that line of code. This percentage is normalized for the file being collected, so the numbers should add up to 100 percent regardless of what else was running at the same time.

Closing Remarks about OProfile

I barely scratched the surface of what OProfile can do. In particular, I didn't examine any other types of events that OProfile is capable of monitoring. The exact events are different on every processor, and you can see what your processor is capable of with the following command:

```
$ opcontrol --list-events
```

The output should be lengthy. The default event is good for application profiling, but for system profiling, you will want to explore some of the other events available to you. You can find more information at the OProfile home page.[14]

9.4   Multiprocessor Performance

The term for an operating system that runs on more than one CPU is *Symmetric Multiprocessing* (SMP), and it has been around for many years.[15] When SMP is used, overall system throughput on a busy server increases because the scheduler can distribute processes across the CPUs. An individual single-threaded application, on the other hand, does not run any faster on a multiprocessor machine because it can run on only one processor at a time. Applications that benefit the most from SMP are multithreaded applications, which allow the OS to distribute threads across processors to realize higher throughput.

Recently, microprocessor vendors have been offering multicore and multithreaded CPUs. This means that many desktop and laptop machines now need SMP operating systems to take advantage of these new processors. Before, only servers and high-end workstations used SMP hardware.

9.4.1   Types of SMP Hardware

SMP comes in a few varieties, and new ones are on the way. Each SMP approach has advantages and drawbacks. Understanding these can help you design code that will take the most advantage of multiprocessor hardware.

Before I go into the details of SMP implementations, you need some background. If you're already familiar with these terms, you may want to skip the following sections.

9.4.1.1   Some Background in CPU Parallelism

To increase the speed of the fastest CPUs, manufacturers have resorted to several tricks over the years. It helps to understand these tricks so that you can understand why SMP and multicore CPUs are important.

RISC versus CISC

It's hard to imagine, but there once was a time when people didn't trust compilers. Programmers wrote code in assembly, even if a compiler was available. Assembly

---

14. http://oprofile.sourceforge.net
15. Linux 2.0 came out in 1996 and was the first version of Linux that supported SMP.

language was considered to be the most efficient language, and most assembly programmers didn't trust compilers to produce efficient or even correct output.

Most processors of the day were CISC (Complex Instruction Set Computers), which provided a rich instruction set with many addressing modes to make assembly-language programming easier. Two prominent examples of CISC processors are the Motorola 68000 and the Intel 8086. The Motorola processor was the processor used in the original Macintosh computer, whereas the 8086 was the processor used in the IBM PC.[16] The 8086 instruction set survives today as a subset in the IA32 architecture.

Studies by IBM, Stanford, and Berkeley demonstrated that they could use the transistors on a CPU more effectively by creating fewer instructions with limited addressing modes and lower instruction latency. This was the motivation for the creation of the Reduced Instruction Set Computer (RISC) processor. In general, RISC instructions are more compiler friendly than user friendly. Examples of RISC processors include the PowerPC, SPARC, and MIPS processors.

Pipelining and Execution Parallelism

One innovation that allowed CISC and RISC processors to run faster was the use of *pipelining*—the computerized equivalent of the familiar manufacturing assembly line, used by Henry Ford in the early 20th century to speed automobile manufacturing. When the assembly of a car was broken into several steps, each worker could specialize in one particular assembly step. Because all workers were specialists, they could work more efficiently than if they each had to assemble cars from start to finish.

Instead of assembling cars, the CPU pipeline executes instructions one piece at a time. The CPU designer breaks each instruction into discrete steps that can be executed independently. Each step is accompanied by special-purpose hardware dedicated to that step in the pipeline. The specialized hardware is referred to as an execution unit (sometimes a *supersalar* unit). What the pipeline is to the assembly line, the execution unit is to the worker.

The similarity to the assembly line ends there, however. Different instructions require different stages, and some instructions take longer to execute than others. An instruction pipeline would be something like an assembly line that assembles

---

16. Technically, it was the 8088—the 8-bit version of the 8086.

cars, trucks, bicycles, and airplanes on a single line. We call the time it takes for an instruction to go through the pipeline the instruction *latency*.

Each stage of a pipeline completes in one CPU clock, so a CPU with a 20-stage pipeline can require up to 20 clock cycles to complete a single instruction. This seems like a lot until you consider that the CPU can work on 20 instructions at the same time, so the net *throughput* can be one instruction per clock. This theoretical maximum throughput is rarely achieved due to pipeline *stalls.*

A pipeline stall occurs most often as a result of a conditional branch instruction. By the time the branch instruction and its condition have been decoded, there can be several instructions behind it in the pipeline. These instructions may be discarded as a result of the branch. In this case, the throughput drops because the pipeline must be filled before the CPU starts executing instructions again. The depth of the pipeline determines how much of a penalty this will be, as illustrated in Figure 9-3.

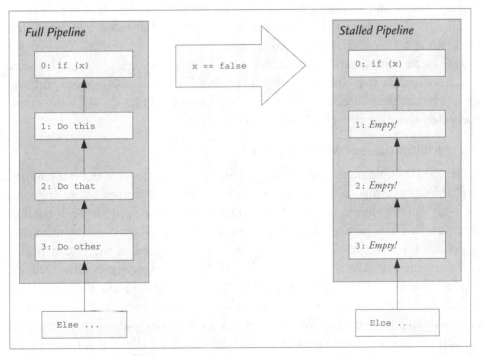

FIGURE 9-3   Simplified Four-Stage Pipeline Stall: When the CPU Knows That x Is False, All the Other Stages of the Pipeline Must Be Flushed and Refilled

Pipeline stalls are unavoidable; you can't write code without `if` statements. Many CPUs come with features that try to minimize the effects of branching, but the results will vary based on the application. In general, the pipeline allows the processor to achieve peak instruction throughput in bursts. In real-world applications, that throughput cannot be sustained.

A common feature of RISC processors is that they have low instruction latencies, requiring short instruction pipelines compared with CISC processors. This means that RISC processors should not suffer as badly from a pipeline stall as CISC processors do. This is one reason why IA32 processors have faster clocks than comparable RISC processors. A deeper pipeline requires a faster clock to keep the latency low in terms of nanoseconds. But sometimes, to make the clocks faster, it's necessary to make the pipeline deeper. It's a vicious cycle.

Cache

I discussed cache in detail in Chapter 5, so I won't dwell on it here. This is an important feature that enables processors to go faster than the DRAM otherwise would allow. Cache allows the core to operate at a very high clock frequency that today's DRAM technology is not capable of.

Because cache is so integral to performance, it's important to understand how the cache is allocated in a multicore design to predict how well your application will perform. The cache architecture of a multicore design could be the deciding factor for you when choosing one chip over another.

9.4.1.2   Multiprocessor Motherboard

The oldest SMP implementation places two or more processors on the same motherboard. The processors use a common FSB, RAM, and north bridge (refer to Figure 9-1), which presents many design challenges. For one thing, it tends to limit the speed of the FSB bus because of the signal-quality issues associated with having many devices on a common bus. As a result, the FSB speed of the fastest multiprocessor systems typically is slower than that of the fastest single-processor systems.

AMD's Opteron CPUs have integrated DRAM controllers on the CPU that allow each CPU on a multiprocessor motherboard to have high-speed access to its own DRAM. In addition, the Opteron replaces the FSB bus with a Hypertransport bus, which is a packet-based point-to-point interface. This eliminates many of the signal-quality issues that exist with a traditional FSB and allows AMD to place many more CPUs on a single motherboard. The drawback to this approach is that unlike FSB speed, which varies all over the map, the Hypertransport bus speed stays constant until the next version of the standard is published. Hypertransport is a published standard that other chip vendors design to, so changes to the standard are infrequent. Likewise, the integrated DRAM controller on the Opteron tends to lag the latest DRAM technology, because adopting a new memory technology requires a new CPU design.

As you can see, each approach has advantages and drawbacks.

9.4.1.3   Symmetric Multithreading (SMT)

This is the generic Linux term for Intel's Hyperthreading feature found in some Pentium and Xeon processors. A processor with Hyperthreading looks like a multiple-core CPU to the operating system. These are not true multicore machines, because the SMT CPUs share most of the on-chip resources and, therefore, contend with one another for them.

Each logical processor has its own register set and instruction pipeline, but that's about it. The processors share the on-chip cache, MMU, TLB, and all the execution units. The upshot of this is that two logical cores, for example, cannot process instructions twice as fast as two single-core processors.

SMT is an opportunity for parallelism unique to CISC processors. Because the pipeline is deeper on a CISC processor, the effect of a pipeline stall is more drastic than on a RISC processor, which has a shorter pipeline. Providing multiple pipelines in the form of multiple logical CPUs is one way to keep the execution units busy in the presence of a pipeline stall.

Hyperthreading (and SMT) got its name because it is most effective at accelerating multithreaded software. Threads, unlike processes, share memory and page table entries, which makes them ideal for distributing across logical CPUs. Because there is only one MMU on an SMT CPU, threads experience more of a performance boost than processes do.

9.4.1.4   Multicore CPUs

CPU vendors say they have reached the limit of how fast they can make a single CPU run in terms of clock frequency. The problem is largely with the amount of heat the fast processors produce. When multiple cores are used, the chip can run at a lower clock frequency but execute more code in the same number of clocks. A dual-core CPU can run with a slower clock but still claim to be faster than a single-core CPU running at a faster clock rate.

By the time you read this book, multicore CPUs should be available for almost every architecture. To keep the discussion simple, I will refer exclusively to the Intel-architecture implementations from AMD and Intel. The issues addressed by both manufacturers apply to all architectures and should provide a good basis of understanding.

The first generation of multicore CPUs from Intel and AMD are dual core. Functionally, a dual-core CPU is equivalent to two single-core CPUs (for example, on a multiprocessor motherboard). Each core has its own registers, cache, instruction pipeline, execution units, MMU, and so on. A dual-core processor should, in principle, perform as well as an SMP system with two single-core processors running at the same clock frequency.

Future dual-core and quad-core CPUs will share the on-chip cache at some level, which has drawbacks and advantages. On one hand, it limits the amount of cache a single CPU can access without contending with another CPU. On the other hand, sharing the cache cuts down on the number of cycles used to synchronize separate caches. So some applications will benefit from sharing cache across multiple processors, and some will suffer. There is no simple answer as to which is the better approach.

9.4.2   Programming on an SMP Machine

Most applications never need to know that they are running on a machine with multiple CPUs. Most of the details are dealt with in hardware and the operating system. The operating system is responsible for distributing tasks and balancing the load across CPUs. There are some applications, however, in which user space should be aware of the number and types of CPUs to make most efficient use of the hardware.

9.4.2.1   Linux Scheduler and SMP

Linux introduced SMP in version 2.0 of the kernel. The SMP scheduler tries to distribute tasks and threads efficiently across CPUs, making the most effective use of the hardware. The heuristics involved are based on several assumptions, the most basic of which is that all CPUs are equal. Indeed, that's what the *symmetric* in *Symmetric Multiprocessing* means.

This assumption is being challenged by innovations such as SMT and multicore processors. In advanced multiprocessor architectures, it is often left up to the application to understand the nature of the hardware and clue in the scheduler.

The SMP scheduler tends to keep the process on the same CPU, because (thanks to lazy TLB flushes) there is a good probability that it will be able to reuse TLBs. In fact, with an SMT CPU, this is a waste, because both logical CPUs use the same MMU and cache. This could mean that a process will be forced to wait for one CPU because the scheduler thinks it will be more costly to queue the process on the other CPU.

One of the ways that user applications can give the scheduler a clue is via the *affinity mask.* The scheduler maintains an affinity mask for each process (and thread) in the system. It is a bitmap with 1 bit for each CPU in the system. The default affinity mask is all ones, which means that any processor may execute the process.

When the scheduler finds a task in the runnable state, it checks to see which CPUs are available to execute code. Then it compares this against the affinity mask of the process to determine which CPU will execute the process. You can restrict a process to executing on one or more processors by setting the affinity mask appropriately.

As the kernel matures, the scheduler catches up to the technology. In Linux 2.6.7, the scheduler added support for SMT[17] in addition to SMP. So presumably, the scheduler can make smarter choices when it comes to choosing CPUs for execution.

9.4.2.2   Using Affinity to Force a Process to Use a Particular CPU

The `schedutils` package includes the `taskset` command, which can be used to set the affinity mask for a particular process. It can be applied to a running process or a single command. You can use the `taskset` command, for example, to force a process to run only on the first processor of an SMP system by setting bit 0 of the affinity mask and no others:

```
$ taskset 1 ./myprogram                    Set the affinity mask to 1.
```

You can use `taskset` to set or examine the affinity mask on running processes as well as by using the `-p` option:

```
$ taskset -p 1234
pid 1234's current affinity mask: 1
```

Linux allows any user to inspect the affinity mask of any process, but only `root` can change the affinity mask of a process, regardless of who owns it.

---

17. Available under *Processor Type and Features* in the kernel configuration menu.

9.4.2.3   When and Why to Modify Process Affinity

Whenever possible, it is preferable to leave the affinity mask alone and leave scheduling up to the Linux scheduler. Hard-coding process affinity into an application is likely to embed many assumptions in your design. Most likely, the code will run fine on whatever target you are testing on but may be suboptimal on a newer or different architecture.

Changing the affinity mask is called for in only a few circumstances. One example would be if you have a memory-intensive application that you want to keep on a single processor. Although the Linux scheduler tries to keep this on a single CPU, there is no guarantee that it will stay on one CPU. If you have two such processes running on a dual-CPU system, it may make sense to lock them down on individual processors.

Another good use of affinity would be when you have dedicated hardware, such as an embedded computer. In this case, the underlying hardware is well understood beforehand, and the code running on the computer is under full control of the system designers. Using affinity can be an excellent way to make sure that the underlying hardware is utilized most efficiently.

9.4.2.4   Process Affinity API

Processes and threads can inspect and modify their affinity mask via system calls defined for this purpose, but they, too, must have root privileges to change the affinity mask. A process can inspect the affinity mask of itself or another process by using the following GLIBC extensions:

```
int sched_setaffinity(pid_t  pid,  size_t setsize,  cpu_set_t *cpuset);
int sched_getaffinity(pid_t  pid,  size_t setsize,  cpu_set_t *cpuset);
```

These functions return 0 for success and –1 when there is an error. The cpu_set_t is the bit mask I discussed earlier, and the setsize parameter is the size of the mask. cpu_set_t is defined to provide a bit mask that allows many more CPUs than can fit in an unsigned long. As a result, you need special macros to set and clear the bits in this mask. These are defined as follows:

```
CPU_ZERO(p)     - Clears the mask pointed to by p.
CPU_SET(n,p)    - Sets the bit for CPU n in mask pointed to by p.
CPU_CLR(n,p)    - Clears the bit for CPU n in the mask pointed to by p.
CPU_ISSET(n,p)  - Returns nonzero when bit n of the mask pointed to by p is set.
```

To call one of the `setaffinity` functions, you must use these macros to initialize a `cpu_set_t`. The process must have root privileges; otherwise, the function will return an error. These functions should not be used for threads. GLIBC provides extensions to the POSIX `pthreads` API for this purpose.

9.4.2.5 Thread Affinity API

The GNU Native POSIX Threads Library (NPTL) contains functions to support thread affinity. With these functions, you can restrict a running thread to one or more CPUs in the system. This can be helpful for maximizing performance by keeping threads that use common memory on one CPU, which could help reduce cache misses.

The POSIX `pthreads` standard does not currently accommodate affinity, so the functions in NPTL are extensions, as indicated by the _np (non-POSIX) suffix. These functions are defined as follows:

```
int pthread_setaffinity_np(pthread_t tid, size_t setsize, cpu_set_t *cpuset);
int pthread_setaffinity_np(pthread_t tid, size_t setsize, cpu_set_t *cpuset);
```

The functions above require a running thread, given by `tid`, to operate correctly. To affect the currently running thread, the caller can pass the return value of `pthread_self` as the value for `tid`. If you want to initialize the affinity *before* the thread is launched, you can do this via the thread attributes. Given a properly initialized `pthread_attr_t` object, you can set the affinity with the following functions:

```
int pthread_attr_setaffinity_np(pthread_attr_t *attr, size_t setsize, cpu_set_t *cpuset);
int pthread_attr_getaffinity_np(pthread_attr_t *attr, size_t setsize, cpu_set_t *cpuset);
```

Note that these functions do not take a thread ID as an argument. The caller provides the storage for `attr` and uses it as an argument to `pthread_create`. The thread created will have the affinity mask set to the value set in the attributes.

9.5 Summary

This chapter covered the basics of performance monitoring and tuning. It also covered some basic concepts of multiprocessing (SMP) and things you can do to tune your applications to make the most of multiprocessor and multicore machines.

9.5.1   Performance Issues in This Chapter

- Bus contention—I looked at some example architectures based on PCI and illustrated what to look out for to identify bus contention in your system.

- Interrupts—I examined the interrupt architecture of the typical PC and explored some of the interrupt-related issues that software encounters.

- Memory, page faults, swapping—I described how these issues affect your application and how to measure them.

9.5.2   Terms Introduced in This Chapter

- Affinity—a technique used by the operating system to lock a process to a sub-set of the CPUs in a multiprocessor system

- Multicore—a chip with more than one CPU

- Multiprocessor—a computer with more than one CPU

- SMP, SMT (Symmetric Multiprocessing, Symmetric Multithreading)—terms used to describe an operating system that runs on a multiprocessor machine

9.5.3   Tools Used in This Chapter

- `gprof`, `gcov`—used to help optimize code at the source level

- OProfile—a powerful system tool (I demonstrated how it can be used to help optimize applications)

- `strace`, `ltrace`—used to monitor code behavior with minimum invasiveness

- `time`, `top`, `vmstat`, `iostat`, `mpstat`—used to identify memory issues and system throughput issues

9.5.4   Online Resources

- http://sourceforge.net/projects/procps—the home page for the `procps` project, which provides many useful tools for tracking process and system resources

- http://sourceforge.net/projects/strace—the home page for the `strace` project

9.5.5   References

- Dowd, K., and C. Severance. *High Performance Computing, RISC Architectures, Optimization & Benchmarks.* Sebastopol, Calif.: O'Reilly Media, Inc., 1998.

Chapter 10

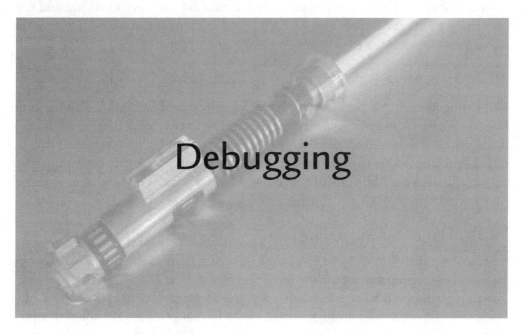

Debugging

10.1   Introduction

This chapter explores some of the most common debugging tools and techniques for Linux.

Once upon a time, there were no debuggers to speak of, and programmers relied almost exclusively on printed messages to the terminal. In some embedded environments today, there is not enough memory or CPU power to do anything else. This technique is always valuable, no matter what the environment is. In this chapter, I discuss some techniques to use printed messages effectively.

I also present a detailed look at the features of the gdb debugger by example. Although a few excellent GUIs are available that enhance gdb's functionality, the text interface is still exceptionally powerful and full featured. Unfortunately, the GUIs do not expose all the capabilities of gdb. Many programmers never take the time to learn this interface, which is still available in the GUI versions.

In this chapter, I compare several tools available for memory checking and discuss the features and limitations of each. Finally, I present some unconventional techniques that you can use when other debugging techniques fail.

10.2   The Most Basic Debugging Tool: printf

Many programmers fall back on `printf` debugging out of laziness. When the code is small, it often is easier to type a couple of `printf` statements than to bring up a debugger, set breakpoints, and peek at variables. In an embedded system, it may be difficult or impossible to run the code under a debugger. In this environment, a printed message may be your only method of debugging. This is also how kernel developers do most of their debugging, by the way.

10.2.1   Problems with Using printf

The first problem with using `printf` is the clutter it leads to. If you rely on `printf` exclusively, you probably are adding `printf` statements in several places in the code. Most programmers are loath to remove a useful message after it has served its purpose; there's always a chance that it will come in handy again. A thoughtful programmer might at least comment out the message so that it doesn't clutter the screen, but more often than not, these messages scroll by on the screen at an alarming rate.

Cluttering the code with messages (even if they're commented out) can distract programmers who may be trying to understand the code and fix bugs. Cluttering the screen with messages alarms and confuses unsuspecting users and programmers alike. Worse, it can affect performance.

10.2.1.1   Performance Effects of Using printf

Depending on the output device you are using, a `printf` statement can affect your code's performance. Pseudoterminals go a long way toward sheltering you from this impact. When your code prints to an X terminal, chances are that it's writing to a deep pipe:

```
$ time od -v /dev/zero -N200000
                              Many, many lines later . . .
0606440 000000 000000 000000 000000 000000 000000 000000 000000
0606460 000000 000000 000000 000000 000000 000000 000000 000000
0606500

real    0m1.257s
user    0m0.052s
sys     0m0.092s
```

This command took 1.257 seconds to execute, which is misleading. Because it ran on an X terminal, the actual time it took for all the data to scroll by was a bit longer than the runtime of the program. Because of buffering in the pseudoterminal, the text continues to scroll by after the program has terminated. The same command redirected to `/dev/null` runs much faster:

```
$ time od -v /dev/zero -N200000 > /dev/null

real    0m0.059s
user    0m0.048s
sys     0m0.012s
```

Although this is an extreme example, the point is that text output, in any form, affects your performance.

10.2.1.2   Synchronization Issues with printf

When I looked at IPC in Chapter 7, I discussed the issue of buffering. When the program printout is directed at the screen, you take it for granted that the text appears when the code is run. This generally is true for any short message that ends with a newline, but this behavior usually changes when the output is redirected to another device. Consider this simple example:

```
for (i = 0; i < 3; i++) {
    printf("Hello World\n");
    sleep(1);
}
```

When you run this command, you see `Hello World` printed once per second for 3 seconds. Now pretend that this is a program you are debugging, and you want to save the output to a file while you are watching it. The tool for this is the `tee` command, which allows you to do exactly that. But there's a surprise in store:

```
$ ./hello | tee hello.out
```

You should see nothing for 3 seconds, followed by three lines of `Hello World`. If you were expecting your messages to show up when the `printf` statement was executed, you would be wrong. The problem is that the C standard library uses streams built on top of plain file descriptors. These streams are used for standard I/O and any file that uses a `FILE*` pointer. The C library maintains a buffer for each stream and uses different buffering strategies based on whether or not the output is a terminal. When the output is a terminal, file streams use what is called *line buffering*. This causes the stream to defer writing characters to the device until a newline is encountered. Then all the characters up to and including the newline are printed. Because most messages you print to the screen have a newline, this fools you into thinking that your `printf` statements will be synchronous all the time. When the output is not a terminal, characters are not sent to the device until the buffer is full or the program explicitly flushes the buffer with `fflush`.

10.2.1.3   Buffering and C File Streams

It is always more efficient to send characters to a device in blocks of characters rather than one character at a time. The user-space buffers allow the driver to send characters to the output device in blocks. Because terminal devices are often character devices, they do not have buffering the way a block device (such as a disk) does. The user-space buffer is a workaround for this.

Buffering doesn't always work well with terminals, because humans expect to see their output immediately when they press a key, rather than after they type some number of bytes. To accommodate this, the C library allows the buffering strategy to be tuned to the type of device attached to the file stream. C file streams allow three basic strategies that can be selected with the `setvbuf` function, which is defined as follows:

```
int setvbuf(FILE *stream, char *buf, int mode, size_t size);
```

The `stream` argument tells the function which stream you want to modify—for example, `stdout`. The `buf` and `size` arguments allow you to provide your own buffer for streaming purposes. There are some applications for which this is desirable, but it's easiest to allow the C library to allocate the buffer for you. To use the defaults, you can pass `NULL` for the `buf` and `0` for the `size`. The interesting argument, however, is the `mode` argument, which takes one of three values:

- `_IONBF`—unbuffered. No buffering is done on the stream. Characters are written one at a time.

- `_IOLBF`—line buffered. Characters are buffered up to the first newline character.

- `_IOFBF`—fully buffered. Characters are buffered until the buffer is full.

The default behavior of `stdout` is to use line buffering (`_IOLBF`) when it is attached to a terminal. When you redirect `stdout` to a file or a pipe (as I did above), the behavior changes to fully buffered (_IOFBF). Most of the time, this is what you want. The penalties you pay for writing to the terminal are diminished by the use of buffering.

If you really want to force your printouts to be synchronous, you have a couple of choices. One option is to force buffering back to line-buffering mode with setvbuf as follows:

```
setvbuf(stdout,NULL,_IOLBF,0);
```

You also could turn off buffering altogether with _IONBF, but either way, you force your code to run slower than it would with buffering. This is true even if you redirect to /dev/null. It's not due to a bug in /dev/null; the fact is that turning off buffering causes your code to make more system calls—specifically, write calls. So intuitively, fully buffered streams are faster than line-buffered streams because they require fewer system calls, regardless of the device. Likewise, a line-buffered stream is faster than an unbuffered stream because it also requires fewer system calls.

A second option to force synchronous output is to flush the buffer manually using the fflush command. The advantage of this is that you can target specific printouts for flushing and take advantage of buffering at other times. You may want to print a message when a counter hits a certain value and see it instantly, for example. A single fflush call in this case is a good solution. The disadvantage of fflush is that it adds more lines of code and clutter.

10.2.1.4   Buffering and File Systems

In addition to the user-space buffers that the C library provides, the file system maintains buffers in the kernel. Figure 10-1 shows a diagram of where the buffers reside and the library calls that move the data among them. Note that flushing the user-space buffer with fflush does not flush the file-system buffer. The data is not written to disk until the system determines that it needs to write it or the application calls fsync.

When the program you are using to view the file runs on the same system where the file is written, this is not a big issue. The file-system cache is visible to every process on the system, so every process in the system sees the data just as though it had been written to disk. It just may not have been written to the physical media yet.

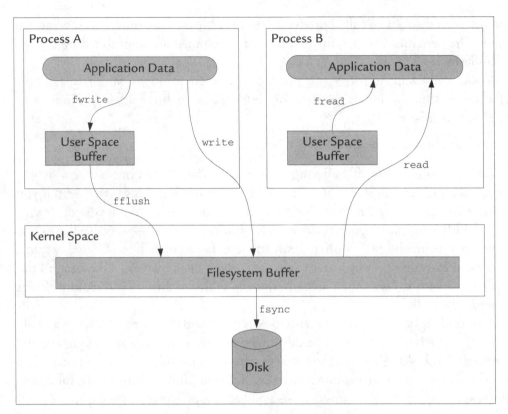

FIGURE 10-1   I/O Buffering Overview

File-system buffering can be a problem when you are looking at a file from a different computer. Perhaps the media resides on a remote NFS server. In this case, what you see is only as up to date as the most recent write to the media. Data sitting in the file-system cache on another client is not visible to you. This sort of problem is an issue only in very specific circumstances, but when it happens, you can force updates to the file system with the `fsync` and `fdatasync` functions, which are defined as follows:

```
int fsync(int fd);
int fdatasync(int fd);
```

Both functions force the user data to be written from the file-system cache to the device. Both block the caller until the device driver indicates that the data has been

written to the device.[1] The difference is that fdatasync writes the only user data
to the device, whereas fsync updates the file-system metadata as well.

Note that these functions take a file descriptor, not a file stream, as an argument,
so these functions do not replace the fflush or setvbuf calls for file streams but
are required in addition to them. You can get the file descriptor for any C file stream
with the fileno function. One pattern to follow is as follows:

```
printf("Hello World\n");
fflush(stdout);                          Flush the file stream buffer (in user space); must be done first.
fsync(fileno(stdout));                   Flush the file-system buffer (in kernel space).
```

It is interesting to note that fread does not behave as you might expect based on
Figure 10-1. GLIBC does not use the user-space buffer as a cache in the traditional
sense; it is used only to coalesce reads and writes so that the underlying system calls
use larger blocks. Although it is possible to get stale data from the buffer, you can
prevent this by calling fseek before calling fread, which will cause fread to
refresh the data in the buffer.

10.2.2   Using printf Effectively

Based on the previous discussion, perhaps one of the most important things to
know about using printf is knowing when not to use it. If you can't avoid it, you
can at least turn it off when you don't need it.

10.2.2.1   Preprocessor Help

The C preprocessor can be very helpful for formatting and controlling debug messages. One useful pattern is to wrap calls to printf in a macro, which can be used
to cut down on clutter and also allows you remove the messages easily when they're
not needed. For example:

```
#ifdef DEBUG
#define DEBUGMSG(...) printf(__VA_ARGS__)      /* Uses a C99 / GNU extension */
#else
#define DEBUGMSG /* nop */
#endif
```

---

1. Devices such as hard drives have internal cache as well, which may not be flushed when this function
    returns. There is no standard way to control the drive's internal cache.

Using variable argument lists in macros began as a GNU extension but was adopted by the C99 standard as well. If you are using a non-GNU compiler or one that does not support C99 extensions, there is a more clumsy alternative syntax that gives you the effect of variable argument lists:

```
#define DEBUGMSG(msg) printf msg        /* Caller passes in the parentheses. */

/* Only works like this ... */
DEBUGMSG(("Hello World %d\n",123));    /* becomes printf("Hello World %d\n",123);
*/
```

Note the double parentheses enclosing the arguments. The inner parentheses become part of the macro argument, which is why they are left off in the definition. This is a bit awkward, a bit ugly, and hard to explain, but it is a useful substitute for variable argument lists in macros.

Wrapping `printf` calls in a macro also allows you to hide much ugliness that can otherwise be useful. You can include a filename and line number in each message as follows:

```
#define DEBUGMSG(fmt,...) printf("%s %d " fmt, __FILE__,__LINE__, ## __VA_ARGS__)
```

The double pound sign, used in this context, is another GNU-only extension. Normally, this is used for string concatenation inside a macro, but in this context, GNU assigns a different meaning. When used with __VA_ARGS__ it strips the trailing comma for you when you use the macro with a format string that takes no arguments. That is, if __VA_ARGS__ is empty, `gcc` will remove the trailing comma for you. Without this extension, you would be required to provide at least one argument even when the format strings take no arguments.

Note that the format string `"%s %d"` is concatenated with the `fmt` argument by the C compiler—not the C preprocessor. Concatenating fixed strings like this has been a feature of C since the original ANSI (1989) standard.

Quick and Dirty Preprocessor Tricks

Here are some of my favorite `printf` tricks using the C preprocessor.

Printing Variables to the Screen with Minimal Typing

```
#define PHEX(x)printf("%#10x %s\n", x, #x)
...
PHEX(foo);
PHEX(bar);
PHEX(averylongname);
```

The trick here is using the # character to wrap a macro argument in quotes. The preprocessor expands arguments that are preceded with a # by enclosing this in quotes. This can save some typing. The following line

```
PHEX(averylongname);
```

expands to

```
printf("%#10x %s\n", averylongname, "averylongname");
```

The other trick is to put the values in a fixed-width field on the left. I find that the output is much easier to read, because the variable names can vary all over the map but the values always line up. For example:

```
       0x1 foo
       0x2 bar
0xdeadbeef averylongname
```

I used hexadecimal in this example, but you can use this trick for whatever format you like. The magic is on the right side of the format string.

Inline Synchronization

Based on the earlier discussion of synchronization, it's possible to wrap this ugliness in a macro to cut down on clutter. One solution could look like this:

```
#define DEBUGMSG(...) \
        do { \
        printf(__VA_ARGS__);\
        fflush(stdout);\
        } while(0)
```

You can stuff anything you need to in this block of code. If this block of code grows over time, it may start to affect the size of your code. It may be time to create a function instead.

Using do / while(0) in macros

This pattern is used extensively in the Linux kernel source. When a macro contains more than one statement, it is dangerous to define it without enclosing braces. Suppose that you want to print a message before exiting. The following simple macro is syntactically correct but defective:

```
#define EXITMSG(msg)   printf(msg); exit(EXIT_FAILURE)
```

This will compile fine, but a typical use case is likely to behave incorrectly. Consider this example:

```
if ( x != 0 ) EXITMSG("x is not zero\n");
```

The resulting code after preprocessing is equivalent to this:

```
if ( x != 0 ) printf("x is not zero\n");
exit(EXIT_FAILURE);
```

When used this way, the exit call is unconditional. The code will always exit at this point, which clearly is not what was intended. An intuitive fix might look like the following definition:

```
#define EXITMSG(msg)   { printf(msg); exit(EXIT_FAILURE); }
```

The addition of the braces allows the macro to behave as a single statement. This works in most cases, but it still has problems in some contexts. For example:

```
if ( x != 0 )
   EXITMSG("x is not zero\n");
else
   printf("no problem\n");
```

This does not compile. After expansion, it looks like this:

```
if (x != 0)
   { printf("x is not zero\n"); exit(1); };
else                            /* Syntax error here! */
   printf("no problem\n");
```

The semicolon following the closing brace terminates the if statement. The else clause looks like a stand-alone statement to the compiler, which of course is incorrect.

The fix for this is to place the bracketed code inside a do/while statement. The behavior of the do/while block is to execute the code inside the block at least once.

The condition (following the `while` keyword) is evaluated after the block is executed. So when you use a condition of 0 (false), the block is executed once and only once. The redefined macro looks like this.

```
#define EXITMSG(msg) \
     do { printf(msg); exit(EXIT_FAILURE); } while(0)
```

The code inside the block is perfectly encapsulated so that it can be used in any context. Because the condition is a literal, the optimizer is able to omit any looping code that it otherwise would have generated.

10.2.2.2   Using a Wrapper Function

There are drawbacks to using the preprocessor exclusively to control printed output. In the most recent example, I wrapped a block of code inside a macro. This is a primitive form of function inlining. The drawback of this is that macros don't have a function signature, so there is no argument checking in the macro. Any syntax errors that occur while calling one of these macros can produce misleading error messages.

The alternative is to wrap this code in a function. This may be unattractive on some architectures because of the increase in overhead due to function calls. This drawback is minimized thanks to the `inline` keyword supported in C++, C99, and `gcc` in general. An *inline function* is a function that isn't actually called. Instead, each time the compiler encounters a call to an inline function, it places the compiled instructions at that spot in the code. In effect, the function produces the same code that the macro produces, except that now there are function signature for enhanced error checking and warnings. Inlining saves the overhead of a function call but increases the code size because the compiled instructions appear many times in the object file instead of only once. For this reason, inlining is treated as a compiler hint (not a directive). The optimizer is free to use its own heuristics to decide when inlining is beneficial.[2]

The second hurdle to overcome using a wrapper function is variable argument lists. The `printf` function uses a variable argument list to support formatted strings

---

2.   `gcc` does not use inlining unless compiled using `-O3` or explicitly directed via the `-finline-functions` option.

that can take any number of arguments. The API for using variable arguments is defined in `stdarg.h`. A simple wrapper can look like this:

```
inline int myprintf( const char *fmt, ... )
{
    int n;
    va_list ap;                    va_list holds the information needed for the API.
    va_start(ap, fmt);             Indicate where the variable arguments start (i.e.. after fmt).
    n = vprintf(fmt,ap);           vprintf takes a format string and a va_list.
    va_end(ap);                    Must call this before exiting the function.
    return n;
}
```

This function adds no value but illustrates how to use variable arguments to create your own `printf` wrapper. The key is that the underlying functions you are calling must take a `va_list` as an argument. The C standard library contains equivalents for virtually all the `printf`-like functions. You can recognize these by the fact that they all begin with v: `vprintf`, `vsprintf`, `vfprintf`, and so on.

Creating a function wrapper for `printf` has the drawback of disabling type checking for the variable arguments. You don't have this problem with a macro, because in all the examples, the format string is a string literal and is never stored in a variable. So the expanded macro contains a call to `printf` with the format in a string literal and all the arguments. As you shall see, GNU provides an extension to get around this drawback.

`printf` is the exception when it comes to checking variable arguments. Normally, the compiler cannot make any assumptions about the type or number of arguments in a variable argument list. In a `printf` call, these can be inferred from the format string. The `gcc` compiler has the ability to parse literal format strings and check them against the variable arguments for correctness. `vprintf` and other `stdarg`-friendly functions cannot check format strings because they take only a `va_list` to hold the arguments to the format string. What's more, in `myprintf`, you pass a string variable to `vprintf` instead of a string literal, so the compiler is unable to parse the format string.

GNU allows you to apply `printf` format checking to any function by using the `__attribute__` directive. This syntax is the same used in `stdio.h` for `printf` and friends. For `myprintf`, you could add the attribute to the function prototype as follows:

```
inline int myprintf( const char *fmt, ... )
        __attribute__ ((format (printf, 1, 2)));
```

The __attribute__ directive is a general-purpose directive. This instance specifically tells the compiler that the function follows the printf formatting rules and that the format string is in argument 1, with the first format argument starting at argument 2. Note that the __attribute__ directive is available only on GNU compilers and is not standard; therefore, it is not portable to other compilers.

10.2.2.3   Don't Ignore the printf Format Warnings

The addition of format warnings to printf is useful, but unfortunately, the majority of these warnings are portability issues and not necessarily bugs. One of the most common warnings you will see involves mismatched integer types, which look like the following:

```
warning: int format, long int arg (arg 2)
warning: long unsigned int format, int arg (arg 2)
```

The C standard is vague on how big an int or a long should be, so these messages are cautious. In fact, with gcc virtually all 32-bit architectures use the same size for long and int. Because printf uses variable arguments, the compiler promotes all small integral values to int and all floating-point values to double. So although printf has format support for these other types, there is no danger of seeing the wrong value in the output due to the argument size.

There are warnings you should pay attention to, however; they could be embedded in the noise from these earlier warnings. There are data-type mismatches that will garble your output or possibly crash your program.

64-Bit Types

The off_t type, for example, is used in the POSIX APIs such as lseek and mmap. It can be either a 32-bit size or a 64-bit size, depending on compiler flags. By default, you get a 32-bit type, but GNU allows you to replace off_t with a 64-bit type by compiling with the flag

```
-D_FILE_OFFSET_BITS=64
```

When a 64-bit type appears as an argument to an integer or long integer format, the output will not be correct. Worse, because the size is different, subsequent arguments will also be incorrect or could even cause your application to crash. The warning in this case differs in different versions of gcc:

```
gcc 3.x: warning: int format, different type arg
gcc 4.x: warning: format '%x' expects type 'unsigned int', but argument 2 has type 'off_t'
```

This warning is relevant whether you are compiling on 64-bit or 32-bit architectures. The type `long long` has been used by `gcc` and other compilers to represent 64-bit types on 32-bit architectures. The format for a `long long` type is `ll`, for example:

```
printf("%lld\n", x);
```

The situation is a bit messy. On x86_64 architectures, `gcc` recognizes both `long` and `long long` as 64-bit types. And wouldn't you know, `printf` requires the format to match the type, even though the types are the same size. On IA32, for example, `gcc` implements C99's `int64_t` type as a `long long`, but on x86_64, `gcc` uses type `long`. So to build on IA32 without warnings, a `printf` format requires `"%lld"`, whereas the same code compiled on x86_64 requires `"%ld"`.

Floating-Point Types

Mixing floating-point and integer types is just as dangerous as mixing 64-bit and 32-bit types. That's because the double type is 64 bits. Interestingly though, mixing float with double arguments is not a problem, because C promotes a float to a double when it appears in a variable argument list. For the same reason, using a `float` argument to an integer format can be catastrophic, because the `float` is promoted to `double`, and integer arguments are all 32-bits. Again the warning is slightly different in different versions of `gcc`:

```
gcc 3.x: warning: int format, double arg (arg 2)
gcc 4.x: warning: format '%d' expects type 'int', but argument 2 has type 'double'
```

Note that in both cases, the actual argument was `float`, but the compiler warning takes into account the fact that the compiler promotes it to `double`.

String Types

String types are perhaps the most likely sources of error, because they take pointers as arguments, and pointers can go wrong in so many ways. Again, the warning varies from one release to the next of `gcc`:

```
gcc 3.x: warning: format argument is not a pointer (arg 2)
gcc 3.x: warning: char format, different type arg (arg 2)
gcc 4.x: warning: format '%s' expects type 'char *', but argument 2 has type 'int'
gcc 4.x: warning: format '%s' expects type 'char *', but argument 2 has type 'int *'
```

The code responsible for these warnings is likely to produce crashes at runtime. If you see one of these warnings, you should inspect the code and fix it. If the code is correct as is, use an explicit type cast to remove the warning.

10.2.2.4   Tips for Creating Good Debug Messages

A formatting convention can give you indication at a glance of what is going on without requiring you to read every line of printout.

Use an Easily Recognizable Format

Adults read by recognizing the shapes of words, not by sounding out every letter in a word. A consistent format will take advantage of this fact by giving "good" messages one shape and "bad" messages another. Consider this rubbish, which could have come from your favorite program:

```
 debug>   The  LAST  time I  cHecked,   the DVD drive is  within   DEfined
tolerances.
 Relax,   THE hard   drive  is  runniNg.
 -- The   USB   port   is  not  In   flames.
It's  a good thing   that  the pcI  bus is  running.
 I'm optimistic   because the  usb  port is better.
 Don't paNic, but   the DVd  Drive is going tO  explode.
  The   last  time   I  checKed,  THE   heap  is   OptImal.

 debug> The  moUse IS  not   in   flames.

 *** EverythinG's  fine, I checked anD the memory is   running   at  full   speed.
```

The same text, using a uniform format, easily highlights the errors, no matter how silly:

```
info - The last time I checked, the DVD drive is within defined tolerances.
info - Relax, the hard drive is running.
info - The USB port is not in flames.
info - It's a good thing that the PCI bus is running.
info - I'm optimistic because the USB port is better.
**** ERROR - Don't panic, but the DVD drive is going to explode.
info - The last time I checked, the heap is optimal.
info - The mouse is not in flames.
info - Everything's fine, I checked and the memory is running at full speed.
```

Creating your own `printf` wrapper is ideal for enforcing predictable formats in your output. It can't help you separate the relevant from the irrelevant information, though.

One Line Per Message

Messages can get cryptic when you try to squeeze them on a single line, but there are advantages to doing so. If your program dumps a great deal of printout to a file, for example, you can use a simple `grep` command to look for particular messages.

If the information you need is on more than one line, you may have to resort to manual inspection.

Keep Chattiness to a Minimum

It's fun to keep things lighthearted, but when chat starts to clutter the screen or worse, slow the application, it's time to cut back.

10.2.3   Some Final Words on printf Debugging

Using `printf` is not without side effects, as I have demonstrated. One side effect that I have not mentioned is inadvertent synchronization. This is more often a problem in multithreaded code but can be an issue in single-threaded code as well. Perhaps you have encountered a bug that went away when `printf` was turned on. This can happen when a strategically placed `printf` hides a race condition in a multithreaded application. In single-threaded applications, a `printf` can cause the compiler to store a float in memory that otherwise was in a register. Because floating-point registers on IA32 have higher precision than an IEEE float, the addition of a `printf` may change your numerical results, as the example in Listing 10-1 illustrates.

LISTING 10-1   side-effects.c: A Demonstration of printf Side Effects on IA32

```
 1 #include <stdio.h>
 2 #include <string.h>
 3 #include <stdlib.h>
 4 #include <math.h>
 5
 6 int main(int argc, char *argv[])
 7 {
 8     // Make argument a volatile variable. This prevents
 9     // the optimizer from taking any shortcuts.
10     volatile double arg = 7.0;
11
12     // Square root of a prime is 'irrational';
13     // i.e. digits go on forever. On IA32, x
14     // will be in an 88-bit floating point register.
15     double x = sqrt(arg);
16
17 #ifndef NOPRINT
18     // If we print it, x must be stored on the stack.
19     // double has only 64-bits so we lose precision
20     printf("x    = % 0.20f\n", x);
21 #endif
22
```

```
23        // By calling printf, we changed the value of x,
24        // which will show up as a non-zero diff.
25        volatile double diff = sqrt(arg) - x;
26        printf("diff = % 0.20f\n", diff);
27
28        if (diff == 0.0) {
29            printf("Zero diff!\n");
30        }
31        else {
32            printf("Nonzero diff!!!\n");
33        }
34 }
```

I compiled this program with gcc 4.0.1, both with and without the macro
NOPRINT defined as follows:

```
$ cc -o print    -O2            -lm side-effects.c
$ cc -o noprint  -O2 -DNOPRINT -lm side-effects.c

$ ./noprint
diff =  0.00000000000000000000
Zero diff!

$ ./print
x     =  2.64575131106459071617
diff = -0.00000000000000012577
Nonzero diff!!!
```

As the annotation in the code shows, simply calling printf changes the behavior of the program enough to change the results. It forces the compiler to store the
variable x in memory, which has less precision than the internal floating-point registers on the IA32. As a result, the value stored in x no longer is the same as what
was stored in the register.[3]

10.3   Getting Comfortable with the GNU Debugger: gdb

gdb is a text-based debugger with intuitive commands. Most Linux programmers
have had at least some experience with it. Every command can be abbreviated—
some with only one letter. More often, you need to type the first few letters of the
command. gdb needs enough letters to identify the command uniquely, so when

---

3. Assembly output can vary from one version of gcc to the next. Your results may vary. You can avoid this
    sort of error by using -ffloat-store option to gcc, which forces the compiler not to use floating-
    point registers for storage.

you don't type enough letters, gdb will give you a helpful hint. Type **sh** at the gdb prompt, for example, and you will see the following message:

```
(gdb) sh
Ambiguous command "sh": sharedlibrary, shell, show.
```

After typing a few letters, you can press Tab, which will complete the command based on the letters you have already typed, if possible. If no completion is offered, you can press Tab again to see a list of matching commands. For example:

```
(gdb) b<Tab><Tab>
backtrace   break       bt
(gdb) b
```

I typed **b**, and gdb offered backtrace, break, and bt as possible completions.[4] I return to the gdb prompt with the letters I just typed. I still need to type enough letters for gdb to identify the command unambiguously.

10.3.1   Running Your Code with gdb

When you launch gdb, you can specify your program on the command line or just start gdb and load your program. Either pattern works:

```
$ gdb ./hello  ... or

$ gdb
(gdb) file ./hello
Reading symbols from /home/john/hello...done.
```

Both commands read your file and its symbols into memory. The latter form also allows you to switch programs without exiting gdb.

At the gdb prompt, you can jump into your code with the run command, if you like. This is useful if you already know that it's going to crash. When it crashes, you can get a stack backtrace to see where the code died. More often, you want to step through the code or set a breakpoint.

Here are the basic commands you need to know for starting your code in gdb:

- set args—a special case of the set command used to pass command-line arguments. gdb stores the arguments you specify for use with subsequent calls

---

4. Note that b by itself is the abbreviation for break and that bt is the abbreviation for backtrace.

to the `run` command, although you can specify new arguments with each call to `run`. To clear the arguments after they have been set, however, you must use `set args`.

- `run`—starts the program from the beginning. The program executes with the arguments specified here or whatever was set by the most recent call to `set args`. Execution continues until the program exits, aborts, or hits a breakpoint.

- `start`—the same as `run` except that the program stops as though a breakpoint were set in `main`. This allows you to single-step from the beginning of the program.

- `step`—executes a single line of code. If the line contains a function that is compiled with debugging, `gdb` will step into that function. You must start your program with the `run` or `start` command before you can use this command.

- `next`—the same as `step` except that `gdb` will not step into functions, regardless of whether they are compiled with debugging.

- `kill`—terminates your program. This is not equivalent to the `kill` *system call*, which sends a signal to the running program. For that, see the `signal` command.

10.3.2 Stopping and Restarting Execution

You can stop a running program at any time by pressing `Ctrl+C`. This tells `gdb` to stop the currently running program but does not send the program a `SIGINT`, so you can continue program execution from where it left off. Some applications actually lend themselves to this kind of debugging without breakpoints, but most don't. For those that don't, explicit breakpoint commands are available from the `gdb` prompt.

Here are the basic commands:

- `break`, `tbreak`—set a breakpoint (`break`) or temporary breakpoint (`tbreak`). With no arguments, the commands set a breakpoint at the next instruction to be executed; more often, you specify a function or line number at which to stop. These commands also can be followed by a logical expression to create a *conditional breakpoint* (see the section "Using Conditional Breakpoints" later in this chapter).

- watch—similar to a breakpoint but uses hardware registers (if available) to monitor a particular location for a change. This can allow your program to execute much more quickly than a conventional breakpoint (see the section "Using Watchpoints" later in this chapter).

- continue—resumes program execution from where it stopped. The continue command allows an optional numeric argument (N) that tells gdb to ignore the following N-1 breakpoints. In other words, "Continue until the process hits the breakpoint for the Nth time."

- signal—sends a signal to your program and continues. The command takes a single argument, which can be the signal number or the signal name. You can see a list of signal names by typing info signal.

- info breakpoints—lists the currently active breakpoints and watches.

- delete—deletes all breakpoints. To delete a single breakpoint, use info breakpoints to get the breakpoint number, and pass that number to the delete command.

10.3.2.1   Breakpoint Syntax

The breakpoint command is abbreviated as b because it is used so frequently. The argument to the breakpoint command is always an instruction address, which can be provided in one of the following ways:

```
(gdb) b                          Break at the next instruction in the current stack frame.
(gdb) b foo                      Break at function foo.
(gdb) b foobar.c:foo             Break at function foo defined in foobar.c.
(gdb) b 10                       Break at line 10 in the current module.
(gdb) b foobar.c:10              Break at line 10 in foobar.c.
(gdb) b *0xdeadbeef              Break at address 0xdeadbeef.
```

Breakpoints can be set almost anywhere in memory. The underlying code does not need to be compiled with debug, although it helps. Listing 10-2 creates a buggy program that overruns the heap upon request.

LISTING 10-2   nasty.c: A Nasty Buggy Program

```
 1 #include <stdio.h>
 2 #include <string.h>
 3 #include <stdlib.h>
 4
 5 void *nasty(char *buf, int setlen)
 6 {
 7     // We don't check setlen! Naughty!
 8     return memset(buf, 'a', setlen);
 9 }
10
11 // Use a fixed buffer length...
12 const int buflen = 16;
13
14 int main(int argc, char *argv[])
15 {
16     char *buf = malloc(buflen);
17
18     // Default to same length as buffer
19     int len = buflen;
20     if (argc > 1)
21         // Allow command line arguments to override buffer length.
22         len = atoi(argv[1]);
23
24     // If len > buflen, then this corrupts the heap.
25     nasty(buf, len);
26
27     // Some versions of glibc detect errors here, but not always.
28     free(buf);
29
30     // Get here and everything should be okay.
31     printf("buflen=%d len=%d okay\n", buflen, len);
32     return 0;
33 }
```

You set a breakpoint on memset, which is the offending function, even though memset is part of the standard library, which is not compiled with debug. A debug session would look like this:

```
$ gdb ./nasty
GNU gdb Red Hat Linux (6.1post-1.20040607.43.0.1rh)
Copyright 2004 Free Software Foundation, Inc.
GDB is free software, covered by the GNU General Public License, and you are
welcome to change it and/or distribute copies of it under certain conditions.
Type "show copying" to see the conditions.
```

```
There is absolutely no warranty for GDB.  Type "show warranty" for details.
This GDB was configured as "i386-redhat-linux-gnu"...Using host libthread_db
library "/lib/tls/libthread_db.so.1".

(gdb) b memset
Function "memset" not defined.
Make breakpoint pending on future shared library load? (y or [n]) y

Breakpoint 1 (memset) pending.
(gdb) run 100
Starting program: /home/john/examples/ch-10/debug/nasty 100
Reading symbols from shared object read from target memory...done.
Loaded system supplied DSO at 0xffffe000
Breakpoint 2 at 0xb7e4e050
Pending breakpoint "memset" resolved

Breakpoint 2, 0xb7e4e050 in memset () from /lib/tls/libc.so.6
(gdb) bt
#0  0xb7e4e050 in memset () from /lib/tls/libc.so.6
#1  0x0804844e in nasty (buf=0x804a008 "", setlen=100) at nasty.c:8
#2  0x080484b5 in main (argc=2, argv=0xbf836564) at nasty.c:25
```

This session illustrates several concepts. First, when you load your program, the
shared libraries are not yet loaded. gdb does not recognize memset because it is part
of the standard C library, which is implemented as a shared library and has not been
loaded yet. gdb prompts you with the option of setting a *pending* breakpoint, which
means that it will look for this symbol as each shared library is loaded. When gdb
encounters the pending breakpoint in the shared library, it will set the breakpoint
you requested. If gdb never sees the symbol from the pending breakpoint (say, you
misspelled memset), you will hear nothing more from gdb about it.

You start the program by using the run command with an argument of 100,
which will cause memset to overrun the buffer. The program stops on memset as
expected, but you can't see anything useful in this stack frame because memset is
not compiled with debug. You can use the bt command (the abbreviation for
backtrace) to see the call stack. This shows you the arguments passed to the
nasty function, which called memset. This also shows the offending length that
was passed to nasty.

10.3.2.2   Using Conditional Breakpoints

You also could debug the program in Listing 10-2 by using a conditional breakpoint.
You can stop on the nasty function whenever setlen is greater than buflen, for

example. The syntax for this is to include an `if` statement after the breakpoint, as follows:

```
(gdb) b nasty if setlen > buflen
Breakpoint 1 at 0x804843e: file nasty.c, line 8.
(gdb) run 100
Starting program: /home/john/examples/ch-10/debug/nasty 100
Reading symbols from shared object read from target memory...done.
Loaded system supplied DSO at 0xffffe000

Breakpoint 1, nasty (buf=0x804a008 "", setlen=100) at nasty.c:8
8            return memset(buf, 'a', setlen);
```

You can include any address or condition in the conditional breakpoint. The only restriction is that any variables used must be in the same scope as the address of the breakpoint. The following conditional breakpoint does not work:

```
(gdb) b nasty if len > buflen
No symbol "len" in current context.
```

In this case, `len` is a local variable inside `main` and is not in scope when the `nasty` function is called, so `gdb` does not allow it. You can specify the scope explicitly by using C++-style scoping operations. The same conditional breakpoint can be set as follows:

```
(gdb) b nasty if main::len > buflen
Breakpoint 1 at 0x804845e: file nasty.c, line 8.
```

Notice that the code does not need to be written in C++ for you to use this syntax.

10.3.2.3   Setting Breakpoints with C++ Code

C++ programs can be challenging to debug. With namespaces, overloading, and templates, it can be hard to narrow down symbols for breakpoints. Fortunately, `gdb` provides some helpful shortcuts to make debugging easier.

Try debugging the program in Listing 10-3. This is particularly difficult due to the long function names, which are very similar. On top of that, the program places them all in a namespace and overloads one of them to maximize the amount of typing required. `gdb` allows tab completion of all commands and symbols, which is very helpful for cutting down the amount of typing you need to do and eliminating opportunities for typos. Unfortunately, because all the functions are in a namespace, you must know the namespace before you can use tab completion. Just typing **annoy<Tab>** will not work.

LISTING 10-3   cppsym.c: Only a C++ Programmer Could Love This

```
1  // Three inconveniently named functions
2  // wrapped inside a namespace, just to make them more annoying.
3  // And for good measure, we overload one of the functions.
4
5  namespace inconvenient {
6      void *annoyingFunctionName1(void *ptr) {
7          return ptr;
8      };
9      void *annoyingFunctionName2(void *ptr) {
10         return ptr;
11     };
12     void *annoyingFunctionName3(void *ptr) {
13         return ptr;
14     };
15     void *annoyingFunctionName3(int x) {
16         return (void *) x;
17     };
18 };
19
20 // Too bad the 'using' statement is not an option in gdb...
21 using namespace inconvenient;
22
23 int main(int argc, char *argv[])
24 {
25     annoyingFunctionName1(0);
26     annoyingFunctionName2(0);
27     annoyingFunctionName3(0);
28     annoyingFunctionName3((int) 0);
29 }
```

Because this module is so small, it's easy to see that these functions are in a namespace. In real-world examples, this is normally not the case. For those times, the info command is very helpful. For example:

```
(gdb) info function  annoy          Look for any function with the word "annoy" in it.
All functions matching regular expression "annoy":

File cppsym.cpp:
void *inconvenient::annoyingFunctionName1(void*);
void *inconvenient::annoyingFunctionName2(void*);
void *inconvenient::annoyingFunctionName3(int);
void *inconvenient::annoyingFunctionName3(void*);
```

This shows the namespace as well as all the matching function names. Now that you know the namespace, you can set a breakpoint using tab completion, but here's one more trick to know: Tab completion works for the namespace (inconvenient), but stops there, because gdb's tab completion does not include the colons that are part of the namespace. To work around this, you need to begin the function name with a single quote and then use tab completion, as follows:

```
(gdb) b 'inc<Tab><Tab>
inconvenient
inconvenient::annoyingFunctionName1(void*)
inconvenient::annoyingFunctionName2(void*)
inconvenient::annoyingFunctionName3(int)
inconvenient::annoyingFunctionName3(void*)
```

The Tab gets you as far as the first colon. Pressing Tab again shows you a list of possible matches. To get any further with tab completion, you must type the two colons by hand and then use tab completion to continue. For example:

```
(gdb) b 'incon<tab>                          becomes b 'inconvenient
(gdb) b 'inconvenient::<Tab>                  becomes b 'inconvenient::annoyingFunctionName
(gdb) b 'inconvenient::annoyingFunctionName3<Tab><Tab>
inconvenient::annoyingFunctionName3(int)
inconvenient::annoyingFunctionName3(void*)
(gdb) b 'inconvenient::annoyingFunctionName3(
```

Finally, when you picked the function you want, you must close the quotes and press Enter. The complete command would look like this:

```
(gdb) b 'inconvenient::annoyingFunctionName3(void*)'
Breakpoint 2 at 0x804836f: file cppsym.cpp, line 13.
```

Tab completion sure beats all that typing.

10.3.2.4   Using Watchpoints

Many processors come with special purpose registers to assist in breakpoint debugging. gdb makes registers available to you via the watchpoint command. A *watchpoint* allows you to stop the program whenever a specific memory location is read or written. Contrast this with a breakpoint, which takes an instruction address as an argument and stops when the code at that location is executed. Watchpoints are especially useful when you're looking for memory corruption by defective code.

gdb also implements watchpoints for architectures that don't have supporting hardware. In this case, gdb will single-step your executable and monitor the memory with each step. This causes your code to run orders of magnitude slower than normal.

To set a watchpoint to stop the program any time it changes the value of a variable named `foo`, simply use the following command:

```
(gdb) watch foo
```
Watch the value of `foo` for changes.

Beware: Watchpoints trigger only when the value in memory changes. If the initial value of `foo` is `123` and the code writes `123`, for example, this watchpoint will not trigger. Notice that the `watch` command automatically takes the address of `foo` to be used as the watchpoint. If `foo` happens to be a pointer to a location that you want to monitor, you would need to use the following syntax:

```
(gdb) watch *foo
```
Watch the location pointed to by `foo` for changes.

If you forget the asterisk, you will end up monitoring the value of the pointer! These watchpoints stop whenever the variable in the expression is modified, no matter where the program is. That means that you could wind up breaking in a module that was compiled without debugging. In this case, you can go up the stack and (ideally) find a frame that has useful debugging information.

Watchpoints can be combined with logical conditions to create conditional watchpoints. You can stop any time `foo` is written with the value `123`, as follows:

```
(gdb) watch foo if foo == 123
```

This syntax is identical to the conditional breakpoint syntax I discussed earlier in the chapter. The condition does not have to contain the value being watched. You could just as easily use an expression like this:

```
(gdb) watch foo if someflag == true
```

Any logical statement works, provided that all the scoping requirements are met when the watchpoint is hit. Because watchpoints can trigger anywhere in your code, gdb makes no assumptions about the scope of the variables in the condition statement and does not check their scope when you set the watchpoint. If a variable in the conditional expression is not in scope when the watchpoint is hit, the watchpoint simply does not trigger.

A Detailed Example Using Watchpoints

A more detailed example should illustrate the usefulness of watchpoints. Listing 10-4 contains a defective program that overruns a heap buffer, but only sometimes. This is the sort of bug that can be very hard to catch, even with a debugger.

I created a function called ovrrun that is a thin wrapper around memcpy. Because there is no bounds checking inside this function, there is opportunity to overrun the target buffer. I added a memcpy to slow things and simulate a processing-intensive program. The target buffer is allocated from the heap using buflen as a size. I artificially created a 1-in-800,000 chance of overrunning the target buffer by 1 byte. This sort of overrun often has no side effects due to the padding that the malloc function typically performs. You can detect the overrun after the fact by using strlen, but normally, that would be too late. If this were a very large overrun, it could cause the program to crash.

Without watches, your first inclination may be to set a conditional breakpoint. You can stop whenever the ovrrun function is called with a msglen greater than buflen. The syntax for this would be

```
(gdb) b ovrrun if msglen > buflen
```

This works as expected, but it is extremely slow. The reason is that *every* call to msglen causes the program to stop and transfer control to gdb. gdb examines the value of msglen and compares it with buflen each time, deciding whether to continue or stop the program. Because this program calls ovrrun 800,000 times, the overhead of this conditional breakpoint affects performance dramatically. On my 1.7 GHz P4, the overrun program takes only about 700 ms to execute when running under gdb with no breakpoints. With the conditional breakpoint set, the program takes more than 2 minutes and 17 seconds.

The same thing done with a watchpoint does not affect the code at all; the code runs as fast as it does under gdb with no watchpoints. The watchpoint is set as follows:

```
(gdb) watch buf[buflen]
```

Here, you are looking for a write to the byte at location buf+buflen, which would indicate an overrun. The reason why this is so fast is that the trigger is controlled in the processor hardware, and the processor does not generate a trigger until the write takes place. So instead of stopping the program 800,000 times, gdb stops the program only once.

Watchpoints come in three flavors:

- watch—breaks when the location is written by the program and the value changes

- rwatch—breaks when the location is read by the program

- awatch—breaks when the location is read or written by the program

gdb manages watchpoints just like breakpoints. Watchpoints are listed with the info watchpoints command, which is a synonym for info breakpoints. Just like breakpoints, watchpoints can be removed with the delete command.

LISTING 10-4   overrun.c: Defective Code Example to Illustrate Watchpoints

```
 1 #include <stdio.h>
 2 #include <string.h>
 3 #include <stdlib.h>
 4 #include <time.h>
 5
 6 // Source text for copying
 7 const char text[] = "0123456789abcdef";
 8
 9 // This function will overrun if you tell it to.
10 void ovrrun(char *buf, const char *msg, int msglen)
11 {
12     // Pointless memcpy - just to slow us down and illustrate
13     // the usefulness of watchpoints
14     char dummy[4096];
15     memset(dummy, msglen, sizeof(dummy));
16
17     // Here's the culprit...
18     memcpy(buf, msg, msglen);
19 }
20
21 // Carefullly chosen malloc size.
22 // malloc a small buffer so that space comes from the heap (not mmap).
23 // malloc will also pad the buffer, which means that a one-byte overrun
24 // should not cause the program to crash.
25 const int buflen = 13;
26
27 int main(int argc, char *argv[])
28 {
29     char *buf = malloc(buflen);
30     int i;
```

```
31
32       // Seed the random number generator so that each run is different.
33       srand(time(NULL));
34
35       // Loop count - a nice high number.
36       int n = 800000;
37
38       // We want the chance of overrun to be 1 in N just to make this hard
39       // to catch.
40       int thresh = RAND_MAX / n;
41
42       for (i = 0; i < n; i++) {
43           // Overrun if the random number is less than the threshold
44           int len = (rand() < thresh) ? buflen + 1 : buflen;
45           ovrrun(buf, text, len);
46       }
47
48       // Overrun is easy to detect but hard to catch.
49       int overran = (strlen(buf) > buflen);
50       if (overran)
51           printf("OVERRUN!\n");
52       else
53           printf("No overrun\n");
54
55       free(buf);
56       return overran;
57 }
```

10.3.3   Inspecting and Manipulating Data

gdb has very powerful features for inspecting data using only a few commands with rich syntax. Before you explore them, I'll go over the basic commands involved:

- print—provides a unique, rich formatting syntax that lets you display all types of data, such as including strings and arrays. The objects printed can be objects in memory or any valid C or C++ expression.

- x—short for *examine* and similar to the print command except that x works with memory addresses and raw data, whereas print can handle abstract expressions. Both commands accept modifiers, discussed in the next section.

- printf—just like the C function of the same name. It follows identical rules for formatting. Don't forget to include a newline in your format string unless you really don't want one.

- whatis—tells you everything gdb knows about the type of a given symbol.

- `backtrace`—shows the call stack of the current program, including local variables, if desired.

- `up`, `down`—changes the stack frame so you can examine local variables in different parts of the call stack.

- `frame`—an alternative to the `up` and `down` commands that allows you to specify exactly which frame to go to. Frames are specified using the numbers listed in the `backtrace` command.

- `info locals`—a subcommand of the `info` command that shows all the local variables in the current stack frame.

10.3.3.1   print Expression Syntax

Printing a single variable or dumping memory is done with the `print` and `x` commands. (`print` is abbreviated as `p`.) The `print` command can take almost any valid C or C++ expression as an argument,[5] whereas the `x` command takes an address as an argument and displays the memory at that address. When you use a variable as an argument to the `x` command, it is treated as an address even if the variable is not a pointer. For example:

```
(gdb) whatis foo
type = long long int
(gdb) p foo
$2 = 4096                                         The value of foo is 0x1000.
(gdb) x foo
0x1000: Cannot access memory at address 0x1000    foo is treated as an address!
(gdb) x &foo
0xbf9af240:     0x00001000                        Memory is dumped as 32-bit (default).
```

In this case, the variable `foo` is a 64-bit integer that contains the value `4096`. The `print` command works as expected, but when you pass `foo` to the `x` command, it fails, because the value of `x` in this case is an invalid address. When you use the address of `foo` as the argument, you get a dump of the memory in hexadecimal using the default word size.

Defaults are made to be changed, however, and `gdb` makes it easy to change the default behavior of these commands. Both `print` and `x` allow you to provide modifiers to change the output behavior. `x` allows you to specify a count as well. For

---

5. gdb also understands expressions in languages other than C/C++. See `info gdb languages support` for details.

both commands, gdb requires that you separate the modifiers from the command with a forward slash. For example,

```
(gdb) p/x foo                          Print foo using hexadecimal.
$2 = 0x1000
(gdb) x/d &foo                         Dump memory at location &foo in decimal.
0x22eec4:       4096
```

The complete list of modifiers is shown in Table 10-1.

TABLE 10-1   Output Modifiers for the print and x Commands

Modifier	Format	print	x
x	Hexadecimal	Yes	Yes
d	Signed decimal	Yes	Yes
u	Unsigned decimal	Yes	Yes
o	Octal	Yes	Yes
t	Binary	Yes	Yes
a	Address	Prints hexadecimal and shows its relationship to nearby symbols.	Prints hexadecimal and shows its relationship to nearby symbols.
c	Character	Least significant byte.	Dumps memory in pairs—an ASCII character with a decimal byte.
f	Floating point	Display memory as double.	Display memory in floating point, using the current word size. Use g for IEEE double and w for IEEE float on 32-bit machines.
i	Instructions	No	Disassembly memory at the given location.
s	Null-terminated ASCII string	No	Display memory as an ASCII string. Output stops at the first NUL character.

In addition, x allows you to specify the word size used when dumping memory as well as the number of words to dump. The count is specified immediately after the slash. For example:

```
(gdb) x/8bx &foo                          Dump 8 bytes in hexadecimal at address &foo.
0x22eec4:       0x00     0x10    0x00    0x00    0xd8    0xef    0x22    0x00
```

Because the x command dumps memory, it uses a fixed word size to display the data. This word size can be specified with one of the suffixes listed in Table 10-2. Here, I used x with the word size specified with the b flag. print, on the other hand, knows the size of the data from the type of the variable.

gdb remembers your modifiers for the next time you use the command, so you need only specify the modifiers once. If that's what you want to use for the remainder of the session, you do not need to specify any modifiers again. The modifiers following the count may occur in any order, so 8bx is the same as 8xb.

10.3.3.2   Print Examples

Using Table 10-1 and Table 10-2, I'll show some quick examples. I mentioned earlier in the chapter that print can take any valid C syntax as an argument. gdb also can call functions, which means that you can do some interesting things from the gdb command line:

```
(gdb) p getpid()                          Print the process ID of the current process.
$1 = 12903
(gdb) p kill(getpid(),0)                  Test to see if the process exists.
$2 = 0
(gdb) p kill(getpid(),9)                  Kill the process via the C API. (gdb will not be happy.)

Program terminated with signal SIGKILL, Killed.
The program no longer exists.
The program being debugged stopped while in a function called from GDB.
When the function (kill) is done executing, GDB will silently
stop (instead of continuing to evaluate the expression containing
the function call).
```

print uses the type of the variable it is printing to format the output, whereas x dumps memory using an explicit word size as specified by the format. You can demonstrate this with the following C variables:

```
double dblarr[] = {1,2,3,4};
float  fltarr[] = {1,2,3,4};
int    intarr[] = {1,2,3,4};
```

TABLE 10-2   Word Sizes Used with the x Command

Suffix	Word Size
b	Byte (8 bits)
h	Half word (2 bytes)
w	Word (4 bytes)
g	Giant (8 bytes)

Now see the difference between x and print in gdb:

```
(gdb) p intarr
$5 = {10, 20, 30, 40}                 Output is formatted as an array of ints.

(gdb) x/4wx intarr                    Output is in 32-bit hex (as requested).
0x8049610 <intarr>:      0x0000000a     0x00000014     0x0000001e
0x00000028

(gdb) x/2gx intarr                    Output is in 64-bit hex (as requested).
0x8049610 <intarr>:      0x000000140000000a     0x000000280000001e
```

Using x with floating-point numbers can get weird if you are not careful. An IEEE float is 4 bytes, for example, but if you inadvertently use an 8-byte word size (g) with a float, you get gibberish. An IEEE double is 8 bytes, so the same format looks fine with the array of doubles:

```
(gdb) p fltarr                        p has no problem with floats.
$7 = {10, 20, 30, 40}

(gdb) x/4wf fltarr                    Word size w happens to be the same as sizeof(float).
0x8049600 <fltarr>:      10      20      30      40

(gdb) x/2gf fltarr                    Word size g is too big for floats.
0x8049600 <fltarr>:      134217760.5625   34359746808

(gdb) x/4gf dblarr                    Word size g is just right for doubles.
0x80495e0 <dblarr>:      10      20
0x80495f0 <dblarr+16>:   30      40
```

In these examples, I specified the format explicitly, which is a good idea when you can remember to do it. The problem is when you forget to specify the format and can't understand the results. In that case, you should check and recheck to make sure that you are using the correct format before jumping to any conclusions.

These are just a few of the many variations you can apply when printing data. `print` allows even more flexibility with variables because it allows you to use C syntax. With arrays, for example, you can use C syntax to print individual values, or you can print out multiple elements by using the ampersand suffix:

```
(gdb) p *intarr          Just like C, array can be used like a pointer.
$4 = 10
(gdb) p intarr[1]        Use C subscript notation to look at the second element in the array.
$5 = 20
(gdb) p intarr[1]@2      Use a combination of subscripts and @ to look at two elements starting at element 1.
$6 = {20, 30}
```

There are some subtle differences to be aware of when you print strings, however. Some formats recognize ASCII NULs, and some ignore them. Consider these declarations:

```
const char ccarr[] = "This is NUL terminated.\00ops! you shouldn't see this.";
const char *ccptr = ccarr;
```

The `ccarr` is an array, with a NUL character in the middle of some ASCII text. `ccptr` is a pointer that points to the same memory. Notice that the `print` command distinguishes between the two variables based on their types, whereas the `x` command, with an explicit `/s` modifier, treats both types the same:

```
(gdb) p ccarr            Array type does not recognize ASCII NUL.
$1 = "This is NUL terminated.\000Oops! you shouldn't see this."

(gdb) p ccptr            Pointer to char recognizes NUL.
$2 = 0x8048440 "This is NUL terminated."

(gdb) x/s ccarr          /s explicitly tells x to print a null-terminated string.
0x8048440 <ccarr>:       "This is NUL terminated."
```

With `print`, you can coerce the types using regular C syntax to force the output to look the way you want. For example:

```
(gdb) p (char*) ccarr
$3 = 0x403040 "This is NUL terminated."
```

Finally, you may never need it, but you can disassemble machine code anywhere in memory by using the `i` format with the `x` command:

```
(gdb) x/10i main
0x401050 <main>:         push    %ebp
0x401051 <main+1>:       mov     %esp,%ebp
0x401053 <main+3>:       sub     $0x28,%esp
0x401056 <main+6>:       and     $0xfffffff0,%esp
0x401059 <main+9>:       mov     $0x0,%eax
0x40105e <main+14>:      add     $0xf,%eax
0x401061 <main+17>:      add     $0xf,%eax
0x401064 <main+20>:      shr     $0x4,%eax
0x401067 <main+23>:      shl     $0x4,%eax
0x40106a <main+26>:      mov     %eax,0xffffffe4(%ebp)
```

This could come in handy if you are trying to look for buffer overflow attacks.

10.3.3.3 Calling Functions from gdb

gdb allows you to call any function that is visible in your program. The function executes in the context of your running process and consumes stack and other resources from the process being debugged. Although this is cool, it can have unintended side effects if not used carefully.

A function call can be included as an argument to almost every command. I used this earlier in the chapter to illustrate use of the print command, where I called the kill function as an argument to print. If you simply want to call a function and nothing else, use the call command:

```
(gdb) call getpid()
$1 = 27274
```

The value $1 is a temporary value that is allocated by gdb to hold the return value of the function. This memory resides in gdb's space (not the running program). gdb allocates these variables automatically for you whenever it needs to store a return value. You can use these values as arguments to functions. You can pass the previous result of getpid to the kill command as follows:

```
(gdb) call kill($1,0)
$2 = 0
```

If you want to modify values in the running program's space, you can use the set command. set takes many different arguments, but like most gdb commands, it accepts almost any valid C expression as an argument. Due to gdb's free syntax, you can set a variable using any command that allows C expressions as an argument, not just the set command. It's easy to remember to use set with assignment expressions.

10.3.3.4   Some Notes about the C++ and Templates

C++ templates pose a unique debugging challenge. Templates allow a programmer to define code in a generic fashion such that the compiler can generate source code from a more abstract specification. Consider the following trivial example, which swaps two values:

```
template <class Typ>
void swapvals( Typ &a, Typ &b)
{
        Typ tmp = a;
        a = b;
        b = tmp;
}
```

The token `Tmp` is a placeholder for a type name. Defining this template in your source will not generate any code until you use it. When you use it, you must specify a type that will take the place of `Typ`. This is called *instantiation*. To create a function to swap two doubles, you would call this function as follows:

```
swapvals<double>(a,b);
```

This causes the compiler to create a `swapvals` function that works exclusively with `double`s. If you need to swap two variables of type `int`, you can use `swapvals<int>`, which causes the compiler to generate a completely different function with a unique function signature. Because the template defines a whole family of functions, setting a breakpoint on a function defined by a template requires some finesse. Start by looking for the function with gdb's `info functions` command:

```
(gdb) info func swapvals
All functions matching regular expression "swapvals":

File templ.cpp:
void void swapvals<Foo>(Foo&, Foo&);              gdb 6.3 prints 'void' twice, for some reason.
void void swapvals<double>(double&, double&);
void void swapvals<int>(int&, int&);          .
```

Notice that there is a unique function for each type. There is no command that will apply a breakpoint on all functions generated by this template. You can set a breakpoint on only one of these functions at a time. To set a breakpoint on the `int` version, you can start with an open quote and use the tab expansion:

```
(gdb) b 'void swap<Tab>
(gdb) b 'void swapvals<<Tab>
(gdb) b 'void swapvals<int>(int&, int&)'
Breakpoint 3 at 0x8048434: file templ.cpp, line 8.
```

The closest you can come to setting a breakpoint on all functions that match a template is the `rbreak` command. This sets a breakpoint on all functions that match a given regular expression. For example:

```
(gdb) rbreak swapvals
Breakpoint 2 at 0x8048456: file templ.cpp, line 8.
void void swapvals<Foo>(Foo&, Foo&);
Breakpoint 3 at 0x8048400: file templ.cpp, line 8.
void void swapvals<double>(double&, double&);
Breakpoint 4 at 0x8048434: file templ.cpp, line 8.
void void swapvals<int>(int&, int&);
```

If your template has a short name that matches many other functions, you may end up setting unintended breakpoints. Use this carefully.

10.3.3.5   Some Notes about the C++ Standard Template Library

Although C++ includes the ANSI C standard library, C++ adds its own standard library implemented almost exclusively with templates. Technically, the *Standard Template Library* (STL) is now the C++ standard library, although many programmers still refer to it as *STL*.

One of the features in the standard template library is the container. A *container* is a template that implements dynamic storage. Containers can save a great deal of coding by implementing common storage algorithms such as lists, queues, and maps. Debugging code that uses containers can be a challenge, however.

The problem is that C++ containers go to great lengths to hide the underlying implementation from the user. Data inside a container is accessible only via method calls. You can use gdb to call these methods just like functions. This way, you can inspect containers at run time.

Look at one of the simplest C++ containers: the vector. The vector is designed to behave like a regular C array except that the storage is dynamic. Compare the two by using a type int:

```
int myarray[3];                        C array of three ints
std::vector<int> myvector(3);          C++ vector of three ints
```

When you debug code that has these two declarations, you can find out what you are looking at by using the `whatis` command:

```
(gdb) whatis myarray
type = int [3]                          Size is fixed.
(gdb) whatis myvector
type = std::vector<int,std::allocator<int> >  Size is dynamic—not reported.
```

All C++ containers have a `size` method that tells you how many elements are stored in the container. You can call this method from `gdb` just like any other function:

```
(gdb) p myvector.size()
$1 = 3
```

There is a catch, however: C++ templates do not generate code unless the code is used (instantiated). So unless your code actually uses the `size` method above, it will not be instantiated, and there will be no `size` method in the executable to call. In this case, you might see a message like the following:

```
(gdb) p myvector.size()
Cannot evaluate function -- may be inlined
```

To make matters more confusing, the method could get instantiated indirectly by using other methods. So you might be able to use this technique to debug in one program but not another. To make your life easier, you can consciously add super-fluous method calls to your code for the purpose of debugging. Also note that instantiation must be done for each unique type, so instantiating `vector<int>::size` does not instantiate `vector<float>::size`.

Note that `gdb` is able to treat containers of `std::vector` as regular arrays, so most syntax that works with arrays also works with vectors. Most other containers require help from method calls and iterators. Recall that an *iterator* is the C++ equivalent of a pointer used to access data in containers. Iterators use the same syntax as pointers, but they are not pointers. Luckily, `gdb` understands iterators, so you can print data using equivalent syntax. Consider the following code fragment:

```
std::list<int> mylist;
...
std::list<int>::iterator x = mylist.begin();
```

When x is instantiated inside the code, you can print use the same syntax with this iterator as you would with a pointer inside gdb:

```
(gdb) p *x
$1 = (int &) @0x804c1f8: 100
```

That's about as much as you can do with an iterator inside gdb. You cannot use pointer math or walk through a sequence container by using the ++ operator in gdb. If you need to see data inside C++ containers (other than a vector) from gdb, you will need to add some code to facilitate this.

10.3.3.6   The display Command

display prints the specified expression each time the program stops. You can display as many expressions as you want and format each expression using the same syntax as the x command.

Compile and run the program in Listing 10-5 with gdb. This program also demonstrates using gdb with containers.

LISTING 10-5   permute.cpp: A C++ Program to Demonstrate gdb's display Command

```
 1 #include <stdio.h>
 2 #include <string>
 3 #include <algorithm>
 4
 5 int main(int argc, char *argv[])
 6 {
 7     int i = 0;
 8     std::string token = "ABCD";
 9
10     // Simple loop goes through every permutation of a string
11     // using std::next_permutation.
12     do {
13         i++;
14     } while (std::next_permutation(token.begin(), token.end()));
15
16     printf("%d permutations\n", i);
17     return 0;
18 }
```

`token` is a four-character string that this program permutes using the C++ algorithm `std::next_permutation`. The laws of combinatorics states that there are four factorial[6] (4!) permutations of this string. You set a breakpoint on line 13 so you can watch what it does with the `display` command:

```
Breakpoint 2, main (argc=1, argv=0xbffce1a4) at permute.cpp:13
13                    i++;
(gdb) display/xw token.c_str()                           Display four chars as a longword.
1: x/xw token.c_str ()  0x804a014:       0x44434241
(gdb) display/s token.c_str()                            Display same thing as ASCII.
2: x/s token.c_str ()  0x804a014:          "ABCD"
(gdb) cont
Continuing.


Breakpoint 2, main (argc=1, argv=0xbffce1a4) at permute.cpp:13
13                    i++;
2: x/s token.c_str ()  0x804a014:          "ABDC"
1: x/xw token.c_str ()  0x804a014:       0x43444241
(gdb)                                                    No need to retype "cont."
Continuing.


Breakpoint 2, main (argc=1, argv=0xbffce1a4) at permute.cpp:13
13                    i++;
2: x/s token.c_str ()  0x804a014:          "ACBD"
1: x/xw token.c_str ()  0x804a014:       0x44424341

etc...

Breakpoint 2, main (argc=1, argv=0xbffce1a4) at permute.cpp:13
13                    i++;
2: x/s token.c_str ()  0x804a014:          "DCBA"    Final permutation.
1: x/xw token.c_str ()  0x804a014:       0x41424344
(gdb)
Continuing.
24 permutations                                          4 factorial = 24
```

You created two displays, which `gdb` numbers 1 and 2 for reference. Each time the program stops, both expressions are evaluated. In this case, `gdb` calls the `c_str` method of `std::string` once for each display. You can stop these displays at any time. To stop displaying the ASCII string in this example, you could type `undisplay 2` to remove display 2.

---

6. For the math impaired: N! = N * (N-1) * (N-2) ... * 2, so 4! = 4 * 3 * 2 = 24.

10.3.4 Attaching to a Running Process with gdb

From the command line, you can attach to a running process with `gdb` using the following syntax:

```
$ gdb programname pid
```

The `pid` is the process ID of the process you want to attach to, and the `programname` is the filename of the executable. These must match for the debugging session to be relevant. If you try to work with an executable that has been recompiled since the process was launched, there is no guarantee that the results you get will make any sense.

If you want to debug a different program, you don't need to quit `gdb` or terminate the currently running process. You can stop debugging and let the process continue running by using the `detach` command. This terminates the debugging session without terminating your process. When `gdb` is detached, you can change the program and debug a different process with the `attach` command. If necessary, you can use the `file` command to set the executable to match the new process.

You could use these commands as an alternative to starting `gdb` the way you did earlier in the chapter, as follows:

```
(gdb) file programname
(gdb) attach pid
```

Note that if the process is compiled with `debug`, it may be possible to skip the `file` command and let `gdb` figure out where the executable is.

10.3.5 Debugging Core Files

When a process dumps a core file, it leaves behind the state of its virtual memory. Core files are always the result of a signal. The most common core-file-generating signals encountered while debugging include

- `SIGSEGV`—segmentation violation. This signal is generated when a process attempts to read from or write to an invalid memory address; it also can occur when attempting to write to a read-only page or read from a page with no read permission.

- `SIGFPE`—floating-point error. Oddly enough, this signal usually is *not* generated by floating-point functions. Instead, you will see `SIGFPE` on the x86 architecture when a process attempts an *integer* divide by zero.

- SIGABRT—abort; used by the abort and assert functions.

- SIGILL—illegal instruction. This signal is most likely to occur in hand-coded assembly routines that attempt to use privileged instructions from user mode.

- SIGBUS—bus error, but not in the hardware sense. This signal can be the result of a page fault that could not complete, such as running out of swap space.

The core file includes information about which signal caused the core file. As long as you have a copy of the *same* executable that generated the core file (as well as all the same shared objects), you can debug the program using the core file. To debug, use the following command line:

```
$ gdb exec-filename core-filename
```

Traditionally, core files are named simply core, although many distributions setup the kernel to dump core files with the process ID as part of the name—for example, core.pid.[7] When you bring up a file for *postmortem debugging* in this way, one of the first things gdb tells you is what caused the core dump. If it can, gdb will place you at the line of source where the signal occurred. For example:

```
$ gdb seldomcrash core.27078
...
Reading symbols from shared object read from target memory...done.
Loaded system supplied DSO at 0xffffe000
Core was generated by './seldomcrash'.
Program terminated with signal 8, Arithmetic exception.

...
#0  0x0804836c in main (argc=1, argv=0xbfc9acd4) at seldomcrash.c:10
10              return someint / 0;          Oops, divided by 0!
(gdb)
```

As you might expect, you can bring up programs for postmortem debugging from within gdb by using the file command followed by the core-file command.

When a program severely corrupts the stack, the core file that is generated often is of limited use with gdb, because gdb needs the stack to navigate the local variables. Even when the stack is corrupt, however, global and static variables will still be useful.

---

7. This feature is disabled by the command sysctl -w kernel.core_uses_pid = 0.

Knowing that your program corrupted the stack is useful information, but unfortunately, gdb doesn't come right out and tell you this. The only clue you get to this event is when the functions listed in the backtrace command make no sense for the program you are running, or gdb might just tell you no stack.

The most common cause of stack corruption is a buffer overflow of a local variable. You might declare an array on the stack and use memset or memcpy to initialize the array to too large a size. In general, any time you take a pointer to a local variable and give it to another function, you create the risk of an overrun. This opportunity for buffer overflow is possible with scanf, read, and many other functions.

The program in Listing 10-6 is an implementation of the factorial function I described earlier in the chapter. This is commonly used in statistical applications and in computer-science classes as an example of recursive programming.[8]

LISTING 10-6   factorial.c: An Example of Stack Corruption

```
 1  #include <stdio.h>
 2  #include <string.h>
 3  #include <stdlib.h>
 4
 5  // factorial function. Traditional programming example
 6  // of a recursive function.
 7  int factorial(int x)
 8  {
 9      int overflow;
10      static int depth = 0;
11
12      if (x <= 1)
13          return 1;
14
15      if (++depth > 6) {
16          // Overflow n bytes. Will cause a SIGSEGV, but we don't know where.
17          int n = 0x100;
18          memset((char *) &overflow, 0xa5, sizeof(overflow) + n);
19      }
20
21      return x * factorial(x - 1);
22  }
23
```

continues

---

8. Infinite recursion is a common programming bug that leads to a SIGSEGV but not necessarily to stack corruption.

```
24 int main(int argc, char *argv[])
25 {
26     int n = 3;
27     printf("Command line argument > 7 will cause stack corruption\n");
28     if (argc > 1) {
29         n = atoi(argv[1]);
30     }
31     printf("%d! == %d\n", n, factorial(n));
32     return 0;
33 }
```

In this contrived example, you deliberately trash the stack after the function has called itself seven times. To do this, you write 256 bytes to the address of an integer local variable. Here it is in action:

```
$ ./factorial 7
Command line argument > 7 will cause stack corruption
7! == 5040
$ ./factorial 8
Command line argument > 7 will cause stack corruption
Segmentation fault (core dumped)                    Told you so!
$ gdb ./factorial core
GNU gdb Red Hat Linux (6.3.0.0-1.21rh)
...
Core was generated by `./factorial 8'.
Program terminated with signal 11, Segmentation fault.
...
#0  0xa5a5a5a5 in ?? ()                             This is not looking good.
(gdb) bt                                            Let's look at the backtrace.
#0  0xa5a5a5a5 in ?? ()
#1  0xa5a5a5a5 in ?? ()
#2  0xa5a5a5a5 in ?? ()
#3  0xa5a5a5a5 in ?? ()
...                                                 OK, that wasn't helpful.
#21 0xa5a5a5a5 in ?? ()
#22 0xa5a5a5a5 in ?? ()
---Type <return> to continue, or q <return> to quit---q
Quit
(gdb)p factorial::depth                             Static variables are still OK.
$1 = 7
```

After the program dumps core, you use gdb to attempt postmortem debugging and find that the stack is unusable. Your clue is that the backtrace command (bt) shows nothing useful. You can still use this core file, however. You only need stack frames to look at local variables. All static and global variables are still visible. To look at the static variable depth defined inside the function factorial, use C++ syntax: factorial::depth. Examining this value tells you that you called factorial seven times recursively. In this case, that's almost as good as a stack trace.

Unfortunately, most programs aren't this easy to debug. If you are debugging a program that is exhibiting stack corruption, you can consider adding global or static variables for the purpose of postmortem debugging. I explore this idea further in the section "Creating Your Own Black Box" later in this chapter.

10.3.6   Debugging Multithreaded Programs with gdb

Debugging programs with multiple threads can be a difficult task. gdb is thread aware and provides several features to make this task easier.

All multithreaded programs start out single threaded, so debugging is straightforward until the threads are created. The default behavior of gdb in a multithreaded program probably is what you would expect. When you're at the command prompt, all threads are stopped. When you single-step through the code, gdb attempts to stay in the current thread. If a breakpoint occurs in a different thread, however, the command prompt will switch to that thread's stack frame.

The `info threads` command shows you the currently running threads. This is illustrated below with the code omitted:

```
(gdb) info threads
  4 Thread -1225585744 (LWP 6703)   0x0804854c in the_thread (ptr=0x2)
    at thread-demo.c:17
  3 Thread -1217193040 (LWP 6702)   0x0804854c in the_thread (ptr=0x1)
    at thread-demo.c:17
  2 Thread -1208800336 (LWP 6701)   0x0804854c in the_thread (ptr=0x0)
    at thread-demo.c:17
* 1 Thread -1208797504 (LWP 6698)   main (argc=1, argv=0xbf940e84)
    at thread-demo.c:45
```

The first column is a gdb-defined thread identifier. These are simple incrementing values that gdb uses to make switching between threads easier for the user. The number increases with each new thread, which can be helpful for identifying which thread is which. The large negative number is the pthread_t used by the pthreads API.

At the command prompt, gdb uses the stack frame of the current thread for local variables. The *current thread* is wherever gdb happened to stop. To switch from one thread to another, use the `thread` command followed by the gdb identifier of that thread.

Any breakpoint you set without a qualifier applies to all threads. The first thread that hits the breakpoint will stop the program, and gdb will make that thread the current thread. To make a breakpoint apply to only one thread, use the `thread` qualifier to the `break` command. If you want to stop at function `foo` in thread 3, use the following command:

```
(gdb) break foo thread 3
```

Whenever `gdb` hits a breakpoint, the thread that caused the breakpoint becomes the current thread. Any single-stepping from that point occurs in the current thread.

Using gdb's scheduler-lock Feature with Threads

When you're single-stepping in a multithreaded program using the `step` or `next` commands, it's important to know that other threads will execute while the current thread single-steps. Usually, this is what you want, because it provides some degree of simultaneity among threads while you single-step through the application.

There are occasions when this might be undesirable, however. While you are stepping through the code with `gdb` in one thread, the other threads can execute and hit breakpoints. If this happens `gdb` will switch threads automatically. To prevent this, you can modify the scheduler behavior while stepping through the code with the `set scheduler-lock` command. This takes one of three settings:

```
set scheduler-lock off
set scheduler-lock on
set scheduler-lock step
```

The default setting is `off`, which I just described. The `on` setting causes `gdb` to disable all other threads while you single-step through code. The other threads do not run until you resume execution with the `continue` command.

The `step` setting causes the threads to stop during a `step` but not during a `next` command—that is, other threads do not run during single stepping unless you step *over* a function in the current thread with the next function.

10.3.7   Debugging Optimized Code

`gcc` allows you to compile code with optimization and debugging, although these options seem mutually exclusive. There are times when the performance penalty for not using optimization is unacceptable. At the same time, the behavior of optimized code running under the debugger can be downright bizarre. Sometimes, you can compromise by compiling only selected modules without optimization, but that's not always possible.

Optimization is architecture specific, so there are no hard and fast guidelines that I can give you. There are some typical things to look out for:

- Unused variables—The optimizer is free to remove unused variables from the code, which can be confusing when running under debug. Sometimes programmers set aside variables to store data that you look at only while debugging. Such a write-only variable is a prime candidate for removal by the optimizer. That makes debugging harder, of course. To protect such variables from the optimizer, declare them volatile.

- Inline functions—This is a typical optimization that compilers make to save the overhead of a function call. When a function is inlined, it will not appear on the call stack. To disable function inlining, compile your code using the gcc flag -fno-inline.

- Out-of-order steps—Single-stepping through an optimized function can challenge your sensibilities. Where unoptimized code proceeds nicely from top to bottom, an optimized function often jumps all over the place with no rhyme or reason because the optimizer rearranges the code to execute in a more efficient manner.

Sometimes, looking at the assembly language can help. gdb does not provide listings of source and assembly together, but you can see what the compiler is telling gdb with the objdump command. Consider this screwed-up function:

```
 1 void vscale2(double *vec, int len, double arg)
 2 {
 3     int i;
 4
 5     // Temporaries to confuse the reader...
 6     double a, b, c;
 7     for (i = 0; i < len; i++) {
 8
 9         // Don't ask me what this does
10         a = arg * arg;
11         b = arg * a / 2;
12         c = a * b * arg;
13         vec[i] *= c;
14     }
15 }
```

The temporary variables defined on line 6 serve only to confuse the reader. By reusing the temporary variables on multiple lines, you give the optimizer opportunities to combine these lines into a single operation. Compiling this function with optimization and running it through `objdump` shows that all these references are collapsed into one line of code from the debugger's point of view—that is, the optimizer is able to realize these are temporary variables and exploit this by combining all this code.

The `objdump` command can be helpful here. It can produce a dump of the machine code, disassembly, and debug information annotated with the original C source. When we run this on our object file compiled with optimization and debug, we can see things more clearly. For example:

```
$ objdump -S -l vscale2.o

vscale2.o:      file format elf32-i386

Disassembly of section .text:

00000000 <vscale2>:
vscale2():
/home/john/examples/ch-10/debug/vscale2.c:2    Line numbers show where gdb can set breakpoints.
void vscale2(double *vec, int len, double arg)
{
   0:   55                      push   %ebp
   1:   89 e5                   mov    %esp,%ebp
   3:   8b 4d 0c                mov    0xc(%ebp),%ecx
   6:   dd 45 10                fldl   0x10(%ebp)
/home/john/examples/ch-10/debug/vscale2.c:7    The following code is attributed to line 7.
    int i;

    // Temporaries to confuse the reader...
    double a, b, c;
    for (i = 0; i < len; i++) {
   9:   85 c9                   test   %ecx,%ecx
   b:   7e 25                   jle    32 <vscale2+0x32>
   d:   d9 c0                   fld    %st(0)
   f:   d8 c9                   fmul   %st(1),%st
  11:   d9 c1                   fld    %st(1)
  13:   d8 c9                   fmul   %st(1),%st
  15:   d8 0d 00 00 00 00       fmuls  0x0
  1b:   de c9                   fmulp  %st,%st(1)
  1d:   de c9                   fmulp  %st,%st(1)
  1f:   31 d2                   xor    %edx,%edx
  21:   8b 45 08                mov    0x8(%ebp),%eax
/home/john/examples/ch-10/debug/vscale2.c:13   Notice that there is no code attributed to lines 8–12!
```

```
              // Don't ask me what this does     This gibberish has been optimized away.
              a = arg * arg;
              b = arg * a / 2;
              c = a * b * arg;
              vec[i] *= c;
  24:    d9 c0                       fld     %st(0)
  26:    dc 08                       fmull   (%eax)
  28:    dd 18                       fstpl   (%eax)
/home/john/examples/ch-10/debug/vscale2.c:7
  2a:    42                          inc     %edx
  2b:    83 c0 08                    add     $0x8,%eax
  2e:    39 d1                       cmp     %edx,%ecx
  30:    75 f2                       jne     24 <vscale2+0x24>
  32:    dd d8                       fstp    %st(0)
/home/john/examples/ch-10/debug/vscale2.c:15
      }
}
  34:    c9                          leave
  35:    c3                          ret
  36:    89 f6                       mov     %esi,%esi
```

What this shows is that when you run this code, you cannot set breakpoints on lines 10, 11, and 12 because the temporaries have been coalesced by the optimizer. If you try to set a breakpoint on line 10, for example, the debugger will appear to comply, but the code will actually stop on line 15. As you might expect, there is no storage allocated for a, b, or c, so you can't try to print these variables at runtime. If you try, gdb will respond with a message like this:

```
No symbol "a" in current context.
```

There is no trace of these variables in the debug output (try info locals from inside vscale2 as well). Again, if you feel you need to keep these temporary values for debugging, declare them volatile. But use the volatile keyword sparingly, because it degrades your performance.

10.4 Debugging Shared Objects

Shared objects have many names on different platforms, but the concept is the same. Microsoft Windows calls these *dynamic linked libraries,* whereas many UNIX tools refer to them as *dynamic libraries.* The generic term is *shared objects* because these need not be libraries, although that is how they are most commonly used. Debugging code in a shared object is not much different from debugging a normal program. Sometimes, however, getting the correct binary into memory can be a challenge.

10.4.1   When and Why to Use Shared Objects

By default, all Linux applications use shared objects for the standard libraries, because this is the most efficient way to use memory. You can see this with the `ldd` command.[9] Try this on any `Hello World` application:

```
$ ldd hello
        linux-gate.so.1 =>  (0xffffe000)
        libc.so.6 => /lib/libc.so.6 (0xb7e32000)
        /lib/ld-linux.so.2 (0xb7f69000)
```

Here, you can see that the file was linked against the standard library `libc.so`, and the runtime version can be found at `/lib/libc.so.6`. The program also must be linked with the dynamic linker itself, which is `/lib/ld-linux.so.2` in this executable. `linux-gate.so.1` is a pseudo shared object that appears on Intel architectures. It allows shared libraries to use the faster `sysenter` and `sysexit` opcodes if the processor supports it. This is faster than the normal mechanism for making system calls, which uses a software interrupt.

Normally, shared objects are used to share a library of routines among many processes. This saves physical memory, because the read-only segments of the shared library can occupy the same physical memory across processes.

Although most programmers do not write code that will be shared by many processes, there are other reasons to use shared objects. One use for shared objects is to provide extensions to scripting languages. Perl and Python, for example, allow programmers to create shared libraries that can be called from scripts. This gives you the flexibility of a script while keeping the efficiency of C for processor-intensive parts. The shared object is pulled in as a module, and the functions within are visible to the script interpreter.[10]

Another, less common application is to use shared objects to implement overlays. Overlays once were a common technique used to save memory on 16-bit platforms without virtual memory. Today, such techniques are hardly necessary, but just in case, POSIX has an API for you. Interested readers should look at the `dlopen(3)` man page.

---

9. *LDD* stands for *list dynamic dependencies.*
10. Sound interesting? Check out www.swig.org.

10.4.2 Creating Shared Objects

Conceptually, the only difference between a shared object and a program is that the shared object typically does not have a `main` function. This is not a requirement, however. You can create shared objects that can be called just like an executable while retaining the ability to be linked dynamically into a larger program. The dynamic linker itself is just such a shared object; it is used by the `ldd` command I introduced earlier in the chapter.

Creating a simple shared object is easy enough; just build it as though it were a program, but use the `-shared` and `-fpic` flags. For example:

```
$ cc -shared -fpic -o libmylib.so mylib1.c mylib2.c
```

The `-shared` flag is for the linker, which tells it to produce a shared object instead of an executable. The `-fpic` flag informs the compiler to generate *position-independent code*. This is important because unlike those of a conventional executable, the shared object's virtual addresses are not known until runtime.

Linking a program with a shared object is deceptively simple:

```
$ cc -o myprog myprog.o -L . -lmylib
```

Here, I informed the linker that my shared library is located in the current directory with the `-L` option. The problem is that the runtime linker `ld-linux.so` needs to know where to find this shared object as well. This is a problem, as you can see when you try to run this program:

```
$ ./myprog
./myprog: error while loading shared libraries: libmylib.so: cannot open shared
object file: No such file or directory
```

The problem is that the system has no clue where the shared object is located. Programs linked with shared objects do not contain any information about where to find the shared objects. This is deliberate, because shared objects are located in specific locations on every system. If this application were to run on a different system, it should make no assumptions about where to find a shared object. Instead, each shared object provides what is called a *soname*, which is the name that the dynamic linker uses to identify the object. The library you created does not have an soname, because you did not specify one. This is optional, because the dynamic linker will fall back to using the filename if it does not recognize the soname.

10.4.3   Locating Shared Objects

Locating shared objects is the job of the dynamic linker `ldlinux.so`, located in
`/lib`. The dynamic linker will always search in the standard paths `/lib` and
`/usr/lib`. If you want to store shared objects in different places, you can use the
environment variable `LD_LIBRARY_PATH`. More often, systems have shared libraries
in several places. To prevent the dynamic linker from having to search through
many paths, the system keeps a cache of sonames and the shared object locations in
`/etc/ld.so.cache`. This cache is created and updated by the `/sbin/ldconfig`
program, which searches the directories listed in `/etc/ld.so.conf`.

Whenever you install new libraries, it is necessary to run the `ldconfig` program
to update the cache. In addition, `ldconfig` creates symbolic links so that the filenames of the shared object files can be uniquely different from the sonames. Using
the `hello` program on my Fedora Core 3 machine, `libc.so.6` points to a file
named `libc-2.3.6.so`:

```
$ ls -l /lib/libc.so.6
lrwxrwxrwx  1 root root 13 Jul  2 16:03 /lib/libc.so.6 -> libc-2.3.6.so
```

`libc.so.6` is a generic soname encountered by the compiler, whereas
`libc-2.3.6.so` is the filename used by the GNU C library package (`glibc`). In
principle, you don't need to use `glibc` to provide `libc.so.6`. You could substitute your own library. As long as it uses the correct soname and is found in the
path, the dynamic linker will use it. In reality, replacing `glibc` probably would
break all the GNU tools that require `glibc` extensions.

10.4.4   Overriding the Default Shared Object Locations

Unprivileged users can use the environment variable `LD_LIBRARY_PATH` to tell the
dynamic linker where to look. You can finally get the `myprog` example to run as
follows:

```
$ LD_LIBRARY_PATH=./ ./myprog
```

This tells the dynamic linker to look in the current directory for shared objects,
which is where `libmylib.so` is located. For objects that have a soname, you can
save a little typing by using the `LD_PRELOAD` environment variable as follows:

```
$ LD_PRELOAD=libc.so.6 ./hello-world   libc.so.6 is the soname of glibc on my system.
```

This tells the dynamic linker specifically to link against `libc` before linking the rest of `hello-world`. This particular technique can be useful if your program links with a library that re-implements a vital function from `libc`. LD_PRELOAD works only with libraries that have `sonames` listed in `/etc/ld.so.cache`.

Both these techniques are very useful for debugging shared objects, because they allow you to create a shared object in a private directory. There, you can link with the shared object without interfering with other processes that may be using an installed version of the same shared object. You can debug a new version of the object without fear of crashing other processes.

10.4.5 Security Issues with Shared Objects

I have discussed the benefits of shared objects, but shared objects also pose a serious security risk if used improperly. Some shared objects are shared by many programs, such as `libc`, which is used by virtually every system command. These objects are used by many programs, including many that run with root privilege. If a malicious programmer can compromise a commonly used shared object, he can compromise your whole system.

Suppose that you create a program with `setuid root` privileges to allow ordinary users on your system to do some routine maintenance task. Whenever an ordinary user runs this program, the process will execute with `root`'s privileges. Perhaps this program uses a shared object that is located in an insecure location. A malicious programmer theoretically could replace that shared object with malware. Your original program remains untouched but unknowingly compromises the system by calling one of the functions in this hijacked shared object.

For this reason, the dynamic linker goes to great lengths to make sure that shared objects pulled in by such programs are secure. Only objects in the standard path are allowed, for example (LD_LIBRARY_PATH is ignored), and all shared objects must have root ownership and read-only permissions.[11]

10.4.6 Tools for Working with Shared Objects

The Linux dynamic linker is itself a command-line tool. For historical reasons, the man page is listed under `ld.so(8)`, although the actual program name used in current

---

11. For more details, see `ld.so(8)`.

distributions is `ld-linux.so.2`. When invoked from the command line, the linker takes several options and understands many environment variables, which you can use to understand your program better. These options are described in the `ld.so(8)` man page, but in most cases the preferred tool is `ldd`, which is actually a wrapper script that calls `ld-linux.so.2` and has some more user-friendly options.

10.4.6.1 List Shared Objects Required by an Executable

With no options, `ldd` will show you all the shared objects required by an executable:

```
$ ldd hello
        linux-gate.so.1 =>   (0xffffe000)
        libm.so.6 => /lib/libm.so.6 (0xb7f1b000)
        libpthread.so.0 => /lib/libpthread.so.0 (0xb7f09000)
        libc.so.6 => /lib/libc.so.6 (0xb7de0000)
        /lib/ld-linux.so.2 (0xb7f4e000)
```

Strictly speaking, this is a list of objects that the file was linked with—not necessarily the objects that the executable requires. In this case, I deliberately linked a `Hello World` program with the math library and the `pthread` library, neither of which is required:

```
$ gcc -o hello hello.c -lm -lpthread
```

Unlike static libraries, the linker does not remove shared object code from the executable. Recall that a static library is just an archive. The linker uses the archive to pull in object files that it needs and only the object files that it needs. In this way, the static linker is able to eliminate unneeded object files from the executable. When you specify a shared object on the command line, the linker includes it in the executable whether it's necessary or not.

You can see this with the `ldd` command you used earlier in the chapter. In this case, you happen to know that `libpthread.so` and `libm.so` are not required, but what if you didn't know that? The `-u` option will show you unused dependencies, as follows:[12]

```
$ ldd -u ./hello
Unused direct dependencies:

        /lib/libm.so.6
        /lib/libpthread.so.0
```

---

12. Curiously, the `-u` option is missing from the `ldd` man page but shows up with `--help`.

It's up to you to do the mental gymnastics to figure out *how* those shared objects found their way into your executable. Knowing the naming convention for libraries is one way to work backward into the command-line options that got you here. Many open source projects use the `pkg-config` tool to create the command-line options that are used to link a project. In some cases, these rules can pull in extra shared objects.

10.4.6.2 Why Worry about Unused Shared Objects?

For each shared object a program links with, the dynamic linker must search the object for unresolved references and call initialization routines. This increases the amount of time it takes for your program to start. On a fast desktop machine, unused shared objects probably don't amount to much extra time, but if there are many of them, it could add up to a significant delay.

Another issue with unused shared objects is the resources they consume. Whether it is used or not, a shared object may allocate and initialize a large amount of physical memory. If initialized and left unused, this memory eventually will find its way to the swap partition. Objects that don't consume physical memory may consume virtual memory. This is memory that is allocated but uninitialized. If never used, it will never be swapped and will never consume physical RAM, but it limits the number of available virtual addresses that can be used by a program. Usually, this is a problem only in applications on 32-bit architectures that require very large datasets—on the order of gigabytes of RAM.

As a rule, it's always a good idea to avoid unnecessary shared objects. In particular, if you have a system with a slow CPU or limited RAM, you should be extra careful not to link with shared libraries you do not need. On a modern server or desktop system, none of these issues is a serious problem by itself. Nevertheless, when many applications use many shared objects that they don't need, the system as a whole can start to feel the effects.

10.4.6.3 Looking for Symbols in Shared Objects

Occasionally, you might download some source code that compiles but does not link because it is missing a symbol. The `nm` and `objdump` commands are the tools of choice for looking at program symbol tables. In addition, there is the `readelf` command. All these tools do basically the same thing, but you may find that based on what you need to know, only one of these tools can help.

Suppose that you have a shared object file and want to know its soname before you install it. Recall that the `ldconfig` command does the job of reading sonames and putting them in the cache. Before you install this library, you may want to know whether it conflicts with any existing sonames. You can look at the cache at any time with `ldconfig p`. To find the soname of a single (uninstalled) shared object, you need to look at the so-called DYNAMIC section. The `nm` tool is not suited for this, but `objdump` and `readelf` are:

```
$ objdump -x some-obj-1.0.so | grep SONAME
   SONAME       libmylib.so

$ readelf  -a libmylib.so |grep SONAME
 0x0000000e (SONAME)                          Library soname: [libmylib.so]
```

Another problem that arises is when the linker complains about unresolved symbols. This occurs perhaps most often due to a missing library or attempting to link with the wrong version of a library. There are many ways this can happen. In C++, the problem can be caused by a function signature that has changed or perhaps just a typo.

All three tools can print out symbol tables, but `nm` may be the easiest to use. To look through the object code to find references to a particular symbol, use the following command:

```
$ nm -uA *.o | grep foo
```

The `-u` option restricts the output to unresolved symbols in each object file. The `-A` option displays the filename information with each symbol, so that when you pipe the output to the `grep` command, you can see which object file contains that symbol. For C++ code, there is also the `-c` option, which demangles the symbols for you as well. This can help in debugging libraries that may have unwisely chosen function signatures, such as the following:

```
int foo(char p);
int foo(unsigned char p);
```

C++ allows both functions to have unique signatures but silently typecasts the input parameters to use one if the other is missing.[13] To look for libraries that have

---

13. By the way, if you change the input argument types to `const` references, the input types are strictly enforced.

these functions, just drop the -u option. Adding the -C option never hurts unless you really want to see mangled function names:

```
$ nm -gCA lib*.a | grep foo
libFoolib.a:somefile.o:00000000 T foo(char)
libFoolib.a:somefile.o:00000016 T foo(unsigned char)
```

As you might guess, the objdump and readelf commands can do the same thing as well. The equivalent of the nm command using objdump is

```
$ objdump -t
```

objdump also has a -C option to demangle symbol names. The equivalent readelf command is

```
$ readelf -s
```

Unlike nm and objdump, readelf has no options to demangle symbol names as of version 2.15.94. All three utilities are available as part of the binutils package.

10.5   Looking for Memory Issues

Problems with memory can take many forms, from buffer overflows to memory leaks. Many tools try to help, but there are limits to what you can do. Nevertheless, some tools are easy enough to use that they're worth a try. Sometimes when one tool doesn't work, another will. Even glibc has features to help you debug dynamic memory issues.

10.5.1   Double Free

Freeing a pointer twice is an easy-enough mistake to make, but the consequences can be dire. The problem is that until recently, glibc would not check your pointers for you and would blindly accept any pointer you give it. Freeing a pointer to an invalid virtual address will cause a SIGSEGV at the point where it occurred. That's easy to find. Freeing a pointer that points to a valid virtual address can be much more difficult to find.

Most often, the invalid pointer being freed is one that was initialized by a malloc call but already freed with a free call. It is possible that freeing the pointer twice will corrupt the free list that glibc uses to track dynamic memory allocations. When this happens, you will get SIGSEGV, but it might not occur until the *next* free or malloc call! That's more difficult to find.

Some idiosyncrasies in `glibc` make finding such errors more difficult. Blocks above a certain size are allocated using `mmap` calls instead of a conventional heap, for example. Traditionally, the heap is a large pool of memory that grows and shrinks as the process requires. `glibc` uses anonymous `mmaps` to allocate large blocks and a traditional heap for small blocks. This creates different failure modes for different block sizes that may be difficult to interpret.

Recent versions of `glibc` include checking for invalid free pointers that cause a program to terminate with a core dump no matter what the circumstances. I look at this topic in detail later in the chapter.

10.5.2   Memory Leaks

A memory leak occurs when a process allocates a block of memory, discards it, and then neglects to free it. Often, small leaks are harmless, and the program continues to run with no ill effects. Given time, though, even a small leak can grow to become a problem. A simple utility that executes for a short time can tolerate small leaks because it discards its heap after it exits. A daemon process that may run for months cannot tolerate any leaks, however, because they accumulate over time.

The effect of a memory leak is that your process's memory footprint continues to grow. When allocated memory has not been touched, the leaked memory may consume only virtual addresses. As long as your program doesn't run out of user-space virtual addresses (typically, 3GB on a 32-bit machine), you will never see any ill effects. In most cases, the leaked memory has been modified by the program, so these pages must consume physical storage (either RAM or swap). As the unused memory pages age and the demand for system memory increases, these pages get paged out to disk.

The swapping is perhaps the most insidious side effect of memory leaks, because a single leaky program can slow the entire system. Fortunately, memory leaks are not very hard to find. Following are some tools to help.

10.5.3   Buffer Overflows

A buffer overflow occurs when an application writes beyond the end of a block of memory, overwriting memory that may be in use for other purposes. An overflow may result in writing to unmapped or read-only memory, which will result in a `SIGSEGV`. Overflows are a common type of error and can occur in any type of memory: stack, dynamic, or static. There are several tools for detecting overflows in dynamic memory, but detecting overflows in static memory and local variables is harder.

The best advice for dealing with overflows is to avoid them. Certain standard library functions present ample opportunities for overflows to occur and should be avoided. In most instances, a safer alternative is available. A good tool that can uncover vulnerabilities is `flawfinder`.[14] This is a Python script that parses your source code for dangerous functions and reports them to you.

10.5.3.1   Stack Buffer Overflows

A stack buffer overflow represents a security risk. Several attackers have used overflow vulnerabilities in commercial software to implant malware on otherwise-secure systems.

A typical vulnerability involves a text input field defined as a local variable using a function that has no overflow checking. When the input consists of plain text or garbage, the program will simply crash. This is bad enough, but a clever attacker can input binary machine code into a text field to overflow the input buffer. With some trial and error, a clever attacker can figure out just the right bytes to write to coax the program to run his code and take over the process.

The precise details of how this occurs are beyond the scope of this book, but it is important to know that stack buffer overflows are a security risk. Under normal circumstances, a stack buffer overflow is difficult to find when it occurs. The typical signature of a stack buffer overflow is a `SIGSEGV` followed by a core dump that includes no useful backtrace. When this occurs, it may be quicker to do a code review looking for known problem functions than to try debugging it.

10.5.3.2   Heap Buffer Overflows

When a program overflows a heap buffer, the consequences are not always immediate. When `malloc` uses an `mmap` call to allocate a block of memory (as it does for large blocks), it pads the requested block size so that it is a multiple of the page size. Therefore, if the requested block size is not an integral number of pages, the amount of space allocated for the block includes extra bytes. Your code can overrun

---

14. www.dwheeler.com/flawfinder

the end of the block, and you may never know. Only when your code overruns into the address beyond the end of the last page will it terminate with a SIGSEGV. The good news is that it terminates immediately, and there is no opportunity for such an overrun to corrupt the heap. With smaller blocks, that do not use mmap, the problem can be more difficult.

With small blocks, a small overflow can go undetected as well. Most heap implementations will pad the block size so that it falls on an efficient boundary in memory. This allows you to overrun a few bytes occasionally with no ill effects. Such an error may cause a crash only sometimes. The details depend on the implementation of the standard library, the size of the block, and the size of the overflow.

When the code overflows a small block beyond end of the padding, it corrupts the internal lists that malloc and free use to maintain the heap. Typically, such an overflow isn't detected until the next malloc or free call. To make matters more confusing, the free call that fails need not be freeing the block that has overflowed. If the overflow is large enough, it may extend into invalid virtual addresses, in which case you will get a SIGSEGV.

The problems of dynamic memory overflows are essentially the same for C++. At the core of the default operators for new and delete is a conventional heap that may even use the C library versions of malloc and free. The GNU implementation of new and delete appears to be intolerant of even a single-byte overflow, although like C, you don't find out about it until the delete operation. C++ allows you to overload these operators, however. When you do this, you create new failure modes for overflows. This is one reason why the decision to overload operator new and delete should not be taken lightly.

Several tools are available to check for heap overflows; I look at them later in this chapter.

10.5.4   glibc Tools

The GNU standard library (glibc) has had built-in debugging features for dynamic memory for a long time. Until recently, these features were turned off by default and enabled only by the environment variable MALLOC_CHECK_. The rationale for not checking the heap with each allocation and free was that it decreased efficiency. Some checks are inexpensive enough that recent versions of glibc have some of these basic checks turned on by default.

10.5.4.1   Using MALLOC_CHECK_

glibc inspects the environment variable MALLOC_CHECK_ and alters its behavior as follows:

- MALLOC_CHECK_=0—disables all checking

- MALLOC_CHECK_=1—prints a message to stderr when an error is detected

- MALLOC_CHECK_=2—aborts when an error is detected; no message is printed

When MALLOC_CHECK_ is not set, older versions of glibc behave as though MALLOC_CHECK_ were set to 0. Newer versions behave as though MALLOC_CHECK_ were set to 2. It will dump core as soon as it detects an inconsistency and print a lengthy traceback as well. The default output is more verbose than the output you get when you set MALLOC_CHECK_ to 2. Here is the output from a trivial program (not shown) I created that does a double-free and links with glibc version 2.3.6:

```
$ ./double-free                              MALLOC_CHECK_ not set
*** glibc detected *** ./double-free: double free or corruption (top): 0x0804a008 ***
======= Backtrace: =========
/lib/libc.so.6[0xb7e8f1e0]
/lib/libc.so.6(__libc_free+0x77)[0xb7e8f72b]
./double-free[0x80483f8]
/lib/libc.so.6(__libc_start_main+0xdf)[0xb7e40d7f]
./double-free[0x804832d]
======= Memory map: ========
08048000-08049000 r-xp 00000000 fd:00 576680    /home/john/examples/ch-10/memory/double-free
08049000-0804a000 rw-p 00000000 fd:00 576680    /home/john/examples/ch-10/memory/double-free
                                                 [ rest of memory map omitted ]
```

The memory map may seem like overkill, but recall that for large block sizes, glibc will use mmap instead of a conventional heap. The stack trace is not as user friendly as a gdb stack trace,[15] but because this is a SIGABRT, there should be a core file to go with it. Then you can use gdb in postmortem mode to view the backtrace as well as any variable values.

10.5.4.2   Looking for Memory Leaks with mtrace

mtrace is a tool provided with glibc that Fedora packages with the glibc-utils package. This may not be installed by default on your system. On other distributions,

---

15. See also addr2line(1) from binutils.

it may be packaged similarly. The main purpose of `mtrace` is to look for leaks. There are better tools for this purpose, but because this one comes as part of `glibc` it's worth mentioning.

To use the `mtrace` utility, you must instrument your code with the `mtrace` and `muntrace` functions provided by `glibc`. In addition, you must set the environment variable `MALLOC_TRACE` to the name of a file where `glibc` will store data for the `mtrace` utility. After you run your code, data is stored in the file you specify. This data is overwritten with each run. I'll skip the listing here just to show you how `mtrace` runs:

```
$ MALLOC_TRACE=foo.dat ./ex-mtrace        mtrace data will be stored in foo.dat.
leaking 0x603 bytes
leaking 0x6e2 bytes
leaking 0x1d8 bytes
leaking 0xd9f bytes
leaking 0xc3 bytes
leaking 0x22f bytes
$ mtrace ./ex-mtrace foo.dat               mtrace needs the name of the executable and the data.

Memory not freed:
-----------------
   Address      Size     Caller
0x0804a378      0x603    at /home/john/examples/ch-10/memory/ex-mtrace.c:23
0x0804a980      0x6e2    at /home/john/examples/ch-10/memory/ex-mtrace.c:23
0x0804b068      0x1d8    at /home/john/examples/ch-10/memory/ex-mtrace.c:23
0x0804b248      0xd9f    at /home/john/examples/ch-10/memory/ex-mtrace.c:23
0x0804bff0      0xc3     at /home/john/examples/ch-10/memory/ex-mtrace.c:23
0x0804c0b8      0x22f    at /home/john/examples/ch-10/memory/ex-mtrace.c:23
```

While `mtrace` works with C++ code, it's not very useful. It correctly reports the number and size of memory leaks in C++ code, but it fails to identify the line number of the leak. Perhaps this is because `mtrace` follows the `malloc` call but not the `new` call. Because `malloc` is called by the C++ standard library, the return pointer does not point to a module with debugging symbols.

10.5.4.3 Gathering Memory Statistics with memusage

To use the `memusage` utility, you do not need to instrument your code at all. This utility also comes with the `glibc-utils` package in Fedora. It tells you how much memory your program is using in the form of a histogram. The default output goes to the standard output and uses ASCII text to show a graphical histogram. Here is an example:

```
$ memusage awk 'BEGIN{print "Hello World"}'   Show the memory usage of awk.
Hello World

Memory usage summary: heap total: 3564, heap peak: 3548, stack peak: 8604
         total calls    total memory    failed calls
  malloc|        28            3564               0
 realloc|         0               0               0   (in place: 0, dec: 0)
  calloc|         0               0               0
    free|        10              48
Histogram for block sizes:
    0-15         21   75% ==================================================
   16-31          3   10% =======
   32-47          1    3% ==
   48-63          1    3% ==
  112-127         1    3% ==
 3200-3215        1    3% ==
```

Like all the functions in glibc-utils, memusage has no man page and no info
page. The --help option indicates some useful features, such as the ability to trace
mmap and munmap calls in addition to malloc and free:

```
$ memusage --help
Usage: memusage [OPTION]... PROGRAM [PROGRAMOPTION]...
Profile memory usage of PROGRAM.

   -n,--progname=NAME     Name of the program file to profile
   -p,--png=FILE          Generate PNG graphic and store it in FILE
   -d,--data=FILE         Generate binary data file and store it in FILE
   -u,--unbuffered        Don't buffer output
   -b,--buffer=SIZE       Collect SIZE entries before writing them out
      --no-timer          Don't collect additional information though timer
   -m,--mmap              Also trace mmap & friends

   -?,--help              Print this help and exit
      --usage             Give a short usage message
   -V,--version           Print version information and exit

 The following options only apply when generating graphical output:
   -t,--time-based        Make graph linear in time
   -T,--total             Also draw graph of total memory use
      --title=STRING      Use STRING as title of the graph
   -x,--x-size=SIZE       Make graphic SIZE pixels wide
   -y,--y-size=SIZE       Make graphic SIZE pixels high

Mandatory arguments to long options are also mandatory for any corresponding
short options.

For bug reporting instructions, please see:
<http://www.gnu.org/software/libc/bugs.html>.
```

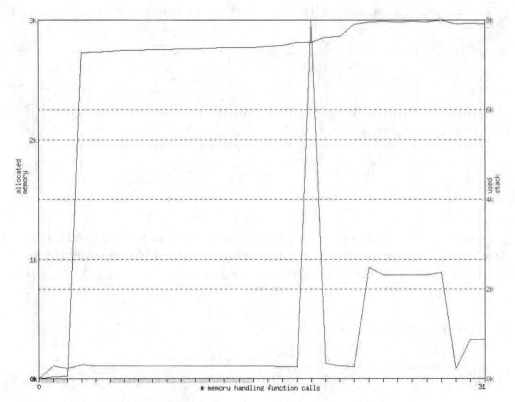

FIGURE 10-2   Graphical Output from `memusage`

One interesting feature is the ability to graph the output into a PNG file.[16] An example of this is shown in Figure 10-2.

Finally, the `memusagestat` utility produces a PNG file from the data produced with the d option of `memusage`. These tools appear to be works in progress.

10.5.5   Using Valgrind to Debug Memory Issues

In Chapter 9 I used Valgrind[17] to demonstrate its ability to debug cache issues, but it's more commonly used for debugging memory issues. This is in fact the default

---

16. *PNG* stands for *Portable Network Graphics,* an open format for sharing images (www.libpng.org).
17. www.valgrind.org

option for the `valgrind` command if you do not specify the `--tool` option. Calling `valgrind` with no arguments is equivalent to the following command:

```
$ valgrind --tool=memcheck ./myprog
```

The advantage of Valgrind is that you do not need to instrument your code to debug your application. The price you pay for this is performance. Valgrind causes your code's performance to drop dramatically. The other disadvantage of using a tool like Valgrind is that some results do not show up until the program exits. Specifically, leaks by nature cannot always be detected until the program exits.

10.5.5.1   Using Valgrind to Detect Leaks

With no arguments, the `valgrind` command will print a summary of what it believes are leaks when the program exits. To get more details, use the `--leakcheck=full` option. Listing 10-7 contains examples of two types of memory leaks that Valgrind looks for.

LISTING 10-7   leaky.c: Leak Example

```c
 1 #include <stdio.h>
 2 #include <string.h>
 3 #include <stdlib.h>
 4
 5 char *possible_leak(int x)
 6 {
 7     // Static pointer - valgrind doesn't know if this is needed.
 8     static char *lp;
 9     char *p = (char *) malloc(x);
10     lp = p + x / 2;
11     return p;
12 }
13
14 int main(int argc, char *argv[])
15 {
16     // Definitely lost.
17     char *p1 = malloc(0x1000);
18
19     // Possibly lost
20     char *p2 = possible_leak(0x1000);
21     return 0;
22 }
```

The first type of leak that Valgrind reports is a simple leak. In Listing 10-7, pointer p1 is allocated and discarded without being freed. Because p1 goes out of scope, the block is *definitely* leaked. The second allocation occurs inside the function possible_leak. This time, I included a static pointer that points to somewhere in the middle of the most recently allocated block. This could be a value that will be used on the next call, or it could just be an oversight in programming. Valgrind can't tell the difference, so it reports it as *possibly* leaked:

```
$ valgrind --quiet --leak-check=full ./leaky
==22309==
==22309== 4,096 bytes in 1 blocks are possibly lost in loss record 1 of 2
==22309==    at 0x40044C9: malloc (vg_replace_malloc.c:149)
==22309==    by 0x804838D: possible_leak (leaky.c:9)
==22309==    by 0x80483E8: main (leaky.c:20)
==22309==
==22309==
==22309== 4,096 bytes in 1 blocks are definitely lost in loss record 2 of 2
==22309==    at 0x40044C9: malloc (vg_replace_malloc.c:149)
==22309==    by 0x80483D5: main (leaky.c:17)
```

Notice that the *possible* leak points the finger at the possible_leak function as the source of the leak. When you encounter this in your code, now you'll know what to look for.

10.5.5.2 Looking for Memory Corruption with Valgrind

Valgrind is capable of looking for heap memory corruption as well as memory leaks. Specifically, Valgrind can detect single-byte overruns that might go unnoticed by glibc. Listing 10-8 shows a program with a single-byte overflow.

LISTING 10-8   new-corrupt.cpp: Example of Heap Corruption in a C++ Program

```
1 #include <string.h>
2
3 int main(int argc, char *argv[])
4 {
5     int *ptr = new int;
6     memset(ptr, 0, sizeof(int) + 1);        // One byte overflow
7     delete ptr;
8 }
```

Running this program with the valgrind command uncovers this flaw:

```
$ valgrind --quiet ./new-corrupt
==14780== Invalid write of size 1
```

```
==14780==    at 0x80484B9: main (new-corrupt.cpp:6)
==14780== Address 0x402E02C is 0 bytes after a block of size 4 alloc'd
==14780==    at 0x4004888: operator new(unsigned) (vg_replace_malloc.c:163)
==14780==    by 0x80484A9: main (new-corrupt.cpp:5)
```

It's important to point out that the overflows that Valgrind detects are in heap only. There is no way for Valgrind to detect overflows of stack or static memory.

10.5.5.3 Heap Analysis with Massif

The massif tool that comes with Valgrind is useful for showing a summary of heap usage by function. To illustrate this, I need an example. The program in Listing 10-9, called funalloc, contains two functions that simply leak memory.

LISTING 10-9   funalloc.c: Memory Allocation Functions

```
 1 #include <stdio.h>
 2 #include <string.h>
 3 #include <stdlib.h>
 4 #include <unistd.h>
 5
 6 void func1(void)
 7 {
 8     malloc(1024);              // Deliberate leak
 9 }
10
11 void func2(void)
12 {
13     malloc(1024);              // Deliberate leak
14 }
15
16 int main(int argc, char *argv[])
17 {
18     srand(0);
19     int i;
20     for (i = 0; i < 256; i++) {
21         int r = rand() % 100;
22         if (r > 75) {
23             func2();           // Called about 25% of the time
24         }
25         else {
26             func1();           // Called about 75% of the time
27         }
28         // Space out the samples on the graph.
29         usleep(1);
30     }
31 }
```

The `funalloc` program uses a pseudorandom sequence to make it unpredictable, but statistically it will call `func1` about 75 percent of the time. Because both functions allocate the same amount of memory, you should see that `func1` accounts for about 75 percent of the heap in use.

To run the example, use the following command line:

```
$ valgrind --tool=massif ./funalloc
```

This creates two files: `massif.PID.ps` and `massif.PID.txt`. The text file shows what you already knew:

```
Command: ./funalloc

== 0 ============================
Heap allocation functions accounted for 97.9% of measured spacetime

Called from:
  73.5% : 0x8048432: func1 (funalloc.c:8)

  24.4% : 0x804844A: func2 (funalloc.c:13)
```
(additional data deleted)

The graph is also interesting to look at and is shown in Figure 10-3. Each color represents one of the functions in the program. The height of the graph represents the total heap in use. Dwarfed by the heap allocations is the stack usage, which can be especially important in multithreaded applications.

10.5.5.4   Valgrind Final Thoughts

With all the Valgrind tools, line number information is available only for modules compiled with debugging. Without debugging, you still get a summary of errors. In many cases, it's preferable to redirect the output to a log file for viewing in an editor. The option for this is `--log-file`.

Valgrind is a big gun. I only scratched the surface of what Valgrind is capable of. In some cases, the performance penalties of Valgrind may make you want to leave it on the shelf. Other tools are faster and provide rough answers, but for fine-grained details, few tools compare with Valgrind.

In addition to `memcheck`, `massif`, and `cachegrind`, you can use `callgrind` and `helgrind`. `callgrind` is a function profiler similar to `gprof`, although it combines some of the features of `cachegrind` as well. `helgrind` claims to look for data race conditions in multithreaded programs. These tools are too complex to cover in this book, but you can explore them on your own system.

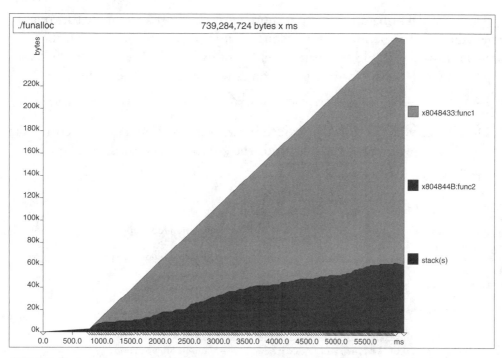

FIGURE 10-3   Heap Usage by Function Created by Massif

10.5.6   Looking for Overflows with Electric Fence

Electric Fence uses some clever techniques to find overflows in heap memory when they happen, unlike `glibc`, which can detect overflows only after the fact. Although Valgrind does this as well, Electric Fence uses the Memory Management Unit (MMU) to trap the offending code. Because the MMU does the real work, the performance penalty of using Electric Fence is minimal.

You do not need to instrument your code to use Electric Fence. Instead, it provides a dynamic library that implements alternative versions of the dynamic allocation functions. A wrapper script called `ef` is provided to take care of the necessary `LD_PRELOAD` environment variable setting. As with Valgrind, all you do is invoke your process with the `ef` command. You can run the `new-corrupt` program in Listing 10-8 with Electric Fence as follows:

```
$ ef ./new-corrupt

  Electric Fence 2.2.0 Copyright (C) 1987-1999 Bruce Perens <bruce@perens.com>
/usr/bin/ef: line 20: 23227 Segmentation fault      (core dumped) ( export
LD_PRELOAD=libefence.so.0.0; exec $* )
```

Then you can bring up `gdb` in postmortem mode to get an accurate backtrace of where the overflow occurred. If you don't want to use a core file, you can run your program in `gdb` with Electric Fence in either of two ways. One way is to link your application with the static library that comes with Electric Fence, as follows:

```
$ g++ -g -o new-corrupt new-corrupt.cpp -lefence          libefence.a is linked in.
```

Otherwise, you can use dynamic libraries from within `gdb` by setting the `LD_PRELOAD` environment variable inside the `gdb` command shell, as follows:

```
$ gdb ./new-corrupt
...
(gdb) set environment LD_PRELOAD libefence.so
(gdb) run
Starting program: /home/john/examples/ch-10/memory/new-corrupt

  Electric Fence 2.2.0 Copyright (C) 1987-1999 Bruce Perens <bruce@perens.com>
Reading symbols from shared object read from target memory...done.
Loaded system supplied DSO at 0xffffe000

  Electric Fence 2.2.0 Copyright (C) 1987-1999 Bruce Perens <bruce@perens.com>

Program received signal SIGSEGV, Segmentation fault.
0x080484b9 in main (argc=1, argv=0xbfb8a404) at new-corrupt.cpp:7
7               memset(ptr,0,sizeof(int)+1);
(gdb)
```

This prevents the core file that you otherwise would get when you run this program. Intuitively, you might be inclined to run `gdb` under Electric Fence with the `ef` command. Actually, this does not work in version 2.2.2 of Electric Fence because of the way the `ef` script is written and because `gdb` 6.3 contains `mallocs` of 0 bytes:

```
$ ef gdb ./new-corrupt

  Electric Fence 2.2.0 Copyright (C) 1987-1999 Bruce Perens <bruce@perens.com>

ElectricFence Aborting: Allocating 0 bytes, probably a bug.
/usr/bin/ef: line 20: 23307 Illegal instruction     (core dumped) ( export
LD_PRELOAD=libefence.so.0.0; exec $* )
```

This can be prevented by setting the environment variable `EF_ALLOW_MALLOC_0`, which tells `libefence` to relax about 0-byte allocations. You can set several other environment variables to alter the behavior of Electric Fence, as described in the `man` page `efence(3)`.

Another feature of Electric Fence is the ability to detect underruns as well as overruns. An underrun occurs when a process writes to an address preceding a block of memory. This type of error can happen with pointer arithmetic, such as the following:

```
char *buf = malloc(1024);
...
char *ptr = buf + 10;               It's poor style, but you can use negative indexes with ptr.
...
*(ptr - 11) = '\0';                 You asked for it: an underrun!
```

To detect this underrun with Electric Fence, you must set the environment variable EF_PROTECT_BELOW:

```
$ EF_PROTECT_BELOW=1 ef ./underrun

  Electric Fence 2.2.0 Copyright (C) 1987-1999 Bruce Perens <bruce@perens.com>
/usr/bin/ef: line 20:  4644 Segmentation fault      (core dumped) ( export
LD_PRELOAD=libefence.so.0.0; exec $* )
```

The complete example is not shown, but the debugging mechanism is exactly the same as before. The error causes a SIGSEGV, which leads to the line of code that generated the error.

Electric Fence works by allocating an extra read-only page after each allocated block for the purpose of causing a SIGSEGV when the code overruns. Because it allocates an extra page for every block, regardless of its size, the library can make your code use much more memory than normal. Applications that allocate many small blocks will see their heap usage increase dramatically.

Another problem occurs because of block alignment in the allocation libraries. It is very difficult to detect a single-byte overrun under some circumstances, such as example in Listing 10-4. Electric Fence fails to detect this overrun as well.

Finally, the only mechanism Electric Fence uses to inform you of errors is a SIGSEGV, which is not very informative. So although you may find a problem by using Electric Fence, you may need to use another tool to understand the problem. Nevertheless, Electric Fence provides a quick-and-dirty way to check your code for serious errors.

10.6   Unconventional Techniques

With all the tools available for debugging, there are still occasions when unconventional techniques are called for. For some applications, running under a debugger is too difficult, or using replacement libraries causes problems.

10.6.1   Creating Your Own Black Box

You probably are familiar with the so-called black box in commercial airliners. This is the device that crash investigators search for to determine the cause of an accident. It contains a history of measurements from some time in the past up to the point of the crash. By examining the history leading up to the crash, it may be possible to determine the cause.

You can create the software equivalent of a black box for use with your applications. There are advantages to using this technique instead of a debugger:

- It gives you fine-grained control over what gets logged and what doesn't. In this way, you can preserve performance while keeping some debugging information available.

- You can use this technique with optimized executables; you don't necessarily need to compile with debugging.

- This technique can be especially effective when you are trying to debug a stack overflow. Recall that a stack overflow typically causes your traceback information to be invalid, making debugging almost useless.

Listing 10-10 contains a complete example of a program that creates a black box in the form of a *trace buffer* (the more common term for this technique when used in software).

LISTING 10-10   trace-buffer.c: A Complete Example Using a Software Black Box

```
 1 #include <stdio.h>
 2 #include <string.h>
 3 #include <stdlib.h>
 4 #include <stdarg.h>
 5
 6 // Global message buffer. Give it a name that's easy to remember.
 7 // Pick a size that works for you.
 8 char tracebuf[4096] = "";
 9 char *mstart = tracebuf;
10
11 // Prototype for our printf-like function. We use the GNU __attribute__
12 // directive to include format checking for free.
13 int dbgprintf(const char *fmt, ...)
14     __attribute__ ((__format__(__printf__, 1, 2)));
15
16 // Printf-like function sends data to the trace buffer.
```

```
17 int dbgprintf(const char *fmt, ...)
18 {
19     int n = 0;
20
21     // ref. stdarg(3)
22     va_list ap;
23     va_start(ap, fmt);
24
25     // Number of chars available for snprintf
26     int nchars = sizeof(tracebuf) - (mstart - tracebuf);
27
28     if (nchars <= 2) {
29         // Circular buffer.
30         mstart = tracebuf;
31         nchars = sizeof(tracebuf);
32     }
33
34     // Write the message to the buffer
35     n = vsnprintf(mstart, nchars, fmt, ap);
36     mstart += n + 1;
37
38     va_end(ap);
39     return n;
40 }
41
42 int defective(int x)
43 {
44     int y = 1;
45     dbgprintf("defective(%u)", x);
46     if (x == 10) {
47         dbgprintf("time to corrupt the stack!");
48
49         // Overflow the stack by 128 bytes (that should be enough).
50         memset(&y, 0xa5, sizeof(y) + 128);
51
52         // Most likely won't die until we try to return.
53         dbgprintf("I'm still here; returning now.");
54         return 0;
55     }
56
57     return defective(x + 1);
58 }
59
60 int main(int argc, char *argv[])
61 {
62     defective(1);
63     dbgprintf("exiting...");
64     return 0;
65 }
```

The function `dbgprintf` is a `printf`-like function that writes to a block of global memory instead of writing to the standard output. The memory is used as a circular buffer so that when the buffer is full, the oldest messages are overwritten by the newest messages. The amount of history you get is determined by the size of the memory you allocate.

The rest of the program contains a single function that will overflow the stack under the right conditions. It's a recursive function that increments its input parameter and calls itself with the new value. When this value reaches 10, the program will overflow the stack. The result, as you might expect, is a core file. As you also might expect, the core file does not contain a usable backtrace. For example:

```
$ cc -g -o trace-buffer trace-buffer.c
./trace-buffer
Segmentation fault (core dumped)
$ gdb ./trace-buffer core.25347
...
#0  0xa5a5a5a5 in ?? ()              Senseless address is the first sign of trouble!
(gdb) bt                            Try a backtrace and see what you get...
#0  0xa5a5a5a5 in ?? ()
#1  0xa5a5a5a5 in ?? ()
...                                 More of the same
#22 0xa5a5a5a5 in ?? ()
---Type <return> to continue, or q <return> to quit---q
Quit
(gdb) x/15s &tracebuf              Look at the first 15 messages in tracebuf.
0x8049720 <tracebuf>:     "defective(1)"
0x804972d <tracebuf+13>:        "defective(2)"
0x804973a <tracebuf+26>:        "defective(3)"
0x8049747 <tracebuf+39>:        "defective(4)"
0x8049754 <tracebuf+52>:        "defective(5)"
0x8049761 <tracebuf+65>:        "defective(6)"
0x804976e <tracebuf+78>:        "defective(7)"
0x804977b <tracebuf+91>:        "defective(8)"
0x8049788 <tracebuf+104>:       "defective(9)"
0x8049795 <tracebuf+117>:       "defective(10)"
0x80497a3 <tracebuf+131>:       "time to corrupt the stack!"
0x80497be <tracebuf+158>:       "I'm still here; returning now."
0x80497dd <tracebuf+189>:       ""
0x80497de <tracebuf+190>:       ""
0x80497df <tracebuf+191>:       ""
(gdb)
```

In this example, you can see that the stack is useless thanks to the `defective` function, but the global data is intact. You take advantage of this by looking at the trace buffer with `gdb`. The messages give you a history of what took place before the crash. There's no guarantee that this is going to tell you what you need to know, but you can always modify the content to help. This also works in code compiled for optimization. You don't necessarily need the debugger, either; you can use the `strings` command to dump all the ASCII strings from the core file and see these messages in the order in which they were written.

The implementation in Listing 10-10 is not perfect, but it is simple. When the buffer is full, for example, the last message will be truncated. If you never fill the buffer, this is not a problem. If you do fill the buffer, you probably will truncate one message. Making it more robust than this is left as an exercise.

10.6.2   Getting Backtraces at Runtime

The simplest way to get a backtrace of your program is to use `gdb`. The drawback here is that attaching to a running process with the debugger requires it to stop the process, type some commands, and restart the process. This stop time can be quite invasive if you need to do it often. `gdb` comes with an undocumented script called `gstack`, which does this for you and cuts down the time required to get a traceback. To get the traceback for a running process, the syntax is

```
$ gstack pid          All you supply is the pid.
```

The advantage of `gstack` is that it requires much less time to execute than it would take you to type interactively in `gdb`. `gstack` prints only the function names in the stack trace, so your executable need not be compiled with `debug` to get useful output.

There are times when you might want to include backtrace information in your program output, such as in an error handler. In this case, you do not want to rely on the programmer to enter any commands; you want to produce the backtrace automatically. `glibc` provides some unique functions for this purpose. The `backtrace`[18] function gives you an array of pointers that are the program counters pulled off the stack. The prototype for `backtrace` is as follows:

```
int backtrace (void **BUFFER, int SIZE)
```

---

18. Reference: `info libc backtrace`.

By themselves, the pointers don't help much. You probably want to see symbols. glibc provides a function called `backtrace_symbols` that ostensibly translates the pointers from `backtrace` into symbols. Unfortunately, `backtrace_symbols` appears only to lookup symbols in `libc`—that is, it does not appear to be intended for general usage. No problem, though; you can use the `addr2line` utility to translate the output into line numbers, provided that your executable is compiled with debug. Even without `debug`, you can still see function names. An example of a traceback function that calls `addr2line` could look like the following:

```
void print_trace(void)
{
    int i;
    const int NTRACE = 32;        // Maximum call stack depth.
    void *traceback[NTRACE];      // Will hold instruction pointers

    // Use a shell command to lookup addresses.
    // Ref. addr2line(1), which is part of binutils.
    char cmd[128] = "addr2line -f -e ";

    // Use the symlink /proc/self/exe to get the name of the executable.
    // This prevents us from having to keep a copy of argv[0] somewhere.
    char *prog = cmd + strlen(cmd);
    int r = readlink("/proc/self/exe",prog,sizeof(cmd)-(prog-cmd)-1);

    // ... error checking omitted for brevity

    // Run the shell command - ref. popen(3)
    FILE *fp = popen(cmd, "w");

    // ... error checking omitted for brevity

    int depth = backtrace(traceback, NTRACE);

    for (i = 0; i < depth; i++) {
        // Send the addresses to addr2line.
        // addr2line prints to stdout.
        fprintf(fp, "%p\n", traceback[i]);

        // ... error checking omitted for brevity
    }
    fclose(fp);
}
```

`addr2line` accepts pointers from the standard input, which is what you take advantage of here. You must specify the executable with the `-e` option. In this case, I took the path of least resistance by reading the symlink in `/proc/self/exe` to keep the listing short. With no options, `addr2line` attempts to produce line-number information for each pointer, which is available only when the executable is compiled with `debug`. Without debugging information, the information you get is useless. That is why I include the `-f` option in the command, which prints the closest function to each pointer. This should be valid even with debugging turned on.[19]

10.6.3   Forcing Core Dumps

It seems paradoxical that you should want your code to generate a core file, but for hard-to-catch bugs, this can be very useful. One such situation might be a regression test that runs overnight. In this case, you may not be able to predict what will fail, but if something does fail, you want as much information as possible. The core file will provide you as much information as you can get.

Recall that most new distributions disable core files by default. To enable core-file generation in `bash`, use the following command:

```
$ ulimit -c unlimited
```

The system limit can most likely be found in `/etc/rc.local`, but as I discussed in Chapter 6, there are good reasons to disable core files by default.

10.6.3.1   abort and assert

These two functions will terminate your program and generate a core file. Specifically, they both work by generating a `SIGABRT` signal. Calling `abort` is equivalent to calling

```
raise(SIGABRT);
```

You should use this when you believe that the program state is unknown (perhaps because of some memory overflows) and it is unwise to continue. You could just as well call `exit`, but that wouldn't leave a core file for you to examine. The typical pattern for using `abort` looks like this:

```
if ( ! program is sane ) abort();
```

With that in mind, ANSI C defines the `assert` macro, which wraps this up into a single line. `assert` takes a single argument, which is evaluated as a Boolean

---

19. Beware: Optimization can alter your call stack in unexpected ways.

expression. When the expression is false, it calls `abort`. The output includes the line number and expression that failed:

```
assert(!insane);
```

When `insane` is true, the output looks like this:

```
$./foo
assert: foo.c:7: main: Assertion '!insane' failed.
Aborted (core dumped)
```

You can disable `assert` by compiling your code with the preprocessor macro `NDEBUG` defined. When `assert` is disabled in this way, the expression inside the parentheses is discarded before the compiler sees it. This could lead to side effects caused by turning off `assert`. Do yourself a favor: Keep your assertions simple.

10.6.3.2   Using gcore

Normally, a core dump is produced by the kernel as the result of an abnormal termination. `gdb` allows you to dump a core file without terminating the process. The command for this in `gdb` is `gcore`. When you execute the `gcore` command from `gdb`, it writes a core file to a file named `core.pid` or any name you choose. `gdb` comes with a shell script named `gcore`, which attaches to a process with `gdb` and dumps the core using the `gcore` command; then it disconnects and allows the process to continue.

`gcore` takes one or more process IDs as arguments and allows you to change the core filename with the `-o` option.

10.6.4   Using Signals

A common use for signals is to dump some debugging information when a particular signal is received. You can, for example, force a program to dump core by sending it a core-generating signal such as `SIGBART`.[20] This way, you can exert control from the shell without necessarily instrumenting your code. More proactively, you can create a signal handler that responds to one of the user-defined signals

---

20. You actually can send any `core`-generating signal, such as `SIGSEGV` or `SIGBUS`, and the process will terminate with a `core` dump.

(SIGUSR1, SIGUSR2), prints some debugging information at the time of the signal, and allows the program to continue to run.

Another idea is to facilitate just-in-time debugging by using SIGSTOP and SIGCONT. In some examples in this book, I used SIGSTOP to pause the process and allow you to examine the process state before it terminated. This is as simple as adding the following line to your code:

```
raise(SIGSTOP);
```

This is equivalent to pressing Ctrl+Z for a foreground process in the shell. You can stop a background process by sending it SIGSTOP from the shell as follows:

```
$ kill -STOP pid
```

After you stop a process, you must send it a SIGCONT to allow it to continue running. From the shell, this is just as simple:

```
$ kill -CONT pid
```

While the process is stopped, you can examine the state of the process without any inherent race conditions—that is, you can look at things without them changing from underneath you. In particular, you probably will be interested in the /proc file system.

10.6.5 Using procfs for Debugging

Recall that procfs refers to the file-system driver that is used to report process information and is mounted on /proc. This file system contains a great deal of system information, but it also contains one directory for each running process. Each subdirectory is named for the process ID and contains the process-specific information. One exception is /proc/self, which is a symbolic link to the process directory of the currently running process. More precisely, when a process opens files in /proc/self, it actually is opening files in its own process-specific directory.

Most of the information about process state is available from the ps command and from commands in the procps package. You are strongly encouraged to use these commands whenever possible, but a few things that are found uniquely in the /proc file system, and they can be invaluable for debugging.

A running process is a moving target, of course, and when using values from procfs, you must keep this in mind. It is always preferable to make sure that the process is in a nonrunning state when you are examining values. The process does not need to be stopped; it can just as easily be sleeping or blocking in a system call. As long as it is not executing when you look at the data, you can trust the data that you see.

10.6.5.1   Memory Maps

Earlier in the book, I introduced the useful pmap command for looking at a process's memory map. This can be helpful in tracking down memory leaks, which usually lead to fragmentation. In particular, when malloc uses mmap calls to allocate blocks, these blocks can be visible in the memory map. The blocks *may* map directly to allocated blocks in your program.

The raw unfiltered data that pmap gets comes from /proc/PID/maps. In most cases, the pmap command is preferable. For details on the procfs maps format, consult proc(5).

10.6.5.2   Process Environment

Inside each directory is useful information about the process environment, including the environment variables as well as the current working directory and filename of the executable. Environment variables are stored in /proc/PID/environ as a flat array of characters with NUL characters separating each environment variable. The easiest way to look at this from the shell is with the strings command, as follows:

```
$ strings -n1 /proc/PID/environ
MANPATH=:/home/john/usr/share/man
HOSTNAME=redhat
TERM=xterm
SHELL=/bin/bash
HISTSIZE=1000 ...                        Output continues.
```

This file is read-only, which means that you cannot modify the environment of a running process from the shell. I use the -n1 option to the strings command because by default, strings will filter out strings fewer than four characters in length. Here, I tell it to show strings as short as one character—that is, all strings.

Another useful file is `/proc/cmdline`, which stores the process's command line in the same format. This allows you to see exactly what the process's `argv` vector looked like when it was executed. For example:

```
$ strings -n1 /proc/self/cmdline | cat -n
    1   strings                              Contents of argv[0]
    2   -n1                                  Contents of argv[1]
    3   /proc/self/cmdline                   Contents of argv[2]
```

A little mental arithmetic is required, because line 1 contains `argv[0]`, but you get the idea.

10.6.5.3   Open Files

The `/proc` directory of the process also tells you about open files and directories. `/proc/PID/exe` contains a symbolic link to the executable file that was used to launch the process. For example:

```
$ ls -l /proc/self/exe
lrwxrwxrwx  1 john john 0 Jul 30 11:53 /proc/self/exe -> /bin/ls
```

Similarly, `/proc/PID/cwd` is a symbolic link to the current working directory of the process. This is useful when connecting to a server process that is writing data to its current working directory. It may not tell you where that is; you can use `procfs` to find out for yourself.

Finally, you can see every file a process has open by looking at its file descriptors in `/proc/PID/fd`. This is a subdirectory that contains a symbolic link for each open file descriptor. The name of the link is the pathname of the open file if the file resides on a file system. If the file is a socket or pipe, a `readlink` of the file typically contains some textual indication of the nature of the file descriptor. For example:

```
$ ls -l /proc/self/fd | tee /dev/null
total 4
lrwx------  1 john john 64 Jul 30 12:00 0 -> /dev/pts/3
l-wx------  1 john john 64 Jul 30 12:00 1 -> pipe:[33209]
lrwx------  1 john john 64 Jul 30 12:00 2 -> /dev/pts/3
lr-x------  1 john john 64 Jul 30 12:00 3 -> /proc/5487/fd
```

Note that file descriptors 0 and 2 (standard input and standard error, respectively) point to the pseudoterminal device. The standard output is piped to the `tee` command, so file descriptor 1 shows up as `pipe:[33209]`. This is not a file you can open, but it does tell you that this is a pipe and that 33209 happens to be the inode number of this pipe. File descriptor 3 is an open directory. This is actually /proc/self/fd, which in this case points to /proc/5487/fd.

In Chapter 6, I introduced the tools lsof and fuser, both of which use this information extensively. Which tool you prefer depends on the circumstances, but sometimes, a simple ls command in /proc tells you everything you need to know.

10.7   Summary

This chapter covered some of the tools and issues involved with debugging user code. I covered several techniques for using printf to debug your code, and I also looked at some of the undesirable side effects of this debugging technique.

Also in this chapter, I took a detailed look at the GNU debugger (gdb) and covered some basic and not-so-basic usage. I demonstrated how to make most efficient use of gdb in circumstances where otherwise, it may slow your code drastically. I looked at some issues unique to debugging C++ code with gdb.

This chapter also looked at some of the unique problems associated with shared objects, which can be challenging to debug. I looked at how to run a process temporarily with a specific shared object that may be under development without having to replace the systemwide copy of that object. I also demonstrated how to do this using gdb.

Finally, I demonstrated several tools for resolving memory issues in your code, such as memory overflows and corrupted stacks. I looked at some popular tools as well as a few unconventional techniques.

10.7.1   Tools Used in This Chapter

- Electric Fence—a tool to look for memory overruns and underruns that uses the MMU

- gdb—the GNU debugger; used for interactive debugging of a process

- mtrace—part of glibc that allows you to look for memory leaks after your code has run

- Valgrind—a powerful tool that can look for memory leaks, memory corruption, and many other things

10.7.2   Online Resources

- http://duma.sourceforge.net—a fork of Electric Fence

- http://perens.com/FreeSoftware/ElectricFence—the original home of Electric Fence

- www.valgrind.org—the home page of the Valgrind project

10.7.3   References

- Robbins, A. *GDB Pocket Reference.* Sebastopol, Calif.: O'Reilly Media, Inc., 2005.

Index

THIS BOOK IS SAFARI ENABLED

INCLUDES FREE 45-DAY ACCESS TO THE ONLINE EDITION

The Safari® Enabled icon on the cover of your favorite technology book means the book is available through Safari Bookshelf. When you buy this book, you get free access to the online edition for 45 days.

Safari Bookshelf is an electronic reference library that lets you easily search thousands of technical books, find code samples, download chapters, and access technical information whenever and wherever you need it.

TO GAIN 45-DAY SAFARI ENABLED ACCESS TO THIS BOOK:

- Go to **http://www.prenhallprofessional.com/safarienabled**
- Complete the brief registration form
- Enter the coupon code found in the front of this book on the "Copyright" page

If you have difficulty registering on Safari Bookshelf or accessing the online edition, please e-mail customer-service@safaribooksonline.com.

PRENTICE HALL